Museum of Anthropology, University of Michigan
Memoirs, Number 45

Prehispanic Settlement Patterns in the Northwestern Valley of Mexico

The Zumpango Region

Jeffrey R. Parsons

with contributions by Larry J. Gorenflo,
Mary H. Parsons, and David J. Wilson

Ann Arbor, Michigan
2008

©2008 by the Regents of the University of Michigan
The Museum of Anthropology
All rights reserved

Printed in the United States of America
ISBN 978-0-915703-70-8

Cover design by Katherine Clahassey

The University of Michigan Museum of Anthropology currently publishes two monograph series, Anthropological Papers and Memoirs, as well as an electronic series in CD-ROM form. For a complete catalog, write to Museum of Anthropology Publications, 4013 Museums Building, 1109 Geddes Avenue, Ann Arbor, MI 48109-1079, or see www.lsa.umich.edu/umma/

Library of Congress Cataloging-in-Publication Data

Parsons, Jeffrey R.
  Prehispanic settlement patterns in the northwestern Valley of Mexico : the Zumpango region / Jeffrey R. Parsons ; with contributions by Larry J. Gorenflo, Mary H. Parsons, and David J. Wilson.
    p. cm. -- (Museum of Anthropology, University of Michigan memoirs ; no. 45)
  Includes bibliographical references.
  ISBN 978-0-915703-70-8 (alk. paper)
  1. Indians of Mexico--Mexico--Mexico, Valley of--Antiquities. 2. Land settlement patterns, Prehistoric--Mexico--Mexico, Valley of. 3. Mexico, Valley of (Mexico)--Antiquities. 4. Zumpango Region (Mexico)--Antiquities. 5. Mexico--Antiquities. I. Gorenflo, L. J. (Larry J.) II. Parsons, Mary Hrones. III. Wilson, David J. (David John), 1941- IV. University of Michigan. Museum of Anthropology. V. Title.
  F1219.1.M53P374 2008
  972'.52--dc22
                        2008050989

The paper used in this publication meets the requirements of the ANSI Standard Z39.48-1984 (Permanence of Paper)

*Dedicated to the memory of
William T. Sanders (1926-2008):
mentor, colleague, friend, and a source
of inspiration for nearly fifty years.*

Contents

LIST OF TABLES, *vii*
LIST OF FIGURES, *viii*
LIST OF PLATES, *xi*
PREFACE, *xvii*
ACKNOWLEDGMENTS, *xviii*

CHAPTER 1. INTRODUCTION, *1*
    Overall Scope and Objectives, *1*
    The First Valley of Mexico Conference, 1960, *1*
    Working Out the Survey Methodology, 1960–1964, *2*
    A Critique, *6*
    The Organization of this Monograph, *8*

CHAPTER 2. THE NATURAL ENVIRONMENT, *9*
    The Zumpango Region in the Valley of Mexico, *9*
    Environmental Zones in the Zumpango Region, *10*
    Modern and Historic Climate in the Zumpango Region, *14*
    Paleoclimatological Studies, *25*

CHAPTER 3. THE HISTORICALLY DOCUMENTED OCCUPATION OF THE ZUMPANGO REGION:
      SIXTEENTH THROUGH TWENTIETH CENTURIES, *29*
    Introduction, *29*
    The Twentieth Century, *29*
    The Zumpango Region on the Eve of Spanish Conquest, *33*
    The Colonial Period (1521–1810), *36*
    The Nineteenth Century, *44*
    Summary and Conclusions, *48*

CHAPTER 4. FIELD AND LABORATORY METHODOLOGY, *51*
    Surface Conditions—Potentials and Problems for Regional Surface Survey in the Zumpango
      Region, *51*
    Survey Methodology, *52*
    Laboratory Procedures in Mexico, *57*
    Laboratory Procedures in Ann Arbor, *58*
    Site Classification, *58*
    Chronology, *60*

CHAPTER 5. THE PATTERNING OF SETTLEMENT, *by J.R. Parsons and L.J. Gorenflo, 61*
    Trends in Numbers of Sites, Numbers of Occupied Hectares, and Population, *61*
    Occupation by Environmental Zone, *77*
    Occupation by Site Type, *83*
    The Spatial Configuration of Settlement, *84*
    Overall Summary and Conclusions, *96*

CHAPTER 6. FUTURE RESEARCH NEEDS, *101*
    Chronology, *101*
    Stylistic Variability in Coeval Regional Ceramic Assemblages within and around the Valley
        of Mexico, *101*
    Geoarchaeological Study, *101*
    Paleoclimatological Study, *102*
    Definition of Settlement Systems, *102*
    More Attention to Lithics, *102*
    Study of Lime Resources, *102*
    Study of Aquatic Resources, *102*
    Study of Water-Control Technology, *102*
    Investigation of Pre-Formative and Aceramic ("Off-Site") Occupation, *103*
    Extending Regional Surveys into the Pachuca Region, *103*
    Maintenance and Restudy of Curated Collections, *103*
    Can We Proceed in the Face of Massive Site Destruction and Landscape Transformation?, *104*

CHAPTER 7. RESUMEN EN ESPAÑOL DE LOS PRINCIPALES CONCLUSIONES, *translated by A.H. Parsons*, 105

BIBLIOGRAPHY, *109*

APPENDIX A. THE SITE DESCRIPTIONS, *by J.R. Parsons, M.H. Parsons, and D.J. Wilson*, 119
    Late Formative Site, *120*
    Terminal Formative Sites, *120*
    Classic Sites, *131*
    Early Toltec Sites, *170*
    Late Toltec Sites, *189*
    Aztec Sites, *255*

APPENDIX B. CERAMIC CHRONOLOGY, *by J.R. Parsons, M.H. Parsons, and D.J. Wilson*, 349
    The Late Formative, *349*
    Terminal Formative (Tzacualli Phase), *350*
    Classic, *356*
    Early Toltec, *371*
    Late Toltec, *378*
    Early and Late Aztec, *389*

Tables

2.1. Environmental zones in the Zumpango Region, *14*
2.2. Environmental zones of meteorological stations, *18*
2.3. Average monthly rainfall for Zumpango and Tula, *18*
2.4. Average monthly rainfall for Pachuca, Tizayuca, and Teoloyucan, *18*
2.5. Total annual rainfall for Teoloyucan, Pachuca, Tizayuca, Tula, Hueypoxtla, and Huehuetoca, *18*
2.6. Monthly rainfall for Pachuca, *19*
2.7. Monthly rainfall for Tizayuca, *20*
2.8. Monthly rainfall for Tula, *21*
2.9. Monthly rainfall for Apaxco, *21*
2.10. Monthly rainfall for Cuautitlan, *21*
2.11. Monthly rainfall for Huehuetoca, *22*
2.12. Monthly rainfall for Hueypoxtla, *23*
2.13. Monthly rainfall for Teoloyucan, *24*
2.14. Monthly rainfall for Tepotzotlan, *25*
2.15. Monthly rainfall for Tequixquiac, *26*
2.16. Monthly rainfall for Zumpango, *26*
2.17. Years with rainfall shortfalls during planting and growing season, *27*
2.18. Reported frosts during April, May, June, and August, *27*
3.1. Modern settlement populations in the Zumpango Region, *30*
3.2. Modern (1960) settlements: environmental contexts and demography, *32*
3.3. Modern and prehispanic population densities, *33*
3.4. Comparison of modern and prehispanic settlement/site population densities, *34*
3.5. Tribute paid to the Triple Alliance from the Hueypuchtla province, *35*
3.6. Population of the Citlaltepec jurisdiction, *44*
3.7. Number of Indian tributaries in the Citlaltepec jurisdiction, *44*
3.8. Surface areas of lakes in the Valley of Mexico in the early nineteenth century, *45*
3.9. Lake surface areas and water depths in 1861, *45*
3.10. Lake measurements in 1866, *46*
3.11. Modern communities listed and not listed in sixteenth-century documents, *48*
4.1. Zumpango Region surveyed area, *57*
4.2. Prehispanic chronology in the Zumpango Region, *60*
5.1. Summary of number of sites, occupied hectares, and population, *62*
5.2. Population densities at different periods in the Zumpango Region compared with overall densities for other surveyed regions in the Valley of Mexico, *62*
5.3. Expected and actual population, and population density, by environmental zone, *82*
5.4. Number of sites by environmental zone in the Zumpango Region, *82*
5.5. Number of occupied hectares by environmental zone in the Zumpango Region, *82*
5.6. Numbers and percentages of sites in each site type in the Zumpango Region, *85*
5.7. Percentages of numbers of hamlets, villages, and centers in the Zumpango Region, *85*
5.8. Numbers and percentages of occupied hectares in each site type in the Zumpango Region, *85*
5.9. Percentages of occupied hectares in hamlets, villages, and centers in the Zumpango Region, *86*
5.10. Numbers and percentages of population in each site type in the Zumpango Region, *86*
5.11. Percentages of population in hamlets, villages, and centers in the Zumpango Region, *86*
5.12. Comparison of percentages of site types in Zumpango Region and Valley of Mexico, *87*
5.13. Comparison of percentages of populations in different site types, *87*
A1. Summary of Zumpango Region site data, *335*

Figures

1.1. Mesoamerica, *2*
1.2. The Valley of Mexico, showing principal towns, *3*
1.3. The Valley of Mexico, showing the Zumpango Region and other surveyed regions, *4*
1.4. The Zumpango Region, showing its position between greater Mexico City and the Tula Region, *5*
2.1. Internal drainage basins in the Mexican Mesa Central, *10*
2.2. The Zumpango Region, showing survey borders and modern cultural features, *11*
2.3. Environmental zones in the Zumpango Region, *12*
2.4. Geomorphic elevated zones along the north shore of Lake Xaltocán-Zumpango, *13*
2.5. Rainfall isohyets of average annual rainfall in the Valley of Mexico, *17*
3.1. The Zumpango Region, showing modern settlements, *31*
3.2. Enrico Martinez's map of the Valley of Mexico in 1628, *37*
4.1. Two members of a survey crew, *54*
4.2. Recording information on the 1:5000 airphoto, *54*
4.3. A conversation with local people, *55*
4.4. Encounter with a territorial dog, *55*
4.5. Surface collecting, *56*
5.1. Prehispanic population profile in the Zumpango Region, *63*
5.2. Early Formative occupation in the Valley of Mexico, *64*
5.3. Middle Formative occupation in the Valley of Mexico, *65*
5.4. Late Formative occupation in the Zumpango Region, *66*
5.5. Late Formative occupation in the Valley of Mexico, *67*
5.6. Terminal Formative occupation in the Zumpango Region, *68*
5.7. Terminal Formative occupation in the Valley of Mexico, *69*
5.8. Classic occupation in the Zumpango Region, *70*
5.9. Classic occupation in the Valley of Mexico, *71*
5.10. Early Toltec occupation in the Zumpango Region, *73*
5.11. Early Toltec occupation in the Valley of Mexico, *74*
5.12. Late Toltec occupation in the Zumpango Region, *75*
5.13. Late Toltec occupation in the Valley of Mexico, *76*
5.14. Late Aztec occupation in the Zumpango Region, *78*
5.15. Late Aztec occupation in the Valley of Mexico, *79*
5.16. Prehispanic population densities in the Valley of Mexico over time, *80*
5.17. Population density in 1 × 1 km cells in the Zumpango Region, *81*
5.18. Histogram of Terminal Formative site area in the Zumpango Region, *87*
5.19. Histogram of Classic site area in the Zumpango Region, *88*
5.20. Histogram of Early Toltec site area in the Zumpango Region, *88*
5.21. Histogram of Late Toltec site area in the Zumpango Region, *91*
5.22. Distribution of Aztec II-III Black/Orange pottery in the Zumpango Region, *93*
5.23. Histogram of Late Aztec site area in the Zumpango Region, *94*
5.24. Histogram of Late Aztec site population in the Zumpango Region, *95*
5.25. Distribution of Aztec IV Black/Orange pottery in the Zumpango Region, *97*
5.26. Areas of population loss and gain from one period to another in the Zumpango Region, *98*

A1. Map of Late Formative sites in the Zumpango Region, *121*
A2. Map of Terminal Formative sites in the Zumpango Region, *123*
A3. Map of Classic sites in the Zumpango Region, *132*
A4. Map of Early Toltec sites in the Zumpango Region, *171*
A5a. Zu-ET-12, sketch plan of ceremonial-civic core of site, *176*
A5b. Zu-ET-12, sketch plan of Feature CH plaza area, *177*
A5c. Zu-ET-12, sketch plan of Feature BW complex, *178*
A6a. Zu-ET-12, sketch plan and profile of Feature BK complex, *178*
A6b. Zu-ET-12, sketch plan of Feature BU complex, *179*
A7. Map of Late Toltec sites in the Zumpango Region, *190*
A8. Map of Aztec sites in the Zumpango Region, *256*
A9. Zu-Az-36, sketch plan of base of structure at Feature AQ, *265*
A10. Zu-Az-47, sketch plan of site areas, *269*

B1. Late Formative Red and Plainware shouldered bowls, *351*
B2. Late Formative Plainware ollas with flaring necks, and bowl-basin, *352*
B3. Terminal Formative Plainware simple bowls and Plainware shouldered bowls, *353*
B4. Terminal Formative (Tzacualli phase) Plainware wedge-rim ollas, *354*
B5. Terminal Formative Plainware wedge-rim and flaring-rim ollas, *355*
B6. Classic Red/Buff hemispherical bowls, *356*
B7. Classic Red/Buff flaring-rim bowls, *357*
B8. Classic Red/Buff flaring-rim bowls, no rim sherds, *358*
B9. Classic Red/Buff flaring-rim bowls, *359*
B10. Classic Monochrome hemispherical bowls, *360*
B11. Classic Monochrome bowls with flaring rims, *361*
B12. Classic Monochrome ollas with slight-everted rims, *362*
B13. Classic Monochrome ollas with medium-everted rims, *363*
B14. Classic Monochrome ollas with wide-everted rims, *364*
B15. Classic Utilitarian Ware, Red/Buff olla/basins, *365*
B16. Classic Utilitarian Ware, Red/Buff olla/basins, *366*
B17. Classic Utilitarian Ware, Monochrome basins, *368*
B18. Classic Utilitarian Ware, comales and Rose-on-Granular, *369*
B19. Classic Specialty Ware, Thin Orange, *369*
B20. Classic Specialty Ware, censer flange and figurines, *370*
B21. Classic Specialty Ware, Monochrome Matte bowls, *370*
B22. Early Toltec Service Ware, Monochrome bowls, *371*
B23. Early Toltec Service Ware, Red/Buff bowls (Coyotlatelco), *373*
B24. Early Toltec Service Ware, Red/Buff bowls (Coyotlatelco), *374*
B25. Early Toltec Utilitarian Ware, beveled-rim basins with scraped exterior, *375*
B26. Early Toltec Utilitarian Ware, wedge-rim ollas, *376*
B27. Early Toltec Utilitarian everted-rim ollas, *377*
B28. Early Toltec Utilitarian Ware, low-neck, rolled-rim ollas, *378*
B29. Late Toltec Service Ware, Monochrome bowls, *380*
B30. Late Toltec Service Ware, Red/Buff bowls, wide-band variant, *381*
B31. Late Toltec Service Ware, Red/Buff bowls, wavy-line variant, *382*

B32. Late Toltec Service Ware, Red/Buff bowls, wavy-line variant, *383*
B33. Late Toltec Service Ware, Orange/Cream (Joroba) bowls, *384*
B34. Late Toltec Utilitarian Ware, beveled-rim ollas, *385*
B35. Late Toltec Utilitarian Ware, basins with scraped exterior, *386*
B36. Late Toltec Utilitarian Ware, comales and ink-stamped jars, *388*
B37. Aztec Orange Service Ware, Monochrome bowls, *391*
B38. Aztec Orange Service Ware, Aztec II-III Black/Orange bowl-basin, *391*
B39. Orange Service Ware, Aztec III Black/Orange bowls, *392*
B40. Aztec Orange Service Ware, Aztec III Black/Orange bowls, *393*
B41. Aztec Orange Service Ware, Aztec III Black/Orange dishes, *394*
B42. Aztec III Black/Orange molcajetes, *395*
B43. Aztec III Black/Orange molcajetes, *396*
B44. Aztec IV Black/Orange molcajetes, *397*
B45. Aztec Orange Utilitarian Ware: jars and basins, *398*
B46. Aztec Orange Utilitarian Ware, comales, *400*
B47. Aztec Red Service Ware, Monochrome bowls, *401*
B48. Aztec Red Service Ware, Black/Red bowls, *402*
B49. Aztec Red Service Ware, Black/Red bowls, *403*
B50. Aztec Red Service Ware, Black-and-White/Red bowls, *404*
B51. Aztec Red Service Ware, Black-and-White/Red bowls, *405*
B52. Aztec Specialty Ware, Huastec Black-and-Purple/Cream Tradeware, *405*

Plates

2.1. Maize field created by stone check dam in barranca, *15*
2.2. Maize fields created by stone check dams in barranca, *15*
2.3. Mammoth skull from modern sand quarry near ancient shoreline of Lake Zumpango, *16*
3.1. Entrance to the Gran Canal de Desagüe tunnel under construction near Zumpango, *34*
5.1. Example of Aztec II Black/Orange sherd from Zu-Az-46, *92*

A1. Zu-LF-1, facing SE over Location 5, *122*
A2. Zu-TF-5, facing NW over Location 44, *124*
A3. Zu-TF-8, facing west over Location 67, *125*
A4. Zu-TF-9, facing west over Location 66, *126*
A5. Zu-TF-20, facing north over Location 68, *128*
A6. Zu-TF-22, facing east over Location 78, *130*
A7. Zu-TF-25, facing SW over Location 75, *130*
A8. Zu-Cl-1, facing north over Location 20, *133*
A9. Zu-Cl-2, facing SW over Location 10, *133*
A10. Zu-Cl-3, facing south over Location 9, *134*
A11. Zu-Cl-4, facing NE at Location 7, *134*
A12. Zu-Cl-6, facing SW over site area, *135*
A13. Zu-Cl-10, facing north over Location 24, *136*
A14. Zu-Cl-11, general site area, *137*
A15. Zu-Cl-11, facing north at Feature AU, *137*
A16. Zu-Cl-11, facing SE at Feature AV, *138*
A17. Zu-Cl-13, facing east over Location 29, *139*
A18. Zu-Cl-15, facing north at Feature AD, *139*
A19. Zu-Cl-20, facing west over Location 21, *141*
A20. Zu-Cl-21, facing west over Location 22, *141*
A21. Zu-Cl-26, canal cutting through field near Location 15, *142*
A22. Zu-Cl-27, facing SE over Location 55, *143*
A23. Zu-Cl-31, facing SE over site area, *144*
A24. Zu-Cl-33, facing south over Location 9, *146*
A25. Zu-Cl-34, facing south over Location 88, *146*
A26. Zu-Cl-38, facing north over site area, *148*
A27. Zu-Cl-40, facing ENE over site area, *148*
A28. Zu-Cl-40, facing north over Location 40, *149*
A29. Zu-Cl-42, facing south over Location 41, *149*
A30. Zu-Cl-48, facing west over Location 48, *151*
A31. Zu-Cl-53, facing NE over Location 31, *152*
A32. Zu-Cl-55, facing NW over Location 53, *154*
A33. Zu-Cl-59, facing east over Location 41, *154*
A34. Zu-Cl-61, facing east over Location 97, *156*
A35. Zu-Cl-63, facing north over Location 83, *156*
A36. Zu-Cl-64, facing NE over Location 89, *157*
A37. Zu-Cl-70, facing east over Location 65, *159*
A38. Zu-Cl-71, facing east over Location 47, *159*
A39. Zu-Cl-73, facing SW over Location 71, *159*

A40. Zu-Cl-75, facing south over Location 72, *160*
A41. Zu-Cl-77, facing south over Location 69, *161*
A42. Zu-Cl-80, facing NE over Location 84, *162*
A43. Zu-Cl-81, facing east over Location 85, *163*
A44. Zu-Cl-82, facing SW over Location 81, *163*
A45. Zu-Cl-84, facing SE over site area, *165*
A46. Zu-Cl-85, facing WSW over site area, *165*
A47. Zu-Cl-86, facing SE over Location 95, *165*
A48. Zu-Cl-89, facing west over general site area, *167*
A49. Zu-Cl-89, facing north at Feature DE, *167*
A50. Zu-Cl-90, facing north over Location 55, with Tultepec Island in background, *167*
A51. Zu-Cl-90, plastered floor in ditch profile, near Location 55, *168*
A52. Zu-Cl-90, facing west over Location 57, *168*
A53. Zu-Cl-90, facing south over Location 58, showing heavy surface pottery, *169*
A54. Zu-Cl-90, facing SE over Location 60, *169*
A55. Zu-ET-1, facing SW over site area, *172*
A56. Zu-ET-8, facing south over Location 10-M, *173*
A57. Zu-ET-12, facing SW at northern half of Cerro de la Mesa Grande, *174*
A58. Zu-ET-12, section of site's ceremonial-civic core, *176*
A59. Zu-ET-12, Feature BH, showing stone wall exposed in looter's pit, *179*
A60. Zu-ET-12, facing SW at Feature BK, *180*
A61. Zu-ET-12, facing north at Feature BR, *180*
A62. Zu-ET-12, facing NW over platform supporting Feature BW, *181*
A63. Zu-ET-12, Feature BX, from top of Feature BZ, *181*
A64. Zu-ET-12, facing south at Features BZ, CB, and CD, *182*
A65. Zu-ET-12, facing north over Feature CG (depression), *182*
A66. Zu-ET-12, petroglyph at base of cliff below site, *183*
A67. Zu-ET-12, petroglyph at base of cliff below site, *184*
A68. Zu-ET-20, facing NE over site area, *186*
A69. Zu-ET-20, facing NE over Location 84, *187*
A70. Zu-LT-1, facing north over Location 22, *191*
A71. Zu-LT-6, facing south at Feature W, *192*
A72. Zu-LT-13, facing west at Feature AG, *193*
A73. Zu-LT-16, facing NNW over Location 31, *194*
A74. Zu-LT-17, facing north at Feature AG, *195*
A75. Zu-LT-22, facing south over Location 33, *197*
A76. Zu-LT-28, facing south at Feature AF, *197*
A77. Zu-LT-29, facing north at Feature AE, *197*
A78. Zu-LT-30, facing north over Location 23, *199*
A79. Zu-LT-31, facing east over Location 6, *199*
A80. Zu-LT-33, facing south over Location 8, *199*
A81. Zu-LT-35, facing north at Feature M, *200*
A82. Zu-LT-40, facing NW at Feature N, *202*
A83. Zu-LT-41, facing south over general site area, *202*
A84. Zu-LT-41, facing west over Location 1, *202*
A85. Zu-LT-46, facing south over general site area, *203*
A86. Zu-LT-49, facing SW at Feature CI, *205*
A87. Zu-LT-52, facing SW over Location 27, *206*

A88. Zu-LT-53, facing north over Location 86, *206*
A89. Zu-LT-62, facing east at Feature AX, *210*
A90. Zu-LT-63, facing south over site area, *210*
A91. Zu-LT-65, facing NW at Feature BB, *211*
A92. Zu-LT-69, facing north at Feature AB, *211*
A93. Zu-LT-69, facing west at Feature AC, *211*
A94. Zu-LT-72, Location 13 area, *212*
A95. Zu-LT-74, facing SW at Feature CN, *214*
A96. Zu-LT-74, stone wall exposed in looter's pit at Feature CN, *214*
A97. Zu-LT-75, facing north over general site area, *215*
A98. Zu-LT-75, facing NW at Feature E, *215*
A99. Zu-LT-76, facing SW at Feature V, *216*
A100. Zu-LT-80, facing NW at Feature A, *217*
A101. Zu-LT-80, rubble fill in looter's pit at Feature A, *218*
A102. Zu-LT-80, facing east at Feature C, *218*
A103. Zu-LT-80, facing east over Location 1, *219*
A104. Zu-LT-82, facing west at Feature CP, *220*
A105. Zu-LT-82, facing north at Feature CQ, *220*
A106. Zu-LT-85, facing east at Feature BE, *221*
A107. Zu-LT-86, facing north over Location 44, *222*
A108. Zu-LT-87, facing SE over general site area, *223*
A109. Zu-LT-87, facing east at Feature BF, *223*
A110. Zu-LT-87, facing SW at Feature BM, *224*
A111. Zu-LT-101, stone wall base on Feature AJ, *226*
A112. Zu-LT-106, facing NW at Feature AS, *227*
A113. Zu-LT-109, facing SE at Feature BB, *228*
A114. Zu-LT-117, facing SE at Feature BD, *230*
A115. Zu-LT-134, facing west at Feature BP, *233*
A116. Zu-LT-135, facing west over general site area, *234*
A117. Zu-LT-135, facing south at Feature EI, *234*
A118. Zu-LT-151, facing SW at Feature DG, *237*
A119. Zu-LT-169, facing north over Location 70, *240*
A120. Zu-LT-174, facing east over Location 74, *242*
A121. Zu-LT-176, facing SE over general site area, *242*
A122. Zu-LT-176, facing NE over Location 76, *242*
A123. Zu-LT-178, facing north over Location 82, *243*
A124. Zu-LT-179/-180/-181/-182/-183, facing SE over Location 79, *244*
A125. Zu-LT-191, facing north over Location 80, *245*
A126. Zu-LT-196, facing west over Location 90, *247*
A127. Zu-LT-203, facing SE over Location 86, *249*
A128. Zu-LT-209, facing SW over Location 51, *250*
A129. Zu-LT-210, facing east over general site area, *251*
A130. Zu-LT-210, facing east at Feature DG, *251*
A131. Zu-LT-211, facing north at Feature EG, *252*
A132. Zu-LT-211, facing east at Feature EH, *253*
A133. Zu-LT-211, heavy sherd cover at Location 81, *253*
A134. Zu-LT-212, facing west over site, *254*
A135. Zu-LT-213, facing SW over site, *255*

A136. Zu-Az-5, facing south over Location 21, *257*
A137. Zu-Az-18, facing SE over Location 12, *260*
A138. Zu-Az-19, facing east at Feature O, *261*
A139. Zu-Az-19, looter's pit in Feature O, *261*
A140. Zu-Az-24, facing NW over Location 3, *262*
A141. Zu-Az-35, facing north over Location 32, *264*
A142. Zu-Az-36, facing north at Feature AQ, *265*
A143. Zu-Az-37, facing NE at Feature AL, *267*
A144. Zu-Az-39, facing west at Feature AR, *267*
A145. Zu-Az-44, facing west at Feature BC, *267*
A146. Zu-Az-44, stone wall exposed in looter's pit at Feature BC, *268*
A147. Zu-Az-47, stucco floor exposed in looter's pit at Feature AE, *269*
A148. Zu-Az-47, stucco floor in plaza area, *270*
A149. Zu-Az-49, facing south at Feature X, with Cerro de la Mesa Grande in background, *271*
A150. Zu-Az-56, example of earth-faced terrace, *272*
A151. Zu-Az-68, facing west over Location 35, *275*
A152. Zu-Az-71, facing NE over Location 9, *276*
A153. Zu-Az-72, facing NE over Location 37-M, *276*
A154. Zu-Az-73, facing north over Location 38, *277*
A155. Zu-Az-78, facing SW at Feature L, *279*
A156. Zu-Az-79, facing south at Feature D, *279*
A157. Zu-Az-80, facing north at Feature A, *280*
A158. Zu-Az-87, facing NW at Feature CM, *282*
A159. Zu-Az-99, facing north at Feature AU, *284*
A160. Zu-Az-103/-104, facing north over general site area, *285*
A161. Zu-Az-103/-104, facing south at Feature DR, *286*
A162. Zu-Az-103/-104, facing SE at Feature DT, *286*
A163. Zu-Az-105, facing north at Feature DQ, *286*
A164. Zu-Az-115, facing west over Location 51, *289*
A165. Zu-Az-115, example of Aztec II B/O sherd, *289*
A166. Zu-Az-116, facing west over Location 52, *289*
A167. Zu-Az-130/-131, facing SW over general site area, *293*
A168. Zu-Az-130/-131, facing west at Feature AK, *293*
A169. Zu-Az-130/-131, Feature AM, *295*
A170. Zu-Az-138, facing NW at Feature CL, *295*
A171. Zu-Az-155, facing SE at Feature AW, *297*
A172. Zu-Az-155, stone wall base at Feature AW, *298*
A173. Zu-Az-155, surface collecting in progress at Location 28, *299*
A174. Zu-Az-157, facing SW at Feature BA, *299*
A175. Zu-Az-157, wall base at Feature BA, *300*
A176. Zu-Az-169, facing east over general site area, *301*
A177. Zu-Az-169, facing north at Feature DA, *301*
A178. Zu-Az-172, facing west over general site area, *302*
A179. Zu-Az-172, facing south at Feature CS, *303*
A180. Zu-Az-172, facing south at Features CU (foreground) and CV (background), *303*
A181. Zu-Az-172, pitted surface of Feature CV, *304*
A182. Zu-Az-196, facing north at Feature DB, *307*
A183. Zu-Az-204, facing south at Feature DF, *309*

A184. Zu-Az-214, facing east over general site area, *311*
A185. Zu-Az-224, facing west at Feature DI, *313*
A186. Zu-Az-236, facing north over general site area, *315*
A187. Zu-Az-237, facing west at Feature DL, *317*
A188. Zu-Az-237, plastered surfaces at Feature DL, *317*
A189. Zu-Az-249, facing NE over site area, *319*
A190. Zu-Az-249, facing north over Location 49, *319*
A191. Zu-Az-253, facing north over general site area at edge of Lake Zumpango, *320*
A192. Zu-Az-259/-260, facing SE over general site area, *321*
A193. Zu-Az-259/-260, facing SE over Location 94, *322*
A194. Zu-Az-274, facing south at Feature DU, *325*
A195. Zu-Az-275, surface at Feature DV, *325*
A196. Zu-Az-276, facing south over part of Xaltocán Island, from adjacent lakebed, *327*
A197. Zu-Az-276, facing NE at modern Xaltocán, *327*
A198. Zu-Az-276, facing east across old lakebed east of Xaltocán, *327*
A199. Zu-Az-289, facing north over site area, *329*
A200. Zu-Az-289, facing west at Feature DJ, *330*
A201. Zu-Az-289, looter's pit in Feature DJ, *330*
A202. Zu-Az-298, facing north over site area, *332*
A203. Zu-Az-299, view of Feature DF, *333*
A204. Zu-Az-300, facing north over site, *333*
A205. Zu-Az-302, facing SE at Feature CM, *334*

B1. Tzacualli figurine, *407*
B2. Classic Red/Buff bowl, *407*
B3. Classic Red/Buff bowls, *408*
B4. Classic Red/Buff bowl, with incised lines, *409*
B5. Classic Monochrome olla, with wide everted rim, *409*
B6. Classic Monochrome olla, with low neck, *409*
B7. Classic Monochrome olla, with rolled rim, *409*
B8. Classic Red/Buff olla, with single red band, *410*
B9. Classic Red/Buff olla with wide red band, *410*
B10. Classic Red/Buff olla, rim with red upper surface, *410*
B11. Classic Rose/Granular, *410*
B12. Classic Thin Orange, *411*
B13. Classic figurines, *412*
B14. Classic candelero, *412*
B15. Early Toltec, low frequency decorated types, *413*
B16. Early Toltec Coyotlatelco Red/Buff, *414*
B17. Late Toltec Monochrome bowl supports, *415*
B18. Late Toltec Monochrome bowl, striated interior base, *416*
B19. Late Toltec Wide-Band Red/Buff bowl supports, *416*
B20. Late Toltec Wide-Band Red/Buff bowl design variants, *417*
B21. Late Toltec Wavy-Line Red/Buff bowl design variants, *418*
B22. Late Toltec Orange/Cream bowls, *420*
B23. Late Toltec Utilitarian basin with scraped exterior, *420*
B24. Late Toltec comal with handle, *420*
B25. Late Toltec Ink-Stamped jar, *421*

B26. Late Toltec Plumbate Ware, *421*
B27. Late Toltec Sillon Incised Orange, *421*
B28. Late Toltec Orange Stamped, *421*
B29. Late Toltec Blanco Llevantado (Tula Watercolored), *422*
B30. Late Toltec figurines, *422*
B31. Colonial glazed pottery, *422*
B32. Aztec II-III Black/Orange bowl/basins, *423*
B33. Aztec III Black/Orange bowl/basin design variants, *424*
B34. Aztec II Black/Orange plates, *425*
B35. Aztec II-III Black/Orange dish/plates, *425*
B36. Aztec III Black/Orange dish/plates, *426*
B37. Aztec II-III Black/Orange molcajete, *426*
B38. Aztec III and IV Black/Orange molcajetes, *427*
B39. Aztec IV(?) Black/Orange molcajete (unique design), *428*
B40. Aztec IV Black/Orange dishes and molcajetes, *428*
B41. Aztec IV Black/Orange slab supports, *429*
B42. Aztec Black/Red bowls with comb design, *430*
B43. Aztec Black/Red bowls with geometric designs, *431*
B44. Aztec Black and White/Red bowls with vertical panels, *432*
B45. Aztec Black and White/Red bowls with triangular panels, *433*
B46. Aztec Black and White/Red bowls with complex designs, *434*
B47. Aztec Yellow/Red bowl, *434*
B48. Aztec Huastec Tradeware, *435*
B49. Aztec Huastec Tradeware with strap handle, *436*
B50. Aztec Texcoco Fabric Marked, *436*
B51. Aztec Texcoco Fabric Marked, whole vessel, *436*
B52. Aztec Chalco-Cholula Polychrome, *437*
B53. Aztec censers, *437*
B54. Aztec censer, *438*
B55. Aztec censer, *438*
B56. Aztec censer, *438*

Preface

This monograph is long overdue. We completed our fieldwork in the Zumpango Region in December 1973, and over the next few years we tabulated much of the data, prepared some maps and figures, wrote the first drafts of the final site descriptions, and then filed everything away as we became involved in other tasks. Some general highlights of the Zumpango Region survey data have already been considered in at least three earlier syntheses (Parsons 1974; Wolf 1976; Sanders et al. 1979), and the data themselves have been published in outline form (Parsons et al. 1983). Over the past three decades the Zumpango Region, along with much of the entire Valley of Mexico, has changed dramatically: most of the sites described in this monograph have been destroyed by several different forms of the landuse intensification, and much of the landscape itself has been radically altered in physical appearance. Contemporary occupation in and around the survey area changed from something like a traditional peasant society to something very different—a kind of post-industrial suburb at the edge of one of the world's largest urban megapolises.

I finally returned to full-time work on this monograph at the time of my retirement from the University of Michigan in 2006. Getting back to this material has been a bit like time-traveling as I dusted off the old file folders and maps, revised the site descriptions, retabulated much of the site data, and scanned the old black-and-white survey negatives into a digital format and reprinted them as memory aids. Because I had been away from the surface collections for so long, I returned twice to our storage facility in Mexico in order to reexamine the surface pottery: the first time, in 1996, when Robert Cobean helped me better understand the Late Toltec assemblage, and a second time in 2007 when I went back over all our Zumpango Region surface collections and photographed many of the decorated sherds. Gradually most of it came back to me as I reworked my way through all these materials.

The main purpose of, and justification for, this monograph is to provide a description of the Zumpango Region survey data that is sufficiently detailed to serve as a basic data source for future study—obviously this is something that should have happened years ago, but "better late than never." Because it is often difficult to anticipate the needs of future scholars, I have opted to err on the side of presenting too much, rather than too little, information. Because so many of the sites described in this monograph have been destroyed and the landscapes so radically altered, I have included a large number of photographs in order to give the reader a reasonable sense of what we encountered in the field in 1973. This seems additionally justified in view of the fact that so many of these sites can never be revisited and restudied in the future.

Acknowledgments

The general strategy for systematic archaeological regional survey in the Valley of Mexico was initially conceived and implemented by the late William T. Sanders in the Teotihuacan Valley in 1960. The Zumpango Region survey was a direct outgrowth of Sanders' pioneering antecedent work, and his inspiration and encouragement over the years have played a major role in bringing this monograph to fruition.

Our field headquarters in 1973 was at the Posada La Carreta in Ajacuba, Hidalgo, and our landlords/hosts there, Jose Careaga and Acela Benitez de Careaga, went out of their way to make our stay both pleasant and productive. During the time of our fieldwork, several colleagues were working in the nearby Tula Region, and we profited greatly by interaction with them: Richard Diehl, Robert Cobean, Dan Healan, and Guadalupe Mastache. In later years we also benefited greatly by discussions about matters of mutual interest in and around the Zumpango Region with Elizabeth Brumfiel, Thomas Charlton, Charles Frederick, Raul García, Kenneth Hirth, Leah Minc, Deborah Nichols, Teresa Rojas, Mari Carmen Serra, and Yoko Sugiura.

Our 1973 fieldwork was funded by a major grant from the National Science Foundation (Grant GS-31911), with additional funding from the University of Michigan Museum of Anthropology (then directed by the late James B. Griffin, who provided his own particular brand of encouragement and support). We are grateful to the students who assisted us so capably in our fieldwork in 1973: Cheryl Barris, Terence D'Altroy, James Lockhart, Ellen Messer, Naomi Miller, Clemence Overall, Michael Whalen, David Wilson, and Diana Wilson.

Special thanks are due to the late Arquitecto Ignacio Marquina, then Director of the Departamento de Monumentos Prehispanicos, and Arqueólogo Eduardo Matos (then Marquina's assistant), for the courtesies they extended in granting permits for our fieldwork. We also thank the numerous municipial authorities throughout the Zumpango Region who formally sanctioned our surveys, and the many local people who were typically so hospitable and understanding as we walked over their fields for six months.

In 1987 we spent several days revisiting the Zumpango Region and evaluating the condition of the landscape and archaeological sites. This was made possible by the help and encouragement of Dra. Mari Carmen Serra, at that time Director of the Insituto de Investigaciones Antropológicas, Universidad Nacional Autónoma de México, who provided us with a vehicle and the opportunity to participate in a field seminar with several UNAM and ENAH students. It was at that time that we began to be more aware of the rapidly deteriorating condition of the archaeological record in the Zumpango Region and throughout the Valley of Mexico.

In the early 1990s, the late Mary Hodge and Leah Minc helped us reorganize our numerous surface collections from the Zumpango Region and other parts of the Valley of Mexico. This helped pave the way for Bob Cobean's restudy of the Late Toltec components of our Zumpango Region collections in 1996.

Finally, we are very grateful to Kay Clahassey for her expertise and skill in preparing many of the figures in this monograph; to Larry Gorenflo for his generous help in putting together many of the maps included in Chapter 5 and elsewhere in this monograph; to Naomi Miller for her marvelous drawings included in Chapter 4; to Jill Rheinheimer for her care and diligence in editing the manuscript; and to Apphia H. Parsons for her help with the translations.

Chapter 1

Introduction

The Zumpango Region is situated in the far northwestern corner of the Valley of Mexico on the southern edge of the Mexican *Mesa Central* (Figs. 1.1–1.3). It lies between the northern edge of the Mexico City megapolis and the southeastern borders of the adjacent Tula Region (Fig. 1.4). This long-delayed publication is the penultimate of the monographs that have presented data collected during the regional surveys in the Valley of Mexico during the 1960s and 1970s.[1] It seems appropriate to consider how our research design developed during that period and with the considerable benefit of hindsight, offer a critique of its strengths and weaknesses.

Overall Scope and Objectives

As the heartland of several major prehispanic urban civilizations, the Valley of Mexico has been an ideal natural laboratory for systematic regional archaeology that studies the development of preindustrial complex society. Survey archaeologists wanted to provide a regional perspective on major ancient urban centers in central Mexico—Teotihuacan in particular, but also Tula, Tenochtitlan, Cuicuilco, Cholula, Xochicalco, and others. They wanted to estimate population, define administrative hierarchies, and better understand land use, craft production, and exchange in their regional contexts, and they strove to understand the ecological basis for cultural development (e.g., Sanders 1956, 1957, 1962, 1968, 1972; Palerm and Wolf 1961).

In the 1960s and 1970s, the surficial archaeological record in the Valley of Mexico was nearly ideal for systematic regional surface survey: high visibility, with limited natural vegetation in a semiarid and intensively cultivated landscape where frequent plowing with shallow, horse-drawn implements annually produced a rich harvest of potsherds and other archaeological remains at the ground surface. Because modern road building and construction projects were underway throughout the region (albeit on a much smaller scale than later), new exposures of long buried archaeological artifacts and architecture were often available for inspection along many ditches and road cuts.

The First Valley of Mexico Conference, 1960

The first conference devoted to planning long-term archaeological research in the Valley of Mexico was held in 1960. The conference chairman (Eric R. Wolf) drew up a list of thirteen specific research objectives (tabulated in Parsons 1971:1):

1) Changes in the natural and man-made environment of the Valley of Mexico over time and the possible correlation of these changes with cultural factors.
2) The antiquity, development, and relative importance of major and minor patterns of land use over time.
3) The characteristics of settlement in the Valley and changes in settlement patterns over time and related population problems.
4) The nature of relationships between hamlets, villages, towns, cities, and similar units at various periods including a discussion of relations between specific sites.
5) Problems of urbanization.

---

[1] The last monograph, *Prehispanic Settlement Patterns in the Temascalapa Region, Mexico*, by L. Gorenflo and W. Sanders, will appear shortly in the Pennsylvania State University series.

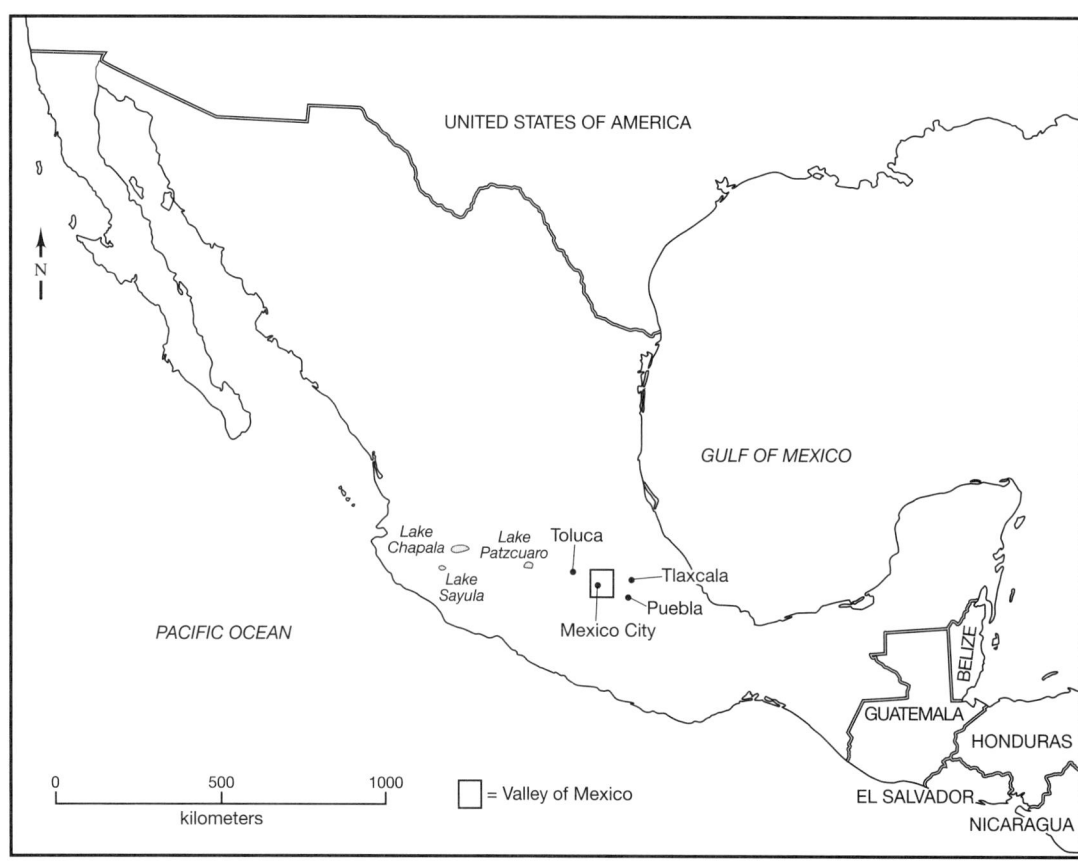

Figure 1.1. Mesoamerica.

6) The characteristics of symbiotic regions in the Valley in various periods of time and their social consequences.

7) The relevance of environment to agriculture and settlement patterns, and to the problems of social control at various levels.

8) Patterns of ceremonial control at various time levels.

9) Patterns of political control at various time levels.

10) Patterns of warfare in the prehispanic period.

11) Effects of the Spanish conquest and colonization on social and cultural groups in the Valley of Mexico.

12) Cultural persistence or change in major patterns throughout all known time periods within the Valley.

13) Causal or functional relationships between various cultural patterns at different time periods.

With these objectives in mind, William Sanders and Rene Millon initiated their complementary studies of the Teotihuacan Valley in 1960: Sanders directed his attention to the regional level, while Millon focused on urban Teotihuacan.

Working Out the Survey Methodology, 1960–1964

In the early 1960s, the systematic study of regional settlement patterns was still a radical new approach in archaeology. William Sanders was one of the few doing it.[2] He had the overall strategy clearly in mind, but the field tactics were still to be worked out. When I joined his project in 1961, I became involved in some of the early efforts to devise a field survey methodology to produce the data we required.

As a newcomer to archaeology in 1961, I had no idea that I was intersecting with research both radical and innovative. I had just graduated from Penn State with a B.S. degree in geology. In the summer of 1960, I had worked with one of my professors, Robert Scholten, on his geological mapping project in the Rocky Mountains of southwestern Montana and adjacent Idaho (Scholten and Ramspott 1968; Parsons 2002). Based on my experience in Montana and Idaho, regional mapping of surface features

---

[2] Robert M. Adams (1961) was carrying out comparable fieldwork at the same time in Chiapas, southeastern Mexico.

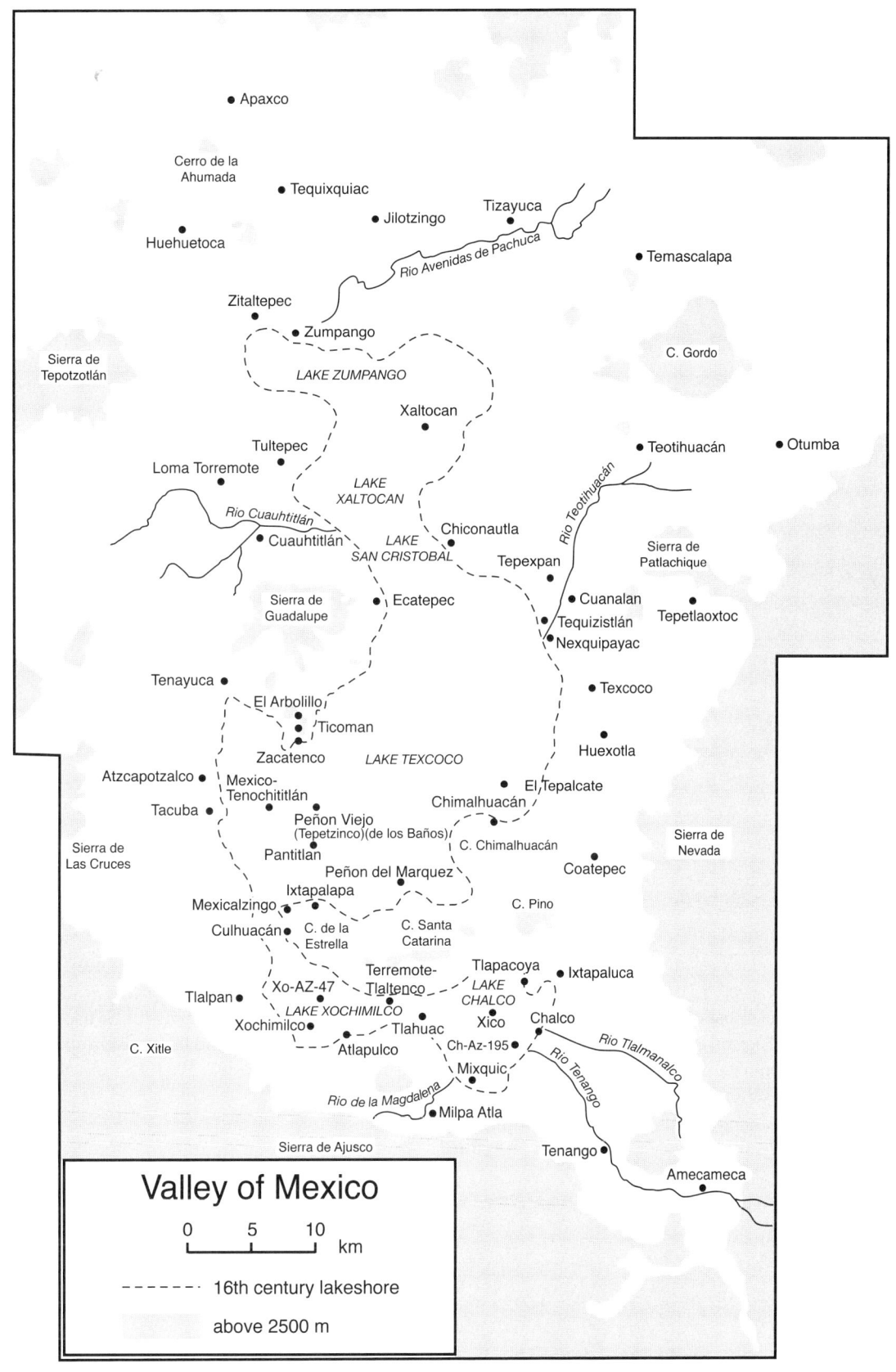

Figure 1.2. The Valley of Mexico, showing principal towns.

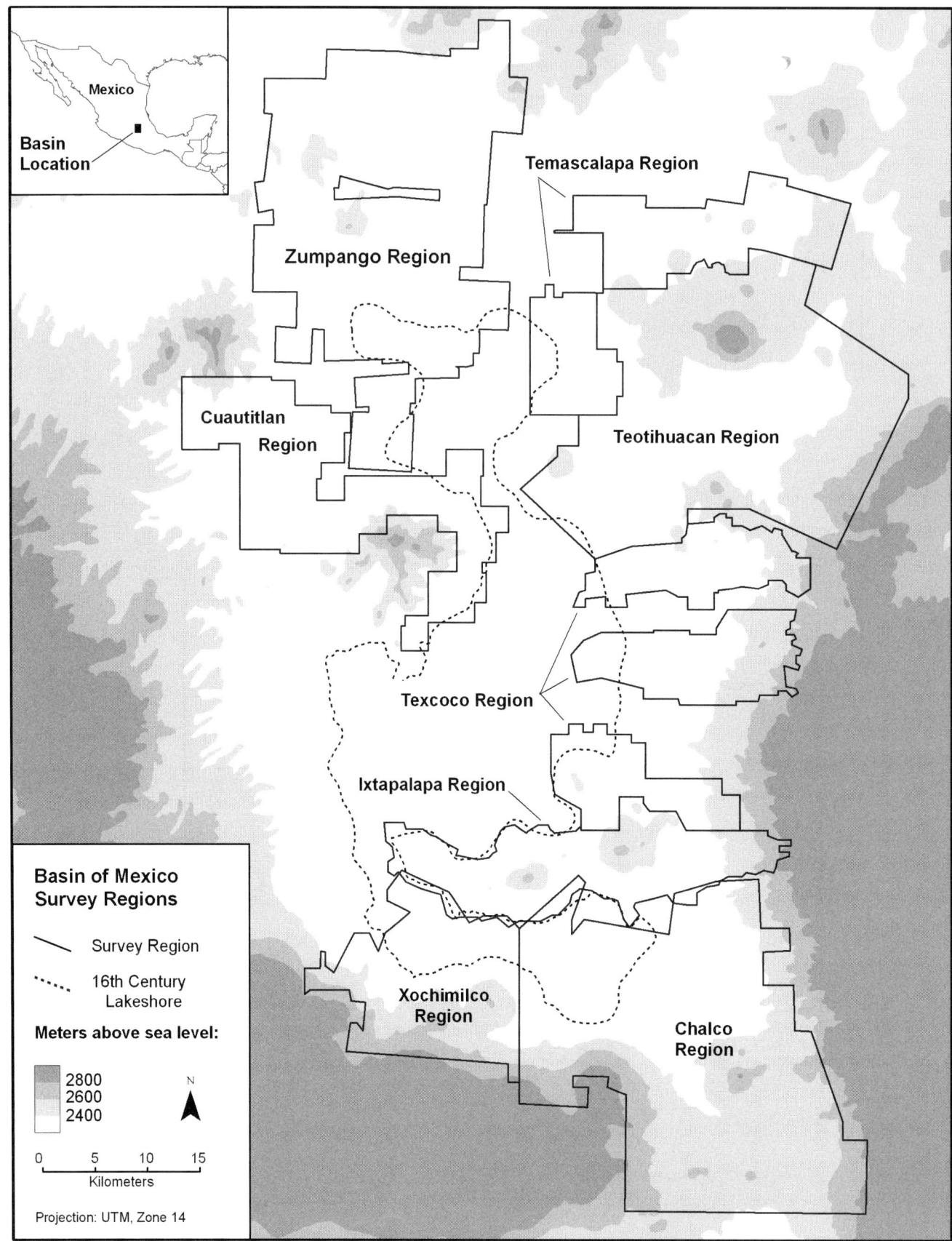

Figure 1.3. The Valley of Mexico, showing the Zumpango Region and other surveyed regions.

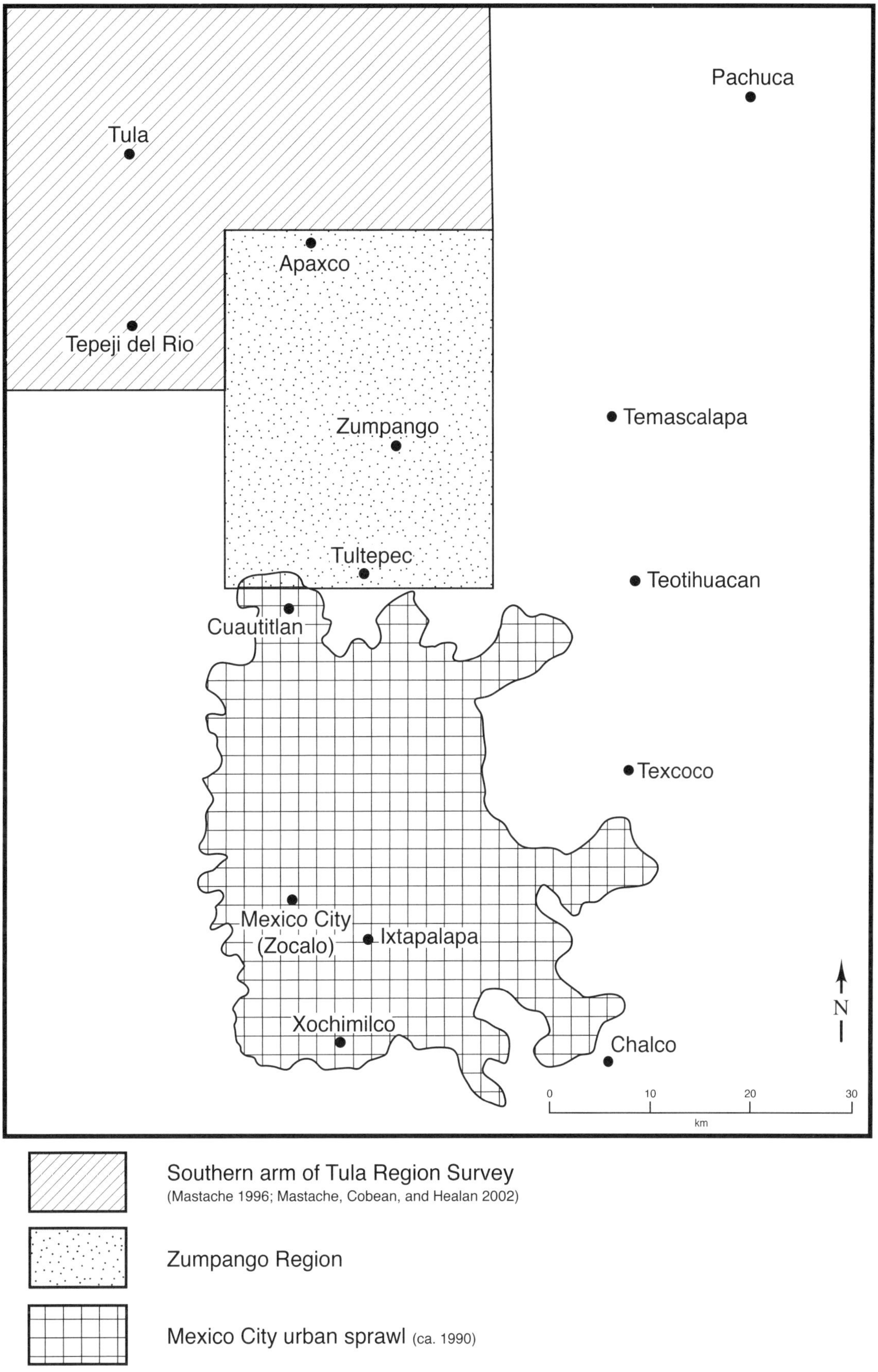

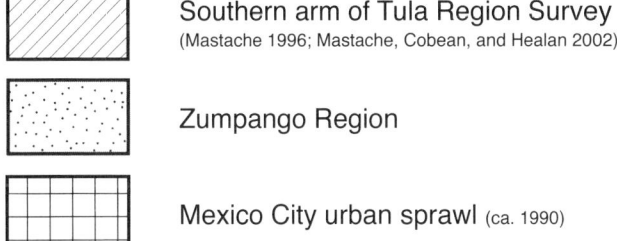

Figure 1.4. The Zumpango Region, showing its position between greater Mexico City and the Tula Region.

seemed natural and normal to me: walking systematically over the landscape, with airphotos as guides and base maps, plotting the distribution of surface features in order to develop ideas about long-term change. In 1960, it was surficial geological features and ideas about geological dynamics in the northern Rockies (or, as Rob Scholten used to put it, trying to figure out "what made the mountains"); in 1961 and subsequently, it was surficial archaeological remains and long-term ancient cultural change in central Mexico. Once I adjusted to looking for potsherds and mounds instead of rock formations and their weathered products, regional geological mapping and regional archaeological survey seemed methodologically much the same to me.

By 1963, we had developed the essentials of an effective regional survey methodology. Much as a field geologist maps rock formations on the ground surface and infers the underlying structural forces that produced them on the basis of their spatial configuration, we worked out procedures for walking systematically over the landscape, using airphotos for guidance and for plotting the distributions of precolumbian surface pottery, the mounded remnants of architecture, canals, terraces, and other ancient features. We inferred relative chronology from the different pottery types we encountered where ancient houses and public buildings had once stood. Once the distributions of these material remains had been discerned and plotted on base maps, we could develop hypotheses about long-term cultural change on the basis of changing regional settlement patterns.

Right from the start we attempted to do what is now often called "full coverage" survey; it never occurred to us to do anything else. This was, of course, some years before the concept of regional sampling began to be developed in archaeological regional studies, and we were not part of that effort after it did begin in the later 1960s (Parsons 1972, 1990, 2004).

A Critique

The surveys accomplished a great deal, but, at the same time, failed in some ways to realize their potential. In this section I highlight my notion of these strengths and weaknesses.

Strengths

Defining the "big picture"

Because the surveys were full-coverage and systematic, they detected where sites were and where they were not over large, contiguous blocks of terrain. Because surface pottery (and in many cases rock rubble) densities could be recorded with some accuracy, site areas could be determined and credible (albeit rough) population estimates made. We could measure inter-site distances and spatially relate specific sites to each other and to different kinds of environmental features. Because remnants of public architecture were usually detectable on the ground surface in the form of relatively high and large mounds, it was possible to make reasonable inferences about the relative sociopolitical importance of different sites based on the differential distribution of ceremonial-civic structures. Site hierarchies, using site area and volume of public architecture as proxies, could be generated and used to develop hypotheses about sociopolitical organization.

Because the spatial relationships could be established between human occupation and different kinds of natural resources (agricultural, hydraulic, forest, lacustrine, and mineral), reasonable hypotheses could be developed about land and resource use. Because occupation gaps could be discerned, absences of settlement could be used to help develop ideas about natural and cultural factors that may have discouraged the establishment of permanent habitations. Because different periods of time could be compared on the basis of the same variables, it was possible to develop important hypotheses about long-term changes in all these parameters.

In other words, the surveys provided an excellent vision of the "big picture" and generated a whole series of important new questions and hypotheses that might be evaluated and tested by future research. Compare, for example, the archaeological empirical richness of the post-survey synthesis by Sanders et al. (1979) with overviews of comparable scope written at a time before these survey data were available (e.g., Vaillant 1941).

Use of survey data by other scholars

Because the survey data were robust, they could provide the empirical foundation for follow-up studies by scholars who developed and evaluated hypotheses often completely unrelated to the objectives of the original surveyors themselves. Examples of such studies include Brumfiel (1976), Earle (1976), Parsons (1976), Alden (1979), Steponaitis (1981), and Gorenflo (2006). Similarly, years later, the original surveyors could reflect on their old data in light of new ideas and information from the Valley of Mexico and elsewhere (e.g., Parsons 2006b).

Use of curated collections in new research

The curated surface collections accumulated during the surveys have provided the empirical basis for several important analytical studies over the past thirty-five years. Examples include M. Parsons' (1972a, 1972b, 1975) study of the spatial distributions of different kinds of spindle whorls; the typological, neutron activation, and spatial studies of Aztec ceramics undertaken by Mary Hodge and Leah Minc (Hodge and Minc 1990; Hodge et al. 1993; Minc 1994, 1999; Minc et al. 1994); Christopher Garraty's (2006) study of the spatial variability of Aztec ceramics; Destiny Crider et al.'s (2007) on-going study of the spatial variability of Epiclassic and Early Postclassic ceramics; and the continuing efforts of Larry Gorenflo and Kenneth Hirth to compile large-scale, computerized databases that can eventually be shared and used by scholars to develop and test new hypotheses (e.g., Smith 2002).

Research design of new field projects

The survey data have also been important in the design and implementation of several subsequent field investigations in the

Valley of Mexico. These include Deborah Nichols' (1980, 1982, 1987) studies of Formative agricultural intensification; Paul Tolstoy's excavations and syntheses of Early and Middle Formative occupation in the southern Valley of Mexico (Tolstoy 1975; Tolstoy and Fish 1975; Tolstoy et al. 1977); Elizabeth Brumfiel's (1976a) refined surficial study of Aztec Huexotla; Robert Santley's (1977) excavations at the Formative Loma Torremote site on the shore of Lake Xaltocán; Parsons et al.'s (1985) excavations of chinampa-related sites in Lake Chalco-Xochimilco; Susan Evans' (1988) excavations of the Aztec community at Cihuatecpan; Mari Carmen Serra's (1988) excavations at the Formative Terremote-Tlaltenco site in Lake Xochimilco, and her subsequent excavations at the Formative Temamatla site on the southeastern shore of Lake Chalco (Ramírez et al. 2000); Maria Castillo's (1994) and Carlos Lazcano's (1995) excavations (under the direction of Mari Carmen Serra) of chinampa-related sites in western Lake Xochimilco; the Instituto Nacional de Antropología e Historia (INAH) excavations at the Xo-Az-46 and Xo-Az-47 chinampa sites in Lake Xochimilco undertaken in 1988 (Gonzalez 1988; Corona 1996) and 1993 (Ávila 1995); Charles Frederick's geoarchaeological studies of landscape change and chinampa development in the southeastern Valley of Mexico (Frederick 2007); and Nadia Vélez's (2007) comprehensive study of rural Classic-period settlement in the Valley of Mexico.

Some Thoughts On What We Might Have Done Differently

Starting in the opposite corner of the Valley of Mexico: The Cuicuilco Region

The decision to begin systematic regional survey in the Teotihuacan Valley was made primarily because of Sanders' great interest at that time in developing a regional context for urban Teotihuacan, and because of the obvious complementarity between Sanders' regional study and Millon's focus on urban Teotihuacan itself. In retrospect, however, it has become clear to us that we should have initiated the regional surveys in the opposite, southwestern corner of the Valley of Mexico in what we might then have called the Cuicuilco Region. This is because in the early 1960s, this latter region was still relatively uncovered by the urban sprawl that overwhelmed it only a few years later, long before a similar fate had overtaken the Teotihuacan Valley and other parts of the eastern Valley of Mexico.

The Cuicuilco Region definitely had survey potential in the early 1960s. In 1956, for example, Eric Wolf and Angel Palerm had located what appeared to be ancient canals that seemed to extend beneath the lava overlying Cuicuilco (Wolf and Palerm 1956; Palerm 1961). Inspired by Wolf and Palerm's study, in 1962 Charles Kolb and I attempted a weekend survey of the Cuicuilco site and its surroundings, working with airphotos to locate areas that remained uncovered by the Xitle lava flow (there were many such places, and some contained archaeological surface remains). We commuted laboriously back and forth from Teotihuacan on public transport for a couple of weekends until we gave it up because of the sheer logistical difficulties. A full-scale regional survey in the southwestern Valley of Mexico in the early 1960s would certainly have produced a large amount of important regional information that is now simply unavailable. Comparable efforts could have also been made in the western Valley of Mexico, beginning just north of what was then the northern edge of Mexico City in the vicinity of Tenayuca—another area that soon afterwards disappeared under dense urban sprawl, much earlier than did the eastern Valley of Mexico.

Going beyond our emphasis on chronology and ceramics

Early on we concluded that we could deal effectively with some issues (e.g., population estimation, site size, occupational chronology, architectural complexity), but less well with others (e.g., intra-site variability, site function, production, exchange, cosmology). Consequently, we soon abandoned any systematic effort to collect surface data that might provide a basis for studying activity areas, social or economic variability, or ritual practices. Rather, we focused almost entirely on occupational chronology, and employed intuitive grab sampling of surface pottery as the best means to control this key variable. We also committed ourselves to defining the "big picture," opting to maximize extensive areal coverage at the expense of more intensive surface collection and test excavations within sites. Because we believed them to be chronologically undiagnostic, we paid little attention to lithics, thereby missing a great deal of potential insight into function.

I suspect that we should have sacrificed some areal coverage to do more in-depth work at a few carefully selected sites so as to refine chronology and illuminate site function and intra-site variability. Such a strategy could have provided us with a better understanding of what our settlement patterning meant (that is, a better definition of settlement systems), and may have given us a basis for devising new survey techniques to deal with emerging questions.

In retrospect, we should have done this simply because so many of the sites that warranted more intensive study have now disappeared due to the overall intensification of modern land use (mechanized agriculture [land leveling and deep plowing], reforestation and land reclamation [chisel plowing and terrace building with bulldozers], urban sprawl, and so on). Due to our limited ability to specify function, our settlement-site typology, based as it is on only a few variables, remains imprecise and essentially untested; unfortunately, this typology *is still too often accepted much less critically than it ought to be*. In particular, I suspect that many (most?) of the sites in our "Small Hamlet" category are not permanent settlements at all, but probably represent intermittently occupied localities where a much more narrow range of activities were carried out.

Obviously, beginning in the mid-1970s, when there were still a lot of intact sites and landscapes in the Valley of Mexico, we should have initiated a series of follow-up field studies aimed at answering the kinds of questions I have just posed. A few such studies were carried out at that time (e.g., Brumfiel 1976a), but why didn't we do a lot more of this? A major factor was that the principal investigators in the Valley of Mexico surveys (Sanders, Blanton, and Parsons) were attracted to other research areas at exactly this period: Sanders to the Maya region, Blanton to the Valley of Oaxaca, and Parsons to the Peruvian Andes.

Sanders returned to the Valley of Mexico in the early 1980s for excavations at Tlajinga in the southern part of urban Teotihuacan. A decade later, Sanders hoped to develop a new field project at Aztec Tepetlaoxtoc (Tx-Az-24) to complement Barbara Williams' and Herbert Harvey's (Harvey 1985; Williams 1991, 1994; Williams and Harvey 1997) ethnohistorical research. But, alas!, by that time the Tepetlaoxtoc archaeological site had been so degraded by urban sprawl, mechanized agriculture, and land reclamation that it was no longer possible to undertake systematic research (Sanders 1997).

I returned to the Valley of Mexico in the early 1980s for excavations in the chinampa area, but due to administrative commitments at the University of Michigan, found it impossible to direct any sustained archaeological field research. I turned to ethnographic studies—less demanding in terms of time and funding commitments—and became so interested in these investigations that I continued them into the early 1990s. By that time, most of the archaeological sites that had interested me had disappeared.

Getting more geoarchaeological input

Our implicit assumption throughout the surveys was that archaeological materials on the ground surface adequately reflect the underlying subsurface remains. Although we occasionally questioned this assumption, it was never adequately tested, particularly within the deep alluvial soil at the juncture of the lower piedmont and the lakeshore plain where there is a major break-of-slope and where alluvial deposits are most likely to have covered archaeological remains. Surveys have detected archaeological sites in such settings, some of them substantial, but without a fuller understanding of their geomorphological context, their significance remains unclear. Full-fledged geoarchaeological studies are the only way out of this conundrum. Although small beginnings have been made in studies by Charles Frederick (Frederick et al. 2005) and Carlos Córdova (1997; Córdova and Parsons 1997), these promising investigations represent only a bare beginning of what is needed.

Figuring out how to deal with the invisible Archaic (preceramic) and the unaddressed problem of the Archaic-Formative transition

Our survey methodology was incapable of dealing with preceramic remains in any meaningful way. Consequently, the regional surveys have made virtually no contribution to the definition of occupation during the millennia prior to about 1000 B.C. Consequently, we still have little idea of how or why hunter-gatherer populations began living in sedentary settlements focused on agriculture and using pottery. At the regional level, we still understand very little about the nature of hunter-gatherer lifeways during any time period (both Archaic and post-Archaic). The Early and Middle Formative in the Valley of Mexico can never be fully understood until regionally oriented fieldwork can be directed at the underlying Archaic and Archaic-Formative transition. Similarly, the economies of Formative and post-Formative periods will remain inadequately described until we are able to better discern (at the regional level) their nonagricultural components (hunters, fishers, collectors, saltmakers, miners, foresters, and so on).

The Organization of this Monograph

Chapter 2 provides a geographic description of the Zumpango Region, with emphasis on landforms and climate, and gives a general overview of paleoenvironmental change to the limited extent that available information permits. Chapter 3 considers the historic-period occupation of the survey area, beginning with twentieth-century census data and settlement maps, and summarizing demographic and settlement data from earlier centuries as far back as the sixteenth-century descriptions recorded by Spanish administrators. Chapter 4 details our survey methodology, and in Chapter 5 we consider the implications of our settlement data for long-term cultural development in and around the Zumpango Region. Chapter 6 presents some thoughts on future research needs, and Chapter 7 provides a brief Spanish-language summary of our main conclusions. The archaeological sites are described in detail in Appendix A, and Appendix B describes the highlights of our ceramic chronology.

No authorship is specifically indicated for those chapters authored exclusively by myself. The co-authors of other chapters and appendices are identified under the initial chapter headings. Unless otherwise specified, references to past and present time are relative to our 1973 fieldwork.

Chapter 2

The Natural Environment

The Zumpango Region in the Valley of Mexico

The Valley of Mexico is a large internal-drainage basin that measures about 8000 square kilometers in surface area (around 110 km north-to-south by 80 km east-to-west). It is one of several internal-drainage basins that occur within the central Mexican volcanic axis, or *Mesa Central* (Fig. 2.1). Lacking natural external drainage, the Valley of Mexico forms a great natural saucer, rimmed by higher ground that surrounds a central depression. Artificial drainage begun in the early seventeenth century was not completed for over 300 years (Garay 1888; Gurría 1978; Lemoine 1978; Ramirez 1976). In earlier centuries, rainfall on the surrounding slopes and plains drained into the lowest part of the basin to form a series of interconnected shallow lakes and marshes: from north to south, Lake Zumpango, Lake Xaltocán, Lake San Cristobal, Lake Texcoco, Lake Xochimilco, and Lake Chalco (Fig. 1.2). Of these, Lake Texcoco, with its bed at slightly below 2235 m asl, was the lowest. The bed of Lake Zumpango was some 6 m elevated, while the floors of Lakes San Cristobal and Xaltocán were about 3.5 m higher; to the south, the bottoms of Lakes Chalco and Xochimilco were about 3 m above the bed of Lake Texcoco (Beltran 1958:14-15). Lake Texcoco, at the bottom of the drainage gradient, was saline; Lakes Zumpango, Xaltocán, and San Cristobal were fresh to brackish, while Lakes Chalco and Xochimilco were freshwater, in part due to the abundance of springs along their southern margins.

Based on his study of sixteenth-century documentary sources, Gardiner (1956:59) estimated that at the time of initial Spanish contact in 1519, the entire lake surface (Lake Texcoco plus the northern and southern lakes) covered some 442 square miles (approximately 1132 km^2), about 20% of the entire Valley of Mexico basin area below the encircling mountain slopes and ridges. A surface area of about 1000 km^2 is commonly used by modern authors (e.g., García Sanchez 1998:37).

The Zumpango Region is at the far northwestern corner of the Valley of Mexico (Figs. 1.2, 1.3). Hydrographically, the northern half of the Zumpango Region as we have defined it is actually outside the drainage limits of the Basin of Mexico, overlapping into the upper drainage of the Río Salado, a tributary of the Río Tula that ultimately drains into the Gulf of Mexico (Fig. 2.2). Thus, although the Zumpango Region is usually considered to be part of long-term cultural development within the Valley of Mexico, approximately half of our archaeological survey area lies outside the hydrographic Basin of Mexico, just north of the drainage divide between the Basin and the neighboring Mezquital region (sometimes referred to as the Tula Region). Throughout this monograph I use "Valley of Mexico" when discussing cultural phenomena while reserving "Basin of Mexico" for more strictly environmental, and especially hydrographic, contexts.

The borders of the Zumpango Region survey area are more arbitrary than most other survey regions within the Valley of Mexico. Unlike previously surveyed regions farther south (Teotihuacan, Texcoco, Ixtapalapa, Chalco, Xochimilco, and Cuautitlan), the Zumpango Region lacks well-defined mountain ranges, or subranges, along most of its perimeter; such ranges occur only along parts of the western survey border. On the north and northeast there are only low, discontinuous hill ranges (principally the Cerro Buenavista massif on the north, and the Cerro Aranda massif on the northeast) that provide some semblance of a topographic border. On the east and south our survey limits were completely arbitrary, defined only by the distances over which we were able to extend our surveys across the broad piedmont, lakeshore, and lakebed plains in the time available to us.

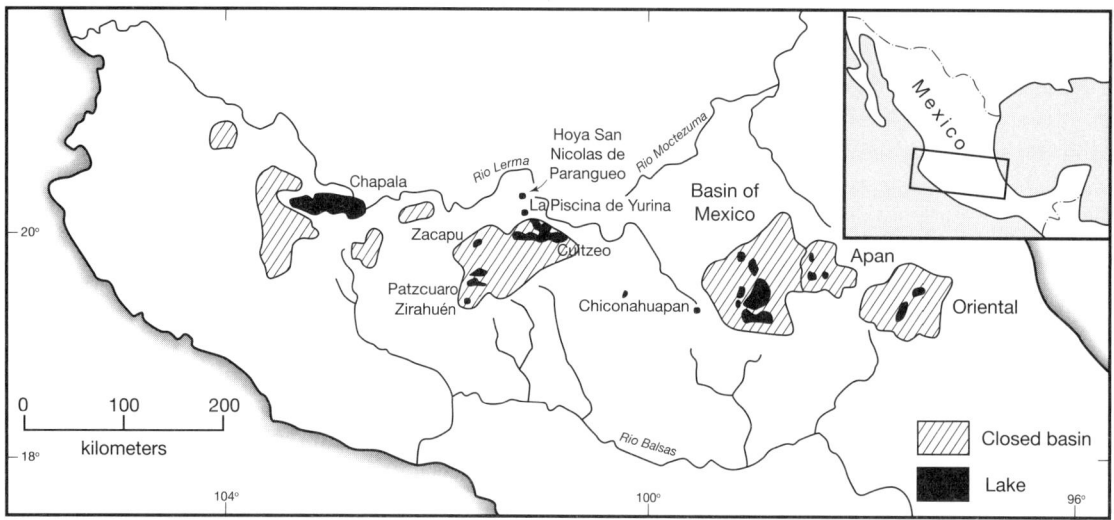

Figure 2.1. Internal drainage basins in the Mexican *Mesa Central* (adapted from Metcalfe et al. 1989:21).

Environmental Zones in the Zumpango Region

We define four major zones within our survey area (Fig. 2.3): (1) the Upper Salado Drainage (USD) (ca. 2200–2275/2400 m asl), north of the drainage divide between the Mezquital and the Basin of Mexico (BOM); (2) the Basin of Mexico Lower Piedmont (BOMLP) (ca. 2270–2400 m asl), south of the drainage divide and north of the Lakeshore Plain; (3) the Lakeshore Plain (LP) (ca. 2245–2270 m asl) in the BOM drainage; and (4) the Lakebed (LB) (below ca. 2245 m asl) in the BOM drainage. The USD and BOMLP are both extensively and severely eroded, with large patches of bare tepetate (subsoil), and with soil depths exceeding 50 cm only along the floodplains of the two main waterways (the Río Salado and Río Pachuca; see below). The Lakeshore Plain and Lakebed zones, by contrast, have deep soil cover (usually at least 1 m, but sometimes much deeper), where soil alluviation may have obscured some archaeological remains.

Recent geoarchaeological studies (Frederick et al. 2005) have revealed the presence of two ancient beach ridges and one extensive strand plain along the northern border of Lake Xaltocán (Fig. 2.4). Their "high beach ridge" stands at 10 to 16 m above the present level of the lakebed, and their "low beach ridge" is approximately 2 to 3 m higher than the lakebed surface. The ages of the beaches are uncertain, but the higher, older feature is believed to date to the last lacustrine highstand of 32,000 to 35,000 years B.P., while the younger beach appears to be several thousand years old. Lying between these beach ridges is an extensive ancient "strand plain," whose undulating surface is elevated about 5 to 6 m above the lakebed. As will be seen in Chapter 5, most of our prehispanic near-lake settlements occupy these ancient elevated surfaces along the northern shore of Lake Xaltocán.

There are two large hill massifs (Cerro de Mesa Grande [CMG], ca. 2400–2555 m asl; Cerro Jalpa [CJ], ca. 2400–2650 m asl) inside the survey area, and three massifs that partially border the area on the west (Cerro Colorado [CC], ca. 2400–2650 m asl) and on the northeast (Cerro Buenavista [CB], ca. 2350–2460 m asl; Cerro Aranda [CA], ca. 2400–2700 m asl). A large natural island, Cerro Tultepec (TI) (attaining a maximum elevation of about 80 m above the level of the surrounding Lakebed), lies near the far southern limit of our survey, and a small, artificial island (Xaltocán, attaining a maximum elevation of about 5 m above the level of the surrounding Lakebed) lies just beyond the southeastern edge of the survey area.

Table 2.1 gives the area of each environmental zone in the Zumpango Region. In this table, the small sections of Cerro Colorado and Cerro Aranda that fall within our survey area are included in the Upper Salado Drainage zone, and Xaltocán Island is included within the Lakebed zone.

Two permanent streams—much modified from their original aspect—flow through parts of our survey area: the Río Salado in the northwest and the Río Pachuca (formally Avenidas de Pachuca) in the east. The Río Salado drains northwestward into the Río Tula, and most of its volume is now composed of treated sewage (*agua negra*) that enters the riverbed from two large, underground tunnels running beneath the drainage divide that drains northward from Mexico City through the Gran Canal de Desagüe and the Canal de Costura (Fig. 2.2). The Río Pachuca formerly drained southwestward into what used to be Lake Zumpango, but now disappears into a massive underground drainage tunnel at the modern town of Zumpango, and from there flows to the north and into the Río Salado. Prior to the early seventeenth century, another permanent river, the Río Cuautitlán, also entered Lake Zumpango from the southwest, but for some four centuries this

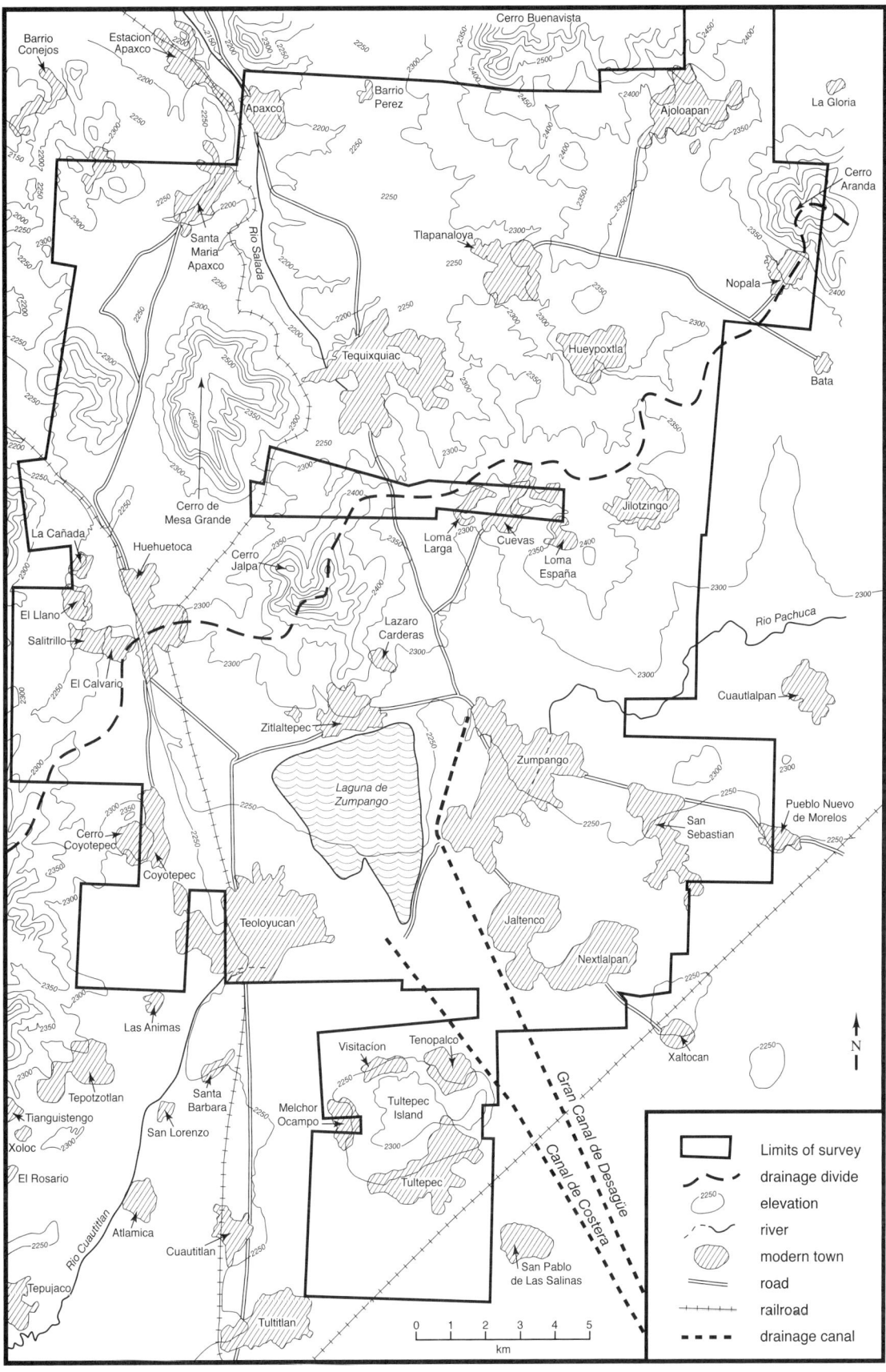

Figure 2.2. The Zupango Region, showing survey borders and modern cultural features.

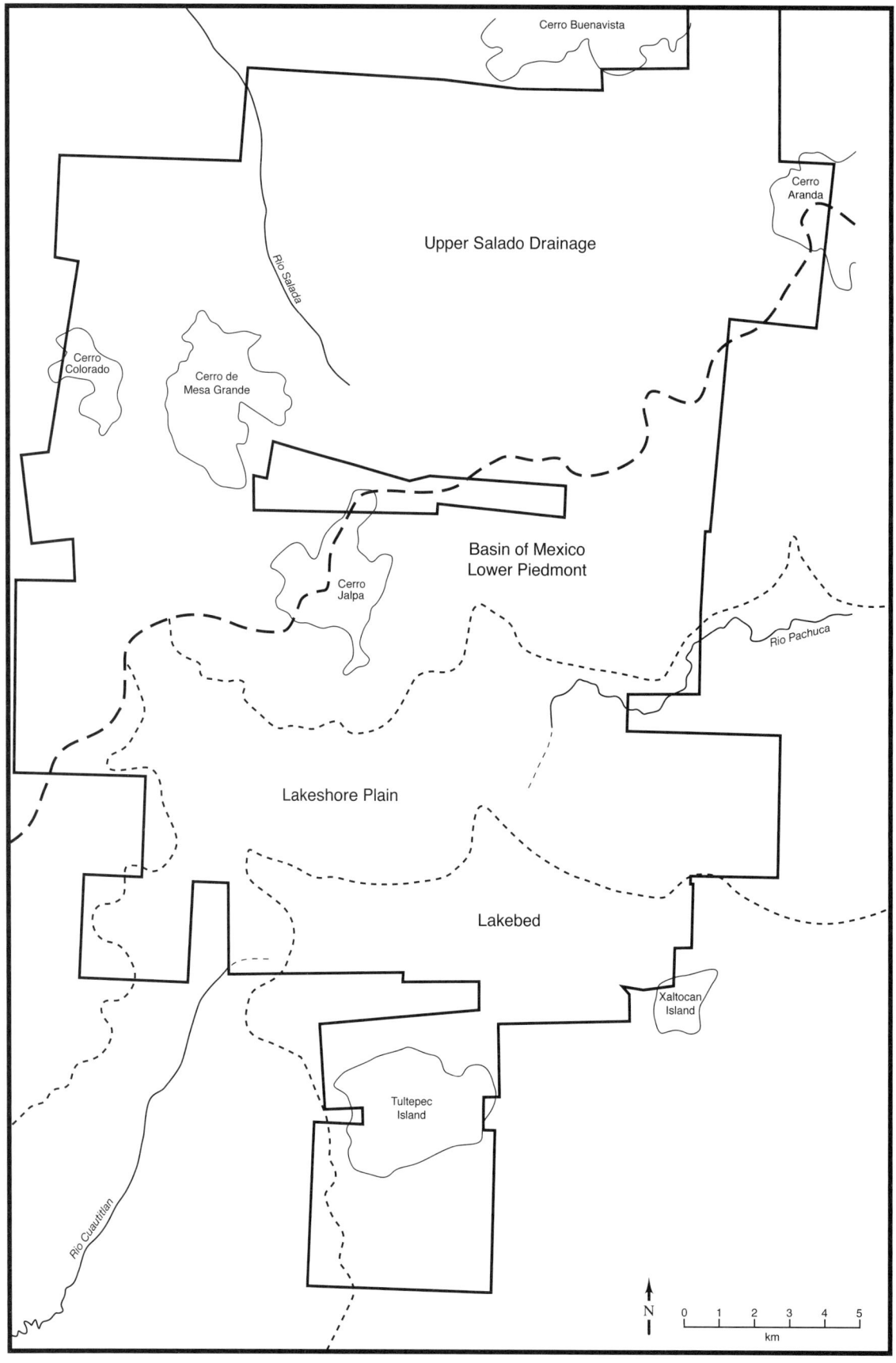

Figure 2.3. Environmental zones in the Zumpango Region.

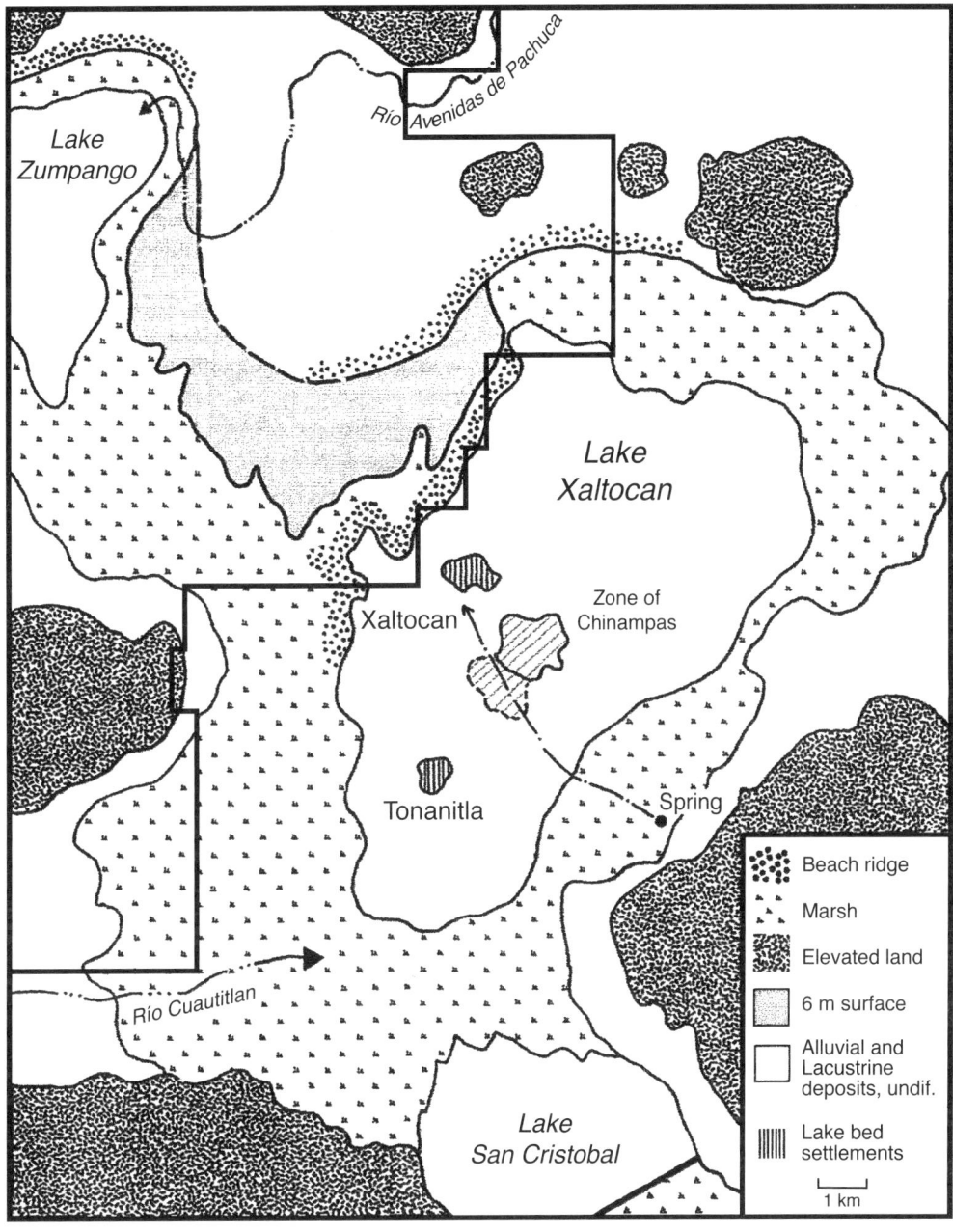

Figure 2.4. Geomorphic elevated zones (ancient beach ridges and strand plain) along the north shore of Lake Xaltocán-Zumpango (adapted from Frederick et al. 2005:75, Fig. 3.2).

Table 2.1. Environmental zones in the Zumpango Region.

Zone	Area (km²)	Percent of Total Zumpango Region
Upper Salado Drainage (USD)	288.06	47.3
Cerro de Mesa Grande (CMG)	10.96	1.8
Cerro Jalpa (CJ)	9.74	1.6
Basin of Mexico Lower Piedmont (BOMLP)	101.70	16.7
Lakeshore Plain (LP)	115.71	19.0
Lakebed (LB)	70.04	11.5
Tultepec Island (TI)	12.79	2.1

waterway, one of the largest in the entire Basin of Mexico, has been diverted northward through canals and tunnels out of the BOM drainage (Rojas et al. 1974).

The processes of erosion and alluviation have operated very differently in the environmental zones we have defined. In Chapter 3, I will discuss some of the highlights of Melville's (1994) archival study that details the extreme environmental degradation that occurred over much of the Zumpango Region during 1530 to 1610—a compelling demonstration that the modern scene differs environmentally and ecologically in many important ways from conditions that prevailed during the late prehispanic period. In 1973, despite severe gully and sheet erosion over much of the USD and BOMLP, most of these two zones, together with the Lakeshore Plain and Tultepec Island, were devoted to rainfall-based agriculture (maize, beans, barley, and alfalfa the principal crops, with many stands of maguey and nopal, usually along field borders). In some cases, complex terrace systems that capture runoff during the rainy season have been devised for cultivating crops along seasonal waterways (*barrancas*) (Plates 2.1, 2.2). Irrigation agriculture was much more limited, restricted mainly to low-lying fields along the Río Salado (using mainly *agua negra*) and Río Pachuca. Higher ground in the hill massifs was used primarily for pasturing sheep, goats, and a few cattle; these domestic animals also grazed extensively in fallow fields and along canals, ditches, and field borders.

As a result of massive modern drainage projects over the past century, the northern Lakebed zone is now also devoted to rainfall-based agriculture, with some irrigation cultivation. The more saline southern Lakebed is less useful for agriculture, and in 1973 was devoted to pasture for domestic animals, with some stretches of wasteland to the southeast and beyond Xaltocán. In prehispanic times, of course, the entire Lakebed, and much of the lower Lakeshore Plain as well, would have been marshland and open water, with some seasonal and long-term variability (as discussed in Chap. 3). Such wetland conditions also prevailed in far more ancient times, as indicated by our discovery of a mammoth skull that had been unearthed some years previously by workers in a modern sand quarry along the former lakeshore near the modern village of San Sebastian (Plate 2.3) (not formally designated by us as an archaeological site).

Modern and Historic Climate in the Zumpango Region

The modern climate of the Valley of Mexico features a highly seasonal distribution of rainfall and temperature. The fundamental division is between a four-month rainy season (June through September) and an eight-month dry season (October through May). Roughly 80% of the average annual rainfall of 600 to 1000 mm falls during the rainy season months; cloud cover is significantly greater during this period as well. The oldest rainfall data I have found are from A.D. 1855 to 1875: during that period, the average annual rainfall (at an unspecified measuring station, probably in or near Mexico City) was 603 mm, with a low of 355 mm in 1860 and a high of 924 mm in 1865 (Reyes 1878).

As seen in Figure 2.5, average annual rainfall within the Valley of Mexico increases from lower to higher elevation and from north to south. Today in the Zumpango Region, average annual rainfall varies between 600 and 700 mm, the western half being somewhat drier than the eastern sector (Secretaria de Programación y Presupuesto 1981). This is comparable to rainfall in the entire northern half of the Valley of Mexico; south of about Texcoco in the east-central Valley, rainfall increases notably, attaining an annual average of approximately 1000 mm in the far south and southeast.

In the Valley of Mexico, there is little variation in average *maximum* daily or monthly temperatures over the entire annual cycle. However, the average *minimum* temperatures are decidedly lower from November through March than during the rest of the year (e.g., Parsons 1971:6-7). There is also a great deal of variability in the onset of the summer rainy season (normally late May or early June, but occasionally delayed until mid-June), the first killing frosts in the fall (usually early November, but occasionally as early as mid-October), and the last frosts in early spring (usually March, but occasionally well into April or even later). There is also great variability in the amount of annual rainfall. This combined uncertainty in rainfall and frost means that rainfall-based agriculture is fraught with uncertainty, especially in the drier northern half of the Valley of Mexico, and, most especially, in the drier western half of the Zumpango Region. The availability, either naturally or through artificial means (for example, canal irrigation, swamp drainage), of naturally existing moisture suitable for cultivation would always have had high priority (e.g., Sanders 1957; Palerm 1973; Rojas et al. 1974; Feldman 1974).

Meteorological data reported between 1906 and 1938 from stations in and around the Zumpango Region (see Table 2.2, which lists the environmental zones of the reporting meteorological stations) provide details about the generalizations noted above (Tables 2.3–2.18). I have also noted the number of days per month with recorded frosts for those stations providing such

Plate 2.1. Maize field created by stone check dam in *barranca*, in a severely eroded section of the Upper Salado Drainage.

Plate 2.2. Maize fields created by stone check dams in *barranca*, in a severely eroded section of the Upper Salado Drainage.

Plate 2.3. Mammoth skull from modern sand quarry near ancient shoreline of Lake Zumpango.

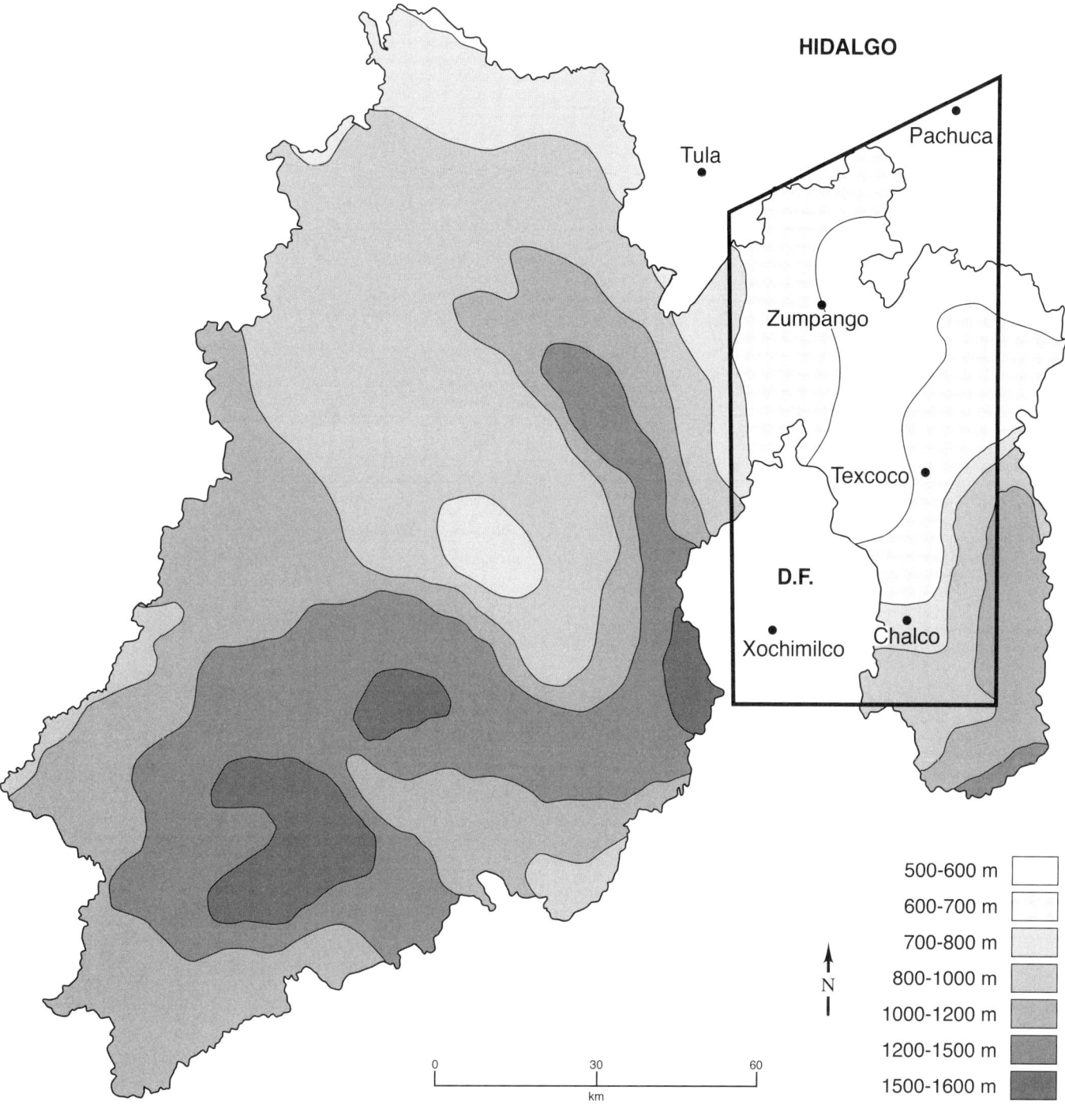

Figure 2.5. Rainfall isohyets of average annual rainfall (mm) in the Valley of Mexico (adapted from Secretaria de Programación y Presupuesto 1981). The Valley of Mexico is outlined.

Table 2.2. Environmental zones of meteorological stations.

Inside Zumpango Region			Outside Zumpango Region		
Upper Salado Drainage	*Lakeshore Plain*	*Lakebed*	*Basin of Mexico Lower Piedmont*	*Lakeshore Plain*	*Mezquital*
Apaxco	Zumpango	Teoloyucan	Pachuca	Cuautitlan	Tula
Tequixquiac			Tizayuca		
Hueypoxtla			Tepotzotlan		
Huehuetoca					

Table 2.3. Average monthly rainfall (in mm) for Zumpango and Tula, 1906–1910.

Month	Station	
	Zumpango	*Tula*
January	0.5	3.8
February	17.5	15.1
March	13.6	4.6
April	30.6	54.6
May	71.3	104.1
June	80.6	89.9
July	119.1	70.3
August	125.2	108.9
September	101.7	52.9
October	27.7	44.8
November	7.8	9.6
December	5.0	9.9
Total	*600.6*	*568.5*

(Compiled from Servicio Meteorológico Mexicano, 1924)

Table 2.4. Average monthly rainfall (in mm) for Pachuca, Tizayuca, and Teoloyucan, 1921–1925.

Month	Station		
	Pachuca	*Tizayuca*	*Teoloyucan*
January	2.9	14.2	1.0
February	17.7	20.9	15.4
March	21.3	36.8	13.3
April	28.2	20.6	25.2
May	33.1	37.9	47.4
June	100.8	125.9	149.8
July	56.3	105.2	121.2
August	46.3	67.9	95.4
September	81.1	120.6	135.6
October	62.0	50.1	45.1
November	25.5	27.4	19.3
December	8.1	15.1	8.1
Total	*642.6*	*642.6*	*676.2*

(Compiled from Servicio Meteorológico Mexicano, 1925)

Table 2.5. Total annual rainfall (in mm) for Teoloyucan, Pachuca, Tizayuca, Tula, Hueypoxtla, and Huehuetoca.

Station	Year									
	1919	*1920*	*1921*	*1923*	*1928*	*1929*	*1930*	*1931*	*1932*	*1936*
Teoloyucan	646.0	653.8	505.1	609.8	558.2	543.6	755.8	811.5		734.3
Pachuca			371.9	490.2	468.8					301.9
Tizayuca			422.7		491.5	476.0	603.0	560.0		
Tula					630.0			848.4	660.3	661.1
Hueypoxtla						604.8	579.5	811.5		
Huehuetoca									611.1	627.2

(Compiled from Servicio Meteorológico Mexicano)

Table 2.6. Monthly rainfall (in mm) for Pachuca, 1921–1938.

Month	Year									
	1921	*1923*	*1928*	*1929*	*1930*	*1931*	*1933*	*1936*	*1937*	*1938*
January	0.0	no data	no data	14.0	3.0	16.4 11 days*	0.5 11 days*	3.0 16 days*	no data	0.0 19 days*
February	3.7	no data	no data	0.0	no data	0.0 6 days*	14.3 1 day*	10.8 8 days*	no data	11.0 15 days*
March	20.0	no data	32.5	0.0	0.0	2.2 2 days*	3.7	1.7 2 days*	no data	2.9 3 days*
April	29.0	no data	7.5	2.0	19.0	18.5 1 day*	no data	18.9 3 days*	26.5 2 days*	12.3 2 days*
May	1.3	no data	45.5	45.5	49.5	38.5	no data	28.4	87.7	46.7
June	15.3	no data	35.5	49.0	80.0	43.3	no data	4.8	31.8	96.1
July	63.3	44.3	89.0	49.4	45.0	82.7	87.5	45.2	61.1	no data
August	64.0	29.9	45.0	40.5	41.7	46.8	146.1	129.1	52.9	no data
September	81.5	13.3	101.5	105.5	16.9	130.5	108.2	52.8	23.0	no data
October	52.3	61.1	18.3	2.0	179.0	no data	21.4 7 days*	2.4 4 days*	no data	no data
November	33.0	24.4	52.5	no data	11.2	5.7 12 days*	8.7 14 days*	4.8 4 days*	no data	no data
December	8.5	0.0	1.0	15.0	0.0	4.2 14 days*	0.0 11 days*	0.0 10 days*	no data	no data
Total	*371.9*	*inc.*	*inc.*	*inc.*	*inc.*	*inc.*	*inc.*	*301.9*	*inc.*	*inc.*

(Compiled from Servicio Meteorológico Mexicano)
*Number of days with frost.

Table 2.7. Monthly rainfall (in mm) for Tizayuca, 1921–1931.

Month	Year						
	1921	*1922*	*1923*	*1928*	*1929*	*1930*	*1931*
January	0.0	no data	no data	no data	0.0	5.5	no data
February	0.0	no data	no data	no data	0.0	no data	0.0 20 days*
March	10.5	no data	no data	no data	0.0	0.0	0.0 20 days*
April	14.0	no data	12.0	no data	0.0	36.0	11.5 3 days*
May	0.0	no data	14.4	no data	63.0	95.6	41.0
June	85.2	92.5	146.8	31.5	75.5	143.5	66.0
July	131.3	no data	103.1	89.0	152.0	77.0	148.0
August	62.6	76.6	70.5	63.0	92.0	78.0	146.0
September	55.7	153.8	51.5	138.5	35.0	39.5	108.5
October	35.2	36.2	72.0	30.5	0.0	91.5	no data
November	28.2	47.8	38.0	23.0	no data	12.5	0.0 11 days*
December	0.0	11.7	0.0	0.0	21.0	0.0	24.0 15 days*
Total	422.7	*inc.*	*inc.*	*inc.*	*inc.*	*inc.*	*inc.*

(Compiled from Servicio Meteorológico Mexicano)
*Number of days with frost.

Table 2.8. Monthly rainfall (in mm) for Tula, 1928–1938.

Month	Year							
	1928	*1929*	*1930*	*1931*	*1933*	*1936*	*1937*	*1938*
January	no data	0.0	7.5	35.6 15 days*	0.0 11 days*	12.3 10 days*	no data	0.0 18 days*
February	no data	0.0	no data	0.0 9 days*	5.5 9 days*	0.03 3 days*	no data	12.2 6 days*
March	no data	0.0	0.0	0.0 11 days*	27.5 6 days*	17.7	no data	1.5
April	no data	1.5	52.3	24.5 1 day*	no data	15.7	26.8	66.2
May	no data	96.8	70.4	88.0	no data	44.3	63.0	39.6
June	66.0	25.0	167.5	127.2	no data	16.2	72.3	110.2
July	164.5	no data	71.7	221.1	153.0	280.7	142.6	no data
August	71.0	no data	165.5	157.0	187.5	96.4	70.9	no data
September	129.0	131.0	no data	137.7	190.5	135.7	122.8	no data
October	50.0	9.0	167.2	no data	13.6 4 days*	29.9	no data	no data
November	31.0	no data	19.9	0.0 13 days*	18.0 14 days*	17.2 2 days*	no data	no data
December	0.0	0.0	0.4	25.8 20 days*	1.5 28 days*	0.0 7 days*	no data	no data
Total	*inc.*	*inc.*	*inc.*	*inc.*	*inc.*	666.1	*inc.*	*inc.*

(Compiled from Servicio Meteorológico Mexicano)
*Number of days with frost.

Table 2.9. Monthly rainfall (in mm) for Apaxco, 1928–1930.

Month	Year		
	1928	*1929*	*1930*
January	no data	5.4	8.0
February	no data	0.0	no data
March	6.0	0.0	0.0
April	15.1	no data	11.0
May	34.6	no data	107.5
June	62.7	no data	127.9
July	226.2	no data	136.4
August	37.4	no data	no data
September	94.6	82.2	no data
October	4.0	0.0	no data
November	63.9	no data	no data
December	0.0	0.0	no data

(Compiled from Servicio Meteorológico Mexicano)

Table 2.10. Monthly rainfall (in mm) for Cuautitlan, 1928–1930.

Month	Year		
	1928	*1929*	*1930*
January	no data	8.0	8.0
February	no data	0.0	no data
March	14.0	no data	no data
April	7.5	no data	no data
May	88.0	no data	no data
June	45.0	no data	no data
July	115.0	no data	187.5
August	94.5	no data	no data
September	125.0	114.5	24.7
October	27.0	0.0	152.3
November	41.0	no data	6.0
December	0.0	no data	no data

(Compiled from Servicio Meteorológico Mexicano)

Table 2.11. Monthly rainfall (in mm) for Huehuetoca, 1929–1938.

Month	Year					
	1929	*1930*	*1931*	*1936*	*1937*	*1938*
January	8.8	0.0	no data	3.3 10 days*	no data	0.0 23 days*
February	no data	no data	no data	3.6 16 days*	no data	20.3 7 days*
March	no data	0.0	0.0 13 days*	0.0 22 days*	no data	16.6 2 days*
April	no data	47.2	2.5	17.9 1 day*	20.3	61.1
May	40.5	120.9	42.5	74.3 2 days*	144.7	82.1 1 day*
June	no data	147.0	130.0	15.2	104.2	107.5
July	155.7	162.1	216.0	175.1	no data	no data
August	144.1	115.8	94.0	119.1	143.4	no data
September	90.3	57.9	32.3	139.1	164.0	no data
October	7.3	140.5	no data	57.0 1 day*	no data	no data
November	no data	no data	0.0 8 days*	21.3 3 days*	no data	no data
December	7.8	2.0	no data	1.3 29 days*	no data	no data
Total	*inc.*	*inc.*	*inc.*	*627.2*	*inc.*	*inc.*

(Compiled from Servicio Meteorológico Mexicano)
*Number of days with frost.

Table 2.12. Monthly rainfall (in mm) for Hueypoxtla, 1928–1936.

Month	Year					
	1928	*1929*	*1930*	*1931*	*1933*	*1936*
January	no data	10.5	0.0	0.0 13 days*	0.0 31 days*	no data
February	no data	0.0	no data	0.0 12 days*	6.5 25 days*	0.0 29 days*
March	34.2	0.0	0.0	no data	22.5 27 days*	2.0 22 days*
April	34.5	5.5	2.0	no data	no data	17.0 7 days*
May	71.5	69.7	101.0	23.8	no data	64.0 3 days*
June	54.0	82.9	138.5	73.6	no data	0.0 3 days*
July	123.3	189.9	63.0	162.5	49.5	110.2
August	54.1	129.7	74.0	50.3 3 days*	157.5	no data
September	148.2	44.5	27.5	no data	82.0	no data
October	11.5	18.5	144.5	no data	67.5 7 days*	no data
November	34.5	no data	5.0	no data	13.0 18 days*	no data
December	0.0	9.6	3.0	7.2 13 days*	0.0 31 days*	no data

(Compiled from Servicio Meteorológico Mexicano)
*Number of days with frost.

Table 2.13. Monthly rainfall (in mm) for Teoloyucan, 1919–1938.

Month	1919	1920	1921	1922	1923	1928	1929	1930	1931	1933	1936	1938
January	91.2	10.2	0.0	0.0	0.0	no data	0.5	6.5	no data	0.0 17 days*	13.2 16 days*	no data
February	0.2	0.0	0.0	no data	26.7	no data	0.0	no data	6.2 14 days*	5.7 13 days*	5.7 no data	13.0 18 days*
March	4.2	0.0	13.2	22.4	4.5	no data	0.0	0.0	0.0 7 days*	26.5 7 days*	5.0	0.0 18 days*
April	13.1	0.0	28.8	no data	21.9	no data	2.5	31.4	10.0 9 days*	no data	25.2	20.2 1 day*
May	5.4	113.5	12.8	no data	33.2	43.9	47.7	94.6	91.5	no data	62.0 1 day*	48.0 2 days*
June	111.8	158.2	111.2	124.2	221.6	28.9	64.7	153.2	149.2	no data	16.7	94.5 1 day*
July	165.1	126.0	108.4	no data	104.2	111.0	135.9	206.7	216.5	69.4	179.5	no data
August	48.5	118.5	94.3	66.3	93.5	74.5	142.7	136.5	145.5	176.0	209.0	no data
September	91.7	51.5	68.7	152.3	55.3	143.3	86.2	29.7	144.2	87.0	128.6	no data
October	61.0	11.0	35.3	13.7	40.2	38.2	0.0	83.7	no data	20.5 4 days*	70.9 1 day*	no data
November	47.3	21.7	25.9	17.2	8.7	48.2	no data	2.0	6.2 12 days*	1.5 11 days*	10.5 3 days*	no data
December	6.5	43.2	6.5	3.2	0.0	0.0	16.7	0.0	27.2 14 days*	10.2 27 days*	8.0 14 days*	no data
Total	646.0	653.8	505.1	inc.	609.8	inc.	inc.	inc.	inc.	inc.	734.3	inc.

(Compiled from Servicio Meteorológico Mexicano)
*Number of days with frost.

data (Tables 2.6–2.8, 2.11–2.15). These data were compiled by the Servicio Meteorológico Mexicano and published in their annual *Boletín*.

Although they are not fully complete, I have utilized these records for two reasons: (1) they were readily accessible to me at the University of Michigan library (where earlier and later data were not available), and (2) they were collected from a period of time that should be sufficiently long enough to provide insight into general patterns of temperature and rainfall behavior within our study area during the first third of the twentieth century—a time prior to the massive industrialization and urbanization that has occurred over the past half century, and that may better reflect earlier climatic conditions than would more recent data.

As incomplete as they are, the data on rainfall and frost days (Tables 2.3–2.16) clearly illustrate several important dimensions of twentieth-century climate within the Zumpango Region and immediately around its borders:

(1) The months between November and March consistently have many days with frost. Like the rest of the Valley of Mexico and adjacent parts of the Mexican *Mesa Central*, this means there is only one growing season for seed-based annual crops (maize, amaranth, beans, squash, and so on).

(2) There is considerable (and unpredictable) rainfall variability at individual measuring stations, both in terms of total precipitation from one year to the next, and in the amount of rainfall within the same month in successive years. This unpredictable variability is especially critical for the planting season (April–June) when some years show rainfall well below average (Table 2.17).

(3) Although the months between November and March consistently have many days with frost, individual measuring

Table 2.14. Monthly rainfall (in mm) for Tepotzotlan, 1929–1938.

Month	Year						
	1929	*1930*	*1931*	*1933*	*1936*	*1937*	*1938*
January	no data	1.5	9.1 14 days*	0.0 18 days*	3.2 24 days*	no data	no data
February	no data	no data	0.0 13 days*	0.0 14 days*	0.0 20 days*	no data	15.6 19 days*
March	no data	0.0	0.0 7 days	13.1 9 days*	0.0 4 days*	no data	5.6 14 days*
April	no data	30.2	6.7 28 days*	no data	no data	18.6 1 day	62.3 4 days*
May	61.8	87.7	112.0	no data	no data	141.4	70.3 4 days*
June	no data	176.6	174.2	no data	5.6	159.6	91.7 4 days*
July	180.3	168.5	189.2	46.4	66.3	240.1	no data
August	136.1	92.0	181.7	217.7	78.0	145.9	no data
September	150.9	56.8	83.3	112.5	54.8	156.6	no data
October	2.0	55.4	no data	29.8 4 days*	35.0 1 day*	no data	no data
November	no data	2.9	3.8 8 days*	0.0 13 days*	6.3 2 days*	no data	no data
December	13.0	0.0	9.4 13 days*	1.5 24 days*	0.0 22 days*	no data	no data

(Compiled from Servicio Meteorológico Mexicano)
*Number of days with frost.

stations indicate considerable variability in the number of days with frost during the critical months of April through June (planting season) and October (late growing season). Frosts have even been reported in June and August, the heart of the annual growing season for seed-based crops (Table 2.18).

(4) As noted above, this unpredictability in the timing of both rainfall and frost creates major problems for rainfall-based cultivation of annual crops that must be seeded early enough each year so they mature before the onset of fall frosts. We might expect that this stress would stimulate innovation in artificial water control (drainage and canal irrigation) and the development of cultigens (like maguey) that are more resistant to drought and frost than are annual seed crops. The relative importance of artificial water control may have been even greater in the Zumpango Region and elsewhere in the relatively drier northern Valley of Mexico than in the comparatively more humid central and southern sectors.

Paleoclimatological Studies

It is more difficult to assess climate in prehispanic time although Bradbury's (1989:75) study of diatoms indicates that the historic lake levels were established roughly 5000 years ago, following an interval of widespread volcanic ash eruption (also Bradbury 2000; Caballero et al. 1999; Lozano-García and Xelhuantzi-López 1997; Niederberger 1976:253; Watts and Bradbury 1982:56; Frederick et al. 2005). While still far from definitive, several more recent studies across central and western Mexico of ancient lacustrine deposits, pollen, ostracods, diatoms, and oxygen isotope ratios have all pointed to a relatively more arid period beginning after about 1000 A.D. and extending well into the eighteenth century (Berres 2000; Bridgewater et al. 1999; Caballero and Ortega 1998; Davies et al. 2004; Lozano-García et al. 1993; Lozano-García

Table 2.15. Monthly rainfall (in mm) for Tequixquiac, 1928–1938.

Month	Year							
	1928	*1929*	*1930*	*1931*	*1933*	*1936*	*1937*	*1938*
January	no data	no data	no data	18.0 13 days*	0.0 22 days*	7.5 17 days*	no data	no data
February	no data	0.0	no data	0.0 20 days*	11.8 15 days*	1.0 5 days*	no data	11.7 13 days*
March	no data	0.0	0.0	0.0 18 days*	16.2 12 days*	3.5	no data	19.3 4 days*
April	no data	10.5	11.5	19.0 10 days*	no data	21.5	12.7 3 days*	21.0
May	65.8	37.0	149.5	77.5	no data	50.5 2 days*	76.9	67.3 3 days*
June	43.7	93.3	126.6	85.0	no data	13.0 1 day*	113.5	188.7
July	134.7	225.0	146.3	223.7	35.0	269.9	no data	no data
August	58.5	no data	90.0	142.5	182.1	160.3	87.1	no data
September	132.0	no data	42.5	185.5	112.3	125.0	100.7	no data
October	15.5	10.0	131.8	no data	no data	53.7	no data	no data
November	no data	no data	5.0	no data	0.5 10 days*	9.7 4 days*	no data	no data
December	no data	no data	1.5	no data	0.0 25 days*	0.0 15 days*	no data	no data
Total	*inc.*	*inc.*	*inc.*	*inc.*	*inc.*	715.6	*inc.*	*inc.*

(Compiled from Servicio Meteorológico Mexicano)
*Number of days with frost.

Table 2.16. Monthly rainfall (in mm) for Zumpango, 1929 and 1930.

Month	Year	
	1929	*1930*
January	no data	6.7
February	no data	no data
March	no data	0.0
April	no data	18.2
May	28.4	38.9
June	161.9	27.7
July	196.8	23.9
August	105.8	31.0
September	81.7	2.1
October	4.5	no data
November	no data	no data
December	9.0	no data

(Compiled from Servicio Meteorológico Mexicano)

and Ortega-Guerrero 1993, 1994, 1997; Metcalfe et al. 1989, 2000; O'Hara et al. 1994), although some investigators have concluded that the fourteenth through seventeenth centuries were relatively wetter (O'Hara and Metcalfe 1997). These findings accord reasonably well with studies in North America and Europe that indicate a period of significant, long-term drought between approximately A.D. 800 and 1350, commonly referred to as the "Medieval Climatic Anomaly" (Jones et al. 1999). There is also some indication that episodes of intensive volcanism may have produced changes in water levels that were independent of other climatic causes (Lozano-García and Ortega-Guerrero 1998).

Córdova (1997:485–86) provides somewhat more refined paleoclimatic data from several excavations he undertook in the bed of southeastern Lake Texcoco; these data indicate that the Terminal Formative (ca. 250 B.C.–A.D. 100) was a time of falling lake levels, with rising levels during the subsequent Classic and Epiclassic periods (ca. A.D. 100–900), and with falling levels again by A.D. 1100.

Table 2.17. Years with precipitation shortfalls during the annual planting and growing season (May–September).

Station	Years and Months with Unusually Low Reported Rainfall
Pachuca	1921: May, June 1923: July, August 1928: June, August 1929: June, August 1930: August, September 1931: June, August 1936: July 1937: June, July
Tizayuca	1928: June 1929: June 1931: June
Tula	1928: June 1929: June 1936: June 1937: June
Tepotzotlan	1936: June, July, August
Cuautitlan	1928: June
Apaxco	1928: June
Huehuetoca	1936: June
Hueypoxtla	1928: June 1931: June, August 1933: July
Teoloyucan	1928: June 1929: June
Tequixquiac	1928: June, August
Zumpango	1930: June, July, August 1931: September

(Compiled from Servicio Meteorológico Mexicano)

Table 2.18. Reported frosts during April, May, June, and August.

Station	Number of Days with Frost								
	April				May		June		August
	1931	1936	1937	1938	1936	1938	1936	1938	1931
Pachuca	1	3	2	2	-	-	-	-	-
Tizayuca	3	-	-	-	-	-	-	-	-
Tula	1	-	-	-	-	-	-	-	-
Tepotzotlan	28	-	1	4	28	-	-	4	-
Huehuetoca	-	1	-	-	-	1	-	-	-
Hueypoxtla	-	7	-	-	-	7	3	-	3
Teoloyucan	9	-	-	-	9	-	-	1	-
Tequixquiac	10	-	3	-	10	-	1	-	-

(Compiled from Servicio Meteorológico Mexicano)

Aside from external climatic forces, in the densely populated lake basins of central Mexico the anthropogenic component of landscape development and change must always be considered. Some have argued that the increased erosion associated with precolumbian deforestation and agricultural intensification may have played a major role in changing lake levels (Davies et al. 2004; Metcalfe et al. 1989; O'Hara et al. 1993; O'Hara et al. 1994). As noted above, other studies suggest that "catastrophic geological events" (such as volcanic eruptions) probably played a significant role in these processes (Fisher et al. 2003; Israde-Alcántara et al. 2005; Lozano-García and Ortega-Guerrero 1998). The steep decline of the native population after Spanish contact, combined with extensive erosion and deforestation caused by introduced sheep pastoralism, resulted in serious environmental degradation in highland central Mexico after the mid-sixteenth century (Frederick 1995; Melville 1994).

At this point in our overall understanding, the available data imply that lake levels across central Mexico would have been somewhat higher during Middle and Late Formative, and Classic times, than they were in the Terminal Formative, Postclassic, and Early Colonial periods. The Epiclassic (ca. A.D. 650–900) appears to have been an era transitional between relatively wetter and relatively drier conditions. Berres (2000) has recently suggested that lowered lake levels after A.D. 1100 could have produced expanded marshlands and expanded insect collecting, together with intensified fishing and waterfowl hunting (with more efficient seines and large nets replacing earlier reliance on spearing, hooks, lines, and small dip nets).

Lacustrine surface area in the Valley of Mexico is closely related to water depth. On the basis of historical sources, Rojas (1985:2) estimated that throughout the later prehispanic and Colonial periods, average water depth in the lake system as a whole oscillated between 1 and 3 m, with a few pockets where water was as deep as 5 m (northeastern Lake Chalco). The nineteenth-century documentary sources considered in Chapter 3 indicate the complicated interrelationship between water depth and surface area of the lakes and marshes.

Chapter 3

The Historically Documented Occupation of the Zumpango Region: Sixteenth through Twentieth Centuries

Introduction

At the time of our fieldwork in 1973, the Zumpango Region had not yet been completely overwhelmed by urban sprawl, although it was on the verge of it. Most of our survey area was still devoted to agriculture and the grazing of sheep, goats, and some cattle. Agriculture was partly mechanized, but was still mainly carried out with horse-drawn plows and other comparatively traditional forms of technology, much of which had been in place for centuries. Large-scale programs of land reclamation—the construction (using bulldozers) of huge terraces, and extensive reforestation atop these terraces, designed to reduce the serious sheet erosion that over the centuries had so greatly reduced the region's agricultural potential—were then only just beginning. Even though extensive new barrios of dispersed residences had begun to appear around the margins of older, long-established settlements (especially around Apaxco, Huehuetoca, and Cuevas) by the 1950s, most local communities in the Zumpango Region in 1973 were still relatively nucleated settlements, many of which had been originally established as nodes in the Spanish Colonial administrative hierarchy, and some of which had clear (although not always well defined) prehispanic antecedents.

When I revisited the area for several days in 1987, I found that much had changed; in many ways, the region as we knew it in 1973 no longer existed. It is probably fair to say that the 1973 fieldseason fell near the end of one way of life in the Zumpango Region (essentially a variant of peasant society) and the beginning of another (the transition to an industrial, or perhaps even post-industrial, society). This monograph does not attempt to deal with the radical transformations in population size and distribution, and in the very character of the landscape, that occurred after the mid-1970s—transformations that had less to do with local and regional considerations than they did with national and international issues of globalization, population explosion, mega-urbanization, urban and suburban sprawl, and the mechanization and full commercialization of most kinds of production and exchange.

In this chapter, my objective is to trace the main outlines of the historically documented developmental trajectory that led to the settlement system we encountered during our 1973 fieldseason. This effort seems useful in order to better understand the degree to which modern (that is, pre-1980s twentieth century) demography and landuse may (or may not) provide useful analogies for interpreting our prehispanic/prehistoric archaeological data.

The Twentieth Century

In 1973, the Zumpango Region contained some thirty-one comparatively nucleated settlements (pueblos, some of which included detached, dependent barrios), plus a scattering of dispersed agricultural enterprises (ranchos, rancherias, and haciendas) and a few small mining operations (limestone quarries) (Fig. 2.2). Most of the pueblo settlements had been established during the Colonial Period, and all are included in twentieth-century federal census tabulations (Table 3.1). Figure 3.1 indicates how relatively stable these settlements remained between 1900 and 1960.

At the time of our survey, the population densities of these modern settlements ranged between 4.1 and 88.4 people/hectare (Table 3.2). Assuming no significant errors in our measurements of settlement area, this extreme demographic variability

Table 3.1. Modern settlement populations (1900–1960) in the Zumpango Region (not including scattered rancherias, ranchos, and haciendas), listed in approximate north-to-south order, with municipio centers in boldface.

Pueblo	Year					
	1900	*1921*	*1930*	*1940*	*1950*	*1960*
Apaxco, Estacion Apaxco, & Barrio Perez	1746	1181	1591	3078	3718	
Apaxco & Estacion Apaxco						4961
Barrio Perez						240
Sta. Maria Apaxco	-	434	430	809	1009	1316
Tlapanaloya	1134	1009	1198	1397	1599	1881
Ajoloapan	506	1713	2328	2639	2724	3437
Nopala	86	113	416	582	608	2068
Hueypoxtla	955	1116	1022	1253	1236	1265
Tequixquiac	1859	2264	2675	3880	3990	5463
Cuevas	1055	1087	1136	1453	1619	1884
Loma Larga						
Loma España						
Jilotzingo	1152	1291	1517	1479	1953	1941
Huehuetoca	2545	1070	2437	3499	4021	5490
La Cañada						
El Llano						
Salitrillo						
El Calvario						
Zitlaltepec	2027	2367	3115	3821	4453	5680
Lázaro Cárdenas	-	-	-	-	-	318
Zumpango	5942	5405	4484	5583	6539	8371
Coyotepec	2818	2597	3463	4159	4471	5967
Teoloyucan	3619	1015	992	1167	1703[a]	2239
Jaltenco	1270	1186	1203	1464	1727	1965
Nextlalpan	1870	344	1524	1556	1670	2329
San Sebastian	252	515[a]	778	719	841	1002
Xaltocán	288	293	339	353	420	567
Tenopalco	523	470	814	544	501	570
Visitación	655	781	1016	1019	1398	1867
Melchor Ocampo	?[b]	1789	2252	2584	3016	3958
Tultepec	2119	2398	2769	2566	4058	5601
Population totals[c]	*32,421*	*30,438*	*37,499*	*45,604*	*53,274*	*70,380*
Overall population density (people/km²)	*53.2*	*50.0*	*61.6*	*74.9*	*87.5*	*115.6*

(Based on published census figures [México, Dirección General de Estadística, 1901, 1925, 1932, 1943, 1953, 1963]. The 1910 and 1970 censuses did not tabulate figures for individual settlements.)
[a]Census data uncertain. Figure estimated by averaging decade-earlier and decade-later census figures.
[b]Melchor Ocampo is not listed in the 1900 census. If it appears under another name (unknown to us), the 1900 population figure should be revised slightly upward.
[c]Figures should probably be increased by 10% to account for population in scattered barrios, rancherias, ranchos, and haciendas that is not included in these tabulations.

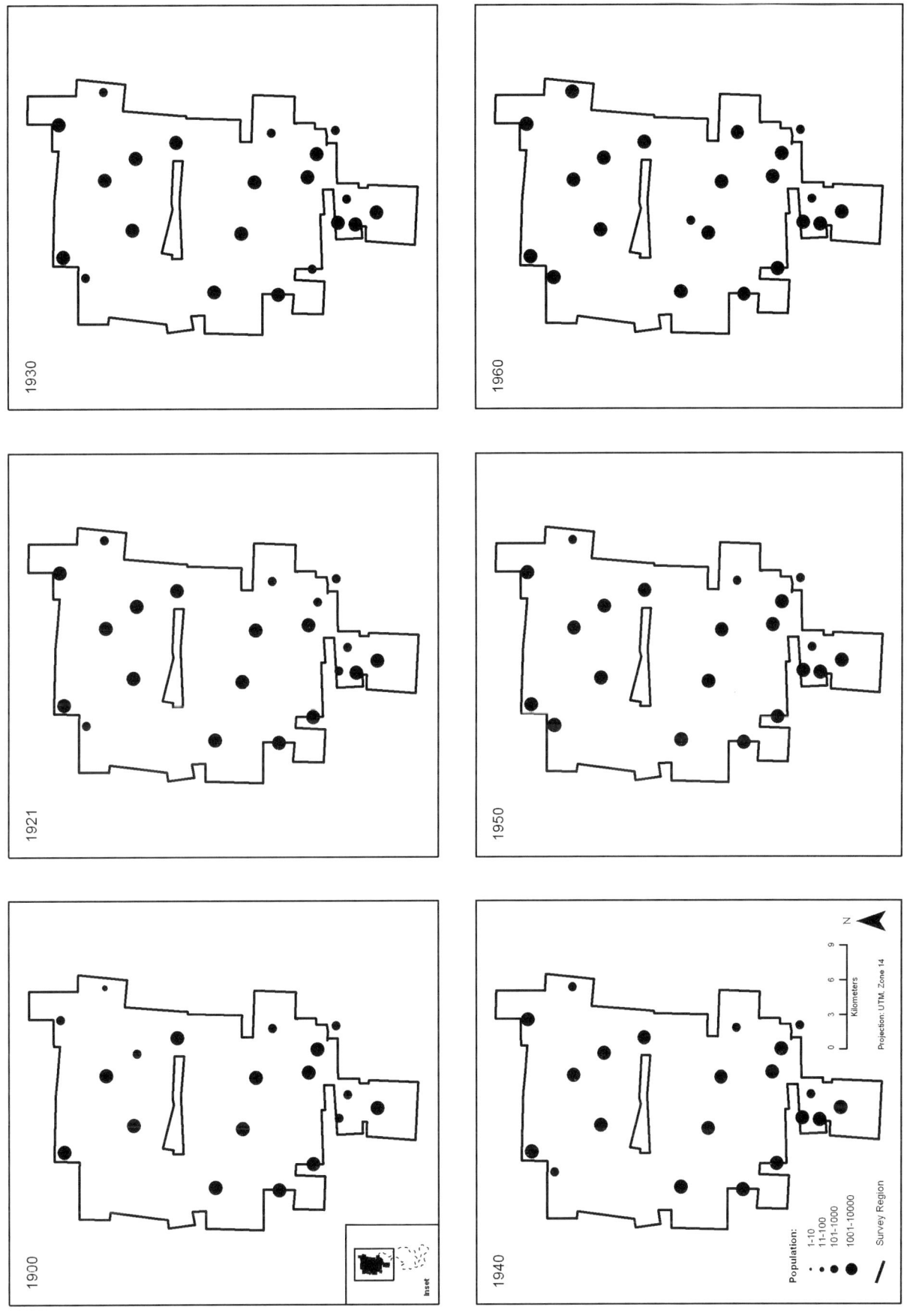

Figure 3.1. The Zumpango Region, showing modern settlements, 1900–1960 (courtesy Larry Gorenflo).

Table 3.2. Modern (1960) settlements: environmental contexts and demography.

Settlement	Mean Elevation (m asl)	Zone	Population	Surface Area* (ha)	Population Density (people/ha)
Apaxco & Estacion Apaxco	2180	USD	4961	152.5	32.5
Barrio Perez	2270	USD	240		
Sta. Maria Apaxco	2200	USD	1316	147.5	8.9
Tlapanaloya	2280	USD	1881	205.0	9.2
Ajoloapan	2375	USD	3437	365.0	9.4
Nopala	2360	USD	2068	77.5	26.7
Hueypoxtla	2320	USD	1265	115.0	11.0
Tequixquiac	2240	USD	5463	447.5	12.2
Cuevas Loma Larga Loma España	2300	BOMLP	1884	237.5	7.9
Jilotzingo	2360	BOMLP	1941	165.0	11.8
Huehuetoca La Cañada El Llano Salitrillo El Calvario	2260	USD	5490	445.0	12.3
Zitlaltepec	2290	Lakeshore Plain	5680	230.0	24.7
Lázaro Cárdenas	2320	BOMLP	318	22.5	14.1
Zumpango	2250	Lakeshore Plain	8371	602.5	13.9
Coyotepec	2300	BOMLP (CC)	5967	67.5	88.4
Teoloyucan	2245	Lakeshore Plain	2239	434.5	5.2
Jaltenco	2245	Lakeshore Plain	1965	482.2	4.1
Nextlalpan	2245	Lakeshore Plain	2329	283.6	8.2
San Sebastian	2245	Lakeshore Plain	1002	132.5	7.6
Xaltocán	2250	Lakebed	567	78.5	7.2
Tenopalco	2250	Tultepec Island	570	138.7	4.1
Visitación	2250	Tultepec Island	1867	47.9	39.0
Melchor Ocampo	2250	Tultepec Island	3958	70.4	56.2
Tultepec	2250	Tultepec Island	5601	140.8	39.8
Total:			70,380	5089.1	$\mu = 19.8 \pm 20.2$

Key: USD = Upper Salado Drainage; BOMLP = Basin of Mexico Lower Piedmont; CC = Cerro Colorado.
*Computed with compensating polar planimeter from 1:25,000 topographic maps (México, Depto. Cartográfico Militar 1957).

Table 3.3. Modern and prehispanic population densities (609 km² for modern; 536 km² for prehispanic).

Date	Population*	Overall Pop. Density (people/km²)
1960	70,380+	115.6+
1950	53,274	87.5
1940	45,604	74.9
1930	37,499	61.6
1921	30,438	50.0
1900	32,421	53.2
Late Aztec ca. A.D. 1500	42,505	78.9
Early Aztec ca. A.D. 1250	negligible	negligible
Late Toltec ca. A.D. 1000	18,060	34.3
Early Toltec ca. A.D. 750	5145	9.8
Classic ca. A.D. 400	8290	15.8
Terminal Formative (Tzacualli) ca. A.D. 100	740	1.4
Late Formative ca. 300 B.C.	30	0.1

*Maximum estimates used for prehispanic periods.

must reflect a variety of factors, including length of settlement (some dependent barrios are of comparatively recent origin) and functional diversity (the larger and denser settlements typically include residential, civic, ritual, and commercial activities).

Table 3.3 indicates how overall regional population density has changed between 1900 and 1960, and compares twentieth-century population density with our archaeologically derived estimated densities for different prehispanic periods. Prehispanic densities comparable to those of the twentieth century were achieved only during the Late Aztec period; all other periods were characterized by much lower figures. However, when population densities of individual modern settlements are compared with our estimates for prehispanic sites (Table 3.4), the figures for people/occupied hectare are, not surprisingly, much more similar.

In 1973, although undoubtedly some people commuted to jobs in shops, offices, schools, and factories in Mexico City or nearby larger towns, most people in the Zumpango Region still made their living from agriculture, with pastoralism and limestone quarrying as secondary occupations. Most agriculture was rainfall-based, and the only extensively irrigated zones were along the course of the Río Salado in the northwestern section of our survey area and, to a lesser degree, in the south along the Río Pachuca. Most irrigation was done with treated sewage (*agua negra*) that flowed northward out of the Valley of Mexico through huge canals and tunnels (Plate 3.1) and into the Río Tula drainage; a much smaller quantity of something like *agua negra* was similarly acquired for more modest irrigation from the Río Pachuca, which had its source in the environs of Pachuca to the northeast. It was clear, as we walked over the landscape from late May into early December in 1973, that only these irrigated lands were highly and dependably productive.

The Zumpango Region on the Eve of Spanish Conquest

Gibson's (1964), Carrasco's (1999), and Hicks' (2005) syntheses of historical sources indicate that most of our Zumpango Region survey area was within the Tepaneca domain of the Triple Alliance during the fifteenth century, but came to be increasingly dominated by the Mexica and Acolhua polities centered at Tenochtitlan and Texcoco, respectively, during the early sixteenth century. The documentary sources indicate that the Late Aztec period was a time of sociopolitical instability in the Zumpango Region; in many cases, the inhabitants of our survey area were governed by, and paid tribute to, different imperial overlords in Atzcapotzalco, Tacuba, Tenochtitlan, and Texcoco—often at the same time.

The Matricula de Tributos and Codex Mendoza (ca. early 1520s)

The *Matricula de Tributos* and *Codex Mendoza*, lists of provinces tributary to the Triple Alliance, have been discussed and explicated by Barlow (1949), and further studied by Gibson (1964) and Carrasco (1999). These documents were probably prepared shortly after the Spanish conquest in 1521 to facilitate the flow of tribute into the newly established Spanish capital in Tenochtitlan/Mexico City (Barlow 1949:4). Much of the Zumpango Region fell into the Hueypuchtla (Hueypoxtla) and Citlaltepec (modern Zitlaltepec) tributary provinces. In addition to several places outside our study area, these provinces included several towns whose names survived into modern times: Hueypoxtla, Tlapanaloya, Tequixquiac, Zitlaltepec, Zumpango, Apaxco, and Xaltocán (Barlow 1949:48-50; Carrasco 1999:103-4, 125-28).

The nature and quantity of tribute is suggestive of the kinds of products and labor services available in this region during the final decades prior to Spanish conquest (Table 3.5). Maguey products ("henequen" fiber and "maguey honey") are particularly notable in these tribute lists, as is the quantity of labor that must have been involved in collecting and processing these raw materials. Carrasco (1999:107) also notes that the Citlaltepec province's tribute included "decorated cotton cloths, birds, feathers, *chalchihuites*, fish, mats, other small items, and slaves captured in war." The inclusion of cotton textiles, exotic green stones (*chalchihuites*), and war captives indicates that some tribute items were locally obtained and/or manufactured from imported raw materials that

Table 3.4. Comparison of modern (1960) and prehispanic settlement/site population densities.

Period	Number of Sites	Total Occupied Hectares	Population*	Overall Settlement Population Density (people/occupied ha)
Modern (1960)	31+	5089.1	70,380+	13.8
Late Aztec	302	1574.5	42,505	23.0
Late Toltec	213	703.3	18,060	25.7
Early Toltec	30	156.4	5145	32.9
Classic	90	307.3	8290	27.0
Terminal Formative	26	69.1	740	15.3
Late Formative	1	3.0	30	10.0

*Maximum estimates used for prehispanic periods.

Plate 3.1. Entrance to the Gran Canal de Desagüe tunnel under construction near Zumpango, ca. 1900 (photo by C.B. Waite, courtesy Institut Iberocamericana, Berlin).

Table 3.5. Tribute paid to the Triple Alliance from the Hueypuchtla province.

Category	Items
Clothing	400 little decorated mantles
	400 henequen mantles with black-and-white border
	800 white henequen mantles
	62 warriors' costumes, with shields
Food	4 wooden cribs (1 each of maize, beans, chian, and huauhtli)
	400 jars of thick maguey honey

(After Barlow 1949:50)

could have been acquired only through participation in regional exchange networks (Hicks 1987). The abundance and widespread distribution of small ceramic spindle whorls suitable for spinning fine cotton thread (Parsons 1972a, 1975) attest archaeologically to the quantities of cotton cloth that were produced throughout the Zumpango Region, and elsewhere in the Valley of Mexico, where cotton itself could not be locally produced.

Indigenous Land Tenure in 1519

Gibson (1964:257) has discerned five major categories of land holdings that existed within each community in the Valley of Mexico at the time of initial Spanish contact in 1519 (all of which were radically altered during the subsequent Colonial period):

(1) *teotlalli*, or land of the temples and gods; (2) *tecpantlalli*, or land of the community houses; (3) *tlatocatlalli*…, or land of the tlatoque [ruler]; (4) *pillalli* and *tecuhtlalli*, or land of the nobles…; (5) *calpullalli*, or land of the calputin [commoners].

Gibson (1964:270) notes that besides agricultural plots, a community's lands might also include lacustrine and marshland wetland zones, plus "a forest (*monte*) used for stone or firewood or pasturage or protection against a neighbor." Each community territory tended to incorporate within its borders the full range of environmental diversity within its local region.

Gibson's first four categories of land were worked primarily on a communal basis by commoners as part of their labor tribute obligations to different overlords. Because such lands were usually embedded within the holdings of each local community, it might be possible to discern them archaeologically, at least in a general and roughly approximate way, by noting the distribution of the remnants of public architecture (that is, relatively large mounds) and assuming that lands designated for the support of public institutions, and the elites associated with these institutions, would have tended to cluster in the general vicinity of such physical symbols of authority.

Gibson's fifth land category, *calpullalli*, is of particular interest since it was the economic foundation of the great mass of commoners (*maceguales*) organized into territorially based local *calpulli* communities. Gibson (1964:267) found that this *calpullalli* designation

> signified both the house sites and the agricultural plots of calpulli members, no matter how distributed. Although the calpullalli might be identified [in the Spanish colonial documents] as 'common' land, it was not worked in common but was subdivided into individual plots. . . . [the head of a commoner household] possessed usufruct privileges so long as he cultivated it and paid his tribute from it. He had the traditional privilege of bequeathing his *tlalmilli* [agricultural plot] and his house to his descendants, but he forfeited his tenure if he failed to work the plot or moved elsewhere. If escheatment to the community took place, a tlalmilli might be reissued to a new user. Plots not worked for two years might be worked temporarily by the community, so that the tribute due on them might be paid, and this circumstance may have underlain, at least in part, the common plantings for caciques and principales. Unassigned plots were retained for those about to marry or for others who had no lands. Calpulli land in some cases also supported the non-agricultural population: craftsmen, hunters, fishermen, masters of singing and dancing, and others. Control over the allocation of plots appears to have been exercised . . . by tlatoque, tequitlatos, elders (viejos), and other calpulli officers.

Eyewitness Observations of Hernán Cortés and Bernal Diaz del Castillo in 1519–1521

In the course of his military campaigns against Tenochtitlan in 1521, Hernán Cortés and his forces passed by Xaltocán. His third letter to the King of Spain, dated May 15, 1522, provides this description:

> Y llegamos a una población que se dice Xaltoca, que está asentada en medio de la laguna, y alrededor de ella hallamos muchas y grandes acequias llenas de agua y hacían la dicha población muy fuerte, porque los de caballo no podían entrar a ella, y los contrarios daban muchas gritas, tirándonos muchas varas y flechas; y los peones, aunque con trabajo, entránronlos dentro, y echáronlos fuera, y quemaron mucha parte del pueblo. Y aquella noche nos fuimos a dormir una legua de allí; y en amaneciendo tomamos nuestro camino, y en él hallamos los enemigos, y de lejos comenzaron a gritar, como lo suelen hacer en la guerra, que cierto es cosa espantosa oirlos, y nosotros comenzamos a seguirlos; y siguiéndolos, llegamos a una grande y hermosa ciudad que se dice Goatitan [Cuautitlán?], y hallámosla despoblada. [Cortés 1963:134]

[English translation by Apphia H. Parsons] And we arrived at a town called Xaltoca, which is situated in the middle of the lake, around which we found many large channels filled with water, that made this town very strong, because men on horseback could not enter, and the enemy yelled and threw many lances and arrows at us; and the foot soldiers, with effort, entered inside and threw them outside and they burned much of the town. And that night we left the town and slept one league away; and in the morning, we set out on our road, and there we encountered the enemies, and from far away they began to yell, as they do in war, and it truly is frightening to hear them, and we began to follow them, and doing so we arrived at a large and beautiful city which is called Goatitan [Cuautitlán?] and we found it deserted.

Bernal Diaz del Castillo, a soldier in Cortés' army, described the Xaltocán campaign in more detail:

> although the houses [at Xaltocán] were built in the waters of a lake, there was an entrance from the land.... [enroute to Xaltocán from Texcoco, the Spanish forces passed through] a thickly peopled country.... [as the Spaniards approached Xaltocán] the Mexicans and the people of Saltocan began to attack our troops when they were close to the pueblo, and they shot many darts and arrows at them and slung stones from their slings, from the canals where they were posted, ... our horsemen could do them no hurt for they could not gallop nor cross the creeks which were full of water. The causeway and road by which they were used to enter the town from the land had been destroyed and broken down by hand only a few days before, and they so flooded it that it was as full of water as the ditches. Owing to this, our soldiers found no way by which they could enter the town, or do any damage to its defenders.... [Finally, through great effort, the Spanish forces were able to directly assault and burn the town, and] ... much cotton cloth and gold and other spoil was taken, but, as the town was built in the lake, the Mexicans and the inhabitants soon got into their canoes with all the property they were able to carry and went off to Mexico [Tenochtitlán].... [The Tlaxcalan Indian troops allied with the Spanish] came out of it rich with cloaks and salt and gold and other spoil. Then they went to sleep at some huts near the limekilns, about a league distant from Saltocan. [Diaz del Castillo 1910:31-34]

The Colonial Period (1521–1810)

During the sixteenth and seventeenth centuries, the following communities in the Zumpango Region were important places, many with named *tlatoani* overlords in 1519, and all had *cabecera* status within the Spanish colonial administrative hierarchy (Gibson 1964:41, 43): Citlaltepec, Huehuetoca, Hueypoxtla, Tequixquiac, Xaltocán, Xilotzingo, and Zumpango (Fig. 3.2). All these places survived into the twentieth century as towns or villages, some as municipal capitals.

By the Late Colonial period (eighteenth and early nineteenth centuries), the western portion of the Zumpango Region was administered within the Cuauhtitlan *corregimiento* jurisdiction, with Huehuetoca as a dependent community. The central sector of the Zumpango Region was within the Citlaltpec jurisdiction, with Tequixquiac, Zumpango, Xaltenco, and Xaltocán as dependent communities. The northeastern sector of the Zumpango Region was in the Hueypoxtla jurisdiction (no dependent communities show on Gibson's map) (Gibson 1964:88-89, Map 5). By the early nineteenth century, a number of Early Colonial communities (primarily dependent barrios) had apparently disappeared, at least from archival sources.

Gibson (1964) suggests a high degree of continuity between the form and placement of late prehispanic and Colonial administrative districts, and this lakeshore-to-interior configuration is clearly apparent for the Cuauhtitlan and Citlaltepec jurisdictions in the Zumpango Region survey area.

> The organization of corregimiento jurisdictions... displays the familiar sector pattern, with the several areas fanning out from the central lakes.... Characteristic corregimientos... possessed frontages of lakeshore and widened as they extended outward to the edges of the Valley [of Mexico]. The pattern was derived, as is obvious, from the original Indian cabecera and estancia locations. [Gibson 1964:88-89, Map 5]

There is significant continuity between the mid-sixteenth century and the twentieth century in terms of the locations of many named communities that endured throughout this long period and into the twentieth century. Nevertheless, Elinor Melville's (1994) archival study of sixteenth-century environmental change in the Mezquital region—including most of the Zumpango Region and extending some 80 km farther to the north and west—has clearly shown how Spanish administrative policies and economic practices radically altered the prehispanic environment, ecology, and lifeways in our survey region within less than a century after the 1520s. Key interrelated factors included the following:

(1) The severe decline of Indian population caused primarily by introduced Old World diseases (especially smallpox, measles, cholera, and influenza), and by the onerous demands upon Indian labor for Spanish-directed mining, textile workshops, and large-scale drainage and flood-control operations. This decline occurred throughout the Valley of Mexico, the whole of Colonial New Spain, and the entire Western Hemisphere as the sixteenth and seventeenth centuries unfolded, often with astonishing rapidity (e.g., Gibson 1964:136-47; Crosby 1967; Dobyns 1976; Denevan 1992). For the Valley of Mexico as a whole, Gibson (1964:141) estimates "an initial [Indian] population at the time of conquest of about 1,500,000; a decline to about 325,000 by 1570; a further decline to about 70,000 in the mid-seventeenth century; an increase to about 120,000 in 1742; and a further increase to about 275,000 by 1800."

Gibson (1964:141) has also noted that the demographic recovery that was underway by A.D. 1700 in the Valley of Mexico as a whole was significantly less rapid in the northern third (including the Zumpango Region) than in the central and southern sectors of the Valley. He suggested that "[t]he difference is probably to be attributed to the decreasing moisture of the northern part of the Valley, and to the preservation of the southern lakes, and changes in birth rate and migration may both be involved" (Gibson 1964:140).

(2) The *congregación* policy, whereby scattered Indian groups were increasingly concentrated after the mid-sixteenth century into nucleated, gridded settlements, many of which have survived into modern times. Gibson (1964:286-87, Table 22) has noted the archival documentation for the implementation during the late sixteenth century of *congregaciones* in Citlaltepec, Huehuetoca, Hueypoxtla, Tequixquiac, Xaltocán, and Zumpango.

(3) The occupation of former Indian lands by Spanish ranchos and haciendas, many concerned with raising sheep—an exotic Old World species, newly introduced into the Zumpango Region and other parts of central Mexico in large numbers by the

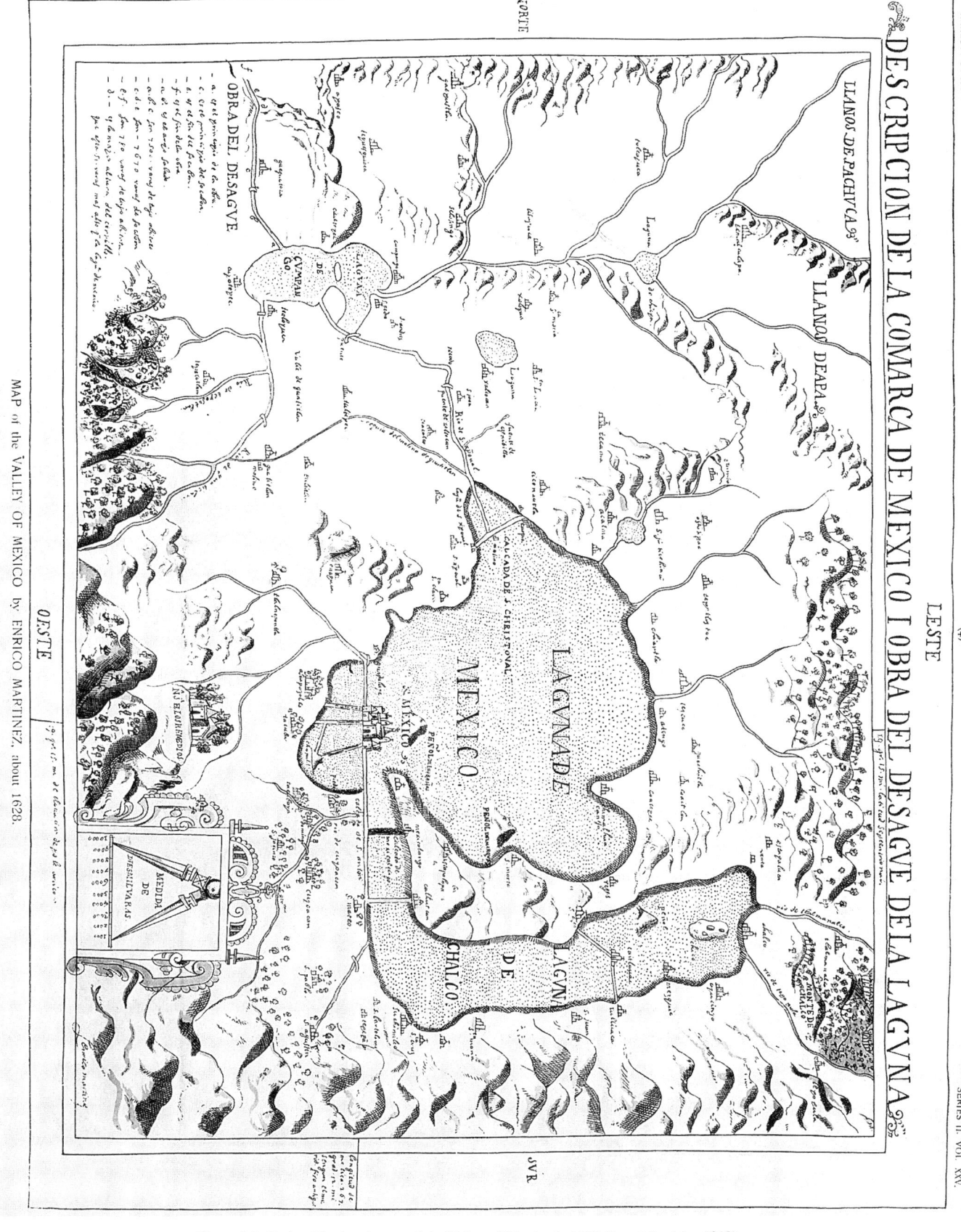

Figure 3.2. Enrico Martinez's map of the Valley of Mexico in 1628 (from Maudslay 1910).

1530s. Some Spanish holdings were in the form of very large enterprises, such as the huge Jesuit hacienda of Santa Lucia on the plains of eastern Lake Xaltocán and adjacent lakeshore zone (Konrad 1980). In general, traditional indigenous land tenure was radically altered during the Early Colonial period (Gibson 1964:257-99). For example,

> [b]y 1600 much land formerly cultivated by the Indians of Xaltocan in the higher ground toward Ozumbilla [east of the Lake Xaltocán shore] had been abandoned, and the town's agriculture had come to be concentrated in the lower chinampa area [a zone recently studied archaeologically by Nichols and Frederick (1993)]. [Gibson 1964:268]

And, in more general terms,

> with the development of the new Indian municipal governments, the community representatives... operated everywhere as agents in the alienation of common lands. With progressive depopulation, and with continuous Spanish demands for tribute payments, it was a natural step for gobernadores not to reissue calpullalli to surviving macegueles but rather to sell or rent it to Spaniards. [Gibson 1964:268]

Indian labor for agricultural production (especially wheat farms), mining, textile workshops, and massive drainage projects was heavily taxed and forcibly recruited throughout the long Colonial period (Gibson 1964:220-56). Particularly onerous for the native population of the Zumpango Region were heavy demands for labor in the excavation of large drainage canals and the construction of dams and causeways as Spanish authorities sought to provide more effective drainage and flood control (Gibson 1964:240-42). Because the Valley of Mexico was bordered by high, impenetrable mountain ranges on all other sides, it was precisely through the low drainage divide through the Zumpango Region that the large canals (the massive *Gran Canal de Desagüe*, *Canal de Costera*, and *Tajo de Nochistongo*) for external drainage had to pass (Fig. 2.2).

(4) A great expansion of lime making (for construction of new buildings in Mexico City and elsewhere) and mining (for silver production in the nearby Pachuca mines), both of which required vast quantities of firewood and brush for fuel (Bargallo 1955).

(5) Greatly accelerated erosion—the product of overgrazing, deforestation, and the abandonment of intensive indigenous agricultural practices (such as terracing)—that substantially reduced the suitability of the region for intensive agriculture in subsequent centuries.

Several passages from Melville's study nicely set the stage for our attempt to bridge the gap between modern and sixteenth-century occupations of the Zumpango Region. An inescapable conclusion is that the late prehispanic past was environmentally and ecologically quite distinct from that of the subsequent 500 years.

In the following quotation, Melville's "Southern Plain" sub-area comprises most of our Zumpango Region:

Tula and the Southern Plain, lying along the northern edge of the Valley of Mexico, were two of the most densely populated and fertile areas in the Valle del Mezquital. They were the first of the sub-areas to be intensively exploited by grazing, and they were the most degraded by the end of the [sixteenth] century. The Spaniards were attracted by the excellent resources for both agriculture and pastoralism, by the limestone hills (as sources of lime), and by the proximity to Tenochtitlan (Mexico City). The major changes in land use were conversion of lands to grazing ... and the accelerated exploitation of limestone quarries.... Exploitation of these rich sub-areas by grazing was especially intense: grazing rates in the 1570s reached their highest regional levels here.... by the end of the century between 81.6 and 93.6 percent of the total surface of these areas was formally converted to grazing.... [T]he extent of land moved into the Spanish land tenure system by the end of the century becomes overwhelming....

During the period of the 1550s and 1560s croplands and hillsides were converted to grasslands and some ground was left bare of vegetation. These grasslands and denuded soils were subsequently invaded by secondary growth consisting primarily of armed species of plants: wild maguey (*lechugilla*: Agave lechugilla), yucca (*palmas sylvestres*: Yucca spp.), cacti (*tunal, nopal*: prickly pear cactus: Opuntia spp.), thorn bushes (*espinos*: possibly ocotillo: Fouqueria spp.), mesquite (*mesquites*: Prosopis spp.), and *cardones* (possibly the introduced thistle Cynara cardunculus). The process of environmental change was further complicated by deforestation for lime and charcoal manufacture. By the last two decades of the sixteenth century extensive sheet erosion to hardpan (*tepetate, calichal*) was recorded for the hillsides and flatlands in both sub-areas, as were failing springs in the Southern Plain....

Flocks of sheep accelerated the removal of the vegetative cover of the Southern Plain by trampling shrubs and eating out palatable herds and grasses. The Indians of Tlapanaloya complained bitterly that sheep trampled the stalks of the shrub *tlacotl*, which was used as a wood substitute in the production of lime. They argued that destruction of this shrub jeopardized lime production—and therefore tributes [that they were required to pay to Spanish overlords]....

By the time of the geographic descriptions of 1579, the woods that had covered the slopes surrounding Tezcatepec in the Southern Plain in 1548 had receded to the tops of the mountains between Tezcatepec and Axacuba. The deforestation of these northern hills can be ascribed primarily to the activities of lime workers who needed fuel for their kilns. Spaniards applied for grants of limestone quarries in the limestone hills north of Tlapanaloya and east of Apaxco to supply demand for lime to rebuild the city of Tenochtitlan. Deforestation of the woodlands in these hills was noticeable as early as 1562. By the 1570s the woods east of Apasco and on the hills north of Tlapanaloya were also depleted by cutting and burning,... As the lime workers ranged farther afield to collect fuel, they were undoubtedly instrumental in maintaining this sub-area relatively free of the woody secondary growth that grew so thickly in other areas by the end of the century. The Indians also complained that sheep ate the leaves of the plants *camal, cacomitl*, and *hueycamitl* so that the roots could not be harvested.

By the 1560s spiny and arid-zone plants began to invade this sub-area, followed by woody species. At first there were reports of abandoned croplands and untended magueys, then the yucca appeared; this was followed by the wild maguey and mesquite at the end of the century. The fertility of the soils on the piedmont of the Southern Plain deteriorated over the same period. In 1579 the undulating lands of Tequixquiac, Tlapanaloya, and Hueypoxtla were reported as open, cleared, and suitable for the production of cereals. During the following two decades there are increasing references to stony soils, and by 1606 the lands near Hueypoxtla were eroded *tepetate* badlands where only mesquite, yuccas, and wild magueys grew.... The processes that led eventually to the severe erosion in this area, namely the removal of the ground cover by overgrazing—leading to increased overland flow of water—also reduced groundwater recharge. By 1595 the springs in Tequixquiac and Hueypoxtla, which fed the tributaries of the north-flowing stream, the Rio Salado, were failing. [Melville 1994:89-95]

The Relaciones Geográficas 1579–1582

The *Relaciones Geográficas* are compilations of a royal questionnaire distributed to local administrators by Spanish viceregal authorities throughout New Spain in 1579–1582, seeking several kinds of information about individual indigenous communities. The most recent publication of these questionnaires is that edited by Acuña (1985, 1986a, 1986b); there is an earlier version edited by Paso y Troncoso (1905). Bernal (1957) published some reports that pertain to the Zumpango Region, and Strauss (1974) utilized several unpublished documents from the larger corpus in his study of the utilization of the resources of Lake Xaltocán-Zumpango during the Colonial period.

Numerous relevant passages that I quote below indicate that many modern settlements in the Zumpango Region have sixteenth-century roots. However, as suggested above, it is important to realize that not all of these documented sixteenth-century settlements necessarily had direct prehispanic antecedents: by the late sixteenth century, the ravages of introduced European diseases resulted in massive declines of Indian population, and Spanish *congregación* policies resulted in "the resettlement of scattered Indian families or of entire *sujetos* into compact communities" (Gibson 1964:282). It is important to remember that the environmental degradation discussed by Melville (above) was well underway by the time these questionnaires were being filled out ca. 1580.

In the following paragraphs, the original Spanish texts are followed by English translations by Apphia H. Parsons.

The Chiconautla District

The center of the modern town (now expansive urban sprawl) of Chiconautla is approximately 10 km southeast of the southeastern corner of the Zumpango Region survey area (Fig 1.2). In the late 1570s, the Chiconautla district included, besides the principal *cabecera* of Chiconauhtlan (modern Chiconaulta) itself, the secondary centers of Tecama (modern Tecamac), Xaltocán, and Ecatepeque (modern Ecatepec), each of which contained numerous dependent communities (barrios). The Chiconautla, Tecamac, and Ecatepec communities are all outside our survey area, but at least two of the Xaltocán barrios (Nextlalpan and Caltengo [modern Xaltenco]) fall within the borders of our survey area (Fig. 2.2). Xaltocán contained 420 "tributaries" (heads of household) (Acuña 1985:230).

The area is described as agriculturally productive, with maguey as an important crop:

> Es tierra abundosa de pastos y no es falta de aguas, y, en algunas partes desta jur[isdicci]ón, beben de pozos; y es abundosa de maíz y frijoles (como habas), y chile y tomates chicos y grandes. Y, en esta jur[isdicci]ón, hay membrillos y cerezas y algunas peras; hay gran calidad de un árbol que llaman maguey, que es a manera de unos cardos que llaman en *Castilla la vieja*, tobas, del cual se saca vino y vinagre y se hace conserva del cogollo, y, el zumo dél, caliente, es medicina muy principal para heridas; y, ansimismo, dél hacen vestidos e hilo para coser cosas, bastas, y sogas. [Acuña 1985:233-34]

[English translation] It is a land of rich pastures, not lacking in water, and in parts of this area they drink from wells, and there is abundant corn and beans (such as broad beans) and chiles and large and small tomatoes. And, in this area, there are quince and cherries and some pears; there are high quality trees called *magueys*, that are similar to the spiney plants called *tobas* in *Castilla la vieja* [region of northern Spain], from which they produce wine and vinegar and they preserve the heart, and the juice, when hot, is an important medicine for treating injuries. And from this same plant they make clothing and thread for sewing, stitching and rope.

Agriculture was complemented by fishing and hunting:

> los indios siembran y cogen maíz y frijoles y chile, y otras legumbres, y pescan y cazan, y desto se sustentan; y pagan su tribute con maíz y dineros. [Acuña 1985:238]

[English translation] the Indians plant and harvest maize and beans and chiles and other vegetables, and they fish and hunt, and from this they sustain themselves, and they pay their tribute with maize and money.

Another passage speaks about the severe depopulation since the time of initial Spanish contact in the 1520s and the subsequent concentration of surviving Indians (including both *Nahuatl* and *Otomi* speakers) into Spanish-organized settlements (some of which have survived into modern times):

> Esta comarca y jur[iscicci]ón tiene como dos mil y qui[nient]os indios, que son muy pocos, porque dicen los indios antiguos, y así se ve por las poblaciones antiguas, que solía haber en esta jur[isdicci]ón, en cada pueblo de las cabeceras arriba nombradas, tantos indios como ahora hay en la jur[isdicci]ón toda. Y, los que ahora están pobladas, están en sus pueblos formados, con sus iglesias permanentes. Los indios desta jur[isdicci]ón son indios de buen entendimi[en]to y de razón, y de buenos y vivos ingenios. Son algunos, mercaderes y tratan unos con otros, y otros entre ellos son inclinados a [la] caza, y otros a [la] pesquería, y otros a las labores de los frutos que cogen en esta tierra.... Y hay, en esta jur[isdicci]ón, dos géneros de lenguas: *mexicana* y *otomit[e]*, y la más se usa es la *mexicana*. [Acuña 1985:234]

[English translation] This region has around 2500 Indians, which is very few. The old Indians say that there used to be, in each town of the *cabeceras* named above, as many Indians as now live in the entire region, and one can see this in the old towns. In the places that remain inhabited, people live in their established

towns with their permanent churches. The Indians of this area possess good understanding and reason and are intelligent and inventive. Some are merchants, trading amongst each other, and others dedicate themselves to hunting or fishing and others to the labor of fruits which are gathered in this land.... And there are, in this region, two types of language: *mexicana* and *otomi*, and the more common is *mexicana*.

Another passage notes some of the consequences for settlement organization and the appearance of regional depopulation:

> como se han muerto muchos indios, están los pueblos desbaratados y sin orden de calles, porque hay pocas casas y derramadas. [Acuña 1985:235]

> *[English translation]* as many Indians have died, the villages are in ruins and without ordered streets, because there are few houses and they are scattered.

Another consequence of regional depopulation was the decay of the agricultural infrastructure based on canal irrigation:

> en la ribera y valle por donde enfrente deste pueblo, baja el río que tengo referido, se podría regar con el agua dél mucha tierra, y se podrían plantar y hacer muchas huertas y buenas heredades. Y al presente no hay ninguna. [Acuña 1985:236]

> *[English translation]* along the river bank and in the valley where the river descends, facing the town, you could irrigate much land, and plant and cultivate many gardens and establish good farms. And at this time there are none.

The hunting of wild game was apparently confined to birds, hares, and rabbits, while newly introduced sheep and goats flourished (probably with the expense of significant habitat destruction, as discussed in Melville 1994):

> hay gran cantidad de caza de volatería; caza de campo, hay liebres y conejos.... y, ovejas y cabras, se crían bien en esta jur[isdicci]ón. [Acuña 1985:237]

> *[English translation]* there is much hunting of fowl; there are hares and rabbits for field hunting.... and sheep and goats do well when raised here.

Saltmaking around the lakeshore was important, and apparently saltmakers were specialists who lived from their craft:

> hay una manera de salinas: que, en los salitrales junto a la laguna, los indios cogen la tela de la tierra, y la echan en agua y la cuecen, y sacan unos panes redondos de sal negra como piedra, y con ésta se sustentan. [Acuña 1985:237]

> *[English translation]* there is a type of salt marsh: in which in the salt beds near the lake, the Indians gather the topsoil and throw it in water and boil it and remove round loaves of salt, black like rocks, and with this they support themselves.

Indians lived in flat-roofed structures made of adobes:

> usan los indios casas bajas, las paredes de adobes, cubiertas de terrados con ruines maderas, las cuales traen de los montes más cercanos. [Acuña 1985:238]

> *[English translation]* the Indians live in low houses, with walls made of mud brick, covered with flat roofs of small timbers that they bring from the nearest forests.

The Tequixquiac District

This Colonial administrative unit included both *Nahuatl* and *Otomi* speakers, and contained several communities in the survey area that have survived into the twentieth century: Tequixquiac itself, Hueypoxtla, Tlapanaloya, and Xilotzingo. The latter three are mentioned, but not specifically described (Acuña 1986a:191).

Tequixquiac, which means "lugar de agua salobre [place of salty water]," was said to be named for a saline springs within a marshy area:

> Este pueblo de Tequixquiac está fundado en un valle muy llano que está en medio de unas lomas, que tiene, por los lados, a un cerro grande que cae a la p[ar]te de occidente [now called Cerro de Mesa Grande]. Y, por el dicho valle, corren unos arroyos de agua salobre, de donde tomó el nombre de Tequixquiac. Es lugar malsano, por ser el suelo muy húmedo y casi todo de ciénegas. [Acuña 1986a:193]

> *[English translation]* This town of Tequixquiac is located in a very flat valley, in the middle of some hills. On one side is a large hill that slopes down to the west [now called Cerro de Mesa Grande]. And in this valley, run several streams of salty water, for which Tequixquiac was named. It is an unhealthy place, for the ground is very damp and swampy.

This was apparently a densely populated area with productive agriculture, but maguey, nopal, and wild plant and animal foods were also important, as were many introduced species of cultivated plants and animals:

> Las comidas de su gentilidad era yerbas y raíces del campo y frutas silvestres, y aves y sabandijas y culebras, y cosas de montería y otras sabandijas. Muchos dellos comían maíz, aunquye no todos, por ser tantos. Ahora comen todos, maíz y frijoles y chile, y casi todo lo que la gente Española come, como es pan, y carne de vaca y carenero, y aves y cosas de montería;... Usan mucho la miel del maguey,... hacen della vino, que ellos llaman pulque. [Acuña 1986a:193]

> *[English translation]* The foods of these pagans were grasses and roots of the field and wild fruits and birds and insects and snakes and things that were hunted and other small creatures. Many of the people ate corn, but not all of them, being so many. Today all the people eat corn and beans and chiles and almost everything that Spanish people eat—bread, beef, mutton, birds and other hunted animals... They often use the sap of the *maguey*,... from which they make wine they call *pulque*.

> En este pueblo hay muchos árboles silvestres de fruta muy buena, como es el de la tuna [fruit of the nopal].... Y, asimismo,

hay otra fruta q[ue] llaman calpuli, que es como cereza de España.... Hay otra árbol que llaman el maguey, que es el major y de más provecho de cuantos hay en estas p[ar]tes, porque da sobre veinte frutos, como son vino, vinagre, miel, diacitrón de la tierra, hilo, agua, clavos, leña, y madera p[ar]a subrir casas. ... Frutas de Castilla, hay duraznos, membrillos, albaricoques, peras, manzanas, higos, uvas, y todo género de hortaliza, como es coles, lechugas, cebollas, rábanos, yerbabuena, perejil, culantdro, alcauciles, nobos, zanahorias, chirivías, escaroles, [y] mucho rosa de Castilla, clavelinas, y otros géneros de yerbas y rosas y flores de n[uest]ra España. Y los naturals se dan mucho a sembrarlo y cogerlo, con otras muchas semillas de la tierra, como son chile y chian y huauhtli, y otras legumbres a su modo. ...

Los dichos naturales no tienen género de animal doméstico, si no es perrillos pequeños. Aves, tienen gallinas y patos y ánsares, y también crían puercos y ovejas y cabras. Animales bravos, hay en los campos y ceros deste pue[b]lo, como son venados, liebres, conejos, zorrillos, leones, comadrejas [y] tuzas, que habitan debajo de la tierra, y, raposos, lobos casi al modo de los de España. Suelen venire por Navidad grullas, ánsares y otros géneros de aves, y, en este pue[b]lo, hay de ordinario patos reales; [y] bravos, corvejones, cuervos, buharros, gavilanes, halcones, mochuelos, gaviotas, garazs y codornices, y otros muchos géneros de aves campesinas. [Acuña 1986a:195-96]

[English translation] There are many wild trees in this town, which bear very good fruit, such as the *tuna* [fruit of the nopal].... There are also other fruits called *calpuli*, which are like Spanish cherries.... There is another tree they call *maguey*, which is the most important and most beneficial for the great number that exist in these parts, because it produces more than twenty products, such as wine, vinegar, honey, candied cactus, thread, needle, nails, firewood and wood for making houses.... Of the fruits we know in Spain, there are peaches, quinces, apricots, pears, apples, figs, grapes and all kind of vegetables, such as cabbages, lettuce, onions, radishes, *yerbabuena*, parsley, cilantro, artichokes, turnips, carrots, chives, escarole, and many roses of Castile [rosa gallica], carnations and other types of grasses, roses, and flowers of our Spain. And the natives spend a lot of time planting and gathering them, with many other native seeds, such as their chiles, amaranth and other vegetables of that type....

These natives do not have any type of domesticated animals, except for small dogs. For birds, they have hens, ducks, and geese and they also raise pigs, sheep, and goats. There are wild animals in the fields and hills of this town, such as deer, hares, rabbits, skunks, lions, weasels, and gophers, which live underground, and foxes and wolves nearly the same as those in Spain. Near Christmastime, cranes, geese and other types of birds arrive, and in this town there are usually ducks [mallards], wild loons, ravens, crows, sparrowhawks, falcons, small owls, gulls, herons, and quail, and many other kinds of country birds.

Indian houses and pre-Christian burial customs are briefly described:

La forma de las casas q[ue] los naturals tienen son pequeñas de adobes y cubiertas de paja. Son muy humosas, por no tener buena traza y ser ellos poco curiosos en el edificio dellas. [Acuña 1986a:196]

[English translation] The natives have small adobe houses, covered with straw. They are very smoky, due to poor layout and because the inhabitants are not neat in building them.

[A]l que moría enterraban luego, sentado en una sepultura honda, y allí le ponían mantas, y comida y dos o tres cántaros de vino de la tierra [pulque]. [Acuña 1986a:192]

[English translation] They later buried the person who died, placed in a deep grave, and there they put blankets and food and two or three carafes of local wine [*pulque*].

In the 1570s, Indians of the Tequixquiac District were active traders:

Los naturales deste pue[bl]o tratan en muchas menudencias a su modo, como es en miel, calabazas, chile, [he]nequén, maíz, sal, y, algunos que pueden, tratan en cosas de mercadería de Castilla, como es papel, chchillos, jabon, cuentezuelas y otras menudencias, de que pagan sus tributes y se sustentan. [Acuña 1986a:196]

[English translation] The natives of this town trade in many small items in their way, such as honey, squash, chilis, *henequén* fiber, corn, salt and those who can trade Spanish merchandise, such as paper, planks, soap, spearheads, and other small items, from which they pay their tributes and make their living.

The Paso y Troncoso (1905) edition of the *Relaciones Geográficas* includes brief descriptions of the pueblos of Gueypustla (Hueypoxtla), Tequisquiaque (Tequixquiac), Tlapanaloya, and Apazco (Apaxco). These descriptions include length and width measurements of each pueblo's terrain (which appear to include settlement area as well as agricultural and grazing lands). These measurements are given in leagues (leguas)—which I have converted to kilometers following Haggard (1941:78), who determined that in Colonial Mexico, one Spanish league equals 2.6 miles (4.19 km).

Hueypoxtla (Paso y Troncoso 1905:110)
Tiene de largo este pueblo dos leguas [ca. 8.4 km] y una y media de ancho [ca. 6.3 km] [this obviously refers to both the settlement and its dependent lands].... Tiene este pueblo con su estancia seiscientos y quarenta y siete casas, y en ellas mill y nouecientos y veynte y siete casados y dozientos y ochenta y siete solteros y mill y trezientos y quarenta y ocho muchachos de ocho años para arriba. No tiene tierras de regadio: son tierras altas y frias y muy sugetas a [h]eladas; ay buenas piedras para molinos y para hazer cal; ay muchas tunas y magueys y desto y de sus labrancas tienen los naturals mucha grangeria.

[English translation] This town measures two leagues [8.4 km] in length by one and a half [6.3 km] in width [this obviously refers to both the settlement and its dependent lands].... The town, including its farm settlement (*estancia*), contains 647 houses, inhabited by 1927 married men, 287 single adults, and 1348 children over the age of eight. There is no irrigated land; the land is high and cold and subject to frosts; there are good rocks for mills and for making lime; there are many *nopales* and *magueys* and the natives make much use of these plants and their stalks.

Based on his study of archival sources, Gibson (1964:270) has characterized early sixteenth-century Hueypoxtla as an example of a common type of indigenous community "with scattered house sites and agricultural lands." This suggests that archaeologically we might expect to find considerable evidence for dispersed, rather than nucleated, residential occupation during the Late Aztec period. Indeed, this is precisely what the Late Aztec settlement configuration looks like in the vicinity of modern Hueypoxtla (Appendix A: Sites Zu-Az-130, -132, and so on).

Tequixquiac (Paso y Troncoso 1905:207)
Tiene este pueblo ochocientas y treinta casas y en ellas ay mill y noventa hombres casados y dozientos y quarenta y tres solteros y mill dozientos y sesenta y siete muchachos de diez años para abaxo. Tiene este pueblo de largo legua y media [ca. 6.3 km] y mas de vna legua de ancho [ca. 4.2+ km], pasa por vn arroyo de agua todo el año, en el qual se puede hacer un molino: pueden regar mill y seiscientas brazas de tierra de largo y ciento y cinquenta de ancho, y antes mas que menos. Demas desto tienen dos fuentes que riegan con ellas vna poca de tierra, y toda la demas tierra es buena para sembrar de seco, en que ay muy buenos pedazos de tierra humeda; yelanse muchas veces alli las semillas. Es tierra muy bien poblada de gentes y sementeras; ay piedras para hacer cal y desto se aprovechan los naturals; ay baldios en que puede haber tres mill ovejas.

[English translation] This town has 830 houses, with 1090 married men, 243 single adults and 1267 children under the age of ten. The town measures one and a half leagues in length [6.3 km] by more than one league [4.2+ km] in width, with a stream passing through, which has water all year round and on which a mill can be built. They are able to water an area 1600 fathoms in length by 150 fathoms in width, and previously more than that. In addition, from this stream they have two fountains with which they water a small part of the land, and the rest of the land is good for planting dry seeds, as it contains good patches of moist land; they often throw seeds there. This is a land well-populated with people and with planted seeds; there are rocks for making lime, of which the natives take advantage; there is open, un-worked land, enough for 3000 sheep.

Tlapanaloya (Paso y Troncoso 1905:208)
Este pueblo tiene vna estancia que se dize Xomeyuca, la qual está a quatro leguas [ca. 16.8 km] de la cabecera.... Tienen todos juntos sesenta casas y en ellas ciento y diez y ocho casados y treynta solteros y cinquenta muchachos.... Es tierra alta y fragosa y tiene mucha piedra de cal; ay mucha tierra desocupada para ganado ovejuno y en ella lleue poco y yelo mucho.

[English translation] This town has a farm settlement called Xomeyuca, which is four leagues [16.8 km] from the main settlement.... All together, there are 70 houses, with 118 married men, 30 single adults and 50 children.... It is high, rugged land, with many limestone rocks; there is much unoccupied land for raising sheep, where it rains little and frosts often.

Apaxco (Paso y Troncoso 1905:17-18)
Este pueblo tiene 231 casas y en ellas quinientos y treynta y dos hombres casados y sesenta y dos biudos y dozientos y cinquenta y un muchachos que comienzan a seruir y cinquenta y nueve niños de cinco años para abajo. Tiene de largo dos leguas [ca. 8.4 km], y vna en ancho poco mas o menos [ca. 4.2 km]; passa por el vn arroyo de agua en que se puede hazer un molino que muela todo el año y pueden regar con el cerca de tres mill brazas de tierra en largo y mas de ciento y cinquenta en ancho.... La tierra que se riega es muy buena, la demas tier[ra] es vn poco de monte de enzinas bien poco. Ay vnas lomas de piedra de cal; ay muy buenas tierras para sembrar de seco pero son muy sugetas al yelo.

[English translation] This town has 231 houses, in which live 1532 married men, 62 widowers and 251 young men coming of age, and 59 children under the age of five. The town measures two leagues [8.4 km] in length by one league [4.2 km], more or less, in width. A stream flows through the town, on which a mill could operate all year round, and they can water nearly 3000 fathoms of land in length by more than 150 in width.... The land that is irrigated is very good; the rest of the land is partially forested, with a small number of oak trees. There are some limestone hills; there are good lands for planting dry seeds, but they are very prone to frosts.

The Citlaltepec District

This lakeshore community, which included both *Nahuatl* and *Otomi* speakers, contained five dependent barrios (Acuña 1986a:196-97) (none of whose names survive on modern maps or in modern census records). The surviving nearby settlements of Tlapanaloya, Xilotzingo, and Apaxco are also mentioned, but not specifically described (Acuña 1986a:197).

Lacustrine resources were very important in late sixteenth-century subsistence and exchange, and the lake itself included both saline and freshwater sectors:

Este dicho pue[bl]o [Citlaltepec] está fundado junto a una laguna grande que trendá más de seis leguas de boj [6 measured leagues = 25.1 km], la mayor parte de la cual es agua dulcísima y, la demás, de agua salobre y gruesa. La dulce nunca jamás disminuye ni se seca, sino que está en un ser, porque, demás de un río que en ella entra de ordin[ari]o, afirman estos indios que, en el medio y golfo della, tiene un ojo grande. Y así lo da a entender la grandeza de la dicha laguna, y por ser en partes muy honda y de agua clarisima, y el suelo arenisco y limpio.... Tiene los deste pue[bl]o grandísimos aprovechami[ent]os desta d[ic]ha laguna, y los demás que en contorno della y de las demás están, porque toman grandísima suma de pescado blanco, del tamaño y forma de truchas, que es el major y más sano que en esta tierra se come, y [el] más preciado en ella. Y, asimismo, toman otros géneros de pescados, ... y muchas ranas, y grandísima suma de patos, ánsares, grullas, garzas y otros géneros de aves, que toman con redes y lazos, de que son muy aprovechados, y sacan mucha suma de dinero. Y no lo son menos, de las esteras q[ue] hacen del tulle o 'juncos' que por la vera de las dichas lagunas, hay, [de] las cuales de ordinario traen estos indios mucha cantidad [en] canoas, que así las llaman, [que] son unas barquillas pequeñas de una pieza, a manera de artesas, y con éstas van de unas p[ar]tes a otras grandísima ligereza, remando con un remo a manera de pala de horno. Usan anzuelos para pescar, y redes. Tienen, en las dichas lagunas, muchos y diversos géneros de yerbas y raíces, con que se sustentan, y cogen mucho salitre de los pedazos de laguna que se secan, y, de otras muchas cosas, tienen mismo aprovechami[ent]o....
Los naturales deste pue[bl]o y sus sujetos tienen, por principal trato y granjería, vender pescado y esteras, y otras cosas q[ue] de la dicha laguna sacan de cosas de caza. [Acuña 1986a:201-2, 204]

[English translation] This town [Citlaltepec] is located near a large lake with a perimeter of more than six leagues [25.1 km],

the majority of which is fresh water, the rest is brackish and hard. The fresh water never diminishes nor dries up, but is always there, for in addition to a river which flows into the lake, these Indians say that in the middle of the lake and along the gulf, there is a large spring. Thus one understands the largeness of this lake, and it being very deep and clear in places, and the ground sandy and clean. . . . The people of this town make great use of this lake, and people in the surrounding area as well, for they catch a great number of white fish—the size and shape of trout—which are the best and healthiest eaten here and the most valued. They also catch other types of fish, . . . and many frogs and many ducks, geese, cranes, herons, and other types of birds, which they catch with nets and traps. They make great use of these birds, and the birds bring great sums of money. And not least, the rush mats that they make from the rushes found along the edges of these lakes, which the Indians collect in large numbers in canoes, which is what they call the small, one-piece boats, in which they travel from place to place very quickly, rowing with a paddle like an oven shovel. They use bait and nets to fish. These lakes contain many diverse kinds of grasses and roots, on which the natives subsist, and they gather a lot of saltpetre from the lake, which they dry, and they make use of many other things. . . .

The natives of this town and others like them live primarily by trade and farming, selling fish and rush mats, and other items they get from the lake and from hunting.

In addition to the lacustrine resources, the cultivation of indigenous plants (maize, beans, squash, nopal, maguey) and many kinds of introduced grains, vegetables, fruits and livestock, and the hunting of wild animals (deer, rabbits, hares, birds), were also important (Acuña 1986a:202-3).

Indian houses were flat-roofed, with adobe-brick walls and thatched roofs (Acuña 1986a:203). In pre-Christian times, commoners were said to have been buried in deep tombs ("sepulturas hondas"), but Indian elites apparently were cremated and their ashes buried (Acuña 1986a:198).

The Xilotzingo District

Besides Xilotzingo itself, this district included four dependent barrios, none of whose names survive on modern maps or in modern census records. Within our survey area, the surviving settlements of Apaxco, Hueypoxtla, Tequixquiac, Tlapanaloya, and Citlaltepec are also mentioned (the first four are not specifically described; the latter is described elsewhere [see above]).

Xilotzingo was situated in a

loma alta, llana [y] descubierta de todas partes, y, por la p[ar]te de la caída, tiene muchos valles y llanadas que se riegan en tiempo de aguas, y hay muchas estancias de ganados menores y mayors. Llámase esta comarca, por espacio de quince o veinte leguas, la Teot[l]alpa, que quiere decir 'la tierra de los dioses.' [Acuña 1986a:206]

[English translation] high rise, flat and open on all sides, and on the downhill part has many valleys and flatlands which they water in the rainy season, and there are many farm settlements with smaller or larger herds of animals. They call this area, for a space of fifteen or twenty leagues, Teotlalpa, which means 'the land of the gods.'

Indigenous cultigens (maize, amaranth, squash, chile, maguey, and nopal) and turkeys ("gallinas de la tierra"), and introduced crops (wheat, fava beans, numerous fruits and vegetables) and domesticated animals (sheep, goats, and poultry) were important in the local diet, as were waterfowl and a large number of wild animals (deer, hares, rabbits, carnivores, and numerous species of nonaquatic birds) (Acuña 1986a:206-9).

Several local products appear to have been particularly important for producing wealth for making tribute payments:

miel de maguey . . . gallinas y [he]nequén y cal, y sal, chile y otras menudencias de poco momento. [Acuña 1986a:209]

[English translation] maguey honey . . . hens and *henequén* fiber and lime and salt, chilis and other small things.

Indigenous elites were said to have been formerly buried in

una boveda grande, sentado y con mucha comida y vino de la tierra, y mantas y cacao y coas y cotaras. [Acuña 1986a:205-6]

[English translation] a large vault, seated and with much food and local wine and blankets and cacao and digging sticks and quilted armor.

Paso y Troncoso (1905) also includes a description of Xilotzingo:

Este pueblo esta partido en quarto barrios, que son Xilocingo, Teztongo, Guantala y Cicinique. Estan todos en termino de dos leguas [ca. 8.4 km] y son todos novecientos y diez y nueve casas, y en ellas setecientos y veinto hombres y ochenta solteros y noventa y ocho muchachos. Tiene una legua [ca. 4.2 km] de termino en largo y otra en ancho: es tierra seca, beuen de pozos y xagueyes; ay piedra de cal que grangean; quando llueve se da bien qualquier cosa; es muy sujeto a eladas. [Paso y Troncoso 1905:296-97]

[English translation] This town is divided into four neighborhoods, which are Xilocingo, Teztongo, Guantala, and Cicinique. All are encompassed within two leagues [8.4 km] and contain in total 919 houses, 720 men, 80 single adults and 98 children. The area measures one league [4.2 km] in length and another in width; it is dry land, with many wells and ditches; there is limestone, which they mine; when it rains, things go well; it is very prone to frosts.

The Seventeenth and Eighteenth Centuries

By the end of the eighteenth century, the size and composition of population in the core of the Zumpango Region can be approximated by Gibson's figures for the Citlaltepec jurisdiction (Table 3.6).

Similarly, the overall trend of the Indian population profile for the Zumpango Region from 1570 until about 1804 can probably be approximated by Gibson's tabulation of changes in the number of Indian tributaries in the Citlaltepec jurisdiction (Table 3.7). Gibson calculated total population for 1797–1804 by using

Table 3.6. Population of the Citlaltepec jurisdiction, 1790–1804.

Indian Tributaries	Total Indians	Non-Indian Groups					% Non-Indian
		Spaniards	*Mestizos*	*Castas*	*Pardos*	*Total Non-Indians*	
1362	6534	500	988	304	38	1830	22.0

(From Gibson 1964:146, Table 11)

Table 3.7. Number of Indian tributaries in the Citlaltepec jurisdiction, 1570–1804.

Jurisdicion	Year							
	1570	*1644*	*1692*	*1742*	*1761-1765*	*1782*	*1787-1794*	*1797-1804*
Citlaltepec	6600	661	720	1206	1021	902	745	1362

(From Gibson 1964:142, Table 10)

a multiplier of 4.8, but he notes that different multipliers must be used for earlier periods due to changing demographic, social, and economic conditions. Gibson suggests a multiplier of 2.8–3.3 for the sixteenth century; by the late eighteenth century, however, he favors a multiplier of 4.06–5.79 (1964:140).

These figures clearly indicate, at least in general terms, the great (nearly unimaginable) magnitude of population loss in the Zumpango Region during the century and a half following 1521. By the early nineteenth century, a degree of recovery was underway, but regional population remained far below that of the sixteenth century.

The Nineteenth Century

By the beginning of the nineteenth century, more serious attention began to be paid to the growing imbalance in the Valley of Mexico between the numbers and configuration of people, on the one hand, and the control and utilization of water and aquatic resources, on the other. By this time, serious efforts to provide an external drainage outlet for the entire Basin of Mexico so as to control flooding had been underway for upwards of two centuries (Rojas et al. 1974; Ramirez 1976; Gurría 1978; Lemoine 1978), and these efforts were to continue through the nineteenth century and into the early decades of the twentieth century.

There are also indications from archival sources that significant water-control projects, particularly efforts to control the flow of both the Río Cuautitlan and the Río Pachuca into Lake Xaltocán-Zumpango, were undertaken under the hegemony of the Triple Alliance during the Late Aztec period, at least as early as 1435 and perhaps somewhat earlier (Palerm 1973:147, 155, 177, 191, 219, 229-44; Strauss 1974:139-54). Because so little is known of these prehispanic drainage efforts, Rojas et al. (1974:12) called for archaeological study to delineate their nature and time depth (would that we had followed their advice at the time it was offered!).

Because the exploitation of wetlands and aquatic resources was formerly so important in the southern half of the Zumpango Region, it is useful to outline the main changes in the nature of the former lacustrine and marshland zones that once existed in part of our survey area.

At the beginning of the nineteenth century, Alexander von Humboldt (1984) estimated the lake areas in the Valley of Mexico (Table 3.8). A survey carried out by the Comisión del Valle de México in 1861 (Gonzalez 1902:IV, cited in García Sanchez 1998:37) measured the surface areas and water depths of the different lakes as indicated in Table 3.9. A survey by M. Iglesias in 1866, cited in Niederberger (1987:1:88, 93), revealed the area, depth, and volume measurements found in Table 3.10.

Humboldt described the northern lakes (San Cristobal, Xaltocán, and Zumpango) as he observed them in the early years of the nineteenth century. Particularly interesting are the mentions of raised *calzadas* (walkways, said to be of prehispanic origin, and, as we noted above, discussed by Palerm [1973] on the basis of documentary sources) that crossed these lakes and marshlands, connecting communities on different sides of the wetlands and subdividing the lakes themselves into separate hydraulic "compartments," although they were occasionally broken and overrun by unusually severe floods (in particular, during the years 1648, 1675, 1707, 1732, 1748, 1772, and 1795):

El lago de San Cristóbal . . . es separado del lago de Xaltocan por una calzada muy antigua que va a los pueblos de San Pablo [probably modern San Pablo de la Laguna] y de Santo Tomás de Chiconautla. . . . *La calzada de la Cruz del Rey* divide el lago de Zumpango en dos estanques, llamados, el más occidental, Laguna de Citlaltépec, y el más oriental Laguna de Coyotepec. [Humboldt 1984:137-38]

[English translation] Lake San Cristóbal . . . is separated from Lake Xaltocan by a very old walkway, which goes to the towns of San Pablo [probably modern San Pablo de la Laguna] and Santo Tomás de Chiconautla. . . . The *Cruz del Rey* walkway divides

Table 3.8. Surface areas of lakes in the Valley of Mexico at the beginning of the nineteenth century.

Lake	Surface Area (km²)
Chalco-Xochimilco	114.4
Texcoco	177.8
San Cristobal*	63.4
Zumpango	19.4
Total surface area	*375.0*

(Adapted from Humboldt 1984:136)
*Lake San Cristobal here includes Lake Xaltocán.

Table 3.9. Lake surface areas and water depths in 1861.

Lake	Dry Season Area (km²)	Wet Season Area (km²)	Water Depth (m)
Chalco	104.5	114.2	2.40
Xochimilco	47.1	63.4	2.4-3.0
Texcoco	183.3	272.2	0.5
San Cristobal	11.0	11.0	0.6
Xaltocán	54.1	54.1	0.4
Zumpango	17.2	21.7	0.8
Total	*417*	*536.6*	

(Adapted from García Sanchez 1998:37)

Lake Zumpango into two smaller lakes, called Lake Citlaltépec (to the west) and Lake Coyotepec (to the east).

One of the earliest major flood-control projects undertaken by the Spanish authorities in the seventeenth century (in the decades after 1607) was to extend the efforts of prehispanic engineers in shifting the course of the Río Cuautitlan (the largest in the entire Valley of Mexico in terms of its volume of water) so that its waters drained northward through a canal and tunnel cut at Nochistongo near Huehuetoca (Humboldt 1984:140-41; Garay 1888:51), and then flowed into the Río Salado and on into the Atlantic drainage of the Río Tula. This drainage complex extended over a linear distance of 20.6 km (Humboldt 1984:148), attaining a maximum depth of up to 60 m and a width of up to 110 m—a remarkable engineering feat, and one that was achieved through the deployment of an extraordinary amount of forced Indian labor.

This seventeenth-century project was subsequently expanded and improved during the subsequent eighteenth and nineteenth centuries (Humboldt 1984:149; Garay 1888), and continued intermittently until the early twentieth century (*New York Times* 1894; Gurría 1978; Lemoine 1978) (Plate 3.1). As a result, after the early seventeenth century, Lake Xaltocán-Zumpango received much less water than it had previously, and so shrank considerably relative to its prehispanic condition. In fact, so intense and enduring were the late nineteenth efforts to improve the massive drainage infrastructure that for several decades, Zumpango assumed the aspect of a real boom town as it

se convirtió en la verdadera 'capital de las obras de desagüe' ... Porque fue ahí donde se establecieron las oficinas de la administración del desagüe, los almacenes para la guarda y reparto de los implementos y maquinaria de trabajo, y los talleres de herrería y carpintería para la fabricación y reparación de los útiles e instrumentos que se iban necesitando.... Zumpango presentó la imagen de una colmena humana, particularamente animada en los dias 'de raya.' [Lemoine 1978:57-58]

[English translation] became the true 'capital of drainage works' ... because it was there that they established the administrative offices for drainage, the stores for the maintenance and repair of tools and machinery and the forges and carpentry workshops for the making and repairing of tools and necessary instruments, ... Zumpango gave the impression of a human beehive, especially busy on 'paydays.'

In the early 1860s, Manuel Orozco y Berra described Lakes Xaltocán and Zumpango, then in fairly advanced stages of drainage:

Era el mes de marzo [near end of the dry season], y las aguas se habian agotado de tal manera que Almaraz [one of the project engineers] pudo atravesar a pié enjuto desde Santa Inés hasta Tonanitla [both pueblos to the south of our survey area], sin encontrar mas de un pequeño charco hacia San Pablo, con tan corta profundidad que el pasto nacido en el fondo asomaba sobre el superficie del líquido; entre Tonanitla y Xaltocan se hallaba otro charco en condiciones iguales al anterior, y solo al N. de Xaltocan habia una porción algo considerable de agua, cuya altura no pasaba en los lugares mas profundos de 0.12 m.
En el lago de Zumpango quedaron observados mas de treinta puntos, encontrándose el fondo de un barro negro que hace el vaso sumamente atascoso. [Orozco y Berra 1864:35]

[English translation] It was the month of March [near the end of the dry season], and the waters had been exhausted to such an extent that Almaraz could cross on foot from Santa Inés to Tonanitla [both pueblos to the south of our survey area], without encountering more than a small pond near San Pablo, with such little depth that the grasses growing at the bottom appeared to be on the surface of the water; between Tonanitla and Xaltocan another small pond was found, similar to the first one, and only north of Xaltocan was there any considerable quantity of water, but with a level no deeper than 0.12 meters.
In Lake Zumpango more than thirty places were observed where the bottom was of black mud, making the water extremely boggy.

Table 3.10. Lake measurements in 1866.

Lake	Area (km²)	Average Depth (m)	Volume (m³)
Texcoco	239	1.80	429,372,000
San Cristobal-Xaltocán	121	0.39	47,360,430
Zumpango	26	0.55	14,478,200
Total	*386*		*491,210,630*

(Adapted from Niederberger 1987:1:88, 93)

Orozco y Berra also provided a description of Xaltocán and its neighboring villages, their domestic economies, and the hunting of waterfowl in the remnants of Lake Xaltocán:

> Xaltocan está compuesto de ruinas y miserables chozas amontonadas en la isla, advirtiéndose por todas partes escombros y soledad; la iglesia misma casi está por tierra, sin culto y sin adornos. Los habitants viven durante el invierno, de los productos, de la caza de los patos, de los chichicuilotes, de las agachonas etc.; mientras duran las aguas en el lago se mantienen con la pesca del pescado blanco, de los juiles, de los charalitos y mexlapiques, de los atepocates etc, que se encuentran solo en los lugares por donde entran en vaso las aguas dulces; recogen tambienel ahuautle, el puxi y el cuculito; mas cuando se enjuta el lago y se agotan tan precarious medios de subsistencia, los infelices indígenas tienen que emigrar, de una vez huyendo de tierra tan ingrate, o por tiempo determinado para encontrar trabajo en alguna otra parte.
> Tonanitla [a pueblo ca. 4 km south of Xaltocan] es el transunto de Xaltocan: de ambos pueblos parten hacia el O. pequeñas calzadas, que los comunican con la tierra firme: la comunicación se interrumpe cuando las cubren en su crecimiento las aguas. Los charquetales persisten durante las secas, en la proximidad de los dos pueblos; las aguas estancadas alli impregnan el suelo con sus sales, lo reblandecen con sus infiltraciones, y forman atascaderos o pantanos que reciben el nombre de barreales....
> Nextlalpan es la cabecera de los pueblos cercanos; aquellos terrenos son poco a proposito para el cultivo y producen cortas cosechas de maiz, frijol, haba, cebada, y algun tomate. Los habitants beben el agua salobre de los pozos, se dedican a la agricultura y a la arriería, se empeñan en la onerosa servidumbre de peones de las haciendas, y los de Nextlalpan y de Xaltenco fabrican algun salitre.
> La caza del pato se hace en este lago por medio de armadas, y por el método particular llamado aquí de parejas. Consiste en doce o quince hombres armados, que en chalupas y en orden de batalla, se acercan silenciosamente hasta el punto mas cercano que las aves no los perciben, a una voz disparan, y a fuerza de remo se lanzan sobre la presa muerta o herida, para que nada se escape de lo caido. [Orozco y Berra 1864:170-71]

> *[English translation]* Xaltocan is composed of ruins and wretched huts piled up on the island, with debris and loneliness all around; the church itself is almost fallen down, without shrines or adornments. During the winter, the inhabitants live by hunting ducks, curlew and other aquatic birds; while water remains in the lake, they support themselves by catching white fish, *juiles*, *charalitos*, *mexlapiques*, and *atepocates*, etc., which are found only in the areas where fresh water enters the basin. They also gather aquatic insect eggs (*ahuautle*), brine flies (*puxi*), and algae (*cuculito*). When the lake diminishes and they exhaust these precarious means of subsistence, the unhappy natives must emigrate, fleeing the harsh land one time, or for a set period of time to look for work in other parts.
> Tonanitla [a *pueblo* ca. 4 km south of Xaltocán] is an exact copy of Xaltocan: from both towns, small walkways lead westward, connecting them with the mainland. Communication is interrupted when the rising waters cover these walkways. Small wet areas remain during the dry season, near the two towns; the salt from the stagnant waters permeate into the soil and soften it with their infiltrations, forming bogs or marshes, which are called *barreales*....
> Nextlalpan is the main settlement of the area; those lands are little-suited to cultivation and produce scanty harvests of corn, kidney beans, broad beans, barley and a few tomatoes. The inhabitants drink salty water from the wells, their work consists of agriculture and raising beasts of burden; they enslave themselves in the burdensome and servile work as laborers on *haciendas*, and those from Nextlalpan and Xaltocan make some saltpetre.
> The hunting of ducks on this lake is done using fleets of boats, and by the specific method called *parejas*. It consists of twelve or fifteen armed men, in small boats and in battle formation, who silently approach the birds, getting as close as possible without the birds noticing them. Then, all at once, they shoot, and with the strength of their paddles they throw themselves at their wounded or dead prey, so that none gets away.

Orozco y Berra also described nearby Lake Zumpango and the life of the people who lived around its shores in the early 1860s:

> La figura del lago es del todo irregular, y la sinuosidad de sus orillas no le presta semejanza con ninguna de las figuras geométricas regulares: su superficie es de 0.98 leguas cuadradas [ca. 16.8 km²].
> ... antiguamente recibia este lago el caudal del rio de Cuautitlan, reputado como el mas importante del Valle; por ese hecho la superficie se extendia a distancias considerables, de manera que por el O. se encontraban sus orillas cercanas al pueblo de Teoloyuca. Despues que aquella corriente fué sacada por el tajo de Nochistongo, la estensión del Zumpango disminuyó mucho, encontrándose hoy ritirado mas de tres mil metros del espresado Teoloyuca. Tampoco existe el canal que formaba el desagüe directo del recipiente, de manera que, ahora determinan sus variaciones, las crecientes que recibe en la estación lluviosa, en cuya época llega a su maximum, y el tiempo seco, en que toca a su minimum, agotadas las aguas por la evaporacion y demas fenómenos análogos. El fondo es fangoso: en Marzo de 1862 [near the end of the annual dry season] el nivel del líquido variaba desde 0.08 m en las orillas hasta medio metro en la parte mas profunda....
> En medio del lago hay una pequeña isla oblonga, cuyo nombre es Zatlatelco [almost certainly the same place, still called by the same name, that we were told about in 1973—see description of Zu-Az-253]; presenta la particularidad de ser salitrosa, mientras los terrenos del rededor del vaso son bastante feraces [fertile].
> Las aguas son casi dulces.... Los terrenos vecinos, enlamados con el limo de las crecientes, son propios para la agricultura

y rinden abundantes cosechas. Los habitantes acostumbran ir sembrando, principalmente maiz, en las tierras descubiertas por el líquido y a medida que éste se disminuye por la evaporacion, manera por la cual, no solo aprovechan los jugos, sinto tambien casi toda la estension del vaso. Esto presenta el grave inconveniente de que si las lluvias adelantan, el lago crece rápidamente, sepultando en su seno los frutos de una cosecha próxima a ser recogida.

La desecacion annual del recipiente impide el desarrollo de los peces, por lo cual la pesca es insignificante.

Los pueblos principales inmediatos al lago son Zumpango, Citlaltepec, San Pedro barrio de Zumpango, Teoloyuca, Coyotepec, y la hacienda de Xalpa. Los habitantes se dedican principalmente a la agricultura; siembran maiz, alverjon, haba, frijol, cebada, centeno y trigo aventurero, o dependiente de las lluvias para su riego, de cuyas semillas, maiz sobre todo, recogen abundantes cosechas. Usan de agua de pozos, dulces si están abiertos en los lugares altos, salitrosos si están en los bajos. [Orozco y Berra 1864:171-72]

[English translation] The lake's shape is irregular, the curves of its shore resembling no regular geometric figure: it has an area of 0.98 square leagues [ca. 16.8 km^2].

. . . In previous times, this lake received the flow from the Cuautitlan river, reputed to be the most important in the Valley; because of this influx of water, the area of the lake extended a considerable distance, so that to the west its shores reached near the town of Teoloyuca. After the flow from the Cuautitlan river was blocked by the Nochistongo dike, the expanse of Lake Zumpango decreased greatly; its borders now stand more than 3000 meters from Teoloyuca. Neither does the canal exist which once allowed for direct drainage, so that today's variances are determined—the high water levels in the rainy season and the low levels in the dry season—by water that disappears through evaporation, and other similar phenomena. The depths are muddy: in March of 1862 [near the end of the annual dry season] the water level varied between 0.08 meter along the shore to half a meter in the deepest part. . . .

In the middle of the lake there is a small oblong island, whose name is Zatlatelco [almost certainly the same place, still called by the same name, that we were told about in 1973—see description of Zu-Az-253 in Appendix A]; this island presents the peculiarity of having salty soil while the lands around the lake are very fertile.

The waters are nearly freshwater. . . . The neighboring lands, enriched with mud from when the lake rises, are suitable for agriculture and yield abundant harvests. The inhabitants regularly plant seeds, mostly corn, in the lands uncovered by the water, and to the extent that evaporation reduces the water level, they are able to make use of nearly the whole basin, not just the most fertile areas. This presents the great disadvantage that if the rains come early, the lake grows rapidly, burying the fruits of the next harvest in its waters before they can be gathered.

The annual drying up of the lake impedes the development of fish, and for this reason, fishing is insignificant here.

The principal towns adjoining the lake are Zumpango, Citlaltepec, the San Pedro neighborhood of Zumpango, Teoloyuca, Coyotepec, and the *hacienda* of Xalpa. The inhabitants' primary work is agriculture; they sow corn, peas, broad beans, kidney beans, barley, rye and wheat, and from these seeds they gather abundant harvests, especially corn, as long as the rains provide ample irrigation for the crops. They use water from wells, if they are open; freshwater in higher lands, salty water in the low-lying areas.

Writing near the end of the nineteenth century, Francisco de Garay offered a vivid description of the changes in lifeways produced by the ongoing projects that removed the large volume of water that had previously flowed into Lake Xaltocán-Zumpango through the Río Cuautitlan:

Con el desvio de la corriente del río, se hirió de muerte toda la comarca. Hoy el pueblo de Xaltocan, encaramado sobre un pequeño isla, domina durante los meses de la seca, un llano inmenso lleno de eflorescencias salinas; es un desierto. Los míseros habitantes del lugar, no teniendo ni agua que beber, huyen a otras tierras hasta que vuelva la estación de las aguas. Entónces la pesca, y despues la caza del pato, los atrae de nuevo a sus hogares. En 1600 era uno de los pueblos más ricos en riegos, como lo atestiguan los naturals con los títulos que conservan *en el sagrado* de su ruinoso templo; hoy no tienen ni un campo. Más al sur, en el mismo lago, en un islote, se halla el pueblo de Tonanitla. A una legua de distancia al Este, sobre la orilla, está la hacienda de Ojo de Agua, donde brota un hermoso manantial, el único que existe en el vaso de este lago. Gracias a los derrames de esa fuente, cuidadosamente recogidos por los indígenas, por bordos atravezados de Sureste a Nordoeste, el agua forma unas dos lagunetas permanents durante la seca, que sirven de viveros para el pescado blanco; al venire las aguas y extenderse éstas en los vasos de Xaltocan y de San Cristóbal, el pescado aumenta prodigiosamente, y es el elemento principal de vida para todos los pueblos de los contornos; de agricultores, las obras del Desagüe los ha convertido en pescadores. Algunos aun conservan su antigua industria de fabricantes de *petates*, de *chiquihuites* y de otros productos del *tule*, pero no encontrándose ya éste en los terrenos salados del Norte, los industriales tienen que irlo a buscar a diez o doce leguas [ca. 40-50 km] de distancia en el lago de Xochimilco. Sin embargo, . . . llevan una vida precaria y miserable, y la población ha disminuido con los elementos de vida que han desaparecido.

Los lagos de Xaltocan y de San Cristobal no se atierran notablemente, pues no reciben en su vaso ningun rio o arroyo. Algunas torrenteras del cerro de Chiconautla, y de los llanos inmediatos, son los que lo alimentan. Durante los meses de calor, su lecho se seca y los vientos reinantes del Norte levantan densas nubes de polve, que pasan al Sur, hacienda desaparecer los atierres que se hayan formado. [Garay 1888:64-65]

[English translation] With the diversion of the river current, the entire region was devastated. Today during the dry months, the town of Xaltocan, raised up on a small island, looks out over an immense plain full of salt dust; it is a desert. The miserable inhabitants of this place, without even water to drink, flee to other lands until the rainy season returns, when fishing and then duck-hunting bring them back to their homes. In 1600, this was one of the most water-rich towns in the area, as the natives attest with the titles preserved in the sacred confines of their ruined temple; today they lack even a field. Further south on the same lake, on an island, is the town of Tonanitla. One league from here, to the east and on the shore, is a *hacienda* called *Ojo de Agua* where a beautiful spring wells up, the only one in the basin of this lake. Thanks to the waters from this spring, carefully gathered by the natives by means of embankments laid from southeast to northwest, the water forms two small lakes that remain during the dry season, serving as hatcheries for white fish; when the waters return and these lakes expand into the basins of Lakes Xaltocan and San Cristóbal, the fish grow rapidly and become the principal life-sustaining element for all the towns in the surrounding

area. The drainages have turned farmers into fishermen. Some still practice the old industry of making woven mats and baskets and other products from rushes, but since they no longer find the rushes in the salty lands of the north, they must go in search of them some ten or twelve leagues [ca. 40-50 km] away, in Lake Xochimilco. Nevertheless, . . . they live a precarious and miserable life, and the population has diminished along with the ways of life that have disappeared.

Lakes Xaltocan and San Cristóbal do not silt up noticeably, for they are not supplied by any river or stream. They receive their waters instead from floods from Cerro Chiconautla and from the nearby plains. During the hot months, the lakebed dries out and the north winds bring dense clouds of dust that blow to the south, eliminating the buildups of soil that have formed.

Garay noted that the sizes of Lakes Xaltocán, Zumpango, and San Cristobal varied considerably over the course of an annual cycle:

> En el estiaje [dry season] los vasos de Zumpango, Xaltocan, San Cristobal y del mismo Texcoco, con excepción de algunas charcales, se secan por completo. En tiempo de aguas la de Zumpango generalmente mide una superficie de una legua; la de Xaltocan de tres, y la de San Cristóbal de dos. [Garay 1888:69]

[English translation] In the dry season, the basins of Zumpango, Xaltocan, San Cristóbal and also Texcoco, with the exception of a few ponds, dry up completely. In the rainy season, the waters of Lake Zumpango generally measure one league in area; those of Lake Xaltocan, three leagues, and those of Lake San Cristóbal, two leagues.

The impact of the rerouting of the Ríos Cuautitlan and Pachuca was particularly detrimental to the wetlands of Lake Xaltocán-Zumpango since, with only one exception (the above-noted spring at Ojo de Agua in eastern Lake Xaltocán), these northern lakes lacked the numerous permanent springs that fed into Lakes Texcoco, Xochimilco, and Chalco farther south in the Valley of Mexico (Garay 1888:70; Peñafiel 1884:79-81).

Summary and Conclusions

The names of many, but far from all, modern settlements have survived since the sixteenth century (Table 3.11); several of these settlements today function as municipio capitals. As far as I can determine, there are no *significant* communities named in the sixteenth-century sources that have failed to survive into the twentieth century (ignoring a number of places listed as dependent barrios in the sixteenth-century sources).

We know that many names of Colonial and even Late Aztec communities have survived into the late twentieth century, and it seems safe to assume that these named communities have remained in *approximately* the same places over the past 500 years. What we do not know is the degree to which these fifteenth- and sixteenth-century settlements resembled their modern namesakes in terms of precise location, physical configuration, population size, population density, sociopolitical status, and functional characteristics. My impression (to be further developed and explicated in subsequent sections of this monograph) is that Late Aztec settlements were much less nucleated than their Colonial and modern counterparts—that is, residential, ritual, civic, and economic functions were spatially more dispersed in Late Aztec times relative to the historic period. An altogether much more complicated matter is the degree to which elements of the Colonial and Late Aztec settlement systems can be projected farther back into prehispanic times. As will be discussed in subsequent sections of this monograph, the radical changes in regional settlement configuration at several junctures in the prehispanic past imply that historic and ethnographic patterns may not always provide good analogies for prehistoric times.

In any case, the historical sources, and our own observations in 1973, indicate that the following interrelated considerations must be taken into account in any effort to interpret archaeological data in the light of these sources and observations:

(1) Although many sixteenth-century community names have survived into the present, it seems clear that the main features of historic settlement patterning in the Zumpango Region is largely a product of Spanish *congregación* policies. There is no *necessary* relationship between the specific loci and physical or functional characteristics of modern settlements and their sixteenth-century namesakes.

Table 3.11. Modern communities in the Zumpango Region listed and not listed in sixteenth-century documents (discounting modern dependent barrios).[a]

Listed in Early Sixteenth-Century Documents[b]	Listed in *Relaciones Geográficas*, 1579-1582[c]	Not Listed in Sixteenth-Century Documents
Apaxco	**Apaxco**	Ajoloapan
Hueypoxtla	Coyotepec	Cuevas
Tlapanaloya	**Huehuetoca**	**Melchor Ocampo**
Xaltocán	**Hueypoxtla**	Nopala
Zitlaltepec	**Jaltenco**	San Sebastian
Zumpango	Jilotzingo	Tenopalco
	Nextlalpan	**Teoloyucan**
	Tequixquiac	**Tultepec**
	Tlapanaloya	Visitación
	Xaltocán	
	Zitlaltepec	
	Zumpango	

[a]Modern spellings used; listed in alphabetical order. Names in boldface indicate modern municipio capitals.
[b](Barlow 1949; Gibson 1964; Carrasco 1999; Hicks 2005)
[c](Acuña 1986; Paso y Troncoso 1905)

(2) The modern physical environment is severely degraded relative to late prehispanic times, and this degradation was already well underway by the late sixteenth century. Principal factors in this degradation have been the introduction and intensification of sheep raising and deforestation after the 1520s, and the great loss of Indian population that reached its nadir in the mid-seventeenth century and the consequent abandonment, or severe decline, of intensive land use in much of the area.

(3) Although the cultivation of indigenous and introduced crops has been the primary foundation of subsistence and the domestic economy for centuries, the productivity of rainfall-based agriculture has always been uncertain and unpredictable. The only highly productive agricultural lands today are irrigated fields, mainly along the course of the Río Salado as it flows northward into the Río Tula. Because of deforestation and massive sheet erosion, it is difficult to know the earlier irrigation potential of other parts of the Zumpango Region—particularly the broad Upper Salado Drainage east of Apaxco and Tequixquiac and north of Huehuetoca, and the Basin of Mexico Lower Piedmont north of the Río Pachuca.

(4) The massive drainage projects that began in the early seventeenth century and continued for over 300 years have radically altered the prehispanic hydrology of the Zumpango Region. Archival studies (Palerm 1973; Strauss 1974) indicate that there were also major efforts during late prehispanic times to control water levels for flood control and agricultural production (for example, the development of chinampas around Xaltocán and other communities in southern Lake Xaltocán-San Cristobal). Although these precolumbian undertakings remain poorly understood, they did not involve any drainage out of the Basin of Mexico. The two principal rivers (Cuautitlan and Pachuca) that once fed directly into Lake Xaltocán-Zumpango have long been diverted out of the Basin of Mexico watershed. Consequently, the former wetland zones in the southern half of our survey area had almost vanished by 1973, and this desiccation process had been underway at an accelerating pace for centuries before that. Much of the terrain in the southern half of the Zumpango Region that is now devoted primarily to agriculture and grazing was formerly exploited for such products as salt, waterfowl, fish, reeds, edible insects, algae, reeds, and numerous other aquatic resources, in addition to substantial zones of agricultural chinampas—nearly all of which had vanished by the time of our fieldwork in 1973.

(5) Although available evidence is skimpy, Gibson's (1964) archival studies indicate a deliberate Colonial policy to maximize access to the full range of available resources within each regional administrative jurisdiction—that is, to configure the territory of administrative districts such that its inhabitants would have a degree of direct access to agricultural and grazing lands, forest zones, and wetland resources. This echoes points subsequently raised in Pedro Carrasco's (1980) archivally based discussion of Mesoamerican "verticality" (the incorporation of different ecological zones within a single political economy), with clear suggestions of prehispanic antecedents. Obviously, in the Zumpango Region, this "verticality" strategy would have been most fully feasible for territories bordering the lakeshores.

Complementing and extending such efforts as might have been made to ensure a degree of territorial economic autonomy, the Colonial documentary sources, especially those of the sixteenth century, also indicate the importance of interregional exchanges of complementary products and services within the Valley of Mexico via water-borne transport through marketplace networks. Such water-borne linkages almost certainly had prehispanic antecedents. In this fashion, the inhabitants of the Zumpango Region interacted in local and regional exchange networks with consumers and producers throughout the Valley of Mexico—as recent archaeological studies of Middle and Late Postclassic ceramic distributions have indicated (Nichols et al. 2002; Brumfiel and Hodge 1996; Hodge and Neff 2005).

With these considerations in mind, we now turn to the archaeological survey data, beginning in Chapter 4 with a discussion of how we designed and implemented our fieldwork in 1973, and how we subsequently processed the information in the laboratory.

Chapter 4

Field and Laboratory Methodology

Surface Conditions—Potentials and Problems for Regional Surface Survey in the Zumpango Region

The reliability and productivity of our surface survey are closely tied to certain specific characteristics of the ground surface in the Zumpango Region. Much of the surface below approximately 2450 m asl has been plowed, at least occasionally, for several centuries. A great deal of this terrain was almost certainly cultivated in prehispanic times as well, albeit with a technology that lacked horse- or ox-drawn plows. This continual, long-term disturbance and reworking of the ground surface has maintained a steady churning up of archaeological materials within the plow zone and has ensured renewed exposure of ceramic and lithic artifacts in many localities. Furthermore, intensive cultivation has also removed much natural vegetation that might otherwise have obscured surficial archaeological remains.

In much of the Zumpango Region, the soil cover is presently less than one meter deep. This is especially true for the Upper Salado Drainage (USD) and the Basin of Mexico Lower Piedmont (BOMLP), where extensive erosion has often reduced soil cover to depths of less than 50 cm, and there are even many large patches of bare subsoil (*tepetate*). Much deeper soil characterizes the Lakeshore Plain and Lakebed zones in the southern half of our study area (Fig. 2.3). In the latter two areas, we suspect that alluviation may have obscured some archaeological remains. Elsewhere, the combination of thin soil cover, limited alluviation, extensive plowing, and moderate to severe erosion has created an almost ideal situation in which surface remains can be used with confidence to infer occupational chronology, the borders of ancient settlements, and the presence of certain other kinds of prehispanic occupation (for instance, stone-faced terracing). While our confidence is lower in the Lakeshore Plain and Lakebed zones, the fact that we have recovered abundant surficial remains of prehispanic occupation in both these sectors indicates that even in such deep-soil locations, the archaeological surface materials reflect a good deal about the more deeply buried subsurface remains.

The post-depositional impact of erosion on archaeological surface remains should also be considered. One might expect, for example, that since erosion has been severe in some sloping areas, there would have been significant lateral movement of surface artifacts over time and, consequently, some uncertainty in relating surface finds to their original locations. We do occasionally find some badly water-worn sherds in *barranca* beds where they are obviously well removed from their original locations. However, it appears that the great majority of sherds and stone artifacts do not travel very far from their original loci. Even in those areas where all topsoil has been stripped away by massive sheet erosion, the stone wall bases of ancient structures often remain partially intact (functioning like small terraces), and associated ceramic and lithic materials appear to have settled virtually in place onto the underlying subsoil. Very few sherds that we find outside of actual *barranca* beds, for example, show any indication of having been transported by water.

This is not to say that there are no problems in inferring prehispanic occupation on the basis of archaeological surface remains over most of our survey area. Surface visibility of such occupation can significantly change seasonally as a field is plowed, planted, cultivated, and allowed to lie fallow. Impressions of artifact density can vary depending on the point in the modern land-use cycle in which the archaeologist makes observations. Some fields are left fallow for varying lengths of time, and the lack of annual plowing can affect the apparent density of surface pottery relative to fields that are plowed every year. Some expanses of terrain have seldom, or never, been plowed. In such a situation (such as occurs at the hilltop site of Zu-ET-12), even a fairly large, nucleated site may have a sparse sherd cover. In some areas, relict stands of oak-conifer or thick grassy-bushy vegetation may seriously obscure surface pottery. We have made no systematic endeavor to control for this kind of variability. Hirth (1974) did make such an attempt in his regional surveys in eastern Morelos, south of the Valley of Mexico. He found that archaeological surface manifestations can vary significantly at specific sites within an annual cycle. We should certainly expect some of the same kinds of variation within the Valley of Mexico.

While we unfortunately have no control over this kind of potential variability, we did indicate the character of the site area at the time we observed it, and specifically noted those localities where we believe our impressions may be inadequate. In cases where the ground surface had not been plowed, we made a special effort to observe points where it had been disturbed in other ways (for example, gopher burrows, ant hills, erosion channels, man-made pitting or ditching). In some cases, we have probably missed small sites in unplowed areas or in places where cultivated plants and weed cover were particularly heavy (such as sometimes occurs near the end of the growing season, in October and November). Sites with standing architecture are always visible, although sherd cover may be so scanty as to make evaluation of chronology and occupational intensity (based on relative sherd density) difficult.

Our survey works best where there are few occupational components at any single locality. The greater the number of components at one place, the greater the possibility for errors in our evaluation of each component at that place. At multicomponent sites it can be difficult, or even impossible, to date architectural remains visible on the surface. If one component is very dominant, or particularly intense, other components may be overlooked or underestimated unless considerable care is taken to recognize and recover them. Multicomponent sites are particularly troublesome for our survey, and our impressions of their occupation should be taken with less confidence than for sites that have been occupied less continuously and for shorter periods.

Survey Methodology

With the above considerations in mind, we now discuss the specific techniques we utilized to recover, record, and evaluate the surface remains of prehispanic occupation in the Zumpango Region. Some aspects of this methodology have been described in earlier publications from other parts of the Valley of Mexico (Parsons 1971; Blanton 1972; Sanders et al. 1979; Parsons et al. 1982). For us, a site is a discrete cluster of occupation, defined by the presence of surface pottery and lithic artifacts and/or mounding, that appears to have had a significant "settlement function." We leave aside for now the thorny question of how large such a "cluster" needs to be before it deserves designation as a "site," except to note that since we are interested mainly in "settlements," we have been guided by our thinking that the smallest settlement might be an area suitable for at least a few domestic structures.

Several excavations at sites located or observed during our surveys elsewhere in the Valley of Mexico indicate that such occupational clusters do indeed represent the loci of prehispanic activity at those localities (e.g., Tolstoy and Fish 1975; Santley 1977; Parsons et al. 1985; Serra 1988; Ramírez et al. 2000; García Chávez 1991, 2004; García Chávez and Córdoba 1994; Sanders 1994; Castillo 1994; Lazcano 1995; Parsons and Morett 2004; Brumfiel 2005; Hodge 2008). With a few obvious exceptions (for example, isolated hilltop platform mounds with little or no surface pottery), we believe we are defining residential loci, although we have no control over such critical factors as seasonal or temporary versus permanent residence.

Our efforts have been tremendously facilitated by the availability of good quality, large-scale aerial photographs. Without these, our entire field procedure would have required substantial modification. We used vertical aerial photographs at a scale of 1:5000 for maneuvering in the field and for directly plotting surface archaeological and land-use data. During the summer part of our fieldseason (May through late August), we worked in two teams, each comprising three or four people; during the subsequent fall months (September through early December), we worked in one team of three or four people. For best results, every team member should have a good general knowledge of the regional ceramic sequence. In practice, it is possible to operate, albeit less efficiently, if only one team member is thoroughly familiar with the full details of ceramic variability; in such cases, the more experienced person needs to frequently check on the impressions of the other team members.

The members of the survey team walked in an essentially linear fashion, separated by distances of 20 to 50 meters. This spacing was primarily determined by topographic considerations, the presence of modern settlement (including the presence of dogs defending their well-defined territories), and the complexity of prehispanic occupation. Where multicomponent prehispanic occupation occurs, or where ceramic chronology appears questionable, the interperson spacing contracts so as to ensure accurate observation. Where occupation is clearly single component, or where it is wholly absent, the interval can expand.

The person at the center of the survey line carried the 1:5000 airphoto mounted on a plywood board. This center-person guided the field team through an area and wrote the team's observations (concerning sherd density, mounding, locations of surface collections, and so on) in coded form directly onto the aerial photo. At frequent intervals, the team members along the survey line called out their observations to the center-person (Fig. 4.1), who recorded these observations on the airphoto. The survey team moved at the pace of its slowest member (usually the center-person, who must pause frequently to record both the information along his or her own path and that being relayed by teammates) (Fig. 4.2). Care was taken that the entire team moved at about the same pace to avoid the inevitable loss of cohesion should any member(s) get too far ahead of, or behind, the rest.

Relative sherd density was "eye-balled" directly in the field according to a visual scale described in an earlier study (Parsons 1971:22-23):

> In designating occupational density in the field, we have employed a generalized, subjective visual scale of estimation: very light, light, light-to-moderate, moderate, and heavy.
>
> 1) *Very light*—A wide scattering of surface pottery, with single sherds visible only at intervals of several meters. If no effort is made to search for sherds, one may expect that surface pottery is absent.
> 2) *Light*—Sherds distributed continuously, with single sherds at intervals of several cm, but no significant build up of sherd density beyond this point.
> 3) *Light-to-moderate*—A marked build up of sherd density to a point where sherds are clearly visible everywhere, and there are very few gaps in the distribution of surface pottery. Some one-meter squares selected at random might produce very few sherds, while others might yield up to 100, or so, pieces of pottery.
> 4) *Moderate*—A continuous layer of sherds in a situation where any randomly placed one-meter square would produce a count of roughly 100 to 200 pieces of pottery.
> 5) *Heavy* [rarely encountered]—A continuous layer of sherds in a situation where any randomly-placed one-meter square would produce a count of several hundred pieces of pottery.

While this system has several disadvantages, for our purposes these are counterbalanced by considerable advantages including—most importantly—speed and reasonable reliability and consistency when used by trained field observers. With such field workers, it is possible to move fairly rapidly over large areas and to produce regional maps of relative sherd density that could be duplicated, with only small margins of error, by another comparably trained and experienced survey team working in the same area. Nonetheless, this system is not wholly rigorous, and there is always the potential for uncontrollable and unpredictable variability in the evaluation of sherd density by different observers, even within the same survey team.

Furthermore, although we hope we are measuring relative settlement nucleation by our observations of relative sherd density, in actuality we are unable to evaluate how sherd density at any specific locality may vary with different degrees of occupational time depth or permanence. Just as significantly, our methodology for evaluating sherd density cannot be easily used by people who have not worked with us and who might attempt to evaluate occupational intensity in other areas and compare their results with ours. For such interregional comparative purposes, it would be desirable to have actual sherd counts per square meter, or something similar. Our only excuse for not including such a technique in our survey is that when we did briefly attempt it at an early stage in the Valley of Mexico surveys, it simply proved to be much too time consuming and logistically difficult.

The entire survey team halted its movement whenever an archaeological feature, such as a mound or terrace remnant, was encountered, or when any particular problem arose—usually relating to questions about ceramic chronology or placement of surface collections, but occasionally involving things such as conversations with local people regarding our work (Fig. 4.3), fending off territorially oriented dogs (Fig. 4.4), maneuvering around or through modern settlements, or extricating ourselves from difficult terrain. Every recognizable prehispanic architectural feature (usually a mound) was measured, photographed, and described in the field notebook. The survey team also stopped and pooled its labor to make collections of surface pottery (and a few lithic artifacts). The decision to make a surface collection at any particular location was the product of several considerations.

We attempted to make at least one surface collection at every site we defined. Largely because of our belief that Aztec ceramic chronology was comparatively easy to evaluate on the basis of "eye-balling" observations, we tended to sample single-component Aztec sites less frequently than others. Relatively larger sites and multicomponent sites generally require more surface collections to properly understand chronological variation over time and space at particular localities. Sometimes simple logistical problems governed the frequency of surface collecting. For example, because a survey team could seldom return to a distant vehicle during the course of a day's work, bagged surface collections must usually be carried for several hours. There is a limit to the weight and volume that can be backpacked in this fashion by a small survey team, even when a local worker is hired to assist with this task, and so surface collecting for the day had to be curtailed or postponed after such a limit was reached. In a few cases, we revisited inadequately sampled sites to make additional surface collections, but it was often not practicable to do this.

Although our surface collections from the Zumpango Region and elsewhere in the Valley of Mexico have subsequently proved useful to other archaeologists for different research purposes, at the time of our survey our principal purpose in making these collections was to control for occupational chronology, which accounts for our focus on ceramics at the expense of lithic artifacts. We were less interested in inferring functional and status differences over time and space. Such inferences, we felt, would have to be based on a much more sophisticated and time-consuming sampling strategy than we could implement at this early stage of our regional investigation. Thus, we saw the main function of our surface collections as supplementing our in-the-field "eye-balling" chronological appraisals.

Once we had decided on a collection locality, all the team members congregated at the chosen spot. We attempted to collect between 50 and 150 diagnostic rim and decorated body sherds (including bases and handles). This is the quantity of material that approximately fills a standard cloth bag, and that can be carried around for several hours without undue strain. We determined that this quantity of diagnostic ceramic material can be collected by two to four people within about a twenty-minute period from an area that varies inversely with sherd density—from about 10,000

Figure 4.1. Two members of a survey crew, showing typical spacing configuration and communication procedures (drawing by Naomi F. Miller).

Figure 4.2. Recording information on the 1:5000 airphoto (drawing by Naomi F. Miller).

Figure 4.3. A conversation with local people (drawing by Naomi F. Miller).

Figure 4.4. Encounter with a territorial dog (drawing by Naomi F. Miller).

Figure 4.5. Surface collecting (drawing by Naomi F. Miller).

m² (one hectare) for light sherd cover to about 100 m² for light-to-moderate concentrations. An area of appropriate size is marked off, and the survey team spends about twenty minutes picking up all diagnostic material from within the designated area (Fig. 4.5). We assume that this procedure will produce a representative sample of the subsurface ceramic material at this locality.

The survey proceeded airphoto by airphoto (at 1:5000, photos measuring 50 × 50 cm, the size we normally used, incorporate areas approximately 2.5 × 2.5 km). Each individual airphoto was completed before the next one was begun by a single team working in any given part of the overall survey area. We made no attempt to define sites or to delineate their borders in the field. During earlier field seasons we had attempted to do this, but it generally produced chaos as we invariably drifted off our airphoto as we followed out larger sites or when we tried to keep track of several different site borders in areas of multi-component occupation (we defined our sites on the basis of both chronological and spatial variables, and consequently there are as many separate "sites" as there are significant occupational components at any single locality). Instead, we found it more effective to concentrate on covering one airphoto at a time, and to define individual site borders shortly afterwards when, in our field lab, several adjoining airphotos were traced onto a single large sheet of transparent paper. On such a tracing, regional distributions of coeval archaeological remains can be readily discerned when annotations of occupations from different time periods are underlined with different colors.

Nevertheless, by not defining site boundaries in the field, we sometimes created another problem for ourselves. Because we usually did not know how large or complex a site was while we were actually walking over any one part of it, it was sometimes difficult to organize our surface collecting so as to include all major, or distinctive, parts of the site. Consequently, some sites are undersampled or oversampled, and occasionally we were forced to revisit a site to make additional collections (which we usually did only in the larger and/or more complicated sites).

In the field, we carried small notebooks in which we wrote descriptions of specific archaeological features, the details of surface collection areas, and a detailed record of photographs taken in the course of a day's work. We wrote most other observations (for example, modern land use, drainage features, soil depth) directly onto the airphotos. Most of our airphotos were of fairly recent vintage, and so we had a ready-made record of modern settlements, roads, pathways, agricultural fields and field borders, erosional severity, drainage patterns, and so on. We simply superimposed impressionistic contour lines (eye-balled) onto the airphotos in order to clarify the topography when it came time to make tracings onto paper. Archaeological remains, except for some unusually large mounds, were seldom apparent on the airphotos, but once we had observed them in the field, archaeological details could be readily and accurately drawn onto the photo surfaces.

On the airphotos, we recorded a continuous flow of sherd densities by time period as these were called to the center-person from the surveyors along the survey line, and as the center-person recorded his or her own observations. We also recorded "Locations," usually places where we made surface collections (designated consecutively from #1 by each survey team), and "Features," usually specific concentrations of architectural remains such as mounds or terrace remnants (designated consecutively, beginning with the letter A, by each survey team). Each roll of film (Kodak Plus-X, 36 exposures) was assigned a number; this roll number and each negative number as it was exposed were recorded in the notebook carried by each team as locations, features, and landscapes were photographed.

With a very few exceptions (for example, small areas for which local landowners denied us permission to enter), we surveyed all open terrain within our survey borders. We did not survey systematically within modern settlements, except for an occasional empty houselot or small open field. Occasionally we made more casual observations while walking along streets inside these villages and towns. Working in this fashion, we covered an area of 526 km² (Table 4.1).

Laboratory Procedures in Mexico

As noted above, once the field survey on individual airphotos was completed, we traced the annotated information onto large sheets of transparent paper where site borders were defined and numbered. These provisional field numbers were intended only for purposes of record keeping in the field and laboratory, and were subsequently replaced by final site numbers when the final maps were later prepared for publication (as discussed below). On the tracings, site borders were drawn around areas of roughly continuous coeval occupation where the density of surface pottery measured at least "light" on our visual estimation scale. Certain allowances were made for areas where occupation was almost certainly present, but where the density of surface pottery was depressed as the result of infrequent plowing or heavy veg-

Table 4.1. Zumpango Region surveyed area.

Total area within 1973 survey borders	609 km²
Total area covered by modern settlement (1960)[a]	56 km²
Area of Laguna de Zumpango	16 km²
Area of survey gap[b]	11 km²
Total 1973 surveyed area	526 km²

[a]15% added to total area of main settlements to account for scattered ranchos, rancherias, and haciendas; several unsurveyable plots; and population growth between 1960 and 1973.
[b]The result of an unperceived (while in the field) gap between adjacent airphotos in the central part of the survey area.

etation cover. In a few cases where surface pottery was virtually absent (for example, at isolated hilltop platform mounds), sites were defined on the basis of architecture alone.

In most cases, the delineation of site borders proved to be a relatively straightforward task since surface pottery and mounding are usually concentrated in fairly discrete and well-defined areas. For the Late Aztec period, however, archaeological remains have often proved to be much less clustered, and there is frequently an almost continuous scatter of dispersed occupation over very large areas. In many of the fields we examined, there were often at least a few Late Aztec sherds, so it is difficult to draw a border around discrete sherd concentrations of this period. Consequently, for this last period of the prehispanic sequence, our site definitions have often been made on a more arbitrary basis than we would have preferred.

Our site identification system was developed by W.T. Sanders during the original Teotihuacan Valley surveys and has remained unchanged. Each site (ideally, a discrete cluster of surface pottery and/or architectural remains that belong to a single archaeological period) is identified by a three-part label. The first part of this label identifies the sub-region of the Valley of Mexico: Teotihuacan Region (T), Texcoco Region (Tx), Ixtapalapa Region (Ix), Chalco Region (Ch), Xochimilco Region (Xo), Cuautitlan Region (Cu), Zumpango Region (Zu), Temascalapa Region (Tm). The second part of the site label identifies the period to which the occupation dates (there are no Early or Middle Formative sites in the Zumpango Region): Early Formative (EF), Middle Formative (MF), Late Formative (LF), Terminal Formative (TF), Classic (Cl), Early Toltec (ET), Late Toltec (LT), Aztec (Az). The third part of the site label is a number that specifies the specific site within the total number of sites of a particular period in a particular sub-area. These site numbers appear on our maps showing the sites for each time period, with number "1" at the northeastern corner of the survey area, and proceeding southwestward in order until all the sites for a particular time period have been numbered in sequence from NE to SW. Thus, for example, the forty-eighth Late Toltec site in the Zumpango Region is designated Zu-LT-48.

Our usual procedure, soon after survey on an airphoto was complete, was for one of the team members to remain for a day at the field headquarters to: (1) trace the information contained on that airphoto onto a large sheet of tracing paper; (2) define and number the sites on the tracing paper; and (3) prepare a descriptive report for each defined site on the basis of field notes, information recorded on the airphoto, the writer's own memories, and contact prints of relevant photographs. We had the survey films developed and contact sheets printed at a camera store in Mexico City, and the relevant contact prints were included in each site report.

Although some examination of the surface collections took place daily as we washed and re-bagged the sherds, most of the formal study of these collections occurred over a two-week period at the end of the fieldseason, when Mary H. Parsons and I went through the collections, bag by bag, tabulating the material according to a general type classification. We revisited all these collections over a three-week period in June 2007 at our lab at the Museo Nacional de Agricultura, Universidad Nacional de Chapingo, when we photographed many of the sherds and generally got reacquainted with the material. In 1996, Robert Cobean and I reexamined many of the Late Toltec collections to assess the degree to which that material corresponded with his Tollan phase from nearby Tula (we found a very close correspondence).

Laboratory Procedures in Ann Arbor

Soon after we returned to Ann Arbor in December 1973, we began to process our tabulated field data. This work involved several different tasks that occupied us intensively for about two years, and that extended intermittently over many years after that. There were four basic operations: (1) reducing our original 1:5000 base maps to 1:25,000 maps for each period on which the final site numbers appeared (these 1:25,000 maps were subsequently reduced photographically to a size suitable for publication); (2) computing site areas with a compensating polar planimeter (K&E Model 62-0015); (3) compiling our site information into a computerized database (for example, Parsons et al. 1983); and (4) preparing final site descriptions. Much later, in 2007, I scanned all the original survey photographic negatives (20 rolls, over 700 individual pictures), and I used these digital images extensively in revising and illustrating the site descriptions for this monograph (Appendix A).

Reducing our 1:5000 field maps to 1:25,000 final base maps was complicated and tedious. The 1:25,000 maps were made during the 1950s, and showed modern towns and other settlements, roads, canals, and drainage canals, in addition to ten-meter contour lines and UTM coordinates (México, Depto. de Defensa Nacional 1957). The reduction process was accomplished using an ingenious machine (which worked rather like a photographic enlarger in reverse) in the University of Michigan Department of Geography's cartography lab (sadly, machine, lab, and department have long since vanished from the scene). We placed outlines of individual sites at the 1:5000 scale into a holder in the upper part of the reducer apparatus, adjusted the settings so that a 1:25,000 image would result, and projected this image onto a horizontal easel below the reducer lens. We then retraced these reduced images and placed them onto the 1:25,000 base maps as accurately as we could. Once all sites from each time period had been placed on to separate 1:25,000 base maps, the final site numbers were assigned, going from NE to SW in the manner discussed above, and UTM coordinates were obtained for each site from these same 1:25,000 maps. Years later, these UTM coordinates were converted into latitude-longitude coordinates using a computer program developed by Charles L. Taylor and accessible on the internet (Taylor 2003).

Site Classification

The site classification was developed during the early years of the Valley of Mexico regional surveys (Parsons 1971; Blanton 1972) and with some modifications, it has remained in use since then. It takes into account the interrelated attributes of site area, apparent occupational density (usually measured by relative density of surface pottery), estimated population, and architectural complexity (number and size of mounds). It is modeled, in part, after the partially documented settlement system that existed in the Valley of Mexico at the time of initial Spanish contact (*cabeceras*, *pueblos*, *estancias*, *rancherías*), and, as detailed below, by mid-twentieth-century rural settlement in central Mexico. While this classification has continued to be useful, it has never been rigorously tested, and it remains inherently subjective and intuitive. It suffers most from poor control over site function, and from the sometimes arbitrary manner in which certain site categories are defined. Because the site classification has been so influenced by the sixteenth-century data, its applicability to pre-Aztec periods is apt to be more limited. We continue to use this classification because we think that it remains basically sound at this stage of research, and because we still have nothing better to offer in its place.

One of the principal features of our classification is its reliance on estimated site population, rather than on site area. This differs from common practice in Mesopotamia where regional surveys (e.g., Adams 1965; Adams and Nissen 1972; Johnson 1973) have found it practical and meaningful to classify archaeological sites on the basis of surface area alone. This is because in much of the Near East, ancient occupation has commonly built up over very long periods of time within a restricted area such that an archaeological site can often be defined by the limits of a *tell* (a single mound). The area and height of such a tell vary directly with population size, length of occupation, and the size of architecture. Such tells are rarely present in Mesoamerica, and in the Valley of Mexico we have had to contend with a great range of variation in occupational density within site borders: some sites have remains that are thinly scattered over large areas, while in others, surface pottery and mounding are tightly nucleated over areas of varying size. Therefore, comparing our sites on the basis of surface area alone is not particularly helpful in constructing a site hierarchy that helps define a regional settlement system. Instead, we have combined surface area and occupational density to produce an estimate for site population that we consider a better proxy for site "size" than surface area alone.

The derivation of population estimates has been described in an earlier monograph (Parsons 1971:23):

> In making population estimates we have used Sanders' (1965:50) figures for population densities of modern settlement types characteristic of highland Mesoamerica. At sites where sherd densities are consistently in the light-to-moderate, moderate, and heavy ranges, we have used Sanders' figure of 2500 to 5000 people per square km (or, 25 to 50 per hectare) which characterize his "High-Density Compact Village." For sites where sherds are consistently in the light and light-to-moderate range, we have been guided by his density figures for "Compact Low-Density Village" (1000 to 2500 per square km; or, 10 to 25 per hectare), "Scattered Village" (500 to 1000 per square km; or, 5 to 10 per hectare), and "Compact Rancheria" (200 to 300 per square km; or, 2 to 3 per hectare).

We stress again that our main concern in making these population estimates has been to provide relative indices by which demographic comparisons within and between prehispanic time periods can be made. We do not expect that these estimates are necessarily accurate estimates of actual population sizes at various points in time. There are many obvious problems in translating our survey data into population figures. For example, as our chronological phases are typically several centuries long, we are usually unable to differentiate between loci with continuous occupation over a long time versus loci occupied only briefly within the same ceramic phase. Within a single phase, sherd build up of any particular density may equally well have resulted from a long occupation by a few people, or from a short occupation by many people living closer together, or by any one of several other imaginable possibilities between these two extremes. Furthermore, since we do not adequately control site function, some sites may be special-function loci, occupied only intermittently, seasonally, or occasionally by groups of people whose principal settlements are elsewhere. There are also the problems of the variability in sherd density that may be caused by post-depositional factors such as different land use, erosion, alluviation, and vegetation cover.

Nevertheless, there is some indication that our absolute population estimates may not be wholly unrealistic: using ethnohistoric sources, Sanders (1970) calculated populations in the eastern Valley of Mexico for the period of Spanish contact that are surprisingly close to our archaeologically based estimates for the same area during the Late Aztec period. It is on the basis of these ethnohistorically derived population estimates that we have judged the archaeological estimates as about 20% too low (Sanders et al. 1979).

Our site typology for the Zumpango Region is as follows:

Regional Center. Large surface area, highly nucleated occupation in its core area, abundant monumental public architecture, and an estimated urban population usually exceeding 5000 people.

Local Center. A smaller version of the Regional Center, with less monumental and less abundant public architecture, less nucleated occupation, and an estimated population of less than 2000 people.

Large Nucleated Village. Predominantly light-to-moderate and moderate surface pottery (or heavier), generally lacking monumental public architecture, with an estimated population over 500 people. There is no formal upper limit for estimated population, but this figure rarely exceeds 1500 people.

Small Nucleated Village. Same as Large Nucleated Village, with an estimated population of 100 to 500 people.

Large Dispersed Village. Predominantly light surface pottery, with an estimated population of more than 500 people. Some light-to-moderate sherd concentrations may occur, but this level of sherd density is clearly subordinate to "light." Rarely, if ever, is there any evidence of monumental public architecture.

Small Dispersed Village. Same as Large Dispersed Village, with an estimated population of 100 to 500 people.

Hamlet. Any site lacking public architecture for which we estimate a population between 20 to 100 people.

Small Hamlet. Any site for which we estimate a population of less than 20 people, and where there is no evidence of public architecture. Most of these probably represent isolated household residences or temporary camps, and many could well be temporary occupations rather than enduring, permanently occupied settlements.

Isolated Ceremonial-Civic Precinct. A concentration of one or more platform mounds well separated spatially from any other significant occupation, and which appears to lack permanent residential population. Such sites are typically situated on hilltops, but occasionally are found on lower ground.

Isolated Obsidian Workshop. A concentration of obsidian debris situated well outside the boundaries of a settlement, and for which there is minimal evidence of permanent residential population.

Isolated Saltmaking Workshop. A concentration of "saltmaking" pottery situated well outside the boundaries of a settlement, and for which there is minimal evidence of permanent residential population.

The reader will recognize the assumptions implicit in this site typology. The principal criteria are site size (for which our estimate of population provides a proxy) and the presence or absence of public architecture. The critical assumptions are that important centers (in terms of administration, redistribution, and ritual) will be relatively large and nucleated, and that they will be the loci of the most important political, economic, and religious functionaries (as manifested by the presence of public architecture). We presently have no reason to doubt the validity of these assumptions, but our site typology will certainly be less useful

Table 4.2. Prehispanic chronology in the Zumpango Region.

Absolute Dates	Major Period	Zumpango Region Periods	Phases
1520 A.D.	Late Postclassic	Late Aztec	Aztec IV (?)
1350 A.D.			Aztec III
	Middle Postclassic	Early Aztec	Aztec II
1200 A.D.			Aztec I
	Early Postclassic	Late Toltec	Aztec I
			Mazapan/Tollan
900 A.D.			
	Epiclassic	Early Toltec	Coyotlatelco
650 A.D.			
			Metepec
	Classic	Classic	Xolalpan
			Tlamimilolpa
150 A.D.			Miccaotli
		Late Terminal Formative	Tzacualli
50 B.C.	Terminal Formative		
		Early Terminal Formative	Patlachique
250 B.C.			
	Late Formative	Late Formative	Ticoman
500 B.C.			
	No Early Formative or Middle Formative in the Zumpango Region		

if these assumptions do not hold at one or more points in time. We are especially concerned, for example, by the question of whether "centers" are necessarily nucleated. Since we have only limited control over function, our typology should be regarded as generalized and provisional. Its validity remains to be tested, and it must eventually be considerably refined.

Chronology

Table 4.2 shows our present understanding of how the pottery in our surface collections from the Zumpango Region fit into the ceramic chronology that has been established for the Valley of Mexico over the past several decades. Our chronological inferences are largely based on our understanding of the ceramic chronology as it existed at the time of our fieldwork in 1973. During the intervening decades, several refinements of the ceramic chronology based on large excavated samples have appeared (for example, McBride 1974; Cobean 1990; Hodge and Minc 1991; Sanders 1986, 1995; Rattray 2001). However, we have not gone back through our collections to re-phase them, mainly because of logistical difficulties, but partly because we felt that these collections were generally too small, too badly weathered, and too infrequently made to provide an adequate basis for slicing time into thinner segments. Such refined calibration of occupational chronology at the regional level is one of the most critical problems for future investigations of prehispanic settlement patterning in the Valley of Mexico.

Chapter 5

The Patterning of Settlement

Jeffrey R. Parsons and Larry J. Gorenflo

This chapter examines our archaeological data from several different perspectives in order to illuminate long-term trends in prehispanic demography, economy, and polity within the Zumpango Region, and to consider the significance of these trends within the larger context of the Valley of Mexico and adjacent parts of central Mexico.

Trends in Numbers of Sites, Numbers of Occupied Hectares, and Population

Table 5.1 summarizes number of sites, occupied hectares, and population for each time period in the Zumpango Region as a whole, and Figure 5.1 illustrates the (highly generalized) long-term population profile. For modern demographic comparisons, Table 5.1 includes population and regional density figures for A.D. 1900 and 1960—interestingly, population size and density ca. A.D. 1500 (Late Aztec) were both higher than in A.D. 1900, although substantially below levels attained by 1960 (and subsequently). The principal difference between prehispanic and twentieth-century settlements is the far greater nucleation of the latter. Table 5.2 compares long-term population density in the Zumpango Region with the overall figures for other surveyed regions in the Valley of Mexico and shows that, except for the Late Toltec period, the Zumpango Region was always less densely inhabited than most other parts of the larger region.

As noted in Chapter 2, because of difficulties in recognizing the full extent of Early Aztec occupation, this period remains imprecisely defined. Although our present impression is one of minimal Early Aztec population, we acknowledge that the underlying evidence remains shaky. Similarly, owing to problems of ceramic chronology noted in Chapter 4, we have relatively less confidence in our Early Toltec figures. Unfortunately, until our Classic ceramic chronology is better refined, we must consider this long period as a single block of time.

Formative

The dearth of Formative-period occupation in the Zumpango Region contrasts strikingly with most other surveyed regions in the Valley of Mexico (Figs. 5.2–5.7). Formative occupation is also very limited in other parts of the northern third of the Valley of Mexico: we know of no reported sites in the Pachuca Region to the northeast of the Zumpango Region, and in the nearby Temascalapa Region to the east, the Formative occupation is limited to Terminal Formative (Tzacualli phase) hamlets and likely temporary settlements (Gorenflo and Sanders 2007). In the Tula Region to the west and north, only three Formative sites (all dating to later phases of the Formative) have been reported (Cobean 1974; Mastache and Crespo 1974:73; Mastache, Cobean, and Healan 2002:44-45). The only large Formative site in the Tula Region covers an area of about 15 ha, in a relatively well-watered area near the modern town of Tepeji del Río, about 10 km west of the northwestern border of the Zumpango Region. These northern regions (Zumpango, Temascalapa, and Tula) were clearly marginal to Formative developments farther south. It was not until the late Terminal Formative (Tzacualli phase) that significant occupation became established in the area north of Lake Xaltocán-Zumpango (Figs. 5.6, 5.7), and it was not until the subsequent Classic that the Zumpango Region was occupied at a level comparable to other parts of the Valley of Mexico (Figs. 5.8, 5.9).

Table 5.1. Summary of number of sites, occupied hectares, and population.

Period	Number of Sites	Occupied Hectares	Population Minimum	Population Maximum	Population Density[a] (people/km²)
Early & Middle Formative	none	none	0	0	0.0
Late Formative	1	3.0	15	30	0.1
Terminal Formative (Tzacualli)	26	48.4	363	740	1.4
Classic	90	307.3	4140	8290	15.8
Early Toltec	30	156.4	2582	5145	9.8
Late Toltec	213	703.3	9017	18,060	34.3
Early Aztec	very few	very few	very few	few	very low
Late Aztec[b]	302	1799.90	20,743	41,485	78.9
Modern (1900)	ca. 31	no data	32,421		53.2
Modern (1960)	31+	5089.1	70,380+		115.6

[a]Population densities computed using surveyed area of 526 km², with maximal estimates.
[b]Includes Xaltocán (Zu-Az-276).

Table 5.2. Population densities at different periods in the Zumpango Region compared with overall densities for other surveyed regions in the Valley of Mexico.

Surveyed Region	Area (km²)	Population Densities (people/km²)							
		EF	MF	LF	TF	Cl	ET	LT	L. Az
Zumpango Region	526	0.0	0.0	0.1	1.4[a]	15.8	9.8	34.3	78.9
Rest of the Valley of Mexico	2179	0.4	5.4	22.5	43.1[b]	68.2[c] 22.5[d]	42.8	30.5	145.9

Key: EF = Early Formative; MF = Middle Formative; LF = Late Formative; TF = Terminal Formative; Cl = Classic; ET = Early Toltec; LT = Late Toltec; L. Az = Late Aztec.
[a]Tzacualli phase only.
[b]Patlachique and Tzacualli phases intermingled.
[c]Inclusive of urban Teotihuacan.
[d]Exclusive of urban Teotihuacan.

The Patterning of Settlement

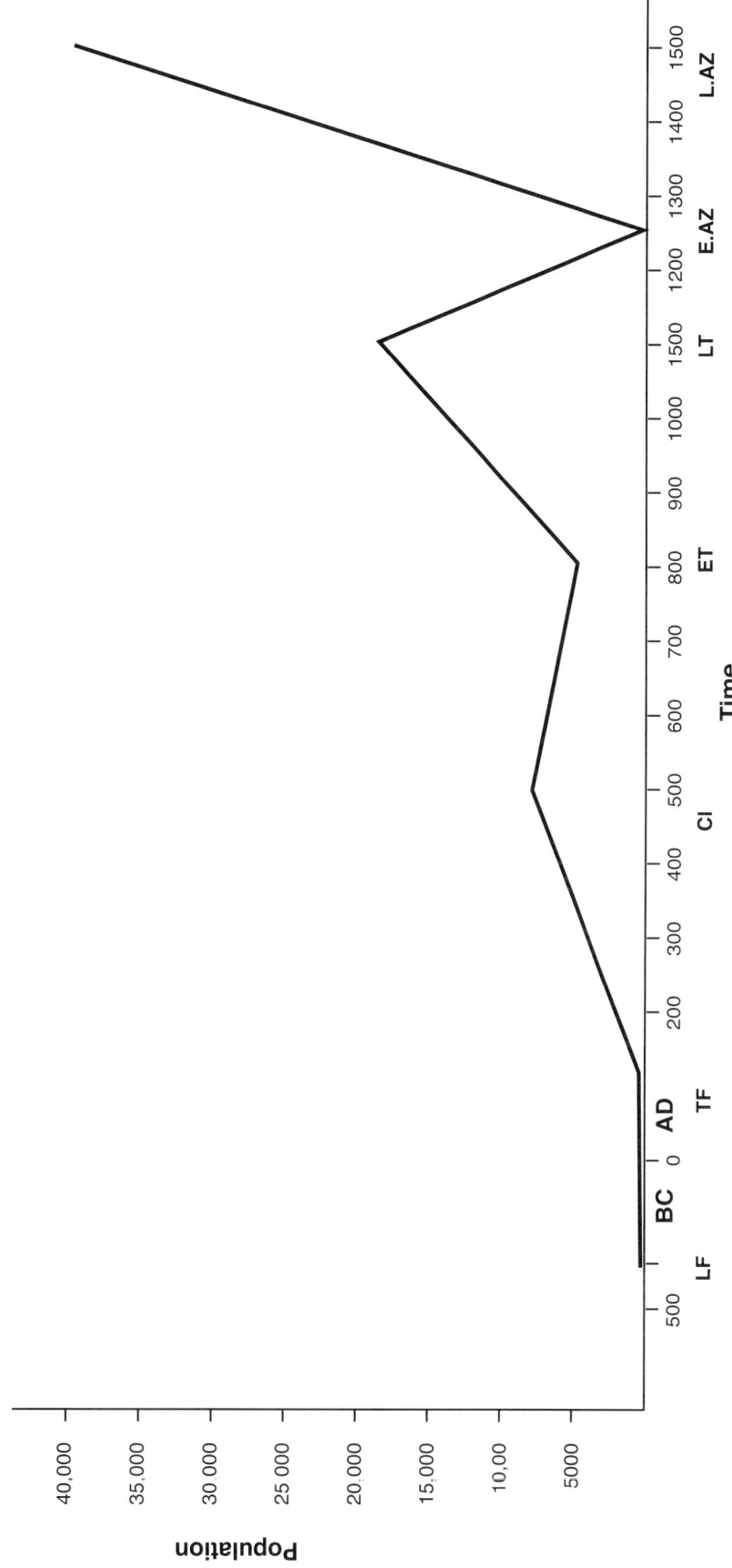

Figure 5.1. Prehispanic population profile in the Zumpango Region.

64 *Prehispanic Settlement Patterns in the Northwestern Valley of Mexico*

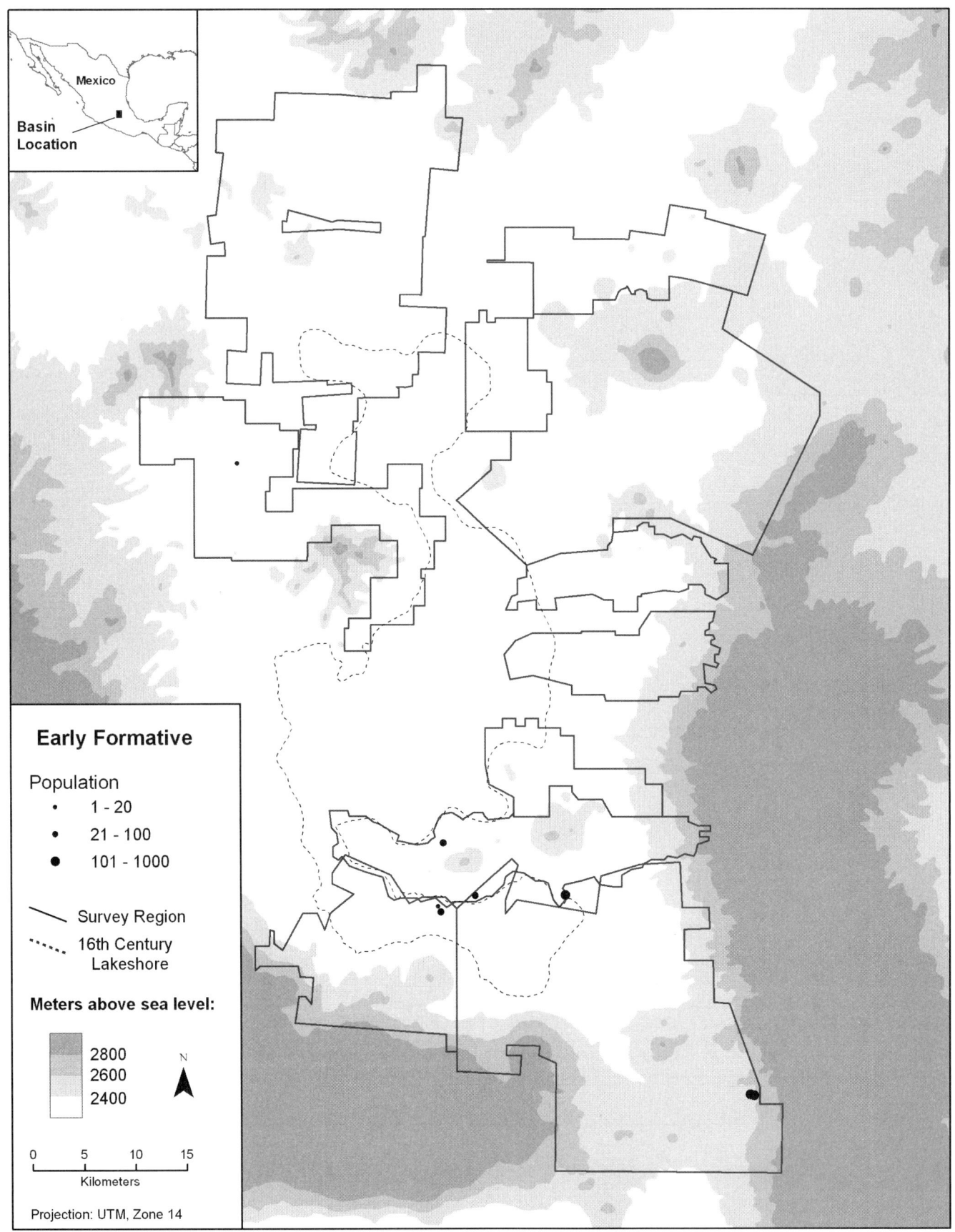

Figure 5.2. Early Formative occupation in the Valley of Mexico.

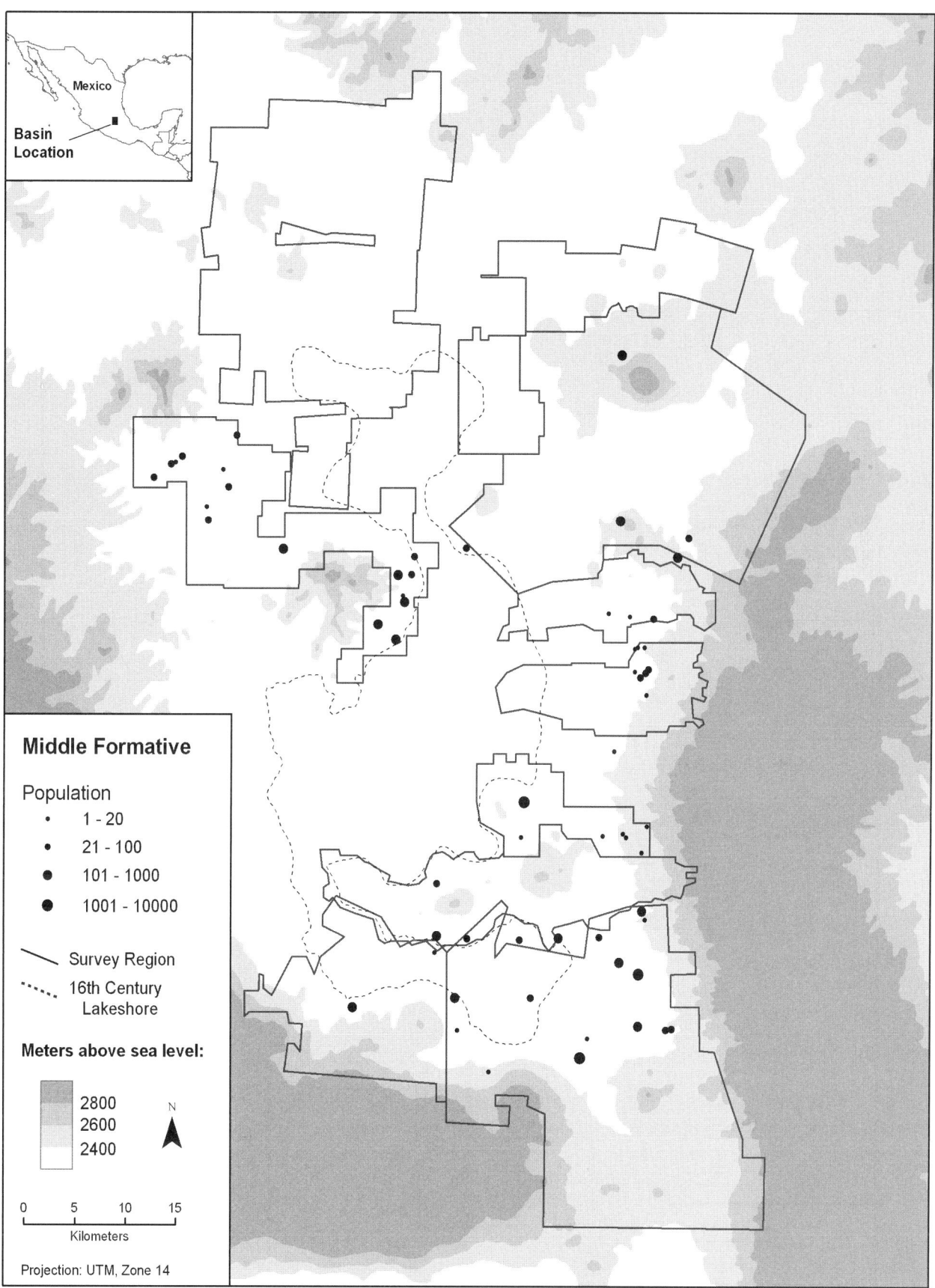

Figure 5.3. Middle Formative occupation in the Valley of Mexico.

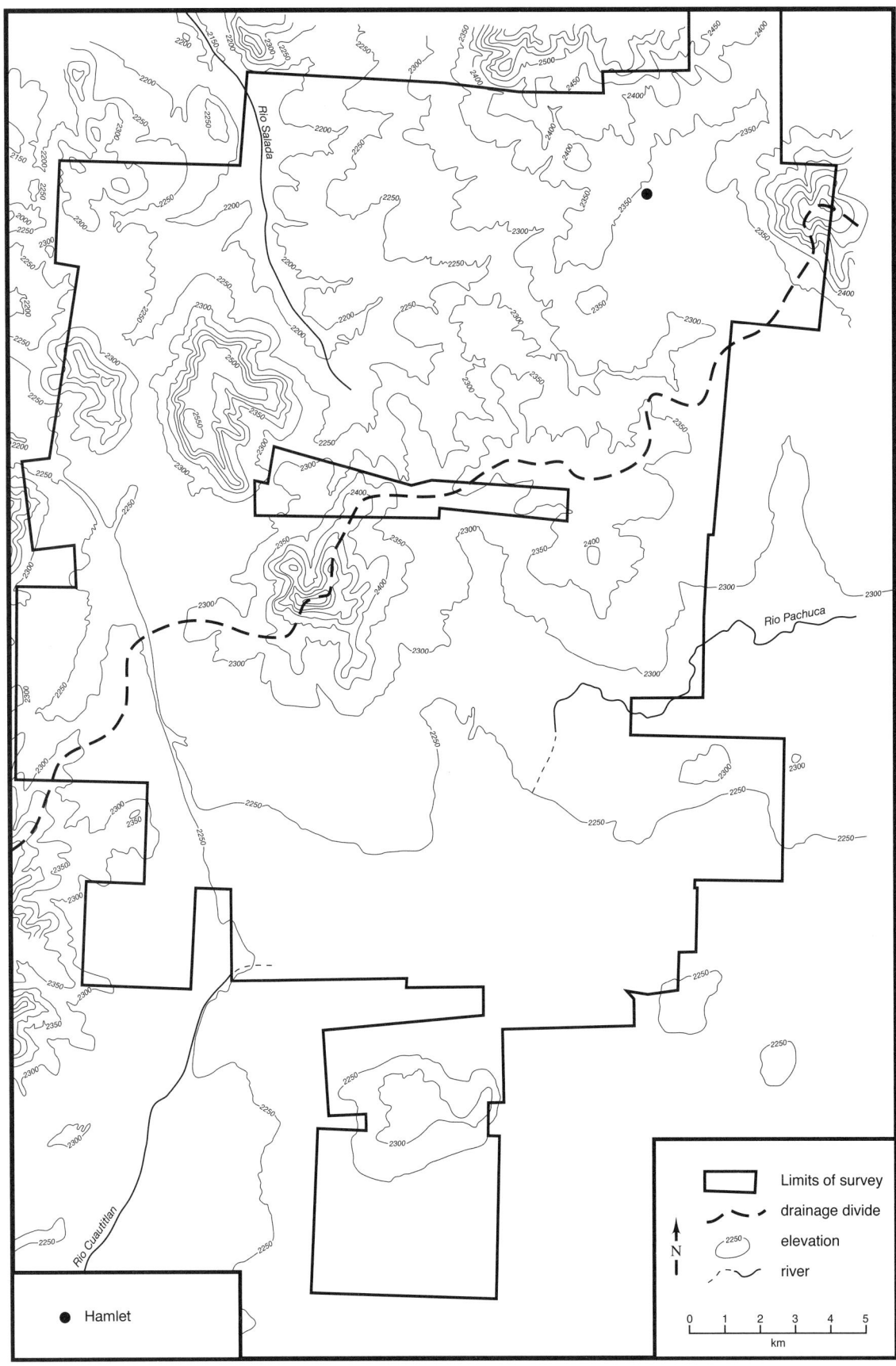

Figure 5.4. Late Formative occupation in the Zumpango Region.

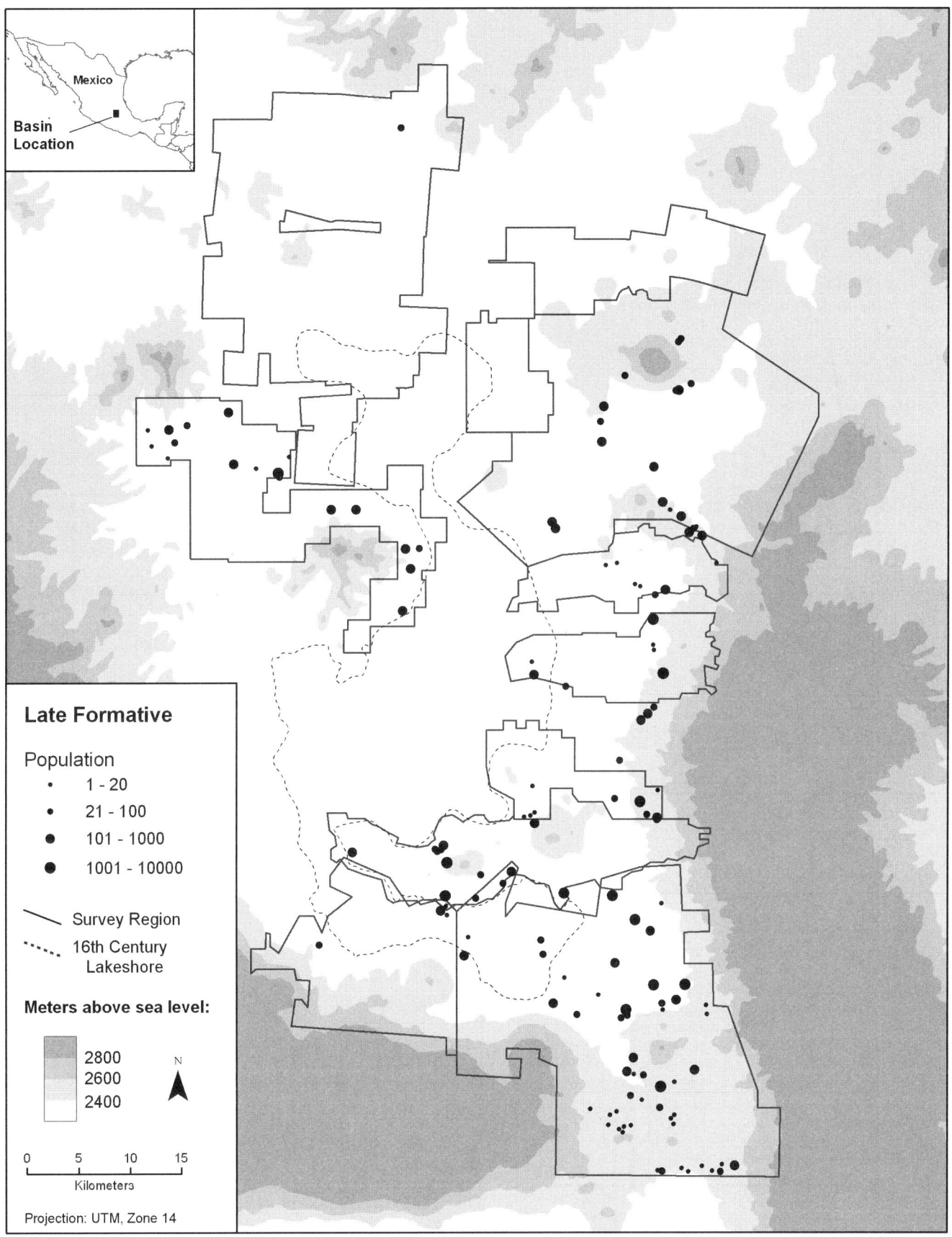

Figure 5.5. Late Formative occupation in the Valley of Mexico.

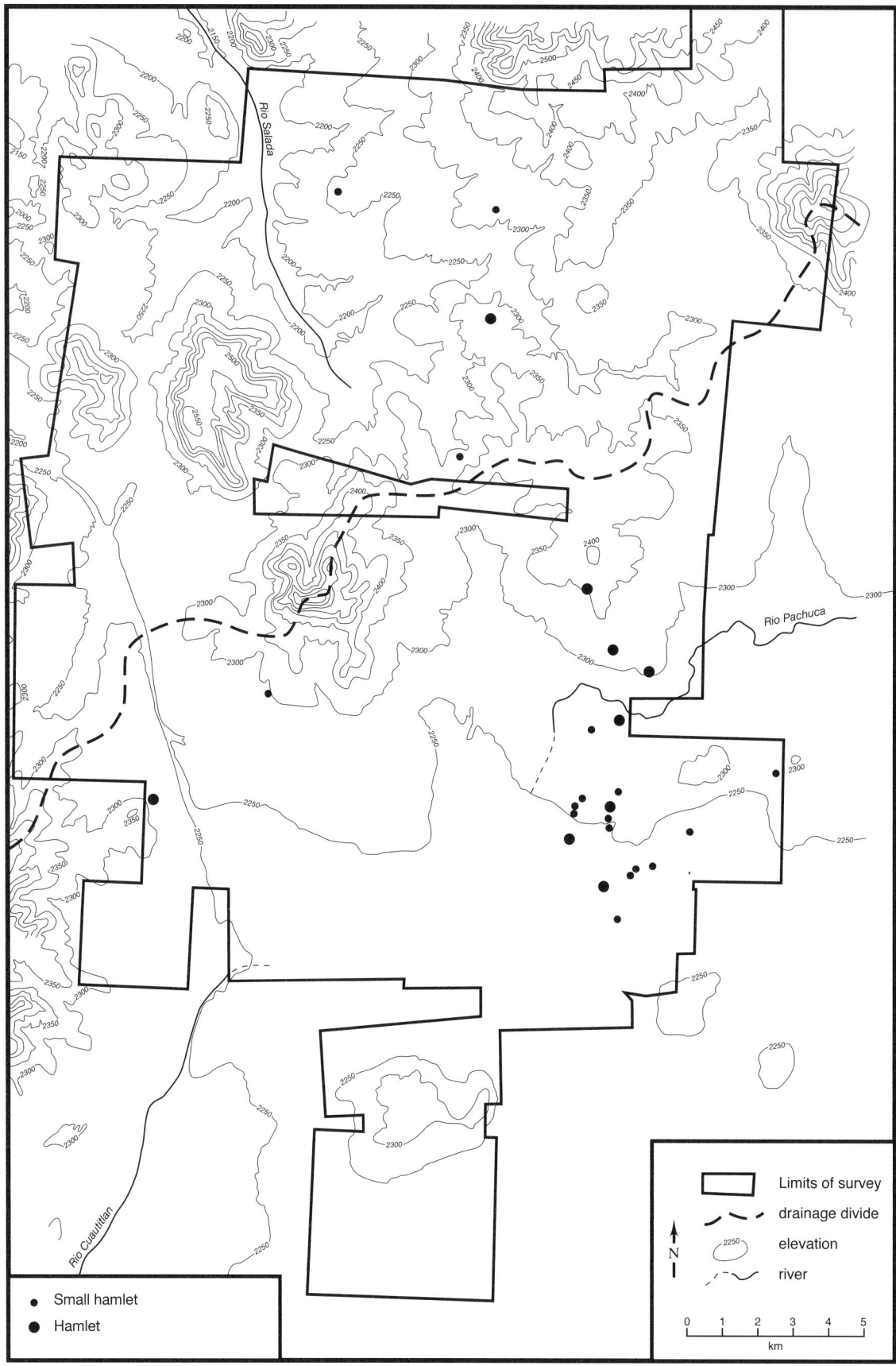

Figure 5.6. Terminal Formative occupation in the Zumpango Region.

The Patterning of Settlement 69

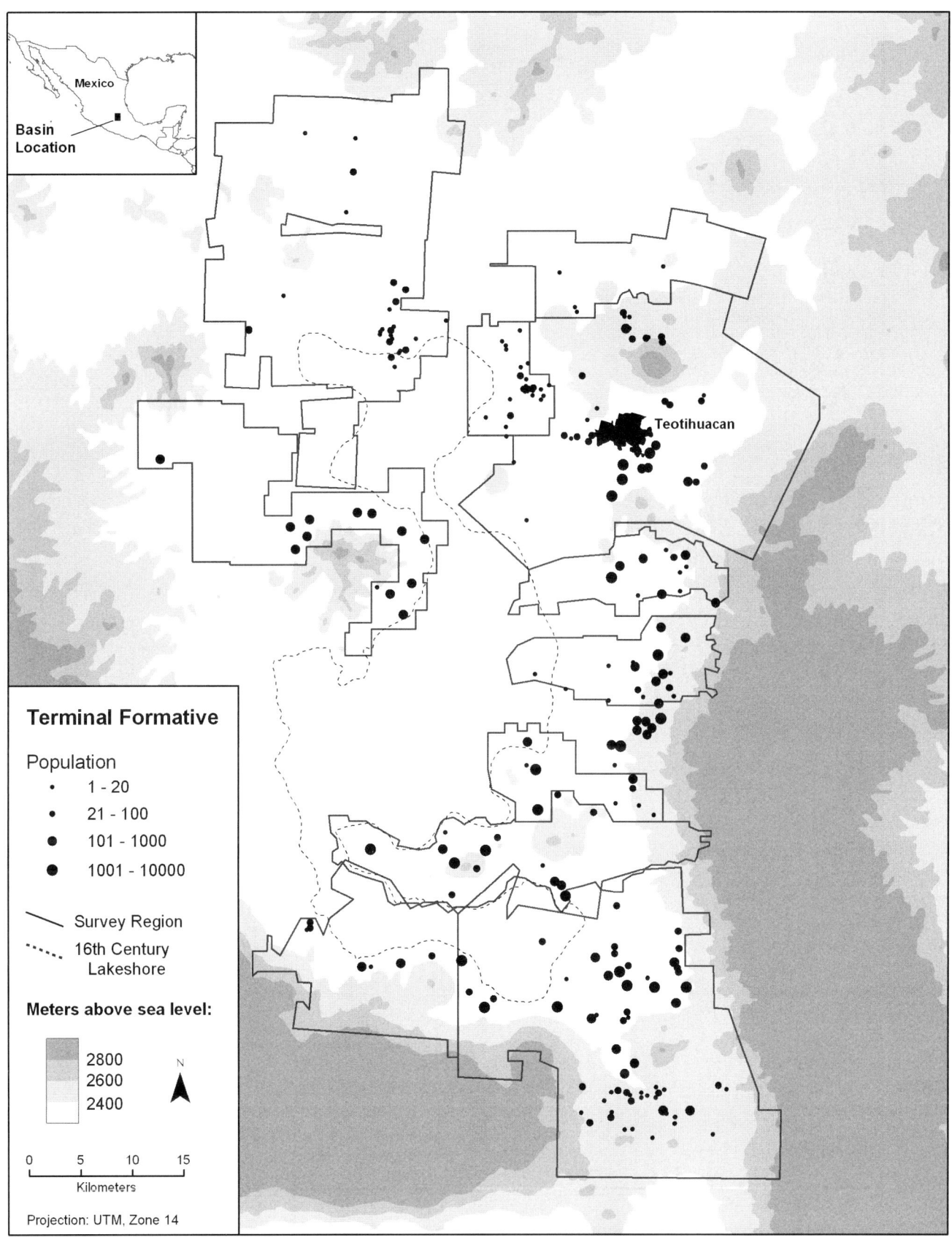

Figure 5.7. Terminal Formative occupation in the Valley of Mexico.

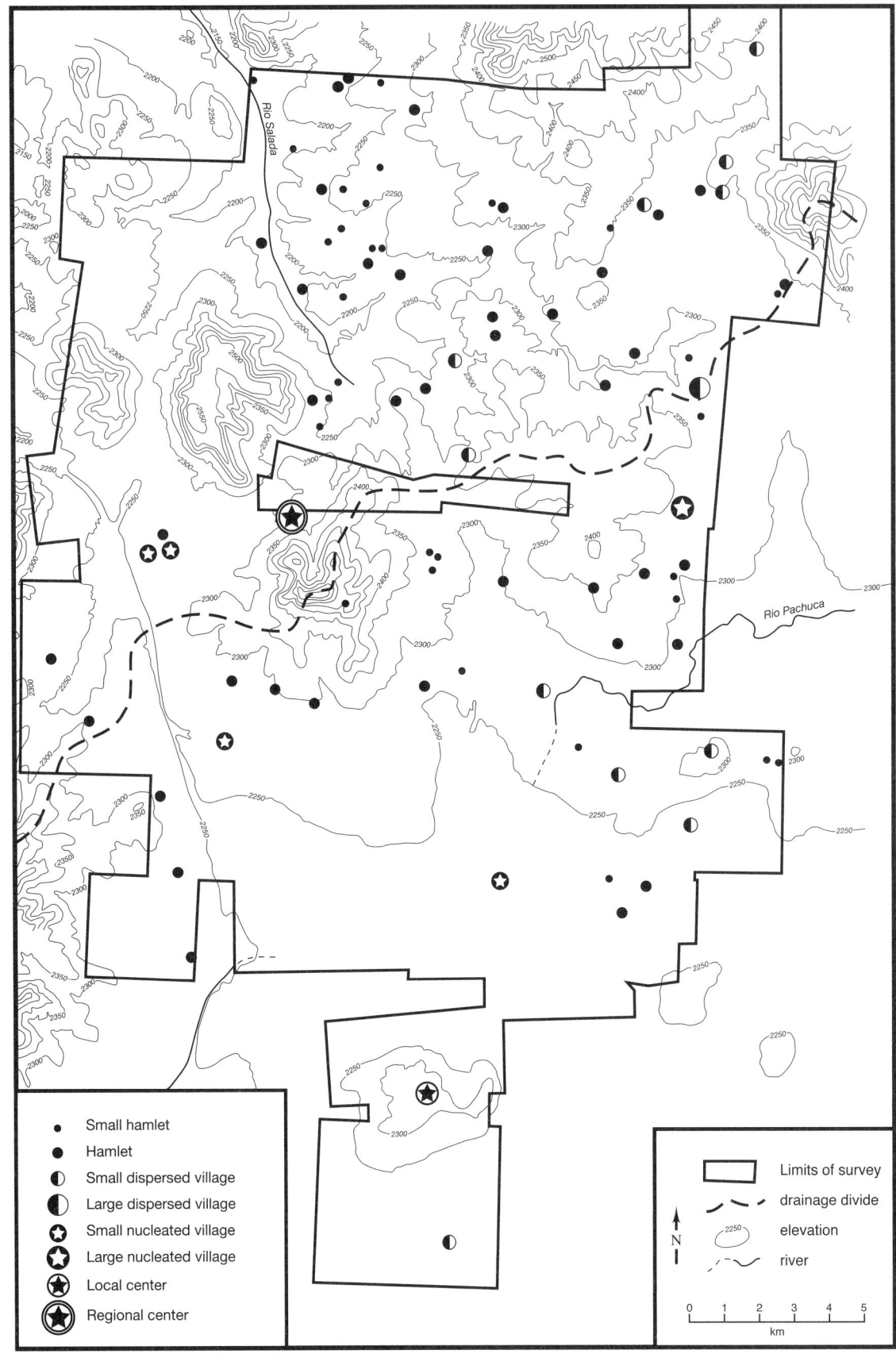

Figure 5.8. Classic occupation in the Zumpango Region.

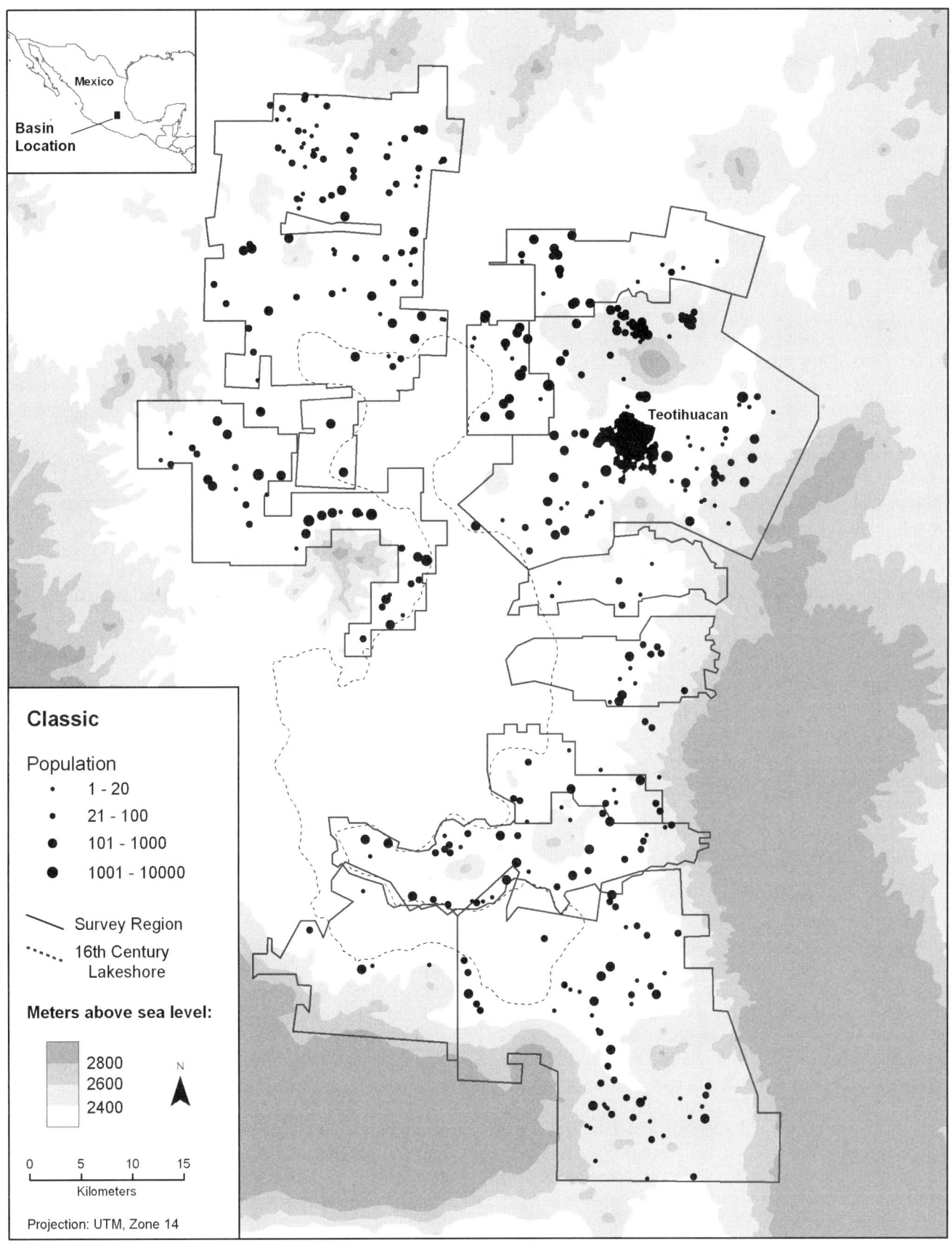

Figure 5.9. Classic occupation in the Valley of Mexico.

Classic

As we now perceive it, there was an explosive expansion of settlement throughout the Zumpango Region during the Classic period. This contrasts notably with the small, lakeshore-focused occupation of the antecedent Terminal Formative. The Classic is also the period for which significant occupation is first reported in the adjacent Tula Region to the north (Diaz 1980; Mastache and Crespo 1982:13-19; Mastache, Cobean, and Healan 2002:51-55), and in the Temascalapa Region to the east (Gorenflo and Sanders 2007). For the first time, all these previously sparsely settled northern regions were occupied by *relatively* large populations.

This major expansion of Classic occupation in the Zumpango Region and adjacent northern areas contrasts notably to what happened at that time in the central and southern Valley of Mexico where, during the explosive growth of the Teotihuacan urban center in the late Terminal Formative (Tzacualli phase) and Early Classic, there was substantial population decline relative to the antecedent earlier Terminal Formative (the Patlachique phase, which is unrepresented in the Zumpango Region). The northern regions, in contrast, had very modest pre-Tzacualli occupations, and growth there occurred as urban Teotihuacan itself was expanding. Instead of drawing population in (as from the central and southern Valley of Mexico), during its florescence Teotihuacan seemed to be placing people in the sparsely settled northern sectors of its heartland. This apparent arrangement of settlement in the north began, very modestly, during the late Terminal Formative (Tzacualli phase), and accelerated greatly during the subsequent Classic. Eventually, with better chronological control, it will be very important to determine if there were any significant occupational differences between the Early and Late Classic in the Zumpango Region. Such a comparison should illuminate the extent to which Teotihuacan's political and economic impact on different parts of its heartland varied over the course of the long Classic period.

Early Toltec

This was a time of radical transformation within the Zumpango Region, with substantial population loss, contraction of relatively diffuse settlement away from the lakeshore zone, and the emergence of a large regional center (Zu-ET-12) in a unique hilltop locale (Cerro de Mesa Grande) (Fig. 5.10). These radical changes must imply a comparably radical transformation of regional polity and economy. Some similar changes occurred at this time in other parts of the Valley of Mexico (Fig. 5.11). However, the hilltop setting of Zu-ET-12 is radically different from anything before or after in the entire Valley of Mexico, where there are no other large hilltop settlements, and where all large Early Toltec sites are found on hillflanks or in low-lying terrain. Zu-ET-12 is also unique among large Early Toltec sites in the Valley of Mexico in that it was unoccupied prior to Early Toltec times, and was rapidly and completely abandoned immediately afterward.

The Early Toltec occupation of the Zumpango Region appears to be more similar to that of the nearby Tula Region, where Mastache, Cobean, and Healan (2002:62-69) report a number of hilltop Epiclassic sites. These include La Mesa, a large center covering approximately 100 ha, although seemingly of low population density. Mapping and excavations at La Mesa revealed the presence of three distinct ceremonial precincts with abundant public architecture and numerous terrace platforms—altogether a site rather comparable to Zu-ET-12, although the latter was considerably smaller in area and probably more densely occupied.

In the Toluca Region to the west, Sugiura (2005) found few important Epiclassic hilltop sites. However, in Puebla-Tlaxcala to the east, two major Epiclassic hilltop sites have been reported: Cacaxtla-Xochitecatl (Serra 1998) and Cerro Zapotecas (Mountjoy 1987; Salomón 2006). To the south of the Valley of Mexico, in Morelos, the major Epiclassic center at Xochicalco occupies a large hilltop (Hirth and Cyphers 1988; Hirth 2000). Thus, it appears that the hilltop setting of Zu-ET-12 is not unusual for major Epiclassic centers in central Mexico generally, however unique it is within the Valley of Mexico. This is a notable contrast, whose significance remains unknown.

These Classic-to-Epiclassic shifts in the Zumpango Region and throughout the Valley of Mexico and central Mexico generally can be understood only within the overall context of Teotihuacan's collapse and the subsequent realignments of political and economic networks across central Mexico and beyond (e.g., Solar 2006). This was also the time when important new centers were beginning to develop in the adjacent Tula Region, including the early stages of Tula itself (Mastache, Cobean, and Healan 2002:60-69).

Late Toltec

With the Early Postclassic (Late Toltec) period, there was another radical transformation in the Zumpango Region: the rapid and complete abandonment of Zu-ET-12; a very large population increase at the regional level; a spread of settlement to all parts of the survey area; and the growth of several important local and regional centers (Fig. 5.12)—in some ways, an expansion and intensification of the earlier Classic-period occupation. All this occurred within the context of Tula's explosive growth as a major regional and supra-regional center (Diehl 1983; Healan 1989; Mastache, Cobean, and Healan 2002). While some of these changes are paralleled in other parts of the Valley of Mexico (Fig. 5.13), there are also important north-to-south differences within this region during Late Toltec times: generally speaking, in the northern Valley of Mexico, there were more people and larger settlements than in the south, and the northern ceramic assemblages appear to correspond more closely with the Tollan phase at Tula itself. This north-south contrast must reflect Tula's expansion and consolidation of its heartland region. In view of the general population dispersal and decline in the central and southern Valley of Mexico, and the decreasing similarities to Tula's Tollan phase ceramics in the coeval pottery assemblages of the southern half of the Valley of Mexico, this Tula heartland region apparently did not extend much beyond Tultepec Island at the southern edge of the Zumpango Region.

The Patterning of Settlement

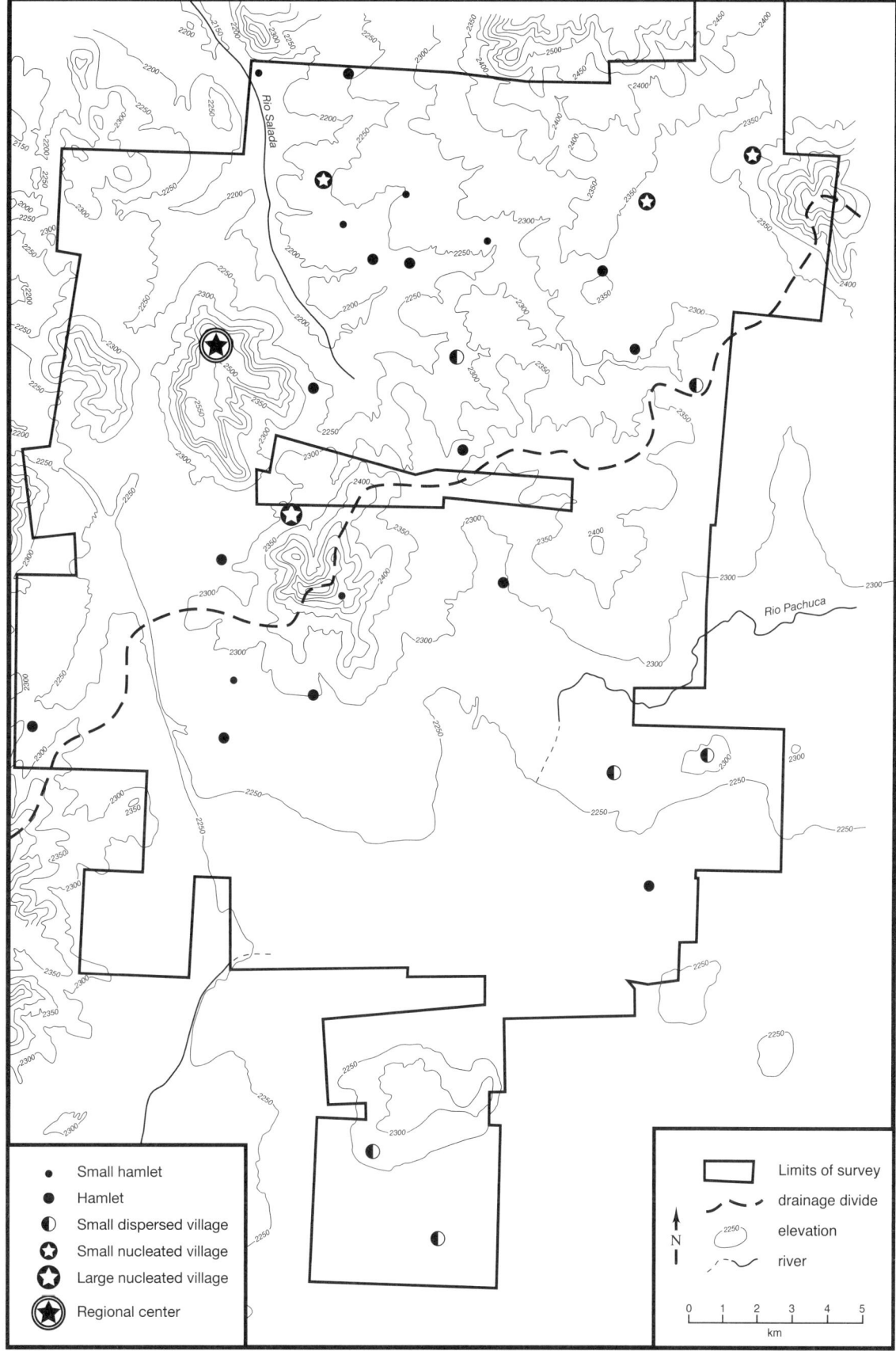

Figure 5.10. Early Toltec occupation in the Zumpango Region.

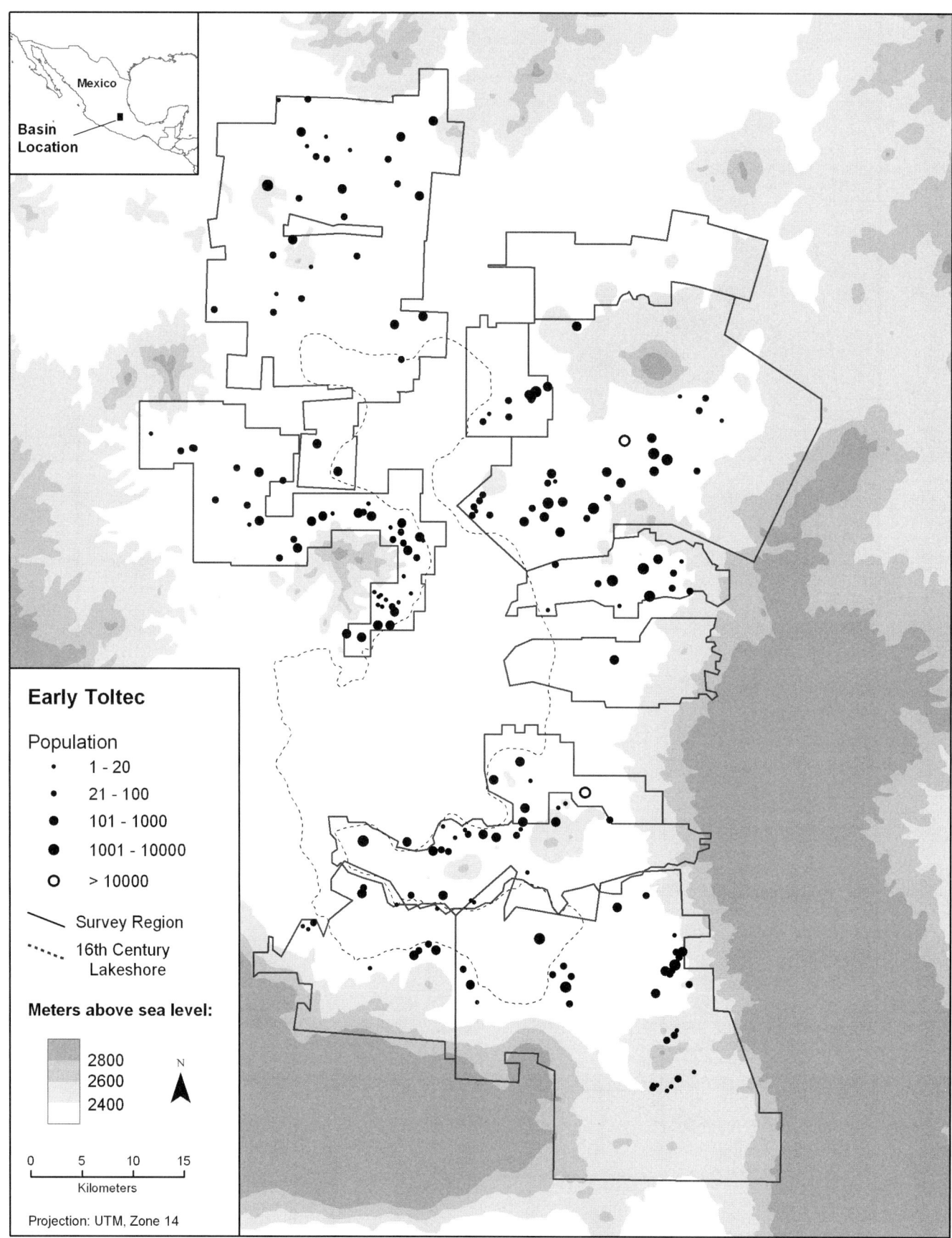

Figure 5.11. Early Toltec occupation in the Valley of Mexico.

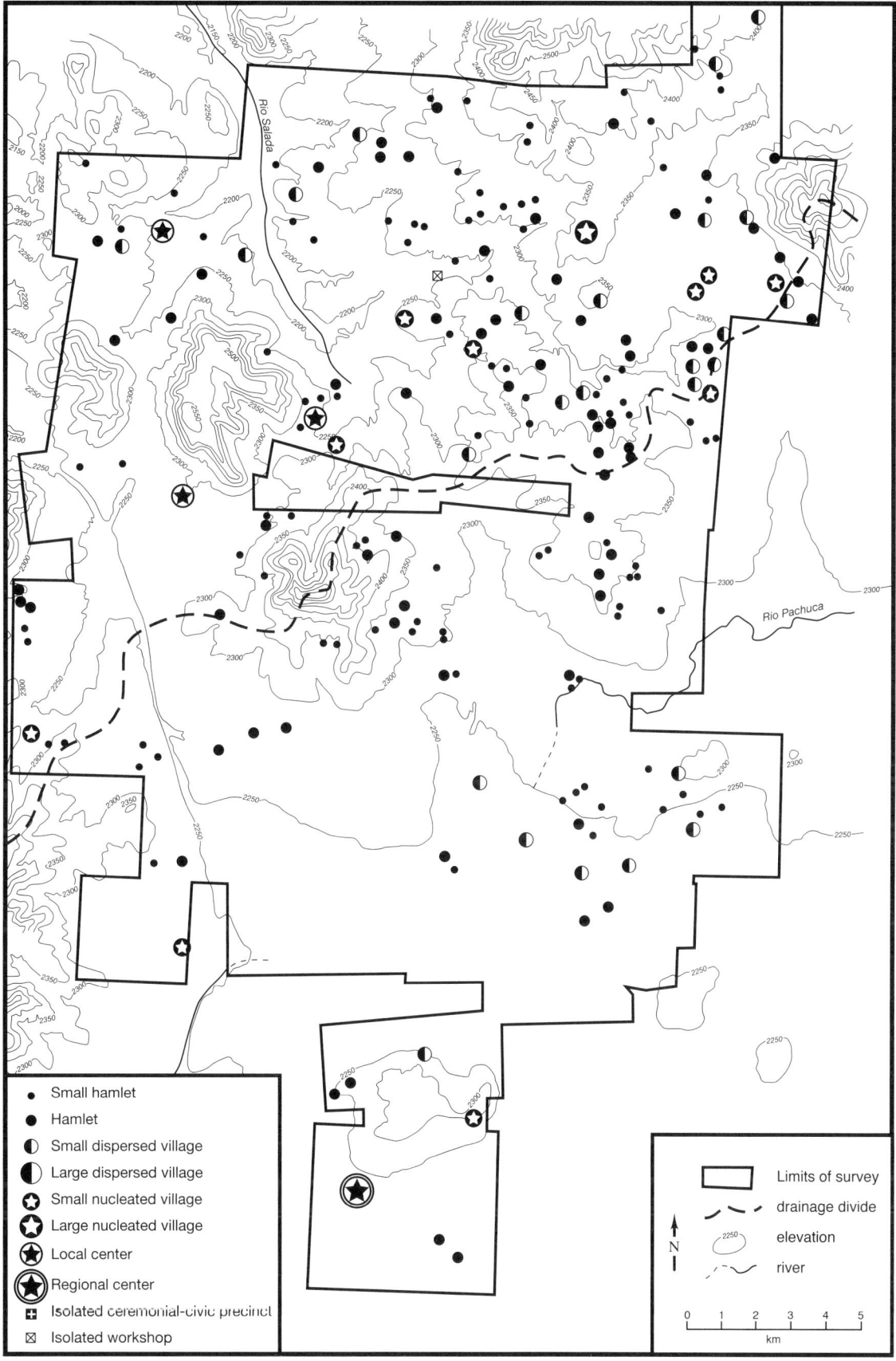

Figure 5.12. Late Toltec occupation in the Zumpango Region.

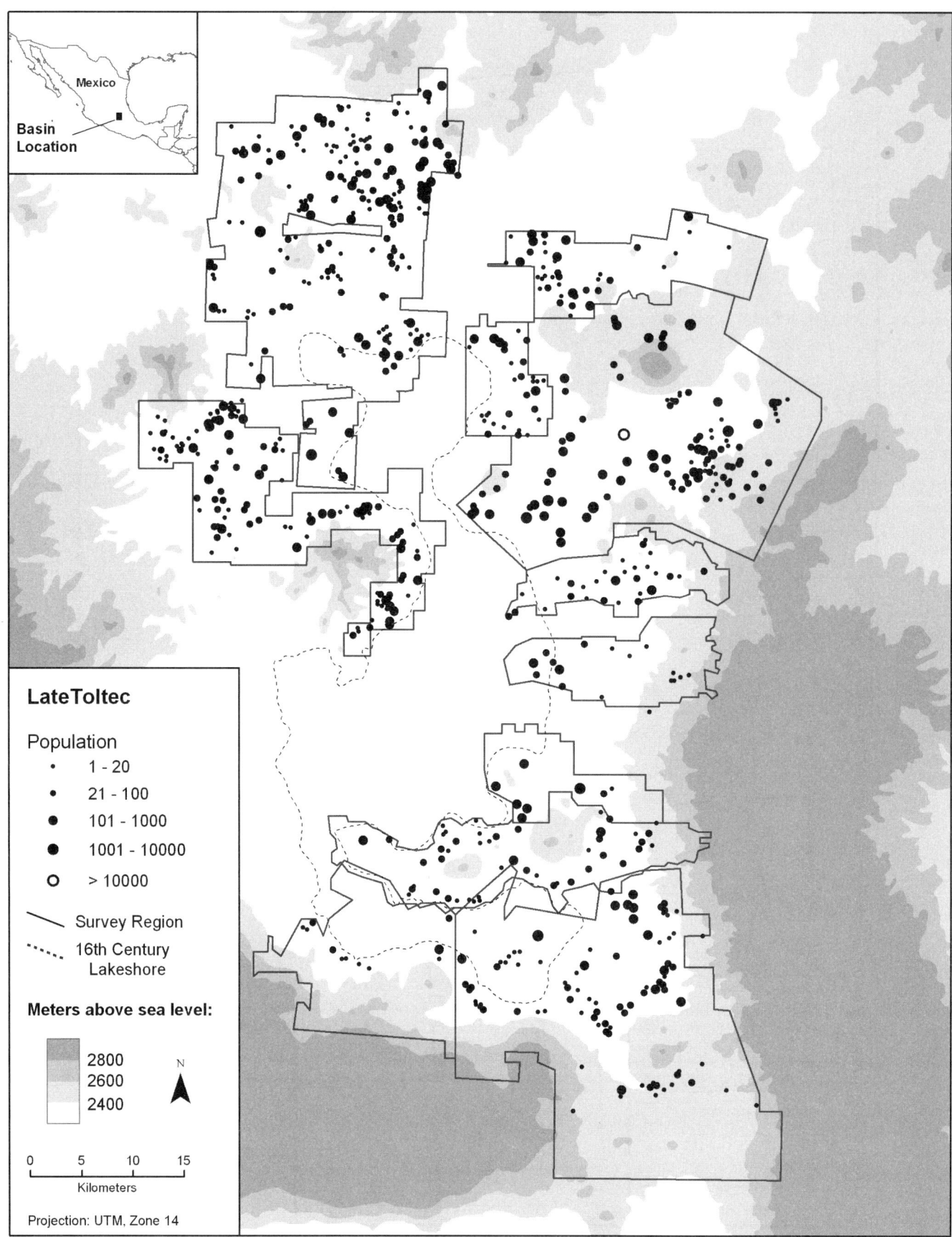

Figure 5.13. Late Toltec occupation in the Valley of Mexico.

Early Aztec

The collapse of Tula as a major center after the Early Postclassic and its immediate aftermath correlates in time with an apparent significant population decline in the Zumpango Region for at least a few generations during the Middle Postclassic (Early Aztec). There are also indications of a similar decline of population and settlement in the nearby Tula Region (Robert Cobean, pers. comm., May 2008), the Temascalapa Region (Gorenflo and Sanders 2007), and probably in the Pachuca Region as well. In other words, most of Tula's Early Postclassic heartland suffered a major demographic collapse during the Middle Postclassic.

We have much to learn about this regional demographic collapse. Although obviously profound and far-reaching, its causes, duration, and intensity all remain uncertain (e.g., Parsons and Gorenflo, in press). The dissolution of Tula-centered socioeconomic networks combined with a continuation of the increased aridity that had apparently already set in across the entire *Mesa Central* after A.D. 1100 (see Chapter 2) may well have produced especially severe short-term difficulties for sedentary agriculturalists throughout Tula's former heartland zone, the relatively driest part of central Mexico, at a time when there was no effective centralized management of the increasingly critical water resources.

Late Aztec

By the Late Postclassic (Late Aztec), the Zumpango Region, like the rest of the Valley of Mexico (Figs. 5.14, 5.15) and the adjacent Tula Region (Cobean 1974; Robert Cobean, pers. comm., May 2008), again filled rapidly with important local and regional centers and a regional population that by the early sixteenth century had attained unprecedented levels of size and density within a sociopolitical context dominated by lakeshore imperial centers in the central Valley of Mexico. Figure 5.16 illustrates prehispanic population densities throughout the surveyed portions of the Valley of Mexico.

Occupation by Environmental Zone

Table 5.3 compares the *actual* population for each time period within each of the seven major environmental zones in the Zumpango Region with the population for those zones that would be *expected* solely on the basis of their proportional representation within the survey area. The table also shows actual population density by environmental zones, and Figure 5.17 graphically illustrates population densities at different periods within an arbitrary grid of 1 × 1 km cells. Tables 5.4 and 5.5 present comparable figures for numbers of sites and occupied hectares.

Late and Terminal Formative

With a single small site, Late Formative occupation in the Zumpango Region was so sparse as to be nearly invisible with our survey methodology. During the subsequent late Terminal Formative, the BOMLP and LP zones are occupied at substantially higher than expected levels, while occupations in the USD and LB zones are lower than would be expected on the basis of proportional areas alone. This suggests a primary orientation toward wetland resources along the northern shores of Lake Xaltocán-Zumpango during a period of pioneering occupation of a relatively arid and previously very sparsely settled region, and prior to the development of large regional economic networks in this part of the Valley of Mexico.

It is also notable that virtually all the near-lakeshore Terminal Formative occupation occupies the surface of an old strand plain and associated beach ridges that are naturally elevated several meters above the general levels of the surrounding Lakeshore Plain and Lakebed surfaces (Frederick et al. 2005:75, Fig. 3.2) (Fig. 2.4).

These small Terminal Formative settlements occupied naturally well-drained terrain in immediate proximity to wetlands and aquatic resources. Comparable site clustering on these same naturally elevated lakeshore surfaces continues through nearly all subsequent periods, except, interestingly, the Late Aztec, when overall prehispanic occupational density peaked in the Zumpango Region.

Classic

During the Classic period, there is a somewhat higher than expected occupation of the USD zone, and a much higher than expected occupation of Tultepec Island (Table 5.3). These patterns indicate the movement of settlement into previously unoccupied or under-utilized terrain, and suggest a diversification of the economy from an earlier primary focus on wetland resources toward more utilization and diversification of agriculture, and perhaps the specialized quarrying of lime in calcareous lands well away from the lakeshore zone.

Lime sources are scarce in the central and southern Valley of Mexico, and the extensive deposits of limey subsoils and rock outcrops in the Zumpango Region would have been the major sources of this essential material for the huge urban community of Teotihuacan. The extensive Classic and post-Classic occupations of the BOMLP and USD zones in the Zumpango Region may have been stimulated by Teotihuacan's need for great quantities of mortar and stucco (an idea developed in Sanders et al. [1979:291], and reinforced by Gibson's [1964:336] historical research that revealed extensive lime production in this same region during the Colonial period). Several major modern cement companies, all of which actively quarry the rich local calcareous deposits in huge open-pit operations, are presently situated on the northern side of the Zumpango Region and in the adjacent Tula Region to the north and west.

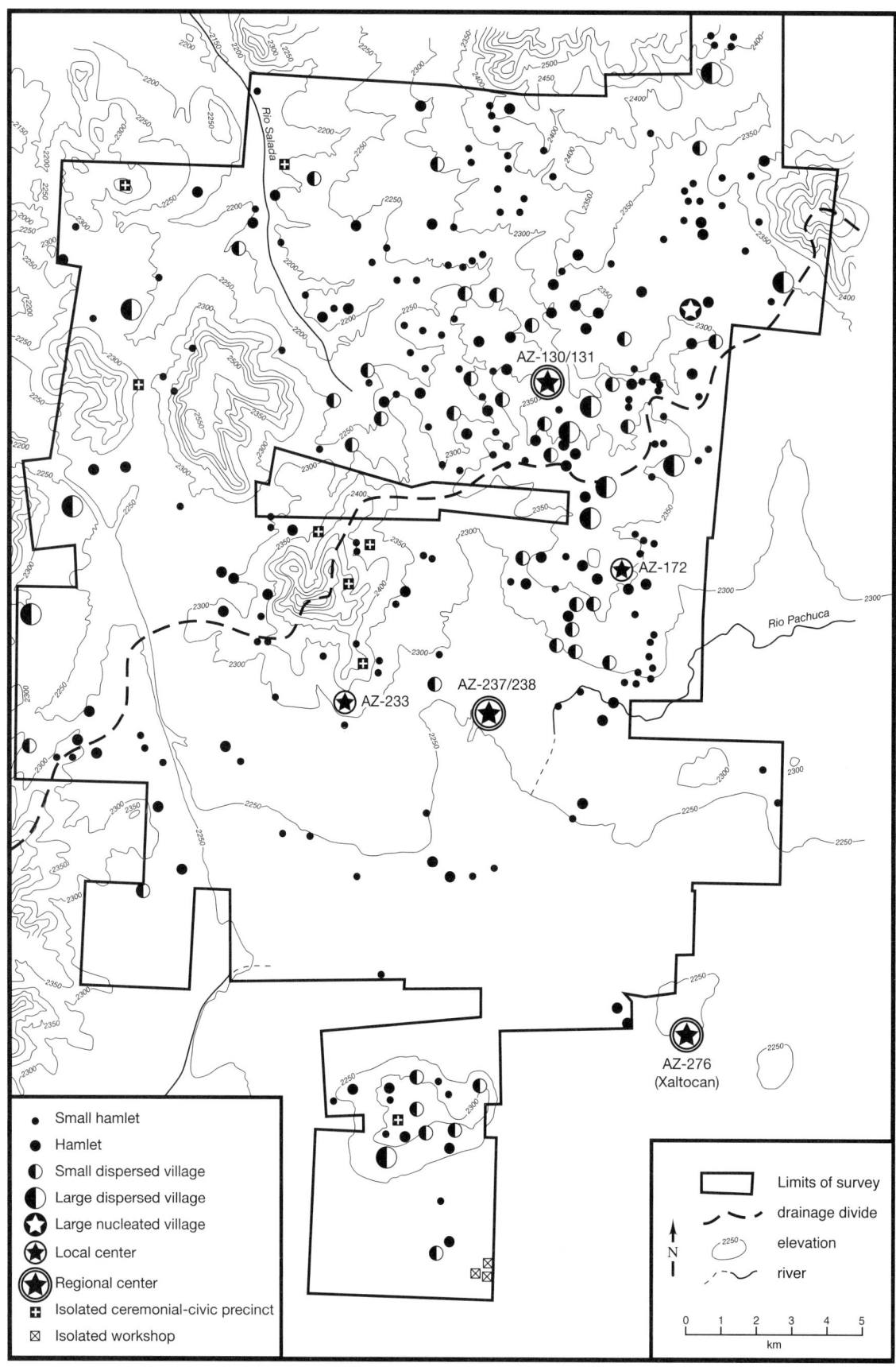

Figure 5.14. Late Aztec occupation in the Zumpango Region.

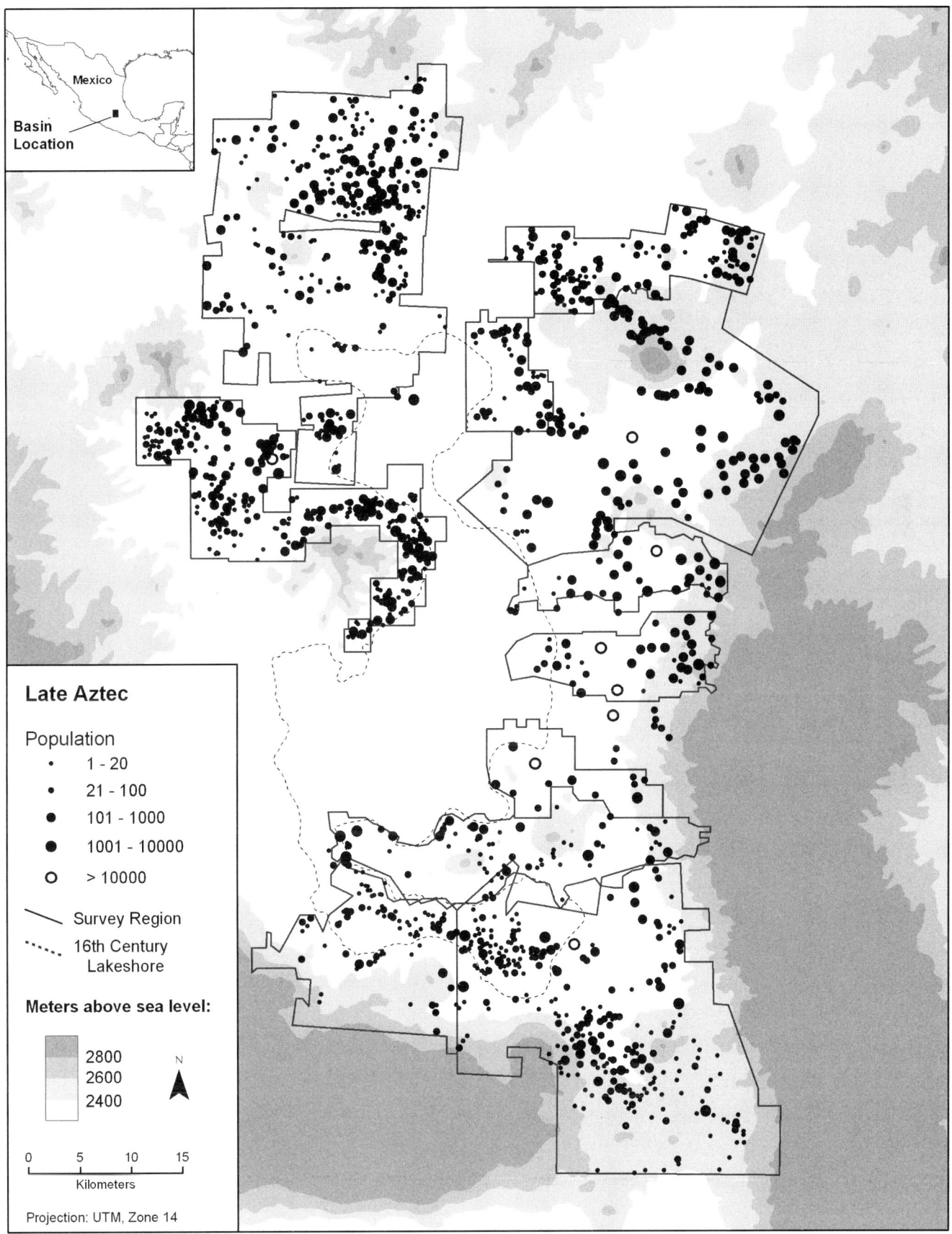

Figure 5.15. Late Aztec occupation in the Valley of Mexico.

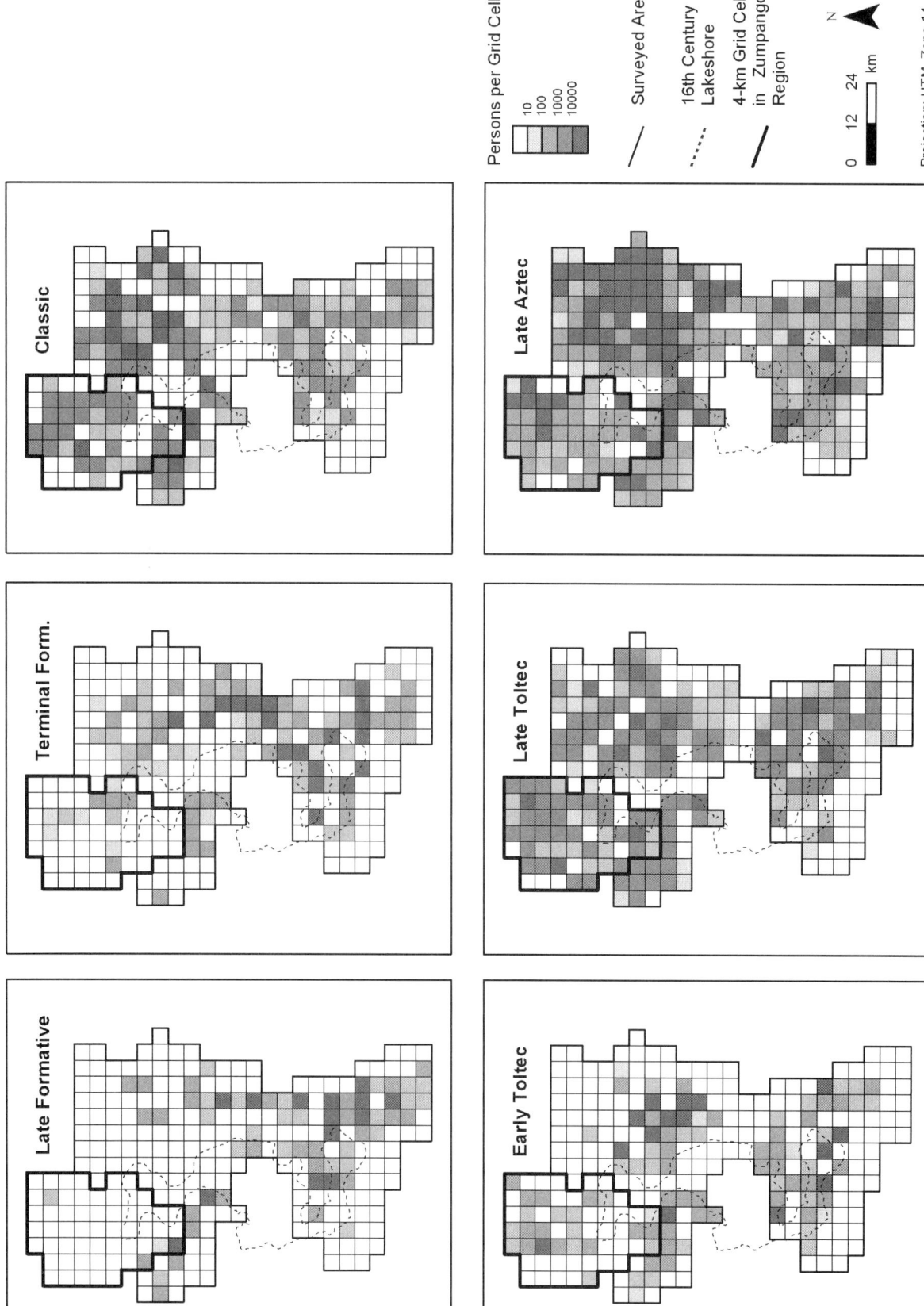

Figure 5.16. Prehispanic population densities in the Valley of Mexico over time, in 4 × 4 km cells. The Zumpango Region is outlined in heavy black.

The Patterning of Settlement

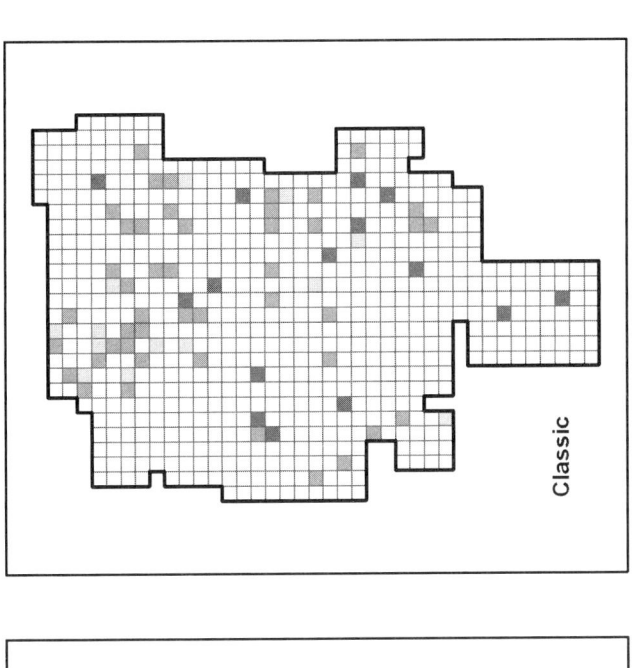
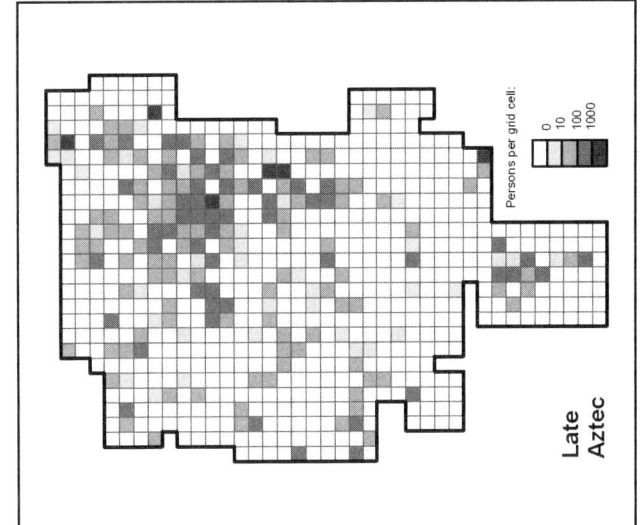
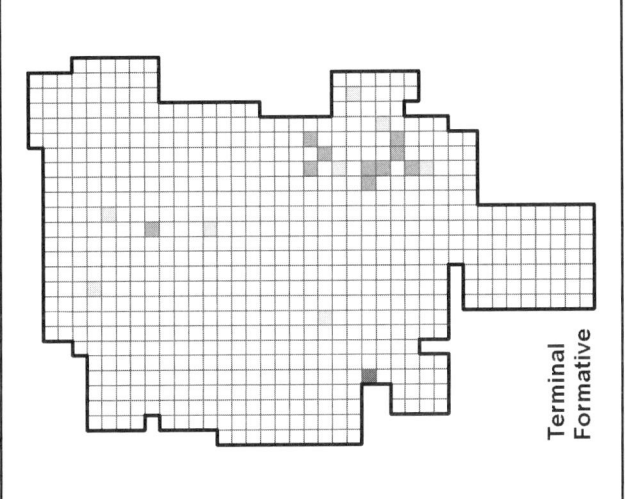
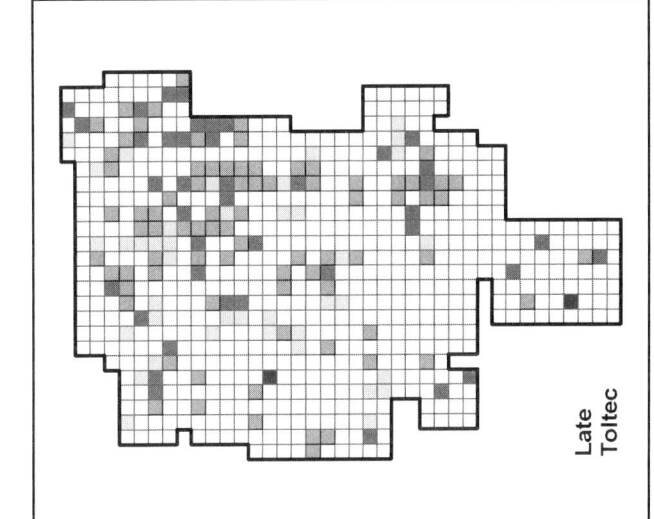
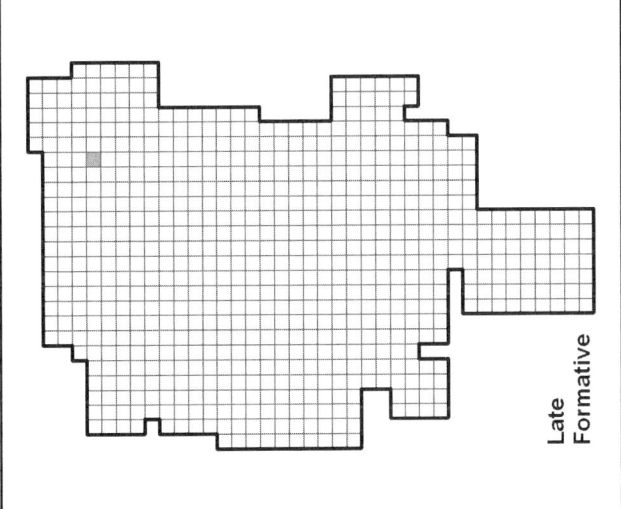
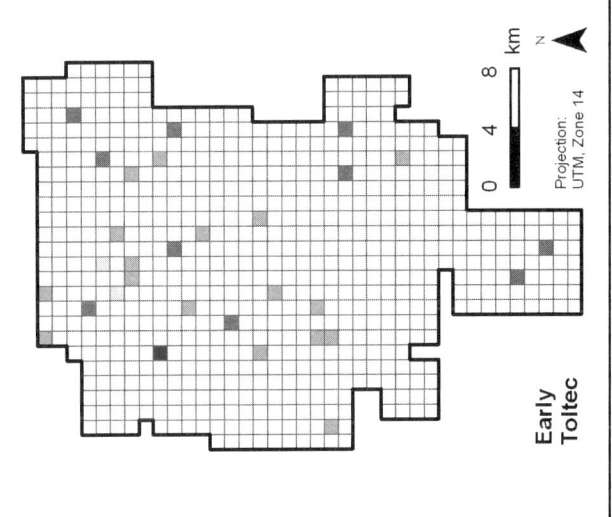

Figure 5.17. Population density in 1 × 1 km cells in the Zumpango Region.

Table 5.3. Expected and actual population, and population density (people/km^2), using maximum estimates, by environmental zone in the Zumpango Region.

Zone	Area (km^2)	% of ZR	LF ZR Pop. = 30			TF ZR Pop. = 740			Cl ZR Pop. = 8290			ET ZR Pop. = 5145			LT ZR Pop. = 18,060			L. Az ZR Pop. = 41,485		
			Exp. Pop.	Actual Pop.	Density	Exp. Pop.	Actual Pop.	Density	Exp. Pop.	Actual Pop.	Density	Exp. Pop.	Actual Pop.	Density	Exp. Pop.	Actual Pop.	Density	Exp. Pop.	Actual Pop.	Density
USD	288.1	47.3	14	**30**	0.1	350	**60**	0.2	3921	**4820**	16.7	2434	2775	9.6	8542	**9820**	34.1	19,620	20,055	69.6
CMG	11.0	1.8	1	0		13	0	0.0	149	0	0.0	93	**1500**	136.4	325	0	0.0	747	0	0.0
CJ	9.7	1.6	1	0		0	0	0.0	133	0	0.0	82	20	2.1	289	0	0.0	664	10	1.0
BOMLP	101.7	16.7	5	0		124	**250**	2.5	1384	1265	12.4	859	**80**	0.8	3016	**1900**	18.7	6927	**10,560**	103.8
LP	115.7	19.0	6	0		141	**430**	3.7	1575	1205	10.4	978	770	6.7	3431	**2280**	19.7	7881	**5015**	43.3
LB	70.0	11.5	3	0		85	**0**	0.0	953	**200**	2.9	592	**0**	0.0	2077	**270**	3.9	4770	4225*	60.4
TI	12.8	2.1	1	0		16	0	0.0	174	**800**	62.5	108	0	0.0	379	**3790**	296.1	871	1615	126.2
Overall	609.0			30	0.05		740	1.2		8290	13.6		5145	8.4		18,060	29.7		41,485	68.1

Key: ZR = Zumpango Region; LF = Late Formative; TF = Terminal Formative; Cl = Classic; ET = Early Toltec; LT = Late Toltec; L. Az = Late Aztec; USD = Upper Salado Drainage; CMG = Cerro de Mesa Grande; CJ = Cerro Jalpa; BOMLP = Basin of Mexico Lower Piedmont; LP = Lakeshore Plain; LB = Lakebed; TI = Tultepec Island.
Boldface indicates notably higher or lower actual relative to expected population.
*Counts Xaltocán (Zu-Az-276).

Table 5.4. Number of sites (N) by environmental zone in the Zumpango Region.

Zone	% of Zumpango Region	LF N = 1		TF N = 26		Cl N = 90		ET N = 30		LT N = 208		L. Az N = 280	
		Exp'd	Actual	Exp'd	Actual	Exp'd	Actual	Exp'd	Actual	Exp'd	Actual	Exp'd	Actual
USD	47.3	-	-	12	**4**	43	54	14	19	99	126	132	**165**
CMG	1.8	-	-	-	-	2	0	-	1	4	0	5	0
CJ	1.6	-	-	-	-	-	1	-	1	3	0	4	3
BOMLP	16.7	-	-	4	5	15	17	5	**2**	35	39	47	58
LP	19.0	-	-	5	**17**	17	16	6	7	40	37	53	**28**
LB	11.5	-	-	3	0	10	**1**	3	**0**	24	**2**	32	**10***
TI	2.1	-	-	-	-	2	1	1	0	4	4	6	**16**

Key: See Table 5.3.
Boldface indicates notably higher or lower actual relative to expected number of sites.
*Counts Xaltocán (Zu-Az-276).

Table 5.5. Number of occupied hectares (N) by environmental zone in the Zumpango Region.

Zone	% of Zumpango Region	LF N = 3.0		TF N = 48.4		Cl N = 307.2		ET N = 156.0		LT N = 704.3		L. Az N = 1808.0	
		Exp'd	Actual	Exp'd	Actual	Exp'd	Actual	Exp'd	Actual	Exp'd	Actual	Exp'd	Actual
USD	47.3	1.4	**30**	22.9	**4.0**	145.4	**174.2**	74.0	83.4	332.7	371.8	854.9	882.4
CMG	1.8	-	0	0.9	0	5.5	0	2.8	**28.6**	12.7	0	32.5	0
CJ	1.6	-	0	0.8	0	4.9	1.0	2.5	1.1	11.3	0	28.9	0.7
BOMLP	16.7	0.5	0	8.1	**16.1**	51.3	46.6	26.1	**5.4**	117.5	**84.2**	301.9	**524.1**
LP	19.0	0.6	0	9.2	**28.3**	58.4	56.8	29.7	37.5	133.6	113.4	343.4	**206.0**
LB	11.5	0.3	0	5.6	0	35.3	**7.6**	18.0	**0**	80.9	**12.8**	207.8	**108.4***
TI	2.1	0.1	0	1.0	0	6.5	**21.0**	3.3	0	14.8	**122.1**	38.0	**86.4**

Key: See Table 5.3.
Boldface indicates notably higher or lower actual relative to expected number of occupied hectares.
*Counts Xaltocán (Zu-Az-276).

Early Toltec

The most unexpected aspect of Early Toltec occupation is the sudden appearance of an unprecedented large settlement (Zu-ET-12) atop Cerro de Mesa Grande—a site that is several orders of magnitude larger than what might be expected solely on the basis of the area of the CMG zone. As noted above, the phenomenon of Zu-ET-12 can be understood only within the context of Teotihuacan's collapse and the extensive realignments of polity and economy that would have occurred throughout central Mexico and beyond. Also notable are the unexpectedly scanty Early Toltec occupations in the BOMLP and LB zones, and the apparent abandonment of Tultepec Island (Table 5.3)—these phenomena must be closely linked to the massive growth of the large new hilltop settlement at Zu-ET-12.

Late Toltec

Except for the major reoccupation of Tultepec Island, the hint of a northerly bias in Early Toltec occupation in the Zumpango Region continues and accelerates into the Late Toltec period: the USD occupation is significantly higher than expected, while that of the BOMLP, the LP, and the LB zones is significantly lower (Table 5.3). This is not surprising in view of the explosive expansion of Tula's size and influence during this period, when the northern Zumpango Region would have been well within the heartland zone of this new Early Postclassic center. Thus, we might expect to see intensification of agriculture in the northern Zumpango Region, an area that would have been highly accessible to Tula on the basis of proximity alone. The unexpectedly large Late Toltec occupation of Tultepec Island at the southern edge of the Zumpango Region might reflect Tula's concerns with accessing the abundant potential for irrigation agriculture in the delta of the Río Cuautitlan on the west and south sides of the island, and the aquatic resources and saltmaking potential along the island's eastern and northern margins.

Tultepec Island proved to be an unusually attractive setting for occupation during the Classic and Late Toltec, although somewhat less so during the Late Aztec. This was especially true for the Late Toltec, when the largest Late Toltec center in the Zumpango Region (Zu-LT-211) was established on the lower southern flanks of Cerro Tultepec. This strategically placed locale sits at the intersection of two important resource zones: (1) the delta of the Río Cuautitlan to the west and south, and (2) the wetlands of Lake Xaltocán-Zumpango to the north and east. In geopolitical terms, during Late Toltec times this may have marked the approximate southern frontier of Tula's heartland. The apparent absence of Formative occupation on Tultepec Island is puzzling. We suspect that such occupation may well exist under the dense overlay of several modern settlements.

Late Aztec

By Late Aztec times, occupation is notably higher than expected in the BOMLP zone and lower than expected in the Lakeshore Plain (Table 5.3). The BOMLP was relatively less densely settled during the antecedent Late Toltec, and seemingly almost depopulated during the Early Aztec. The Late Aztec occupation of the Lakebed zone is notable for the high concentration of population at the Xaltocán center. The unsurveyed lakebed to the southeast of Xaltocán is now known to have been extensively utilized for chinampa agriculture during Late Aztec times (Nichols and Frederick 1993; Frederick et al. 2005). The relatively modest Late Aztec lakeshore/lakebed occupation of the northern part of Lake Xaltocán may reflect a higher concentration of population during this period in the newly developing chinampa zone several kilometers to the southeast.

Occupation by Site Type

Tables 5.6–5.11 show the numbers and proportions of sites, occupied hectares, and estimated population for each site type. Table 5.7 is a simplified version of Table 5.6, collapsing the more complex site typology into hamlets, villages, and centers. Table 5.9 is a simplified version of Table 5.8, and Table 5.11 is a simplified version of Table 5.10.

While small sites predominate for every period in terms of total numbers of sites, there were high proportions of people living in large, relatively nucleated sites (LNV, LC, and RC sites) during all post-Formative periods (Tables 5.10, 5.11) (excepting, of course, the Early Aztec period, when the Zumpango Region was apparently very sparsely populated). The absence of comparatively large, nucleated settlements during Late Formative and Terminal Formative times is another indication that the Zumpango Region was marginal to the Formative developments that were clearly centered well to the south and that included numerous large, nucleated settlements (Figs. 5.5, 5.7, 5.16). It is also true that in every post-Formative period in the Zumpango Region, large numbers of people also resided in smaller and more dispersed settlements (Hamlets and Dispersed Villages) (Tables 5.10, 5.11).

This relatively high proportion of dispersed occupation is generally similar to most other surveyed regions in the Valley of Mexico. One exception is the Teotihuacan Region during the late Terminal Formative and Classic periods, when very high proportions of regional population were concentrated at urban Teotihuacan. Another exception, involving much of the entire Valley, is the Late Aztec period, where in most other surveyed regions within the Valley of Mexico significantly higher proportions of the total population resided in urban communities (Sanders et al. 1979:189, 195, 198, 203).

Table 5.12 compares the relative percentages of different site types in the Zumpango Region with those for the Valley of Mexico as a whole; Table 5.13 presents the same comparison on the basis of population in each of the different site types. These figures show that for most periods, the Zumpango Region had significantly higher proportions of hamlet sites and hamlet inhabitants than virtually all other surveyed parts of the Valley of Mexico; conversely, the Zumpango Region also shows significantly lower proportions over the long term of villages and centers, and of people inhabiting these larger settlements. By comparison with these other regions, the Zumpango Region is decidedly the most rural sector of the Valley of Mexico during the Late Postclassic.

The Spatial Configuration of Settlement

Figure 5.17 provides general impressions of settlement clustering at different periods of time in the Zumpango Region. These impressions are fleshed out in the larger-scale schematic maps shown in Figs. 5.4, 5.6, 5.8, 5.10, 5.12, and 5.14.

The Terminal Formative (Tzacualli Phase)

There is a notable clustering of small settlements near the southeastern corner of the Zumpango Region, along a broad linear transect extending from the northern lakeshore northward into the BOMLP (Figs. 5.6, 5.16). Within the Zumpango Region, there is little Terminal Formative occupation outside this loose cluster. Since there is virtually no antecedent Late Formative occupation in this region of Terminal Formative site clustering, it appears that these TF settlements represent pioneering probes into this very sparsely occupied region, perhaps with a focus on wetland resources. Figure 5.7 suggests that what we see in the Zumpango Region was part of a more generalized movement of small numbers of people around the eastern and northern shores of Lake Xaltocán-Zumpango, perhaps stimulated by policies emanating directly from the rapidly urbanizing new center of Teotihuacan.

The suggestion of a modest site-size hierarchy can be seen in Figure 5.18, which shows that one site (Zu-TF-7, at the upper edge of the Río Pachuca floodplain near the north end of the Terminal Formative settlement cluster) has an area (7.8 ha) nearly twice as large as that of the next largest coeval site (nearby Zu-TF-8, at 4.2 ha). This could mean that Zu-TF-7 was the locus of some sort of local authority figure, perhaps a low-level functionary within the developing Teotihuacan administrative hierarchy, or an emerging high-ranking cluster of chiefly households with comparatively close socioeconomic links to Teotihuacan.

The Classic

Classic occupation is broadly dispersed throughout most of the Zumpango Region, and there is no clearly apparent site clustering. There are only two sectors where there are very few Classic sites: (1) the far northwestern corner, around the flanks of Cerro de Mesa Grande in the USD; and (2) in the Lakeshore Plain and adjacent Lakebed in the southwest (Figs. 5.8, 5.16). In both cases, this phenomenon might be explained by the concentration of regional population into the two largest Classic sites in the Zumpango Region: Zu-Cl-89 on Tultepec Island, and Zu-Cl-60 in the broad pass between Cerro de Mesa Grande and Cerro Jalpa.

In general terms, the overall Classic occupation of the Zumpango Region resembles that of other surveyed parts of the Valley of Mexico outside the highly urbanized Teotihuacan Region (Fig. 5.9). The site-size histogram in Figure 5.19 suggests the development of a bimodal site-size hierarchy, with four unusually large sites (Zu-Cl-89, -60, -40, and -42) that may have been local administrative centers of some type, perhaps closely linked to Teotihuacan. The presence of modest public architecture at Zu-Cl-89 (the only such architecture that can be associated with Classic occupation in the Zumpango Region) reinforces this hypothesis.

The Early Toltec

The reader should keep in mind that, as previously noted, we have a generally lower confidence in our perception of site configuration for the Early Toltec period relative to most others. Nevertheless, what we seem to have is a decline and dispersal of occupation throughout most of the survey area relative to the antecedent Classic, together with a major concentration of population and public architecture at Zu-ET-12 atop Cerro de Mesa Grande (Figs. 5.10, 5.16), a setting that had never been occupied before, and was quickly abandoned prior to the Late Toltec period. Figure 5.11 indicates that these population declines in the Zumpango Region were paralleled in some other parts of the Valley of Mexico, particularly in the portions of the Texcoco and Chalco-Xochimilco Regions to the southeast, and in the northern Temascalapa Region to the east. Nevertheless, most other parts of the Valley of Mexico were much more densely occupied, with major centers measuring up to several hundred hectares.

Figure 5.20 indicates a three-level hierarchy based on site area, with Zu-ET-12 occupying the upper level, and two much smaller sites (Zu-ET-19 and Zu-ET-16) comprising a less well defined second tier. As noted elsewhere, Zu-ET-12 is additionally distinctive in the Zumpango Region for its unique (within the Valley of Mexico) hilltop setting, the relative abundance of its public architecture, and the comparatively high proportion of Coyotlatelco Red/Buff ceramics. All these suggest close linkages at this time with the nearby Tula Region, with its large hilltop centers and abundant Coyotlatelco ceramics.

Table 5.6. Numbers and percentages of sites in each site type in the Zumpango Region.

Period	SH #	SH %	H #	H %	SDV #	SDV %	LDV #	LDV %	SNV #	SNV %	LNV #	LNV %	LC #	LC %	RC #	RC %
LF	-	-	1	100.0	-	-	-	-	-	-	-	-	-	-	-	-
TF	17	65.4	9	34.6	-	-	-	-	-	-	-	-	-	-	-	-
Cl	32	35.6	39	43.3	8	8.9	1	1.1	7	7.7	1	1.1	2	2.2	-	-
ET	6	20.0	13	43.3	5	16.7	-	-	4	13.3	1	3.3	-	-	1	3.3
LT	102	49.0	66	31.7	26	12.5	-	-	9	4.3	1	0.5	3	1.4	1	0.5
L. Az	141	52.4	72	26.8	39	14.5	10	3.7	-	-	1	0.3	3	1.1	3	1.1

Key: SH = Small Hamlet; H = Hamlet; SDV = Small Dispersed Village; LDV = Large Dispersed Village; SNV = Small Nucleated Village; LNV = Large Nucleated Village; LC = Local Center; RC = Regional Center; LF = Late Formative; TF = Terminal Formative; Cl = Classic; ET = Early Toltec; LT = Late Toltec; L. Az = Late Aztec.

Table 5.7. Percentages of numbers of hamlets, villages, and centers in the Zumpango Region.

Period	% Hamlets	% Villages	% Centers
TF	100.0	0.0	0.0
Cl	78.9	18.8	2.2
ET	63.3	33.3	3.3
LT	80.7	17.7	1.9
L. Az	79.2	18.5	2.2

Key: See Table 5.6.

Table 5.8. Numbers and percentages of occupied hectares in each site type in the Zumpango Region.

Period	SH # ha	SH % ha	H # ha	H % ha	SDV # ha	SDV % ha	LDV # ha	LDV % ha	SNV # ha	SNV % ha	LNV # ha	LNV % ha	LC # ha	LC % ha	RC # ha	RC % ha
LF	-	-	3.0	100.0	-	-	-	-	-	-	-	-	-	-	-	-
TF	14.8	30.6	33.6	69.4	-	-	-	-	-	-	-	-	-	-	-	-
Cl	24.6	8.0	108.5	35.3	57.2	18.6	17.2	5.6	42.9	14.0	16.4	5.3	40.5	13.2	-	-
ET	4.5	2.9	35.4	22.6	39.1	25.0	-	-	29.3	18.7	19.5	12.5	-	-	28.6	18.3
LT	76.0	10.8	159.6	22.7	217.1	30.9	-	-	80.3	11.4	16.8	2.4	55.9	7.9	97.5	13.9
L. Az	133.4	7.4	242.9	13.5	418.1	23.2	436.2	24.2	-	-	19.8	1.1	215.3	12.0	327.1	18.2

Key: See Table 5.6.

Table 5.9. Percentages of occupied hectares in hamlets, villages, and centers in the Zumpango Region.

Period	% in Hamlets	% in Villages	% in Centers
TF	100.0	0.0	0.0
Cl	43.3	43.5	13.2
ET	25.5	56.2	18.3
LT	33.5	44.7	21.8
L. Az	20.9	48.5	30.2

Key: See Table 5.6.

Table 5.10. Numbers and percentages of population (maximal estimate) in each site type in the Zumpango Region.

Period	Site Types														
	SH		H		SDV		LDV		SNV		LNV		LC		RC	
	Pop.	%	Pop.	%	Pop.	%	Pop.	%	Pop.	%	Pop.	%	Pop.	%	Pop.	%
LF	-	-	30	100.0	-	-	-	-	-	-	-	-	-	-	-	-
TF	200	27.0	540	73.0	-	-	-	-	-	-	-	-	-	-	-	-
Cl	340	4.1	2090	25.2	1350	16.3	600	7.2	1410	17.0	700	8.4	1800	21.7	-	-
ET	95	1.8	750	14.6	850	16.5	-	-	1150	22.4	800	15.5	-	-	1500	29.2
LT	1180	6.5	3410	18.9	4810	26.6	-	-	2780	15.4	680	3.8	2200	12.2	3000	16.6
L. Az	2025	4.9	4460	10.8	9000	21.7	10,900	26.3	-	-	1000	2.4	4400	10.6	9700	23.4

Key: See Table 5.6.

Table 5.11. Percentages of population in hamlets, villages, and centers in the Zumpango Region.

Period	% in Hamlets	% in Villages	% in Centers
TF	100.0	0.0	0.0
Cl	29.3	48.9	21.7
ET	16.4	54.4	29.2
LT	25.4	45.8	28.8
L. Az	15.7	50.4	34.0

Key: See Table 5.6.

Table 5.12. Comparison of percentages of site types in the Zumpango Region and in the Valley of Mexico as a whole excluding the Zumpango Region.

Period	% Hamlets		% Villages		% Centers	
	VOM	ZR	VOM	ZR	VOM	ZR
LF	54.3	**100.0**	26.0	**0.0**	2.9	**0.0**
TF*	47.6	**100.0**	15.0	**0.0**	2.8	**0.0**
Cl	58.5	**78.9**	23.2	18.8	2.8	2.2
ET	51.9	**63.3**	23.3	**33.3**	5.7	3.3
LT	66.7	**80.7**	15.0	17.7	0.8	**1.9**
L. Az	65.2	**79.2**	20.4	18.5	1.9	2.2

Key: VOM = Valley of Mexico; ZR = Zumpango Region; LF = Late Formative; TF = Terminal Formative; Cl = Classic; ET = Early Toltec; LT = Late Toltec; L. Az = Late Aztec.
Boldface indicates marked differences between Zumpango Region values and those of the overall VOM figures.
*Combines Patlachique and Tzacualli phases for VOM.
Note: The VOM percentage totals do not add up to 100% because there are numerous sites for each time period that fall outside the "Hamlet," "Village," and "Center" classification.

Table 5.13. Comparison of percentages of populations in different site types in the Zumpango Region and in the Valley of Mexico as a whole excluding the Zumpango Region.

Period	% Pop. in Hamlets		% Pop. in Villages		% Pop. in Centers	
	VOM	ZR	VOM	ZR	VOM	ZR
LF	5.4	**100.0**	59.9	**0.0**	34.7	**0.0**
TF*	4.2	**100.0**	33.6	**0.0**	59.6	**0.0**
Cl	4.9	**29.3**	24.5	**48.9**	70.5	**21.7**
ET	3.9	**16.4**	26.4	**54.4**	67.6	**29.2**
LT	17.7	25.4	46.9	45.8	35.4	28.8
L. Az	6.7	**15.7**	31.0	**50.4**	61.2	**34.0**

Key: See Table 5.12.
Boldface indicates marked differences between Zumpango Region values and those of overall VOM averages.
*Combines Patlachique and Tzacualli phases for VOM.

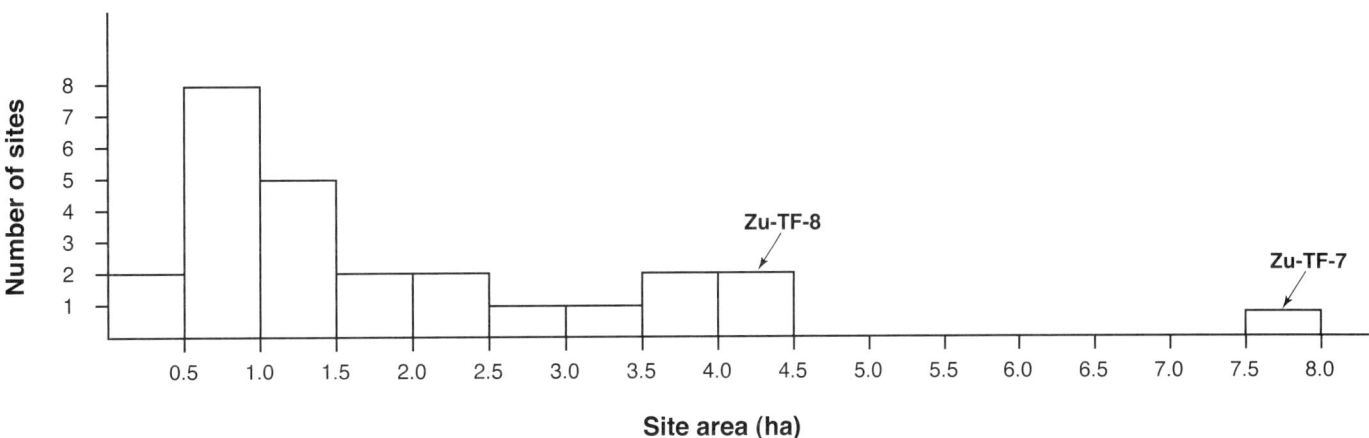

Figure 5.18. Histogram of Terminal Formative site area in the Zumpango Region.

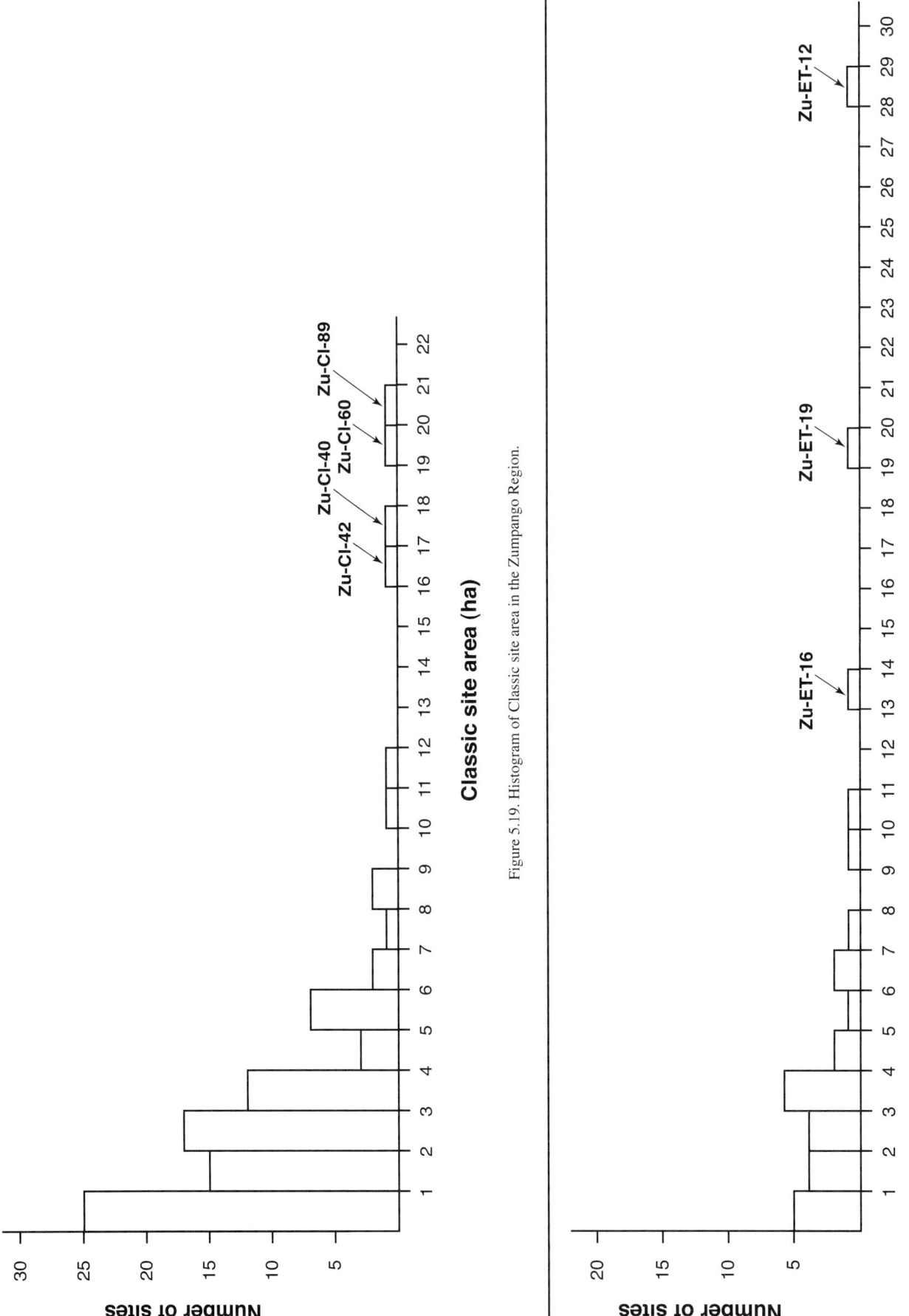

Figure 5.19. Histogram of Classic site area in the Zumpango Region.

Figure 5.20. Histogram of Early Toltec site area in the Zumpango Region.

The Late Toltec

As seen in Figures 5.12 and 5.16, the Late Toltec period witnessed substantial population growth and a general filling in of the regional landscape, particularly within the USD and upper BOMLP zones in the northeastern quadrant of the Zumpango Region. Even the northwest corner of the survey area, sparsely settled during the earlier Classic and Early Toltec periods, now contained substantial occupation, although the western Lakeshore Plain and adjacent Lakebed zones continued to be sparsely settled, as they had been in earlier periods.

Zu-ET-12, the large ET site atop Cerro de Mesa Grande, was quickly abandoned, but substantial new large settlements and their satellites grew up around the southern and eastern flanks of the hill at Zu-LT-135 on the south, and the site cluster centered at Zu-LT-87 on the east. These new settlements, perhaps together with the northwestern site cluster centered at Zu-LT-75 and Zu-LT-80 (both with substantial public architecture), probably replaced the major public functions of Zu-ET-12 during the Late Toltec period.

Several LT site clusters can be discerned. These are most apparent at four localities: (1) a northwestern cluster around Zu-LT-75 and Zu-LT-80; (2) a west-central cluster around Zu-LT-87; (3) a far southern cluster on Tultepec Island, around Zu-LT-211, the largest LT site in the Zumpango Region; and (4) a diffuse cluster comprised of scattered hamlets and small villages, with no apparent principal center, in the southeast, straddling the lakeshore. It is notable that most of this latter Late Toltec occupation (as in the cases of the earlier Terminal Formative, Classic, and Early Toltec in the same area) occupies the broad, naturally elevated surface of the ancient beach ridges and strand plain defined by Frederick et al. (2005) along the north shore of Lake Xaltocán-Zumpango (see Chap. 2). Another western cluster may exist centered at Zu-LT-203, although this lies on our survey border and so is virtually impossible to define clearly.

We are presently unable to distinguish any individual site clusters within the broad scatter of relatively dense settlement in the USD and upper BOMLP in the northeastern quadrant of the Zumpango Region. The "Large Nucleated Village" (Zu-LT-30) at the approximate center of this "mega cluster" might have been a center of public administrative and ceremonial functions (there are indications of public architecture). The presence of several other smaller nucleated settlements scattered across the width of this "mega-cluster" could represent spatially diffuse public functions.

Figure 5.21 shows a distinctly three-tier Late Toltec hierarchy based on individual site area. Nevertheless, because we think that *site clusters* may be more important than individual sites as foci of Late Toltec regional polity and economy, we suspect that this histogram has less significance as a proxy for Late Toltec sociopolitical structure than is probably the case for such histograms presented for earlier periods. This comparative diffusion of population and public functions appears to have carried over into the subsequent Late Aztec period (see below).

Nevertheless, since it is so much larger than any other LT site in the Zumpango Region, it seems likely that Zu-LT-211, at the far southern edge of our survey area, may have had special importance during the Early Postclassic (as hinted at earlier, this site may, for example, have marked the far southern frontier of Tula's heartland zone).

The Early Aztec

We have noted the apparent scarcity of Early Aztec occupation in the Zumpango Region. In another paper (Parsons and Gorenflo, in press), we focused on this issue and explored its implications within the larger context of the Valley of Mexico and adjacent parts of central Mexico. There are four basic questions: (1) was there really a regional Early Aztec occupational collapse in the Zumpango Region; (2) if so, why did it occur; (3) how long did it last; and (4) why and how was this region so successfully reoccupied during the subsequent Late Aztec period?

Our perception of a severe Early Aztec occupational decline rests on the fact that there is almost no definite Aztec II Black/Orange (B/O) pottery (or any of the variants of Black/Red that are known to be closely associated with Aztec I and II Black/Orange in other parts of the Valley of Mexico) in the Zumpango Region. One of the few indisputable Aztec II B/O sherds in our surface collections comes from Zu-Az-46 (Plate 5.1).

As noted in Appendix B, although we conclude that what we define as Aztec II-III Black/Orange pottery dates mainly to the Late Aztec, we suspect that this tradition might actually have begun in late Early Aztec times (as Vaillant [1938] originally suggested some seventy years ago). Figure 5.22 shows two diffuse clusters of Aztec II-III Black/Orange surface pottery in the Zumpango Region: (1) a northern cluster in the Upper Salado Drainage; and (2) a southern cluster in the Lakeshore Plain along the northern shores of Lake Xaltocán-Zumpango, on Tultepec Island, and at Xaltocán (the latter site, where there is also an abundance of Aztec I B/O, lies just beyond the southeastern limits of our survey). Even if Aztec II-III B/O is late Early Aztec in date, there would still be only a very sparse Early Aztec occupation in the Zumpango Region.

Although the precise chronological placement of Aztec II-III B/O pottery remains unclear, we presently prefer to include it within the Late Aztec assemblage. Aztec II-III B/O pottery occurs in some surface collections throughout the Zumpango Region and elsewhere in the Basin of Mexico, but rarely in clear direct association with well-defined Aztec II B/O pottery, and always closely associated with typical Late Aztec ceramic types. To be certain of how Aztec II-III B/O is distributed in time and space, we will eventually need a full-scale reanalysis of the surface collections from all the Valley of Mexico surveys, as well as new stratigraphic excavations at key (surviving) sites.

Several dozen radiocarbon dates relevant to the absolute chronology of Aztec II B/O are now available from several sites in different parts of the Valley of Mexico (Garcia Chávez 2004; Parsons and Gorenflo, in press). These dates suggest that the span of absolute time during which Aztec II B/O was used may have been little more than a century, from the early to mid-fourteenth century into the mid-fifteenth century. This contrasts with the apparently much longer time spans of both Mazapan-Tollan Red/Buff and Aztec I Black/Orange. Thus, the Middle Postclassic depopulation of the northwestern Basin may not have lasted much more than three to five generations. If our Aztec II-III B/O is actually late Middle Postclassic in age, then the regional population abandonment may have endured no more than two generations.

The Late Aztec

The Late Aztec period witnessed rapid population growth and an expansion of occupation throughout most of the Zumpango Region (Figs. 5.14, 5.16). Comparable expansion occurred elsewhere in the Valley of Mexico, including the Temascalapa Region to the east (Fig. 5.15), as well as in the nearby Tula Region just to the north (Robert Cobean, pers. comm., May 2008). This Late Aztec growth in the northern Valley of Mexico and in the Tula Region is all the more impressive since it appears to have occurred after major population declines in these regions during the antecedent Early Aztec—making it the one period of truly rapid population growth in the Valley of Mexico (Gorenflo 2006).

It seems probable that these high levels of Late Aztec population size and density were achieved by substantial immigration. This is another major difference between the northern third and southern two-thirds of the Valley of Mexico: in the center and south, there was a substantial Early Aztec population base, including several important urban centers. That stated, prehispanic settlement data in the Valley of Mexico indicate that considerable internal mobility occurred throughout the region's prehistory (Gorenflo 2006), making migration into the northern part of the Valley possibly a more local example of a very familiar demographic mechanism underlying the ebb and flow of prehistoric population.

Regardless of the presence of possible antecedents, the north-south dichotomy poses four major questions about Postclassic demography in the northern Valley of Mexico and Tula Region that cannot presently be answered: (1) what happened to the large regional Late Toltec population that apparently disappeared by the Early Aztec; (2) from whence did the large and rapid population increase after the Early Aztec come; (3) what caused these fluctuations; and (4) did these fluctuations occur rapidly or gradually?

The only sector of the Zumpango Region that shows a significant Late Aztec population decline relative to the antecedent Late Toltec is the Lakeshore Plain and adjacent Lakebed north and northwest of Xaltocán. Parts of this area—particularly the geomorphic high (the ancient beach ridges and strand plain along the northern shoreline [Frederick et al. 2005])—had been settled since Terminal Formative times (Figs. 5.6, 2.4). As noted above, we attribute this latter population decline to a concentration of Late Aztec population in the newly developed chinampa zone in the unsurveyed lakebed south and southeast of Xaltocán (Nichols and Frederick 1993).

Histograms of Late Aztec site area (Fig. 5.23) and site population (Fig. 5.24) suggest site hierarchies of unprecedented complexity relative to earlier time periods. These Late Aztec histograms must be regarded with a degree of skepticism because they are based on unusually imprecise archaeological measurements of site area for some sites (see Appendix A), and rely more heavily than we would like on ethnohistoric sources. The histograms suggest that one major regional center underlying the modern town of Zumpango (visible to our survey only in small patches at Zu-Az-237 and -238), a secondary regional center at Xaltocán (Zu-Az-276, well defined archaeologically by Brumfiel's [2005] research), and three local centers at Zu-Az-172, Zu-Az-130/131, and Zu-Az-233 (mostly underlying modern Zitlaltepec [ethnohistoric Citlaltepec]) (Fig. 5.13) all appear to have had little or no occupation in earlier centuries.

Three of these new Late Aztec centers are in lakeshore or lakebed locations (Zumpango, Xaltocán, and Citlaltepec), and rapid population nucleation at these places may well have precluded any significant buildup of nearby rural settlements, thus accounting for the relatively few hamlets and villages in their vicinities (Fig. 5.14). If this was the case, then very different forces appear to have been operating around the two smaller Late Aztec local centers farther north (Zu-Az-172 and Zu-Az-130/131), both of which are closely surrounded by numerous smaller villages and hamlets (Fig. 5.14). In other words, during Late Aztec times, the northern two-thirds of the Zumpango Region—the USD and BOMLP zones well away from the lakeshore—had a highly dispersed settlement pattern, while settlement in the southern third of the region—the Lakeshore Plain and Lakebed zones—was much more nucleated. This contrast is also clearly suggested by the late sixteenth-century historical sources discussed in Chapter 3 that refer to an antecedent late prehispanic era of much more dispersed occupation around the nucleated Early Colonial towns and villages that were the products of Spanish-imposed *congregación* policies.

The strength of the break between the Tula-dominated world of the Early Postclassic and the imperial Triple Alliance-dominated polity of the Late Postclassic is nicely illustrated by the fact that the major Late Toltec regional center on Tultepec Island (Zu-LT-211) (Fig. 5.12) was apparently never replaced by any important Late Aztec center. Although Tultepec Island continued to be occupied in Late Aztec times, all settlements there were hamlets and dispersed villages. The strategic Early Postclassic geopolitical significance of this locality, when it may have marked the southern frontier of Tula's heartland zone, had entirely vanished in subsequent centuries. We continue to ponder why a new major center developed in Middle and Late Postclassic times on an artificial island at Xaltocán rather than at the locus of the largest Late Toltec center in the Zumpango Region on Tultepec Island, a previously strategic zone only 6 km to the west of Xaltocán.

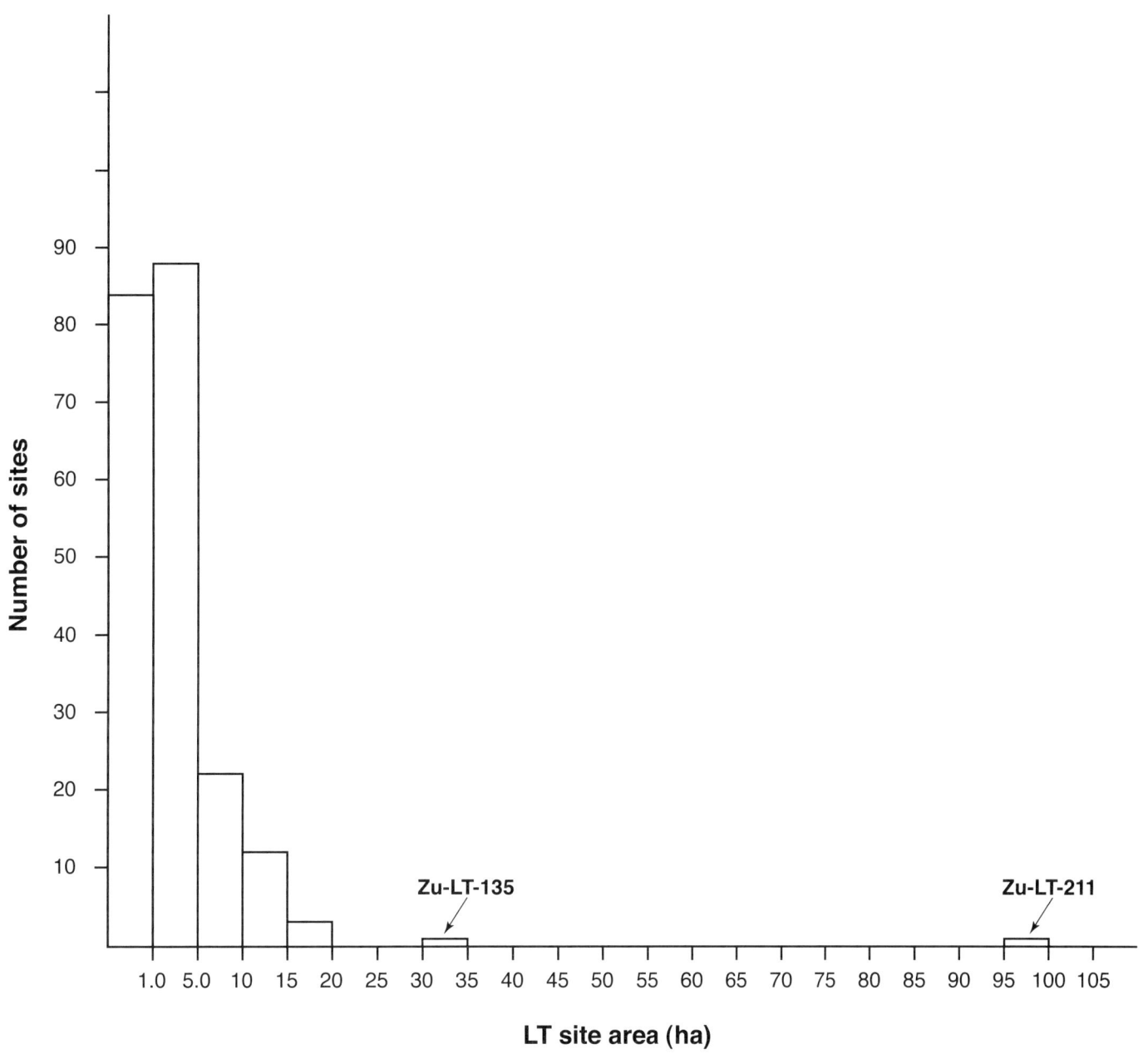

Figure 5.21. Histogram of Late Toltec site area in the Zumpango Region.

Plate 5.1. Example of Aztec II Black/Orange sherd from Zu-Az-46.

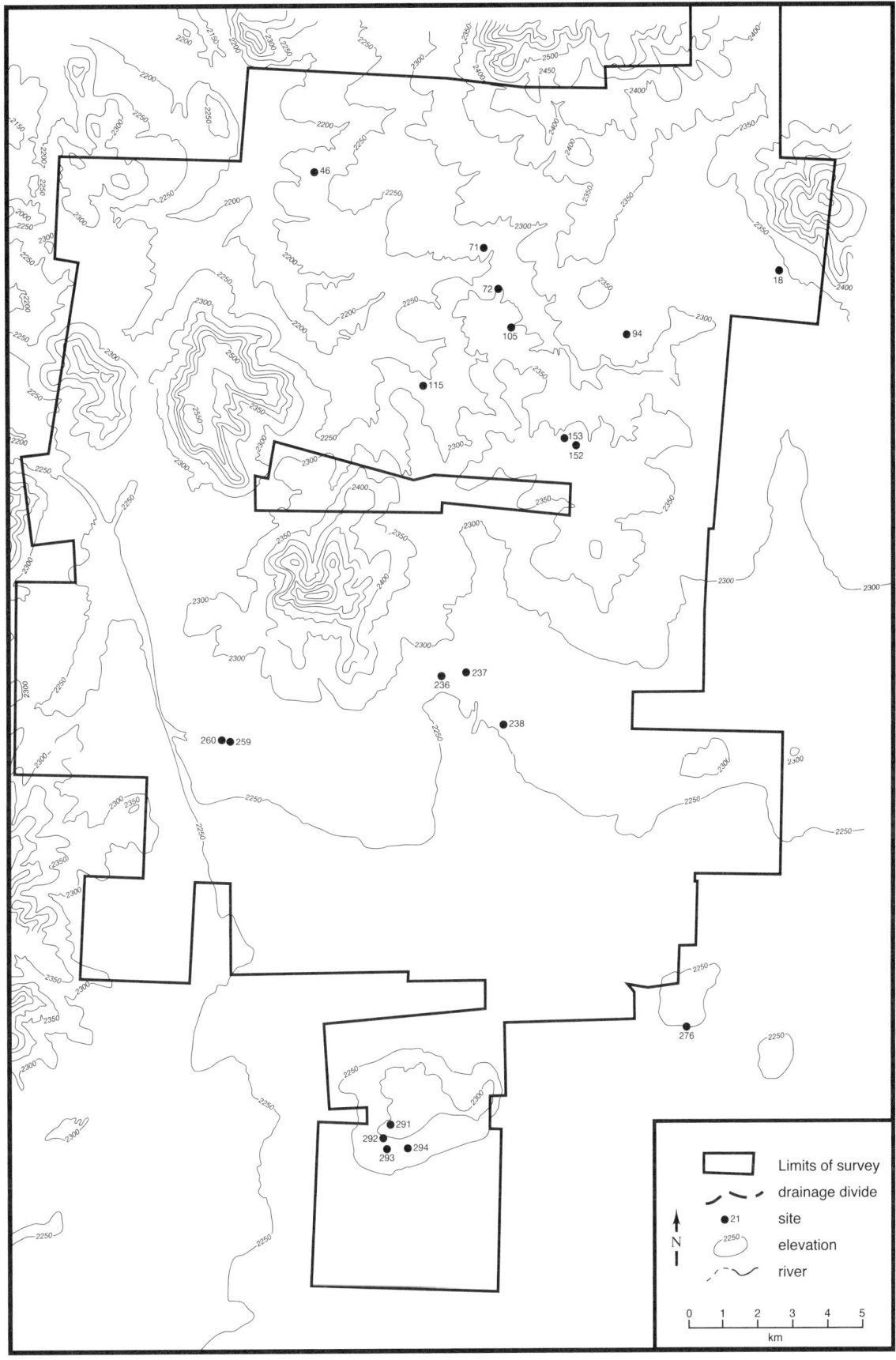

Figure 5.22. Distribution of Aztec II-III Black/Orange pottery in the Zumpango Region.

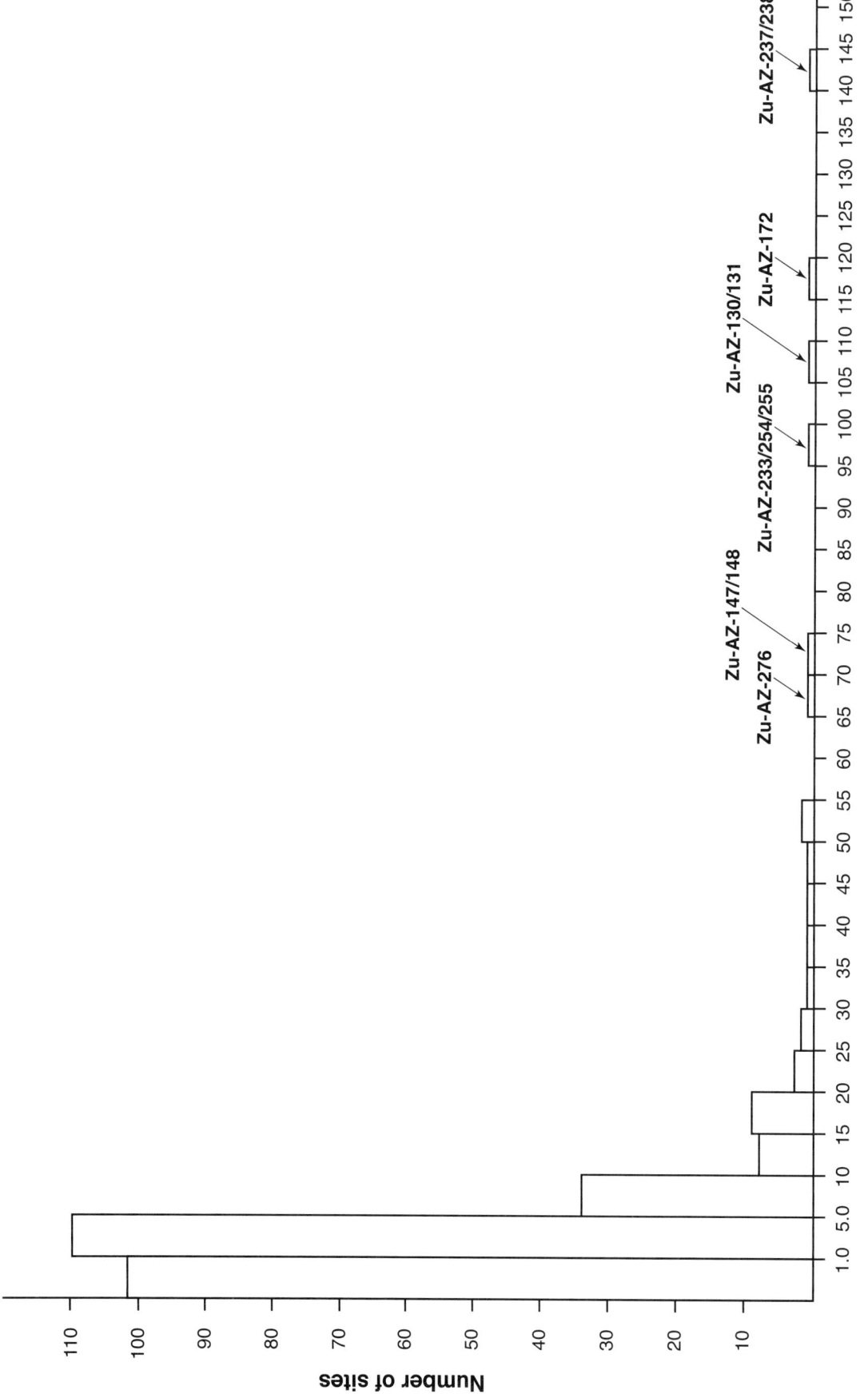

Figure 5.23. Histogram of Late Aztec site area in the Zumpango Region.

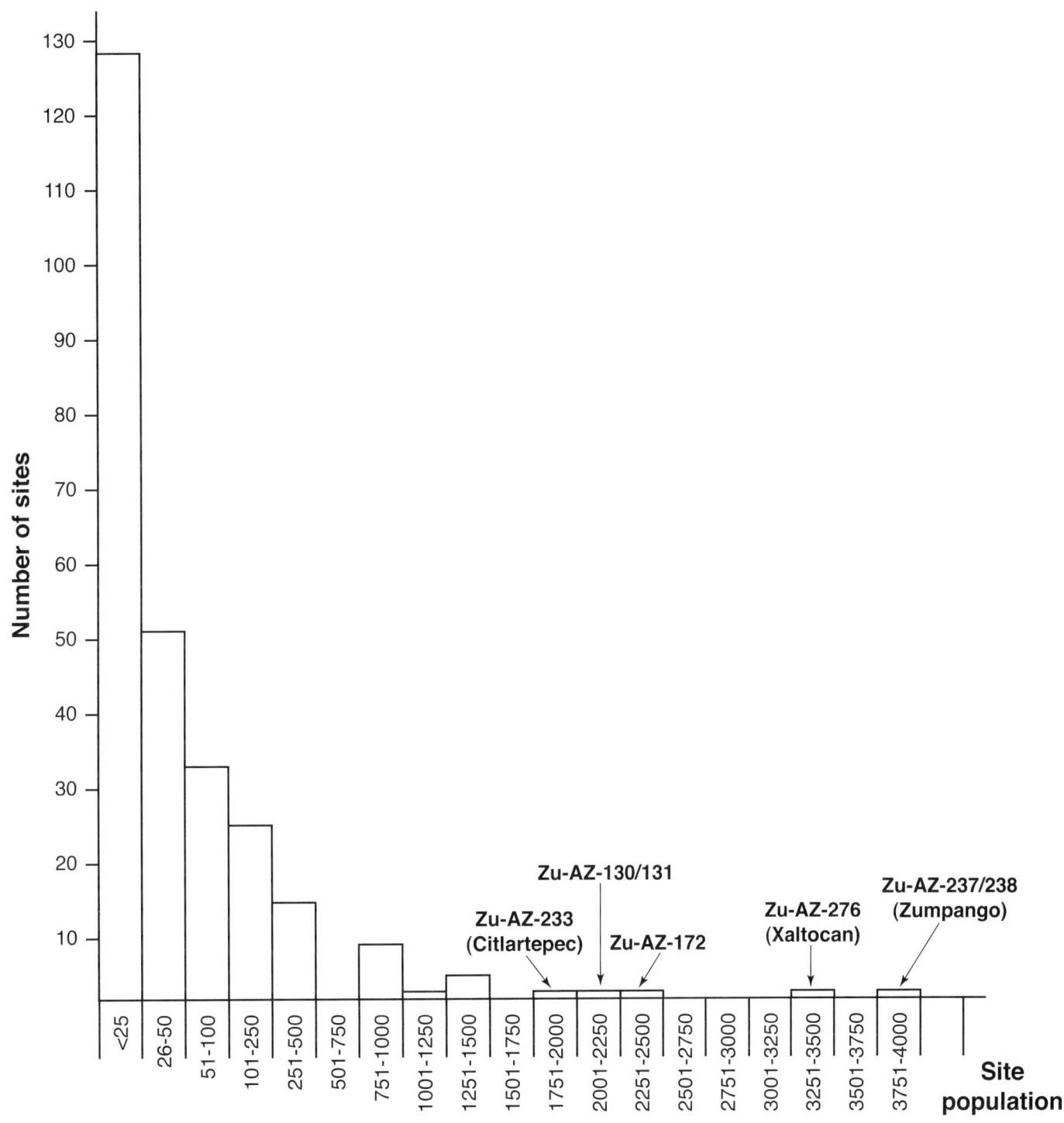

Figure 5.24. Histogram of Late Aztec site population in the Zumpango Region.

The Aztec IV Black/Orange Problem

The surface collections from many of our Late Aztec sites contain sherds of Aztec IV Black/Orange pottery (Fig. 5.25). In virtually all cases, these examples of Aztec IV B/O co-occur with Aztec III B/O ceramics. Uncertainty persists about whether Aztec IV B/O began to be produced and used during late prehispanic times, or whether it might be exclusively post-hispanic. Here we can make no significant contribution to the resolution of this problem, but it concerns us because if Aztec IV B/O is wholly, or primarily, post-hispanic, then our Late Aztec occupation may be somewhat more modest than we presently perceive it to be.

Figure 5.25 shows two clusters of sites with Aztec IV B/O surface pottery in the Zumpango Region: (1) a larger northern cluster in the Upper Salado Drainage and overlapping slightly into the northern edge of the Basin of Mexico Lower Piedmont; and (2) a smaller, southern cluster diffusely scattered across the northern shore of Lake Xaltocán-Zumpango and extending into Tultepec Island and Xaltocán. At present, we have little idea of the significance of these clusters. Their existence hints at a terminal Late Postclassic, possibly Early Colonial, cleavage between wetland- and inland-oriented economies.

Overall Summary and Conclusions

A number of important interrelated points emerge from the data discussed in this chapter (see Fig. 5.26 for a graphical summation of some overall demographic patterns).

(1) Settlement nucleation versus dispersal

Settlement during all prehispanic periods in the Zumpango Region was notably more dispersed that that of the twentieth century. In fact, prehispanic settlement in the Zumpango Region was generally more dispersed and less urbanized (or at least less nucleated) than in any other surveyed region within the Valley of Mexico, with the exception of the nearby Temascalapa Region, also in the north, which had a similar history of sparse prehispanic settlement. Only during Late Toltec times, at the peak of Tula's florescence, did the Zumpango Region attain a level of population size and density that equaled or exceeded the overall demographic averages in the Valley of Mexico as a whole.

(2) The impact of aridity

The Zumpango Region, together with the neighboring Temascalapa, Pachuca, and Tula Regions, is one of the driest parts of highland central Mexico. The northern frontier of Mesoamerica itself, as it is usually defined (Kirchoff 1943), is less than 200 km farther north. The combination of low annual rainfall, variability in annual rainfall, unpredictable onset of the summer rainy season, and unpredictable occurrences of spring and fall frosts make rainfall-based agriculture significantly more risky than in the more favored central and southern parts of the Valley of Mexico. Times of increased regional aridity, such as apparently occurred broadly across the Mexican *Mesa Central* after approximately A.D. 1000, would have required especially effective management of water resources and redistribution between specialized producers, some of whom would have been non-agriculturalists and/or arid-crop (for example, maguey-nopal) cultivators. Such management, in turn, may have been difficult without some degree of centralized sociopolitical organization.

(3) The marginality of the Zumpango Region during the Formative

The Zumpango Region, together with its near neighbors in the northern Valley of Mexico and adjacent Tula Region, was decidedly marginal to Formative developments in the central and southern Valley of Mexico. This marginality can probably be at least partly attributed to the relative aridity of this region. In any case, the Zumpango Region and its nearby northerly neighbors remained very sparsely occupied until the Classic period. The clustering of the very modest Terminal Formative occupation (with its modest site-size hierarchy) along the lakeshore suggests that this pioneering occupation of the Zumpango Region may have been less concerned with agriculture and more oriented toward the exploitation of wetland resources.

(4) Insights into Teotihuacan's early development and its florescence

The major increase of occupation during the Classic period correlates closely with the florescence of the new urban center at Teotihuacan a few dozen kilometers to the southeast. We conclude that the notable Classic population growth and settlement expansion in the previously very sparsely occupied Zumpango Region occurred within the organizational framework deriving from Teotihuacan's needs. These needs probably would have included salt, aquatic resources, and lime, in addition to the development of an agricultural capacity sufficient to sustain a substantial local population, and perhaps, with the development of canal irrigation, to generate a modest surplus for transfer to Teotihuacan itself. The extent to which Teotihuacan itself directly caused and managed these changes remains an open question. An alternative scenario might have these developments taking place in a more undirected way, by individuals and communities who were simply seeking to exploit new opportunities in an "empty niche" within a context of an expanding economy and increased overall wealth.

(5) Insights into Teotihuacan's collapse and its aftermath

The population decline, settlement dislocation, and establishment of a unique new hilltop center during the Early Toltec all point to marked dislocations with the antecedent Classic in the Zumpango Region. In these respects, the Zumpango Region differs from the central and southern Valley of Mexico where regional populations increased relative to Classic times, and where large new Early Toltec centers developed exclusively in hillflank and low-lying settings. Early Toltec settlement patterns in the Zumpango Region are more akin to those in areas around the margins of the Valley of Mexico on the east (Puebla-Tlaxcala), south (Morelos), and north (Tula Region), where large new

The Patterning of Settlement

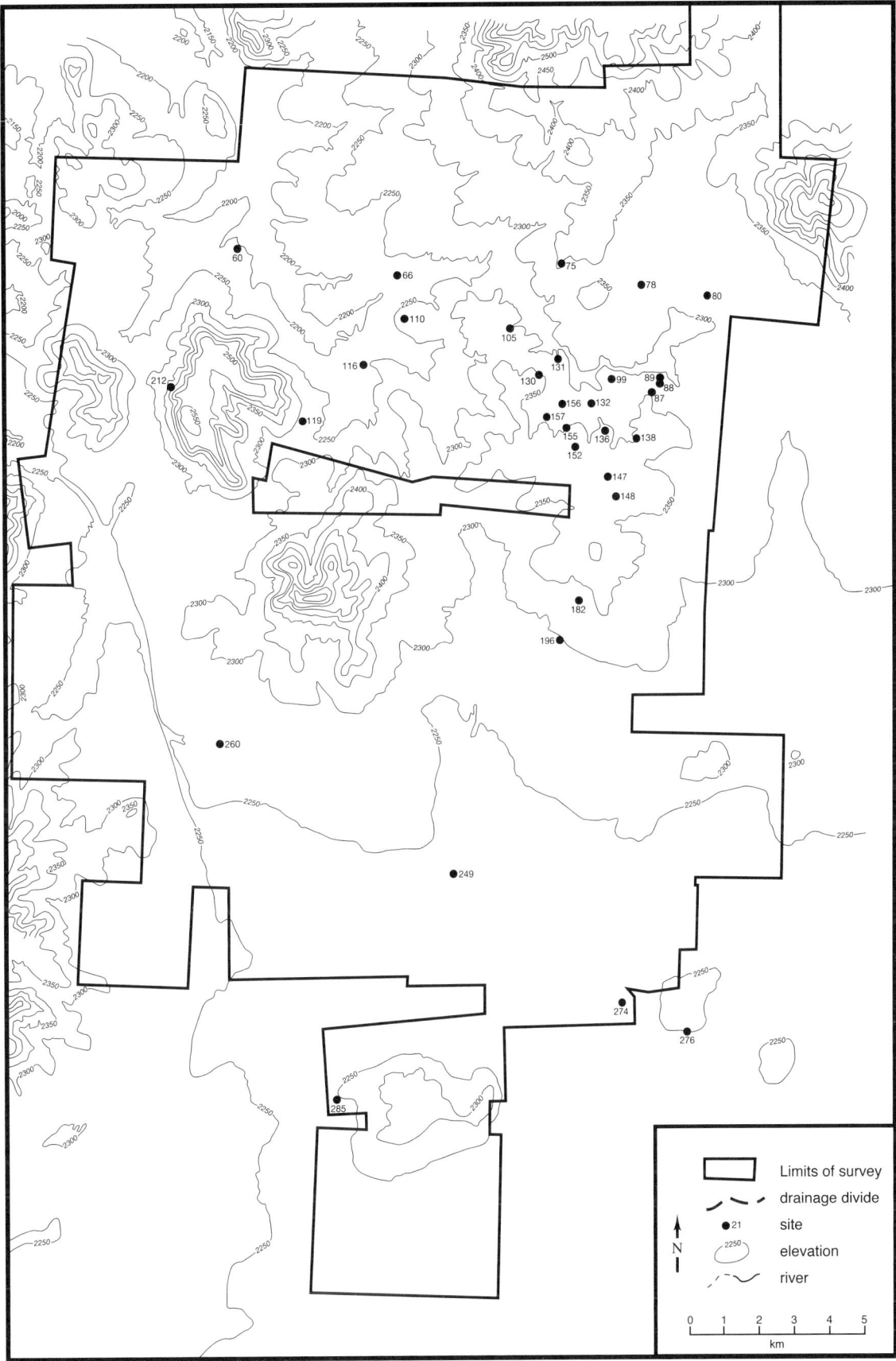

Figure 5.25. Distribution of Aztec IV Black/Orange pottery in the Zumpango Region.

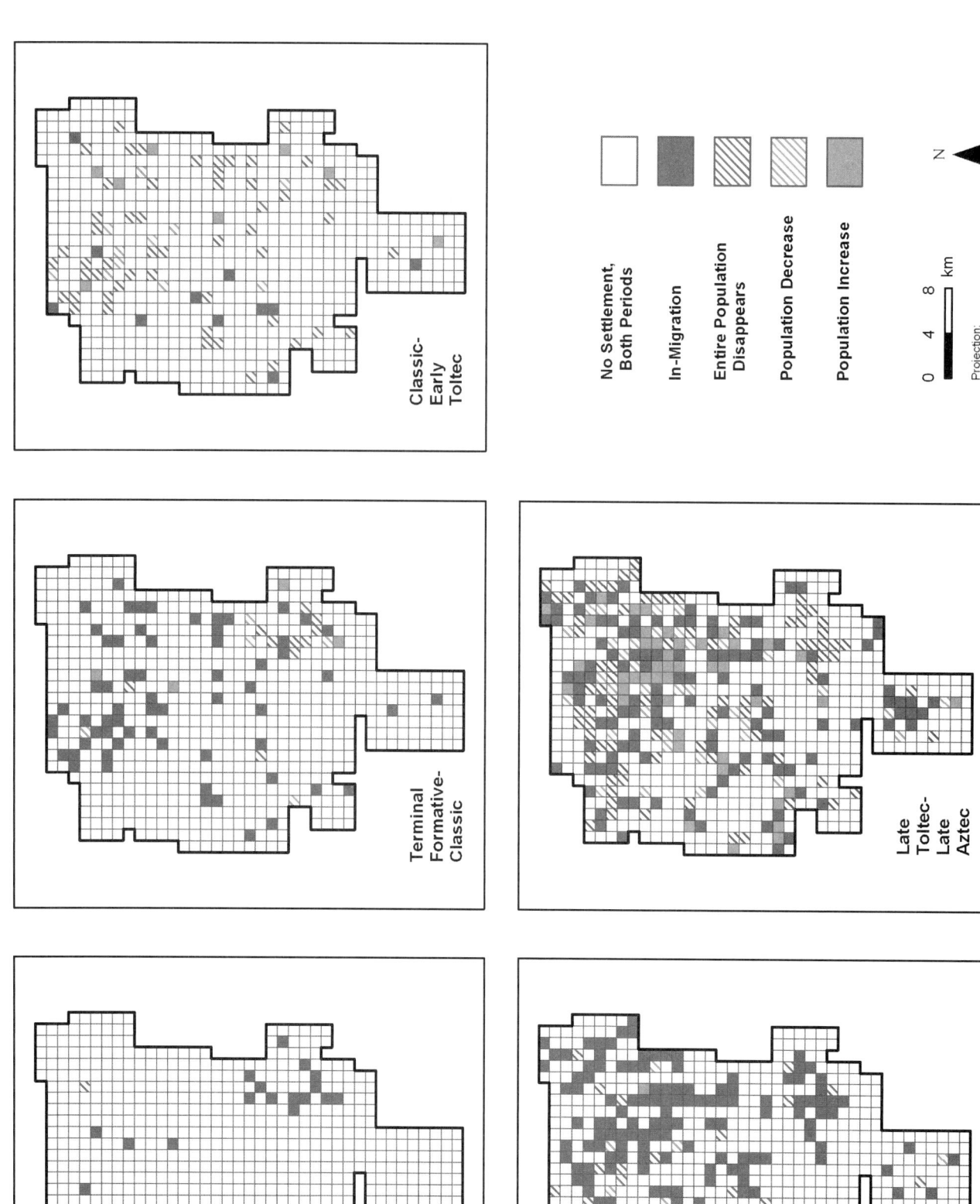

Figure 5.26. Areas of population loss and gain from one period to another in the Zumpango Region, in 1 × 1 km cells.

Epiclassic hilltop centers also developed. These transformations all suggest a collapse of the Teotihuacan-centered political and economic networks that had sustained higher levels of population and regional occupation in the Zumpango Region during the antecedent Classic.

(6) Insights into Tula's early development and subsequent florescence

The new Early Postclassic center of Tula was located only about 20 km from the northwest corner of the Zumpango Region. The large increase of Late Toltec population, the expansion of occupation throughout all parts of the survey area, and the virtual identity of ceramic assemblages in use both at Tula and throughout the Zumpango Region at this time all suggest that the Zumpango Region was incorporated closely and directly into Tula's heartland zone during this period. The occurrence of these developments during a time of increasing overall aridity makes this demographic recovery all the more impressive, and must indicate particularly effective management of water resources and redistribution between specialized, complementary producers during the period of Tula's florescence.

(7) The Early Aztec demographic collapse, the decline of Tula, and the emergence of the Triple Alliance during Late Aztec times

The Early Aztec population decline in the Zumpango Region was almost certainly closely related to the collapse of nearby Tula as a major center by about A.D. 1200. We have emphasized that prehispanic occupation in the comparatively arid northern third of the Valley of Mexico would have been especially risky relative to the more humid central and southern Valley of Mexico. Gorenflo and Sanders (in press) have proposed that any substantial population in the dry northern areas would have required some sort of adaptive specialization consistent with low precipitation, integrated within a broader regional market system that would have provided access to resources not locally available. The collapse of Tula would have significantly reduced the viability of such an adaptive specialization in a dry region that had been experiencing continuing, long-term aridity since approximately A.D. 1000. In light of the remarkable demographic and settlement recovery that occurred in the Zumpango Region during Late Aztec times, this viability obviously must have been restored—seemingly in the absence of any increase in rainfall.

In the Zumpango Region nearly depopulated during Early Aztec times, we probably must invoke significant immigration to account for the large, rapid population growth and settlement expansion that we see during the Late Aztec period. The Late Aztec regional settlement system, dominated by Tenochtitlan and its Triple Alliance partners, with its city-state building blocks, would have provided the basis for regional economic integration during a time when the Zumpango Region was once again densely occupied.

The Late Toltec regional settlement system in the northwestern Valley of Mexico, dominated by nearby Tula, likely also provided a comparable integrated regional economic system, as illustrated by the large and extensive occupation of the Zumpango Region and its northerly neighbors at that time. However, the intervening Early Aztec, a period after the demise of Tula and before the full emergence of the Triple Alliance, would have lacked such regional economic integration, especially within Tula's arid former heartland. The relatively wetter central and southern parts of the Basin of Mexico, a region of persisting Early Aztec occupation, would have provided better opportunities for agriculture and a higher degree of sufficiency than in the north. In the absence of effective water management, and with inadequately administered redistributional networks after Tula's decline, the relatively drier northern Basin would have been limited in the amount of food it could grow, and would not have provided self-sufficiency for any substantial occupation.

(8) Parallels between (a) the Classic, Late Toltec, and Late Aztec versus (b) the Formative, Early Toltec, and Early Aztec periods

The Classic, Late Toltec, and Late Aztec periods were all times of increasing population, expanding settlement, and increased organizational complexity in the Zumpango Region. These were also periods in which major centers outside the Zumpango Region were at the peaks of their power and influence: Classic Teotihuacan, Early Postclassic Tula, and the Late Postclassic Triple Alliance centers at Tenochtitlan, Texcoco, and Tacuba. It is notable that the Late Toltec florescence in the Zumpango Region took place during a period of increasing aridity, when pressure to develop and maintain canal irrigation and other forms of artificial water control would have been very high, and when such challenges were obviously met.

The Formative, Early Toltec, and Early Aztec, on the other hand, were all periods of low and/or rapidly declining population, contraction of settlement, and comparatively un-centralized polity in the Zumpango Region. These were also times when major supra-regional centers (Teotihuacan during the Epiclassic, and Tula during the Middle Postclassic) had collapsed, and when for some centuries there were no new centers that replaced the larger integrating functions of the older primary urban communities. While the Early Aztec decline may have been exacerbated by increasing aridity, there is presently little or no reason to suspect that this problem would have had an adverse impact during Formative and Early Toltec times.

One conclusion seems inescapable: compared to the ecologically more favored (that is, more humid) central and southern portions of the Valley of Mexico, the drier Zumpango Region (and its northerly neighbors) could sustain neither large, dense populations nor a high degree of organizational complexity during periods when there was no major center to administer and enforce centralized political and economic functions. Such large populations and organizational complexity were feasible in this arid region only when there was sufficient organizational capacity in the form of a major supra-regional center to effectively manage the demands of water control (canal irrigation and marshland drainage), and the redistribution of the outputs of specialized production (for example, salt, lime, wetland resources, seed-based agriculture, maguey-based cultivation, and so on).

Chapter 6

Future Research Needs

The previous chapters have presented a large body of empirical data. At the same time, this study has also raised a number of important questions that cannot yet be resolved with these data. We conclude this monograph with a summation of our sense of what archaeologists should consider in their design of future research in and around the Zumpango Region—in part, this revisits some of the criticisms raised in Chapter 1.

Chronology

Although recent research at Tula (e.g., Bey 1986; Mastache, Cobean, and Healan 2002; Cobean 1990) has provided particularly good detail for Late Toltec ceramic chronology in the Zumpango Region, it has all too often been painfully obvious that our artifact chronology for virtually all other periods is simply inadequate to distinguish slices of time short enough to enable us to define many important patterns and processes, or even to suspect their existence. A few outstanding examples of such problem areas include: (a) the distinction between Early versus Late Classic occupations; (b) the proper distinction between Classic and Early Toltec plainwares, and the full definition of the Early Toltec assemblage apart from a few decorated types; (c) the proper definition of the full Early Aztec ceramic assemblage, particularly plainwares; (d) the Late Aztec-to-Colonial period transition; and (e) the definition of Early Colonial occupation, a time of revolutionary change throughout central Mexico that anthropological archaeologists are only beginning to address (e.g., Rodríguez-Alegría 2008). Some progress on chronological refinement can be made with a full-scale restudy of our surface collections (housed at the Museo de Agricultura, Universidad Autónoma de Chapingo). However, chronological refinements are also going to require new stratigraphic excavations and a large series of new radiocarbon dates based on materials collected in such excavations.

Stylistic Variability in Coeval Regional Ceramic Assemblages within and around the Valley of Mexico

In addition to refined ceramic chronology, there is also a great need for more detailed information about the variability in form, paste, technology, and decoration of coeval pottery assemblages within and around the Valley of Mexico. Such information is essential in defining the sociology of pottery production, distribution, and consumption at the regional level. Although promising advances have been made (e.g., Hodge and Minc 1990; Hodge et al. 1993; Minc 1994; Minc et al. 1994; García Chávez 2004; Brumfiel 2005; Crider et al. 2007; Hodge 2008), most of these studies focus on Middle and Late Postclassic assemblages. All too often we are still forced to consider these assemblages in unrealistically monolithic terms, and thereby miss many key insights about prehispanic cultural behavior.

Geoarchaeological Study

Geoarchaeological study is especially needed for the deep-soil portions of the Zumpango Region (the Lakeshore Plain and Lakebed zones) where there is a significant possibility that many remains of ancient occupation may be so deeply buried by overlying sedimentation as to be invisible at the ground surface.

A handful of recent studies of this type have greatly facilitated the ability of archaeologists to better comprehend the full significance of what they can and cannot see at the ground surface, and to understand the anthropogenic components of the past and present landscapes they must deal with (e.g., Córdova 1997; Córdova and Parsons 1997; Frederick et al. 2005).

Paleoclimatological Study

As noted in Chapter 2, there have been a number of important *general-level* studies of ancient environments across central Mexico. However, few of these provide sufficient information about how temperature, rainfall, and landforms have varied over time and space in specific settings to illuminate variability in ancient settlement patterning that may be related to such environmental factors. The main exceptions in the Valley of Mexico are the pioneering geoarchaeological studies of Córdova (1997) and Frederick et al. (2005).

Definition of Settlement Systems

In this study, we have inferred several aspects of site function and the relationships between sites—largely on the basis of relative site size, site location, occupational "intensity" (sherd and mound density), and the presence of non-domestic architecture. These are important and useful interpretations, but they remain incomplete: virtually none are based upon detailed studies of the use and variability of artifact assemblages, domestic activities, architecture, burial patterns, or exchange patterns. Virtually no insights are presently available concerning the presence and meaning of intra-site variability in these characteristics. Advances in settlement-system definition will demand a well-designed program of intensive surface collection and selected testing through small- and large-scale excavation.

More Attention to Lithics

With some important exceptions (e.g., Tolstoy 1971; García Cook 1982; Healan 1986, 1993; Mastache et al. 1990; Pastrana 1998; Cobean 2002; Biskowski 2000), archaeologists working in and around the Valley of Mexico have generally paid much more attention to ceramics than to lithics. This is particularly true for chert, ground-stone, and other non-obsidian materials—artifact classes that have yielded important insights into prehistoric economy and polity in some other parts of Mesoamerica (for example, Parry 1987). During the Zumpango Region survey, we usually noted the general presence of stone artifacts and debitage, but this was done casually and unsystematically, with a focus on obsidian, and our site descriptions cannot be used to derive insights that might complement those provided by other categories of information. Future fieldwork should include the systematic collection and study of lithics as a major research component.

Study of Lime Resources

There is abundant historic and ethnographic documentation about the importance of the Zumpango Region, and the adjacent Tula Region on the north, as a source of lime during the Colonial and modern periods (Gibson 1964; Melville 1994). This important product, used for plaster, stucco, and cement, and in cooking, occurs in much more limited quantities farther south in the Valley of Mexico. Some archaeologists (e.g., Sanders et al. 1979) have suggested that Classic and post-Classic people in the Zumpango Region specialized in the quarrying, processing, and redistribution of lime and lime products. However, this important hypothesis has been based almost exclusively on site location in this lime-rich area, and has never been tested with solid evidence based on the study of artifacts, quarries, kilns, or other types of relevant archaeological remains. Archaeologists should attempt to deal with these important issues in the field.

Study of Aquatic Resources

Recent studies based on historic, ethnographic, and (a few) archaeological sources have emphasized the primary importance of aquatic resources (waterfowl, fish, salamanders, insects, frogs, algae, reeds, and other wetland flora and fauna) in modern, Colonial, and late prehispanic economies in the Valley of Mexico (e.g., Rojas 1985; García Sanchez 1998; Parsons and Morett 2005; Parsons 2006a). Only a few archaeologists have seriously considered these wetland resources in their studies of prehispanic economies in the Valley of Mexico, and most of these efforts have been directed at preceramic/pre-agricultural periods (e.g., Niederberger 1976, 1987). In this monograph, we have suggested that these resources, plus saltmaking, were of primary importance in the prehispanic occupation on and around Lake Xaltocán-Zumpango extending at least as far back as Terminal Formative times. However, as in the case of lime, these suggestions about the procurement, processing, and exchange of aquatic resources still lack solid archaeological testing.

Study of Water-Control Technology

This monograph has emphasized the impact of aridity on prehispanic occupation in the Zumpango Region, the driest part of the Valley of Mexico. We have suggested that water control in the forms of canal irrigation, marshland drainage, and flood control would have been critical for productive agriculture in this region, as indicated by abundant documentary evidence (e.g., Palerm 1973; Rojas et al. 1974) and some archaeological remains of lakebed chinampas (Nichols and Frederick 1993; Frederick et al. 2005). Nevertheless, apart from the lakebed chinampa remnants, there is still no direct archaeological evidence for water-control features of any sort in the Zumpango Region (as Palerm [1974:12] pointed out years ago). Although such features are often notoriously difficult to recover and date, Nichols (1982) has demonstrated that this is feasible in the nearby Cuautitlan Region, and her pioneering effort should be extended throughout the arid northwestern Valley of Mexico.

Investigation of Pre-Formative and Aceramic ("Off-Site") Occupation

Systematic regional survey in the Valley of Mexico has never been able to deal effectively with preceramic (or aceramic) occupation, and this monograph makes no contribution to the pre-Formative millennia, or to most activities that may not be reflected by ceramics on the ground surface, even for periods when ceramics were in use (ancient terracing and chinampa remnants are obvious exceptions). However, we can never expect to understand developments during the earlier part of the Formative era unless we have better insights into their Archaic-period antecedents. Such insights as do exist come primarily from excavations at Tlapacoya in the northeastern corner of Lake Chalco in the southeastern Valley of Mexico (e.g., Niederberger 1976), and from a series of mammoth-butchering sites around the margins of Lake Texcoco (e.g., Aveleyra 1964).

Furthermore, this monograph does not include information on the low-density sherd and lithic scatters that we often did record in the field on our 1:5000 airphotos. We deemed these artifact scatters too ephemeral to include as "sites," but they may well reflect important activities that were carried out beyond the borders of those higher-density artifact concentrations that we have labeled "hamlets," "villages," or "centers." We suspect that such "off-site" archaeological remains might contribute significantly to a better definition of prehispanic settlement systems for all periods. The great challenge is to figure out how to systematically collect and analyze such low-density materials at the regional level—obviously, such investigation must develop new methodology radically different from that we have traditionally employed in the Valley of Mexico surveys (e.g., Parsons and Morett 2004, 2005). The challenge is especially daunting in regions like the Valley of Mexico, where surficial low-density remains from earlier periods are typically overwhelmed by centuries, even millennia, of settlement and landscape modification by dense, urbanized populations. Nevertheless, successful efforts along these lines have been undertaken (e.g., Cipolla and Klink 1997; Ebert 1992; Holdaway et al. 2000; Honeychurch 2003; Klink 1997; Klink and Aldenderfer 1996; Van Leusen and Attema 2002). Archaeologists working at the regional level in the Zumpango Region and elsewhere in the Valley of Mexico should seriously consider how to incorporate studies of "off-site" materials into their research designs.

Extending Regional Surveys into the Pachuca Region

Regional surveys in the 1960s and 1970s covered most non-urbanized portions of the Valley of Mexico. The only major non-surveyed section is the far northeastern corner: the area extending from Pachuca south to the northern border of the Temascalapa Region (we sometimes refer to this as the Pachuca Region). Indications are that, like the nearby Zumpango and Temascalapa Regions, this relatively arid northern region would have had very modest Formative occupation and substantial Classic and Late Aztec settlement, with less predictable Early Toltec and Early Aztec occupations. However, solid empirical regional data from the Pachuca Region are needed to complete and evaluate our current understandings of long-term adaptations to a comparatively arid landscape in the context of major sociopolitical change over two millennia. Our brief reconnaissance in the Pachuca Region over several days in June 2008 indicated that much of this terrain remains open and comparatively unmodified by large-scale bulldozer-terracing and reforestation. Regional survey comparable to that previously undertaken elsewhere in the Valley of Mexico should still be feasible in the Pachuca Region, although for how much longer remains uncertain.

Maintenance and Restudy of Curated Collections

Nearly two decades ago (1991), I detailed the general state of the archaeological record in the Valley of Mexico as I observed it in 1987, and suggested several long-term strategies for dealing with the on-going and accelerating loss of the region's archaeological resources. Since that time, many more sites have been lost, including the great majority of those described in this monograph. In the future, archaeologists will not be able to revisit these obliterated sites to make new collections or observations through surface collection, excavation, or intensified surveys. Consequently, our many hundreds of surface collections, and their accompanying documentation in the form of published reports and unpublished notes and photographs, will remain the only archaeological information available for new studies.

For all their obvious limitations (they were grab samples, made opportunistically and not always consistently), these collections are numerous, substantial, with good provenience, and, above all, still adequately stored and curated at two main locations: (1) the Museo de Agricultura, Universidad Nacional Autónoma de Chapingo, near Texcoco; and (2) the Arizona State University lab in San Juan Teotihuacan. They have already proved useful in several recent studies (e.g., Crider et al. 2007; Garraty 2006; Hodge and Minc 1990, 1991; Hodge et al. 1993; Minc 1994, 1999; Minc et al. 1994). Archaeologists should not forget about these irreplaceable collections, and should make every effort to incorporate them into future research plans wherever relevant.

Can We Proceed in the Face of Massive Site Destruction and Landscape Transformation?

Many of the issues outlined above require access to a variety of surviving archaeological sites, and "non-sites," in order to carry out intensive surface collecting and excavations. We have also alluded to the serious destruction of many archaeological sites, and entire landscapes, during the decades after the original surveys were carried out. We might well ask whether it is realistic to think that we will ever be able to address the essential problems we have defined with the surviving archaeological record in the Valley of Mexico. As noted above, we recently made an effort to provide an answer to this question. Over a two-week period in June and early July 2008, L. Gorenflo, M. Parsons, and I undertook a general reconnaissance throughout most surveyed portions of the Valley of Mexico, including the Zumpango Region, in order to evaluate the general condition of archaeological sites. We found that while there is much really bad news, at the same time there is also a little room for cautious optimism for new archaeological fieldwork in the future.

From an archaeologist's perspective, there have been five principal destructive forces at work at an accelerating pace over the past three decades in the Valley of Mexico: (a) urban and sub-urban sprawl; (b) the mechanization of agriculture, particularly expanding and leveling fields for commercial alfalfa and maize production; (c) the construction of massive terraces in eroded areas using bulldozers, and the reforestation of many of these terraces with thick stands of eucalyptus trees; (d) large-scale quarrying for sand, gravel, and lime; and (e) large trash dumps.

Nevertheless, there are still sites and landscapes that remain sufficiently intact to justify new archaeological study. We plan to present the detailed results of our 2008 reconnaissance in the near future, and in this report we will point to specific sites and areas that future fieldwork might focus on. Still, time is of the essence. Another decade will probably bring an end to all save salvage archaeology in the Zumpango Region and throughout the Valley of Mexico.

Chapter 7

Resumen en Español de los Principales Conclusiones

translated by Apphia H. Parsons

Aparecen unos puntos importantes e interrelacionados en los datos discutidos en esta monografía.

Asentamiento nucleado vs. dispersado

Durante todas las épocas prehispánicas, el asentamiento es notablemente más dispersado que en el siglo veinte. De hecho, el asentamiento prehispánico en la Región de Zumpango es en general más dispersado y menos urbanizado (o por lo menos, menos nucleado) que en cualquier otra región del territorio de reconocimiento arqueológico dentro del Valle de México.

El impacto de la aridez

La región de Zumpango, junto con las regiones cercanas de Temascalapa, Pachuca y Tula, es una de las más secas de las tierras altas en el México central. Se encuentra la frontera norte de Mesoamerica misma, como normalmente definida (Kirchoff 1943), a menos de 200 km más al norte. La agricultura basada en la lluvia tiene bastante más riesgo en esta zona que en los partes más favorables del centro y sur del Valle de México, a causa de una baja precipitación anual, un empiezo del estiaje imprevisible, y heladas de primavera y otoño también imprevisibles. Los tiempos de más aridez regional, cuales por lo visto occurían a traves de la mesa central de México despúes del año 1000 d. de C, habrían requirido una gestión especialmente eficaz de recursos acuáticos y de redistribución entre productores especializados, unos de ellos quien habrían sido no-agrícolas o cultivadores de cosechas de terrenos áridos (como maguey y nopal). Sin cierto nivel de organización sociopolítico centralizado, este dicho gestión quizás era difícil.

La marginalidad de la región de Zumpango durante la época Formativa

La región de Zumpango junto con sus cercanos en el Valle de México del norte y la región contigua de Tula, eran indudablemente marginales en comparación con los desarrollos Formativos en el centro y sur del Valle de México. Probablemente se puede atribuir esta dicha marginalidad a la aridez relativa de la región. En cualquier caso, la región de Zumpango y sus vecinos del norte más cercanos quedaban muy escasamente ocupados hasta la época Clásica. Esta ocupación pionera pre-Clásica quizás era orientada más a la explotación de recursos acuáticos y menos a la agricultura, dado el agrupamiento de ocupación modesta de la época Terminal Formativa a la orilla del lago.

Perspicacias sobre el desarrollo temprano de Teotihuacán y su florescensia

El crecimiento fundamental de ocupación durante la época Clásica está correlacionado estrechamente con la florescencia del nuevo centro urbano en Teotihuacán a unos docenas de kilómetros al sureste. Concluimos que el crecimiento notable durante la época Clásica de la población y la expansión de asentamiento en la zona anteriormente muy escasa ocupada occuría dentro del esquema organizativo basado en los necesidades de Teotihuacán. Estas dichas necesidades probablemente habrían incluido la sal, los reccursos acuáticos, y la cal, además del desarrollo de una capacidad agricultural suficiente para sostener una población local significativa, y quizás con el desarrollo del riego con canales, para generar un sobrante modesto para transmitir hasta Teotihuacán misma. Hasta que punto Teotihuacán causaba y dirigía directamente estes cambios sigue discutible. Con un escenario alternativo, estes desarollos quizás habrían occurido de una manera menos dirigida, por individuos y comunidades tratando de explotar nuevos oportunidades en un "nicho vacío" entre un contexto de una economía en expansión y la enriqueza general.

Perspicacias sobre el derrumbe de Teotihuacán y sus repercusiones

La disminución de la población, la dislocación del asentamiento y el establecimiento de un nuevo centro de cumbre durante la época Tolteca Temprano indican una dislocación marcada con la antecedente época Clásica en la Región de Zumpango. En este sentido, la Región de Zumpango difiere del centro y sur del Valle de México, donde las poblaciones regionales aumentaron en comparación con la época Clásica, y donde grandes nuevos centros del Tolteca Temprano desarrollaron solamente en lugares bajos. El asentamiento de la época Tolteca Temprano en la región de Zumpango es más similar a lo de las áreas al márgen del Valle de México al este (Puebla-Tlaxcala), al sur (Morelos), y al norte (la región de Tula), donde nuevos grandes centros Epiclásicos también desarrollaron en las cumbres. Estas transformaciones sugieren un derrumbe de las redes políticas y económicas basadas en Teotihuacán, que sustenían niveles mas altos de población y occupación regional en la región de Zumpango durante la antecedente época Clásica.

Perspicacias sobre el desarrollo temprano de Tula y su florescensia

El nuevo centro Postclásico Temprano de Tula se ubicara solamente alrededor de 20 km de la esquina noroeste de la Región de Zumpango. El gran aumento de la población en la época Tolteca Tardío, la expansión de ocupación por todo el área del reconocimiento, y la identidad virtual de los ensamblajes de cerámica de Tula y por toda la región de Zumpango a este tiempo—todo sugiere que la Región de Zumpango era incorporado estrechamente y directamente adentro de la zona central de Tula durante este período. Como parece que estos desarrollos occurían durante un tiempo de creciente aridez hace aun más notable esta recuperación demográfica, y tiene que indicar un manejo especialmente effectivo de los recursos acuáticos y la redistribución entre fabricantes especializados y complementarios durante la época de la florescencia de Tula.

El derumbe demográfico del Azteca Temprano, el descenso de Tula, y la aparición de la Alianza Triple durante la época Azteca Tardío

El descenso de la población durante el Azteca Temprano en la Región de Zumpango era casi sin duda estrechamente relacionado al derumbe de la cercana Tula como centro importante después de 1200 d. de C. Hemos subrayado que la ocupación prehispánica en la tercera norteña del Valle de México, que es relativatmente árido, habría sido especialmente riesgosa en comparación con el centro y sur del Valle de México que era una zona más húmeda. Gorenflo y Sanders (2007) han propuesto que alguna población considerable en los áreas secos del norte habría requirido algún tipo de especialización adaptivo consistente con lluvias bajas y que era integrado con un sistema de mercado mas ámplio que habría dado acceso a los recursos no disponible localmente. El derumbe de Tula habría reducido considerablemente la viabilidad de tal especialización adaptiva en una región seca que tenía una aridez duradera y continuada desde hace el año 1000 d. de C. En vista de la sorprendente recuperación demográfica y de asentamiento que occurió en la Región de Zumpango durante la época Azteca Tardío, esta viabilidad tenía que ser restablecido sin algun aumento aparente en la lluvia.

La Región de Zumpango era casi depoblado durante la Azteca Temprana y probablemente tenemos que invocar un inmigración importante para dar cuenta del aumento grande y rápido de la población y la expansión de colonización durante el Azteca Tardío. El sistema regional de asentamiento del Azteca Tardío era dominada por Tenochtitlán y sus socios de la Alianza Triple con sus bloques componentes de ciudad-estado, y este sistema habría proporcionado la base para una integración económica regional durante un período cuando la Región de Zumpango era de nuevo densamente poblada.

Dominado por la cercana Tula, el noroeste del Valle de México tenía un sistema regional de asentamiento durante el Tolteca Tardío que probablemente proporcionaba un sistema económico regional y integrado comparable, como ilustraba la ocupación grande y amplia de la Región de Zumpango y sus vecinos norteños en ese tiempo. Sin embargo, los años de intervalo después del deceso de Tula y antes de la aparición de la Alianza Triple, la época Azteca Temprano faltaba tal integración económica regional, en particular dentro de la antigua corazón árida de Tula. Los partes del centro y del sur del Valle de México eran relativamente más húmedos y por eso habrían proporcionado mejores oportunidades que en el norte para la agricultura y para un nivel más alto de suficiencia. Después del descenso de Tula, a falta de un manejo de agua efectivo y la ausencia de redes de redistribución suficientemente administrados, el Valle norteño, que era relativamente más seca, habría sido limitado en la cantidad de cosechas que podía producir, y no habría proveído ninguna autosuficiencia para una ocupación considerable.

Paralelos entre (a) el Clásico, el Tolteca Tardío, y el Azteca Tardío vs. (b) el Formativo, el Tolteca Temprano, y el Azteca Temprano

En la región de Zumpango, las épocas del Clásico, Tolteca Tardío, y Azteca Tardío eran períodos de aumentación de población, expansión de asentamiento, y creciente complejidad organizativo. También eran períodos de máximo poder e influencia para centros importantes fuera de la Región de Zumpango: Teotihuacan Clásico, Tula del Postclásico Temprano, y los centros del Postclásico Tardío de la Alianza Triple en Tenochititlán, Texcoco, y Tacuba. Es digno de mención que la florescencia durante el Tolteca Tardío en la Región de Zumpango occuría durante un período de aridez creciente, cuando la presión de desarrollar y mantener el riego con canales y otras formas de controlar el agua de manera artificialmente habría sido muy alto, y cuando obviamente esos retos fueron alcanzados.

En la Región de Zumpango, al otro lado, el Formativo, el Tolteca Temprano, y el Azteca Temprano eran épocas de baja población o una población en decliva, una contracción de asentamiento, y una organización política relativamente decentralizada. Eran también períodos cuando los centros supra-regionales (Teotihuacán durante el Epiclásico, y Tula durante el Postclásico Mediano) habían derrumbido, y cuando no había por unos siglos ningun nuevo centro que reemplazaba los antiguos comunidades urbanos primordiales en sus más grandes funciones integrandos. Aunque el descenso de población durante el Azteca Temprano quizás era agravado por la aridez creciente, en este momento hay poco razón de sospechar que este problema habría tenido un impacto adverso durante el Formativo y el Tolteca Temprano.

Una conclusión que parece ineludible es que en comparación con los partes del centro y sur del Valle de México—más húmedos y por eso más beneficiados ecologiamente—la Región de Zumpango, que era más seca, no podía sostener ni grandes densas poblaciones ni un nivel alto de complejidad organizativo durante las épocas cuando no había ningún centro importante para administrar y hacer respetar las funciones centralizadas de política y economía. Las dichas grandes poblaciones y la complejidad organizativa eran viable en esta región árida solamente cuando había una capacidad organizativa en forma de un centro importante supra-regional, suficiente para administrar las exigencias del control de agua (los riegos de canales y el desagüe pantanoso) y la redistribución de las producciones especializadas (por ejemplo, la sal, la cal, los recursos acuáticos, la agricultura basado en semillas [maiz, frijol, amaranto, etc.], y la cultivación basado en maguey y nopal).

Bibliography

Acuña, R. (editor)
1985 *Relaciones Geográficas del Siglo XVI: México, Tomo I*. Universidad Nacional Autónoma de México, México, D.F.
1986a *Relaciones Geográficas del Siglo XVI: México, Tomo II*. Universidad Nacional Autónoma de México, México, D.F.
1986b *Relaciones Geográficas del Siglo XVI: México, Tomo III*. Universidad Nacional Autónoma de México, México, D.F.

Adams, R.M.
1965 *Land Behind Baghdad*. University of Chicago Press, Chicago.

Adams, R.M., and H. Nissen
1972 *The Uruk Countryside*. University of Chicago Press, Chicago.

Aguilera, C.
2001 Algunos aspectos de la cultura del Lago de Zumpango. *Expresión Antropológica*, nueva época, 12:71-83. Colegio Mexiquense, Toluca.

Alden, J.
1979 A reconstruction of Toltec Period political units in the Valley of Mexico. In *Transformations: Mathematical Approaches to Culture Change*, edited by C. Renfrew, pp. 169-200. Academic Press, New York.

Aveleyra Arroyo de Anda, L.
1964 The primitive hunters. In *Natural Environment and Early Cultures*, edited by R. West, pp. 384-412. *Handbook of Middle American Indians, Vol. 1*, R. Wauchope, general editor. University of Texas Press, Austin.

Ávila, R.
1995 *Excavaciones Arqueológicas en San Gregorio Atlapulco, Xochimilco*. Informe, Subdirección de Salvamento Arqueológico, INAH, México, D.F.

2006 *Mexicaltzingo: Arqueología de un Reino Culhua-Mexica*. 2 vols. Instituto Nacional de Anthropología e História, México, D.F.

Baños, E.
1980 *La Industria Salinera de Xocotitlán, Cuenca de México*. Tesis, Escuela Nacional de Antropología e História, México, D.F.

Baños, E., and M. Sanchez
1998 La industria salinera prehispánica en la Cuenca de México. In *La Sal en México, II*, edited by J. Reyes, pp. 65-83. Universidad de Colima, Colima, Mexico.

Barba de Piña Chan, B.
1956 Tlapacoya, Un Sitio de Transición. *Acta Antropológica*, Vol. 1, No. 1. México, D.F.

Barbour, W.
1976 *The Figurines and Figurine Chronology of Ancient Teotihuacan*. PhD dissertation, University of Rochester. University Microfilms, Ann Arbor.
1987 Ceramic figurines from Oxtotipac. In *The Toltec Period Occupation of the Valley. Part 2: Surface Survey and Special Studies*, edited by W.T. Sanders, pp. 697-754. *The Teotihuacan Valley Project Final Report, Vol. 4*. Occasional Papers in Anthropology No. 15, Dept. of Anthropology, Pennsylvania State University, University Park.

Bargallo, M.
1955 *La Minería y la Metalurgía en la América Española durante la Época Colonial*. Fondo de Cultura Económica, México, D.F.

Barlow, R.
1949 *The Extent of the Empire of the Culhua Mexica*. Ibero-Americana No. 28, University of California Press, Berkeley.

Beltran, E.
1958 *El Hombre y su Ambiente: Ensayo sobre el Valle de México*. Fondo de Cultura Económica, México, D.F.

Bernal, I. (editor)
1957 Relacion de Tequixquiac, Citlaltepec, y Xilocingo. *Tlalocan* 3:4:289-309. México, D.F.

Berres, T.
2000 Climate change and lacustrine resources at the period of initial Aztec development. *Ancient Mesoamerica* 11:27-38.

Bey, G.
1986 *A Regional Analysis of Toltec Ceramics, Tula, Hidalgo, Mexico*. PhD dissertation, Tulane University. University Microfilms, Ann Arbor.

Biskowski, M.
2000 Maize preparation and the Aztec subsistence economy. *Ancient Mesoamerica* 11:292-306.

Blanton, R.
1972 *Prehispanic Settlement Patterns in the Ixtapalapa Peninsula Region, Mexico*. Occasional Papers in Anthropology No. 6, Dept. of Anthropology, Pennsylvania State University, University Park.

Blanton, R., and J. Parsons
1971 Ceramic markers used for period designations. In *Prehistoric Settlement Patterns in the Texcoco Region, Mexico*. Memoirs, no. 3, Museum of Anthropology, University of Michigan, Ann Arbor.

Blucher, D.
1970 *Late Preclassic Cultures in the Valley of Mexico: Pre-Urban Teotihuacan*. PhD dissertation, Brandeis University. University Microfilms, Ann Arbor.

Bradbury, J.
1989 Late Quaternary lacustrine paleoenvironments in the Cuenca de México. *Quaternary Science Reviews* 8:75-100.
2000 Limnologic history of Lake Patzcuaro, Michoacán, Mexico for the past 48,000 years: Impacts of climate and man. *Palaeogeography, Palaeoclimatology, Palaeoecology* 163:69-95.

Branstetter-Hardesty, B.
1978 *Ceramics of Cerro Portesuelo, Mexico: An Industry in Transition*. PhD dissertation, University of California at Los Angeles. University Microfilms, Ann Arbor.

Bridgewater, N., T. Heaton, and S. O'Hara
1999 A Late Holocene paleolimnological record from central Mexico, based on faunal and stable-isotope analysis of ostracod shells. *Journal of Paleolimnology* 22:383-97.

Brumfiel, E.
1976a *Specialization and Exchange at the Late Postclassic (Aztec) Community of Huexotla, Mexico*. PhD dissertation, Dept. of Anthropology, University of Michigan, Ann Arbor.
1976b Regional growth in the eastern valley of Mexico: A test of the 'population pressure' hypothesis. In *The Early Mesoamerican Village*, edited by K. Flannery, pp. 234-47. Academic Press, New York.
2005 Ceramic chronology at Xaltocan. In *Production and Power at Postclassic Xaltocan/La Producción Local y el Poder en el Xaltocan Posclásico*, edited by E. Brumfiel, pp. 117-52. Serie Aqueología de México. University of Pittsburgh, Pittsburgh; Instituto Nacional de Antropología e História, México, D.F.

Brumfiel, E. (editor)
2005 *Production and Power at Postclassic Xaltocan/La Producción Local y el Poder en el Xaltocan Posclásico*. Serie Aqueología de México. University of Pittsburgh, Pittsburgh; Instituto Nacional de Antropología e História, México, D.F.

Brumfiel, E., and M. Hodge
1996 Interaction in the Basin of Mexico: The case of Postclassic Xaltocan. In *Arqueología Mesoamericana: Homenaje a William T. Sanders*, edited by G. Mastache, J. Parsons, M. Serra, and R. Santley, pp. 417-37. Instituto Nacional de Antropología e História, México, D.F.

Caballero, M., and B. Ortega
1998 Lake levels since about 40,000 years ago at Lake Chalco, near Mexico City. *Quaternary Research* 50:69-79.

Caballero, M., S. Lozano, B. Ortega, J. Urrutia, and J. Macias
1999 Environmental characteristics of Lake Tecocomulco, northern Basin of Mexico, for the last 50,000 years. *Journal of Paleolimnology* 22(4):399-411.

Carrasco, P.
1980 La aplicabilidad a Mesoamérica del modelo andino de verticalidad. *Revista de la Universidad Complutense* 29:117:237-43. Madrid.
1999 *The Tenocha Empire of Ancient Mexico: The Triple Alliance of Tenochtitlan, Tetzcoco, and Tlacopan*. University of Oklahoma Press, Norman.

Castillo, M.
1994 *Xochimilco Prehispánico: La Vida Cotidiana durante el Postclásico Tardío*. Tesis de Licenciado, Escuela Nacional de Antropología e História, México, D.F.

Charlton, T.
1969 Texcoco Fabric-Marked pottery, tlateles, and salt making. *American Antiquity* 34:73-76.
1971 Texcoco Fabric-Marked pottery and salt making: A further note. *American Antiquity* 36:217-18.

Charlton, T., C. Otis Charlton, and P. Fournier
2005 The Basin of Mexico A.D. 1450-1620: Archaeological dimensions. In *The Postclassic to Spanish-Era Transition in Mesoamerica: Archaeological Perspectives*, edited by S. Kepecs and R. Alexander, pp. 49-62. University of New Mexico Press, Albuquerque.

Cipolla, L., and C. Klink
1997 An Alternative Method for Analyzing Archaic Period Surface Data in the Andean Highlands. Paper presented at the 25th Annual Meeting of the Midwest Conference on Andean and Amazonian Archaeology and Ethnohistory, Madison, Wisconsin, Feb. 1997.

Cobean, R.
1974 Archaeological survey of the Tula Region. In *Studies of Ancient Tollan: A Report of the University of Missouri Tula Archaeological Project*, edited by R. Diehl, pp. 6-10. Monographs in Anthropology No. 1, Dept. of Anthropology, University of Missouri, Columbia.
1978 *The Pre-Aztec Ceramics of Tula, Hidalgo, Mexico*. PhD dissertation, Dept. of Anthropology, Harvard University, Cambridge.
1990 *La Cerámica de Tula, Hidalgo*. Instituto Nacional de Antropología e História, México, D.F.
2002 *Un Mundo de Obsidiana/A World of Obsidian: The Mining and Trade of Volcanic Glass in Ancient Mexico*. Instituto Nacional de Antropología e História, México, D.F.; University of Pittsburgh Press, Pittsburgh.

Córdova, C.
1997 *Landscape Transformations in Aztec and Spanish Colonial Texcoco, Mexico*. PhD dissertation, University of Texas at Austin. University Microfilms, Ann Arbor.

Córdova, C., and J. Parsons
1997 Geoarchaeology of an Aztec dispersed village on the Texcoco piedmont of Central Mexico. *Geoarchaeology* 12:3:177-210.

Corona M., E.
1996 'El Japon,' Xochimilco: Análisis arqueológico de un sitio en la época de la Conquista. *Arqueología* 16:95.

Cortés, H.
1963 [1522] *Cartas y Documentos*. Editorial Porrua, México, D.F.

Crider, D., D. Nichols, H. Neff, and M. Glascock
2007 In the aftermath of Teotihuacan: Epiclassic pottery production and distribution in the Teotihuacan Valley, Mexico. *Latin American Antiquity* 18:123-44.

Crosby, A.
1967 Conquistador y pestilencia: The first New World pandemic and the fall of the great Indian empires. *Hispanic American Historical Review* 47:321-37.

Davies, S., S. Metcalfe, A. MacKenzie, A. Newton, G. Enfield, and J. Farmer
2004 Environmental changes in the Zirahuén Basin, Michoacán, Mexico during the last 1000 years. *Journal of Paleolimnology* 31:77-98.

Denevan, W. (editor)
1992 *The Native Population of the Americas in 1492*. University of Wisconsin Press, Madison.

Departamento Cartográfico Militar
1957 *Cartas Topográficas, Estados Unidos Mexicanos*. Secretaria de la Defensa Nacional, México, D.F.

Diaz, C.
1980 *Chingú: Un Sitio Clásico del Área de Tula, Hidalgo*. Instituto Nacional de Antropología e História, México, D.F.

Diaz del Castillo, B.
1910 [1580] *The True History of the Conquest of New Spain, Vol. IV*, translated by A.P. Maudslay. The Hakluyt Society, London.

Diehl, R.
1983 *Tula: The Toltec Capital of Ancient Mexico*. Thames and Hudson, London.

Diehl, R., R. Lomas, and J. Wynn
1974 Toltec trade with Central America. *Archaeology* 27:3:182-87.

Dobyns, H.
1976 *Native American Historical Demography: A Critical Bibliography*. Indiana University Press, Bloomington.

Earle, T.
1976 A nearest-neighbor analysis of two Formative settlement systems. In *The Early Mesoamerican Village*, edited by K. Flannery, pp. 195-224. Academic Press, New York.

Ebert, J.
1992 *Distributional Archaeology*. University of New Mexico Press, Albuquerque.

Ekholm, G.
1944 *Excavations at Tampico and Panuco in the Huasteca, Mexico*. Anthropological Papers of the American Museum of Natural History, Vol. 38, Pt. 5, New York.

Evans, S.
1988 *Excavations at Cihuatecpan, An Aztec Village in the Teotihuacan Valley*. Publications in Anthropology No. 36, Vanderbilt University, Nashville.

Feldman, L.
1974 Tollan in central Mexico: The geography of economic specialization. In *Studies of Ancient Tollan: A Report of the University of Missouri Tula Archaeological Project*, edited by R. Diehl, pp. 150-89. Monographs in Anthropology No. 1, Dept. of Anthropology, University of Missouri, Columbia.

Fisher, C., H. Pollard, I. Israde-Alcántara, V. Garduño, and S. Banerjee
2003 A re-examination of human-induced environmental change within the Lake Patzcuaro Basin, Michoacán, Mexico. *Proceedings of the National Academy of Sciences* 100(8):4957-62.

Franco, J.
1945 Comentarios sobre tipología y filogenía de la decoración negra sobre color natural del barro en la cerámica 'Azteca II.' *Revista Mexicana de Estudios Antropológicos* 7:163-86.
1949 Algunas problemas relativos a la cerámica Azteca. *El México Antiguo* 7:162-208.
1957 *Motivos Decorativos en la Cerámica Azteca*. Serie Cientifica No. 5. Museo Nacional de Antropología, México, D.F.

Frederick, C.
1995 *Fluvial Responses to Late Quaternary Climatic Change and Land Use in Central Mexico*. PhD dissertation, University of Texas at Austin. University Microfilms, Ann Arbor.
2007 Chinampa cultivation in the Basin of Mexico: Observations on the evolution of form and function. In *Seeking a Richer Harvest: The Archaeology of Subsistence Intensification, Innovation, and Change*, edited by T. Thurston and C. Fisher, pp. 107-24. Springer, New York.

Frederick, C., B. Winsborough, and V. Popper
2005 Geoarchaeological investigations in the northern Basin of Mexico. In *Production and Power at Postclassic Xaltocan/La Producción Local y el Poder en el Xaltocan Posclásico*, edited by E. Brumfiel, pp. 71-115. Serie Aqueología de México. University of Pittsburgh, Pittsburgh; Instituto Nacional de Antropología e História, México, D.F.

Garay, F.
1888 *El Valle de México, Apuntes sobre su Hidrografía*. Secretaria de Fomento, México, D.F.

García Chávez, R.
1991 *Desarrollo Cultural en Azcapotzalco y el Area Suroccidential de la Cuenca de México, desde el Preclásico Medio hasta el Epiclásico*. Tesis de Licenciado, Escuela Nacional de Antropología e História, México, D.F.
2004 *De Tula a Azcapotzalco: Caracterización Arqueológica de los Altepetl de la Cuenca de México del Postclásico Temprano y Medio, a traves del Estudio Cerámico Regional*. Tesis de doctorado, Facultad de Filosofía y Letras, Universidad Nacional Autónoma de México, México, D.F.

García Chávez, R., and L. Córdoba
1994 *Analisis de los Materiales Cerámico y Lítico de Chimalhuacán, Edo. de México*. Instituto Nacional de Antropología e História, Centro Edo. de México, Toluca.

García Cook, A.
1982 *Análisis Tipológico de Artefactos*. Instituto Nacional de Antropología e História, México, D.F.

García Sanchez, M.
1998 *El Comercio de Productos Lacustres: Relaciones de Pervivencia Cultural entre los Valles de Toluca y México, 1880-1970*. Tesis de Maestria en Antropología Social, Centro de Investigaciones y Estudios Superiores en Antropología Social, Instituto Nacional de Antropología e História, México, D.F.

Gardiner, C.H.
1956 *Naval Power in the Conquest of Mexico*. University of Texas Press, Austin.

Garraty, C.
2006 *The Politics of Commerce: Aztec Pottery Production and Exchange in the Basin of Mexico*. PhD dissertation, University of New Mexico, Albuquerque. University Microfilms, Ann Arbor.

Gibson, C.
1964 *The Aztecs under Spanish Rule: A History of the Indians of the Valley of Mexico 1519-1810*. Stanford University Press, Stanford.

Gonzalez, C.
1988 *Proyecto Arqueológico 'El Japon.'* Informe, Archivo Técnico, Subdirección de Estudios Arqueológicos, INAH, México, D.F.

Gonzalez, L.
1902 *Memoria Histórica, Técnica y Administrativa de las Obras del Desagüe del Valle de México, 1449-1900*. 2 vols. Oficina Impresora de Estampillas, Ciudad de México.

Gonzalez Rul, F.
1988 *La Cerámica de Tlatelolco*. Instituto Nacional de Antropología e História, México, D.F.

Gorenflo, L.
2006 The evolution of regional demography and settlement in the prehispanic Basin of Mexico. In *Population and Preindustrial Cities: A Cross-Cultural Perspective*, edited by G. Storey, pp. 295-314. University of Alabama Press, Tuscaloosa.

Gorenflo, L., and W. Sanders
2007 *Archaeological Settlement Pattern Data from the Cuautitlan, Temascalapa, and Teotihuacan Regions, Mexico*. Occasional Papers in Anthropology No. 30, Dept. of Anthropology, Pennsylvania State University, University Park.
in press *Prehispanic Settlement Patterns in the Temascalapa Region, Mexico*. Occasional Papers in Anthropology No. 31, Dept. of Anthropology, Pennsylvania State University, University Park.

Griffin, J., and A. Espejo
1947 La alfararía correspondiente al último periodo de ocupación Nahua del Valle de México, I. *Tlatelolco a Traves de los Tiempos* 6:3-20. México, D.F.
1950 La alfararía correspondiente al último periodo de ocupación Nahua del Valle de México, II. *Tlatelolco a Traves de los Tiempos* 9:3-54. México, D.F.

Gurría, J.
1978 *El Desagüe del Valle de México durante la Época Novohispana*. Instituto de Investigaciones Históricos, Universidad Nacional Autónoma de México, México, D.F.

Haggard, J.
1941 *Handbook for Translators of Spanish Historical Documents*. Archives and Collections, University of Texas, Austin.

Harvey, H.
1985 Household and family structure of Early Colonial Tepetlaoxtoc: An analysis of the Códice de Santa María Asunción. *Estudios de la Cultura Nahuatl* 18:275-94. Instituto de Investigaciones Históricas, Universidad Nacional Autónoma de México, México, D.F.

Healan, D.
1986 Technological and nontechnological aspects of an obsidian workshop excavated at Tula, Hidalgo. In *Economic Aspects of Prehispanic Highland Mexico*, edited by B. Isaac. Research in Economic Anthropology, Supplement 2, JAI Press, New York.
1993 Local vs. non-local obsidian exchange at Tula and its implications for post-Formative Mesoamerica. *World Archaeology* 24:440-66.

Healan, D. (editor)
1989 *Tula of the Toltecs: Excavations and Survey*. University of Iowa Press, Iowa City.

Hicks, F.
1987 First steps toward a market-integrated economy in Aztec Mexico. In *Early State Dynamics, Studies in Human Society*, Vol. 2, edited by H. Claessen and P. Van de Velde, pp. 91-107. E.J. Brill, Leiden.

2005 Mexico, Acolhuacan, and the rulership of Late Postclassic Xaltocan: Insights from an Early Colonial legal case. In *Production and Power at Postclassic Xaltocan/La Producción Local y el Poder en el Xaltocan Posclásico*, edited by E. Brumfiel, pp. 195-206. University of Pittsburgh, Pittsburgh; Instituto Nacional de Antropología e História, México, D.F.

Hirth, K.
1974 *Precolumbian Population Development along the Rio Amatzinac: The Formative through the Classic Periods*. PhD dissertation, University of Wisconsin. University Microfilms, Ann Arbor.

Hirth, K. (editor)
2000 *Ancient Urbanism at Xochicalco: The Evolution and Organization of a Pre-Hispanic Society*. 2 vols. University of Utah Press, Salt Lake City.

Hirth, K., and A. Cyphers Guillén
1988 *Tiempo y Asentamiento en Xochicalco*. Instituto de Investigaciones Antropológicas, Universidad Nacional Autónoma de México, México, D.F.

Hodge, M. (editor)
2008 *Place of Jade: Society and Economy in Ancient Chalco, Mexico*. University of Pittsburgh Press, Pittsburgh; Instituto Nacional de Antropología e História, México, D.F.

Hodge, M., and L. Minc
1990 The spatial patterning of Aztec ceramics: Implications for prehispanic exchange systems in the Valley of Mexico. *Journal of Field Archaeology* 17:415-37.
1991 Aztec-Period Ceramic Distribution and Exchange Systems. Report submitted to the National Science Foundation, Washington, D.C.

Hodge, M., and H. Neff
2005 Xaltocan in the economy of the Basin of Mexico. In *Production and Power at Postclassic Xaltocan*, edited by E. Brumfiel, pp. 319-48. Memoirs in Latin American Archaeology, University of Pittsburgh, Pittsburgh.

Hodge, M., H. Neff, J. Blackman, and L. Minc
1993 Black-on-Orange ceramic production in the Aztec empire's heartland. *Latin American Antiquity* 4:130-57.

Holdaway, S., P. Fanning, and D. Witter
2000 *Report of the Western New South Wales Archaeological Project*. University of Auckland, Auckland, New Zealand.

Holmes, W.
1885 Evidence of the antiquity of man on the site of the City of Mexico. *Transactions of the Anthropological Society of Washington* 3:68-81.

Honeychurch, W.
2003 *Inner Asian Warriors and Khans: A Regional Spatial Analysis of Nomadic Political Organization and Interaction*. PhD dissertation, Dept. of Anthropology, University of Michigan, Ann Arbor.

Humboldt, A.
1984 [1822] *Ensayo Político sobre el Reino de la Nueva España*, edited by J. Ortega y Medina. Editorial Porrua, México, D.F.

Israde-Alcántara, I., V. Garduño-Monroy, C. Fisher, H. Pollard, and M. Rodriguez-Pascua
2005 Lake level change, climate, and the impact of natural events: The role of seismic and volcanic events in the formation of the Lake Patzcuaro Basin, Michoacán, Mexico. *Quaternary International* 135(1):35-46.

Johnson, G.
1973 *Local Exchange and Early State Development in Southwestern Iran*. Anthropological Papers, no. 51, Museum of Anthropology, University of Michigan, Ann Arbor.

Jones, T., G. Brown, L. Raab, J. McVicker, W. Spaulding, D. Kennett, A. York, and P. Walker
1999 Environmental imperatives reconsidered: Demographic crises in western North America during the Medieval Climatic Anomaly. *Current Anthropology* 40:2:137-70.

Kirchoff, P.
1943 Mesoamérica: Sus límites geográficas, composición étnica y carácteres culturales. *Acta Americana* 1:92-107. México, D.F.

Klink, C.
1997 Initial Reconnaissance in the Rio Huenque Valley, Southern Peru. Paper presented at the 25th Annual Meeting, Midwest Conference on Andean and Amazonian Archaeology and Ethnohistory, Madison, Wisconsin, Feb. 1997.

Klink, C., and M. Aldenderfer
1996 Archaic Period Settlement in the Altiplano: Comparisons of Two Recent Surveys in the Southwestern Lake Titicaca Basin. Paper presented at the 24th Annual Meeting, Midwest Conference on Andean and Amazonian Archaeology and Ethnohistory, Beloit, Wisconsin, Feb. 1996.

Koehler, T.
1962 *Late Toltec Ceramics in the Valley of Teotihuacan: A Report on the Maquixco-Mazapan Site*. Master's thesis, Dept. of Anthropology, Columbia University, New York.
1986 Excavations at Maquixco Bajo (TT25A). In *The Toltec Period Occupation of the Valley, Part 1: Excavations and Ceramics*, edited by W. Sanders, pp. 7-52. *The Teotihuacan Valley Project Final Report, Vol. 4*. Occasional Papers in Anthropology No. 13, Dept. of Anthropology, Pennsylvania State University, University Park.

Konrad, H.
1980 *A Jesuit Hacienda in Colonial Mexico: Santa Lucia, 1576-1767*. Stanford University Press, Stanford.

Lazcano, C.
1995 *El Modo de Vida en las Unidades Habitacionales de Xochimilco durante el Postclásico Tardío*. Tesis de Licenciado, Escuela Nacional de Antropología e História, México, D.F.

Lemoine, E.
1978 *El Desagüe del Valle de México durante la Época Independiente*. Instituto de Investigaciones Históricas, Universidad Nacional Autónoma de México, México, D.F.

Linne, S.
1934 *Archaeological Researches at Teotihuacan, Mexico.* Pub. No. 1, The Ethnographical Museum of Sweden, Stockholm.
1942 *Mexican Highland Cultures: Archaeological Researches at Teotihuacan, Calpulalpan, and Chalchicomula in 1934/35.* Pub. No. 7, The Ethnographical Museum of Sweden, Stockholm.

Lozano-García, M., and B. Ortega-Guerrero
1994 Palynological and magnetic susceptibility records of Lake Chalco, central Mexico. *Palaeogeography, Palaeoclimatology, Palaeoecology* 109:177-81.
1998 Late Quaternary environmental changes of the central part of the Basin of Mexico: Correlation between Texcoco and Chalco Basins. *Review of Palaeobotany and Palynology* 99:77-93.

Lozano-García, M., B. Ortega, M. Caballero, and J. Urrutia
1993 Late Pleistocene and Holocene paleoenvironments of Chalco Lake, central Mexico. *Quaternary Research* 40:332-42.

Lozano-García, M., and M. Xelhauntzi-López
1997 Some problems in the Late Quaternary pollen records of central Mexico: The Basin of Mexico and Zacapu. *Quaternary International* 43/44:117-23.

Mastache, A.G.
1996 *Tula y su Área Directa de Interacción: Una Perspectiva Regional sobre el Desarrollo del Estado Tolteca.* Tesis doctorado, Facultad de Filosofía y Letras, Universidad Nacional Autónoma de México, México, D.F.

Mastache, A.G., R. Cobean, and D. Healan
2002 *Ancient Tollan: Tula and the Toltec Heartland.* University of Colorado Press, Boulder.

Mastache, A.G., R. Cobean, C. Rees, and D. Jackson
1990 *Las Industrias Líticas Coyotlatelco en el Área de Tula.* Instituto Nacional de Antropología e História, México, D.F.

Mastache, A.G., and A. Crespo
1974 La ocupación prehispanica en el area de Tula, Hgo. In *Proyecto Tula, 1ª Parte*, edited by E. Matos, pp. 71-104. Instituto Nacional de Antropología e História, México, D.F.
1982 Analisis sobre la traza general de Tula, Hgo. In *Estudios sobre la Antigua Ciudad de Tula*, edited by A.G. Mastache, R. Cobean, A. Crespo, and D. Healan, pp. 13-36. Instituto Nacional de Antropología e História, México, D.F.

Matos, E. (editor)
1999 *Excavaciones en la catedral y el sangrario metropolitanos: Programa de arqueologia urbana.* Instituto Nacional de Antropología e História, México, D.F.

Maudslay, A.P. (translator and annotator)
1910 *The True History of the Conquest of New Spain by Bernal Díaz del Castillo*, Vol. 3. The Hakluyt Society, London.

Mayer-Oakes, W.
1959 A stratigraphic excavation at El Risco, Mexico. *Proceedings of the American Philosophical Society* 103:3:332-73.

McBride, H.
1974 *Formative Ceramics and Prehistoric Settlement Patterns in the Cuauhtitlan Region, Mexico.* PhD dissertation, University of California at Los Angeles. University Microfilms, Ann Arbor.

Melville, E.
1994 *A Plague of Sheep: Environmental Consequences of the Conquest of Mexico.* Cambridge University Press, Cambridge.

Metcalfe, S., S. O'Hara, M. Caballero, and S. Davies
2000 Records of Late Pleistocene-Holocene climatic change in Mexico—A review. *Quaternary Science Review* 19:699-721.

Metcalfe, S., F. Street-Perrott, R. Brown, P. Hales, R. Perrott, and F. Steininger
1989 Late Holocene human impact on lake basins in central Mexico. *Geoarchaeology* 4:119-41.

México, Depto. De Defensa Nacional
1955 *Mapas Topograficas, Escala 1:25,000.* Depto. de Cartográfico Militar, México, D.F.

México, Dirección General de Estadística
1901 *Segundo Censo de Población.* Dirección General de Estadística, México, D.F.
1918 *Tercer Censo de Población.* Dirección General de Estadística, México, D.F.
1925 *Cuarto Censo de Población.* Dirección General de Estadística, México, D.F.
1932 *Quinto Censo de Población.* Dirección General de Estadística, México, D.F.
1943 *Sexto Censo de Población.* Dirección General de Estadística, México, D.F.
1953 *Septimo Censo de Población.* Dirección General de Estadística, México, D.F.
1963 *Octavo Censo de Población.* Dirección General de Estadística, México, D.F.

Minc, L.
1994 *Political Economy and Market Economy Under Aztec Rule: A Regional Perspective Based on Decorated Ceramic Production and Distribution Systems in the Valley of Mexico.* PhD dissertation, Dept. of Anthropology, University of Michigan, Ann Arbor.
1999 The Aztec Salt Trade: Insights from INAA of Texcoco Fabric-Marked Pottery. Paper presented at the 64th annual meeting of the Society for American Archaeology, Chicago.

Minc, L., M. Hodge, and J. Blackman
1994 Stylistic and spatial variability in Early Aztec ceramics: Insights into pre-imperial exchange systems. In *Economies and Polities in the Aztec Realm*, edited by M. Hodge and M. Smith, pp. 133-73. Institute of Mesoamerican Studies, State University of New York at Albany, Albany.

Mountjoy, J.
1987 The collapse of the Classic at Cholula as seen from Cerro Zapotecas. *Notas Mesoamericanas* 10:119-51.

Müller, F.
1990 *La Cerámica de Cuicuilco B: Un Rescate Arqueológica*. Instituto Nacional de Antropología e História, México, D.F.

New York Times
1894 Draining Mexico's Valley—Great Undertaking Rapidly Nearing Completion. *New York Times* May 13, 1895. New York.

Nichols, D.
1980 *Prehispanic Settlement and Land Use in the Northwestern Basin of Mexico: The Cuauhtitlan Region*. PhD dissertation, Dept. of Anthropology, Pennsylvania State University, University Park.
1982 A Middle Formative irrigation system near Sta. Clara Coatitlán in the Basin of Mexico. *American Antiquity* 47:133-44.
1987 Risk and agricultural intensification during the Formative Period in the northern Basin of Mexico. *American Anthropologist* 89:596-616.

Nichols, D., E. Brumfiel, H. Neff, M. Hodge, T. Charlton, and M. Glascock
2002 Neutrons, markets, cities, and empires: A 1000-year perspective on ceramic production and distribution in the Postclassic Basin of Mexico. *Journal of Anthropological Archaeology* 21:25-82.

Nichols, D., and C. Frederick
1993 Irrigation canals and chinampas: Recent research in the northern Basin of Mexico. In *Economic Aspects of Water Management in the Prehispanic New World*, edited by V. Scarborough and B. Isaac, pp. 123-50. Research in Economic Anthropology, Supplement 7, JAI Press, New York.

Niederberger, C.
1976 *Zohapilco—Cinco Milenios de Ocupación Humana en un Sitio Lacustre de la Cuenca de México*. Instituto Nacional de Antropología e História, México, D.F.
1987 *Paleopaysages et Archeologie Pre-Urbaine du Bassin de Mexico (Mexique)*. 2 vols. Centre d'Etudes Mexicaines et Centramericaines, México, D.F.

Noguera, E.
1935 *Tenayuca—Estudio Arqueológico de la Piramide de este Lugar, hecho por el Depto. de Monumentos de La Secretaria de Educación Pública*. Museo Nacional de Arqueología, História y Etnografía, México, D.F.

O'Hara, S., and S. Metcalfe
1997 The climate of Mexico since the Aztec period. *Quaternary International* 43/44:25-31.

O'Hara, S., S. Metcalfe, and F. Street-Perrott
1994 On the arid margin: The relationship between climate, humans, and the environment. A review of evidence from the highlands of central Mexico. *Chemosphere* 29:5:965-81.

O'Hara, S., F. Street-Perrott, and T. Burt
1993 Accelerated soil erosion around a Mexican highland lake caused by prehispanic agriculture. *Nature* 362:48-51.

O'Neill, G.
1962 *Postclassic Ceramic Stratigraphy at Chalco in the Valley of Mexico*. PhD dissertation, Columbia University, New York. University Microfilms, Ann Arbor.

Orozco y Berra, M.
1864 *Memória para la Cartografía Hidrográfica del Valle de México*. Sociedad Mexicana de Geografía y Estadística, Cd. de México.

Palerm, A.
1961 Sistemas de regadio prehispánico en Teotihuacan y en el Pedregal de San Angel. *Revista Interamericana de Ciencias Sociales* 2:1:297-302. México, D.F.
1973 *Obras Hidraúlicas Prehispánicas en el Sistema Lacustre del Valle de México*. Centro de Investigaciones Superiores, Instituto Nacional de Antropología e História, México, D.F.
1974 A manera de presentación. In *Nuevas Noticias sobre las Obras Hidráulicos Prehispánicas y Coloniales en el Valle de México*, edited by T. Rojas et al., pp. 7-17. Centro de Estudios Superiores, Instituto Nacional de Antropología e História, México, D.F.

Palerm, A., and E. Wolf
1961 Ecological potential and cultural development in Mesoamerica. In *Studies in Human Ecology*, edited by A. Palerm and E. Wolf, pp. 1-37. Social Science Monographs III, Pan American Union, Washington, D.C.

Parry, W.
1987 *Chipped Stone Tools in Formative Oaxaca, Mexico: Their Procurement, Production, and Use*. Memoirs, no. 20, Museum of Anthropology, University of Michigan, Ann Arbor.

Parsons, J.R.
1966 *The Aztec Ceramic Sequence in the Teotihuacan Valley, Mexico*. 2 vols. PhD dissertation, Dept. of Anthropology, University of Michigan, Ann Arbor.
1971 *Prehistoric Settlement Patterns in the Texcoco Region, Mexico*. Memoirs, no. 3, Museum of Anthropology, University of Michigan, Ann Arbor.
1972 Archaeological settlement patterns. *Annual Review of Anthropology* 1:127-50.
1974 The development of a prehistoric complex society: A regional perspective from the Valley of Mexico. *Journal of Field Archaeology* 1:81-108.
1976 The role of chinampa agriculture in the food supply of Aztec Tenochtitlán. In *Cultural Change and Continuity: Essays in Honor of James B. Griffin*, edited by C. Cleland, pp. 233-57. Academic Press, New York.
1990 Critical reflections on a decade of full-coverage regional survey in the Valley of Mexico. In *The Archaeology of Regions: A Case for Full Coverage Survey*, edited by S. Fish and S. Kowalewski, pp. 7-31. Smithsonian Institution Press, Washington, D.C.
1991 Arqueología Regional en la Cuenca de México: Una Estrategía para la Investigación Futura. *Anales* 27:157-257. Universidad Nacional Autónoma de México, México, D.F.
2001 *The Last Saltmakers of Nexquipayac, Mexico: An Archaeological Ethnography*. Anthropological Papers, no. 92, Museum of Anthropology, University of Michigan, Ann Arbor.
2002 Geological mapping with Rob Scholten in the Beaverhead Range, SW Montana and adjacent Idaho, summer 1960. *Penn State Dept. of Geosciences Newsletter* 1:4:4, 6, 11. University Park.
2004 Critical Reflections on Forty Years of Systematic Regional Survey. Paper presented at the 69th Annual Meeting of the Society for American Archaeology, Montreal.
2006a *The Last Pescadores of Chimalhuacán, Mexico: An Archaeological Ethnography*. Anthropological Papers, no. 96, Museum of Anthropology, University of Michigan, Ann Arbor.

2006b A regional perspective on Coyotlatelco in the Basin of Mexico: Some new thoughts about old data. In *El Fenómeno Coyotlatelco en el Centro de México: Tiempo, Espacio, y Significado*, edited by L. Solar, pp. 83-96. Instituto Nacional de Antropología e História, México, D.F.

Parsons, J.R., E. Brumfiel, M. Parsons, and D. Wilson
1982 *Prehispanic Settlement Patterns in the Southern Valley of Mexico: The Chalco-Xochimilco Region*. Memoirs, no. 14, Museum of Anthropology, University of Michigan, Ann Arbor.

Parsons, J.R., and L. Gorenflo
in press Why is Aztec II Black/Orange pottery so scarce in the Zumpango Region?: A regional perspective from the Basin of Mexico on Tula's collapse and its aftermath. In *Homenaje a Guadalupe Mastache*, edited by Robert Cobean. Instituto Nacional de Antropología e História, México, D.F.

Parsons, J.R., K. Kintigh, and S. Gregg
1983 *Archaeological Settlement Pattern Data from the Chalco, Xochimilco, Texcoco, and Ixtapalapa Regions, Mexico*. Technical Report, no. 14, Museum of Anthropology, University of Michigan, Ann Arbor.

Parsons, J., and L. Morett
2004 Recursos aquáticos en la subsistencia Azteca: Cazadores, pescadores, y recolectores. *Arqueología Mexicana* 12:68:38-43.
2005 La economía acuática en el Valle de México. In *Etnoarqueología: El Contexto Dinámico de la Cultura Material a Través del Tiempo*, edited by E. Williams, pp. 127-64. El Colegio de Michoacán, Zamora.

Parsons, J.R., M. Parsons, V. Popper, and M. Taft
1985 Chinampa agriculture and Aztec urbanization in the Valley of Mexico. In *Prehistoric Intensive Agriculture in the Tropics*, edited by I. Farrington, pp. 49-96. B.A.R. International Series No. 212, Oxford.

Parsons, M.H.
1972a Spindle whorls from the Teotihuacan Valley, Mexico. In *Miscellaneous Studies in Mexican Prehistory*, pp. 45-80. Anthropological Papers, no. 45, Museum of Anthropology, University of Michigan, Ann Arbor.
1972b Figurines from the Teotihuacan Valley, Mexico. In *Miscellaneous Studies in Mexican Prehistory*, pp. 81-120. Anthropological Papers, no. 45, Museum of Anthropology, University of Michigan, Ann Arbor.
1975 The distribution of Late Postclassic spindle whorls in the Valley of Mexico. *American Antiquity* 40:207-15.

Paso y Troncoso, F. (editor)
1905 *Papeles de Nueva España*. 6 vols. Sucesores de Rivadeneyra, Madrid.

Pastrana, A.
1998 *La Explotación Azteca de la Obsidiana en la Sierra de las Navajas*. Instituto Nacional de Antropología e História, México, D.F.

Peñafiel, A.
1884 *Memoria sobre las Aguas Potables de la Capital de México*. Secretaria de Fomento, Cd. de México.

Plunket, P., and G. Uruñuela
2005 Recent research in Puebla prehistory. *Journal of Archaeological Research* 13:2:89-127.

Ramirez, J.
1976 [1867] *Memória acerca de las Obras e Inundaciones en la Cd. de México*. Instituto Nacional de Antropología e História, México, D.F.

Ramírez, F., L. Gámez, and F. González
2000 *Cerámica de Temamatla*. Instituto de Investigaciones Antropológicas, Universidad Nacional Autónoma de México, México, D.F.

Rattray, E.
1966 An archaeological and stylistic study of Coyotlatelco pottery. *Mesoamerican Notes* 7/8:87-211. Universidad de las Americas, México, D.F.
1973 *The Teotihuacan Ceramic Chronology: Early-Tzacualli to Early-Tlamimilolpa Phases*. PhD dissertation, University of Missouri, Columbia. University Microfilms, Ann Arbor.
1990 New findings on the origins of Thin Orange Ceramics. *Ancient Mesoamerica* 1:2:181-95.
2001 *Teotihuacan: Ceramics, Chronology and Cultural Trends/ Cerámica, Cronología y Tendencias Culturales*. University of Pittsburgh, Pittsburgh; Instituto Nacional de Antropología e História, México, D.F.

Reyes, V.
1878 La ley de periodicidad de la lluvia en el Valle de México. *Boletín de la Sociedad Mexicana de Geografía y Estadística*, 3a época, 4:314-19. Ciudad de México.

Rodríguez-Alegría, E.
2008 Narratives of conquest, colonialism, and cutting-edge technology. *American Anthropologist* 110:33-43.

Rojas, T.
1985 *La Cosecha del Agua en la Cuenca de México*. Cuadernos de la Casa Chata No. 116, Museo Nacional de Culturas Populares, México, D.F.

Rojas, T., R. Strauss, and J. Lameiras (editors)
1974 *Nuevas Noticias sobre las Obras Hidráulicos Prehispánicas y Coloniales en el Valle de México*. Centro de Estudios Superiores, Instituto Nacional de Antropología e História, México, D.F.

Salomón, M.
2006 Cerámicas del Epiclásico en el Valle de Puebla-Tlaxcala: Reflexiones desde el Cerro Zapotecas. In *El Fenómeno Coyotlatelco en el Centro de México: Tiempo, Espacio, y Significado*, edited by L. Solar, pp. 345-59. Instituto Nacional de Antropología e História, México, D.F.

Sanchez, M.
1989 La producción de sal en un sitio del Postclásico Tardío. *Arqueología* 2:81-88.

Sanders, W.T.
1956 The central Mexican symbiotic region: A study in prehistoric settlement patterns. In *Prehistoric Settlement Patterns in the New World*, edited by G. Willey, pp. 115-27. Viking Fund Publications in Anthropology No. 23, New York.

1957 *Tierra y Agua (Land and Water): A Study of the Ecological Processes in the Development of Civilization*. PhD dissertation, Dept. of Anthropology, Harvard University, Cambridge.
1962 Cultural ecology of nuclear Mesoamerica. *American Anthropologist* 64:34-44.
1965 *The Cultural Ecology of the Teotihuacan Valley*. Dept. of Sociology and Anthropology, Pennsylvania State University, University Park.
1968 Hydraulic agriculture, economic symbiosis, and the evolution of states in Central Mexico. In *Anthropological Archaeology of the Americas*, edited by B. Meggers, pp. 88-107. The Anthropological Society of Washington, Washington, D.C.
1970 The population of the Teotihuacan Valley, the Basin of Mexico, and the central Mexican symbiotic region in the 16th century. In *The Natural Environment, Contemporary Occupation, and 16th Century Population of the Valley*, pp. 385-457. *The Teotihuacan Valley Project Final Report, Vol. 1*. Occasional Papers in Anthropology No. 3, Dept. of Anthropology, Pennsylvania State University, University Park.
1971 Settlement patterns in Central Mexico. In *Archaeology of Northern Mesoamerica, Part One*, edited by G. Elkholm and I. Bernal, pp. 3-44. *Handbook of Middle American Indians, Vol. 10*, R. Wauchope, general editor. University of Texas Press, Austin.
1972 Population, agricultural history and societal evolution in Mesoamerica. In *Population Growth, Anthropological Implications*, edited by B. Spooner, pp. 101-53. MIT Press, Boston.
1997 El final de la gran aventura: El ocaso de un recurso natural. *Arqueología*, segunda época, 17:3-20. INAH, México, D.F.

Sanders, W.T. (editor)
1986 *The Toltec Period Occupation of the Valley. Part 1: Excavations and Ceramics; Part 2: Surface Survey and Special Studies. The Teotihuacan Valley Project Final Report, Vol. 4*. Occasional Papers in Anthropology No. 13, Dept. of Anthropology, Pennsylvania State University, University Park.
1994 *The Teotihuacan Period Occupation of the Valley. Part 1: The Excavations. The Teotihuacan Valley Project Final Report, Vol. 3*. Occasional Papers in Anthropology No. 19, Dept. of Anthropology, Pennsylvania State University, University Park.
1995 *The Teotihuacan Period Occupation of the Valley. Part 2: Artifact Analyses. The Teotihuacan Valley Project Final Report, Vol. 3*. Occasional Papers in Anthropology No. 20, Dept. of Anthropology, Pennsylvania State University, University Park.
1996 *The Teotihuacan Period Occupation of the Valley. Part 4: Special Analyses, Miscellaneous Appendices, and Volume Bibliography. The Teotihuacan Valley Project Final Report, Vol. 3*. Occasional Papers in Anthropology No. 24, Dept. of Anthropology, Pennsylvania State University, University Park.

Sanders, W.T., J. Parsons, and R. Santley
1979 *The Basin of Mexico: Ecological Processes in the Evolution of a Civilization*. Academic Press, New York.

Sanders, W.T., M. West, C. Fletcher, and J. Marino
1975 *The Formative Period Occupation of the Valley. Part 1: Texts and Tables; Part 2: Plates and Figures. The Teotihuacan Valley Project Final Report, Vol. 2*. Occasional Papers in Anthropology No. 10, Dept. of Anthropology, Pennsylvania State University, University Park.

Santley, R.
1977 *Intra-Site Settlement Patterns at Loma Torremote and their Relationship to Formative Prehistory in the Cuauhtitlan Region, State of Mexico*. PhD dissertation, Pennsylvania State University. University Microfilms, Ann Arbor.

Scholten, R., and L. Ramspott
1968 *Tectonic Mechanisms Indicated by Structural Framework of Central Beaverhead Range, Idaho-Montana*. Special Paper No. 104, Geological Society of America, Boulder, Colorado.

Scott, S.
1993 *Teotihuacan Mazapan Figurines and the Xipe Totec Statue: A Link Between the Basin of Mexico and the Valley of Oaxaca*. Publications in Anthropology No. 44, Vanderbilt University, Nashville.

Secretaria de Programación y Presupuesto
1981 *Síntesis Geográfica del Estado de México*. Coordinación General de los Servicios Nacionales de Estadistica, Geografía e Informática, México, D.F.

Sejourne, L.
1970 *Arqueología del Valle de México, I: Culhuacan*. Instituto Nacional de Antropología e História, México, D.F.
1983 *Arqueología e História del Valle de México, de Xochimilco a Amecameca*. Siglo Veintiuno Editores, México, D.F.

Serra, M.
1988 *Los Recursos Lacustres de la Cuenca de México durante el Formativo*. Instituto de Investigaciones Antropológicas, Universidad Nacional Autónoma de México, México, D.F.

Serra, M. (editor)
1998 *Xochitecatl*. Gobierno del Estado de Tlaxcala, Tlaxcala, Mexico.

Servicio Meteorológico Mexicano
1919-1938 *Boletín del Servicio Meteorológico Mexicana*. Tacubaya, México, D.F.
1924 *Atlas Termopluviométrico de la República Mexicana, 1906-1910*. Tacubaya, México, D.F.
1925 *Atlas Climatológico de la República Mexicana, 1921-1925*. Tacubaya, México, D.F.

Smith, C.A.
2002 *Concordant Change and Core-Periphery Dynamics: A Synthesis of Highland Mesoamerican Archaeological Survey Data*. PhD dissertation, University of Georgia, Athens. University Microfilms, Ann Arbor.

Solar, L. (editor)
2006 *El Fenómeno Coyotlatelco en el Centro de México: Tiempo, Espacio, y Significado*. Coordinación Nacional de Arqueología, Instituto Nacional de Antropología e História, México, D.F.

Spence, M.
1985 Specialized production in rural Aztec society: Obsidian workshops of the Teotihuacan Valley. In *Contributions to the Archaeology and Ethnohistory of Greater Mesoamerica*, edited by W.J. Folan, pp. 76-125. Southern Illinois University Press, Carbondale.

Steponaitis, V.
1981 Settlement hierarchies and political complexities in nonmarket societies: The Formative Period in the Valley of Mexico. *American Anthropologist* 83:320-63.

Strauss, R.
1974 El area septentrional del Valle de México: Problemas agrohidráulicas prehispánicas y coloniales. In *Nuevas Noticias sobre las Obras Hidráulicas Prehispánicas y Coloniales en el Valle de México*, edited by T. Rojas et al., pp. 135-74. Centro de Estudios Superiores, Instituto Nacional de Antropología e História, México, D.F.

Sugiura, Y.
2005 *Y Atrás Quedó la Ciudad de los Dioses: História de los Asentamientos en el Valle de Toluca*. Instituto de Investigaciones Antropológicas, Universidad Nacional Autónoma de México, México, D.F.

Talavara, E.
1979 *Las Salinas de la Cuenca de México y la Cerámica de Impresión Textil*. Tesis, Escuela Nacional de Antropología e História, México, D.F.

Taylor, C.L.
2003 *Geographic/UTM Coordinate Converter*. HiWAAY Internet Services, http://home.hiwaay.net/~taylorc/toolbox/geography/geoutm.html

Tolstoy, P.
1958 Surface survey of the northern valley of Mexico: The Classic and Postclassic Periods. *Transactions of the American Philosophical Society*, n.s., Vol. 48, Pt. 5, Philadelphia.
1971 Utilitarian artifacts of central Mexico. In *Archaeology of Northern Mesoamerica, Part One*, edited by G. Elkholm and I. Bernal, pp. 270-96. Handbook of Middle American Indians, Vol. 10, R. Wauchope, general editor. University of Texas Press, Austin.
1975 Settlement and population trends in the Basin of Mexico (Ixtapaluca and Zacatenco phases). *Journal of Field Archaeology* 2:331-49.

Tolstoy, P., and S. Fish
1975 Surface and subsurface evidence of community size at Coapexco, Mexico. *Journal of Field Archaeology* 2:97-104.

Tolstoy, P., S. Fish, M. Boksenbaum, and K. Vaughn
1977 Early sedentary communities in the Basin of Mexico. *Journal of Field Archaeology* 4:91-106.

Tovalín, A.
1998 *Desarrollo Arquitectónico del Sitio Arqueológico de Tlapizáhuac*. Instituto Nacional de Antropología e História, México, D.F.

Tozzer, A.M.
1921 *Excavation of a Site at Santiago Ahuitzotla, D.F., Mexico*. Bulletin 74, Bureau of American Ethnology, Smithsonian Institution, Washington, D.C.

Vaillant, G.
1930 *Excavations at Zacatenco*. Anthropological Papers, Vol. 32, Pt. 1, The American Museum of Natural History, New York.
1931 *Excavations at Ticoman*. Anthropological Papers, Vol. 32, Pt. 2, The American Museum of Natural History, New York.
1935 *Excavations at El Arbolillo*. Anthropological Papers, Vol. 35, Pt. 2, The American Museum of Natural History, New York.
1938 Correlation of archaeological and historical sequences in the Valley of Mexico. *American Anthropologist* 40:535-73.
1941 *Aztecs of Mexico: Origin, Rise and Fall of the Aztec Nation*. Doubleday, Doran and Co., Inc., Garden City, New York.

Van Leusen, M., and P. Attema
2002 Regional archaeological patterns in the Sibartide: Preliminary results of the RPC Field Survey Campaign, 2000. *Palaeohistoria* 42/43, Groningen University, The Netherlands.

Vargas, E.
1975 La Cerámica. In *Teotenango: El Antiguo Lugar de la Muralla, Memoria de las Excavaciones Arqueologicas*, Tomo I, edited by R. Piña Chan, pp. 189-265. Dirección de Turismo, Gobierno del Estado de México, Toluca.

Vega, C.
1975 *Forma y Decoración en las Vasijas de Tradición Azteca*. Instituto Nacional de Antropología e História, México, D.F.

Vélez, N.V.
2007 *La Caracterización Socio-Cultural de Sitios Rurales de Teotihuacan dentro de la Cuenca de México*. Tesis de Maestría en Arqueología, Escuela Nacional de Antropología e História, México, D.F.

Watts, W., and J. Bradbury
1982 Paleoecological studies at Lake Patzcuaro on the west-central Mexican plateau and at Chalco in the Basin of Mexico. *Quaternary Research* 17:56-70.

Whalen, M., and J. Parsons
1982 Ceramic markers used for period designations. In *Prehispanic Settlement Patterns in the Southern Valley of Mexico: The Chalco-Xochimilco Region*, pp. 385-460. Memoirs, no. 14, Museum of Anthropology, University of Michigan, Ann Arbor.

Williams, B.
1991 The lands and political organization of a rural tlaxilacalli in Tepetlaoxtoc, ca. A.D. 1540. In *Land and Politics in the Valley of Mexico: A Two-Thousand Year Perspective*, edited by H. Harvey, pp. 187-208. University of New Mexico Press, Albuquerque.
1994 The archaeological signature of local level politics in Tepetlaoxtoc. In *Economies and Polities in the Aztec Realm*, edited by M. Hodge and M. Smith, pp. 73-87. University of Texas Press, Austin.

Williams, B., and H. Harvey
1997 *Códice de Santa María Asunción: Facsimile and Commentary: Households and Lands in Sixteenth Century Tepetlaoxtoc*. University of Utah Press, Salt Lake City.

Wolf, E. (editor)
1976 *The Valley of Mexico: Studies in Pre-Hispanic Ecology and Society*. University of New Mexico Press, Albuquerque.

Wolf, E., and A. Palerm
1956 New Light on the Archaic in the Valley of Mexico. Paper presented at the Annual Meeting of the American Anthropological Association, Los Angeles, Dec. 30, 1956.

Appendix A

Site Descriptions

Jeffrey R. Parsons, Mary H. Parsons, and David J. Wilson

Sites are described in chronological order under standard, self-explanatory headings. Each site description begins with the site's final number, followed in brackets by the original field site number and the designations of any relevant Locations (numbers) and Features (letters) that were assigned in the field. Also in brackets are those site numbers assigned in Parsons et al. 1983 in cases where they differ from the final site numbers in the present monograph—these are sites that we designated as Early Classic (EC) or Late Classic (LC) in the 1983 publication.

Field site numbers were assigned consecutively by the two survey teams: the team headed by J. Parsons used a (J) suffix after each field site number; the team headed by M. Parsons used a (M) suffix to each site number. The original numbers were often applied with black ink to the sherds themselves during our fieldwork, and they are so labelled where they are permanently stored at the Museo de Agricultura, Universidad Autónoma de Chapingo, Texcoco, Edo. de México, Mexico. In some cases, the cloth bags in which the surface collections are stored have had the final site numbers added in red to the original designations in black.

Locations are given in UTM coordinates (easting and northing coordinates, Zone 14), followed by the corresponding north latitude and west longitude coordinates in degrees.

Multiple-component occupations are cross-referenced in the following descriptions. Unless otherwise noted, references to past and present time are relative to the time of our field surveys in May through December, 1973. Abbreviations used include: Late Formative (LF), Terminal Formative (TF), Classic (Cl), Early Toltec (ET), Late Toltec (LT), Early Aztec (E. Az), Late Aztec (L. Az), Aztec (Az).

In the accompanying site maps for each period, sites are numbered consecutively in roughly NE to SW order across the map (with occasional inconsistencies, for which we apologize).

Table A1 (page 335) summarizes the Zumpango Region site data.

Late Formative Site (Fig. A1)

SITE NO. Zu-LF-1 [Zu-LF-1(J); Location 5]
Date of Survey: May 28, 1973
Location: 493700 E, 2206200 N; 19.9523° N, 99.0602° W
Natural Setting: 2345 m asl, on gently sloping ground in the Upper Salado Drainage; medium soil cover and slight erosion.
Modern Land Use: Rainfall-based agriculture. The immediate site area is presently fallow. A modern dirt road borders the east edge of the site.
Archaeological Remains: Light Late Formative surface pottery over an area of ca. 3.00 ha. A trace of Terminal Formative pottery is also present (no TF site designated). We noted a few chert fragments, but very little obsidian. There is very little rock rubble and no discernible structural remains.
We made one surface collection (Location 5) from an area ca. 15 × 30 m in a plowed field (Plate A1), with light LF surface pottery and a few obsidian and chert artifacts.
Discussion: This is the only Late Formative site identified in the entire Zumpango Region survey area. This site and area lack identifiable Middle Formative antecedents, although some occupation may have continued at this site into early TF times. This site apparently represents a pioneering sedentary agricultural settlement in an area where such occupation had previously been absent.
Classification: Hamlet, 15–30 people.

Terminal Formative Sites (Tzacualli Phase) (Fig. A2)

SITE NO. Zu-TF-1 [Zu-Cl-16(M); Location 36; Feature AU]
Date of Survey: June 17, 1973
Location: 489180 E, 2205530 N; 19.9462° N, 99.1034° W
Natural Setting: 2310 m asl, on gently sloping ground in the Upper Salado Drainage; shallow soil cover and severe erosion, with many patches of bare tepetate.
Modern Land Use: Generally wasteland, with very limited rainfall-based cultivation of maguey and maize. A few small stone check dams represent efforts to control erosion.
Archaeological Remains: Light Terminal Formative surface pottery over an area of ca. 0.10 ha. Erosion has exposed several patches of moderate-to-heavy Classic (Zu-Cl-11) and TF pottery. The overlying Classic site extends over a larger area. We noted substantial quantities of obsidian scrapers and blades and one projectile point made of gray obsidian. A few pieces of worked quartzite or chert are also present.
There is a single badly eroded mound (Feature AU), measuring ca. 7 × 13 m and 2.00 m high, with moderate-to-heavy Cl and light TF surface pottery, several obsidian artifacts, and light-to-moderate rock rubble. This is probably a Classic-period feature. This mound with its dark brown soil stands out notably in a field where yellow-brown soil predominates. We made one surface collection over an area ca. 3 × 3 m on the highest part of the mound.
We made one additional surface collection (Location 36) over an area of ca. 3 × 4 m in a fallow field with light-to-moderate Cl and light TF surface pottery, several obsidian artifacts, and light-to-moderate rock rubble.
Discussion: Occupation at this locality is very predominantly Classic.
Classification: Small Hamlet, 2–5 people.

SITE NO. Zu-TF-2 [Zu-Cl-5(M); Location 21]
Date of Survey: June 5, 1973
Location: 484300 E, 2206030 N; 19.9507° N, 99.1500° W
Natural Setting: 2260 m asl, on level ground in the Upper Salado Drainage; medium soil cover and slight erosion.
Modern Land Use: Rainfall-based agriculture. The immediate site area is presently fallow.
Archaeological Remains: Light Terminal Formative surface pottery over an area of ca. 0.50 ha. The TF material is mixed with heavier Classic (Zu-Cl-20) ceramics. We noted several green obsidian blades and chips. There is no rock rubble and no discernible structural remains.
We made one surface collection (Location 21) from an area ca. 25 × 30 m in a fallow field, with light TF and Cl surface pottery, several obsidian artifacts, and no rock rubble.
Discussion: A small TF occupation overlain by a much heavier Classic settlement.
Classification: Small Hamlet, 2–5 people.

SITE NO. Zu-TF-3 [Zu-TF-17(J); Location 88]
Date of Survey: Nov. 1, 1973
Location: 489000 E, 2202380 N; 19.9177° N, 99.1051° W
Natural Setting: 2320 m asl, on nearly level ground on a broad ridge near the juncture of three major *barrancas* in the Upper Salado Drainage; shallow soil cover and moderate to severe erosion, with patches of bare tepetate exposed along the eastern edge of the site.
Modern Land Use: Rainfall-based agriculture, with some maguey semi-terracing.
Archaeological Remains: Light Terminal Formative surface pottery over an area of ca. 2.90 ha. The TF material is mixed with heavier and more extensive Classic ceramics (Zu-Cl-34). We noted a few green obsidian blades. There are no discernible structural remains.
We made one surface collection (Location 88) from an area ca. 10 × 10 m in a recently harvested maize field, with light TF and light-to-moderate Cl surface pottery, a few obsidian artifacts, and moderate rock rubble.
Discussion: A small TF occupation overlain by a larger Classic settlement.
Classification: Hamlet, 20–40 people.

SITE NO. Zu-TF-4 [Zu-Cl-14(J); Location 32]
Date of Survey: July 10, 1973
Location: 488280 E, 2198550 N; 19.8831° N, 99.1120° W
Natural Setting: 2305 m asl, on nearly level ground in the Upper Salado Drainage, just northwest of the divide between the Upper Salado and Basin of Mexico drainages; variable shallow and medium soil cover, with moderate to severe erosion.
Modern Land Use: Fallow agricultural land.
Archaeological Remains: Light-to-moderate Terminal Formative surface pottery over an area of ca. 0.50 ha. The TF material is mixed with approximately equal but more extensive Classic (Zu-Cl-52) ceramics, and there are also traces of Late Toltec and Late Aztec pottery (no LT or Az sites designated). We noted several scrapers, points, blades and flakes of green and gray obsidian, and one basalt mano fragment. There are no discernible structural remains.
We made one surface collection (Location 32) in an unplowed field over an area ca. 20 × 20 m, with light-to-moderate TF and Cl surface pottery, several obsidian artifacts, and light rock rubble.
Discussion: A small TF occupation overlain by a larger Classic settlement.
Classification: Small Hamlet, 5–10 people.

Appendix A: Site Descriptions

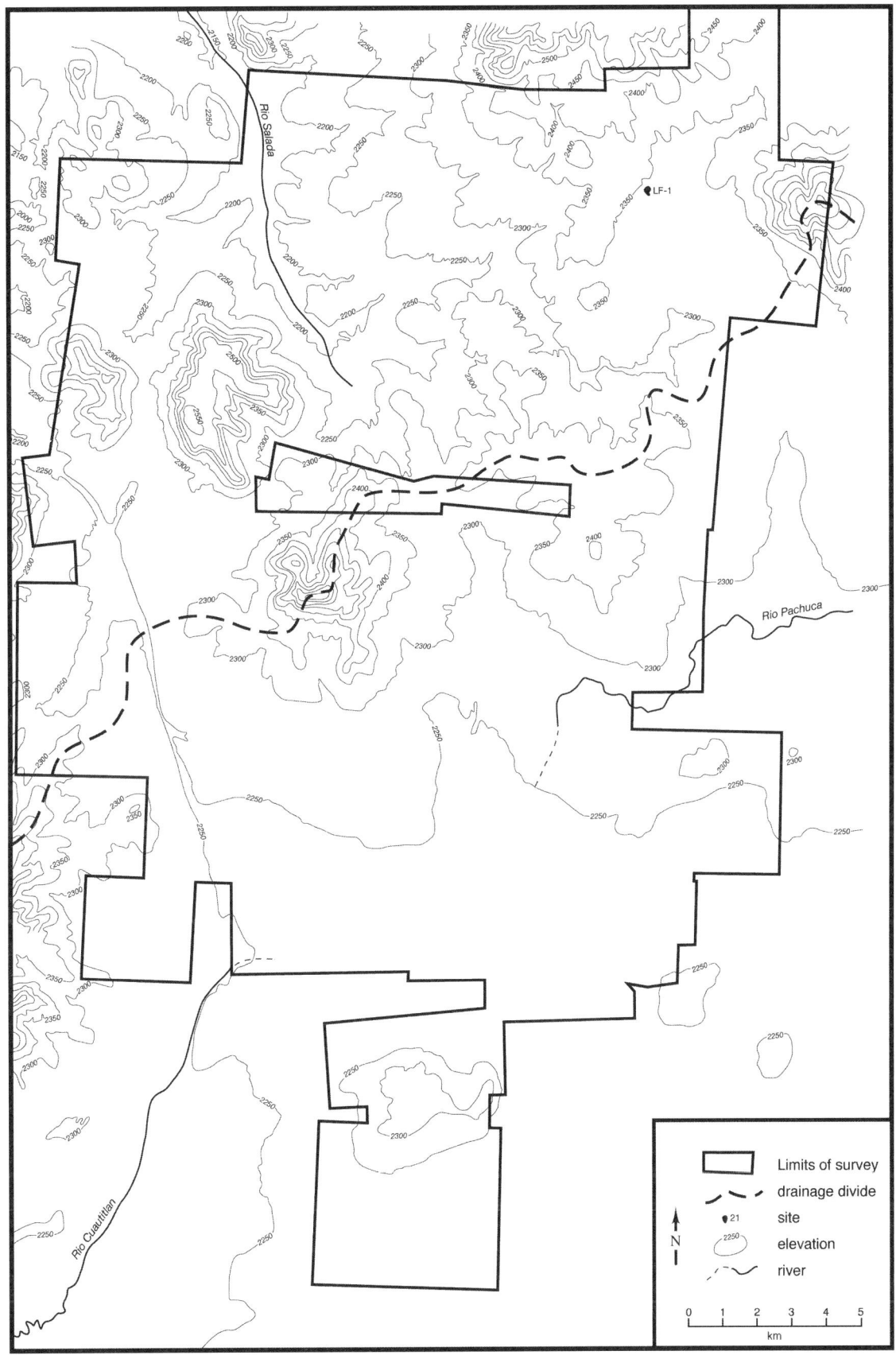

Figure A1. Map of Late Formative sites in the Zumpango Region.

Plate A1. Zu-LF-1, facing SE over Location 5.

Appendix A: Site Descriptions

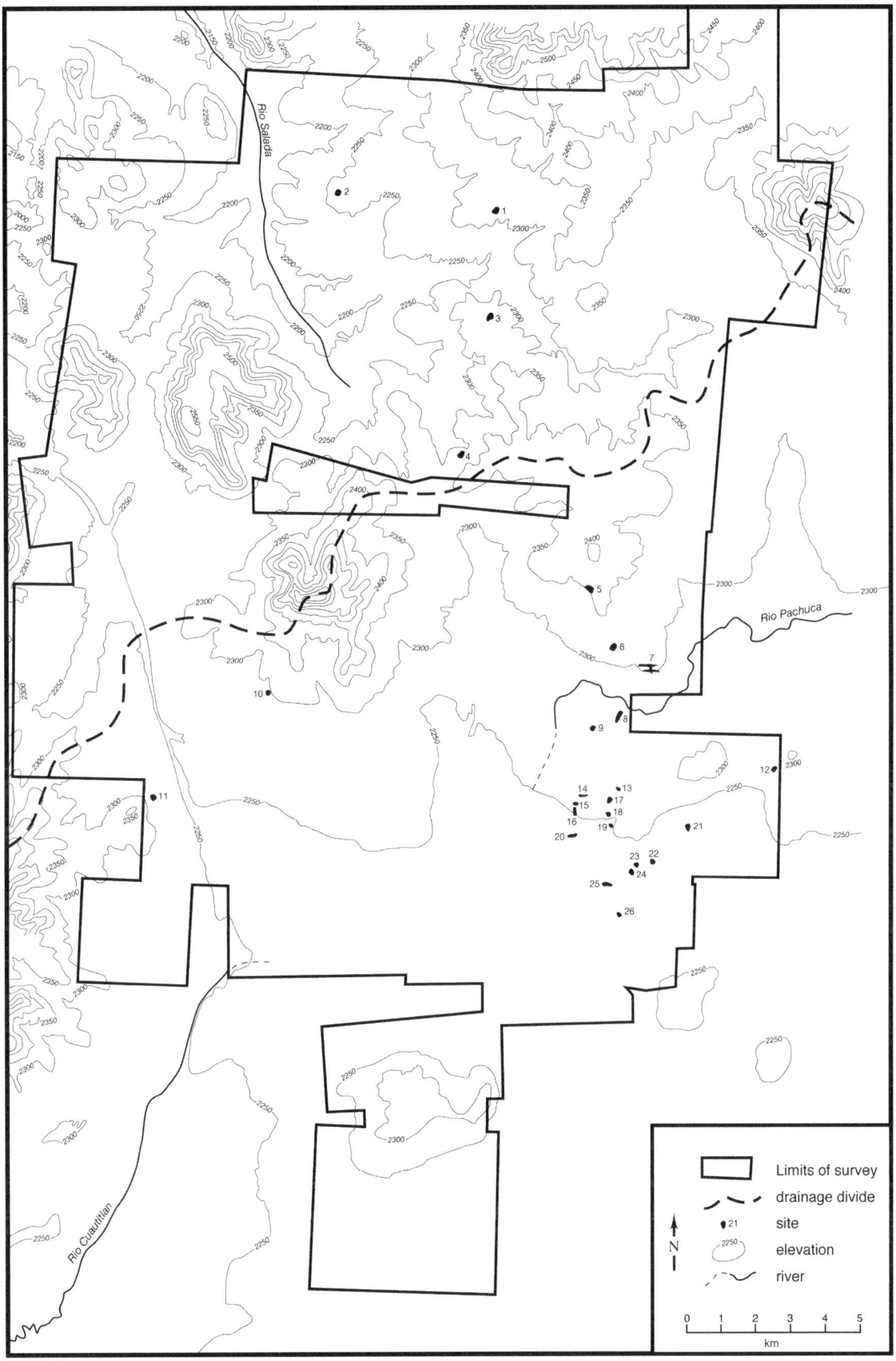

Figure A2. Map of Terminal Formative sites in the Zumpango Region.

Plate A2. Zu-TF-5, facing NW over Location 44.

SITE NO. Zu-TF-5 [Zu-TF-2(J); Location 44]
  Date of Survey: July 24, 1973
  Location: 478820 E, 2187530 N; 19.7834° N, 99.2022° W
  Natural Setting: 2355 m asl, on gently sloping ground in the Basin of Mexico Lower Piedmont; medium soil cover and moderate to severe erosion.
  Modern Land Use: The immediate site area is unplowed pasture, with rainfall-based cultivation in the surrounding terrain.
  Archaeological Remains: Variable light and light-to-moderate Terminal Formative surface pottery and rock rubble over an area of ca. 3.5 ha. The TF material is mixed with approximately equal amounts of Classic (Zu-Cl-24) and lighter Aztec (Zu-Az-181) ceramics. We saw very little obsidian. There is light-to-moderate rock rubble, but no discernible structural remains.
  We made one surface collection (Location 44) in an unplowed field over an area ca. 15 × 15 m, with light-to-moderate TF and Cl surface pottery, very few obsidian artifacts, and light-to-moderate rock rubble (Plate A2).
  Discussion: Mixed TF and Cl occupation.
  Classification: Hamlet, 35–70 people.

SITE NO. Zu-TF-6 [Zu-Cl-25(J); Location 47]
  Date of Survey: July 31, 1973
  Location: 492880 E, 2191930 N; 19.8233° N, 99.0680° W
  Natural Setting: 2320 m asl, on gently sloping ground in the Basin of Mexico Lower Piedmont; shallow soil cover and severe erosion.
  Modern Land Use: The immediate site area is unplowed pasture. Rainfall-based agriculture characterizes the general area.
  Archaeological Remains: Light Terminal Formative surface pottery over an area of ca. 2.3 ha. The TF material is mixed with approximately equal amounts of Classic (Zu-Cl-71) ceramics, and traces of Aztec pottery (no Az site designated). We noted a few obsidian blades and one obsidian scraper. There is very little rock rubble and no discernible structural remains.
  We made one surface collection (Location 47) from an area ca. 15 × 15 m in an unplowed area with light-to-moderate TF and Cl surface pottery, a few obsidian artifacts, and very little rock rubble.
  Discussion: Mixed TF and Cl occupation.
  Classification: Hamlet, 15–30 people.

SITE NO. Zu-TF-7 [Zu-TF-1(J); Location 46]
  Date of Survey: July 29, 1973
  Location: 494030 E, 2191250 N; 19.8172° N, 99.0570° W
  Natural Setting: 2305 m asl, on gently sloping ground in the Basin of Mexico Lower Piedmont; medium soil cover and moderate erosion.
  Modern Land Use: Rainfall-based agriculture, with some terraced fields.
  Archaeological Remains: Light Terminal Formative surface pottery over an area of ca. 7.8 ha. The TF material is mixed with lighter Late Aztec ceramics (Zu-Az-189, Zu-Az-191, Zu-Az-190). We noted a few obsidian blades. There is light-to-moderate rock rubble, but no discernible structural remains.

Plate A3. Zu-TF-8, facing west over Location 67.

We made one surface collection (Location 46) from an area ca. 15 × 20 m in a fallow field, with light TF and very light Az surface pottery, a few obsidian blades, and light-to-moderate rock rubble.

Discussion: Like nearby sites Zu-TF-8, -9, -13–19, and -22–24, this TF site was abandoned prior to the Classic period. This is by far the largest TF site in the Zumpango Region, and may have been a locus of local elite residence.

Classification: Hamlet, 50–100 people.

SITE NO. Zu-TF-8 [Zu-TF-3(J); Location 67]
 Date of Survey: Sept. 25, 1973
 Location: 493070 E, 2190130 N; 19.8070° N, 99.0662° W
 Natural Setting: 2260 m asl, on nearly level ground on the Lakeshore Plain, just south of the Río Zumpango; medium soil cover and slight erosion.
 Modern Land Use: Fallow agricultural land with moderate weed cover. There is rainfall-based agriculture in the general area. A modern dirt road borders the west edge of the site.
 Archaeological Remains: Variable light and light-to-moderate Terminal Formative surface pottery over an area of ca. 4.20 ha. We noted several green and gray obsidian blades and one gray obsidian scraper. There is very little rock rubble and no discernible structural remains.

We made one surface collection (Location 67) from an area ca. 15 × 20 m in a fallow field (Plate A3), with light-to-moderate TF surface pottery, a few obsidian artifacts, and very little rock rubble.

Discussion: Like nearby sites Zu-TF-7, -9, -13–19, and -22–24, this TF site was abandoned prior to the Classic period.

Classification: Hamlet, 20–40 people.

SITE NO. Zu-TF-9 [Zu-TF-4(J); Location 66]
 Date of Survey: Sept. 24, 1973
 Location: 492930 E, 2189380 N; 19.8003° N, 99.0675° W
 Natural Setting: 2260 m asl, on nearly level ground on the Lakeshore Plain; medium soil cover and slight erosion.

Modern Land Use: Rainfall-based agriculture. A recently constructed factory is located northwest of the site area. A modern dirt road borders the north edge of the site.
 Archaeological Remains: Light Terminal Formative surface pottery over an area of ca. 0.70 ha. The TF material is mixed with traces of Late Toltec and Aztec ceramics (no LT or Az sites designated). We noted a few gray obsidian blades. There is very little rock rubble and no discernible structural remains.

We made one surface collection (Location 66) from an area ca. 15 × 20 m in a plowed field (Plate A4), with light TF and traces of LT and Late Az surface pottery, a few obsidian artifacts, and almost no rock rubble.

Discussion: Like nearby sites Zu-TF-7, -8, -13–19, and -22–24, this TF site was abandoned prior to the Classic period. Site Zu-TF-9 may represent a small outlier of the larger Terminal Formative hamlet (Zu-TF-8) 300 m to the northeast.

Classification: Small Hamlet, 5–10 people.

SITE NO. Zu-TF-10 [Zu-Cl-36(M); Location 69]
 Date of Survey: Aug. 2, 1973
 Location: 482220 E, 2190680 N; 19.81193° N, 99.1698° W
 Natural Setting: 2295 m asl, on gently sloping ground at the lower edge of the Basin of Mexico Lower Piedmont, just above the upper edge of the Lakeshore Plain; medium soil cover and slight erosion.
 Modern Land Use: Rainfall-based agriculture. A modern dirt road borders the east edge of the site.
 Archaeological Remains: Light Terminal Formative surface pottery over an area of ca. 0.10 ha. The TF material is mixed with more extensive and slightly heavier quantities of Classic ceramics (Zu-Cl-65). We noted numerous green and gray obsidian blades, several fragments of gray obsidian, and one green obsidian scraper. There is very little rock rubble and no discernible structural remains.

We made one surface collection (Location 69) over an area ca. 6 × 14 m in a plowed maize field (maize ca. 10 cm high), with light TF and light-to-moderate Cl surface pottery, a few obsidian artifacts, and no rock rubble.

Plate A4. Zu-TF-9, facing west over Location 66.

Discussion: A small TF occupation overlain by a larger Classic settlement.
Classification: Small Hamlet, 2–5 people.

SITE NO. **Zu-TF-11** [Zu-TF-2(M); Location 95]
Date of Survey: Dec. 4, 1973
Location: 478820 E, 2187430 N; 19.7825° N, 99.2022° W
Natural Setting: 2290 m asl, on gently sloping ground in the Basin of Mexico Lower Piedmont; shallow soil cover and severe erosion, with patches of bare tepetate.
Modern Land Use: Much of the site area is unplowed pasture, with limited rainfall-based agriculture and maguey semi-terracing. The modern town of Coyotepec encroaches onto the site from the west.
Archaeological Remains: Variable light, light-to-moderate, and moderate Terminal Formative surface pottery over an area of ca. 2.40 ha. The TF material is mixed with approximately equal quantities of Classic ceramics (Zu-Cl-86). Lighter and less extensive quantities of Late Aztec surface pottery (Zu-Az-270) are also present. We noted several green and gray obsidian blades. There is very little rock rubble and no discernible structural remains.

We made one surface collection (Location 95) over an area ca. 10 × 12 m in an unplowed field with light TF and light-to-moderate Cl surface pottery, several obsidian artifacts, and no rock rubble.
Discussion: Because of modern occupation, we were unable to define the western limits of the site. This appears to be another small TF occupation overlain by a larger Classic settlement.
Classification: Hamlet (?), 30–60 people.

SITE NO. **Zu-TF-12** [Zu-Cl-35(J); Location 72]
Date of Survey: Oct. 7, 1973
Location: 497930 E, 2188320 N; 19.7907° N, 99.0198° W
Natural Setting: 2280 m asl, on nearly level ground at the base of a gentle slope leading up towards Loma Coqueme (max. elev. 2310 m asl) to the northeast, at the juncture of the Lakeshore Plain and the Basin of Mexico Lower Piedmont; shallow soil cover and slight erosion.
Modern Land Use: Rainfall-based agriculture. Two modern dirt roads cross the site.
Archaeological Remains: Light Terminal Formative surface pottery over an area of ca. 0.80 ha. The site is located at the eastern border of our survey area and may extend further to the east. The TF material is mixed with lighter Classic (Zu-Cl-75) ceramics. We noted many gray obsidian scrapers and some green obsidian blades. There is very little rock rubble and no discernible structural remains.

We made one surface collection (Location 72) over an area ca. 20 × 25 m in a plowed maize field with light TF and Cl surface pottery, several obsidian artifacts, and little rock rubble.
Discussion: Because we did not define the site's eastern limit, it could be larger than our estimate.
Classification: Small Hamlet (?), 5–10 people.

SITE NO. **Zu-TF-13** [Zu-TF-8(J)]
Date of Survey: Oct. 1, 1973
Location: 492880 E, 2187750 N; 19.7855° N, 99.0680° W
Natural Setting: 2260 m asl, on nearly level ground on the Lakeshore Plain; deep soil cover and slight erosion. Together with sites Zu-TF-14–Zu-TF-26, this site occupies a topographic elevation (ancient beach ridges and intervening strand plain) several meters above the general level of the surrounding Lakeshore Plain (Frederick et al. 2005:75) (Fig. 2.4).
Modern Land Use: The southern three-quarters of the site is devoted to rainfall-based agriculture; the northern quarter is planted in irrigated alfalfa.
Archaeological Remains: Light Terminal Formative surface pottery over an area of ca. 1.30 ha. There is very little rock rubble and no discernible structural remains.

No surface collection made.

Discussion: Like nearby sites Zu-TF-7, -8, -9, -14–19, and -22–24, this site lacks Classic occupation.
Classification: Small Hamlet, 5–15 people.

SITE NO. Zu-TF-14 [Zu-TF-7(J)]
Date of Survey: Oct. 2, 1973
Location: 491800 E, 2187530 N; 19.7835° N, 99.0783° W
Natural Setting: 2260 m asl, on nearly level ground on the Lakeshore Plain; deep soil cover and slight erosion. Together with sites Zu-TF-13 and Zu-TF-15–Zu-TF-26, this site occupies a topographic elevation (ancient beach ridges and intervening strand plain) several meters above the general level of the surrounding Lakeshore Plain (Frederick et al. 2005:75) (Fig. 2.4).
Modern Land Use: Rainfall-based agriculture.
Archaeological Remains: Light Terminal Formative surface pottery over an area of ca. 1.30 ha. The TF material is mixed with approximately equal but somewhat more extensive Late Aztec ceramics (Zu-Az-245). There are no discernible structural remains.
No surface collection made.
Discussion: Like nearby sites Zu-TF-7, -8, -9, and -13–20, this TF site was abandoned prior to the Classic period.
Classification: Small Hamlet, 5–15 people.

SITE NO. Zu-TF-15 [Zu-TF-12(J)]
Date of Survey: Oct. 2, 1973
Location: 491570 E, 2187300 N; 19.7815° N, 99.0805° W
Natural Setting: 2255 m asl, on nearly level ground on the Lakeshore Plain; deep soil cover and slight erosion. Together with sites Zu-TF-13, Zu-TF-14, and Zu-TF-16–Zu-TF-26, this site occupies a topographic elevation (ancient beach ridges and intervening strand plain) several meters above the general level of the surrounding Lakeshore Plain (Frederick et al. 2005:75) (Fig. 2.4).
Modern Land Use: Rainfall-based agriculture.
Archaeological Remains: Light Terminal Formative surface pottery over an area of ca. 1.1 ha. There are no discernible structural remains.
No surface collection made.
Discussion: Like nearby sites Zu-TF-7, -8, -9, -13–19, and -22–24, this TF site was abandoned prior to the Classic period.
Classification: Small Hamlet, 5–10 people.

SITE NO. Zu-TF-16 [Zu-TF-6(J)]
Date of Survey: Oct. 1, 1973
Location: 491550 E, 2187050 N; 19.7792° N, 99.0807° W
Natural Setting: 2250 m asl, on nearly level ground on the Lakeshore Plain; deep soil cover and slight erosion. Together with sites Zu-TF-13–Zu-TF-25 and Zu-TF-17–Zu-TF-26, this site occupies a topographic elevation (ancient beach ridges and intervening strand plain) several meters above the general level of the surrounding Lakeshore Plain (Frederick et al. 2005:75) (Fig. 2.4).
Modern Land Use: Rainfall-based agriculture.
Archaeological Remains: Light Terminal Formative surface pottery over an area of ca. 1.80 ha. The TF material is mixed with approximately equal amounts of Aztec ceramics (Zu-Az-246). The TF occupation is roughly coextensive with, but slightly larger than, the Aztec site. There are no discernible structural remains.
No surface collection made.
Discussion: Like nearby sites Zu-TF-7, -8, -9, -13–19, and -22–24, this TF site was abandoned prior to the Classic period.
Classification: Small Hamlet, 10–20 people.

SITE NO. Zu-TF-17 [Zu-TF-9(J)]
Date of Survey: Oct. 1, 1973
Location: 492600 E, 2187400 N; 19.7824° N, 99.0706° W
Natural Setting: 2260 m asl, on nearly level ground on the Lakeshore Plain; deep soil cover and slight erosion. Together with sites Zu-TF-13–Zu-TF-16 and Zu-TF-18–Zu-TF-26, this site occupies a topographic elevation (ancient beach ridges and intervening strand plain) several meters above the general level of the surrounding Lakeshore Plain (Frederick et al. 2005:75) (Fig. 2.4).
Modern Land Use: Rainfall-based agriculture.
Archaeological Remains: Light Terminal Formative surface pottery over an area of ca. 3.50 ha. There are no discernible structural remains.
No surface collection made.
Discussion: Like nearby sites Zu-TF-7, -8, -9, -13–19, and -22–24, this TF site was abandoned prior to the Classic period.
Classification: Hamlet, 20–40 people.

SITE NO. Zu-TF-18 [Zu-TF-10(J)]
Date of Survey: Oct. 1, 1973
Location: 492600 E, 2187970 N; 19.7875° N, 99.0706° W
Natural Setting: 2255 m asl, on nearly level ground on the Lakeshore Plain; medium soil cover and slight erosion. Together with sites Zu-TF-13–Zu-TF-17 and Zu-TF-19–Zu-TF-26, this site occupies a topographic elevation (ancient beach ridges and intervening strand plain) several meters above the general level of the surrounding Lakeshore Plain (Frederick et al. 2005:75) (Fig. 2.4).
Modern Utilization: Rainfall-based agriculture. Several modern drainage ditches cut through the site area.
Archaeological Remains: Light Terminal Formative surface pottery over an area of ca. 1.00 ha. There are no discernible structural remains.
No surface collection made.
Discussion: Like nearby sites Zu-TF-7, -8, -9, -13–20, and -22–24, this site lacks Classic occupation.
Classification: Small Hamlet, 5–10 people.

SITE NO. Zu-TF-19 [Zu-TF-11(J)]
Date of Survey: Oct. 1, 1973
Location: 492700 E, 2186650 N; 19.7756° N, 99.0697° W
Natural Setting: 2250 m asl, on nearly level ground on the Lakeshore Plain, near the northern edge of Lake Xaltocán-Zumpango; medium soil cover and slight erosion. Together with sites Zu-TF-13–Zu-TF-18 and Zu-TF-20–Zu-TF-26, this site occupies a topographic elevation (ancient beach ridges and intervening strand plain) several meters above the general level of the surrounding Lakeshore Plain (Frederick et al. 2005:75) (Fig. 2.4).
Modern Land Use: Rainfall-based agriculture. Several drainage ditches cut through the area. There are scattered modern residences to the west.
Archaeological Remains: Light Terminal Formative surface pottery over an area of ca. 0.80 ha. There are no discernible structural remains.
No surface collection made.
Discussion: Like nearby sites Zu-TF-7, -8, -9, -13–20, and -22–24, this TF site was abandoned prior to the Classic period.
Classification: Small Hamlet, 5–10 people.

Plate A5. Zu-TF-20, facing north over Location 68.

SITE NO. Zu-TF-20 [Zu-TF-5(J); Location 68]
Date of Survey: Oct. 1, 1973
Location: 492470 E, 2186350 N; 19.7729° N, 99.0719° W
Natural Setting: 2245 m asl, on nearly level ground on the Lakeshore Plain, near the northern edge of Lake Xaltocán-Zumpango; deep soil cover and slight erosion. Together with sites Zu-TF-13–Zu-TF-19 and Zu-TF-21–Zu-TF-26, this site occupies a topographic elevation (ancient beach ridges and intervening strand plain) several meters above the general level of the surrounding Lakeshore Plain (Frederick et al. 2005:75) (Fig. 2.4).
Modern Land Use: Rainfall-based agriculture. Most of the site area is presently lying fallow. A modern dirt road borders the southeast edge of the site.
Archaeological Remains: Variable light and light-to-moderate Terminal Formative surface pottery over an area of ca. 3.00 ha. Mixed with traces of Late Toltec and Late Aztec ceramics (no LT or Az sites designated). We noted a few green and gray obsidian chips. There is no rock rubble and no discernible structural remains.

We made one surface collection (Location 68) over an area ca. 20 × 20 m in a fallow field (Plate A5), with light-to-moderate TF and traces of LT and Az surface pottery, several obsidian artifacts, and very little rock rubble.

Discussion: Like nearby sites Zu-TF-7, -8, -9, -13–19, and -22–24, this TF site was abandoned prior to the Classic period.
Classification: Hamlet, 30–60 people.

SITE NO. Zu-TF-21 [Zu-Cl-37(J); Locations 73, 74]
Date of Survey: Oct. 10, 1973
Location: 495000 E, 2186650 N; 19.7756° N, 99.0477° W
Natural Setting: 2245 m asl, on nearly level ground atop a low elevation that rises to a maximum height of about 1.00 m above the surrounding Lakeshore Plain, near the northern edge of Lake Xaltocán-Zumpango; medium soil cover and slight erosion. Together with sites Zu-TF-13–Zu-TF-20 and Zu-TF-22–Zu-TF-26, this site occupies a topographic elevation (ancient beach ridges and intervening strand plain) several meters above the general level of the surrounding Lakeshore Plain (Frederick et al. 2005:75) (Fig. 2.4).
Modern Land Use: Rainfall-based agriculture. A modern dirt road borders the west edge of the site.
Archaeological Remains: Light Terminal Formative surface pottery over an area of ca. 0.80 ha. Mixed with slightly heavier Classic (Zu-Cl-76), and approximately equal amounts of Late Toltec ceramics (Zu-LT-174). Both the Cl and LT occupations are more extensive than the Terminal Formative. We noted several obsidian blades (both green and gray), and several obsidian fragments. There is light rock rubble and no discernible structural remains.

We made two surface collections (Locations 73, 74):

Location	Area and Context	Content
73	20 × 20 m, in maize field	Light-to-moderate Cl and LT and light TF surface pottery; light rock rubble.
74	10 × 15 m, in maize field	Light-to-moderate LT and light Cl and TF surface pottery; very little rock rubble.

Discussion: A small TF occupation overlain by a larger Classic settlement.
Classification: Small Hamlet, 5–10 people.

SITE NO. Zu-TF-22 [Zu-TF-16(J); Location 78]
   Date of Survey: Oct. 14, 1973
   Location: 494030 E, 2185570 N; 19.7658° N, 99.0570° W
   Natural Setting: 2245 m asl, on nearly level ground on the Lakeshore Plain, near the northern edge of Lake Xaltocán-Zumpango; deep soil cover and slight erosion. Together with sites Zu-TF-13–Zu-TF-21 and Zu-TF-23–Zu-TF-26, this site occupies a topographic elevation (ancient beach ridges and intervening strand plain) several meters above the general level of the surrounding Lakeshore Plain (Frederick et al. 2005:75) (Fig. 2.4).
   Modern Land Use: Rainfall-based agriculture. A modern dirt road skirts the west edge of the site.
   Archaeological Remains: Variable light and light-to-moderate Terminal Formative surface pottery over an area of ca. 1.2 ha. We noted several gray obsidian blades and fragments. There is no rock rubble and no discernible structural remains.
   We made one surface collection (Location 78) over an area ca. 15 × 25 m in a maize field (Plate A6), with light-to-moderate TF, several obsidian artifacts, and no rock rubble.
   Discussion: Like nearby sites Zu-TF-7, -8, -9, -13–20, and -23–24, this TF site was abandoned prior to the Classic period.
   Classification: Small Hamlet, 15–30 people.

SITE NO. Zu-TF-23 [Zu-TF-15(J)]
   Date of Survey: Oct. 11, 1973
   Location: 493470 E, 2185500 N; 19.7652° N, 99.0623° W
   Natural Setting: 2245 m asl, on gently sloping ground atop a broad, low ridge rising about 1.00 m above the general level of the surrounding Lakeshore Plain, near the north edge of Lake Xaltocán-Zumpango; medium soil cover, slight erosion. Together with sites Zu-TF-13–Zu-TF-22 and Zu-TF-24–Zu-TF-26, this site occupies a topographic elevation (ancient beach ridges and intervening strand plain) several meters above the general level of the surrounding Lakeshore Plain (Frederick et al. 2005:75) (Fig. 2.4).
   Modern Land Use: Rainfall-based agriculture.
   Archaeological Remains: Light Terminal Formative surface pottery over an area of ca. 0.90 ha. The TF material is mixed with heavier and more extensive Late Toltec (Zu-LT-176) ceramics. There are no discernible structural remains.
   No surface collection made.
   Discussion: Like nearby sites Zu-TF-7, -8, -9, -13–20, and -22–24, this TF site was abandoned prior to the Classic period. The supporting elevation may be partly, or wholly, artificial. This may be a good location for future excavation in a relatively undisturbed (in 1973) deep-soil deposit.
   Classification: Small Hamlet, 5–10 people.

SITE NO. Zu-TF-24 [Zu-TF -14(J); Location 76]
   Date of Survey: Oct. 11, 1973
   Location: 493350 E, 2185280 N; 19.7632° N, 99.0635° W
   Natural Setting: 2245 m asl, on gently sloping ground atop a low, broad elevation that stands about 1.50–2.00 m above the general level of the surrounding Lakeshore Plain, near the northern edge of Lake Xaltocán-Zumpango; medium to deep soil cover and slight erosion. Together with sites Zu-TF-13–Zu-TF-23, Zu-TF-25, and Zu-TF-26, this site occupies a topographic elevation (ancient beach ridges and intervening strand plain) several meters above the general level of the surrounding Lakeshore Plain (Frederick et al. 2005:75) (Fig. 2.4).
   Modern Land Use: The immediate site area is presently fallow. The general area is devoted to rainfall-based agriculture.
   Archaeological Remains: Light Terminal Formative surface pottery over an area of ca. 1.40 ha. The TF material is mixed with heavier and more extensive Late Toltec (Zu-LT-176) ceramics. We noted several green and gray obsidian blades, flakes, cores, and chips. There is no rock rubble and no definite structural remains.
   We made one surface collection (Location 76) over an area of ca. 20 × 20 m in a fallow field with light TF and light-to-moderate LT surface pottery, several obsidian artifacts, and no rock rubble.
   Discussion: In light of Frederick et al.'s (2005) geoarchaeological study, the supporting elevation is probably mainly natural. This may be a good location for excavation in a relatively undisturbed (in 1973) deep-soil deposit.
   Like nearby sites Zu-TF-7, -8, -9, -13–20, and -22–23, this TF site was abandoned prior to the Classic period.
   Classification: Small Hamlet, 10–20 people.

SITE NO. Zu-TF-25 [Zu-TF-13(J); Location 75]
   Date of Survey: Oct. 11, 1973
   Location: 492630 E, 2184900 N; 19.7598° N, 99.0703° W
   Natural Setting: 2245 m asl, on gently sloping ground on the Lakeshore Plain, near the northern edge of Lake Xaltocán-Zumpango; deep soil cover and slight erosion. Together with sites Zu-TF-13–Zu-TF-24 and Zu-TF-26, this site occupies a topographic elevation (ancient beach ridges and intervening strand plain) several meters above the general level of the surrounding Lakeshore Plain (Frederick et al. 2005:75) (Fig. 2.4).
   Modern Land Use: Rainfall-based agriculture. Several modern dirt roads cross the east and west edges of the site area.
   Archaeological Remains: Light and light-to-moderate Terminal Formative surface pottery over an area of ca. 4.00 ha. Mixed with approximately equal amounts of Classic (Zu-Cl-79) ceramics in the eastern two-thirds of the site. We noted several obsidian blades, flakes, and chips (mainly gray in color). There is no rock rubble and no discernible structural remains.
   We made one surface collection (Location 75) over a triangular area ca. 15 m on a side in a maize field (Plate A7), with light-to-moderate TF and light Cl surface pottery, a few obsidian artifacts, and no rock rubble.
   Discussion: Mixed TF and Cl occupation.
   Classification: Hamlet, 50–100 people.

SITE NO. Zu-TF-26 [Zu-Cl-40(J); Location 85]
   Date of Survey: Oct. 23, 1973
   Location: 492970 E, 2184000 N; 19.7516° N, 99.0671° W
   Natural Setting: 2245 m asl, on gently sloping ground on the Lakeshore Plain, near the northern edge of Lake Xaltocán-Zumpango; deep soil cover and slight erosion.
   Modern Land Use: Rainfall-based agriculture. The northeastern edge of the modern town of Nextlalpan is ca. 100 m to the south.
   Archaeological Remains: Variable very light and light Terminal Formative surface pottery over an area of ca. 0.50 ha. The TF material is mixed with heavier and more extensive Classic ceramics (Zu-Cl-81). We noted several obsidian blades and chips (both green and gray in color). There is no rock rubble and no discernible structural remains.
   We made one surface collection (Location 85) over an area ca. 15 × 20 m in a maize field with light TF and light-to-moderate Cl surface pottery, a few obsidian artifacts, and no rock rubble.
   Discussion: A small TF occupation overlain by a larger Classic settlement.
   Classification: Small Hamlet, 2–5 people.

Plate A6. Zu-TF-22, facing east over Location 78.

Plate A7. Zu-TF-25, facing SW over Location 75.

Classic Sites (Fig. A3)

In an earlier publication (Parsons et al. 1983), we subdivided Classic-period sites into Early Classic (EC) and Late Classic (LC) designations. Even at that time, we were not completely confident of our ability (in 1973) to differentiate clearly between Classic assemblages in our generally small and badly eroded surface collections. In the intervening years, we have realized that we were somewhat inconsistent and premature in making this distinction. To simplify our presentation in the present monograph, we use a single Classic-period site designation (Cl) and number for each Classic site. In most cases, this site number is different from either the EC or LC site numbers in the 1983 publication. In most (but not all) cases, Classic sites appear to have both Early Classic and Late Classic components. In the 1983 monograph, we did not assign both an Early and Late Classic site number to sites where one component was judged to be absent or much lighter than the other; however, we were somewhat inconsistent in this practice. In this chapter, we list the 1983 EC and LC site numbers in brackets after the general Classic site number, and whatever "Location" or "Feature" designations apply, as well as the site's original field number.

SITE NO. Zu-CL-1 [Zu-Cl-8(J); Location 20; Zu-LC-1]
Date of Survey: June 11, 1973
Location: 497050 E, 2210470 N; 19.9909° N, 99.0282° W
Natural Setting: 2390 m asl, on gently sloping ground in the Upper Salado Drainage; medium soil cover and slight erosion.
Modern Land Use: Rainfall-based agriculture.
Archaeological Remains: Variable light and light-to-moderate Classic surface pottery over an area of ca. 5.70 ha. We noted several obsidian blades and fragments (mostly green in color), and one obsidian scraper. There is light rock rubble and no discernible structural remains.
We made one surface collection (Location 20) over an area ca. 15 × 30 m in a fallow field (Plate A8), with light Cl surface pottery, a few obsidian artifacts, and very little rock rubble.
Classification: Small Dispersed Village, 55–110 people.

SITE NO. Zu-Cl-2 [Zu-Cl-4(J); Location 10; Zu-LC-2]
Date of Survey: May 31, 1973
Location: 496030 E, 2207000 N; 19.95945° N, 99.0379° W
Natural Setting: 2360 m asl, on gently sloping ground in the Upper Salado Drainage; medium soil cover and slight erosion over most of the site, and severe erosion along its southern and southwestern edges.
Modern Land Use: Rainfall-based agriculture. Strips of nopal cactus and maguey separate small cultivated fields. A modern dirt road borders the site's southwestern edge.
Archaeological Remains: Variable light, light-to-moderate, and moderate Classic surface pottery over an area of ca. 8.2 ha. Mixed with a trace of Aztec ceramics (no Az site designated). We noted several green obsidian blades. There is moderate rock rubble, but no discernible structural remains.
We made one surface collection (Location 10) over an area ca. 5 × 8 m in a fallow field (Plate A9) with moderate Cl and traces of Az surface pottery, several obsidian artifacts, and moderate rock rubble.
Classification: Small Nucleated Village, 130–260 people.

SITE NO. Zu-Cl-3 [Zu-Cl-5(J); Location 9; Zu-EC-1, Zu-LC-3]
Date of Survey: May 31, 1973
Location: 495850 E, 2206150 N; 19.9518° N, 99.0397° W
Natural Setting: 2350 m asl, on gently sloping ground in the Upper Salado Drainage; medium soil cover and slight erosion.
Modern Land Use: Rainfall-based agriculture. A modern dirt road crosses the southwestern edge of the site.
Archaeological Remains: Variable light, light-to-moderate, and moderate Classic surface pottery over an area of ca. 5.10 ha. We noted a few green obsidian blades and fragments. There is very little rock rubble and no discernible structural remains.
We made one surface collection (Location 9) over an area ca. 20 × 20 m in a fallow field (Plate A10), with light-to-moderate Cl surface pottery, a few obsidian artifacts, and very little rock rubble.
Classification: Small Nucleated Village, 100–200 people.

SITE NO. Zu-Cl-4 [Zu-Cl-3(J); Location 7; Zu-EC-2]
Date of Survey: May 29, 1973
Location: 495250 E, 2206180 N; 19.9521° N, 99.0454° W
Natural Setting: 2340 m asl, on gently sloping ground in the Upper Salado Drainage; medium soil cover and slight erosion.
Modern Land Use: Rainfall-based agriculture. A modern dirt road skirts the eastern edge of the site.
Archaeological Remains: Light-to-moderate Classic surface pottery over an area of ca. 1.70 ha. The Cl material is mixed with a trace of Aztec ceramics (no Az site designated). We noted several green obsidian blades, one gray obsidian scraper, and one gray obsidian projectile point. There are no discernible structural remains.
We made one surface collection (Location 7) over an area ca. 15 × 15 m in a fallow field (Plate A11), with light-to-moderate Cl and traces of Az surface pottery, numerous obsidian artifacts, and moderate rock rubble.
Classification: Hamlet, 30–60 people.

SITE NO. Zu-Cl-5 [Zu-Cl-2(J); Zu-EC-3, Zu-LC-4]
Date of Survey: May 28, 1973
Location: 494000 E, 2205350 N; 19.9446° N, 99.0573° W
Natural Setting: 2340 m asl, on gently sloping ground in the Upper Salado Drainage; medium soil cover and slight erosion.
Modern Land Use: Rainfall-based agriculture. A modern dirt road cuts through the eastern half of the site.
Archaeological Remains: Variable very light and light Classic surface pottery over an area of ca. 3.00 ha. There are no discernible structural remains.
No surface collection made.
Classification: Hamlet, 15–30 people.

SITE NO. Zu-Cl-6 [Zu-Cl-1(J); Location 4; Zu-LC-5]
Date of Survey: May 28, 1973
Location: 493650 E, 2205820 N; 19.9488° N, 99.0607° W
Natural Setting: 2345 m asl, on gently sloping ground in the Upper Salado Drainage (Plate A12); medium soil cover and slight erosion.
Modern Land Use: Rainfall-based agriculture. A modern dirt road crosses the western part of the site.
Archaeological Remains: Variable light, light-to-moderate, and moderate Classic surface pottery over an area of ca. 4.40 ha. The Cl material is mixed with lighter Early Toltec ceramics (Zu-ET-2), and a trace of Aztec pottery (no Az site designated). We noted several green obsidian blades and fragments, and several chert fragments. There is light rock rubble and no discernible structural remains.
We made one surface collection (Location 4) over an area ca. 8 × 10 m in a plowed field with moderate Cl surface pottery, several obsidian and chert artifacts, and light rock rubble.
Discussion: One of the relatively few Classic settlements with continued occupation into the Early Toltec period.
Classification: Small Nucleated Village, 70–140 people.

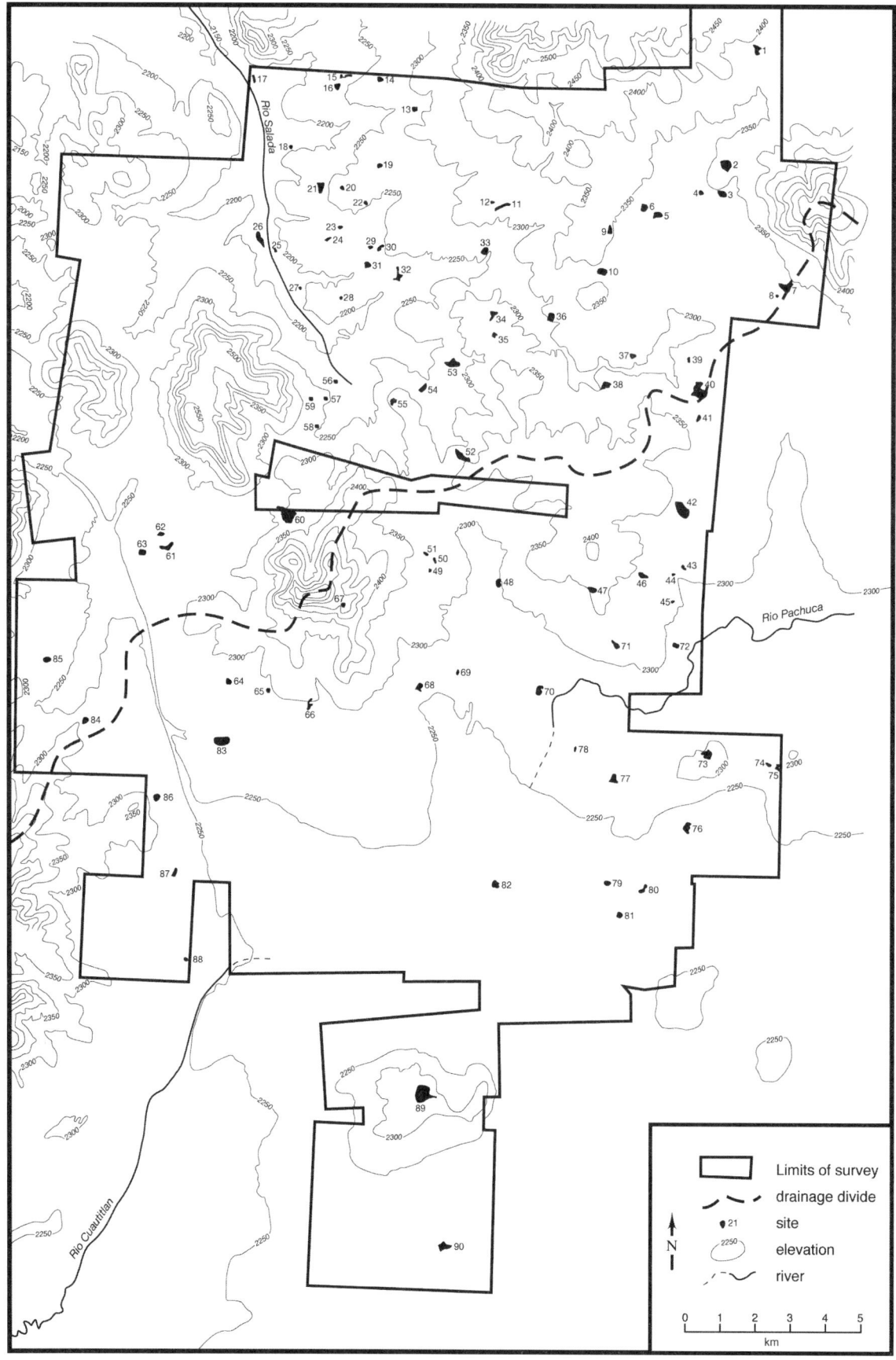

Figure A3. Map of Classic sites in the Zumpango Region.

Plate A8. Zu-Cl-1, facing north over Location 20.

Plate A9. Zu-Cl-2, facing SW over Location 10.

Plate A10. Zu-Cl-3, facing south over Location 9.

Plate A11. Zu-Cl-4, facing NE at Location 7.

Plate A12. Zu-Cl-6, facing SW over site area.

SITE NO. Zu-Cl-7 [Zu-Cl-7(J); Location 13; Zu-EC-4, Zu-LC-6]
  Date of Survey: June 4, 1973
  Location: 497780 E, 2203320 N; 19.9262° N, 99.0212° W
  Natural Setting: 2340 m asl, on gently sloping ground in the Upper Salado Drainage, very close to the divide between the Upper Salado and Basin of Mexico drainages; medium soil cover and slight erosion.
  Modern Land Use: Rainfall-based agriculture. The southwestern edge of the modern town of Nopala is about 50 m from the north edge of the site. Several modern dirt roads running south from Nopala cross the site area.
  Archaeological Remains: Variable light, light-to-moderate, moderate, and heavy Classic surface pottery over a vaguely mounded area of ca. 3.50 ha. The Cl material is mixed with lighter Late Toltec (Zu-LT-38), and approximately equal quantities of Late Aztec (Zu-Az-18) ceramics. There are scattered amorphous concentrations of rock rubble, but no discernible structural remains.
  We made one surface collection (Location 13) over an area of ca. 5 × 5 m in a plowed field, with moderate-to-heavy Classic and very light LT and Az surface pottery, several obsidian artifacts, some chert debris, and moderate rock rubble.
  Classification: Hamlet, 40–80 people.

SITE NO. Zu-Cl-8 [Zu-Cl-6(J); Feature O; Zu-EC-5, Zu-LC-7]
  Date of Survey: June 4, 1973
  Location: 497500 E, 2203100 N; 19.9243° N, 99.0239° W
  Natural Setting: 2330 m asl, on gently sloping ground in the Upper Salado Drainage, very close to the divide between the Upper Salado and Basin of Mexico drainages; medium soil cover and slight erosion.
  Modern Land Use: Rainfall-based agriculture.
  Archaeological Remains: Light Classic surface pottery over an area of ca. 0.50 ha. The Cl material is mixed with approximately equivalent amounts of Late Toltec (Zu-LT-38) and heavier Late Aztec (Zu-Az-19) ceramics.
  There is a single discernible mound (Feature O), which is probably an Aztec feature. This feature measures ca. 35 m in diameter and 1.50 m high, with light-to-moderate Cl, LT, and Late Az surface pottery; several obsidian artifacts; and moderate rock rubble on and around the structure. A large looter's pit in the center of this feature reveals solid earth and rock-rubble construction. We noted several green obsidian blades and fragments.
  We made one surface collection from an area ca. 10 × 10 m around the looter's pit and on the west side of the Feature O mound.
  Discussion: The age of the Feature O mound is uncertain. We suspect its main construction and use dates to the Late Aztec period.
  Classification: Small Hamlet, 5–10 people.

SITE NO. Zu-Cl-9 [Zu-Cl-9(J); Zu-EC-6, Zu-LC-8]
  Date of Survey: June 14, 1973
  Location: 492600 E, 2204850 N; 19.9401° N, 99.0707° W
  Natural Setting: 2355 m asl, on gently sloping ground in the Upper Salado Drainage; medium soil cover and slight erosion.
  Modern Land Use: Rainfall-based agriculture.
  Archaeological Remains: Light Classic surface pottery over an area of ca. 1.80 ha. There are no discernible structural remains.
  No surface collection made.
  Classification: Small Hamlet, 10–20 people.

Plate A13. Zu-Cl-10, facing north over Location 24.

SITE NO. Zu-Cl-10 [Zu-Cl-10(J); Location 24; Zu-EC-7, Zu-LC-9]
Date of Survey: June 14, 1973
Location: 492320 E, 2203650 N; 19.9292° N, 99.0734° W
Natural Setting: 2345 m asl, on gently sloping ground in the Upper Salado Drainage; deep soil cover and slight erosion.
Modern Land Use: Rainfall-based agriculture.
Archaeological Remains: Variable light, light-to-moderate, and moderate Classic surface pottery over an area of ca. 3.00 ha. The Cl material is mixed with approximately equal quantities of Early Toltec ceramics (Zu-ET-3) in the northern half of the site. Traces of Late Toltec and Aztec surface pottery are also present (no LT or Az sites designated). There is very little rock rubble and no discernible structural remains.

We made one surface collection (Location 24) over an area ca. 10 × 15 m in a fallow field (Plate A13), with moderate Cl surface pottery (including one Early Classic figurine), several obsidian artifacts, and very little rock rubble.
Discussion: One of the few Classic sites with continued occupation into the Early Toltec period.
Classification: Hamlet, 35–70 people.

SITE NO. Zu-Cl-11 [Zu-Cl-16(M); Features AU, AV; Location 36; Zu-EC-8, Zu-LC-10]
Date of Survey: June 17, 1973
Location: 489250 E, 2205600 N; 19.9468° N, 99.1027° W
Natural Setting: 2320 m asl, on gently sloping ground in the Upper Salado Drainage; shallow soil cover and severe erosion, with much exposed tepetate (Plate A14).
Modern Land Use: Limited rainfall-based agriculture, with some maguey semi-terracing. Some erosion control has been attempted using small check dams.
Archaeological Remains: Variable light and light-to-moderate Classic surface pottery over an area of ca. 2.40 ha. The Cl material is mixed with lighter Terminal Formative (Zu-TF-1), Late Toltec (Zu-LT-25), and Late Aztec (Zu-Az-29) ceramics. There are substantial quantities of obsidian: chips, several scrapers and blades and one projectile point made of gray obsidian, and several green obsidian blades. We noted a few pieces of worked quartzite or chert.

There are two discernible mounds (Features AU, AV):

Fea.	Area and Context	Height	Content
AU	7 × 13 m, in unplowed area (Plate A15). Badly eroded on west side.	2.00 m	Moderate Cl and TF surface pottery; light rock rubble. One surface collection from area 3 × 3 m on mound surface.
AV	8 × 14 m, in unplowed area (Plate A16).	1.50 m	Light Cl and very light Late Az (both Az III and IV B/O) surface pottery. A looter's pit shows solid earth and rock-rubble construction.

We made a second surface collection (Location 36) in an unplowed area over an area of ca. 3 × 4 m with moderate Cl, light-to-moderate Late Az, and traces of LT surface pottery; several obsidian artifacts; and light-to-moderate rock rubble.
Discussion: The ages of Features AU and AV are uncertain; we suspect their main construction and use are Late Az.
Classification: Hamlet, 25–50 people.

SITE NO. Zu-Cl-12 [Zu-Cl-15(M); Zu-EC-9, Zu-LC-11]
Date of Survey: June 17, 1973
Location: 488950 E, 2205700 N; 19.9477° N, 99.1056° W
Natural Setting: 2320 m asl, on gently sloping ground in the Upper Salado Drainage; shallow soil cover and moderate erosion.
Modern Land Use: Rainfall-based agriculture.
Archaeological Remains: Variable very light and light Classic surface pottery over an area of ca. 0.40 ha. There are no discernible structural remains.

No surface collection made.
Classification: Small Hamlet, 2–5 people.

Plate A14. Zu-Cl-11, general site area.

Plate A15. Zu-Cl-11, facing north at Feature AU.

Plate A16. Zu-Cl-11, facing SE at Feature AV.

SITE NO. Zu-Cl-13 [Zu-Cl-8(M); Location 29; Zu-EC-10, Zu-LC-12]
    Date of Survey: June 10, 1973
    Location: 486470 E, 2208380 N; 19.9719° N, 99.1293° W
    Natural Setting: 2290 m asl, on gently sloping ground in the Upper Salado Drainage; shallow soil cover and moderate erosion.
    Modern Land Use: Rainfall-based agriculture.
    Archaeological Remains: Variable light and light-to-moderate Classic surface pottery over an area of ca. 2.10 ha. We noted several green obsidian artifacts and fragments. There is moderate rock rubble but no discernible structural remains.

We made one surface collection (Location 29) over an area ca. 20 × 20 m in a fallow field (Plate A17), with light-to-moderate Cl surface pottery, several obsidian artifacts, and moderate rock rubble.
    Classification: Hamlet, 20–40 people.

SITE NO. Zu-Cl-14 [Zu-Cl-20(M); Zu-EC-11, Zu-LC-13]
    Date of Survey: June 5, 1973
    Location: 485500 E, 2209350 N; 19.9807° N, 99.1386° W
    Natural Setting: 2260 m asl, on gently sloping ground in the Upper Salado Drainage; medium soil cover and slight erosion.
    Modern Land Use: Rainfall-based agriculture. The northeastern corner of the modern village of Barrio Perez encroaches slightly onto the western edge of the site. There are a few modern drainage ditches in the site area.
    Archaeological Remains: Variable light and light-to-moderate Classic surface pottery over an area of ca. 1.20 ha. Because the survey area terminated south of the site's northern limit, the site's full size could not be determined. There are no discernible structural remains.

No surface collection made.
    Discussion: The surface area of this site remains uncertain.
    Classification: Small Hamlet (?), 5–10 people.

SITE NO. Zu-Cl-15 [Zu-Cl-19(M); Location 26; Feature AD; Zu-EC-12, Zu-LC-14]
    Date of Survey: June 5, 1973
    Location: 484380 E, 2209400 N; 19.9811° N, 99.1493° W
    Natural Setting: 2240 m asl, on gently sloping ground in the Upper Salado Drainage; shallow soil cover and moderate erosion.
    Modern Land Use: Unplowed pasture. There are a few modern drainage ditches in the general area.
    Archaeological Remains: Variable light and light-to-moderate Classic surface pottery over an area of ca. 2.40 ha. The Cl material is mixed with Early Toltec surface pottery (Zu-ET-5) in the western part of the site.

There is a single discernible mound (Feature AD) measuring ca. 20 m in diameter and 1.00 m high, with substantial rock rubble (Plate A18). Surface pottery on the mound is very light Cl, with a trace of Late Az (no Az site designated). We noted several green obsidian flakes, fragments, and one green obsidian projectile point, and one gray obsidian flake tool.

We made one surface collection (Location 26) from an area of unrecorded size in a fallow field with light-to-moderate Cl surface pottery, several obsidian artifacts, and light-to-moderate rock rubble.
    Discussion: The northern limits of the site area were not defined since the site lies at the northern edge of our survey area.
    Classification: Hamlet (?), 20–40 people.

SITE NO. Zu-Cl-16 [Zu-Cl-18(M); Zu-EC-13, Zu-LC-15]
    Date of Survey: June 5, 1973
    Location: 484300 E, 2209050 N; 19.9780° N, 99.1500° W
    Natural Setting: 2240 m asl, on gently sloping ground in the Upper Salado Drainage; shallow soil cover and moderate erosion.
    Modern Land Use: Unplowed pasture.
    Archaeological Remains: Variable light and light-to-moderate Classic surface pottery over an area of ca. 1.60 ha. There are no discernible structural remains, but heavy rock rubble in the northern part of the site may represent the remnants of prehispanic architecture.

No surface collection made.
    Classification: Hamlet, 15–30 people.

Plate A17. Zu-Cl-13, facing east over Location 29.

Plate A18. Zu-Cl-15, facing north at Feature AD.

SITE NO. Zu-Cl-17 [Zu-Cl-17(M); Location 25; Zu-EC-14, Zu-LC-16]
   Date of Survey: June 5, 1973
   Location: 481630 E, 2207130 N; 19.96056° N, 99.1756° W
   Natural Setting: 2170 m asl, on gently sloping ground in the Upper Salado Drainage; deep soil cover and slight erosion.
   Modern Land Use: Rainfall-based agriculture. There are a few modern drainage ditches in the area. A fenced-in area encroaches upon the site from the north and may cover a possible northern extension of the site. The northern edge of the modern town of Apaxco is ca. 100 m to the south.
   Archaeological Remains: Variable light and light-to-moderate Classic surface pottery over an area of ca. 1.10 ha. There are also substantial Early Toltec (Zu-ET-6), and lighter Late Aztec (Zu-Az-48), ceramics. We noted several green obsidian blades and chips, one gray obsidian fragment, and three basalt mano fragments. There is moderate rock rubble, but no discernible structural remains.
   We made one surface collection (Location 25) over an area ca. 8 × 10 m in a fallow field with mixed light-to-moderate Cl and Late Az surface pottery, several obsidian artifacts, and moderate rock rubble.
   Discussion: We were unable to determine the site's northern limits. This is one of the few Cl sites that apparently expanded in size during the subsequent Early Toltec period.
   Classification: Small Hamlet (?), 10–20 people.

SITE NO. Zu-Cl-18 [Zu-Cl-7(M); Zu-EC-15, Zu-LC-17]
   Date of Survey: June 5, 1973
   Location: 482800 E, 2207130 N; 19.9606° N, 99.1644° W
   Natural Setting: 2200 m asl, on gently sloping ground in the Upper Salado Drainage; shallow soil cover and moderate erosion.
   Modern Land Use: Rainfall-based agriculture.
   Archaeological Remains: Light Classic surface pottery over an area of ca. 0.70 ha. There are no discernible structural remains.
   No surface collection made.
   Classification: Small Hamlet, 5–10 people.

SITE NO. Zu-Cl-19 [Zu-Cl-9(M); Location 30; Zu-EC-16, Zu-LC-18]
   Date of Survey: June 11, 1973
   Location: 485500 E, 2206570 N; 19.9556° N, 99.1386° W
   Natural Setting: 2270 m asl, on gently sloping ground in the Upper Salado Drainage; shallow soil cover and severe erosion, with numerous patches of bare tepetate.
   Modern Land Use: Rainfall-based agriculture. The southern part of the site is uncultivated thorn forest.
   Archaeological Remains: Light Classic surface pottery (with a high proportion of ollas) over an area of ca. 1.00 ha. We noted several green obsidian blades and chips, and several basalt mano fragments. There are no discernible structural remains.
   We made one surface collection (Location 30) over an area ca.15 × 20 m at the edge of a plowed field, with light-to-moderate Cl surface pottery, several obsidian artifacts, two basalt mano fragments, and very little rock rubble.
   Classification: Small Hamlet, 5–10 people.

SITE NO. Zu-Cl-20 [Zu-Cl-5(M); Location 21; Zu-EC-17]
   Date of Survey: June 5, 1973
   Location: 484300 E, 2206030 N; 19.9507° N, 99.1500° W
   Natural Setting: 2260 m asl, on nearly level ground in the Upper Salado Drainage; medium soil cover and moderate erosion.
   Modern Land Use: Rainfall-based agriculture. Much of the site area is presently fallow.
   Archaeological Remains: Light Classic surface pottery over an area of ca. 0.50 ha. The Cl material is mixed with lighter Terminal Formative (Zu-TF-2) surface pottery. There are no discernible structural remains.
   We made one surface collection (Location 21) from an area ca. 20 × 25 m in a previously plowed (but currently fallow) field (Plate A19), with light Cl surface pottery, several obsidian artifacts, and very little rock rubble.
   Discussion: One of the few Cl sites in this part of the survey area with antecedent TF occupation.
   Classification: Small Hamlet, 2–5 people.

SITE NO. Zu-Cl-21 [Zu-Cl-6(M); Location 22; Zu-EC-18, Zu-LC-19]
   Date of Survey: June 5, 1973
   Location: 483700 E, 2206070 N; 19.9510° N, 99.1558° W
   Natural Setting: 2240 m asl, on gently sloping ground in the Upper Salado Drainage; medium soil cover and slight erosion.
   Modern Land Use: Rainfall-based agriculture. The site area is presently fallow.
   Archaeological Remains: Variable light, light-to-moderate, and moderate Classic and Early Toltec (Zu-ET-7) surface pottery over an area of ca. 4.5 ha. We noted several green obsidian blades. There is light rock rubble and no discernible structural remains.
   We made one surface collection (Location 22) over an area ca. 5 × 6 m in a fallow field (Plate A20), with moderate Cl surface pottery, several obsidian artifacts, and very little rock rubble.
   Discussion: One of the few Cl sites with continued occupation into the ET period.
   Classification: Hamlet, 50–100 people.

SITE NO. Zu-Cl-22 [Zu-Cl-10(M); Zu-EC-19, Zu-LC-20]
   Date of Survey: June 20, 1973
   Location: 485000 E, 2205570 N; 19.9465° N, 99.1433° W
   Natural Setting: 2255 m asl, on nearly level ground in the Upper Salado Drainage; medium soil cover and slight erosion.
   Modern Land Use: Rainfall-based agriculture.
   Archaeological Remains: Variable light and light-to-moderate Classic surface pottery over an area of ca. 0.70 ha. There are no discernible structural remains.
   No surface collection made.
   Classification: Small Hamlet, 10–20 people.

SITE NO. Zu-Cl-23 [Zu-Cl-4(M); Location 18; Zu-EC-20, Zu-LC-21]
   Date of Survey: June 4, 1973
   Location: 484250 E, 2204880 N; 19.9403° N, 99.1505° W
   Natural Setting: 2230 m asl, on nearly level ground in the Upper Salado Drainage; medium soil cover and slight erosion.
   Modern Land Use: Intensive irrigation cultivation of alfalfa, utilizing *agua negra* pumped from the nearby Río "Gran Canal del Desagüe." This water is distributed to surrounding fields through an extensive system of canals, several of which run through the site.
   Archaeological Remains: Light Classic surface pottery over an area of ca. 0.70 ha. The Cl material is mixed with lighter Early Toltec ceramics (Zu-ET-11). We noted several green obsidian blades, scrapers, and fragments. There are no discernible structural remains.
   We made one surface collection (Location 18) over an area ca. 5 × 20 m in an alfalfa field, with light Cl and ET surface pottery, several obsidian artifacts, and no rock rubble.
   Discussion: Another Cl site with continued occupation into the ET period.
   Classification: Small Hamlet, 5–10 people.

Plate A19. Zu-Cl-20, facing west over Location 21.

Plate A20. Zu-Cl-21, facing west over Location 22.

Plate A21. Zu-Cl-26, canal cutting through field near Location 15.

SITE NO. Zu-Cl-24 [Zu-Cl-3(M); Zu-EC-21, Zu-LC-22]
   Date of Survey: June 4, 1973
   Location: 484030 E, 2204530 N; 19.9371° N, 99.1526° W
   Natural Setting: 2230 m asl, on gently sloping ground in the Upper Salado Drainage; medium soil cover and slight erosion.
   Modern Land Use: Intensive irrigation cultivation of maize, utilizing *agua negra* pumped from the nearby Río "Gran Canal del Desagüe." Water is distributed through an extensive system of canals. A modern dirt road borders the southeast edge of the site.
   Archaeological Remains: Variable very light and light Classic surface pottery over an area of ca. 0.90 ha. There are no discernible structural remains.
   No surface collection made.
   Classification: Small Hamlet, 5–10 people.

SITE NO. Zu-Cl-25 [Zu-Cl-2(M); Location 16; Zu-EC-22, Zu-LC-23]
   Date of Survey: June 3, 1973
   Location: 482280 E, 2204150 N; 19.9337° N, 99.1693° W
   Natural Setting: 2190 m asl, on nearly level ground in the Upper Salado Drainage; deep soil cover and slight erosion.
   Modern Land Use: Intensive irrigation cultivation of alfalfa, utilizing *agua negra* pumped from the nearby Río "Gran Canal del Desagüe" through an extensive network of canals. One of these canals runs north-south through the center of the site. A modern dirt road borders the west edge of the site.
   Archaeological Remains: Light Classic surface pottery over an area of ca. 0.40 ha. We noted several green obsidian fragments. There are no discernible structural remains, and very little rock rubble.
   We made one surface collection (Location 16) over an area ca. 20 × 20 m in an unplowed area along the edge of a large earth *bancal* (associated with local irrigation and drainage), with light Cl surface pottery, several obsidian artifacts, and very little rock rubble.
   Discussion: The site has been extensively disturbed by the modern canal.
   Classification: Small Hamlet, 5–10 people.

SITE NO. Zu-Cl-26 [Zu-Cl-1(M); Locations 15A, 15B; Zu-EC-23, Zu-LC-24]
   Date of Survey: May 31, 1973
   Location: 481750 E, 2204500 N; 19.9368° N, 99.1744° W
   Natural Setting: 2190 m asl, on level ground in the Upper Salado Drainage; deep soil cover and slight erosion.
   Modern Land Use: Intensive irrigation agriculture of maize and alfalfa, utilizing *agua negra* from the nearby Río "Gran Canal del Desagüe" through an extensive network of canals. One of these canals cuts through the western edge of the site. Because of the density of the cultivated crops, the site is detectable mainly by sherds appearing along the edges of the canal (Plate A21), although some surface pottery is also visible in the cultivated fields. A modern dirt road crosses the south edge of the site.

Plate A22. Zu-Cl-27, facing SE over Location 55.

Archaeological Remains: Variable very light and light Classic surface pottery over an area of ca. 4.4 ha. We noted several green obsidian fragments. There is very light rock rubble and no discernible structural remains.

We made two surface collections (Locations 15A, 15B):

Location	Area and Context	Content
15A	3 × 15 m, along edge of maize field	Light Cl surface pottery, several obsidian artifacts, and very light rock rubble.
15B	3 × 20 m, along edge of maize field	Light Cl surface pottery, several obsidian artifacts, and very light rock rubble.

Classification: Hamlet, 20–40 people.

SITE NO. Zu-Cl-27 [Zu-Cl-31(M); Location 55; Zu-EC-24, Zu-LC-25]
Date of Survey: July 16, 1973
Location: 483100 E, 2203070 N; 19.9239° N, 99.1615° W
Natural Setting: 2195 m asl, on nearly level ground at the lower edge of a broad, low ridge in the Upper Salado Drainage; medium soil cover and slight erosion.
Modern Land Use: Intensive irrigation cultivation of maize and alfalfa, using *agua negra* from the Río "Canal del Desagüe" ca. 350 m to the southwest.
Archaeological Remains: Variable light and light-to-moderate Classic surface pottery over an area of ca. 1.40 ha; there are also traces of Early Toltec ceramics (no ET site designated). We noted numerous green obsidian blades, one gray obsidian scraper, and one chert flake. There is no rock rubble and no discernible structural remains.

We made one surface collection (Location 55) from an area ca. 8 × 50 m in an alfalfa field (the alfalfa had recently been cut) (Plate A22), with light-to-moderate Cl surface pottery, several obsidian and chert artifacts, and no rock rubble.
Discussion: Occupation may have continued into the ET period.
Classification: Hamlet, 15–30 people.

SITE NO. Zu-Cl-28 [Zu-Cl-32(M); Zu-EC-25, Zu-LC-26]
Date of Survey: July 16, 1973
Location: 484350 E, 2202700 N; 19.9206° N, 99.1495° W
Natural Setting: 2210 m asl, on nearly level ground atop a low, broad ridge in the Upper Salado Drainage; medium soil cover and slight erosion.
Modern Land Use: Intensive irrigation cultivation of maize and alfalfa, using *agua negra* from the Río "Canal del Desaque" ca. 500 m to the south.
Archaeological Remains: Light Classic surface pottery over an area of ca. 0.40 ha. There are no discernible structural remains.

No surface collection made.
Classification: Small Hamlet, 2–5 people.

SITE NO. Zu-Cl-29 [Zu-Cl-11(M); Zu-EC-26, Zu-LC-27]
Date of Survey: June 20, 1973
Location: 485150 E, 2204250 N; 19.9346° N, 99.1419° W
Natural Setting: 2235 m asl, on nearly level ground in the Upper Salado Drainage; medium soil cover and slight erosion.
Modern Land Use: Rainfall-based agriculture.
Archaeological Remains: Light Classic surface pottery over an area of ca. 0.20 ha. There are no discernible structural remains and very little rock rubble.

No surface collection made.
Classification: Small Hamlet, 2–5 people.

Plate A23. Zu-Cl-31, facing SE over site area.

SITE NO. Zu-Cl-30 [Zu-Cl-25(M); Zu-EC-27, Zu-LC-28]
Date of Survey: June 20, 1973
Location: 485550 E, 2204350 N; 19.9355° N, 99.1381° W
Natural Setting: 2245 m asl, on gently sloping ground in the Upper Salado Drainage; medium soil cover and slight erosion.
Modern Land Use: Rainfall-based agriculture.
Archaeological Remains: Variable very light and light Classic surface pottery over an area of ca. 1.50 ha. There are no discernible structural remains.
No surface collection made.
Classification: Small Hamlet, 5–10 people.

SITE NO. Zu-Cl-31 [Zu-Cl-12(M); Location 40; Feature BD; Zu-EC-28, Zu-LC-29]
Date of Survey: June 20, 1973
Location: 485200 E, 2203820 N; 19.9307° N, 99.1414° W
Natural Setting: 2220 m asl, on nearly level ground in the Upper Salado Drainage; medium soil cover and slight erosion.
Modern Land Use: Rainfall-based agriculture.
Archaeological Remains: Variable light and light-to-moderate Classic surface pottery over an area of ca. 2.40 ha. The Cl material is mixed with lighter Early Toltec (Zu-ET-10) ceramics. We noted several green obsidian blades and chips; several gray obsidian blades, scrapers, knives, and chips; and several basalt mano fragments.
There is a single badly plowed-down mound (Feature BD), measuring ca. 70 by 100 m in area and standing ca. 1.00 m high, with light Cl surface pottery, several obsidian artifacts, three basalt mano fragments, and light-to-moderate rock rubble (chunks of tepetate) on its surface.
We made one surface collection (Location 40) over an area ca. 8 × 10 m at the western edge of Feature BD in a plowed field (Plate A23), with light-to-moderate Cl surface pottery, several obsidian artifacts, one basalt mano, one worked chert core, and very light rock rubble.
Discussion: Another small Cl site where occupation continued into the ET period.
Classification: Hamlet, 25–50 people.

SITE NO. Zu-Cl-32 [Zu-Cl-13(M); Location 39; Features AZ, BA; Zu-EC-29, Zu-LC-30]
Date of Survey: June 18, 1973
Location: 486150 E, 2203450 N; 19.9274° N, 99.1323° W
Natural Setting: 2230 m asl, on gently sloping ground immediately to the north and west of the Río Hueypoxtla in the Upper Salado Drainage; deep soil cover and slight erosion.
Modern Land Use: Rainfall-based agriculture. The paved highway to Tlapanaloya crosses the northern end of the site.
Archaeological Remains: Variable light and light-to-moderate Classic surface pottery over an area of ca. 3.90 ha. The Cl material is mixed with lighter Early Toltec (Zu-ET-9) and Late Aztec (Zu-Az-66) ceramics. There are also traces of Late Toltec ceramics (no LT site designated). We noted several green obsidian blades and chips; several gray obsidian scrapers, blades, and chips; and one obsidian projectile point.
There are two mounds (Features AZ, BA) tightly clustered in the west-central part of the site; they may both be Aztec Structures.

Fea.	Area and Context	Height	Content
AZ	13 × 20 m, in plowed field	0.50 m	Light Cl and ET, and very light Az surface pottery; a few obsidian artifacts; moderate rock rubble.
BA	24 m dia., in partly plowed field	1.50 m	Very light Late Az surface pottery; a few obsidian artifacts; light rock rubble.

We made one surface collection (Location 39) over an area ca. 10 × 15 m in an unplowed field, with light-to-moderate Cl, light Late Az, and traces of LT surface pottery, with numerous obsidian artifacts and moderate rock rubble.
Discussion: A unusually long occupational sequence.
Classification: Hamlet, 40–80 people.

SITE NO. Zu-Cl-33 [Zu-Cl-14(M); Locations 8, 9, 34; Features AT, U; Zu-EC-30, Zu-LC-31]
   Date of Survey: June 14, 1973
   Location: 488720 E, 2204250 N; 19.9346° N, 99.1078° W
   Natural Setting: 2260 m asl, on gently sloping ground in the Upper Salado Drainage; deep soil cover and slight erosion.
   Modern Land Use: Rainfall-based agriculture. There are some drainage ditches and limited terracing in the general area. The northwestern corner of the modern town of Tlapanaloya encroaches onto the eastern side of the site. A modern dirt road crosses the site.
   Archaeological Remains: Variable light and light-to-moderate Classic surface pottery over an area of ca. 3.80 ha. The Cl material is mixed with lighter Late Aztec (Zu-Az-71), Early Toltec (Zu-ET-4), and Late Toltec (Zu-LT-60) ceramics. The Cl surface pottery includes an unusual proportion of fancy decorated ceramics. We noted numerous blades and chips of both green and gray obsidian, one green obsidian projectile point, one gray obsidian projectile point, and one basalt metate fragment.
   Two mounds (Features U, AT) are discernible in the eastern half of the site:

Fea.	Area and Context	Height	Content
U	20 × 30 m, in fallow field, cut by road	1.75 m	Light Cl and ET surface pottery; several obsidian artifacts; moderate rock rubble. One surface collection along roadcut over area ca. 2 × 15 m.
AT	32 m dia., in unplowed area	1.75 m	Light Cl and ET surface pottery; moderate rock rubble.

We made three additional surface collections (Locations 8, 9, 34):

Location	Area and Context	Content
8	6 × 6 m, in fallow field	Light-to-moderate Cl surface pottery; numerous obsidian artifacts; one basalt metate fragment; light-to-moderate rock rubble.
9	8 × 10 m, in fallow field (Plate A24)	Light-to-moderate Cl, LT, light ET, and trace Az surface pottery; numerous obsidian artifacts; light-to-moderate rock rubble.
34	7 × 10 m, in plowed field	Moderate Cl, light ET, light LT, and trace Az surface pottery; abundant obsidian; moderate-to-heavy rock rubble.

   Discussion: Long-term occupation.
   Classification: Hamlet, 40–80 people.

SITE NO. Zu-Cl-34 [Zu-Cl-43(J); Location 88; Zu-EC-31, Zu-LC-32]
   Date of Survey: Nov. 1, 1973
   Location: 489050 E, 2202380 N; 19.9177° N, 99.1046° W
   Natural Setting: 2320 m asl, on nearly level ground atop a broad, ridge near the juncture of three major *barrancas* in the Upper Salado Drainage; shallow soil cover and moderate to severe erosion, with patches of bare tepetate along the eastern edge of the site.
   Modern Land Use: Rainfall-based agriculture, with some maguey semi-terracing.
   Archaeological Remains: Variable light and light-to-moderate Classic surface pottery over an area of ca. 3.50 ha. The Cl material is mixed with lighter Terminal Formative (Zu-TF-3) and Late Aztec (Zu-Az-72) ceramics. We noted a few green obsidian blades and chips. There is moderate rock rubble, but no discernible structural remains.
   We made one surface collection (Location 88) from an area ca. 10 × 10 m in a harvested maize field (Plate A25), with light-to-moderate Cl, light TF, and traces of Az surface pottery, a few obsidian artifacts, and moderate rock rubble.
   Discussion: One of the few Cl sites in this part of the survey area with antecedent TF occupation.
   Classification: Hamlet, 35–70 people.

SITE NO. Zu-Cl-35 [Zu-Cl-42(J); Location 87; Zu-EC-32, Zu-LC-33]
   Date of Survey: Oct. 31, 1973
   Location: 489050 E, 2201750 N; 19.9120° N, 99.1046° W
   Natural Setting: 2330 m asl, on gently sloping ground on a low, broad ridge in the Upper Salado Drainage; shallow soil cover and moderate erosion. Five major *barrancas* head in the area to the north, east and west of the site.
   Modern Land Use: Rainfall-based agriculture, with some maguey semi-terracing.
   Archaeological Remains: Variable light and light-to-moderate Classic surface pottery over an area of ca. 1.70 ha. The Cl material is mixed with approximately equal amounts of Late Toltec (Zu-LT-58) ceramics; there are also possible traces of Early Toltec surface pottery (no ET site defined here). We noted several obsidian blades and fragments. There are no discernible structural remains.
   We made one surface collection (Location 87) from an area ca. 15 m in diameter in a maize field, with light-to-moderate LT and Cl surface pottery, a few obsidian artifacts, and light-to-moderate rock rubble.
   Discussion: The possible presence of ET occupation may indicate long-term settlement at this site.
   Classification: Hamlet, 20–40 people.

SITE NO. Zu-Cl-36 [Zu-Cl-41(J); Location 83; Zu-LC-34]
   Date of Survey: Oct. 21, 1973
   Location: 490750 E, 2202030 N; 19.9146° N, 99.0884° W
   Natural Setting: 2305 m asl, on gently sloping ground along the top and upper slopes of a broad, low ridge in the Upper Salado Drainage; shallow soil cover and moderate to severe erosion.
   Modern Land Use: Rainfall-based agriculture, with some maguey semi-terracing.
   Archaeological Remains: Variable light and light-to-moderate Classic surface pottery over an area of ca. 4.00 ha. The Cl material is mixed throughout with lighter Late Aztec ceramics (Zu-Az-102), and a trace of Late Toltec surface pottery in the southwestern sector (no LT site designated). We noted several green and gray obsidian artifacts and chips. There are some areas of heavy rock rubble, but no discernible structural remains.
   We made one surface collection (Location 83) over an area ca. 10 × 15 m in a plowed field, with light-to-moderate Cl and traces of LT surface pottery, several obsidian artifacts, and heavy rock rubble.
   Classification: Hamlet, 40–80 people.

SITE NO. Zu-Cl-37 [Zu-Cl-11(J); Location 27; Zu-EC-33, Zu-LC-35]
   Date of Survey: June 26, 1973
   Location: 493220 E, 2201100 N; 19.9062° N, 99.0648° W
   Natural Setting: 2310 m asl, on gently sloping ground in the Upper Salado Drainage; shallow soil cover and severe erosion.
   Modern Land Use: Marginal pasture. The modern town of Hucypoxtla borders the northwest edge of the site area and may cover part of the prehispanic occupation. A modern dirt road crosses the south edge of the site.

Plate A24. Zu-Cl-33, facing south over Location 9.

Plate A25. Zu-Cl-34, facing south over Location 88.

Archaeological Remains: Variable light and light-to-moderate Classic surface pottery over an area of ca. 2.10 ha. The Cl material is mixed with heavier Late Toltec (Zu-LT-52) and approximately equal amounts of Early Toltec (Zu-ET-15) ceramics. We noted several obsidian blades and scrapers. There is moderate rock rubble, but no discernible structural remains.

We made one surface collection (Location 27) over an area ca. 25 × 25 m in an unplowed area with light-to-moderate Cl and LT, and traces of Late Az surface pottery; several obsidian artifacts; and moderate rock rubble.

Discussion: We were unable to define the site's northern limits. Another Cl site with long-term occupational continuity.

Classification: Hamlet (?), 25–50 people.

SITE NO. Zu-Cl-38 [Zu-Cl-12(J); Location 26; Zu-EC-34, Zu-LC-36]
Date of Survey: June 26, 1973
Location: 492500 E, 2200250 N; 19.8985° N, 99.0717° W
Natural Setting: 2305 m asl, on moderately sloping ground on the western slopes of Cerro de Cerritos in the Upper Salado Drainage; shallow soil cover and severe erosion, with patches of bare tepetate (Plate A26).
Modern Land Use: Unplowed pasture, with maguey semi-terracing.
Archaeological Remains: Variable light and light-to-moderate Classic surface pottery over an area of ca. 5.30 ha. We noted several green and gray obsidian blades and scrapers, and one projectile point. There are no discernible structural remains, although several moderate concentrations of amorphous rock rubble may represent the remnants of ancient buildings.

We made one surface collection (Location 26) over an area ca. 20 × 20 m in unplowed pasture with light-to-moderate Cl surface pottery, several obsidian artifacts, and very little rock rubble.

Classification: Hamlet, 50–100 people.

Site No. Zu-Cl-39 [Zu-Cl-15(J); Zu-EC-35, Zu-LC-37]
Date of Survey: July 11, 1973
Location: 495100 E, 2200930 N; 19.9046° N, 99.0468° W
Natural Setting: 2325 m asl, on gently sloping ground in the Upper Salado Drainage, just north of the divide between the Upper Salado and Basin of Mexico drainages; shallow soil cover and moderate erosion.
Modern Land Use: Rainfall-based agriculture. The site area is presently fallow.
Archaeological Remains: Light Classic surface pottery over an area of ca. 0.60 ha. The Cl material is mixed with approximately equal amounts of Late Aztec (Zu-Az-83) ceramics. There are no discernible structural remains.

No surface collection made.

Classification: Small Hamlet, 5–10 people.

SITE NO. Zu-Cl-40 [Zu-Cl-16(J); Locations 38, 39, 40; Zu-EC-36, Zu-LC-38]
Date of Survey: July 16, 1973
Location: 495380 E, 2202550 N; 19.9193° N, 99.0441° W
Natural Setting: 2320 m asl, on gently sloping ground atop a low, broad ridge in the Upper Salado Drainage (Plate A27), just north of the divide between the Upper Salado and Basin of Mexico drainages; shallow soil cover and slight erosion.
Modern Land Use: Rainfall-based agriculture.
Archaeological Remains: Variable light and light-to-moderate Classic surface pottery over an area of ca. 17.20 ha. The Cl material is mixed with Early Toltec (Zu-ET-16) and Late Toltec (Zu-LT-48, Zu-LT-49) ceramics in the western half of the Classic site. We noted several green and gray obsidian blades, one gray obsidian projectile point, and seven basalt mano fragments. There is light-to-moderate rock rubble, but no discernible structural remains.

We made three surface collections (Locations 38, 39, 40):

Location	Area and Context	Content
38	15 × 15 m, in fallow field	Light-to-moderate Cl, light Late Az and ET, and very light LT surface pottery; several obsidian artifacts; and light rock rubble.
39	5 × 10 m, in fallow field	Light-to-moderate Cl and LT, light ET, and very light Az surface pottery; several obsidian artifacts; and moderate rock rubble.
40	Collection in plowed field (Plate A28)	Light-to-moderate Cl, light LT and ET, and very light Az surface pottery; several obsidian artifacts; and light-to-moderate rock rubble.

Discussion: Long-term settlement continuity at this relatively large Cl site.
Classification: Large Dispersed Village, 300–600 people.

SITE NO. Zu-Cl-41 [Zu-Cl-17(J); Zu-EC-37, Zu-LC-39]
Date of Survey: July 15, 1973
Location: 495300 E, 2201720 N; 19.9118° N, 99.0449° W
Natural Setting: 2330 m asl, on nearly level ground on a broad, low ridge in the Basin of Mexico Lower Piedmont, just south of the divide between the Upper Salado and Basin of Mexico drainages; shallow soil cover and slight erosion.
Modern Land Use: Rainfall-based agriculture.
Archaeological Remains: Variable light and light-to-moderate Classic surface pottery over an area of ca. 0.60 ha. There are no discernible structural remains.

No surface collection made.

Classification: Small Hamlet, 10–20 people.

SITE NO. Zu-Cl-42 [Zu-Cl-18(J); Location 41; Zu-EC-38, Zu-LC-40]
Date of Survey: July 16, 1973
Location: 494930 E, 2196570 N; 19.8652° N, 99.0484° W
Natural Setting: 2340 m asl, on gently sloping ground in the Basin of Mexico Lower Piedmont; shallow soil cover and moderate erosion.
Modern Land Use: Rainfall-based agriculture and unplowed pasture. Two modern dirt roads run through the site area. The eastern edge of the modern town of Jilotzingo encroaches onto the site from the northwest.
Archaeological Remains: Variable light, light-to-moderate, and moderate Classic surface pottery over an area of ca. 16.40 ha. We noted several obsidian artifacts and fragments, and one ceramic figurine. There is very little rock rubble and no clearly discernible structural remains. However, several areas of vague mounding throughout the site may represent remnants of ancient architecture.

We made one surface collection (Location 41) over a slightly mounded area ca. 10 × 15 m in a plowed field (Plate A29), with moderate Cl surface pottery (including one Early Classic figurine), several obsidian artifacts, and very little rock rubble.

Discussion: The slight mounding at Location 41 may indicate subsurface architecture, possibly fairly well preserved. Although the site's northern limits are not well defined, this is clearly one of the larger Classic sites in the Zumpango Region survey area.
Classification: Large Nucleated Village; 350–700 people.

Plate A26. Zu-Cl-38, facing north over site area.

Plate A27. Zu-Cl-40, facing ENE over site area.

Plate A28. Zu-Cl-40, facing north over Location 40.

Plate A29. Zu-Cl-42, facing south over Location 41.

SITE NO. Zu-Cl-43 [Zu-Cl-21(J); Zu-EC-39]
 Date of Survey: July 22, 1973
 Location: 494970 E, 2194820 N; 19.8494° N, 99.0480° W
 Natural Setting: 2310 m asl, on gently sloping ground in the Basin of Mexico Lower Piedmont; medium soil cover and slight erosion.
 Modern Land Use: Rainfall-based agriculture.
 Archaeological Remains: Variable light and light-to-moderate Classic surface pottery over an area of ca. 1.50 ha. There are no discernible structural remains.
 No surface collection made.
 Classification: Hamlet, 15–30 people.

SITE NO. Zu-Cl-44 [Zu-Cl-20(J); Zu-EC-40, Zu-LC-41]
 Date of Survey: July 22, 1973
 Location: 494650 E, 2194630 N; 19.8477° N, 99.0511° W
 Natural Setting: 2310 m asl, on gently sloping ground in the Basin of Mexico Lower Piedmont; medium soil cover and slight erosion.
 Modern Land Use: Rainfall-based agriculture. A modern dirt road crosses the center of the site.
 Archaeological Remains: Light Classic surface pottery over an area of ca. 0.30 ha. There are no discernible structural remains.
 No surface collection made.
 Classification: Small Hamlet, 2–5 people.

SITE NO. Zu-Cl-45 [Zu-Cl-22(J); Zu-EC-41]
 Date of Survey: July 22, 1973
 Location: 494570 E, 2193500 N; 19.8375° N, 99.0519° W
 Natural Setting: 2310 m asl, on gently sloping ground in the Basin of Mexico Lower Piedmont; medium soil cover and slight erosion.
 Modern Land Use: Rainfall-based agriculture. A canalized *barranca* borders the south edge of the site.
 Archaeological Remains: Variable light and light-to-moderate Classic surface pottery over an area of ca. 0.40 ha. There are no discernible structural remains.
 No surface collection made.
 Classification: Small Hamlet, 5–10 people.

SITE NO. Zu-Cl-46 [Zu-Cl-19(J); Location 43; Features CQ, CR, CS; Zu-EC-42, Zu-LC-42]
 Date of Survey: July 22, 1973
 Location: 493700 E, 2194630 N; 19.8477° N, 99.0602° W
 Natural Setting: 2345 m asl, on nearly level ground on a low, broad ridge in the Basin of Mexico Lower Piedmont; shallow soil cover and severe erosion.
 Modern Land Use: Unplowed pasture.
 Archaeological Remains: Variable light and light-to-moderate Classic surface pottery over an area of ca. 3.90 ha. The Cl material is mixed with Late Toltec (Zu-LT-123) and Late Aztec (Zu-Az-172) surface pottery. We noted substantial quantities of green and gray obsidian blades, and one chert projectile point.
 There are three discernible mounds (Features CQ, CR, CS) in the north-central part of the site, and the numerous concentrations of amorphous rock rubble suggest that several more ancient structures probably existed.

Fea.	Area and Context	Height	Content
CQ	15 m dia., in unplowed area	0.10 m	Light-to-moderate Late Az, light Cl and LT surface pottery; several obsidian artifacts; and moderate rock rubble.
CR	10 × 20 m, in unplowed area	0.50 m	Light-to-moderate Cl and Late Az, very light LT surface pottery; several obsidian artifacts; and moderate rock rubble.
CS	15 × 20 m, in unplowed area	0.25 m	Light Cl and light-to-moderate Late Az surface pottery; several obsidian artifacts; and moderate rock rubble.

We made one surface collection (Location 43) over an area ca. 5 × 5 m in a fallow field with moderate Cl and very light Az surface pottery, several obsidian blades, and moderate rock rubble
 Discussion: The ages of Features CQ, CR, and CS are uncertain; we suspect they are primarily Late Aztec in date.
 Classification: Hamlet, 40–80 people.

SITE NO. Zu-Cl-47 [Zu-Cl-24(J); Location 44; Zu-EC-43]
 Date of Survey: July 24, 1973
 Location: 492180 E, 2194150 N; 19.8434° N, 99.0747° W
 Natural Setting: 2355 m asl, on gently sloping ground in the Basin of Mexico Lower Piedmont; medium soil cover and severe erosion.
 Modern Land Use: Unplowed pasture. A modern dirt road borders the south edge of the site.
 Archaeological Remains: Variable light and light-to-moderate Classic surface pottery over an area of ca. 2.70 ha. The Cl material is mixed with Terminal Formative (Zu-TF-5) and lighter Late Aztec (Zu-Az-181) ceramics. We saw very little obsidian. There is light-to-moderate rock rubble, but no discernible structural remains.
 We made one surface collection (Location 44) over an area ca. 15 × 15 m in an unplowed field with light-to-moderate Cl and TF and traces of Late Az surface pottery, a few obsidian artifacts, and light-to-moderate rock rubble.
 Discussion: This is one of the few Cl sites in this part of the survey area with TF antecedents.
 Classification: Hamlet, 30–60 people.

SITE NO. Zu-Cl-48 [Zu-Cl-26(J); Location 48; Zu-EC-44, Zu-LC-43]
 Date of Survey: Aug. 1, 1973
 Location: 489250 E, 2194130 N; 19.8432° N, 99.1027° W
 Natural Setting: 2295 m asl, on nearly level ground at the lower edge of the Basin of Mexico Lower Piedmont, near the upper edge of the Lakeshore Plain; medium soil cover and slight erosion.
 Modern Land Use: Rainfall-based agriculture.
 Archaeological Remains: Light Classic surface pottery over an area of ca. 2.90 ha. The Cl material is mixed with lighter Early Toltec (Zu-ET-18) ceramics. We noted several obsidian blades and scrapers, and one Classic-period two-hole *candelro*. There is light rock rubble and no discernible structural remains.
 We made one surface collection (Location 48) over an area ca. 8 × 10 m in a plowed field (Plate A30), with light-to-moderate Cl surface pottery, a few obsidian artifacts, and light rock rubble.
 Discussion: One of the relatively few Cl sites with continued occupation into the ET period.
 Classification: Hamlet, 15–30 people.

Plate A30. Zu-Cl-48, facing west over Location 48.

SITE NO. Zu-Cl-49 [Zu-Cl-29(M); Location 58; Zu-EC-45, Zu-LC-44]
   Date of Survey: July 19, 1973
   Location: 487180 E, 2194500 N; 19.8465° N, 99.1224° W
   Natural Setting: 2330 m asl, on gently sloping ground in the Basin of Mexico Lower Piedmont; shallow soil cover and moderate erosion.
   Modern Land Use: Rainfall-based agriculture.
   Archaeological Remains: Variable light-to-moderate and moderate Classic surface pottery over an area of ca. 0.30 ha. We noted numerous obsidian blades, one obsidian scraper, and two gray obsidian fragments. There is very little rock rubble and no discernible structural remains.
   We made one surface collection (Location 58) over an area ca. 3 × 6 m in a plowed maize field, with moderate Cl surface pottery, several obsidian artifacts, and no rock rubble.
   Classification: Small Hamlet, 5–10 people.

SITE NO. Zu-Cl-50 [Zu-Cl-28(M); Zu-EC-46, Zu-LC-45]
   Date of Survey: July 19, 1973
   Location: 487220 E, 2194780 N; 19.8490° N, 99.1221° W
   Natural Setting: 2325 m asl, on gently sloping ground in the Basin of Mexico Lower Piedmont; shallow soil cover and moderate erosion.
   Modern Land Use: Rainfall-based agriculture.
   Archaeological Remains: Light Classic surface pottery over an area of ca. 0.40 ha. In the southern half of the site, the Cl material is mixed with heavier and more extensive Late Toltec (Zu-LT-151) ceramics. There are no discernible structural remains in the Classic site.
   No surface collection made in the Classic site.
   Classification: Small Hamlet, 2–5 people.

SITE NO. Zu-Cl-51 [Zu-Cl-27(M); Zu-EC-47, Zu-LC-46]
   Date of Survey: July 19, 1973
   Location: 487070 E, 2194970 N; 19.8507° N, 99.1235° W
   Natural Setting: 2335 m asl, on gently sloping ground in the Basin of Mexico Lower Piedmont; shallow soil cover and moderate erosion.
   Modern Land Use: Rainfall-based agriculture.
   Archaeological Remains: Very light and light Classic surface pottery over an area of ca. 0.60 ha. The Cl material is mixed with lighter Late Aztec ceramics (Zu-Az-201). There are no discernible structural remains.
   No surface collection made.
   Classification: Small Hamlet, 2–5 people.

SITE NO. Zu-Cl-52 [Zu-Cl-14(J); Locations 32, 33, 34, 35, 36; Features BT, BU; Zu-EC-48, Zu-LC-47]
   Date of Survey: July 10, 1973
   Location: 488220 E, 2198050 N; 19.8786° N, 99.1125° W
   Natural Setting: 2330 m asl, primarily on gently sloping ground along the top of a low, broad ridge in the Upper Salado Drainge, just north of the divide between the Upper Salado and Basin of Mexico drainages; medium soil cover and slight erosion. The northeastern section of the site descends onto a steeper, severely eroded hillslope.
   Modern Land Use: Rainfall-based agriculture on the ridge top, and unplowed pasture on the steeper slopes below. Most of the site area is presently fallow.
   Archaeological Remains: Variable light and light-to-moderate Classic surface pottery over an area of ca. 11.80 ha. The Cl material is mixed with about equal amounts of Early Toltec (Zu-ET-17), Late Toltec (Zu-LT-133) and lighter Terminal Formative (Zu-TF-4) ceramics. We noted several scrapers, points, blades, and flakes of green and gray obsidian, and one basalt mano fragment.

Plate A31. Zu-Cl-53, facing NE over Location 31.

There are two discernible mounds (Features BT, BU):

Fea.	Area and Context	Height	Content
BT	15 m dia., in unplowed field	0.75 m	Very light Cl and light LT surface pottery; several obsidian artifacts; and moderate rock rubble.
BU	20 m dia., in unplowed field	1.00 m	Light LT and Cl surface pottery; several obsidian artifacts; and moderate rock rubble.

We made five surface collections (Locations 32, 33, 34, 35, 36):

Location	Area and Context	Content
32	20 × 20 m, in unplowed pasture	Light-to-moderate Cl and ET, light TF, and very light Az surface pottery; several obsidian artifacts; light rock rubble.
33	4 × 6 m, in fallow field	Moderate Cl and ET surface pottery; several obsidian artifacts; moderate rock rubble.
34	10 × 15 m, in plowed field	Light-to-moderate LT, and light Cl and ET surface pottery; several obsidian artifacts; one basalt mano fragment; moderate rock rubble.
35	10 × 10 m, in plowed field	Moderate Cl and ET surface pottery; several obsidian artifacts; one basalt mano fragment; moderate rock rubble.
36	15 × 15 m, in plowed field	Light-to-moderate LT, and light Cl and ET surface pottery (including one E. Cl figurine); several obsidian artifacts; light-to-moderate rock rubble.

Discussion: The ages of Features BT and BU are uncertain; we suspect they are primarily LT in terms of their main construction and use.

Classification: Small Dispersed Village, 160–320 people.

SITE NO. Zu-Cl-53 [Zu-Cl-13(J); Locations 29, 30, 31; Zu-EC-49, Zu-LC-48]

Date of Survey: July 5, 1973
Location: 487900 E, 2200530 N; 19.9010° N, 99.1156° W
Natural Setting: 2280 m asl, on gently sloping ground in the Upper Salado Drainage; medium soil cover and slight erosion.
Modern Land Use: Rainfall-based agriculture. Modern residential structures at the eastern edge of the modern town of Tequixquiac encroach onto the western side of the site.
Archaeological Remains: Variable light and light-to-moderate Classic surface pottery over an area of ca. 8.20 ha. The Cl material is mixed with lighter Early Toltec (Zu-ET-14) and Late Aztec (Zu-Az-113) ceramics, and there is also a trace of Late Toltec pottery (no LT site designated). We noted several green and gray obsidian blades and scrapers, one gray obsidian projectile point, some obsidian debitage, and three ceramic figurines (one Tzacualli, one Classic, one Aztec). There is light-to-moderate rock rubble, but no discernible structural remains.

We made three surface collections (Locations 29, 30, 31):

Location	Area and Context	Content
29	3 × 15 m, in plowed field	Light-to-moderate Cl and very light Az surface pottery, several obsidian artifacts, light-to-moderate rock rubble.
30	15 × 25 m, in plowed field	Light-to-moderate Cl and very light Az surface pottery, several obsidian artifacts, moderate rock rubble.
31	15 × 15 m, in plowed field (Plate A31)	Light-to-moderate Cl and very light Az surface pottery, several obsidian artifacts, light-to-moderate rock rubble.

Discussion: Despite the encroachment of modern occupation, the archaeological site is fairly well defined. Notable long-term settlement continuity.

Classification: Small Dispersed Village, 120–240 people.

SITE NO. Zu-Cl-54 [Zu-Cl-26(M); Location 50; Zu-EC-50, Zu-LC-49]
Date of Survey: July 11, 1973
Location: 486900 E, 2200030 N; 19.8965° N, 99.1252° W
Natural Setting: 2280 m asl, on gently sloping ground in the Upper Salado Drainage; medium soil cover and slight erosion.
Modern Land Use: Rainfall-based agriculture. Part of the site area is presently fallow. A modern dirt road crosses the north edge of the site. Several modern residential structures at the southern edge of the modern town of Tequixquiac encroach onto the northern side of the site.
Archaeological Remains: Light Classic surface pottery over an area of ca. 3.10 ha. The Cl material is mixed with Late Aztec (Zu-Az-115) and lighter Late Toltec (Zu-LT-91) ceramics. We noted numerous green obsidian blades and fragments, one gray obsidian blade and scraper, and one basalt mano fragment. There is light rock rubble and no discernible structural remains.
We made one surface collection (Location 50) over an area ca. 20 × 20 m in a plowed field with light-to-moderate Cl, light Late Az, and traces of LT surface pottery; several obsidian artifacts; one basalt mano fragment; and light rock rubble.
Classification: Hamlet, 15–30 people.

SITE NO. Zu-Cl-55 [Zu-Cl-30(M); Location 53; Zu-EC-51, Zu-LC-50]
Date of Survey: July 15, 1973
Location: 486070 E, 2199630 N; 19.8929° N, 99.1331° W
Natural Setting: 2305 m asl, on nearly level ground in the Upper Salado Drainage; medium soil cover and slight erosion.
Modern Land Use: Rainfall-based agriculture. Scattered modern residential structures border the site on the west.
Archaeological Remains: Variable light and light-to-moderate Classic surface pottery over an area of ca. 3.40 ha. There is also a trace of Aztec ceramics (no Az site designated). We noted several green and gray obsidian blades, scrapers, projectile points, and fragments, and one basalt metate fragment. There is very light rock rubble and no discernible structural remains.
We made one surface collection (Location 53) over an area ca. 7 × 10 m in a plowed field (Plate A32), with light-to-moderate Cl and traces of Late Az surface pottery, several obsidian artifacts, and very little rock rubble.
Classification: Hamlet, 35–70 people.

SITE NO. Zu-Cl-56 [Zu-Cl-24(M); Zu-EC-52, Zu-LC-51]
Date of Survey: June 25, 1973
Location: 484150 E, 2200180 N; 19.8978° N, 99.1514° W
Natural Setting: 2230 m asl, on gently sloping ground in the Upper Salado Drainage; medium soil cover and slight erosion.
Modern Land Use: Rainfall-based cultivation. The modern town of Tequixquiac encroaches onto the site from the west.
Archaeological Remains: Light-to-moderate Classic surface pottery over an area of ca. 0.20 ha. There are no discernible structural remains.
No surface collection made.
Discussion: We could not accurately define the site's western limits.
Classification: Small Hamlet (?), 2–5 people.

SITE NO. Zu-Cl-57 [Zu -Cl-23(M); Zu-EC-53, Zu-LC-52]
Date of Survey: June 25, 1973
Location: 483950 E, 2199630 N; 19.8928° N, 99.1533° W
Natural Setting: 2255 m asl, on gently sloping ground near the foot of the eastern slopes of Cerro de la Mesa Grande in the Upper Salado Drainage; shallow soil cover and severe erosion, with much exposed tepetate.
Modern Land Use: Wasteland.
Archaeological Remains: Light Classic surface pottery over an area of ca. 0.10 ha. There are no discernible structural remains.
No surface collection made.
Classification: Small Hamlet, 2–5 people.

SITE NO. Zu-Cl-58 [Zu-Cl-22(M); Features BN, BO; Zu-EC-54, Zu-LC-53]
Date of Survey: June 25, 1973
Location: 483750 E, 2198800 N; 19.8853° N, 99.1552° W
Natural Setting: 2260 m asl, on gently sloping ground near the foot of the eastern slopes of Cerro de la Mesa Grande in the Upper Salado Drainage; shallow to medium soil cover and severe erosion, with patches of bare tepetate.
Modern Land Use: Rainfall-based agriculture in those areas with sufficient soil cover. Some attempts have been made to reclaim the badly eroded land by using tepetate blocks to construct small terraces and check dams. Several modern dirt roads pass through the eastern and western sides of the site.
Archaeological Remains: Variable light and light-to-moderate Classic surface pottery over an area of ca. 0.50 ha. The Cl material is mixed with lighter Late Toltec (Zu-LT-87) ceramics. We noted several green and gray obsidian blades, scrapers, flakes, and fragments; several chert flakes; and a bone awl.
There are two discernible mounds (Features BN, BO):

Fea.	Area and Context	Height	Content
BN	25 m dia., in plowed field	1.50 m	Light-to-moderate Cl and LT surface pottery, several obsidian artifacts, light-to-moderate rock rubble. Surface collection made over area 6 × 13 m on mound surface.
BO	25 m dia., in plowed field	1.50 m	Light Cl and LT surface pottery, several obsidian artifacts, and unspecified rock rubble concentration.

Discussion: The ages of Features BN and BO are uncertain; we suspect that their primary construction and use is LT.
Classification: Small Hamlet, 5–10 people.

SITE NO. Zu-Cl-59 [Zu-Cl-21(M); Location 41; Zu-EC-55, Zu-LC-54]
Date of Survey: June 21, 1973
Location: 483570 E, 2199720 N; 19.8936° N, 99.1570° W
Natural Setting: 2270 m asl, on gently sloping ground in the Upper Salado Drainage; shallow soil cover and moderate erosion.
Modern Land Use: Fallow agricultural land. The general area is devoted to rainfall-based agriculture. A railroad line passes through the center of the site.
Archaeological Remains: Light-to-moderate Classic surface pottery over an area of ca. 1.40 ha. The Cl material is mixed with approximately equal quantities of Early Toltec ceramics (Zu-ET-13). We noted several green and gray obsidian blades and scrapers. There is very light rock rubble and no discernible structural remains.
We made one surface collection (Location 41) from an area ca. 4 × 5 m in a plowed field (Plate A33), with light-to-moderate Cl and ET surface pottery, several obsidian artifacts, and very little rock rubble.
Discussion: A small Cl site with continued occupation into the ET period.
Classification: Hamlet, 20–40 people.

Plate A32. Zu-Cl-55, facing NW over Location 53.

Plate A33. Zu-Cl-59, facing east over Location 41.

SITE NO. Zu-Cl-60 [Zu-Cl-33(M); Locations 60, 61; Features DQ, DR; Zu-EC-56, Zu-LC-55]
   Date of Survey: July 23–24, 1973
   Location: 482780 E, 2196000 N; 19.8600° N, 99.1645° W
   Natural Setting: 2330 m asl, on nearly level to gently sloping ground in the Upper Salado Drainage; medium to deep soil cover with slight erosion.
   Modern Land Use: Rainfall-based agriculture. The Hacienda "El Comercio" lies just to the west, and a dirt road leading to the hacienda cuts across the center of the site.
   Archaeological Remains: Variable light, light-to-moderate, and moderate-to-heavy Classic surface pottery over an area of ca. 19.50 ha. This site has the most abundant and best preserved Classic surface pottery in the entire Zumpango Region. The Cl material is mixed with lighter Early Toltec (Zu-ET-19) and Aztec (Zu-Az-208) ceramics. We noted numerous green and gray obsidian blades, scrapers, projectile points, and fragments, and numerous basalt mano and metate fragments.

There are two discernible mounds in the southeastern corner of the site (Features DR, DQ):

Fea.	Area and Context	Height	Content
DQ	10 × 10 m, in unplowed field	0.40 m	Light Cl and ET, and very light Az surface pottery; several obsidian artifacts; and moderate rock rubble. A looter's pit shows earth and rock-rubble fill.
DR	8 × 10 m, in unplowed field	0.40 m	Light Cl, very light ET, and very light Az surface pottery; several obsidian artifacts; and moderate rock rubble.

We made two surface collections (Locations 60, 61):

Location	Area and Context	Content
60	20 × 25 m, in plowed field	Light Cl and ET, and very light Az surface pottery; several obsidian artifacts; and light-to-moderate rock rubble.
61	2.5 × 10 m, in plowed field	Moderate-to-heavy Cl, including an E. Cl figurine, light ET, and traces of LT surface pottery; several obsidian artifacts; and light-to-moderate rock rubble.

   Discussion: The ages of Features DQ and DR are uncertain. However, the preponderance of Classic surface pottery suggests that their primary construction and use date to the Classic period. This is one of the largest Classic sites in the Zumpango Region, slightly larger than Zu-Cl-40. Its size and the presence of so much decorated ceramic ware both suggest a degree of sociopolitical significance at the regional level.
   Classification: Local Center, 500–1000 people.

SITE NO. Zu-Cl-61 [Zu-Cl-40(M); Locations 97, 98; Zu-EC-57, Zu-LC-56]
   Date of Survey: Nov. 8, 1973
   Location: 479150 E, 2195050 N; 19.8514° N, 99.1991° W
   Natural Setting: 2265 m asl, on gently sloping ground in the Upper Salado Drainage; medium to deep soil cover and moderate erosion.
   Modern Land Use: Rainfall-based agriculture.
   Archaeological Remains: Variable light, light-to-moderate, and moderate Classic surface pottery over an area of ca. 5.90 ha. We noted several green and gray obsidian blades and one obsidian projectile point. There are no definite structural remains, but abundant rock rubble throughout the site may represent the remains of prehispanic architecture.

We made two surface collections (Locations 97, 98):

Location	Area and Context	Content
97	10 × 15 m, in harvested maize field	Light-to-moderate Cl surface pottery, several obsidian artifacts, and light rock rubble (Plate A34).
98	10 × 15 m, in harvested maize field	Light-to-moderate Cl surface pottery, several obsidian artifacts, and moderate rock rubble.

   Classification: Small Nucleated Village, 100–200 people.

SITE NO. Zu-Cl-62 [Zu-Cl-39(M); Zu-EC-58, Zu-LC-57]
   Date of Survey: Nov. 8, 1973
   Location: 478950 E, 2195430 N; 19.8548° N, 99.2010° W
   Natural Setting: 2270 m asl, on gently sloping ground in the Upper Salado Drainage; medium soil cover and moderate erosion.
   Modern Land Use: Rainfall-based agriculture.
   Archaeological Remains: Variable light and light-to-moderate Classic surface pottery over an area of ca. 2.30 ha. There are no definite structural remains, although several distinct gray-white soil discolorations associated with abundant rock rubble may represent the remnants of prehispanic architecture.

No surface collection made.
   Classification: Hamlet, 25–50 people.

SITE NO. Zu-Cl-63 [Zu-Cl-38(M); Location 83; Zu-EC-59, Zu-LC-58]
   Date of Survey: Nov. 8, 1973
   Location: 478350 E, 2194880 N; 19.8499° N, 99.2068° W
   Natural Setting: 2260 m asl, on gently sloping ground in the Upper Salado Drainage; medium soil cover and moderate erosion.
   Modern Land Use: Rainfall-based agriculture. A railroad line runs through the eastern edge of the site.
   Archaeological Remains: Variable light, light-to-moderate, and moderate Classic surface pottery over an area of ca. 3.90 ha. The Cl material is mixed with traces of Early Toltec and Aztec ceramics (no ET or Az sites designated). We noted several green and gray obsidian blades and scrapers, and a few chert fragments. There are no discernible mounds, but some vague and irregular elevations with moderate rock rubble may represent loci of subsurface architecture.

We made one surface collection (Location 83) over an area ca. 15 × 20 m in a harvested maize field (Plate A35), with light-to-moderate Cl surface pottery, several obsidian and chert artifacts, and light-to-moderate rock rubble.
   Classification: Small Nucleated Village, 75–150 people.

SITE NO. Zu-Cl-64 [Zu-Cl-44(M); Location 89; Zu-EC-60, Zu-LC-59]
   Date of Survey: Dec. 2, 1973
   Location: 481000 E, 2208450 N; 19.9725° N, 99.1816° W
   Natural Setting: 2280 m asl, on gently sloping ground at the lower edge of the Basin of Mexico Lower Piedmont; deep soil cover and moderate erosion.
   Modern Land Use: Rainfall-based agriculture over most of the general area. There are also some irrigated alfalfa fields to the south of the site. A modern dirt road borders the site on the north.
   Archaeological Remains: Variable light and light-to-moderate Classic surface pottery over an area of ca. 2.70 ha. The Cl material is mixed with lighter Early Toltec (Zu-ET-21) ceramics. There are also traces of Late Toltec and Aztec material (no LT or Az sites designated). We noted several obsidian blades and some debitage, mostly green in color. There are no discernible structural remains.

Plate A34. Zu-Cl-61, facing east over Location 97.

Plate A35. Zu-Cl-63, facing north over Location 83.

Plate A36. Zu-Cl-64, facing NE over Location 89.

We made one surface collection (Location 89) over an area ca. 10 × 10 m in a harvested maize field (Plate A36), with light-to-moderate Cl surface pottery, several obsidian artifacts, and no rock rubble.
Classification: Hamlet, 25–50 people.

SITE NO. Zu-Cl-65 [Zu-Cl-36(M); Location 69; Zu-EC-61]
   Date of Survey: Aug. 2, 1973
   Location: 482150 E, 2208200 N; 19.9703° N, 99.1706° W
   Natural Setting: 2295m asl, on gently sloping ground at the lower edge of the Basin of Mexico Lower Piedmont, just above the upper edge of the Lakeshore Plain; medium soil cover and slight erosion.
   Modern Land Use: Rainfall-based agriculture. A modern dirt road crosses the eastern edge of the site.
   Archaeological Remains: Variable light and light-to-moderate Classic surface pottery over an area of ca. 2.50 ha. The Cl material is mixed with lighter Terminal Formative ceramics (Zu-TF-10). We noted numerous green and gray obsidian blades, several fragments of gray obsidian, and one green obsidian scraper. There is very little rock rubble and no discernible structural remains.
   We made one surface collection (Location 69) over an area ca. 6 × 14 m in a plowed field, with light-to-moderate Cl surface pottery, numerous obsidian artifacts, and no rock rubble.
   Discussion: One of the few Cl sites in this part of the survey area with antecedent TF occupation.
   Classification: Hamlet, 25–50 people.

SITE NO. Zu-Cl-66 [Zu-Cl-37(M); Location 70; Zu-EC-62, Zu-LC-60]
   Date of Survey: Aug. 5, 1973
   Location: 483500 E, 2190470 N; 19.8101° N, 99.1575° W
   Natural Setting: 2300 m asl, on gently sloping ground in the Basin of Mexico Lower Piedmont, just above the upper edge of the Lakeshore Plain; medium soil cover and slight erosion.
   Modern Land Use: Rainfall-based agriculture. Modern residential structures, outliers of the modern town of Zitlaltepec, encroach onto the site from the southwest.

   Archaeological Remains: Variable light and light-to-moderate Classic surface pottery over an area of ca. 3.60 ha. Because of modern occupation, the southwestern limits of the site cannot be defined. The Cl material is mixed with Early Toltec (Zu-ET-24) and much more extensive Late Aztec (Zu-Az-233) ceramics. We noted several obsidian blades and fragments. No discernible structural remains can be associated with the Cl occupation.
   We made one surface collection (Location 70) over an area ca. 8 × 10 m, with light Cl and light-to-moderate Late Az surface pottery, numerous obsidian artifacts, and light-to-moderate rock rubble.
   Discussion: A Cl site with continued occupation into the ET period.
   Classification: Hamlet, 35–70 people.

SITE NO. Zu-Cl-67 [Zu-Cl-34(M); Location 63; Zu-LC-61]
   Date of Survey: July 26, 1973
   Location: 484550 E, 2193180 N; 19.8346° N, 99.1475° W
   Natural Setting: 2505 m asl, on gently to moderately sloping terrain in a saddle between two small hills on the southeastern flanks of Cerro Jalpa; shallow to medium soil cover, with moderate to severe erosion.
   Modern Land Use: Marginal rainfall-based agriculture, with some maguey semi-terracing.
   Archaeological Remains: Variable light and light-to-moderate Classic surface pottery over an area of ca. 1.00 ha. The Cl material is mixed with partially overlapping Early Toltec (Zu-ET-25) material, and a trace of Aztec ceramics (no Az site designated). We noted numerous green obsidian blades, several green obsidian scrapers and fragments, one gray obsidian projectile point, and one chert fragment. There is light-to-moderate rock rubble, but no discernible structural remains.
   We made one surface collection (Location 63) over an area ca. 10 × 15 m in a plowed field, with light-to-moderate Cl and ET surface pottery, several obsidian artifacts, and light-to-moderate rock rubble.
   Discussion: The high elevation and hillside location of this site are unusual; it may have had a non-domestic (possibly ritual?) function. A small Cl site with continued occupation into the ET period.
   Classification: Small Hamlet (?), 10–20 people.

SITE NO. Zu-Cl-68 [Zu-Cl-35(M); Location 67; Zu-EC-63, Zu-LC-62]
Date of Survey: July 30, 1973
Location: 486970 E, 2190800 N; 19.8131° N, 99.1244° W
Natural Setting: 2260 m asl, on gently sloping ground on the Lakeshore Plain, near the northern edge of Lake Xaltocán-Zumpango; medium soil cover and slight erosion.
Modern Land Use: Rainfall-based agriculture. The main paved road into the modern town of Zitlaltepec crosses the northern part of the site. There are a few modern residences scattered within the site area.
Archaeological Remains: Variable light and light-to-moderate Classic surface pottery over an area of ca. 1.70 ha. There are no discernible structural remains.
We made one surface collection (Location 67) over an area of ca. 4 × 8 m in a plowed field (maize 1.00–1.50 m high), with moderate Cl and traces of Az surface pottery, several obsidian artifacts, and light rock rubble.
Classification: Hamlet, 20–40 people.

SITE NO. Zu-Cl-69 [Zu-Cl-29(J); Zu-EC-64, Zu-LC-63]
Date of Survey: Sept. 18, 1973
Location: 488130 E, 2191180 N; 19.8165° N, 99.1133° W
Natural Setting: 2265 m asl, on gently sloping ground on the Lakeshore Plain, near the northern edge of Lake Xaltocán-Zumpango; medium soil cover and slight erosion.
Modern Land Use: Rainfall-based agriculture. The northern edge of the modern town of Zumpango encroaches slightly onto the southeastern edge of the site.
Archaeological Remains: Light Classic surface pottery over an area of ca. 1.30 ha. There are no discernible structural remains.
No surface collection made.
Classification: Small Hamlet, 5–10 people.

SITE NO. Zu-Cl-70 [Zu-Cl-30(J); Location 65; Zu-EC-65, Zu-LC-64]
Date of Survey: Sept. 23, 1973
Location: 490820 E, 2190550 N; 19.8108° N, 99.0877° W
Natural Setting: 2270 m asl, on gently sloping ground on the Lakeshore Plain; medium soil cover and slight erosion.
Modern Land Use: Rainfall-based agriculture. A modern dirt road skirts the southern, eastern, and northern edges of the site.
Archaeological Remains: Variable light and light-to-moderate Classic surface pottery over an area of ca. 5.60 ha. Traces of Terminal Formative and Late Toltec ceramics are also present (no TF or LT sites designated). We noted several obsidian artifacts. There are no discernible structural remains and very little rock rubble.
We made one surface collection (Location 65) over an area of ca. 10 × 20 m in a cultivated field (Plate A37), with light-to-moderate Cl surface pottery, several obsidian artifacts, and no rock rubble.
Classification: Small Dispersed Village, 60–120 people.

SITE NO. Zu-Cl-71 [Zu-Cl-25(J); Location 47; Zu-EC-66]
Date of Survey: July 31, 1973
Location: 492880 E, 2191820 N; 19.8223° N, 99.0680° W
Natural Setting: 2320 m asl, on gently sloping ground in the Basin of Mexico Lower Piedmont; shallow soil cover and severe erosion.
Modern Land Use: The immediate site area is unplowed pasture. The surrounding area is generally devoted to rainfall-based agriculture.
Archaeological Remains: Light Classic surface pottery over an area of ca. 3.10 ha. The Cl material is mixed with approximately equal proportions of Terminal Formative (Zu-TF-6), and lighter Late Aztec (Zu-Az-194) ceramics. We noted a few obsidian blades and one obsidian scraper. There are no discernible structural remains and very little rock rubble.
We made one surface collection (Location 47) from an area ca. 15 × 15 m in an unplowed area (Plate A38), with light-to-moderate Cl surface pottery, a few obsidian artifacts, and no rock rubble.
Discussion: One of the few Cl sites in this area with antecedent TF occupation.
Classification: Hamlet, 15–30 people.

SITE NO. Zu-Cl-72 [Zu-Cl-23(J); Feature CX; Zu-EC-67, Zu-LC-65]
Date of Survey: July 29, 1973
Location: 495000 E, 2191780 N; 19.8220° N, 99.0477° W
Natural Setting: 2295 m asl, on gently sloping ground at the lowermost edge of the Basin of Mexico Lower Piedmont, near the upper edge of the Lakeshore Plain; shallow soil cover and moderate to severe erosion. The Río Zumpango (Avenidas de Pachuca) is ca. 75 m to the east.
Modern Land Use: Rainfall-based agriculture in the eastern half of the site; unplowed pasture in the western half.
Archaeological Remains: Variable light and light-to-moderate Classic surface pottery over an area of ca. 2.40 ha. The Cl material is mixed with traces of Late Toltec and Aztec material (no LT or Az site designated). We noted several green and gray obsidian blades, and one obsidian scraper.
There is one poorly defined mound (Feature CX) in an unplowed pasture area. This feature measures ca. 25 m in diameter and 0.15 m high, with moderate Cl and traces of Late Az and LT surface pottery, several obsidian artifacts, and light rock rubble.
We made one surface collection from the entire mound area.
Classification: Hamlet, 25–50 people.

SITE NO. Zu-Cl-73 [Zu-Cl-33(J); Location 71; Zu-EC-68, Zu-LC-66]
Date of Survey: Oct. 7, 1973
Location: 495630 E, 2188680 N; 19.7939° N, 99.0417° W
Natural Setting: 2310 m asl, on gently sloping ground atop a broad low hill that rises about 25 m above the level of the surrounding Lakeshore Plain; shallow soil cover and moderate erosion.
Modern Land Use: Rainfall-based agriculture in the northern half of the site. The southern half is unplowed pasture. Modern residential structures encroach onto the site from the east and northwest. A modern dirt road borders the site's southern edge.
Archaeological Remains: Variable light and light-to-moderate Classic surface pottery over an area of ca. 6.50 ha. Because of modern occupation, the northwestern limits of the site are impossible to define. In the southern half of the site, the Cl material is mixed with approximately equal quantities of Early Toltec ceramics (Zu-ET-27). There is an unusually high proportion of Classic Thin Orange pottery. We noted several green and gray obsidian artifacts. There are no discernible structural remains and very little rock rubble.
We made one surface collection (Location 71) over an area ca. 10 × 15 m in a fallow field (Plate A39) with moderate Cl surface pottery, several obsidian artifacts, and very little rock rubble.
Discussion: The supporting low hill appears to be a natural feature, but we cannot discount the possibility that part of it is artificial. Continued occupation into the ET period.
Classification: Small Dispersed Village, 60–120 people.

Plate A37. Zu-Cl-70, facing east over Location 65.

Plate A38. Zu-Cl-71, facing east over Location 47.

Plate A39. Zu-Cl-73, facing SW over Location 71.

Plate A40. Zu-Cl-75, facing south over Location 72.

SITE NO. Zu-Cl-74 [Zu-Cl-34(J); Zu-EC-69, Zu-LC-67]
  Date of Survey: Oct. 7, 1973
  Location: 497570 E, 2188380 N; 19.7912° N, 99.0232° W
  Natural Setting: 2260 m asl, on nearly level ground on the Lakeshore Plain, just west of a low hill (Loma Coqueme), near the northern edge of Lake Xaltocán-Zumpango; shallow soil cover and slight erosion.
  Modern Land Use: Rainfall-based agriculture. A modern dirt road borders the north edge of the site.
  Archaeological Remains: Light Classic surface pottery over an area of ca. 0.80 ha. There are no discernible structural remains and no rock rubble.
  No surface collection made.
  Classification: Small Hamlet, 5–10 people.

SITE NO. Zu-Cl-75 [Zu-Cl-35(J); Location 72; Zu-EC-70, Zu-LC-68]
  Date of Survey: Oct. 7, 1973
  Location: 497850 E, 2188350 N; 19.7910° N, 99.0205° W
  Natural Setting: 2280 m asl, on nearly level ground on the Lakeshore Plain, just west of a low hill (Loma Coqueme), near the northern edge of Lake Xaltocán-Zumpango; shallow soil cover and slight erosion.
  Modern Land Use: Rainfall-based agriculture. Two modern dirt roads cross the site.
  Archaeological Remains: Light Classic surface pottery over an area of ca. 1.90 ha. The site is at the eastern border of the survey area, and may extend farther eastward toward Loma Coqueme. In the southern part of the site the Cl material is mixed with approximately equal quantities of Terminal Formative ceramics (Zu-TF-12). We noted several green obsidian blades, four gray obsidian scrapers, and two gray obsidian blades. There are no discernible structural remains and no rock rubble.
  We made one surface collection (Location 72) over an area ca. 20 × 25 m in a cultivated field with thick weed cover (Plate A40), with light Cl and TF surface pottery, several obsidian artifacts, and no rock rubble.
  Discussion: Because we did not define the site's eastern limits, its size is uncertain. One of the few Cl sites with antecedent TF occupation.
  Classification: Small Hamlet (?), 10–20 people.

SITE NO. Zu-Cl-76 [Zu-Cl-37(J); Locations 73, 74; Zu-EC-71, Zu-LC-69]
  Date of Survey: Oct. 10, 1973
  Location: 494970 E, 2186570 N; 19.7749° N, 99.0480° W
  Natural Setting: 2245 m asl, on gently sloping ground atop a low, broad natural (?) elevation on the Lakeshore Plain near the northern edge of Lake Xaltocán-Zumpango; moderate to deep soil cover, slight to moderate erosion. Together with sites Zu-Cl-79–Zu-Cl-82, this site occupies a topographic elevation (ancient beach ridges and intervening strand plain) several meters above the general level of the surrounding Lakeshore Plain (Frederick et al. 2005:75) (Fig. 2.4).
  Modern Land Use: Rainfall-based agriculture. A modern dirt road crosses the western part of the site. The eastern edge of the modern settlement of San Sebastian encroaches onto the western edge of the site area.
  Archaeological Remains: Variable light and light-to-moderate Classic surface pottery over an area of ca. 6.30 ha. The Cl material is mixed with approximately equal amounts of Late Toltec (Zu-LT-174) ceramics in the eastern half of the site, and with lighter Terminal Formative (Zu-TF-21) pottery at the site's northern edge. There is light rock rubble and no discernible structural remains. We noted several obsidian blades (both green and gray).
  We made two surface collections (Locations 73, 74):

Location	Area and Context	Content
73	20 × 20 m, in a cultivated field	Light-to-moderate Cl and LT, and light TF surface pottery; several obsidian artifacts; light rock rubble.
74	10 × 15 m, in a cultivated field	Light-to-moderate LT, and light Cl and TF surface pottery; several obsidian artifacts; light rock rubble.

  Discussion: Because the western limits of the site remain uncertain, we cannot accurately estimate the site size. One of the few Cl sites with antecedent TF occupation.
  Classification: Small Dispersed Village (?), 60–120 people.

Plate A41. Zu-Cl-77, facing south over Location 69.

SITE NO. Zu-Cl-77 [Zu-Cl-32(J); Location 69; Zu-EC-72, Zu-LC-70]
  Date of Survey: Oct. 1, 1973
  Location: 492800 E, 2188030 N; 19.7881° N, 99.0687° W
  Natural Setting: 2270 m asl, on nearly level ground on the Lakeshore Plain, near the northern edge of Lake Xaltocán-Zumpango; deep soil cover and slight erosion.
  Modern Land Use: Rainfall-based agriculture in the southern three-quarters of the site; the northern quarter is devoted to irrigated alfalfa. A modern paved highway runs east-west across the northern half of the site.
  Archaeological Remains: Variable light and light-to-moderate Classic surface pottery over an area of ca. 5.50 ha. Mixed with traces of Early Toltec, Late Toltec, and Aztec material (no ET, LT, or Az sites designated). We noted several green and gray obsidian blades and one gray obsidian scraper. There are no discernible structural remains and very little rock rubble.
  We made one surface collection (Location 69) over an area ca. 10 × 15 m at the edge of a maize field (Plate A41), with light-to-moderate Cl surface pottery, several obsidian artifacts, and very little rock rubble.
  Discussion: Long-term settlement continuity.
  Classification: Small Dispersed Village, 6–120 people.

SITE NO. Zu-Cl-78 [Zu-Cl-31(J); Zu-EC-73, Zu-LC-71]
  Date of Survey: Sept. 24, 1973
  Location: 491630 E, 2188880 N; 19.7957° N, 99.0799° W
  Natural Setting: 2270 m asl, on nearly level ground on the Lakeshore Plain, just south of a small stream, near the northern edge of Lake Xaltocán-Zumpango; deep soil and slight erosion.
  Modern Land Use: Rainfall-based agriculture. Scattered modern residential structures in the eastern outskirts of the modern town of Zumpango surround the site on all sides.
  Archaeological Remains: Light Cl surface pottery over an area of ca. 0.70 ha. There are no discernible structural remains and very little rock rubble.
  No surface collection made.
  Discussion: Because of modern occupation, the limits of the site could not be determined.
  Classification: Small Hamlet (?), 5–10 people.

SITE NO. Zu-Cl-79 [Zu-Cl-39(J); Location 75; Zu-EC-74, Zu-LC-72]
  Date of Survey: Oct. 11, 1973
  Location: 492430 E, 2184930 N; 19.7600° N, 99.0723° W
  Natural Setting: 2245 m asl, on gently sloping to nearly level ground on the Lakeshore Plain, very near the northern edge of Lake Xaltocán-Zumpango; deep soil cover and slight erosion. Together with sites Zu-Cl-77 and Zu-Cl-80–Zu-Cl-82, this site occupies a topographic elevation (ancient beach ridges and intervening strand plain) several meters above the general level of the surrounding Lakeshore Plain (Frederick et al. 2005:75) (Fig. 2.4).
  Modern Land Use: Rainfall-based agriculture. Two modern dirt roads border the site on the east and west.
  Archaeological Remains: Light Classic surface pottery over an area of ca. 2.20 ha. The Cl material is mixed with heavier Terminal Formative pottery (Zu-TF-25). There are no discernible structural remains and no rock rubble.
  We made one surface collection (Location 75) over a triangular area ca. 15 m on a side in a maize field with light-to-moderate TF and light Cl surface pottery, a few obsidian artifacts, and no rock rubble.
  Discussion: One of the few Cl sites with antecedent TF occupation.
  Classification: Small Hamlet, 10–20 people.

SITE NO. Zu-Cl-80 [Zu-Cl-38(J); Location 84; Zu-EC-75, Zu-LC-73]
  Date of Survey: Oct. 22, 1973
  Location: 493630 E, 2184700 N; 19.7580° N, 99.0608° W
  Natural Setting: 2245 m asl, on gently sloping ground on a slight elevation that rises ca. 1.00 m above the general level of the surrounding Lakeshore Plain, near the northern edge of Lake Xaltocán-Zumpango; deep soil cover and no erosion. Together with sites Zu-Cl-76, Zu-Cl-79, Zu-Cl-81, and Zu-Cl-82, this site occupies a topographic elevation

Plate A42. Zu-Cl-80, facing NE over Location 84.

(ancient beach ridges and intervening strand plain) several meters above the general level of the surrounding Lakeshore Plain (Frederick et al. 2005:75) (Fig. 2.4).

Modern Land Use: The immediate site area itself is fallow and thickly weed covered; the surrounding area is used for rainfall-based agriculture. There is a modern house at the southeastern edge of the site.

Archaeological Remains: Variable light and light-to-moderate Classic surface pottery over an area of ca. 3.30 ha. The Cl material is mixed with lighter Early Toltec ceramics (Zu-ET-28). We noted several green and gray obsidian blades and debitage. There is very little rock rubble and no discernible structural remains, although the slight rise upon which the site rests may be partly or wholly of artificial construction.

We made one surface collection (Location 84) over an area ca. 20 × 25 m in a fallow field (Plate A42), with light-to-moderate Cl surface pottery, several obsidian artifacts, and very little rock rubble. A nearby well shows sherds coming out of the wall profile to a depth of ca. 1.00 m.

Discussion: If the slight rise that underlies the surface pottery represents subsurface architecture, the underlying deposits could be very well preserved in this deep-soil area. In 1973, this site had excellent potential for future excavation. Settlement continuity into the ET period.

Classification: Hamlet, 30–60 people.

SITE NO. Zu-Cl-81 [Zu-Cl-40(J); Location 85; Zu-EC-76]
   Date of Survey: Oct. 23, 1973
   Location: 492820 E, 2183950 N; 19.7512° N, 99.0685° W
   Natural Setting: 2245 m asl, on level ground on the Lakeshore Plain, near the northern edge of Lake Xaltocán-Zumpango; deep soil cover and no erosion. Together with sites Zu-Cl-76, Zu-Cl-79, Zu-Cl-80, and Zu-Cl-82, this site occupies a topographic elevation (ancient beach ridges and intervening strand plain) several meters above the general level of the surrounding Lakeshore Plain (Frederick et al. 2005:75) (Fig. 2.4).

Modern Land Use: Rainfall-based agriculture. The modern town of Santa Ana Nextlalpan encroaches onto the site from the south.

Archaeological Remains: Variable light and light-to-moderate Classic surface pottery over an area of ca. 2.90 ha. The Cl material is mixed with lighter Terminal Formative ceramics (Zu-TF-26), and there is also a trace of Late Toltec pottery (no LT site designated). We noted several green and gray obsidian artifacts and debitage fragments. There is no rock rubble and no discernible structural remains.

We made one surface collection (Location 85) over an area ca. 15 × 20 m in a maize field (Plate A43), with light-to-moderate Cl, including one figurine fragment, and very light TF surface pottery; several obsidian artifacts; and no rock rubble.

Discussion: Occupation continuity from antecedent TF.

Classification: Hamlet, 30–60 people.

SITE NO. Zu-Cl-82 [Zu-Cl-36(J); Location 81; Zu-EC-77, Zu-LC-74]
   Date of Survey: Oct. 16, 1973
   Location: 489200 E, 2184880 N; 19.7596° N, 99.1031° W
   Natural Setting: 2245 m asl, on nearly level ground atop a low, broad elevation that rises to 2.00 m above the general level of the surrounding Lakeshore Plain, near the northern edge of Lake Xaltocán-Zumpango; medium to deep soil cover and slight erosion. Together with sites Zu-Cl-76 and Zu-Cl-79–Zu-Cl-81, this site occupies a topographic elevation (ancient beach ridges and intervening strand plain) several meters above the general level of the surrounding Lakeshore Plain (Frederick et al. 2005:75) (Fig. 2.4).

Modern Land Use: Rainfall-based agriculture. A poultry farm encroaches onto the site from the northeast, and a modern dirt road borders the southeastern edge of the site.

Archaeological Remains: Light-to-moderate Classic surface pottery over an area of ca. 5.30 ha. We noted several green and gray obsidian artifacts. There are no discernible structural remains and very little rock rubble.

We made one surface collection (Location 81) over an area ca. 20 × 40 m in a maize field (Plate A44), with light-to-moderate Cl surface pottery and several obsidian artifacts.

Discussion: We assume the supporting elevation is a natural feature, but it could be partly artificial.

Classification: Small Nucleated Village, 80–160 people.

Plate A43. Zu-Cl-81, facing east over Location 85.

Plate A44. Zu-Cl-82, facing SW over Location 81.

SITE NO. Zu-Cl-83 [Zu-Cl-45(M); Locations 91, 92, 93, 94; Zu-EC-78, Zu-LC-75]
Date of Survey: Dec. 2–3, 1973
Location: 480780 E, 2189200 N; 19.7986° N, 99.1835° W
Natural Setting: 2260 m asl, on gently sloping ground atop a low, apparently natural (?) knoll that rises to a maximum height of ca. 5.00 m above the general level of the surrounding Lakeshore Plain; deep soil cover and slight erosion. This site occupies a topographic elevation (ancient beach ridges and intervening strand plain) several meters above the general level of the surrounding Lakeshore Plain (Frederick et al. 2005:75) (Fig. 2.4).
Modern Land Use: Rainfall-based agriculture on the supporting knoll. Much of the surrounding plain is irrigated for maize and alfalfa cultivation. There is a small modern religious shrine at the center of the site.
Archaeological Remains: Variable light and light-to-moderate Classic surface pottery over an area of ca. 10.10 ha. The Cl material is mixed with approximately equal quantities of Early Toltec (Zu-ET-23) and Late Toltec (Zu-LT-197) ceramics, and there is an Aztec component in the southwest corner of the site (Zu-Az-259, Zu-Az-260). We noted several obsidian blades and scrapers, mostly green in color. There is very little rock rubble and no definite structural remains, although the supporting knoll could be partially artificial.

We made four surface collections (Locations 91, 92, 93, 94):

Location	Area and Context	Content
91	15 × 15 m, in a harvested maize field	Light-to-moderate Cl and ET, light LT, and very light Az surface pottery; several obsidian artifacts; very little rock rubble.
92	15 × 15 m, in a harvested maize field	Light-to-moderate Cl and ET, and very light Az surface pottery; several obsidian artifacts; very little rock rubble.
93	8 × 20 m, in a harvested maize field	Light-to-moderate Cl and ET, light LT, and very light Az surface pottery; very little rock rubble.
94	10 × 15 m, in a harvested maize field	Light-to-moderate Cl and ET, light LT, and very light Az surface pottery; several obsidian artifacts; very little rock rubble.

Discussion: This site appears to be more or less continuously occupied from Classic through Late Postclassic times. Such long-term occupational continuity is unusual in this area. This characteristic, together with the protective deep soil cover, suggests that this may be an excellent locality for future stratigraphic excavation, especially if the supporting knoll represents subsurface architecture (if the site area has not been completely destroyed by modern occupation in the decades after our survey).
Classification: Small Nucleated Village, 150–300 people.

SITE NO. Zu-Cl-84 [Zu-Cl-43(M); Location 88; Zu-EC-79, Zu-LC-76]
Date of Survey: Nov. 28, 1973
Location: 476650 E, 2189880 N; 19.8047° N, 99.2229° W
Natural Setting: 2295 m asl, on gently sloping ground near the lower end of a long, low ridge in the Upper Salado Drainage, just above the upper edge of the Lakeshore Plain, and just north of the divide between the Upper Salado and Basin of Mexico drainages; medium soil cover, moderate erosion.
Modern Land Use: Rainfall-based agriculture.
Archaeological Remains: Variable light and light-to-moderate Classic surface pottery over an area of ca. 2.0 ha. There is a lighter admixture of Late Aztec material (Zu-Az-266) along the southern edge of the site. We noted several green obsidian blades. There is substantial rock rubble, but no discernible structural remains.

We made one surface collection (Location 88) over an area ca. 15 × 15 m in a harvested maize field (Plate A45), with light-to-moderate Cl and traces of Az surface pottery, a few obsidian artifacts, and moderate rock rubble.
Classification: Hamlet, 20–40 people.

SITE NO. Zu-Cl-85 [Zu-Cl-42(M); Location 85; Zu-EC-80]
Date of Survey: Nov. 21, 1973
Location: 475450 E, 2191720 N; 19.8213° N, 99.2344° W
Natural Setting: 2275 m asl, on gently sloping ground in the Upper Salado Drainage; medium soil cover and slight erosion.
Modern Land Use: Mainly rainfall-based agriculture, with some irrigated alfalfa. Several drainage ditches and irrigation canals cut through the site area. A modern dirt road borders the western edge of the site. The ground surface is partially obscured by a dense stand of mature maize.
Archaeological Remains: Variable light and light-to-moderate Classic surface pottery over an area of ca. 2.10 ha. We noted several green obsidian blades. There are no discernible structural remains and very little rock rubble.

We made one surface collection (Location 85) of badly weathered pottery over an area ca. 15 m in diameter in a maize field (Plate A46), with light-to-moderate Cl surface pottery and several obsidian artifacts.
Classification: Hamlet, 20–40 people.

SITE NO. Zu-Cl-86 [Zu-Cl-46(M); Location 95; Zu-EC-81, Zu-LC-77]
Date of Survey: Dec. 4, 1973
Location: 478850 E, 2187550 N; 19.7836° N, 99.2019° W
Natural Setting: 2285 m asl, on gently sloping ground in the Basin of Mexico Lower Piedmont, near the lower end of a broad ridge that descends northeastward into the edge of the Lakeshore Plain; shallow soil cover and severe erosion with patches of bare tepetate.
Modern Land Use: The immediate site area is primarily unplowed pasture, with some maguey semi-terracing and minor rainfall-based agriculture. The modern town of Coyotepec surrounds the site on all sides.
Archaeological Remains: Variable light, light-to-moderate, and moderate Classic surface pottery over an area of ca. 2.30 ha. Because of modern occupation, the limits of the archaeological site cannot be defined in any direction. The Cl material is mixed with approximately equal quantities of Terminal Formative ceramics (Zu-TF-11). There is also a lighter admixture of Late Aztec pottery (Zu-Az-270). We noted several green and gray obsidian blades. There are no discernible structural remains and very little rock rubble.

We made one surface collection (Location 95) over an area ca. 10 × 12 m in an unplowed area (Plate A47), with light-to-moderate Cl and light TF and Az surface pottery, and several obsidian artifacts.
Discussion: This could be a much larger site if substantial Classic-period occupation underlies modern Coyotepec. Settlement continuity from antecedent TF period.
Classification: Hamlet (??), 30–60 people.

Plate A45. Zu-Cl-84, facing SE over site area.

Plate A46. Zu-Cl-85, facing WSW over site area.

Plate A47. Zu-Cl-86, facing SE over Location 95.

SITE NO. Zu-Cl-87 [Zu-Cl-47(M); Zu-EC-82, Zu-LC-78]
Date of Survey: Dec. 4, 1973
Location: 479280 E, 2185320 N; 19.7635° N, 99.1978° W
Natural Setting: 2270 m asl, on gently sloping ground at the upper edge of the Lakeshore Plain, close to the northwestern corner of Lake Xaltocán-Zumpango; shallow soil cover, with moderate to severe erosion, with patches of bare tepetate.
Modern Land Use: Rainfall-based agriculture. There is abundant maguey semi-terracing throughout the area. The paved road between Coyotepec and Teoloyucan crosses the northeastern edge of the site. Scattered modern houses encroach onto the site from the south and southeast.
Archaeological Remains: Variable light and light Classic surface pottery over an area of ca. 2.0 ha. There is a possible trace of Early Toltec material at the south end of the site (no ET site defined). Because of modern occupation, the southeastern limits of the site could not be defined. There are no discernible structural remains.
No surface collection made.
Discussion: The site may be somewhat larger if the Classic occupation extends farther southeastward under modern Teoloyucan.
Classification: Hamlet (?), 15–30 people.

SITE NO. Zu-Cl-88 [Zu-Cl-48(M); Zu-EC-83, Zu-LC-79]
Date of Survey: Dec. 5, 1973
Location: 479680 E, 2182700 N; 19.7398° N, 99.1939° W
Natural Setting: 2270 m asl, on gently sloping ground at the upper edge of the Lakeshore Plain, near the northwestern edge of Lake Xaltocán-Zumpango; medium soil cover and moderate erosion.
Modern Land Use: Rainfall-based agriculture.
Archaeological Remains: Light Classic surface pottery over an area of ca. 0.70 ha. There are no discernible structural remains and very little rock rubble.
No surface collection made.
Classification: Small Hamlet, 2–5 people.

SITE NO. Zu-Cl-89 [Zu-Cl-27(J); Location 50; Feature DE; Zu-EC-84, Zu-LC-80]
Date of Survey: Aug. 15, 1973
Location: 486800 E, 2178600 N; 19.7028° N, 99.1260° W
Natural Setting: 2310 m asl, on nearly level ground at the highest point on Tultepec Island (Plate A48); shallow soil cover and moderate erosion.
Modern Land Use: Rainfall-based agriculture.
Archaeological Remains: Variable light and light-to-moderate Classic surface pottery over an area of ca. 21.00 ha. There is a lighter admixture of Late Aztec ceramics (Zu-Az-286) in the northern and southwestern parts of the Classic site.
There is one well defined mound (Feature DE), probably Classic in date, in the eastern sector of the site. This is a flat-topped structure, ca. 15 m in diameter, standing ca. 1.50 m high (Plate A49). A looter's pit in the top of the mound reveals solid earth and rock-rubble construction. The pottery on the mound's surface is very light Cl, with a trace of Az, and a possible trace of Terminal Formative pottery (no TF site defined). We noted several green obsidian blades.
The area immediately surrounding the base of the mound, and particularly along its southern edge, appears to have been built up artificially to form a basal platform perhaps 20 cm high. There are also some vague, irregular mounded areas in the southwestern part of the site that may also represent subsurface architecture.

We made one surface collection (Location 50) over an area ca. 10 × 15 m in a maize field in the lower part of the site, with light-to-moderate Cl surface pottery, several obsidian artifacts, and no rock rubble.
Discussion: This is the largest Classic site in the southern part of the Zumpango Region, and it contains one of the largest Classic public buildings in the survey area.
Classification: Local Center, 400–800 people.

SITE NO. Zu-Cl-90 [Zu-Cl-28(J); Locations 54, 55, 57, 58, 59, 60; Zu-EC-85, Zu-LC-81]
Date of Survey: Aug. 22–23, Sept. 13, 1973
Location: 488000 E, 2174050 N; 19.6617° N, 99.1145° W
Natural Setting: 2245 m asl, atop a low natural (?) elevation rising ca. 1.50 m above the general level of the surrounding bed of Lake Xaltocán-Zumpango (Plate A50); deep soil cover, with slight erosion.
Modern Land Use: Mostly unplowed pasture, with minor rainfall-based agriculture. Several modern drainage ditches and dirt roads cross the site.
Archaeological Remains: Variable light, light-to-moderate, moderate, and moderate-to-heavy surface Classic pottery over an area of ca. 7.60 ha. The Cl material is mixed with lighter Early Toltec (Zu-ET-30) and Late Aztec pottery (Zu-Az-298). The Cl pottery is dominated by large reddish-brown ollas. We noted several green and gray obsidian artifacts, including blades and a few projectile points. There are no discernible structural remains, although the supporting ridge may be partially artificial, and the presence of several amorphous concentrations of rock rubble may be the remnants of ancient structures .
We made six surface collections (Locations 54, 55, 57, 58, 59, 60):

Location	Area and Context	Content
54	10 × 10 m, in a fallow field	Light-to-moderate Cl, light ET, and light Late Az surface pottery; several obsidian artifacts; and light-to-moderate rock rubble.
55	10 × 10 m, in a fallow field (Plate A50)	Moderate Cl and light ET and Late Az surface pottery; and light rock rubble. A nearby ditch profile shows a stucco floor at a depth of ca. 70 cm (Plate A51).
57	2 × 4 m, in a fallow field (Plate A52)	Moderate Cl, light ET, and light Late Az surface pottery; several obsidian artifacts; and moderate rock rubble.
58	5 × 5 m, taken from ditch cut through mounded area (Plate A53)	Moderate-to-heavy Cl, light ET, and very light Az surface pottery; several obsidian artifacts; and light rock rubble.
59	5 × 5 m, in fallow field	Moderate Cl, light ET, and very light Az surface pottery; several obsidian artifacts; and no rock rubble.
60	5 × 5 m, in a fallow field (Plate A54)	Moderate Cl and light ET surface pottery; several obsidian artifacts; and very little rock rubble.

Discussion: Most of the irregular mounding appears to comprise masses of potsherds. The heavy concentration of Texcoco Fabric Marked pottery at two nearby Aztec sites (Zu-Az-297, -298) suggests that site Zu-Cl-90 may have been a saltmaking site during the Classic period, and that saltmaking may have endured here into the ET period. The predominance of a single ceramic form (large reddish-brown ollas) may also indicate a Classic-period saltmaking function (Mayer-Oakes 1959).
Classification: Small Dispersed Village, 100–200 people.

Plate A48. Zu-Cl-89, facing west over general site area.

Plate A49. Zu-Cl-89, facing north at Feature DE.

Plate A50. Zu-Cl-90, facing north over Location 55, with Tultepec Island in background.

(*left*) Plate A51. Zu-Cl-90, stick pointing to plastered floor in ditch profile, near Location 55.
(*below*) Plate A52. Zu-Cl-90, facing west over Location 57.

(*above*) Plate A53. Zu-Cl-90, facing south over Location 58, showing heavy surface pottery.
(*below*) Plate A54. Zu-Cl-90, facing SE over Location 60.

Early Toltec Sites (Fig. A4)

Although it is usually easy to recognize Early Toltec decorated ceramics, the plainwares are much more difficult to identify. It proved especially difficult to separate ET plainwares (especially ollas and basins) from their Classic counterparts. Unlike the situation in our previous surveys in the central and southern Valley of Mexico, many ET sites in the Zumpango Region, including most of the smaller sites, lacked decorated pottery. Consequently, it was often difficult for us to recognize ET occupation in the field, especially during the early part of our fieldseason when we were less familiar with ET plainwares. In many cases, we recognized the presence of ET ceramics in our surface collections only after we examined these collections in greater detail at the end of our 1973 fieldseason.

There are two main consequences of these difficulties:

(1) Our estimates of ET versus Cl site areas in localities where these components co-occur are less precise than we would prefer.

(2) We are unable to specify the presence or absence of ET occupations at many (most?) of those Classic sites where we made no surface collections.

SITE NO. Zu-ET-1 [Zu-ET-1(J); Locations 16, 17, 18]
  Date of Survey: June 7, 1973
  Location: 496720 E, 2207250 N; 19.9618° N, 99.0313° W
  Natural Setting: 2380 m asl, on gently sloping ground in the Upper Salado Drainage; medium soil cover and moderate erosion (Plate A55).
  Modern Land Use: Mixed pasture and rainfall-based agriculture.
  Archaeological Remains: Variable light and light-to-moderate Early Toltec surface pottery over an area of ca. 10.00 ha. The ET material is mixed with lighter Late Aztec ceramics (Zu-Az-10) in the southern part of the site. We noted numerous green and gray obsidian artifacts. There are no definite structural remains, but several poorly preserved stone-faced terraces, of uncertain age, are visible throughout the site. These features measure 10–20 cm high and 10–20 m wide, and there are ET sherds weathering out of the faces of some terraces.

We made three surface collections (Locations 16, 17, 18):

Location	Area and Context	Content
16	15 × 20 m, in unplowed field	Light-to-moderate ET and light Late Az surface pottery, numerous obsidian artifacts, moderate rock rubble.
17	20 × 30 m, in unplowed field	Light-to-moderate ET surface pottery, numerous obsidian artifacts, moderate rock rubble.
18	15 × 20 m, in unplowed field	Light-to-moderate ET and trace Az surface pottery, numerous obsidian artifacts, moderate rock rubble

  Discussion: The age of the terracing is uncertain but because they seem to contain ET pottery within their construction fill, they appear to be post-ET.
  Classification: Small Nucleated Village, 200–400 people.

SITE NO. Zu-ET-2 [Zu-Cl-1(J); Location 4]
  Date of Survey: May 28, 1973
  Location: 493530 E, 2205750 N; 19.9482° N, 99.0618° W
  Natural Setting: 2340 m asl, on nearly level ground in the Upper Salado Drainage; medium soil cover and no erosion.
  Modern Land Use: Rainfall-based agriculture. A modern dirt road skirts the western edge of the site.
  Archaeological Remains: Variable light, light-to-moderate, and moderate Early Toltec surface pottery over an area of ca. 4.40 ha. The ET material is mixed with heavier Classic (Zu-Cl-6) and lighter Late Toltec ceramics (Zu-LT-1). There is also a trace of Aztec pottery (no Az site designated). We noted several obsidian artifacts (mostly green in color), and chert fragments. There is light rock rubble but no discernible structural remains.

We made one surface collection (Location 4) over an area ca. 8 × 10 m in a plowed field, with light-to-moderate Cl and ET surface pottery, several obsidian and chert fragments, and light rock rubble.
  Discussion: Long-term occupational continuity.
  Classification: Small Nucleated Village, 100–200 people.

SITE NO. Zu-ET-3 [Zu-Cl-10(J); Location 24]
  Date of Survey: June 14, 1973
  Location: 492280 E, 2203630 N; 19.9290° N, 99.0738° W
  Natural Setting: 2345 m asl, on gently sloping ground in the Upper Salado Drainage; deep soil cover and slight erosion.
  Modern Land Use: Rainfall-based agriculture.
  Archaeological Remains: Variable light, light-to-moderate, and moderate Early Toltec surface pottery over an area of ca. 3.00 ha. The ET material is mixed with about equal quantities of Classic ceramics (Zu-Cl-10). There are also traces of Late Toltec and Aztec material (no LT or Az sites defined at this locality). There are no discernible structural remains and very little rock rubble.

We made one surface collection (Location 24) over an area ca. 10 × 15 m in a fallow field with moderate Cl and light ET surface pottery, and several obsidian artifacts.
  Discussion: One of relatively few ET sites with antecedent Cl occupation.
  Classification: Hamlet, 45–90 people.

SITE NO. Zu-ET-4 [Zu-Cl-14(M); Location 9; Features U, AT]
  Date of Survey: June 3, 14, 1973
  Location: 488600 E, 2204500 N; 19.9369° N, 99.1089° W
  Natural Setting: 2260 m asl, on gently sloping ground in the Upper Salado Drainage; deep soil cover and slight erosion.
  Modern Land Use: Rainfall-based agriculture. Scattered modern houses on the western side of the modern town of Tlapanaloya encroach onto the site, and there are several modern drainage ditches and terraces in the site area.
  Archaeological Remains: Moderate Early Toltec surface pottery over an area of ca. 0.50 ha. The ET material is mixed with heavier and more extensive Classic ceramics (Zu-Cl-33), and there is partial overlap with a larger Late Toltec site (Zu-LT-60). We noted numerous blades and chips of both green and gray obsidian, one green obsidian projectile point, one gray obsidian projectile point, and one basalt metate fragment.

There are two mounds (Features U, AT), both of which may be Classic-period features:

Fea.	Area and Context	Height	Content
U	20 × 30 m, in unplowed area	1.75 m	Very light to light Cl and ET surface pottery, several obsidian artifacts, and moderate rock rubble. South side partly destroyed by road.
AT	32 m dia., in unplowed area	1.75 m	Light Cl and ET surface pottery, several obsidian artifacts, and moderate rock rubble.

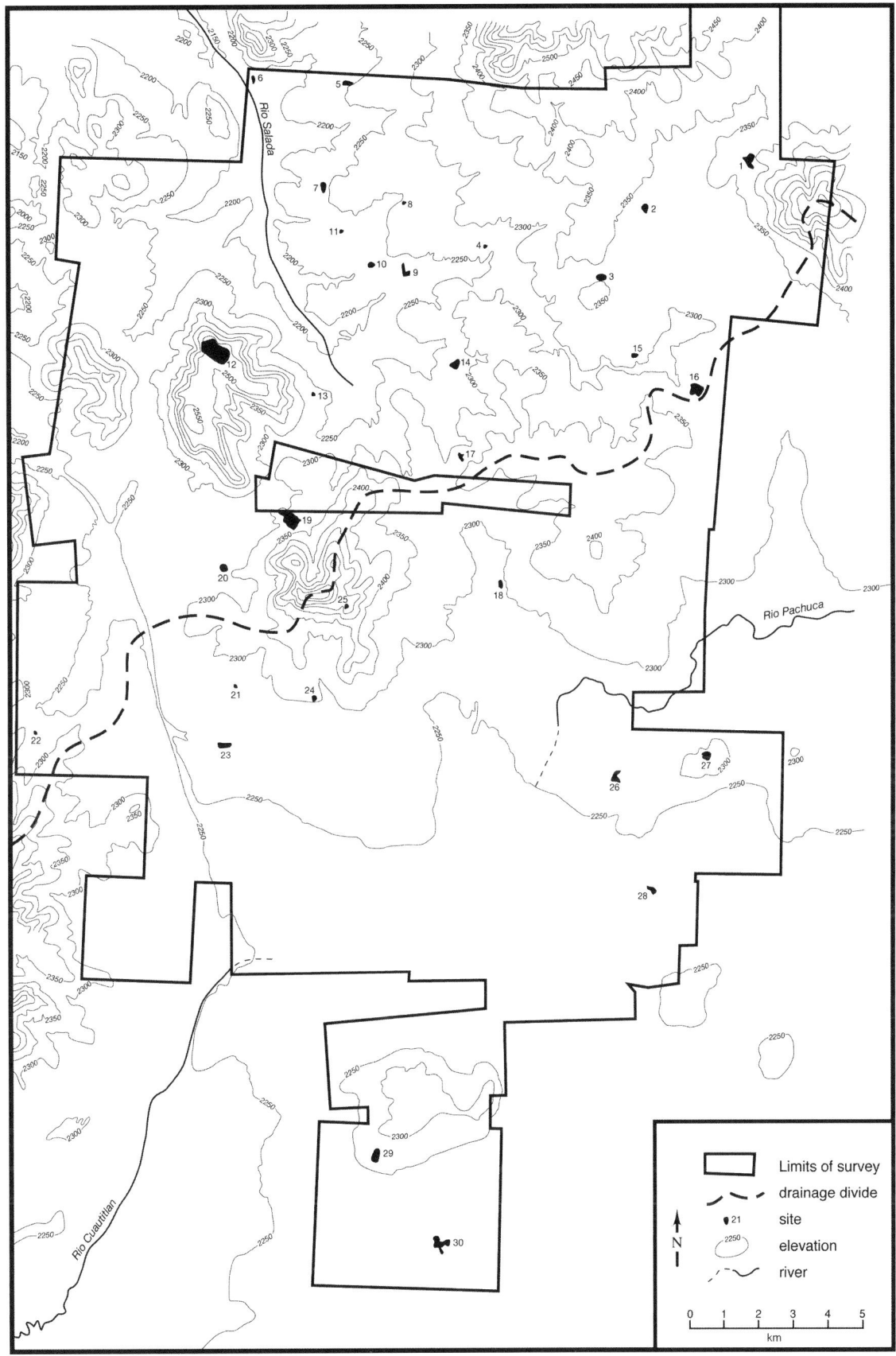

Figure A4. Map of Early Toltec sites in the Zumpango Region.

Plate A55. Zu-ET-1, facing SW over site area.

We made one surface collection (Location 9) in a fallow field, with light-to-moderate Cl and LT and light ET surface pottery, several obsidian artifacts, and light-to-moderate rock rubble.

Discussion: Another small ET site with occupational continuity from the antecedent Cl period.

Classification: Small Hamlet, 10–20 people.

SITE NO. Zu-ET-5 [Zu-Cl-19(M); Location 26; Feature AD]
Date of Survey: June 5, 1973
Location: 484350 E, 2209280 N; 19.9800° N, 99.1496° W
Natural Setting: 2245 m asl, on gently sloping ground in the Upper Salado Drainage; shallow soil cover and moderate erosion.
Modern Land Use: Unplowed pasture. There are a few modern drainage ditches in the site area.
Archaeological Remains: Variable light and light-to-moderate Early Toltec surface pottery over an area of ca. 2.40 ha. The northern limits of the site were not defined, as they extend beyond the northern border of the survey area. The ET material is mixed with approximately equal quantities of Classic ceramics (Zu-Cl-15). There is also a trace of Late Aztec pottery (no Az site designated).

There is one discernible mound (Feature AD). This is an unplowed structure, ca. 20 m in diameter and 1.00 m high. There is light-to-moderate rock rubble on the top and sides of the mound, together with light Cl and ET and a trace of Late Az surface pottery. We noted several green and gray obsidian artifacts, including blades, debitage debris, and one gray obsidian knife.

We made one surface collection (Location 26) over an area of unrecorded size in an unplowed field with light-to-moderate Cl and ET surface pottery, several obsidian artifacts, and light-to-moderate rock rubble.

Discussion: Because the northern site limits were not defined, the size of the site remains uncertain. The age of Feature AD is also uncertain. Another small ET site with antecedent Cl-period occupation.

Classification: Hamlet (?), 25–50 people.

SITE NO. Zu-ET-6 [Zu-Cl-17(M); Location 25]
Date of Survey: June 5, 1973
Location: 481500 E, 2209220 N; 19.9795° N, 99.1768° W
Natural Setting: 2170 m asl, on nearly level ground in the Upper Salado Drainage; deep soil cover and slight erosion.
Modern Land Use: Rainfall-based agriculture. An unsurveyed fenced-in area encroaches onto the site from the north, and part of the site may extend into that area. A few modern drainage ditches cut through the site area.
Archaeological Remains: Variable light and light-to-moderate Early Toltec surface pottery over an area of ca. 1.10 ha. The ET material is mixed with approximately equal quantities of Classic (Zu-Cl-17) and Aztec (Zu-Az-48) ceramics. We noted several green obsidian blades and chips, one gray obsidian fragment, and three basalt mano fragments. There are no discernible structural remains, but amorphous concentrations of rock rubble may represent the remnants of several ancient buildings.

We made one surface collection (Location 25) over an area ca. 8 × 10 m in a fallow field with light-to-moderate Cl, ET, and Az surface pottery; several obsidian artifacts; and light-to-moderate rock rubble.

Discussion: The site area is uncertain because the precise northern limits were not defined. Another ET site with antecedent Cl occupation.

Classification: Small Hamlet (?), 10–20 people.

SITE NO. Zu-ET-7 [Zu-Cl-6(M); Location 22]
Date of Survey: June 5, 1973
Location: 483700 E, 2206200 N; 19.9522° N, 99.1558° W
Natural Setting: 2245 m asl, on gently sloping ground in the Upper Salado Drainage; medium soil cover and slight erosion.
Modern Land Use: Rainfall-based agriculture. The immediate site area is presently fallow.
Archaeological Remains: Variable light, light-to-moderate, and moderate Early Toltec surface pottery over an area of ca. 4.50 ha. The ET material is mixed with heavier Classic ceramics (Zu-Cl-21). We noted several green obsidian blades. There is light rock rubble but no discernible structural remains.

Plate A56. Zu-ET-8, facing south over Location 10-M.

We made one surface collection (Location 22) over an area ca. 5 × 6 m in a plowed field with moderate Cl and ET surface pottery, several obsidian artifacts, and very little rock rubble.

Discussion: Mixed ET and Cl occupation.

Classification: Small Nucleated Village, 75–150 people.

SITE NO. **Zu-ET-8** [No field number; Location 10-M]
  Date of Survey: May 28, 1973
  Location: 486180 E, 2205750 N; 19.9482° N, 99.1321° W
  Natural Setting: 2250 m asl, on nearly level ground in the Upper Salado Drainage; medium soil cover and slight erosion.
  Modern Land Use: Unplowed pasture.
  Archaeological Remains: Light Early Toltec surface pottery over an area of ca. 0.30 ha. The ET material is mixed with a trace of Late Toltec ceramics (no LT site designated). There are no discernible structural remains.

We made one surface collection (Location 10-M) over an area ca. 75 × 75 m in a fallow field (Plate A56), with light ET and traces of LT surface pottery, several obsidian artifacts, and light rock rubble.

Classification: Small Hamlet, 2–5 people.

SITE NO. **Zu-ET-9** [Zu-Cl-13(M); Location 39; Features AZ, BA]
  Date of Survey: June 18, 1973
  Location: 486250 E, 2203630 N; 19.9290° N, 99.1314° W
  Natural Setting: 2240 m asl, on gently sloping ground in the Upper Salado Drainage; deep soil cover and slight erosion.
  Modern Land Use: Rainfall-based agriculture. The modern paved road to Tlapanaloya borders the northern side of the site.
  Archaeological Remains: Variable light and light-to-moderate Early Toltec surface pottery over an area of ca. 3.90 ha. The ET material is mixed with approximately equal quantities of Classic (Zu-Cl-32) and Late Aztec (Zu-Az-66) ceramics. We noted several green obsidian blades and chips; several gray obsidian scrapers, blades, and chips; and one obsidian projectile point.

Two almost contiguous mounds (Features AZ, BA) are located in the west-central part of the site:

Fea.	Area and Context	Height	Content
AZ	13 × 20 m, in unplowed area	0.50 m	Light Cl and ET, traces of Az surface pottery; and moderate rock rubble.
BA	24 m dia., in plowed field	1.50 m	Very light Az surface pottery; and light rock rubble.

We made one surface collection (Location 39) over an area ca. 10 × 15 m in an unplowed field, with light-to-moderate Cl and ET, and light Late Az surface pottery; several obsidian artifacts; and moderate rock rubble.

Discussion: The ages of Features AZ and BA are uncertain; they both may be Aztec structures. Cl to ET settlement continuity.

Classification: Hamlet, 40–80 people.

SITE NO. **Zu-ET-10** [Zu-Cl-12(M); Location 40; Feature BD]
  Date of Survey: June 20, 1973
  Location: 485180 E, 2203880 N; 19.9313° N, 99.1416° W
  Natural Setting: 2225 m asl, on nearly level ground in the Upper Salado Drainage; medium soil cover and slight erosion.
  Modern Land Use: Rainfall-based agriculture.
  Archaeological Remains: Variable light and light-to-moderate Early Toltec surface pottery over an area of ca. 2.40 ha. The ET material is mixed with heavier Classic ceramics (Zu-Cl-31). We noted several green obsidian blades and chips; several gray obsidian blades, scrapers, knives, and chips; and one basalt mano fragment. There is generally very light rock rubble.

There is a single badly plowed-down mound (Feature BD), measuring ca. 70 by 100 m in area and standing 1.0 m high, with light-to-moderate ET and Cl surface pottery and light-to-moderate rock rubble (chunks of tepetate) on its surface.

We made one surface collection (Location 40) over an area ca. 8 × 10 m in an unplowed field, with light ET and light-to-moderate Cl surface pottery, several obsidian artifacts, and very little rock rubble.

Discussion: The age and character of Feature BD are both uncertain. The large size of the slightly mounded area may indicate the presence of several conjoined or tightly clustered ancient structures. Cl to ET settlement continuity.

Classification: Hamlet, 25–50 people.

Plate A57. Zu-ET-12, facing SW at northern half of Cerro de la Mesa Grande.

SITE NO. Zu-ET-11 [Zu-Cl-4(M); Location 18]
Date of Survey: June 4, 1973
Location: 484280 E, 2204850 N; 19.9400° N, 99.1502° W
Natural Setting: 2230 m asl, on nearly level ground in the Upper Salado Drainage; medium soil cover and slight erosion.
Modern Land Use: Intensive cultivation of irrigated alfalfa. The irrigation water is *agua negra* pumped up from the nearby Gran Canal del Desagüe into a large holding tank on a low hilltop south of the site. The irrigation water flows through a network of canals, several of which cut through the site area.
Archaeological Remains: Light Early Toltec surface pottery over an area of ca. 0.70 ha. The ET material is mixed with more abundant Classic ceramics (Zu-Cl-23). We noted several green obsidian blades, scrapers, and fragments. There are no discernible structural remains and very little rock rubble.

We made one surface collection (Location 18) over an area ca. 5 × 20 m in an alfalfa field, with light ET and Cl surface pottery, several obsidian artifacts, and no rock rubble.
Discussion: Cl to ET settlement continuity.
Classification: Small Hamlet, 5–10 people.

SITE NO. Zu-ET-12 [Zu-ET-1(M); Locations 42, 43, 45; Features BH, BI, BJ, BK, BR, BS, BU, BV, BW, BX, BY, BZ, CA, CB, CC, CD, CE, CF, CG, CH, CI, CJ, CK, CL]
Date of Survey: June 24, 26, 1973
Location: 480470 E, 2201180 N; 19.9068° N, 99.1866° W
Natural Setting: 2510 m asl, on the nearly level top of Cerro de la Mesa Grande (Plates A57, A149). The site is situated on gently sloping ground at the north end of the long mesa-like hilltop. There is deep soil cover and slight erosion over most of the site. The terrain descends onto steeper slopes below the site along the western and northern sides of the hill. There is thick grass cover over the entire hilltop, in addition to scattered nopales and thorn bushes (*huarango*).
Modern Land Use: Uncultivated pasture. Extensive remnants of old stone-faced terracing on the south side of the site may have been used for maguey cultivation in the recent past, although there are no maguey plants there today. Although they may be prehispanic, the age of this terracing is uncertain. A nineteenth-century hacienda stone boundary wall runs southeast-northwest along most of the site's long axis.
Archaeological Remains: Because of the dense grass cover, sherd densities are often difficult to ascertain. Nevertheless, there are numerous rodent burrows (*tusas*, or pocket gophers), ant nests, and beetle burrows that have disturbed the surface at many places throughout the site. In such settings, and throughout undisturbed parts of the site as well, surface pottery occurs in light-to-moderate densities, distributed over an area of ca. 28.60 ha. All the visible pottery is Early Toltec, except for traces of Late Aztec and Late Toltec at two locations near the site's eastern edge (no LT or Az sites defined).

There are abundant remains of sizable mounds in the west-central part of the site (Features BH, BI, BJ, BK, BR, BS, BU, BV, BW, BX, BY, BZ, CA, CB, CC, CD, CE, CF, CG, CH, CI, CJ, CK, CL)—these probably represent a ceremonial-civic sector (Plate A58) (Figs. A5a-c, A6a-b). Some of these mounds have been extensively looted. Smaller mounds and irregular concentrations of rock rubble occur throughout much of the rest of the site, and may represent residential structures. Surface pottery is generally denser and more visible in the latter areas.

Mounds BZ, CB, and CD probably comprise the site's ceremonial-civic center. These large mounds are aligned roughly east-west along the southeastern side of an apparent plaza. Immediately to the north of the mounds is a rectangular depression, ca. 25 × 23 m in area and 2 m deep, that may have been a reservoir. Several other substantial mounds cluster in this sector. Of the latter, Feature BK, near the western edge of the site, is of particular interest because of its large size. Associated with Feature BK are a series of well-defined stone-faced terraces, dropping down in four levels toward the steep western slopes.

We noted an unusual quantity of obsidian projectile points at the site. We saw at least 25 such points, and concentrations of blades, chips, and scrapers. There are indications that some of these stone artifacts may have been collected and piled up here by one or more passers-by. Obsidian cores are scarce, but a few are present.

Fea.	Area and Context	Height	Content
BH	20 × 22 m	2.00 m	Very light ET surface pottery; light-to-moderate rock rubble. A looter's pit in center of mound shows stone wall construction (Plate A59).
BI	18 × 15 m	1.50 m	Light ET surface pottery; very light rock rubble. There is a small section of stone wall base.
BJ	9 m dia.	0.50 m	Very light ET on mound, light ET surface pottery around base; no rock rubble.
BK	35 × 25 m (Plate A60)	3.50 m	Very light, light, and light-to-moderate ET surface pottery. Pitting reveals rock-rubble construction. We made one surface collection over entire mound.
BR	7 × 5 m (Plate A61)	0.50 m	Very light ET surface pottery on mound, light ET surface pottery around mound; moderate rock rubble.
BS	4 × 4 m	0.30 m	Light ET surface pottery; heavy rock rubble.
BT	20 × 28 m	3.00 m	Very light and light ET surface pottery; moderate rock rubble. Extensively pitted.
BU	16 × 24 m	3.00 m	Very light ET surface pottery on mound, light ET surface pottery around mound; heavy rock rubble extends out to 2 m from base of mound
BV	4.5 × 6 m	0.40 m	Very light ET surface pottery on mound, light-to-moderate ET surface pottery around mound; heavy rock rubble. Badly pitted.
BW	10 × 13 m mound on 28 × 25 m platform (Plate A62)	0.40 m	Moderate ET surface pottery; heavy rock rubble. A triangular mound associated with a basal platform.
BX	10 × 13 m (Plate A63)	1.00 m	Very light and light ET surface pottery; moderate-to-heavy rock rubble. Looter's pits.

Fea.	Area and Context	Height	Content
BY	25 m dia.	1.00 m	No surface pottery. An amorphous rock pile.
BZ	35 × 40 m (Plate A64)	5.00 m	Very light ET surface pottery; heavy rock rubble. Largest mound at site.
CA	18 × 10 m	1.00 m	No surface pottery; moderate rock rubble.
CB	22 × 27 m	3.50 m	No data on surface pottery; moderate-to-heavy rock rubble.
CC	5 × 10 m	0.50 m	Light ET surface pottery around the mound; moderate-to-heavy rock rubble.
CD	30 × 25 m	1.50 m	Light ET surface pottery; heavy rock rubble. Trapezoidal shape.
CE	7 × 8 m	0.20 m	Very light and light ET surface pottery; heavy rock rubble. Probable domestic structure.
CF	7 × 9 m	0.50 m	No surface pottery; heavy rock rubble.
CG	23 × 25 m	None	This is a depression ca. 2.0 m deep (Plate A65). Very light ET surface pottery; heavy rock rubble.
CH	39 × 40 m plaza	None	Light-to-moderate ET and trace of Az surface pottery; very light rock rubble. This is a plaza surrounded by mounds. One surface collection over entire feature area.
CI	4 × 5 m	0.40 m	Very light and light ET surface pottery; heavy rock rubble. Apparently undisturbed.
CJ	5 × 6 m	0.30 m	Very light and light ET surface pottery; moderate-to-heavy rock rubble. Several looter's pits.
CK	5 × 7 m	0.40 m	Light ET surface pottery around mound, none on mound itself; heavy rock rubble. Apparently undisturbed.
CL	20 × 7 m	1.0 m	Trace of surface pottery; heavy rock rubble. ET figurine found on surface.

Plate A58. Zu-ET-12, section of site's ceremonial-civic core.

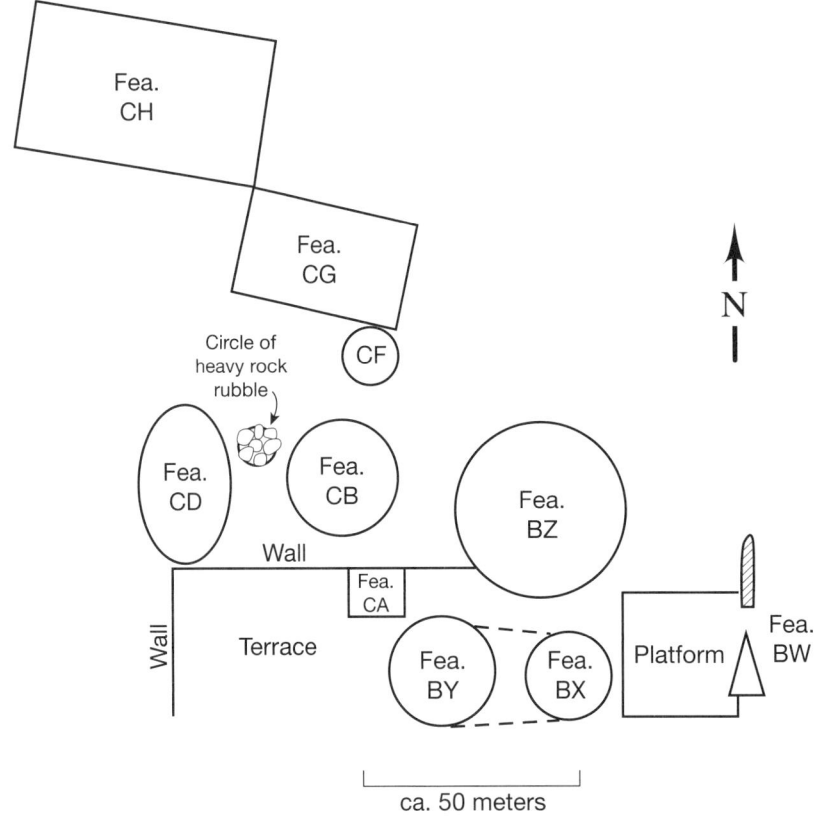

Figure A5a. Zu-ET-12, sketch plan of ceremonial-civic core of site.

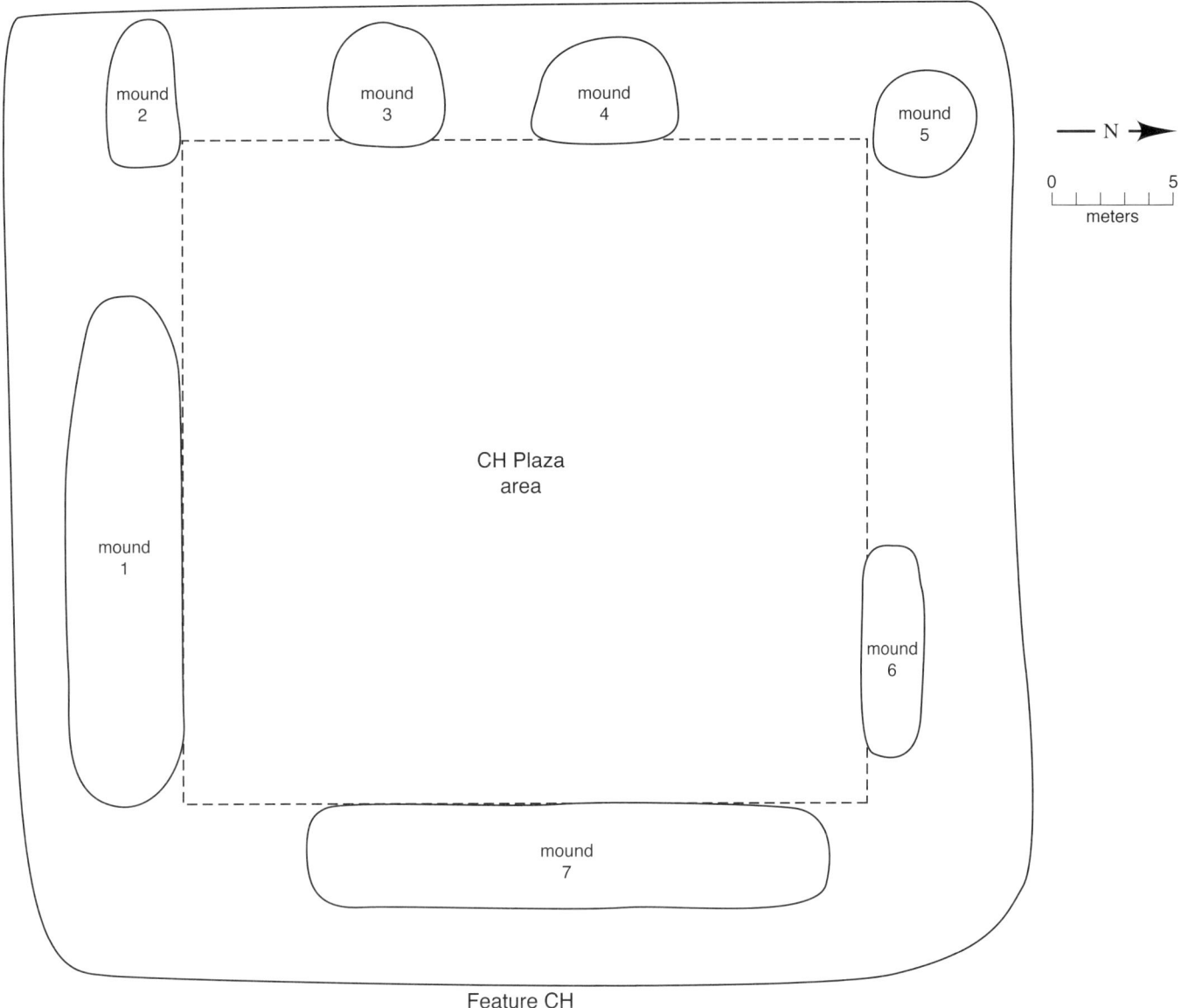

Figure A5b. Zu-ET-12, sketch plan of Feature CH plaza area.

Besides the two surface collections at Features BK and CH, we made three additional surface collections (Locations 42, 43, 45):

Location	Area and Context	Content
42	30 × 45 m, in unplowed area	Light ET surface pottery with several obsidian artifacts; little rock rubble.
43	15 × 35 m, in unplowed area	Light-to-moderate ET surface pottery in scattered patches of bare earth exposed by rodent and insect activity; several obsidian artifacts; little rock rubble.
45	Unrecorded area, in unplowed area near Feature BR	Light ET surface pottery and a few obsidian artifacts; very little rock rubble.

We noted a concentration of petroglyphs carved on rocks along the edge of a cliff face just below the main site area (Plates A66, A67).

Discussion: The age of the petroglyphs below the main site is uncertain, but we presume they are contemporary with the ET occupation on the hilltop. This is by far the largest ET site in the Zumpango Region. Its hilltop location is virtually unique in the entire Basin of Mexico for a site of this size and period.

Classification: Regional Center, 750–1500 people.

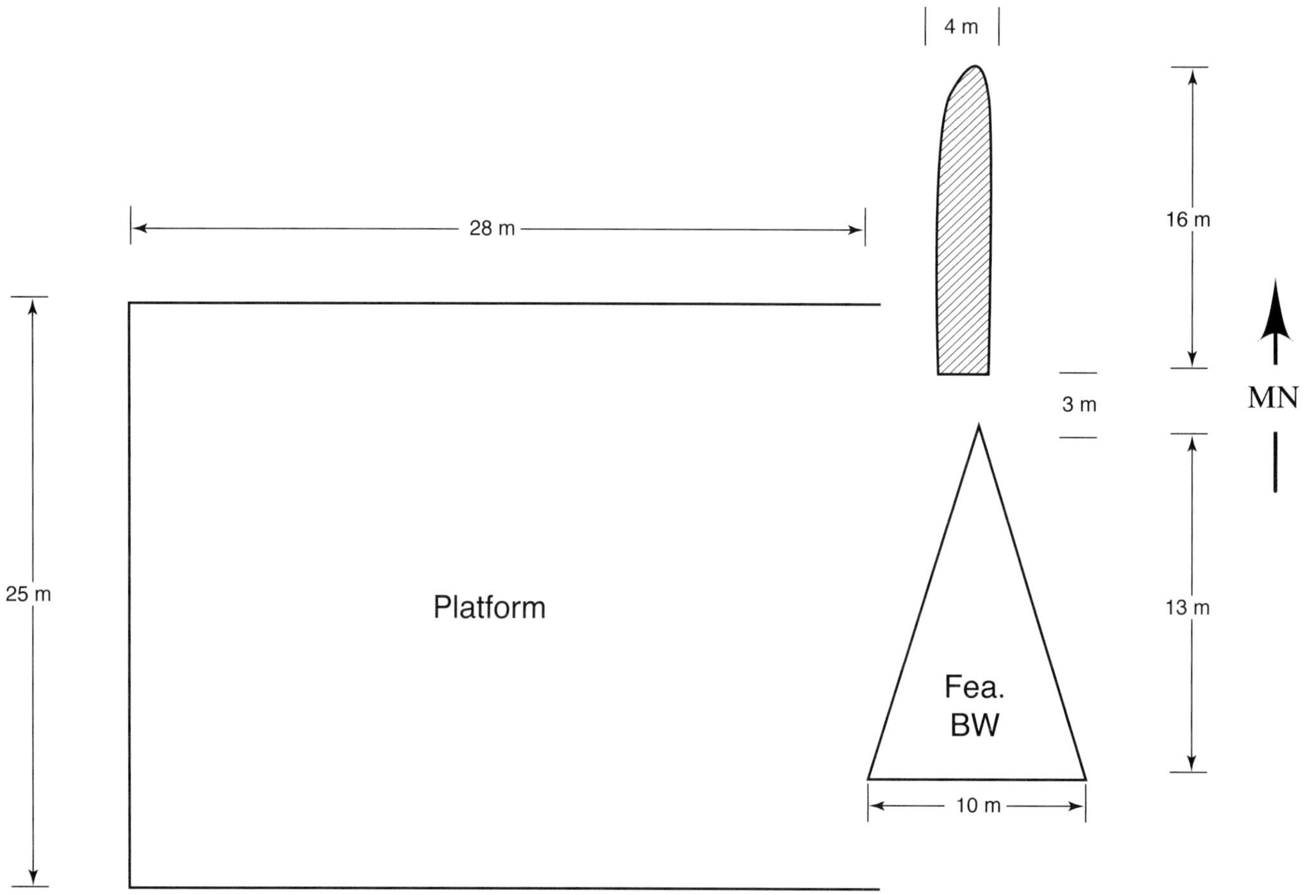

Figure A5c. Zu-ET-12, sketch plan of Feature BW complex.

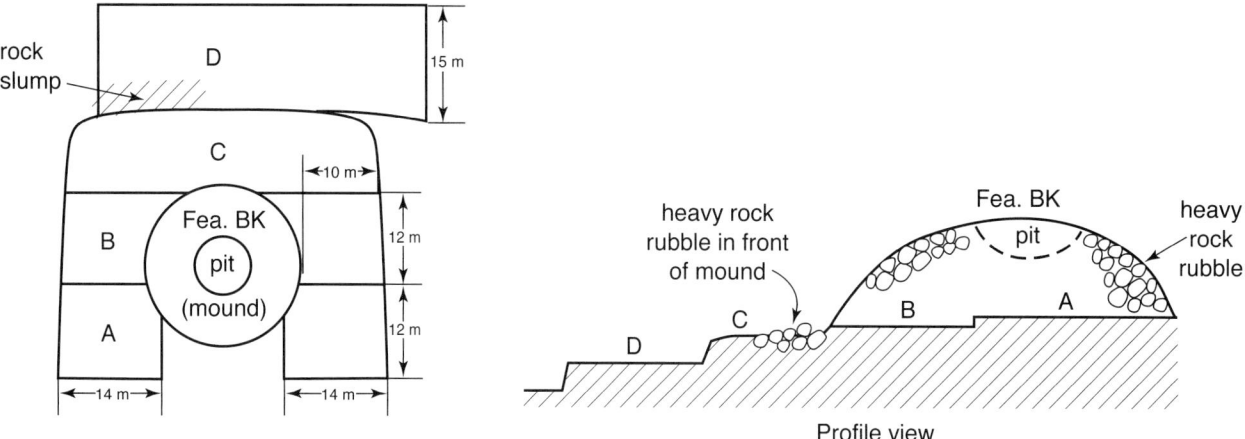

Figure A6a. Zu-ET-12, sketch plan and profile of Feature BK complex.

Appendix A: Site Descriptions

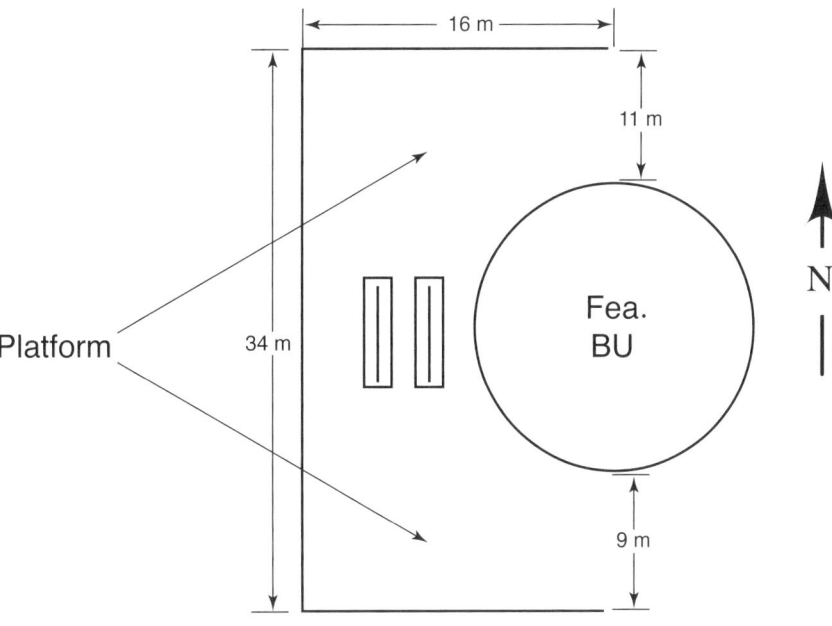

Figure A6b. Zu-ET-12, sketch plan and profile of Feature BU complex.

Plate A59. Zu-ET-12, Feature BH, showing stone wall exposed in looter's pit.

Plate A60. Zu-ET-12, facing SW at Feature BK.

Plate A61. Zu-ET-12, facing north at Feature BR.

Plate A62. Zu-ET-12, facing NW over platform supporting Feature BW, from top of Feature BZ.

Plate A63. Zu-ET-12, Feature BX, from top of Feature BZ.

Plate A64. Zu-ET-12, facing south at Features BZ, CB, and CD.

Plate A65. Zu-ET-12, facing north over Feature CG (depression); Feature CD in foreground.

Plate A66. Zu-ET-12, petroglyph at base of cliff below site.

Plate A67. Zu-ET-12, petroglyph at base of cliff below site.

SITE NO. Zu-ET-13 [Zu-Cl-21(M); Location 41]
   Date of Survey: June 21, 1973
   Location: 483500 E, 2199930 N; 19.8955° N, 99.1576° W
   Natural Setting: 2270 m asl, on gently sloping ground in the Upper Salado Drainage; shallow soil cover and slight erosion.
   Modern Land Use: Rainfall-based agriculture in the general area. The site itself is presently fallow, although it has been plowed in the recent past. A railroad line crosses the center of the site.
   Archaeological Remains: Light-to-moderate surface Early Toltec surface pottery over an area of ca. 1.40 ha. The ET material is mixed with approximately equal quantities of Classic ceramics (Zu-Cl-59). We noted several green and gray obsidian blades and scrapers. There are no discernible structural remains and very little rock rubble.
   We made one surface collection (Location 41) from an area ca. 4 × 5 m in a fallow field, with light-to-moderate ET and Cl surface pottery, several obsidian artifacts, and very light rock rubble.
   Discussion: Cl to ET settlement continuity.
   Classification: Hamlet, 20–40 people.

SITE NO. Zu-ET-14 [Zu-Cl-13(J); Location 30]
   Date of Survey: July 5, 1973
   Location: 487850 E, 2200850 N; 19.9039° N, 99.1161° W
   Natural Setting: 2280 m asl, on gently sloping ground in the Upper Salado Drainage; medium soil cover and slight erosion.
   Modern Land Use: Rainfall-based agriculture. Outlying residences of the modern town of Tequixquiac encroach onto the site from the west and south.
   Archaeological Remains: Variable light and light-to-moderate Early Toltec surface pottery over an area of ca. 6.50 ha. The ET material is mixed with heavier and more extensive Classic (Zu-Cl-53) and lighter Late Aztec ceramics (Zu-Az-113). We noted several green and gray obsidian blades and scrapers, one gray obsidian projectile point, some obsidian debitage, three ceramic figurines (one Tzacualli [no TF site designated], one Classic, one Aztec), and one basalt metate fragment. There is light-to-moderate rock rubble but no discernible structural remains.
   We made one surface collection (Location 30) over an area ca. 15 × 25 m in a plowed field, with light-to-moderate Cl and light ET surface pottery, several obsidian artifacts, one basalt metate fragment, and moderate rock rubble.
   Discussion: Cl to ET settlement continuity.
   Classification: Small Dispersed Village, 75–150 people.

SITE NO. Zu-ET-15 [Zu-Cl-11(J); Location 27]
   Date of Survey: June 26, 1973
   Location: 493220 E, 2201320 N; 19.9082° N, 99.0648° W
   Natural Setting: 2290 m asl, on gently sloping ground in the Upper Salado Drainage; shallow soil cover and severe erosion.
   Modern Land Use: Marginal pasture. The modern town of Hueypoxtla borders the northwestern edge of the site.
   Archaeological Remains: Variable light and light-to-moderate Early Toltec surface pottery over an area of ca. 2.10 ha. Because of modern occupation, the northwestern limits of the site could not be accurately determined. The ET material is mixed with heavier Classic (Zu-Cl-37) and Late Toltec (Zu-LT-52) ceramics. We noted several obsidian blades and scrapers. There is moderate rock rubble but no discernible structural remains.
   We made one surface collection (Location 27) over an area ca. 25 × 25 m in an unplowed area, with light-to-moderate Cl, ET, and LT surface pottery; several obsidian artifacts; and moderate rock rubble.
   Discussion: Long-term settlement continuity.
   Classification: Hamlet, 20–40 people.

SITE NO. Zu-ET-16 [Zu-Cl-16(J); Locations 38, 39, 40]
   Date of Survey: July 16, 1973
   Location: 495400 E, 2200180 N; 19.8979° N, 99.0439° W
   Natural Setting: 2325 m asl, on gently sloping ground atop a broad, low ridge in the Upper Salado Drainage, very close to the divide between the Upper Salado and Basin of Mexico drainages; shallow soil cover and slight erosion.
   Modern Land Use: Rainfall-based agriculture.
   Archaeological Remains: Variable light and light-to-moderate Early Toltec surface pottery over a vaguely mounded area of ca. 13.40 ha. The ET material is mixed with approximately equal quantities of Classic (Zu-Cl-40) and lighter Late Toltec (Zu-LT-48) ceramics. We noted several green and gray obsidian blades, one gray obsidian projectile point, and seven basalt mano fragments. There is light-to-moderate rock rubble, but no discernible structural remains.
   We made three surface collections (Locations 38, 39, 40):

Location	Area and Context	Content
38	15 × 15 m, in plowed field	Light-to-moderate Cl, light ET, and very light LT surface pottery; several obsidian artifacts; one basalt mano fragment; light rock rubble.
39	5 × 10 m, in unplowed area	Light-to-moderate Cl and LT, light ET, and traces of Az surface pottery; one Cl figurine; several obsidian artifacts; moderate rock rubble.
40	Collection area not recorded, in unplowed field	Light-to-moderate Cl, light LT and ET, very light Az surface pottery; several obsidian artifacts; light-to-moderate rock rubble.

   Discussion: Long-term settlement continuity.
   Classification: Small Dispersed Village, 150–300 people.

SITE NO. Zu-ET-17 [Zu-Cl-14(J); Locations 32, 33, 34, 35, 36]
   Date of Survey: July 10, 1973
   Location: 488050 E, 2198180 N; 19.8798° N, 99.1142° W
   Natural Setting: 2325 m asl, on gently sloping ground atop a low, broad ridge in the Upper Salado Drainage, just north of the divide between the Upper Salado Drainage and the Basin of Mexico Lower Piedmont; medium soil cover and slight erosion.
   Modern Land Use: Rainfall-based agriculture. Most of the site is presently fallow.
   Archaeological Remains: Variable light and light-to-moderate Early Toltec surface pottery over an area of ca. 3.30 ha. The ET material is mixed with approximately equal quantities of Classic ceramics (Zu-Cl-52), and there is some overlap with Late Toltec (Zu-LT-133) and Terminal Formative (Zu-TF-4) occupations. We noted several scrapers, points, blades, and flakes of green and gray obsidian, and one basalt mano fragment.
   We made five surface collections (Locations 32, 33, 34, 35, 36):

Location	Area and Context	Content
32	20 × 20 m, in fallow field	Light-to-moderate Cl and ET, light TF, and very light Az surface pottery; several obsidian artifacts; light rock rubble.
33	4 × 6 m, in fallow field	Moderate Cl and ET surface pottery; several obsidian artifacts; moderate rock rubble.
34	10 × 15 m, in plowed field	Light-to-moderate LT, and light Cl and ET surface pottery; several obsidian artifacts; moderate rock rubble.
35	10 × 10 m, in plowed field	Moderate Cl and ET surface pottery; several obsidian artifacts; moderate rock rubble.
36	15 × 15 m, in fallow field	Light-to-moderate LT and light Cl and ET surface pottery; several obsidian artifacts; light-to-moderate rock rubble.

   Discussion: Unusually long settlement continuity at this locality, TF–LT.
   Classification: Hamlet, 35–70 people.

SITE NO. Zu-ET-18 [Zu-Cl-26(J); Location 48]
   Date of Survey: Aug. 1, 1973
   Location: 489300 E, 2194400 N; 19.8456° N, 99.1022° W
   Natural Setting: 2290 m asl, on nearly level ground at the lower edge of the Basin of Mexico Lower Piedmont, just above the upper edge of the Lakeshore Plain; medium soil cover and no erosion.
   Modern Land Use: Rainfall-based agriculture.
   Archaeological Remains: Light Early Toltec surface pottery over an area of ca. 3.60 ha. The ET material is mixed with approximately equal quantities of Classic ceramics (Zu-Cl-48). We noted several obsidian blades and scrapers, and one Cl two-hole *candelero*. There is light rock rubble and no discernible structural remains.
   We made one surface collection (Location 48) over an area ca. 8 × 10 m in a plowed field with light-to-moderate Cl and ET surface pottery, several obsidian artifacts, and light rock rubble.
   Discussion: Cl to ET settlement continuity.
   Classification: Hamlet, 20–40 people.

SITE NO. Zu-ET-19 [Zu-Cl-33(M); Locations 60, 61; Features DQ, DR]
   Date of Survey: July 23–24, 1973
   Location: 482900 E, 2196030 N; 19.8603° N, 99.1633° W
   Natural Setting: 2330 m asl, on nearly level ground in the Upper Salado Drainage. The soil cover varies from deep in the north to medium in the southern part of the site, and erosion has been slight.
   Modern Land Use: Rainfall-based agriculture. A commercial farming complex, the hacienda "El Cenicero," borders the site on the west. A modern dirt road leading to the hacienda runs southeast-northwest across the center of the site.
   Archaeological Remains: Variable light, light-to-moderate, and moderate-to-heavy Early Toltec surface pottery over an area of ca. 19.5 ha. The ET material is mixed with heavier Classic (Zu-Cl-60) and Aztec (Zu-Az-208) ceramics. We noted numerous green and gray obsidian blades, scrapers, projectile points, and fragments, and numerous basalt mano and metate fragments.

Plate A68. Zu-ET-20, facing NE over site area.

There are two mounds in the southeastern corner of the site (Features DR, DQ):

Fea.	Area and Context	Height	Content
DR	8 × 10 m, in unplowed area	0.40 m	Light Cl and very light ET and Az surface pottery; moderate rock rubble.
DQ	10 × 10 m, in unplowed area	0.40 m	Light Cl and ET and very light Az surface pottery; moderate rock rubble. Looter's pit shows earth and rock-rubble fill.

We made two surface collections (Locations 60, 61):

Location	Area and Context	Content
60	20 × 25 m, in plowed field	Light Cl and ET, and very light Az surface pottery; several obsidian artifacts; light-to-moderate rock rubble.
61	2.5 × 10 m, in plowed field	Moderate-to-heavy Cl, light ET, and trace of LT surface pottery; several obsidian artifacts; light-to-moderate rock rubble.

Discussion: Because of the heavy admixture of Cl surface pottery and uncertainties about the nature of ET plainwares at the time of our survey, the surface area of the ET site remains uncertain. In any event, there is Cl to ET settlement continuity.
Classification: Large Nucleated Village (??), 400–800 people.

SITE NO. Zu-ET-20 [Zu-Cl-41(M); Location 84]
Date of Survey: Nov. 13, 1973
Location: 480970 E, 2194570 N; 19.8471° N, 99.1817° W
Natural Setting: 2290 m asl, on gently sloping ground near the lower end of a long, low, broad ridge (Plate A68) in the Upper Salado Drainage; medium soil cover and moderate erosion.
Modern Land Use: Rainfall-based agriculture. The remains of a substantial abandoned floodwater irrigation system extend over lower ground to the west. These remains are probably nineteenth or early twentieth century in age, associated with one of the major haciendas in the area.
Archaeological Remains: Variable light and light-to-moderate Early Toltec surface pottery over an area of ca. 3.40 ha. The ET material is mixed with lighter Aztec ceramics (Zu-Az-219). We noted several green obsidian blades and a few gray obsidian scrapers, and one basalt mano fragment. There are no discernible structural remains.
We made one surface collection (Location 84) over an area ca. 15 × 15 m in a recently harvested maize field (Plate A69), with light-to-moderate ET surface pottery, several obsidian artifacts, and very little rock rubble.
Classification: Hamlet, 35–70 people.

SITE NO. Zu-ET-21 [Zu-Cl-44(M); Location 89]
Date of Survey: Dec. 2, 1973
Location: 481320 E, 2190950 N; 19.8144° N, 99.1784° W
Natural Setting: 2280 m asl, on gently sloping ground on the Lakeshore Plain, near the northern edge of Lake Xaltocán-Zumpango; deep soil cover and slight erosion.
Modern Land Use: Rainfall-based agriculture. Alfalfa is grown in irrigated fields to the south.
Archaeological Remains: Variable light and light-to-moderate Early Toltec surface pottery over an area of ca. 0.80 ha. The ET material is mixed with heavier Classic ceramics (Zu-Cl-64), and traces of Late Toltec and Aztec pottery (no LT or Az sites defined). We noted several obsidian blades and some debitage, mostly green in color. There are no discernible structural remains.
We made one surface collection (Location 89) over an area ca. 10 × 10 m in a recently harvested maize field, with light-to-moderate Cl and light ET surface pottery, several obsidian artifacts, and no rock rubble.
Classification: Small Hamlet, 10–20 people.

SITE NO. Zu-ET-22 [Zu-LT-80(M); Locations 86, 87]
Date of Survey: Nov. 28, 1973
Location: 475320 E, 2189450 N; 19.8008° N, 99.2356° W
Natural Setting: 2280 m asl, on gently sloping ground in the Upper Salado Drainage, near the upper edge of the Lakeshore Plain, just north of the divide between the Upper Salado Drainage and the Basin of Mexico drainages; medium soil cover and slight erosion.
Modern Land Use: Rainfall-based agriculture. A large drainage canal borders the eastern edge of the site.
Archaeological Remains: Light-to-moderate Early Toltec surface pottery over an area of ca. 1.00 ha. The ET material is mixed with heavier

Plate A69. Zu-ET-20, facing NE over Location 84.

Late Toltec (Zu-LT-203) and lighter Aztec ceramics (Zu-Az-269). There are also traces of Classic and Terminal Formative pottery (no Cl or TF sites were defined). We noted several green and gray obsidian blades, scrapers, and some debitage, and some chert debitage. No discernible structural remains can be associated with the ET occupation.

We made two surface collections (Locations 86, 87):

Location	Area and Context	Content
86	5 × 6 m, in recently harvested maize field	Light-to-moderate LT, light ET, and very light Az surface pottery; several obsidian artifacts; light-to-moderate rock rubble.
87	15 × 20 m, in recently harvested maize field	Light-to-moderate LT, light ET, and very light Az surface pottery; several obsidian artifacts; moderate rock rubble.

Discussion: ET to LT settlement continuity.
Classification: Hamlet, 15–30 people.

SITE NO. Zu-ET-23 [Zu-ET-2(M); Locations 91, 92, 93, 94]
Date of Survey: Dec. 3, 1973
Location: 481030 E, 2189180 N; 19.7984° N, 99.1811° W
Natural Setting: 2260 m asl, on gently sloping ground atop a low, apparently natural (?) knoll that rises to a maximum height of ca. 5.00 m above the general level of the surrounding Lakeshore Plain, near the northern edge of Lake Xaltocán-Zumpango; deep soil cover and slight erosion. This site occupies a topographic elevation (ancient beach ridges and intervening strand plain) several meters above the general level of the surrounding Lakeshore Plain (Frederick et al. 2005:75) (Fig. 2.4).

Modern Land Use: Rainfall-based agriculture on the supporting knoll. Much of the surrounding lower ground is devoted to irrigation agriculture. The area is surrounded by the abandoned remains of a nineteenth- or early twentieth-century floodwater irrigation system. There is a small modern religious shrine at the center of the site.

Archaeological Remains: Variable light and light-to-moderate Early Toltec surface pottery over an area of ca. 3.80 ha. The ET material is mixed with approximately equal, but spatially more extensive, quantities of Classic (Zu-Cl-83), Late Toltec (Zu-LT-197), and Late Aztec ceramics (Zu-Az-259, Zu-Az-260). We noted several obsidian blades and scrapers, mostly green in color. There is very little rock rubble and no definite structural remains, although the supporting knoll could be partially artificial.

We made four surface collections (Locations 91, 92, 93, 94):

Location	Area and Context	Content
91	15 × 15 m, in a harvested maize field	Light-to-moderate Cl and ET, and light LT, and very light Az surface pottery; several obsidian artifacts; very little rock rubble.
92	15 × 15 m, in a harvested maize field	Light-to-moderate Cl and ET, and very light Az surface pottery; several obsidian artifacts; very little rock rubble.
93	8 × 20 m, in a harvested maize field	Light-to-moderate Cl and ET, light LT, and very light Az surface pottery; very little rock rubble.
94	10 × 15 m, in a harvested maize field	Light-to-moderate Cl and ET, light LT, and very light Az surface pottery; several obsidian artifacts; very little rock rubble.

Discussion: This site appears to be continuously occupied from Classic through Late Postclassic times. Such long-term occupational continuity is unusual in this area. This characteristic, together with the protective deep soil cover, suggests that this may be an excellent locality for future stratigraphic excavation (if it has not been completely destroyed by modern occupation in the decades after our survey), especially if the supporting knoll represents subsurface architecture.
Classification: Hamlet, 40–80 people.

SITE NO. Zu-ET-24 [Zu-Cl-37(M); Location 70]
 Date of Survey: Aug. 5, 1973
 Location: 483750 E, 2190470 N; 19.8100° N, 99.1552° W
 Natural Setting: 2305 m asl, on gently sloping ground on the southwestern side of a broad ridge in the Basin of Mexico Lower Piedmont; medium soil cover and slight erosion.
 Modern Land Use: Rainfall-based agriculture. Modern houses at the edge of the modern town of Zitlaltepec encroach onto the site from the southwest and southeast.
 Archaeological Remains: Variable light and light-to-moderate Early Toltec surface pottery over an area of ca. 1.80 ha. Because of modern occupation, the southwestern limits of the site could not be accurately defined. The ET material is mixed with heavier and spatially more extensive Classic (Zu-Cl-66) and Late Aztec ceramics (Zu-Az-255). We noted several obsidian blades and fragments. No discernible structural remains can be associated with the Cl or ET occupations.
 We made one surface collection (Location 70) over an area ca. 8 × 10 m in a plowed field in the area of Cl and ET occupation, with light-to-moderate Late Az, and light Cl and ET surface pottery; several obsidian artifacts; and no rock rubble.
 Discussion: Cl to ET settlement continuity.
 Classification: Hamlet, 20–40 people.

SITE NO. Zu-ET-25 [Zu-Cl-34(M); Location 63]
 Date of Survey: July 26, 1973
 Location: 484680 E, 2193500 N; 19.8374° N, 99.1463° W
 Natural Setting: 2505 m asl, on moderately to steeply sloping ground at the edge of a saddle between two peaks on the eastern flank of Cerro Jalpa; shallow to medium soil cover and moderate to severe erosion.
 Modern Land Use: Marginal rainfall-based agriculture, with maguey semi-terracing.
 Archaeological Remains: Variable light and light-to-moderate Early Toltec surface pottery over an area of ca. 1.10 ha. The ET material is mixed with approximately equal quantities of Classic ceramics (Zu-Cl-67), with a trace of Aztec pottery (no Az site defined). We noted numerous green obsidian blades, several green obsidian scrapers and fragments, one gray obsidian projectile point, and one chert fragment. There is light-to-moderate rock rubble, but no discernible structural remains.
 We made one surface collection (Location 63) over an area ca. 10 × 15 m, with light-to-moderate Cl and ET surface pottery, several obsidian artifacts, and light-to-moderate rock rubble.
 Discussion: This site's unusually high elevation and topographic setting suggest that it may have had a non-domestic function. Cl to ET occupational continuity.
 Classification: Small Hamlet (?), 10–20 people.

SITE NO. Zu-ET-26 [Zu-Cl-32(J); Location 69]
 Date of Survey: Oct. 1, 1973
 Location: 492930 E, 2188070 N; 19.7884° N, 99.0675° W
 Natural Setting: 2260 m asl, on nearly level ground on the Lakeshore Plain, near the northern edge of Lake Xaltocán-Zumpango; deep soil cover and slight erosion.
 Modern Land Use: Rainfall-based agriculture in the southern three-quarters of the site; the northern quarter is irrigated alfalfa. The modern paved road to Zumpango crosses the northern half of the site. Two large commercial farms border the site on the east.
 Archaeological Remains: Variable light and light-to-moderate Early Toltec surface pottery over an area of ca. 5.50 ha. The ET material is mixed with heavier Classic ceramics (Zu-Cl-77). There are also traces of Late Toltec and Aztec surface pottery (no LT or Az sites defined). We noted several green and gray obsidian blades and one gray obsidian scraper. There is very little rock rubble and no discernible structural remains.
 We made one surface collection (Location 69) over an area ca. 10 × 15 m at the edge of a maize field with light-to-moderate Cl and light ET surface pottery, several obsidian artifacts, and no rock rubble.
 Discussion: Cl to ET settlement continuity.
 Classification: Small Dispersed Village, 60–120 people.

SITE NO. Zu-ET-27 [Zu-Cl-33(J); Location 71]
 Date of Survey: Oct. 7, 1973
 Location: 495750 E, 2188820 N; 19.7952° N, 99.0406° W
 Natural Setting: 2310 m asl, on gently sloping ground on the top of a low hill that stands ca. 25 m above the general level of the surrounding Lakeshore Plain; shallow soil cover and moderate erosion.
 Modern Land Use: Rainfall-based agriculture in the northern half of the site. The southern half is unplowed pasture. Modern residential structures encroach onto the site from the east and northwest. A modern dirt roads runs along the southern edge of the site.
 Archaeological Remains: Variable light and light-to-moderate Early Toltec surface pottery over an area of ca. 6.50 ha. The ET material is mixed with heavier Classic ceramics (Zu-Cl-73). We noted several green and gray obsidian artifacts. There is very little rock rubble and no discernible structural remains.
 We made one surface collection (Location 71) over an area ca. 10 × 15 m in a fallow field with light-to-moderate Cl and light ET surface pottery, several obsidian artifacts, and very little rock rubble.
 Discussion: Because of modern occupation, we were unable to define the site's precise northwestern limits. Cl to ET settlement continuity.
 Classification: Small Dispersed Village (?), 65–130 people.

SITE NO. Zu-ET-28 [Zu-Cl-38(J); Location 84]
 Date of Survey: Oct. 22, 1973
 Location: 493600 E, 2184740 N; 19.7583° N, 99.0611° W
 Natural Setting: 2245 m asl, on nearly level ground atop a very slight, broad elevation (artificial?) that rises to a maximum height of ca. 1.00 m above the general level of the surrounding Lakeshore Plain, at or near the northern edge of Lake Xaltocán-Zumpango; deep soil cover and no erosion. This site occupies a topographic elevation (ancient beach ridges and intervening strand plain) several meters above the general level of the surrounding Lakeshore Plain (Frederick et al. 2005:75) (Fig. 2.4).
 Modern Land Use: Rainfall-based agriculture. The immediate site area is presently fallow and thickly weed covered. A small modern house encroaches onto the site's southeastern edge. A modern dirt road borders the western edge of the site.
 Archaeological Remains: Variable light and light-to-moderate Early Toltec surface pottery over an area of ca. 3.30 ha. The ET material is mixed with heavier Classic ceramics (Zu-Cl-80). We noted several green and gray obsidian blades and debitage. There is very little rock rubble and no discernible structural remains, although the slight elevation upon which the site rests may be partly or wholly of artificial construction.
 We made one surface collection (Location 84) over an area ca. 20 × 25 m in a fallow, weed-covered field, with light-to-moderate Cl and light ET surface pottery, several obsidian artifacts, and very little rock rubble.
 Discussion: If the underlying elevation represents subsurface architecture, this could be an excellent place for future excavation of well-preserved archaeological deposits.
 Classification: Hamlet, 35–70 people.

SITE NO. Zu-ET-29 [Zu-LT-70(M); Locations 78, 79, 80, 81, 82]
   Date of Survey: Aug. 20–22, 1973
   Location: 485300 E, 2176820 N; 19.6867° N, 99.1403° W
   Natural Setting: 2270 m asl, on gently sloping ground on the lower slopes of Cerro Tultepec, near the edge of the Lakeshore Plain on the western shore of Lake Xaltocán-Zumpango; medium to deep soil cover and slight erosion.
   Modern Land Use: Rainfall-based agriculture. The modern town of Tultepec encroaches onto the site from the east, and may cover part of the archaeological site.
   Archaeological Remains: Variable light and light-to-moderate Early Toltec surface pottery over an area of ca. 7.20 ha. The ET material is mixed with heavier and more extensive Late Toltec ceramics (Zu-LT-211). Because of the heavy LT overlay, it proved difficult to estimate the surface area and sherd density for the ET site. There is also a trace of Aztec surface pottery (no Az site defined). There are numerous green and gray obsidian artifacts and debitage, and we noted one obsidian projectile point. There is very little rock rubble, and no discernible structural remains can be associated with the ET surface pottery.

We made five surface collections (Locations 78, 79, 80, 81, 82):

Location	Area and Context	Content
78	7 × 10 m, in plowed field	Moderate LT, light ET, and traces of Az surface pottery; very little rock rubble.
79	5 × 8 m, in fallow field	Moderate-to-heavy LT, light ET, and traces of Az surface pottery; light rock rubble.
80	Area not recorded, in plowed field	Light-to-moderate LT and traces of ET and Az surface pottery; very little rock rubble.
81	3 × 4 m, in plowed field	Heavy LT, light ET, and traces of Az surface pottery; very little rock rubble.
82	5 × 8 m, in fallow field	Moderate LT, light ET, and traces of Az surface pottery; very little rock rubble.

   Discussion: ET to LT settlement continuity.
   Classification: Small Dispersed Village (?), 75–150 people.

SITE NO. Zu-ET-30 [Zu-Cl-28(J); Locations 54, 55, 57, 58, 59, 60]
   Date of Survey: Aug. 22–23, Sept. 13, 1973
   Location: 487430 E, 2174220 N; 19.6632° N, 99.1199° W
   Natural Setting: 2245 m asl, on a low, natural (?) elevation rising about 1.50 m above the general level of the surrounding Lakeshore Plain south of Tultepec Island, at or close to the northwestern shore of Lake Xaltocán-Zumpango; deep soil cover and slight erosion.
   Modern Land Use: Most of the site area and its surroundings is unplowed pasture, although there is limited rainfall-based agriculture nearby. Several deep drainage ditches and dirt roads cross the site. A railroad line runs southwest-northeast just beyond the site's northwestern edge.
   Archaeological Remains: Variable light, light-to-moderate, and moderate Early Toltec surface pottery over an area of ca. 10.40 ha. The ET material is mixed with much heavier and more extensive Classic ceramics (Zu-Cl-90). There is also lighter Late Aztec pottery (Zu-Az-298). The Cl pottery is dominated by large reddish-brown ollas. We noted several green and gray obsidian blades and a few obsidian projectile points.

There are no definite mounds, but much of the site area is covered with vague, irregular mounding, and there is light-to-moderate rock rubble that may represent the remnants of ancient structures. The supporting elevation may be partially artificial.

We made six surface collections (Locations 54, 55, 57, 58, 59, 60):

Location	Area and Context	Content
54	10 × 10 m, in fallow field	Light-to-moderate Cl, light ET and Late Az surface pottery; light-to-moderate rock rubble.
55	10 × 10 m, in fallow field	Moderate Cl, light ET and Late Az surface pottery; light rock rubble. A nearby ditch profile shows a stucco floor at a depth of ca. 70 cm.
57	2 × 4 m, in fallow field	Moderate Cl, light ET and Late Az surface pottery; moderate rock rubble.
58	5 × 5 m, taken from ditch cut through mounded area	Moderate-to-heavy Cl, light ET, and very light Az surface pottery; light rock rubble.
59	5 × 5 m, in fallow field	Moderate Cl, light ET, and very light Az surface pottery; no rock rubble.
60	5 × 5 m, in fallow field	Moderate Cl and light ET surface pottery; very little rock rubble.

   Discussion: Most of the irregular mounding appears to comprise masses of potsherds. The heavy concentration of Texcoco Fabric Marked pottery at two nearby Az sites (Zu-Az-297, -298) suggests that this ET site may have had a saltmaking function. The predominance of a single ceramic form (large reddish-brown ollas) may also indicate a Classic- and Epiclassic-period saltmaking function (Mayer-Oakes 1959).

Because of the heavy Classic overlay, it remains difficult to define the area of the ET site.
   Classification: Small Nucleated Village (?), 200–400 people.

Late Toltec Sites (Fig. A7)

SITE NO. Zu-LT-1 [Zu-LT-20(J); Location 22]
   Date of Survey: June 12, 1973
   Location: 497630 E, 2210500 N; 19.9911° N, 99.0227° W
   Natural Setting: 2390 m asl, on gently sloping ground in the Upper Salado Drainage; deep soil cover and slight erosion.
   Modern Land Use: Rainfall-based agriculture. There is a still-occupied complex of nineteenth-century hacienda buildings just north of the site.
   Archaeological Remains: Variable light and light-to-moderate Late Toltec surface pottery over an area of ca. 6.40 ha. The LT material is mixed with lighter Classic (Zu-Cl-6) and Early Toltec (Zu-ET-2) ceramics along the northern side of the LT site. We noted several obsidian artifacts (mostly green in color), and chert fragments. There is light-to-moderate rock rubble but no discernible structural remains.

We made one surface collection (Location 22) over an area ca. 8 × 10 m in a fallow field (Plate A70), with light-to-moderate LT, and light ET and Cl surface pottery, several obsidian artifacts, and light-to-moderate rock rubble.
   Classification: Small Dispersed Village, 65–130 people.

SITE NO. Zu-LT-2 [Zu-LT-21(J); Location 21]
   Date of Survey: June 11, 1973
   Location: 495450 E, 2210100 N; 19.9875° N, 99.0435° W
   Natural Setting: 2445 m asl, on gently sloping ground in the Upper Salado Drainage; medium soil cover and moderate erosion.
   Modern Land Use: Rainfall-based agriculture.

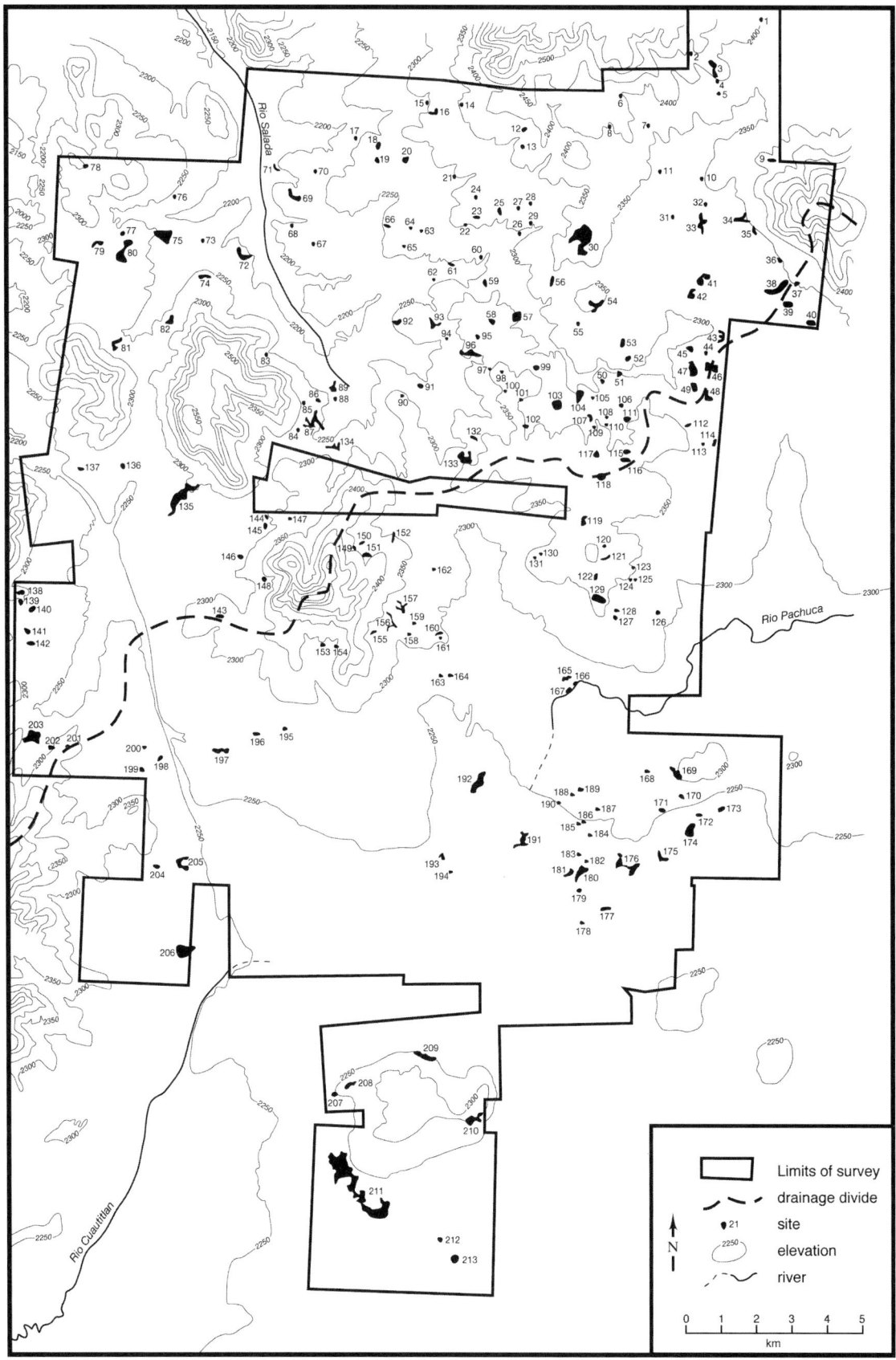

Figure A7. Map of Late Toltec sites in the Zumpango Region.

Plate A70. Zu-LT-1, facing north over Location 22.

Archaeological Remains: Variable light and light-to-moderate Late Toltec surface pottery over an area of ca. 0.70 ha. The LT material is mixed with lighter Late Aztec ceramics (Zu-Az-5). There are no recognizable mounds, although moderate rock rubble in some areas may represent the remnants of former structures. We noted several green obsidian blades, and one maguey spindle whorl.

We made one surface collection (Location 21) over an area ca. 15 m in diameter in a fallow field with light-to-moderate LT and light Late Az surface pottery, several obsidian artifacts, and moderate rock rubble.

Discussion: The apparent absence of Early Aztec surface pottery indicates that this locality was abandoned after LT times and reoccupied during the Late Aztec period.

Classification: Small Hamlet, 5–10 people.

SITE NO. Zu-LT-3 [Zu-LT-19(J)]
  Date of Survey: June 11, 1973
  Location: 496220 E, 2209700 N; 19.9839° N, 99.0361° W
  Natural Setting: 2430 m asl, on gently sloping ground in the Upper Salado Drainage; shallow to medium soil cover; slight to moderate erosion.
  Modern Land Use: Rainfall-based agriculture, with maguey terracing. Maguey semi-terracing occurs throughout the general area. A modern dirt road skirts the northwest edge of the site.
  Archaeological Remains: Variable light and light-to-moderate Late Toltec surface pottery over an area of ca. 7.90 ha. The LT material is mixed with lighter, but more extensive, Late Aztec pottery (Zu-Az-5). There are no discernible structural remains.
  No surface collection made in the LT site.
  Discussion: The apparent absence of Early Aztec surface pottery indicates that this locality was abandoned after LT times and reoccupied during the Late Aztec period.
  Classification: Small Dispersed Village, 80–160 people.

SITE NO. Zu-LT-4 [Zu-LT-18(J); Locations 19, 21]
  Date of Survey: June 10, 1973
  Location: 496350 E, 2209300 N; 19.9803° N, 99.0349° W
  Natural Setting: 2400 m asl, on gently sloping ground in the Upper Salado Drainage; shallow soil cover and moderate erosion.
  Modern Land Use: Rainfall-based maguey cultivation, and unplowed pasture.
  Archaeological Remains: Light Late Toltec surface pottery over an area of ca. 1.40 ha. The LT material is mixed with lighter and more extensive Late Aztec ceramics (Zu-Az-5). This LT site is only 75 m south of the larger Zu-LT-3 site, and might be considered a southern extension of the latter. There are no discernible structural remains.
  We made two surface collections (Locations 19, 21):

Location	Area and Context	Content
19	10 × 15 m, in plowed field	Light-to-moderate Late Az and light LT surface pottery; moderate rock rubble.
21	15 m dia., in fallow field	Light-to-moderate Late Az, light LT; moderate rock rubble.

  Discussion: The apparent absence of Early Aztec surface pottery indicates that this locality was abandoned after LT times and reoccupied during the Late Aztec period.
  Classification: Small Hamlet, 5–10 people.

SITE NO. Zu-LT-5 [Zu-LT-17(J)]
  Date of Survey: June 11, 1973
  Location: 496350 E, 2208900 N; 19.9767° N, 99.0349° W
  Natural Setting: 2380 m asl, on gently sloping ground in the Upper Salado Drainage; shallow soil cover and moderate erosion.
  Modern Land Use: Rainfall-based maguey cultivation, and unplowed pasture. The north edge of the modern village of Santa María Ajoloapan encroaches slightly onto the southern edge of the site. A modern dirt road borders the site's northwestern edge.

Plate A71. Zu-LT-6, facing south at Feature W.

Archaeological Remains: Variable light and light-to-moderate Late Toltec surface pottery over an area of ca. 0.80 ha. The LT material is mixed with lighter and more extensive Late Aztec ceramics (Zu-Az-5). We noted several obsidian artifacts. There are no discernible structural remains.

No surface collection made in the LT site.

Discussion: The apparent absence of Early Aztec surface pottery indicates that this locality was abandoned after LT times and reoccupied during the Late Aztec period.

Classification: Small Hamlet, 10–20 people.

SITE NO. Zu-LT-6 [Zu-LT-24(J); Feature W]
  Date of Survey: June 12, 1973
  Location: 493380 E, 2208820 N; 19.9759° N, 99.0633° W
  Natural Setting: 2405 m asl, on gently sloping ground in the Upper Salado Drainage; medium soil cover and slight erosion.
  Modern Land Use: Rainfall-based agriculture.
  Archaeological Remains: Variable light, and light-to-moderate Late Toltec surface pottery over an area of ca. 0.60 ha. There is a single well preserved mound (Feature W), measuring ca. 25 m in diameter and standing ca. 1.00 m high (Plate A71). The mound surface is covered with moderate rock rubble, light LT pottery, and a trace of Aztec ceramics (no Az site designated here, although there is a possibility that the mound may be an Aztec structure).

No surface collection made.

  Discussion: The age of Feature W is uncertain; it could be an Aztec structure.
  Classification: Small Hamlet, 5–10 people.

SITE NO. Zu-LT-7 [Zu-LT-22(J); Feature X]
  Date of Survey: June 13, 1973
  Location: 494280 E, 2207930 N; 19.9679° N, 99.0547° W
  Natural Setting: 2360 m asl, on gently sloping ground in the Upper Salado Drainage; deep soil cover and slight erosion.
  Modern Land Use: Rainfall-based agriculture. The modern village of Santa María Ajoloapan encroaches onto the site from the east. A modern dirt road borders the northern edge of the site.
  Archaeological Remains: Light-to-moderate Late Toltec surface pottery over an area of ca. 0.50 ha. Because of modern occupation, the eastern site limits could not be accurately determined. The LT material is mixed with approximately equal quantities of Late Aztec pottery (Zu-Az-8). We noted several green obsidian blades.

There is a single badly plowed-down mound (Feature X) near the site's southern edge. This feature measures ca. 20 m in diameter and ca. 0.25 m high. Its surface contains moderate rock rubble and a mixture of LT and Late Az pottery.

No surface collection made.

  Discussion: The age of Feature X is uncertain, as is the site size. The apparent absence of Early Aztec surface pottery suggests that this locality was abandoned after LT times and reoccupied during the Late Aztec period.
  Classification: Small Hamlet (?), 10–20 people.

SITE NO. Zu-LT-8 [Zu-LT-23(J)]
  Date of Survey: June 13, 1973
  Location: 493050 E, 2207930 N; 19.9679° N, 99.0664° W
  Natural Setting: 2400 m asl, on gently sloping ground in the Upper Salado Drainage; deep soil cover and moderate erosion.
  Modern Land Use: Rainfall-based agriculture.
  Archaeological Remains: Variable light and light-to-moderate Late Toltec surface pottery over an area of ca. 2.00 ha. There are no discernible structural remains.

No surface collection made.

  Classification: Hamlet, 20–40 people.

Plate A72. Zu-LT-13, facing west at Feature AG.

SITE NO. Zu-LT-9 [Zu-LT-16(J)]
  Date of Survey: June 7, 1973
  Location: 498000 E, 2206900 N; 19.9586° N, 99.0191° W
  Natural Setting: 2420 m asl, on moderately sloping ground in the Upper Salado Drainage, on the lower northwestern flank of Cerro Aranda; shallow soil cover and moderate erosion.
  Modern Land Use: Unplowed pasture.
  Archaeological Remains: Variable light and light-to-moderate Late Toltec surface pottery over an area of ca. 1.30 ha. There are no discernible structural remains.
  No surface collection made.
  Classification: Hamlet, 15–30 people.

SITE NO. Zu-LT-10 [Zu-LT-2(J)]
  Date of Survey: May 29, 1973
  Location: 495900 E, 2206380 N; 19.9539° N, 99.0392° W
  Natural Setting: 2350 m asl, on gently sloping ground in the Upper Salado Drainage; deep soil cover and slight erosion.
  Modern Land Use: Rainfall-based agriculture. Two modern dirt roads skirt the western and southern edges of the site.
  Archaeological Remains: Variable light and light-to-moderate Late Toltec surface pottery over an area of ca. 1.40 ha. There are no discernible structural remains.
  No surface collection made.
  Classification: Hamlet, 15–30 people.

SITE NO. Zu-LT-11 [Zu-LT-1(J)]
  Date of Survey: May 28, 1973
  Location: 494630 E, 2206550 N; 19.9554° N, 99.0513° W
  Natural Setting: 2340 m asl, on gently sloping ground in the Upper Salado Drainage; deep soil cover and slight erosion.
  Modern Land Use: Rainfall-based agriculture. A modern dirt road skirts the eastern edge of the site.
  Archaeological Remains: Light-to-moderate surface Late Toltec pottery over an area of ca. 0.40 ha. There are no discernible structural remains.
  No surface collection made.
  Classification: Small Hamlet, 5–10 people.

SITE NO. Zu-LT-12 [Zu-LT-32(J)]
  Date of Survey: June 19, 1973
  Location: 490400 E, 2207820 N; 19.9669° N, 99.0918° W
  Natural Setting: 2365 m asl, on gently sloping ground in the Upper Río Salado Drainage; shallow soil cover and severe erosion.
  Modern Land Use: Rainfall-based agriculture.
  Archaeological Remains: Light-to-moderate Late Toltec surface pottery over an area of ca. 0.40 ha. There are no discernible structural remains.
  No surface collection made.
  Classification: Small Hamlet, 5–10 people.

SITE NO. Zu-LT-13 [Zu-LT-31(J); Feature AG]
  Date of Survey: June 19, 1973
  Location: 490380 E, 2207280 N; 19.9620° N, 99.0919° W
  Natural Setting: 2360 m asl, on gently sloping ground in the Upper Salado Drainage; shallow soil cover and severe erosion.
  Modern Land Use: Rainfall-based agriculture.
  Archaeological Remains: The site consists of a single badly eroded mound (Feature AG), measuring ca. 20 m in diameter and standing 0.15 m high (Plate A72). The surface of the mound is covered with moderate rock rubble and light-to-moderate Late Toltec pottery and a trace of Aztec ceramics (no Az site defined here). We noted a few obsidian blades and scrapers.
  We made one surface collection from the entire mound surface.
  Discussion: The age of Feature AG is uncertain; it may be a Late Aztec structure.
  Classification: Small Hamlet, 2–5 people. Probably a single household unit.

Plate A73. Zu-LT-16, facing NNW over Location 31.

SITE NO. Zu-LT-14 [Zu-LT-33(M)]
Date of Survey: June 12, 1973
Location: 488530 E, 2208530 N; 19.9733° N, 99.1096° W
Natural Setting: 2255 m asl, on nearly level ground in the Upper Salado Drainage; medium soil cover and slight erosion, except in the severely eroded southern edge of the site.
Modern Land Use: Rainfall-based agriculture.
Archaeological Remains: Light Late Toltec surface pottery over an area of ca. 0.40 ha. There are no discernible structural remains.
No surface collection made.
Classification: Small Hamlet, 2–5 people.

SITE NO. Zu-LT-15 [Zu-LT-30(M)]
Date of Survey: June 12, 1973
Location: 487530 E, 2208550 N; 19.9735° N, 99.1192° W
Natural Setting: 2300 m asl, on nearly level ground in the Upper Salado Drainage; medium soil cover and slight erosion.
Modern Land Use: Rainfall-based agriculture, with some maguey.
Archaeological Remains: Variable light and light-to-moderate Late Toltec surface pottery over an area of ca. 0.90 ha. There is no discernible mounding, although an area of moderate rock rubble in the southeast corner of the site may represent the remnants of prehispanic architecture.
No surface collection made.
Classification: Small Hamlet, 10–20 people.

SITE NO. Zu-LT-16 [Zu-LT-31(M); Location 31]
Date of Survey: June 12, 1973
Location: 487780 E, 2208300 N; 19.9712° N, 99.1168° W
Natural Setting: 2305 m asl, on nearly level ground in the Upper Salado Drainage; medium soil cover and slight erosion.
Modern Land Use: Pasture and rainfall-based maguey cultivation.
Archaeological Remains: Variable light and light-to-moderate and moderate Late Toltec surface pottery over an area of ca. 1.50 ha. We noted numerous green and gray obsidian blades, scrapers, and debitage, and one exhausted obsidian core, in addition to one LT ceramic figurine. There are no discernible structural remains.
We made one surface collection (Location 31) over an area ca. 7 × 10 m in an unplowed maguey field (Plate A73), with moderate LT surface pottery and light rock rubble.
Classification: Hamlet, 20–40 people.

SITE NO. Zu-LT-17 [Zu-LT-14(M); Features AG, AH, AI, AJ]
Date of Survey: June 10, 1973
Location: 485500 E, 2207470 N; 19.9637° N, 99.1386° W
Natural Setting: 2245 m asl, on nearly level ground in the Upper Salado Drainage; medium soil cover and slight erosion.
Modern Land Use: Rainfall-based agriculture.
Archaeological Remains: Variable light, light-to-moderate, and moderate Late Toltec surface pottery over an area of ca. 5.40 ha. We noted numerous gray and green obsidian blades, scrapers, and some debitage, and one ceramic pestle.
There are four probable residential mounds (Features AG, AH, AI, AJ) dispersed across the eastern two-thirds of the site:

Fea.	Area and Context	Height	Content
AG	30 × 30 m, in unplowed field (Plate A74)	0.30 m	Light-to-moderate LT surface pottery, several obsidian artifacts, moderate rock rubble. One surface collection from entire mound.
AH	23 m dia., in unplowed field	0.30 m	Light-to-moderate LT surface pottery, several obsidian artifacts, light rock rubble. One surface collection from entire mound surface.
AI	9 × 15 m, in unplowed field	1.00 m	Very light LT surface pottery, several obsidian artifacts, light rock rubble. A looter's pit shows earth and rock-rubble fill. Old hacienda marker on top.
AJ	20 × 40 m, in unplowed field	1.00 m	Light-to-moderate LT surface pottery, several obsidian artifacts, moderate rock rubble.

Classification: Small Dispersed Village, 80–160 people.

Plate A74. Zu-LT-17, facing north at Feature AG.

SITE NO. Zu-LT-18 [Zu-LT-16(M)]
Date of Survey: June 10, 1973
Location: 486030 E, 2207280 N; 19.9620° N, 99.1335° W
Natural Setting: 2260 m asl, on gently sloping ground in the Upper Salado Drainage; medium soil cover and slight erosion.
Modern Land Use: Rainfall-based agriculture.
Archaeological Remains: Variable light and light-to-moderate Late Toltec surface pottery over an area of ca. 2.50 ha. There are no definite structural remains, although a concentration of light-to-moderate rock rubble in the northern part of the site may represent the remnants of a prehispanic building.
No surface collection made.
Classification: Hamlet, 25–50 people.

SITE NO. Zu-LT-19 [Zu-LT-15(M); Location 28]
Date of Survey: June 10, 1973
Location: 485970 E, 2206880 N; 19.9584° N, 99.1341° W
Natural Setting: 2270 m asl, on nearly level ground in the Upper Salado Drainage; medium soil cover and slight erosion.
Modern Land Use: Rainfall-based agriculture.
Archaeological Remains: Variable light and light-to-moderate Late Toltec surface pottery over an area of ca. 1.60 ha. The LT material is mixed with traces of Aztec ceramics at the extreme southern edge of the site (no Az site designated). We noted several green and gray obsidian blades, and one basalt mano fragment. There are no discernible structural remains.
We made one surface collection (Location 28) over an area ca. 15 × 20 m in a plowed maize field, with light-to-moderate LT surface pottery, several obsidian artifacts, and no rock rubble.
Classification: Hamlet, 15–30 people.

SITE NO. Zu-LT-20 [Zu-LT-17(M)]
Date of Survey: June 17, 1973
Location: 486850 E, 2206900 N; 19.9586° N, 99.1257° W
Natural Setting: 2280 m asl, on gently sloping ground in the Upper Salado Drainage; medium soil cover and slight to moderate erosion.
Modern Land Use: Rainfall-based agriculture.
Archaeological Remains: Variable light, and light-to-moderate Late Toltec surface pottery over an area of ca. 1.90 ha. The surface pottery occurs in very localized distributions. We noted several green obsidian blades and some obsidian debitage. No structural remains.
No surface collection made.
Classification: Hamlet, 30–60 people.

SITE NO. Zu-LT-21 [Zu-LT-32(M)]
Date of Survey: June 13, 1973
Location: 488380 E, 2206380 N; 19.9539° N, 99.1111° W
Natural Setting: 2300 m asl, on gently sloping ground in the Upper Salado Drainage; medium soil cover and slight to moderate erosion in the immediate site area.
Modern Land Use: The immediate site area is presently fallow. The surrounding terrain is devoted to rainfall-based agriculture.
Archaeological Remains: Variable light and light-to-moderate Late Toltec surface pottery over an area of ca. 0.60 ha. There are no discernible structural remains.
No surface collection made.
Classification: Small Hamlet, 5–10 people.

SITE NO. Zu-LT-22 [Zu-LT-25(M); Location 33]
Date of Survey: June 14, 1973
Location: 488700 E, 2204950 N; 19.9409° N, 99.1080° W

Natural Setting: 2300 m asl, on gently sloping ground in the Upper Salado Drainage; medium soil cover and slight erosion.

Modern Land Use: Rainfall-based agriculture. A modern dirt road skirts the eastern side of the site.

Archaeological Remains: Variable light and light-to-moderate Late Toltec surface pottery over an area of ca. 0.50 ha. The LT material is mixed with a trace of Aztec ceramics in the eastern part of the site (no Az site designated). We noted numerous green and gray obsidian blades, scrapers, and debitage fragments. There are no discernible structural remains.

We made one surface collection (Location 33) over an area ca. 15 m in diameter in a plowed field (Plate A75), with light LT surface pottery, several obsidian artifacts, and very little rock rubble.

Classification: Small Hamlet, 5–10 people.

SITE NO. Zu-LT-23 [Zu-LT-26(M)]

Date of Survey: June 17, 1973

Location: 489030 E, 2205180 N; 19.9430° N, 99.1048° W

Natural Setting: 2310 m asl, on gently sloping ground in the Upper Salado Drainage; medium soil cover and slight erosion.

Modern Land Use: Rainfall-based agriculture. A modern paved road crosses the western part of the site.

Archaeological Remains: Variable light and light-to-moderate Late Toltec surface pottery over an area of ca. 0.80 ha. There are no discernible structures, although an area of moderate rock rubble in the eastern part of the site may be the remnants of a prehispanic building.

No surface collection made.

Classification: Small Hamlet, 10–20 people.

SITE NO. Zu-LT-24 [Zu-LT-34(M)]

Date of Survey: June 17, 1973

Location: 489000 E, 2205380 N; 19.9448° N, 99.1051° W

Natural Setting: 2315 m asl, on nearly level ground in the Upper Salado Drainage; medium soil cover and slight erosion.

Modern Land Use: Rainfall-based agriculture.

Archaeological Remains: Light-to-moderate surface Late Toltec pottery over an area of ca. 0.30 ha. There are no discernible structural remains, although an area of light rock rubble near the northern edge of the site may represent the remnants of prehispanic architecture.

No surface collection made.

Classification: Small Hamlet, 5–10 people.

SITE NO. Zu-LT-25 [Zu-LT-27(M)]

Date of Survey: June 17, 1973

Location: 489720 E, 2205380 N; 19.9448° N, 99.0982° W

Natural Setting: 2310 m asl, on gently sloping ground in the Upper Salado Drainage; shallow soil cover and severe erosion, with patches of bare tepetate.

Modern Land Use: Marginal rainfall-based agriculture with some maguey semi-terracing. A few small check dams of brush and stone have been built to help control the erosion.

Archaeological Remains: Light-to-moderate Late Toltec surface pottery over an area of ca. 1.00 ha. The LT material is mixed with heavier and more extensive Classic (Zu-Cl-11) and Late Aztec (Zu-Az-29) ceramics, and with lighter Terminal Formative (Zu-TF-1) surface pottery. We noted substantial quantities of obsidian: chips, several scrapers and blades and one projectile point made of gray obsidian, and several green obsidian blades. A few pieces of worked quartzite or chert also present. No discernible structural remains can be associated with the LT occupation.

No surface collection made in the LT site.

Discussion: The apparent absence of Early Aztec surface pottery indicates that this locality was abandoned after LT times and reoccupied during the Late Aztec period.

Classification: Small Hamlet, 10–20 people.

SITE NO. Zu-LT-26 [Zu-LT-28(M)]

Date of Survey: June 17, 1973

Location: 490070 E, 2205320 N; 19.9443° N, 99.0949° W

Natural Setting: 2300 m asl, on gently sloping ground in the Upper Salado Drainage; shallow soil cover and severe erosion, with some patches of bare tepetate.

Modern Land Use: Marginal rainfall-based agriculture.

Archaeological Remains: Variable light and light-to-moderate Late Toltec surface pottery over an area of ca. 0.30 ha. There are no discernible structural remains.

No surface collection made.

Classification: Small Hamlet, 5–10 people.

SITE NO. Zu-LT-27 [Zu-LT-30(J)]

Date of Survey: June 18, 1973

Location: 490300 E, 2205470 N; 19.9457° N, 99.0927° W

Natural Setting: 2315 m asl, on gently sloping ground in the Upper Salado Drainage; shallow soil cover and severe erosion.

Modern Land Use: Marginal pasture.

Archaeological Remains: Light-to-moderate Late Toltec surface pottery over an area of ca. 0.60 ha. There are no discernible structural remains.

No surface collection made.

Classification: Small Hamlet, 5–10 people.

SITE NO. Zu-LT-28 [Zu-LT-29(J); Feature AF]

Date of Survey: June 18, 1973

Location: 490550 E, 2205630 N; 19.9471° N, 99.0903° W

Natural Setting: 2320 m asl, on gently sloping ground in the Upper Salado Drainage; shallow soil cover and severe erosion.

Modern Land Use: Marginal pasture.

Archaeological Remains: The site consists of a single badly eroded mound (Feature AF). This feature measures ca. 25 m in diameter and has very little elevation (Plate A76). The surface pottery on and around the mound is light-to-moderate Late Toltec, mixed with traces of Aztec ceramics (no Az site designated). We noted numerous chert fragments and one spindle whorl. There is light-to-moderate rock rubble.

No surface collection made.

Classification: Small Hamlet, 2–5 people.

SITE NO. Zu-LT-29 [Zu-LT-28(J); Feature AE]

Date of Survey: June 18, 1973

Location: 490400 E, 2204680 N; 19.9385° N, 99.0917° W

Natural Setting: 2295 m asl, on gently sloping ground in the Upper Salado Drainage; shallow soil cover and severe erosion, with patches of bare tepetate.

Modern Land Use: Unplowed pasture.

Archaeological Remains: Light-to-moderate Late Toltec surface pottery over an area of ca. 2.00 ha. There is one discernible mound (Feature AE). This feature measures ca. 35 m in diameter and 0.75 m high (Plate A77). There is moderate-to-heavy rock rubble on the mound, and its surface is covered with light-to-moderate LT ceramics, and traces of Classic and Aztec pottery (no Cl or Az sites designated).

We made one surface collection from the entire mound area.

Classification: Hamlet, 30–60 people.

Plate A75. Zu-LT-22, facing south over Location 33.

Plate A76. Zu-LT-28, facing south at Feature AF.

Plate A77. Zu-LT-29, facing north at Feature AE.

SITE NO. Zu-LT-30 [Zu-LT-27(J); Location 23; Features Y, Z, AD]
Date of Survey: June 14, 1973
Location: 492380 E, 2204630 N; 19.9381° N, 99.0728° W
Natural Setting: 2360 m asl, on nearly level ground in the Upper Salado Drainage; medium soil cover and slight erosion.
Modern Land Use: Rainfall-based agriculture. A modern dirt road crosses the site.
Archaeological Remains: Variable light, light-to-moderate, and moderate Late Toltec surface pottery over an area of ca. 16.80 ha. Over the southern half of the site the LT material is mixed with approximately equal quantities of Late Aztec ceramics (Zu-Az-74). We noted several obsidian artifacts.

There are three widely spaced mounds (Features Y, Z, AD):

Fea.	Area and Context	Height	Content
Y	20 m dia., in plowed field	0.75 m	Light LT surface pottery, several obsidian artifacts, moderate rock rubble.
Z	20 m dia., in plowed field	0.75 m	Light LT surface pottery, several obsidian artifacts, moderate rock rubble.
AD	20 m dia.	0.50 m	Light LT and Late Az surface pottery, several obsidian artifacts, moderate rock rubble.

We made one surface collection (Location 23) over an area of ca. 10 × 15 m (Plate A78), with moderate LT surface pottery, numerous obsidian artifacts, and light-to-moderate rock rubble.
Discussion: The age of Feature AD is uncertain; it could be Late Aztec. Features Y and Z appear to be LT. The apparent absence of Early Aztec ceramics suggests that this locality was abandoned after LT times and reoccupied during the Late Aztec period.
Classification: Large Nucleated Village, 340–680 people.

SITE NO. Zu-LT-31 [Zu-LT-5(J); Location 6]
Date of Survey: May 29, 1973
Location: 495030 E, 2205180 N; 19.9431° N, 99.0475° W
Natural Setting: 2340 m asl, on gently sloping ground atop a low ridge in the Upper Salado Drainage (Plate A79); medium soil cover and severe erosion in the immediate site area.
Modern Land Use: Rainfall-based agriculture.
Archaeological Remains: Variable light-to-moderate and moderate Late Toltec surface pottery over an area of ca. 1.40 ha. The LT material is mixed with a trace of Aztec ceramics (no Az site designated). We noted numerous green obsidian blades. There are no discernible structural remains.

We made one surface collection (Location 6) from an area ca. 10 × 10 m in a plowed field with moderate LT surface pottery, numerous obsidian blades, and moderate rock rubble.
Classification: Hamlet, 25–50 people.

SITE NO. Zu-LT-32 [Zu-LT-3(J)]
Date of Survey: May 29, 1973
Location: 496050 E, 2205050 N; 19.9419° N, 99.0377° W
Natural Setting: 2340 m asl, on gently sloping ground in the Upper Salado Drainage; medium soil cover and slight erosion.
Modern Land Use: Rainfall-based agriculture. A modern dirt road borders the southwestern edge of the site.
Archaeological Remains: Variable light and moderate surface Late Toltec pottery over an area of ca. 1.10 ha. There are no discernible structural remains.
No surface collection made.
Classification: Small Hamlet, 10–20 people.

SITE NO. Zu-LT-33 [Zu-LT-4(J); Location 8]
Date of Survey: May 30, 1973
Location: 495900 E, 2205000 N; 19.9414° N, 99.0392° W
Natural Setting: 2335 m asl, on gently sloping ground in the Upper Salado Drainage; shallow soil cover and moderate erosion.
Modern Land Use: Rainfall-based agriculture. Some parts of the site have been plowed so far this year, and others are fallow. A modern dirt road borders the western edge of the site.
Archaeological Remains: Variable light and light-to-moderate Late Toltec surface pottery over an area of ca. 10.70 ha. The LT material is mixed with approximately equal quantities of Late Aztec ceramics (Zu-Az-21, Zu-Az-22). We noted numerous green obsidian blades and one basalt metate fragment. There are no discernible structural remains.

We made one surface collection (Location 8) over an area ca. 10 × 10 m in a plowed field (Plate A80), with moderate LT surface pottery, numerous obsidian artifacts, and light-to-moderate rock rubble.
Discussion: The apparent absence of Early Aztec surface pottery suggests that this locality was abandoned after LT times and reoccupied during the Late Aztec period.
Classification: Small Dispersed Village, 125–250 people.

SITE NO. Zu-LT-34 [Zu-LT-15(J); Features P, R, S, T]
Date of Survey: June 6, 1973
Location: 497180 E, 2205150 N; 19.9428° N, 99.0269° W
Natural Setting: 2345 m asl, on gently sloping ground in the Upper Salado Drainage; shallow soil cover and severe erosion, with patches of bare tepetate.
Modern Land Use: Marginal pasture.
Archaeological Remains: Variable light, light-to-moderate, and moderate Late Toltec surface pottery over an area of ca. 6.80 ha. The LT material is mixed with traces of Aztec ceramics in the central part of the site (no Az site designated). We noted numerous green obsidian blades (especially around the four mounds) and one gray obsidian projectile point.

There are four mounds (Features P, R, S, T) in the northern part of the site:

Fea.	Area and Context	Height	Content
P	40 m dia., in unplowed area	0.20 m	Moderate LT surface pottery, several obsidian artifacts, moderate rock rubble. Very badly eroded.
R	35 m dia., in unplowed area	0.20 m	Moderate LT surface pottery, several obsidian artifacts, moderate rock rubble. Badly eroded.
S	15 × 35 m, in unplowed area	1.00 m	Light-to-moderate LT surface pottery, several obsidian artifacts, moderate-to-heavy rock rubble.
T	10 m dia., in unplowed area	0.75 m	Light-to-moderate LT surface pottery, several obsidian artifacts, moderate rock rubble. Well preserved.

No surface collection made.
Classification: Small Dispersed Village, 100–200 people.

SITE NO. Zu-LT-35 [Zu-LT-13(J); Features M, Q]
Date of Survey: June 3, 6, 1973
Location: 497500 E, 2204800 N; 19.9396° N, 99.0239° W
Natural Setting: 2345 m asl, on gently sloping ground in the Upper Salado Drainage; shallow soil cover and severe erosion. A large *barranca* has severely damaged one of the two surviving prehispanic mounds.
Modern Land Use: Marginal pasture.

Appendix A: Site Descriptions 199

Plate A78. Zu-LT-30, facing north over Location 23.

Plate A79. Zu-LT-31, facing east over Location 6.

Plate A80. Zu-LT-33, facing south over Location 8.

Plate A81. Zu-LT-35, facing north at Feature M.

Archaeological Remains: Variable light and light-to-moderate Late Toltec surface pottery over an area of ca. 2.60 ha. The LT material is mixed with traces of Aztec ceramics (no Az site designated). We noted numerous green obsidian blades.

There are two preserved mounds (Features M, Q), one at either end of the site:

Fea.	Area and Context	Height	Content
M	20 m dia., in unplowed area (Plate A81)	Very low	Light-to-moderate LT and trace Az surface pottery, several obsidian artifacts, moderate-to-heavy rock rubble.
Q	40 m dia., in unplowed area	1.00 m	Light-to-moderate LT and trace Az surface pottery, several obsidian artifacts, moderate rock rubble.

No surface collection made.
Classification: Hamlet, 25–50 people.

SITE NO. Zu-LT-36 [Zu-LT-12(J); Location 14]
Date of Survey: June 5, 1973
Location: 498280 E, 2203950 N; 19.9319° N, 99.0164° W
Natural Setting: 2345 m asl, on gently sloping ground in the Upper Salado Drainage, just north of the divide between the Upper Salado and Basin of Mexico drainages; shallow soil cover and slight erosion.
Modern Land Use: Rainfall-based agriculture. A modern dirt road crosses the site. The modern settlement of Nopala encroaches slightly onto the site from the east.
Archaeological Remains: Variable light and light-to-moderate Late Toltec surface pottery over an area of ca. 1.30 ha. The LT material is mixed with lighter and more extensive Late Aztec ceramics (Zu-Az-18). We noted numerous green obsidian blades. There are no discernible structural remains.

We made one surface collection (Location 14) from an area ca. 10 × 10 m in a plowed field with light-to-moderate LT and light Late Az surface pottery, several obsidian artifacts, and light-to-moderate rock rubble.
Discussion: Owing to the encroachment of modern Nopala, we were unable to estimate the site's eastern limits. The apparent absence of Early Aztec surface pottery suggests that this locality was abandoned after LT times and reoccupied during the Late Aztec period.
Classification: Hamlet (?), 15–30 people.

SITE NO. Zu-LT-37 [Zu-LT-14(J)]
Date of Survey: June 5, 1973
Location: 498780 E, 2203250 N; 19.9256° N, 99.0117° W
Natural Setting: 2350 m asl, on gently sloping ground in the Basin of Mexico Lower Piedmont, just south of the divide between the Upper Salado and Basin of Mexico drainages; shallow to medium soil cover and slight to moderate erosion. A major *barranca* cuts through the site from northeast to southwest.
Modern Land Use: Rainfall-based agriculture. The modern village of Nopala is ca. 50 m to the north.
Archaeological Remains: Variable light and light-to-moderate Late Toltec surface pottery over an area of ca. 2.30 ha. In the western part of the site, the LT material is mixed with approximately equal quantities of Late Aztec ceramics (Zu-Az-18).

No surface collection made in the LT site.
Discussion: The apparent absence of Early Aztec surface pottery suggests that this locality was abandoned after LT times and reoccupied during the Late Aztec period.
Classification: Hamlet, 25–50 people.

SITE NO. Zu-LT-38 [Zu-LT-10(J), Zu-LT-11(J); Locations 11, 12, 15; Feature O]
Date of Survey: June 4, 1973
Location: 498220 E, 2203100 N; 19.9243° N, 99.0170° W
Natural Setting: 2340 m asl, on gently sloping ground in the Upper Salado Drainage, just north of the divide between the Upper Salado and Basin of Mexico drainages; medium soil cover and slight erosion.
Modern Land Use: Rainfall-based agriculture. A modern dirt road crosses the east end of the site.
Archaeological Remains: Variable light, light-to-moderate, and moderate Late Toltec surface pottery over an area of ca. 15.70 ha. The LT material is mixed with traces of Terminal Formative, Classic and Aztec ceramics (no TF, Cl, or Az sites designated).

There is a single mound (Feature O) in the western part of the site. This feature measures ca. 35 m in diameter and 1.50 m high. A large looter's pit in the center of the mound reveals solid earth and rock-rubble construction, and there is moderate rock rubble on the mound surface. We made one surface collection from the mound area. The surface pottery is primarily LT, with traces of Cl and Az ceramics. We noted several green obsidian blades.

We made three additional surface collections (Locations 11, 12, 15):

Location	Area and Context	Content
11	15 × 15 m, in plowed field adjacent to Feature O	Light-to-moderate LT surface pottery, several obsidian artifacts, little rock rubble.
12	15 × 15 m, in plowed field	Light-to-moderate LT and very light Az surface pottery, several obsidian artifacts, light rock rubble
15	10 × 10 m, in plowed field	Light-to-moderate LT and very light Az surface pottery, several obsidian artifacts, light-to-moderate rock rubble

Classification: Small Nucleated Village, 250–500 people.

SITE NO. Zu-LT-39 [Zu-LT-9(J)]
Date of Survey: June 4, 1973
Location: 498530 E, 2202630 N; 19.9200° N, 99.0140° W
Natural Setting: 2340 m asl, on gently sloping ground in the Basin of Mexico Lower Piedmont, just south of the divide between the Upper Salado and Basin of Mexico drainages; medium soil cover and slight erosion.
Modern Land Use: Rainfall-based agriculture. A modern dirt road crosses the eastern part of the site.
Archaeological Remains: Variable light and light-to-moderate Late Toltec surface pottery over an area of ca. 7.00 ha. There are traces of Aztec ceramics in the north-central part of the site (no Az site designated). There are no definite structural remains, but a concentration of light-to-moderate rock rubble in the northeastern corner of the site may represent the remnants of prehispanic architecture.
No surface collection made.
Classification: Small Dispersed Village, 75–150 people.

SITE NO. Zu-LT-40 [Zu-LT-8(J); Feature N]
Date of Survey: June 4, 1973
Location: 499220 E, 2202070 N; 19.9150° N, 99.0075° W
Natural Setting: 2340 m asl, on gently sloping ground in the Basin of Mexico Lower Piedmont (Plate A82); medium soil cover and slight to moderate erosion. A major *barranca* borders the site on the north and northwest.
Modern Land Use: Rainfall-based agriculture.

Archaeological Remains: Variable light and light-to-moderate Late Toltec surface pottery over an area of ca. 4.40 ha. We noted several green obsidian blades. The site extends beyond the limits of the survey area to the east and south, and so its borders in those directions could not be defined.

We discerned a single mound (Feature N) in a plowed field on the south edge of the site. This feature measures ca. 25 m in diameter and 1.5 m high (Plate A82), with light-to-moderate LT surface pottery, several obsidian artifacts, and moderate rock rubble.
No surface collection made.
Discussion: Because its eastern and southern limits were not defined, the size of this site remains uncertain.
Classification: Hamlet (?), 45–90 people.

SITE NO. Zu-LT-41 [Zu-LT-7(J); Location 1]
Date of Survey: May 23, 1973
Location: 495900 E, 2203350 N; 19.9265° N, 99.0392° W
Natural Setting: 2320 m asl, on gently sloping ground in the Upper Salado Drainage (Plate A83); deep soil cover and slight erosion.
Modern Land Use: Rainfall-based agriculture. A modern dirt road crosses the southwestern edge of the site.
Archaeological Remains: Variable light, light-to-moderate, and moderate Late Toltec surface pottery over an area of ca. 10.80 ha. We noted numerous green obsidian blades, a few obsidian scrapers, one basalt mano fragment, and one fragment of marine shell. There are no discernible structural remains.

We made one surface collection (Location 1) from an area ca. 5 × 10 m in a plowed field (Plate A84), with moderate LT surface pottery, several obsidian artifacts, and moderate rock rubble.
Classification: Small Nucleated Village, 200–400 people.

SITE NO. Zu-LT-42 [Zu-LT-6(J); Location 2]
Date of Survey: May 24, 1973
Location: 495500 E, 2202880 N; 19.9223° N, 99.0430° W
Natural Setting: 2310 m asl, on gently sloping ground in the Upper Salado Drainage; shallow to medium soil cover and moderate erosion.
Modern Land Use: Rainfall-based agriculture. A modern dirt roads borders the site on the west and northeast.
Archaeological Remains: Variable light, light-to-moderate, and moderate Late Toltec surface pottery over an area of ca. 5.70 ha. The LT material is mixed with approximately equal quantities of Late Aztec ceramics (Zu-Az-79); the Az surface pottery extends over a larger area. We noted numerous green obsidian blades, and one small (cotton) spindle whorl. No definite structural remains can be associated with the LT occupation, but vague, amorphous, irregular low mounding and moderate rock rubble throughout the site may represent the remnants of several prehispanic structures.

We made one surface collection (Location 2) from an area ca. 10 × 10 m in a plowed field with light-to-moderate LT and light Late Az surface pottery, and moderate rock rubble.
Discussion: The apparent absence of Early Aztec surface pottery suggests that this locality was abandoned after LT times and reoccupied during the Late Aztec period.
Classification: Small Nucleated Village, 85–170 people.

SITE NO. Zu-LT-43 [Zu-LT-61(J); Feature CF]
Date of Survey: July 12, 1973
Location: 496570 E, 2201430 N; 19.9092° N, 99.0328° W
Natural Setting: 2305 m asl, on gently sloping ground in the Upper

Plate A82. Zu-LT-40, facing NW at Feature N.

Plate A83. Zu-LT-41, facing south over general site area.

Plate A84. Zu-LT-41, facing west over Location 1.

Plate A85. Zu-LT-46, facing south over general site area.

Salado Drainage, just northwest of the divide between the Upper Salado and Basin of Mexico drainages; medium soil cover and slight erosion.

Modern Land Use: Rainfall-based agriculture.

Archaeological Remains: Variable light and light-to-moderate Late Toltec surface pottery over an area of ca. 8.20 ha. The LT material is mixed with approximately equal quantities of Late Aztec ceramics (Zu-Az-81). We noted several obsidian artifacts.

There is a single mound (Feature CF) in a plowed field near the western edge of the site. This feature measures ca. 20 m in diameter and 0.25 m high, with light-to-moderate LT and Late Az surface pottery, several obsidian artifacts, and moderate rock rubble.

Discussion: The apparent absence of Early Aztec surface pottery suggests that this locality was abandoned after LT times and reoccupied during the Late Aztec pereiod.

Classification: Small Dispersed Village, 80–160 people.

SITE NO. Zu-LT-44 [Zu-LT-59(J); Feature BY]
Date of Survey: July 11, 1973
Location: 496050 E, 2201100 N; 19.9062° N, 99.0378° W
Natural Setting: 2315 m asl, on gently sloping ground in the Upper Salado Drainage, near the divide between the Upper Salado and Basin of Mexico drainages; deep soil cover and slight erosion.

Modern Land Use: Rainfall-based agriculture. A modern dirt road borders the north edge of the site.

Archaeological Remains: Variable light and light-to-moderate Late Toltec surface pottery over an area of ca. 1.40 ha. The LT material is mixed with traces of Aztec ceramics (no Az site designated). We noted a few obsidian artifacts.

There is a single mound (Feature BY) in an otherwise plowed field near the southeastern corner of the site. This unplowed feature measures ca. 15 × 25 m in area and 0.40 m high, with light LT surface pottery, several obsidian artifacts, and light-to-moderate rock rubble.

No surface collection made.

Classification: Hamlet, 15–30 people.

SITE NO. Zu-LT-45 [Zu-LT-60(J); Feature CD]
Date of Survey: July 11, 1973
Location: 495600 E, 2201200 N; 19.9071° N, 99.0420° W
Natural Setting: 2310 m asl, on gently sloping ground in the Upper Salado Drainage; shallow soil cover and severe erosion.

Modern Land Use: Marginal pasture. A modern dirt road crosses the center of the site.

Archaeological Remains: Variable light and light-to-moderate Late Toltec surface pottery over an area of ca. 2.90 ha. In the northern part of the site, the LT material is mixed with approximately equal quantities of Late Aztec ceramics (Zu-Az-82). We noted a few obsidian blades.

A single badly eroded mound (Feature CD) is visible at the approximate center of the site. This feature measures ca. 15 m in diameter and 0.10 m high, with moderate LT and very light Az surface pottery, several obsidian artifacts, and moderate rock rubble.

No surface collection made.

Discussion: The apparent absence of Early Aztec surface pottery suggests that this locality was abandoned after LT times and reoccupied during the Late Aztec period.

Classification: Hamlet, 30–60 people.

SITE NO. Zu-LT-46 [Zu-LT-57(J); Features BV, BW, BX]
Date of Survey: July 11, 1973
Location: 496220 E, 2200680 N; 19.9024° N, 99.0361° W
Natural Setting: 2335 m asl, on gently sloping ground in the Upper Salado Drainage (Plate A85), at the divide between the Upper Salado and Basin of Mexico drainages; deep soil cover and slight erosion.

Modern Land Use: Rainfall-based agriculture.

Archaeological Remains: Variable light and light-to-moderate Late Toltec surface pottery over an area of ca. 10.40 ha. We noted several obsidian artifacts.

Three mounds (Features BV, BW, BX) are discernible in the eastern part of the site. These features are spaced about 75 m apart, distributed in a roughly semicircular configuration.

Fea.	Area and Context	Height	Content
BV	45 m dia., in unplowed field	0.75 m	Light-to-moderate LT surface pottery, several obsidian artifacts, moderate rock rubble.
BW	25 m dia., in plowed field	0.75 m	Light-to-moderate LT surface pottery, several obsidian artifacts, moderate-to-heavy rock rubble.
BX	40 m dia., in plowed field	0.50 m	Light-to-moderate LT surface pottery, several obsidian artifacts, moderate-to-heavy rock rubble.

Classification: Small Dispersed Village, 105–210 people.

SITE NO. Zu-LT-47 [Zu-LT-58(J); Features BZ, CA, CB, CC]
Date of Survey: July 11, 1973
Location: 495700 E, 2200700 N; 19.9026° N, 99.0411° W
Natural Setting: 2325 m asl, on gently sloping ground in the Upper Salado Drainage, near the divide between the Upper Salado and Basin of Mexico drainages; medium soil cover and moderate erosion.
Modern Land Use: Rainfall-based agriculture. The site area is presently fallow.
Archaeological Remains: Variable light and light-to-moderate Late Toltec surface pottery over an area of ca. 8.70 ha. In the southwestern part of the site, the LT material is mixed with approximately equal quantities of Late Aztec ceramics (Zu-Az-83, Zu-Az-84).

Four mounds (Features BZ, CA, CB, CC) are discernible in the north-central part of the site:

Fea.	Area and Context	Height	Content
BZ	40 m dia., in plowed field	0.20 m	Light-to-moderate LT and very light Az surface pottery, several obsidian artifacts, moderate rock rubble.
CA	15 m dia., in unplowed field	0.15 m	Light-to-moderate LT surface pottery, several obsidian artifacts, moderate rock rubble.
CB	15 m dia., in unplowed field	0.10 m	Light LT and Late Az surface pottery, several obsidian artifacts, moderate rock rubble.
CC	8 × 10 m, in plowed field	0.20 m	Light-to-moderate LT surface pottery, several obsidian artifacts, moderate rock rubble. Surface collection over whole mound.

Discussion: The ages of Features BZ, CA, CB, and CC are uncertain; their main construction and use may date to the Late Aztec period. The apparent absence of Early Aztec surface pottery suggests that this locality was abandoned after LT times and reoccupied during the Late Aztec period.
Classification: Small Dispersed Village, 90–180 people.

SITE NO. Zu-LT-48 [Zu-LT-62(J); Locations 39, 40]
Date of Survey: July 16, 1973
Location: 496070 E, 2199820 N; 19.8946° N, 99.0375° W
Natural Setting: 2335 m asl, on nearly level ground atop a broad, low ridge in the Basin of Mexico Lower Piedmont, just south of the divide between the Upper Salado and Basin of Mexico drainages; shallow soil cover and slight to moderate erosion.
Modern Land Use: Rainfall-based agriculture.
Archaeological Remains: Variable light, light-to-moderate, and moderate Late Toltec surface pottery over an area of ca. 5.10 ha. In the western sector of the site, the LT material is mixed with approximately equal quantities of Classic ceramics (Zu-Cl-40) and lighter amounts of Early Toltec (Zu-ET-16); there are also traces of Aztec surface pottery (no Az site designated at this locality).

We made two surface collections (Locations 39, 40) within the borders of the LT site:

Location	Area and Context	Content
39	5 × 10 m, in fallow field	Light-to-moderate Cl and LT, light ET, and traces of Az surface pottery; several obsidian artifacts; moderate rock rubble.
40	Collection area not recorded, in plowed field	Light-to-moderate Cl, light LT and ET, and traces of Az surface pottery; several obsidian artifacts; light-to-moderate rock rubble.

Discussion: Long-term settlement continuity, Cl–LT.
Classification: Small Nucleated Village, 100–200 people.

SITE NO. Zu-LT-49 [Zu-LT-63(J); Locations 37, 39, 40; Feature CI]
Date of Survey: June 23, 1973
Location: 495700 E, 2200130 N; 19.8974° N, 99.0412° W
Natural Setting: 2330 m asl, on nearly level ground atop a broad, low ridge in the Upper Salado Drainage, just north of the divide between the Upper Salado and Basin of Mexico drainages; shallow soil cover and slight to moderate erosion.
Modern Land Use: Rainfall-based agriculture.
Archaeological Remains: Variable light and light-to-moderate Late Toltec surface pottery over an area of ca. 5.60 ha. The LT material is mixed with approximately equal quantities of Classic ceramics (Zu-Cl-40) and lighter Early Toltec (Zu-ET-16) and Late Aztec (Zu-Az-88) pottery. We noted several green and gray obsidian blades, one gray obsidian projectile point, seven basalt mano fragments, and one basalt metate fragment.

A single mound (Feature CI) is visible in the northwestern part of the site. This unplowed feature measures ca. 20 m in diameter and 1.50 m high, with very light LT surface pottery and moderate rock rubble (Plate A86). A looter's pit indicates solid rock-rubble construction. We found one spindle whorl at the edge of the mound.

We made three surface collections (Locations 37, 39, 40) in the area of the LT site:

Location	Area and Context	Content
37	15 × 20 m, in plowed field	Light-to-moderate LT and light Late Az surface pottery; several obsidian artifacts; moderate rock rubble.
39	5 × 10 m, in unplowed field	Light-to-moderate Cl and LT, light ET, and very light Late Az surface pottery; moderate rock rubble.
40	Area not recorded, in unplowed field	Light-to-moderate Cl, light LT and ET, and very light Late Az surface pottery; several obsidian artifacts; light-to-moderate rock rubble.

Discussion: Although the surface pottery on Feature CI appears to be exclusively LT, the presence of Late Az material in the surrounding field suggests that this feature could date to the Late Aztec period. The apparent absence of Early Aztec surface pottery suggests that this locality was abandoned after LT times and reoccupied during the Late Aztec period. Overall long-term settlement continuity Cl–LT.
Classification: Small Dispersed Village, 55–110 people.

SITE NO. Zu-LT-50 [Zu-LT-38(J)]
Date of Survey: June 23, 1973
Location: 492930 E, 2200250 N; 19.8985° N, 99.0675° W
Natural Setting: 2310 m asl, on gently sloping ground in the Upper Salado Drainage; shallow soil cover and severe erosion.
Modern Land Use: Pasture.
Archaeological Remains: Light-to-moderate Late Toltec surface pottery over an area of ca. 0.40 ha. The LT material is mixed with approximately equal quantities of Late Aztec ceramics (Zu-Az-99). There are no discernible structural remains.

No surface collection made.
Discussion: The apparent absence of Early Aztec surface pottery suggests that this locality was abandoned after LT times and reoccupied during the Late Aztec period.
Classification: Small Hamlet, 5–10 people.

Plate A86. Zu-LT-49, facing SW at Feature C1.

SITE NO. Zu-LT-51 [Zu-LT-34(J)]
Date of Survey: June 25, 1973
Location: 493450 E, 2200500 N; 19.9008° N, 99.0626° W
Natural Setting: 2300 m asl, on gently sloping ground in the Upper Salado Drainage; shallow soil cover and severe erosion.
Modern Land Use: Marginal pasture. The modern town of Hueypoxtla encroaches slightly onto the site from the north.
Archaeological Remains: Light Late Toltec surface pottery over an area of ca. 1.40 ha. The LT material is mixed with approximately equal quantities of Late Aztec ceramics (Zu-Az-99). There are no discernible structural remains.
No surface collection made.
Discussion: The apparent absence of Early Aztec surface pottery suggests that this locality was abandoned after LT times and reoccupied during the Late Aztec period.
Classification: Small Hamlet, 5–10 people.

SITE NO. Zu-LT-52 [Zu-LT-33(J); Location 27]
Date of Survey: June 26, 1973
Location: 493700 E, 2200950 N; 19.9048° N, 99.0602° W
Natural Setting: 2310 m asl, on gently sloping ground in the Upper Salado Drainage; shallow soil cover and severe erosion.
Modern Land Use: Marginal pasture. Two modern dirt roads cross the site. The eastern edge of the modern town of Hueypoxtla borders the site on the west.
Archaeological Remains: Variable light and light-to-moderate Late Toltec surface pottery over an area of ca. 2.20 ha. The LT material is mixed with somewhat lighter Classic (Zu-Cl-37) and Early Toltec (Zu-ET-15) ceramics. We noted several obsidian blades and scrapers. There is moderate rock rubble, but no discernible structural remains
We made one surface collection (Location 27) over an area ca. 25 × 25 m in an unplowed area (Plate A87), with light-to-moderate LT and Cl surface pottery, several obsidian artifacts (blades and scrapers), and moderate rock rubble.
Classification: Hamlet, 20–40 people.

SITE NO. Zu-LT-53 [Zu-LT-114(J); Location 86]
Date of Survey: Oct. 31, 1973
Location: 493500 E, 2201400 N; 19.9089° N, 99.0621° W
Natural Setting: 2320 m asl, on gently sloping ground in the Upper Salado Drainage; shallow soil cover and moderate to severe erosion.
Modern Land Use: Rainfall-based agriculture, with some maguey semi-terracing. Several modern residences on the eastern side of Hueypoxtla encroach onto the site from the west.
Archaeological Remains: Variable light and light-to-moderate Late Toltec surface pottery over an area of ca. 3.00 ha. In the northern part of the site, the LT material is mixed with lighter Late Aztec ceramics (Zu-Az-94). We noted numerous green obsidian blades and some obsidian debitage. There are no discernible structural remains. Because of modern occupation, the western limits of the site could not be defined.
We made one surface collection (Location 86) over an area ca. 15 × 25 m in an unplowed field (Plate A88), with light-to-moderate LT surface pottery.
Discussion: The site may be significantly larger if any significant prehispanic occupation underlies modern Hueypoxtla immediately to the west. The apparent absence of Early Aztec surface pottery suggests that this locality was abandoned after LT times and reoccupied during the Late Aztec period.
Classification: Hamlet (?), 30–60 people.

SITE NO. Zu-LT-54 [Zu-LT-25(J)]
Date of Survey: June 17, 1973
Location: 492700 E, 2202530 N; 19.9191° N, 99.0698° W
Natural Setting: 2350 m asl, on gently sloping ground in the Upper Salado Drainage; shallow soil cover and severe erosion.
Modern Land Use: Rainfall-based agriculture.
Archaeological Remains: Variable light and light-to-moderate Late Toltec surface pottery over an area of ca. 5.90 ha. The LT material is mixed with approximately equal quantities of Late Aztec ceramics (Zu-Az-100). There are no discernible structural remains.
No surface collection made.
Discussion: The apparent absence of Early Aztec surface pottery suggests that this locality was abandoned after LT times and reoccupied during the Late Aztec period.
Classification: Small Dispersed Village, 60–120 people.

Plate A87. Zu-LT-52, facing SW over Location 27.

Plate A88. Zu-LT-53, facing north over Location 86.

SITE NO. Zu-LT-55 [Zu-LT-113(J)]
Date of Survey: Oct. 31, 1973
Location: 492150 E, 2201970 N; 19.9140° N, 99.0750° W
Natural Setting: 2340 m asl, on gently sloping ground in the Upper Salado Drainage; shallow soil cover and severe erosion, with some patches of bare tepetate.
Modern Land Use: Mixed pasture and marginal rainfall-based agriculture in scattered small fields, with some maguey semi-terracing.
Archaeological Remains: Variable light and light-to-moderate Late Toltec surface pottery over an area of ca. 1.40 ha. There are no discernible structural remains.
No surface collection made.
Classification: Hamlet, 15–30 people.

SITE NO. Zu-LT-56 [Zu-LT-26(J); Feature AB]
Date of Survey: June 17, 1973
Location: 491320 E, 2203300 N; 19.9260° N, 99.0829° W
Natural Setting: 2330 m asl, on gently sloping ground in the Upper Salado Drainage; shallow soil cover and severe erosion.
Modern Land Use: Rainfall-based agriculture.
Archaeological Remains: Variable light and light-to-moderate Late Toltec surface pottery over an area of ca. 1.50 ha. The LT material is mixed with lighter Late Aztec ceramics (Zu-Az-76).
There is a single badly eroded mound (Feature AB) in the southern part of the site. This recently plowed feature measures ca. 25 m in diameter and 0.20 m high, with light LT and Late Az surface pottery and moderate rock rubble.
Discussion: The age of Feature AB is uncertain; it may be an Aztec-period structure. The apparent absence of Early Aztec surface pottery suggests that this locality was abandoned after LT times and reoccupied during the Late Aztec period.
Classification: Hamlet, 15–30 people.

SITE NO. Zu-LT-57 [Zu-LT-111(J); Features DR, DS, DT]
Date of Survey: Oct. 21, 1973
Location: 490300 E, 2202200 N; 19.9161° N, 99.0927° W
Natural Setting: 2300 m asl, on gently sloping ground between two major *barrancas* in the Upper Salado Drainage; shallow soil cover and severe erosion, with some patches of bare tepetate.
Modern Land Use: Rainfall-based agriculture, with considerable maguey terracing and semi-terracing.
Archaeological Remains: Variable light and light-to-moderate Late Toltec surface pottery over an area of ca. 6.00 ha. In the southern part of the site, the LT material is mixed with approximately equal quantities of Late Aztec ceramics (Zu-Az-104). We noted numerous obsidian blades, scrapers, and debitage, mostly green in color but with some gray pieces.
There are three distinct mounds (Features DR, DS, DT) along the northern edge of the site:

Fea.	Area and Context	Height	Content
DR	15 m dia., in unplowed field	3.75 m	Very light LT and Late Az surface pottery, heavy rock rubble. Probably a temple platform.
DS	15 m dia., in unplowed field	1.75 m	Very light LT and trace Late Az surface pottery. A looter's pit reveals tepetate-block construction.
DT	15 m dia., in unplowed field	2.00 m	Light LT surface pottery, moderate rock rubble (mostly tepetate chunks). Substantial amounts of obsidian.

Discussion: The architectural complex defined by Features DR, DS, and DT appears to represent a well-defined ceremonial-civic precinct. The construction and use of this complex is uncertain; it may date primarily to the Late Aztec period. If any significant part of the complex dates to the LT, then this site, despite its modest size, may have supra-local significance. In terms of its area and population, this would be a Small Dispersed Village. However, the ceremonial-civic architecture suggests that it may be a small Local Center.
The apparent absence of Early Aztec surface pottery suggests that this locality was abandoned after LT times and reoccupied during the Late Aztec period. This may be another factor in favor of a Late Aztec date for the ceremonial-civic complex.
Classification: Small Dispersed Village (?), 100–200 people.

SITE NO. Zu-LT-58 [Zu-LT-112(J); Location 87]
Date of Survey: Oct. 31, 1973
Location: 489530 E, 2202200 N; 19.9161° N, 99.1000° W
Natural Setting: 2315 m asl, on nearly level ground atop a broad, low hill in the Upper Salado Drainage; shallow soil cover and moderate erosion.
Modern Land Use: Rainfall-based agriculture, with some maguey semi-terracing.
Archaeological Remains: Variable light and light-to-moderate Late Toltec surface pottery over an area of ca. 2.30 ha. The LT material is mixed with approximately equal quantities of Classic ceramics (Zu-Cl-35). Traces of Terminal Formative and Early Toltec pottery also occur (no TF or ET sites designated). We noted several obsidian blades and fragments. There is little rock rubble and no discernible structural remains.
We made one surface collection (Location 87) from an area ca. 15 m in diameter in a plowed field, with light-to-moderate LT and Cl surface pottery and moderate rock rubble.
Classification: Hamlet, 25–50 people.

SITE NO. Zu-LT-59 [Zu-LT-29(M); Location 37]
Date of Survey: June 18, 1973
Location: 489320 E, 2203200 N; 19.9251° N, 99.1020° W
Natural Setting: 2370 m asl, on nearly level ground atop a broad, low ridge in the Upper Salado Drainage; medium soil cover and moderate erosion.
Modern Land Use: Rainfall-based agriculture, with some maguey semi-terracing. The site area is presently fallow. Scattered modern houses at the southwestern corner of Tlapanaloya surround the site area, but do not appear to encroach significantly onto the archaeological remains.
Archaeological Remains: Light Late Toltec surface pottery over an area of ca. 0.80 ha. The LT material is mixed with heavier and more extensive Aztec ceramics (Zu-Az-72) (mostly Late Aztec, but including some Aztec II–III Black/Orange). We noted several green and gray obsidian artifacts. There are no discernible structural remains.
We made one surface collection (Location 37) over an area ca. 15 m in diameter in an unplowed field with light LT and light-to-moderate Aztec surface pottery, several obsidian artifacts, one basalt metate fragment, and very little rock rubble.
Discussion: This is one of the few localities in the Zumpango Region where the presence of Aztec II-III Black/Orange surface pottery suggests continuity of occupation from LT times into the Early and Late Aztec periods.
Classification: Small Hamlet, 5–10 people.

SITE NO. Zu-LT-60 [Zu-LT-24(M); Locations 9, 34]
Date of Survey: June 3, 14, 1973
Location: 489250 E, 2204500 N; 19.9369° N, 99.1027° W
Natural Setting: 2255 m asl, on gently sloping ground in the Upper Salado Drainage; deep soil cover and slight erosion.
Modern Land Use: Rainfall-based agriculture, with some earth- and stone-faced and maguey semi-terracing terracing in the general area. Outlying residences of the modern town of Tlapanaloya encroach onto the site from the northeast. A modern dirt road crosses the central part of the site.
Archaeological Remains: Variable light and light-to-moderate Late Toltec surface pottery over an area of ca. 3.10 ha. The LT material is mixed with heavier Classic ceramics (Zu-Cl-33), and approximately equal quantities of Early Toltec (Zu-ET-4) and Late Aztec (Zu-Az-71) pottery. We noted numerous blades and chips of both green and gray obsidian, one green obsidian projectile point, one gray obsidian projectile point, and one basalt metate fragment.

Although there are two discernible mounds (Features U, AT) in the eastern part of the site, neither appears to be associated with LT surface pottery (see Zu-Cl-33 and Zu-ET-4 site descriptions).

We made two surface collections (Locations 9, 34) in the LT site area:

Location	Area and Context	Content
9	8 × 10 m, in fallow field	Light-to-moderate Cl, LT, light ET, and trace Az surface pottery; numerous obsidian artifacts; light-to-moderate rock rubble.
34	7 × 10 m, in plowed field	Moderate Cl, light ET, light LT, and trace Az surface pottery; abundant obsidian; moderate-to-heavy rock rubble.

Discussion: The long-term occupation of this locality is notable, although the apparent absence of Early Aztec surface pottery suggests that this locality was abandoned after LT times and reoccupied during the Late Aztec period.
Classification: Hamlet, 30–60 people.

SITE NO. Zu-LT-61 [Zu-LT-22(M); Location 35]
Date of Survey: June 14, 1973
Location: 488250 E, 2203800 N; 19.9306° N, 99.1123° W
Natural Setting: 2250 m asl, on gently sloping ground in the Upper Salado Drainage; medium soil cover and slight to moderate erosion.
Modern Land Use: Rainfall-based agriculture. A drainage ditch borders the south edge of the site.
Archaeological Remains: Variable light and light-to-moderate Late Toltec surface pottery over an area of ca. 0.60 ha. The LT material is mixed with approximately equal quantities of Late Aztec ceramics (Zu-Az-68). We noted numerous green obsidian blades, one spindle whorl, and one basalt metate fragment. There are no definite structural remains, but several concentrations of moderate-to-heavy rock rubble may represent the remnants of prehispanic architecture.

We made one surface collection (Location 35) over an area ca. 15 × 15 m in a recently plowed (but fallow) field with light-to-moderate LT and light Late Az surface pottery, several green obsidian artifacts, and moderate-to-heavy rock rubble.
Discussion: The apparent absence of Early Aztec surface pottery suggests that this locality was abandoned after LT times and reoccupied during the Late Aztec period.
Classification: Small Hamlet, 5–10 people.

SITE NO. Zu-LT-62 [Zu-LT-23(M); Features AX, AY]
Date of Survey: June 18, 1973
Location: 487720 E, 2203320 N; 19.9262° N, 99.1173° W
Natural Setting: 2245 m asl, on gently sloping ground in the Upper Salado Drainage; medium to deep soil cover and slight to moderate erosion.
Modern Land Use: Rainfall-based agriculture.
Archaeological Remains: This site consists of a concentration of obsidian debris, both debitage and larger worked pieces, over an area of ca. 15 × 30 m (Feature AX) (Plate A89). Both green and gray obsidian occurs, with gray dominant. We did not determine the full extent of the obsidian debris since it extended eastward beyond the edge of the airphoto. There is also light Late Toltec surface pottery.

We made one surface collection from the area of Feature AX.

We noted a paved stone floor (Feature AY) ca. 10 × 10 m in area and situated atop a low knoll near the obsidian concentration. This floor could be a Colonial-period feature. A large quantity of obsidian debris is eroding from the southwest side of the knoll that supports the floor.
Discussion: This is an unusual site, virtually unique in our survey area. It may be a detached obsidian workshop, or simply a dump for waste from a workshop situated in a nearby settlement.
Classification: Isolated Obsidian Workshop or waste dump. No permanent residence.

SITE NO. Zu-LT-63 [Zu-LT-21(M); Location 11]
Date of Survey: June 19, 1973
Location: 487350 E, 2204750 N; 19.9391° N, 99.1209° W
Natural Setting: 2270 m asl, on gently sloping ground atop a low knoll (natural or artificial?) in the Upper Salado Drainage (Plate A90); medium soil cover and slight to moderate erosion.
Modern Land Use: Rainfall-based agriculture. Presently fallow.
Archaeological Remains: Light-to-moderate Late Toltec surface pottery over an area of ca. 0.40 ha. We noted some gray obsidian artifacts, including one projectile point. There are no definite structural remains, but moderate rock-rubble concentrations may represent the remnants of prehispanic architecture.

We made one surface collection (Location 11) over an area ca. 10 × 15 m in an fallow field with light-to-moderate LT surface pottery, several obsidian artifacts (including one gray obsidian projectile point), and light-to-moderate rock rubble.
Classification: Small Hamlet, 5–10 people.

SITE NO. Zu-LT-64 [Zu-LT-20(M)]
Date of Survey: June 19, 1973
Location: 487030 E, 2204820 N; 19.9398° N, 99.1239° W
Natural Setting: 2270 m asl, on gently sloping ground in the Upper Salado Drainage; medium soil cover and slight to moderate erosion.
Modern Land Use: Rainfall-based agriculture. The site area had recently been plowed and planted at the time of our survey.
Archaeological Remains: Light Late Toltec surface pottery over an area of ca. 0.20 ha. There are no discernible structural remains.
No surface collection made.
Classification: Small Hamlet, 2–5 people.

SITE NO. Zu-LT-65 [Zu-LT-19(M); Feature BB]
Date of Survey: June 19, 1973
Location: 486820 E, 2204280 N; 19.9349° N, 99.1259° W
Natural Setting: 2260 m asl, on gently sloping ground in the Upper Salado Drainage; medium soil cover and slight to moderate erosion.

Modern Land Use: Rainfall-based agriculture. The site area had been recently plowed and planted at the time of our survey.

Archaeological Remains: Variable light and light-to-moderate Late Toltec surface pottery over an area of ca. 0.40 ha. The LT material is mixed with a trace of Aztec ceramics (no Az site designated).

There is a single discernible mound (Feature BB) at the south edge of the site. This much plowed-down feature measures ca. 25 × 35 m in area, and 0.35 m high (Plate A91), with light-to-moderate LT surface pottery, a few obsidian artifacts, and moderate rock rubble.

No surface collection made.

Classification: Small Hamlet, 5–10 people.

SITE NO. Zu-LT-66 [Zu-LT-18(M)]

Date of Survey: June 19, 1973

Location: 486320 E, 2204900 N; 19.9405° N, 99.1307° W

Natural Setting: 2250 m asl, on gently sloping ground in the Upper Salado Drainage; medium soil cover and moderate erosion.

Modern Land Use: Rainfall-based agriculture. The site area had recently been plowed and planted at the time of our survey.

Archaeological Remains: Light Late Toltec surface pottery over an area of ca. 0.90 ha. There are traces of Aztec ceramics near the western edge of the site (no Az site designated).

No surface collection made.

Classification: Small Hamlet, 5–10 people.

SITE NO. Zu-LT-67 [Zu-LT-13(M); Feature Z]

Date of Survey: June 4, 1973

Location: 484030 E, 2204350 N; 19.9355° N, 99.1526° W

Natural Setting: 2220 m asl, on nearly level ground in the Upper Salado Drainage; medium soil cover and slight erosion.

Modern Land Use: Irrigation agriculture, using *agua negra* pumped from the Gran Canal del Desagüe (ca. 600 m to the south). Several irrigation canals cut through the general area.

Archaeological Remains: The site consists of a single mound (Feature Z) that measures ca. 10 × 7 m in area and ca. 1.00 m high, with light Late Toltec surface pottery, several obsidian artifacts, and moderate rock rubble.

No surface collection made.

Classification: Small Hamlet, 2–5 people.

ITE NO. Zu-LT-68 [Zu-LT-9(M); Feature Y]

Date of Survey: June 4, 1973

Location: 483400 E, 2204930 N; 19.9407° N, 99.1586° W

Natural Setting: 2200 m asl, on gently sloping ground in the Upper Salado Drainage; deep soil cover and slight erosion.

Modern Land Use: Irrigation cultivation of maize and alfalfa.

Archaeological Remains: Light Late Toltec surface pottery over an area of ca. 0.40 ha. The LT material is mixed with a trace of Aztec ceramics (no Az site designated). We noted several obsidian artifacts.

There is a single discernible mound (Feature Y). This unplowed feature measures ca. 12 × 12 m in area and 0.50 m high. A looter's pit has exposed a subsurface stone wall. There is light LT surface pottery around the base of the mound, and very little on the mound's surface.

Classification: Small Hamlet, 2–5 people.

SITE NO. Zu-LT-69 [Zu-LT-10(M); Locations 23, 24; Features AA, AB, AC]

Date of Survey: June 5, 1973

Location: 483400 E, 2205750 N; 19.9481° N, 99.1586° W

Natural Setting: 2215 m asl, on gently sloping ground in the Upper Salado Drainage; deep soil cover and slight erosion.

Modern Land Use: Rainfall-based agriculture. Most of the site area had recently been plowed and planted at the time of our survey. The south edge of the site is bordered by the paved highway between Apaxco and Tequixquiac.

Archaeological Remains: Variable light, and light-to-moderate Late Toltec surface pottery over an area of ca. 5.50 ha. The LT material includes two Plumbate sherds. There is also a trace of Aztec ceramics in the eastern part of the site (no Az site designated). We noted numerous green obsidian blades, a few gray obsidian scrapers, one gray obsidian knife, one obsidian trilobal eccentric, one maguey spindle whorl, and two basalt mano fragments.

Three mounds (Features AA, AB, AC) are discernible in the southern part of the site:

Fea.	Area and Context	Height	Content
AA	27 × 35 m, in plowed field	1.00 m	Very light LT surface pottery, several obsidian artifacts, moderate rock rubble.
AB	18 × 18 m, in plowed field (Plate A92)	0.25 m	Light LT surface pottery, several obsidian artifacts, light-to-moderate rock rubble.
AC	13 × 15 m, in plowed field (Plate A93)	0.30 m	Light LT surface pottery, several obsidian artifacts, light-to-moderate rock rubble.

We made two surface collections (Locations 23, 24):

Location	Area and Context	Content
23	15 × 15 m, in unplowed field	Light-to-moderate LT surface pottery, several obsidian artifacts, moderate rock rubble.
24	6 × 15 m, in unplowed field	Moderate LT surface pottery, several obsidian artifacts, light-to-moderate rock rubble.

Classification: Small Dispersed Village, 60–120 people.

SITE NO. Zu-LT-70 [Zu-LT-12(M); Location 27]

Date of Survey: June 5, 1973

Location: 484050 E, 2206500 N; 19.9549° N, 99.1524° W

Natural Setting: 2230 m asl, on nearly level ground in the Upper Salado Drainage; shallow soil cover and slight erosion.

Modern Land Use: Rainfall-based agriculture.

Archaeological Remains: Variable light-to-moderate and moderate Late Toltec surface pottery over an area of ca. 0.80 ha. The LT material is mixed with more extensive Aztec ceramics (Zu-Az-46) (the Az component includes both Az II-III and III Black/Orange pottery). We noted numerous green and gray obsidian blades, scrapers, and debitage fragments. There are no discernible structural remains.

We made one surface collection (Location 27) in a part of the site with predominantly Aztec surface pottery over an area ca. 10 × 10 m in a plowed field with light-to-moderate Az and light LT surface pottery, several obsidian artifacts, and light rock rubble.

Discussion: This is one of the few sites in the Zumpango Region with both Aztec II-III and III Black/Orange surface pottery.

Classification: Hamlet, 15–30 people.

Plate A89. Zu-LT-62, facing east at Feature AX.

Plate A90. Zu-LT-63, facing south over site area.

Plate A91. Zu-LT-65, facing NW at Feature BB.

Plate A92. Zu-LT-69, facing north at Feature AB.

Plate A93. Zu-LT-69, facing west at Feature AC.

Plate A94. Zu-LT-72, Location 13 area.

SITE NO. Zu-LT-71 [Zu-LT-11(M); Location 19; Feature AF]
   Date of Survey: June 5, 1973
   Location: 482850 E, 2206630 N; 19.9561° N, 99.1639° W
   Natural Setting: 2200 m asl, on gently sloping ground in the Upper Salado Drainage; medium soil cover and slight erosion.
   Modern Land Use: Rainfall-based agriculture. The southern edge of the modern town of Apaxco is ca. 100 m to the northwest.
   Archaeological Remains: Light Late Toltec surface pottery over an area of ca. 0.90 ha. We noted several green obsidian blades.
   A single mound (Feature AF) is discernible in a plowed field at the north end of the site. This features measures ca. 24 × 26 m in area and 1.00 m high, with very light LT surface pottery and light-to-moderate rock rubble. A looter's pit has exposed earth and rock-rubble fill.
   We made one surface collection (Location 19) over an area ca. 20 m in diameter in a fallow field, with light LT surface pottery, several obsidian artifacts, and light rock rubble.
   Classification: Small Hamlet, 2–5 people.

SITE NO. Zu-LT-72 [Zu-LT-8(M); Locations 13, 14]
   Date of Survey: May 31, 1973
   Location: 481780 E, 2203950 N; 19.9319° N, 99.1741° W
   Natural Setting: 2205 m asl, on gently sloping ground in the Upper Salado Drainage; medium soil cover and moderate erosion.
   Modern Land Use: Agriculture, both rainfall-based and irrigated. A railroad crosses the eastern edge of the site. There is a modern house in the southwestern corner of the site.
   Archaeological Remains: Variable light and light-to-moderate Late Toltec surface pottery over an area of ca. 6.10 ha. The LT material is mixed with lighter Late Aztec ceramics (Zu-Az-60). Comales are unusually abundant, and we saw two spindle whorls (one maguey, one cotton). Green obsidian blades are abundant. There are no discernible structural remains.
   We made two surface collections (Locations 13, 14):

Location	Area and Context	Content
13	10 × 16 m, in unplowed field (Plate A94)	Light-to-moderate LT surface pottery, several obsidian artifacts, light rock rubble.
14	2 × 20 m, in unplowed field	Moderate LT and very light Az surface pottery, several obsidian artifacts, light rock rubble.

   Discussion: The apparent absence of Early Aztec surface pottery suggests that this locality was abandoned after LT times and reoccupied during the Late Aztec period.
   Classification: Small Dispersed Village, 60–120 people.

SITE NO. Zu-LT-73 [Zu-LT-6(M); Location 6]
   Date of Survey: May 29, 1973
   Location: 480630 E, 2204400 N; 19.9359° N, 99.1851° W
   Natural Setting: 2225 m asl, on gently sloping ground in the Upper Salado Drainage; medium soil cover and slight erosion.
   Modern Land Use: Irrigation agriculture of maize and alfalfa. Irrigation water is *agua negra*, taken from the nearby Gran Canal del Desagüe through an extensive network of canals. The immediate site area is presently fallow.
   Archaeological Remains: Variable light and light-to-moderate Late Toltec surface pottery over an area of ca. 0.70 ha. We noted several green and gray obsidian blades. There are no discernible structural remains.
   We made one surface collection (Location 6) over an area 9 × 11 m in an unplowed field, with light-to-moderate LT surface pottery, several obsidian artifacts, and very little rock rubble.
   Classification: Small Hamlet, 5–10 people.

SITE NO. Zu-LT-74 [Zu-LT-43(M); Feature CN]
  Date of Survey: July 1, 1973
  Location: 480700 E, 2203350 N; 19.9264° N, 99.1844° W
  Natural Setting: 2255 m asl, on gently sloping ground in the Upper Salado Drainage; medium soil cover and slight erosion.
  Modern Land Use: Rainfall-based agriculture. At the time of our survey, the site area had recently been plowed and planted.
  Archaeological Remains: Variable light and light-to-moderate Late Toltec surface pottery over an area of ca. 4.10 ha; there is also a trace of Aztec ceramics (no Az site designated). We noted several green and gray obsidian blades, flakes, and some obsidian debitage. The site lies immediately south of a gap in the airphoto coverage, and may extend somewhat to the north.
  There is a single mound (Feature CN) at the edge of a plowed field near the north edge of the site. This feature measures ca. 21 × 23 m in area and 2.00 m high (Plate A95). Three looter's pits have exposed a mortared tabular-stone wall that appears to enclose a mass of rock-rubble fill (Plate A96). The mound's surface pottery is very light LT, and there is a trace of Az ceramics to the southwest of the mound.
  No surface collection made.
  Classification: Hamlet, 40–80 people.

SITE NO. Zu-LT-75 [Zu-LT-5(M); Features D, E, F, G, H, I, J, K, L, R, S, T; Locations 4, 5, 7]
  Date of Survey: May 23, 29, 1973
  Location: 479400 E, 2204600 N; 19.9377° N, 99.1969° W
  Natural Setting: 2240 m asl, on gently sloping ground in the Upper Salado Drainage (Plate A97); shallow to medium soil cover and generally slight to moderate erosion, with severe erosion in the southern and western sections (where there are patches of bare tepetate).
  Modern Land Use: Mainly rainfall-based agriculture. The preserved mounds are uncultivated. There is some maguey semi-terracing in the southern part of the site. A paved road borders the eastern edge of the site.
  Archaeological Remains: Variable light, light-to-moderate, and moderate Late Toltec surface pottery over an area of ca. 10.70 ha. We noted numerous green and gray obsidian artifacts, and one green obsidian trilobal eccentric.
  There are twelve preserved mounds scattered throughout the site (Features D, E, F, G, H, I, J, K, L, R, S, T):

Fea.	Area and Context	Height	Content
D	11 m dia., in unplowed field	0.80 m	Light LT surface pottery, several obsidian artifacts, light rock rubble.
E	25 × 45 m, in unplowed field (Plate A98)	2.00 m	Trace LT surface pottery, moderate rock rubble. Looter's pit shows earth and rock-rubble construction.
F	30 × 45 m, in unplowed field	2.50 m north 4.00 m south	Very light LT surface pottery, moderate rock rubble.
G	16 × 16 m, in unplowed field	1.50 m	Light LT surface pottery, light-to-moderate rock rubble. Looter's pit shows tepetate rubble construction.
H	18 × 18 m, in unplowed field	1.50 m	Very light LT surface pottery, very little rock rubble. Looter's pit shows layers of tepetate blocks and rock rubble.
I	15 × 15 m, in unplowed field	2.00 m	Light LT surface pottery, very little rock rubble. Looter's pit shows rock-rubble construction.
J	25 m dia., in unplowed field	1.50 m	Light LT surface pottery, moderate rock rubble.
K	40 m dia., in unplowed field	2.00 m, with flat top	Light LT surface pottery, light-to-moderate rock rubble.
L	Platform/plaza, 60 × 15 m, in plowed field	3.00 m N-S, 0-3.00 m E-W	Very light LT surface pottery, light rock rubble. Feature L is apparently a stone retaining wall that defines a platform, or plaza, measuring ca. 15 × 60 m, between two mounds (Features I and K). This wall seems to have been about 3 m high along its longest (eastern) side. A large looter's pit indicates that the wall is constructed of rock rubble and tepetate blocks. A circular stone-cobble threshing floor, ca. 21 m in diameter and of either modern or Colonial-period date, has been constructed near the southern edge of the platform/plaza. This feature may overlie another prehispanic mound.
R	14 m dia., in unplowed field	0.10 m	Light LT surface pottery, very little rock rubble. Two obsidian trilobal eccentrics.
S	7 m dia., in unplowed field	0.20 m	Light LT and trace Az surface pottery, light-to-moderate rock rubble.
T	20 m dia., in unplowed field	2.00 m	No surface pottery, light rock rubble.

We made three surface collections (Locations 4, 5, 7):

Location	Area and Context	Content
4	14 × 14 m, in unplowed field	Light-to-moderate LT surface pottery, numerous obsidian artifacts, moderate rock rubble.
5	10 × 10 m, in unplowed field	Light-to-moderate LT and trace of Late Az surface pottery, numerous obsidian artifacts, one basalt mano fragment, moderate rock rubble.
7	8 × 10 m, in plowed field	Moderate LT and trace of Late Az surface pottery, numerous obsidian artifacts, moderate rock rubble.

  Discussion: This is one of the largest LT sites in the Zumpango Region. Its large size and the presence of a substantial ceremonial-civic complex suggest a degree of supra-local sociopolitical significance. Although we doubt it, the trace of Late Aztec surface pottery (no Az site defined here) could mean that some of the mound features may date to that period.
  Classification: Local Center, 300–600 people.

SITE NO. Zu-LT-76 [Zu-LT-7(M); Feature V]
  Date of Survey: May 30, 1973
  Location: 479700 E, 2205720 N; 19.9478° N, 99.1940° W
  Natural Setting: 2245 m asl, on gently sloping ground in the Upper Salado Drainage; medium soil cover and slight erosion.
  Modern Land Use: Rainfall-based agriculture. The site area is presently fallow.

(*above*) Plate A95. Zu-LT-74, facing SW at Feature CN.
(*left*) Plate A96. Zu-LT-74, stone wall exposed in looter's pit at Feature CN.

Plate A97. Zu-LT-75, facing north over general site area.

Plate A98. Zu-LT-75, facing NW at Feature E.

Plate A99. Zu-LT-76, facing SW at Feature V.

Archaeological Remains: This site consists of a single mound in an unplowed field (Feature V). This feature measures ca. 25 × 25 m in area and 1.50 m high (Plate A99), with light Late Toltec surface pottery and moderate rock rubble. The presence of some glazed ceramics suggests that this might be, at least in part, a post-hispanic structure.

No surface collection made.

Discussion: The function of Feature V is problematic. Its height and relatively light surface pottery suggest a non-domestic function, but the height may be exaggerated by recent looting.

Classification: Small Hamlet (?), 5–10 people.

SITE NO. Zu-LT-77 [Zu-LT-4(M)]
  Date of Survey: May 28, 1973
  Location: 478150 E, 2204630 N; 19.9380° N, 99.2088° W
  Natural Setting: 2260 m asl, on gently sloping ground in the Upper Salado Drainage; medium soil cover and moderate erosion.
  Modern Land Use: Rainfall-based agriculture.
  Archaeological Remains: Variable light and light-to-moderate Late Toltec surface pottery over an area of ca. 0.80 ha. There are no discernible structural remains.
  No surface collection made.
  Classification: Small Hamlet, 10–20 people.

SITE NO. Zu-LT-78 [Zu-LT-1(M); Feature B]
  Date of Survey: May 21, 1973
  Location: 477000 E, 2206630 N; 19.9560° N, 99.2198° W
  Natural Setting: 2350 m asl, on gently sloping ground in the Upper Salado Drainage; medium soil cover and moderate erosion.
  Modern Land Use: Rainfall-based agriculture. The site area is presently fallow, but has been plowed in recent years.
  Archaeological Remains: Light Late Toltec surface pottery over an area of ca. 0.80 ha. We noted one green obsidian projectile point.
  There is a single mound (Feature B), near the western edge of the site. This feature measures 16 × 19 m in area and 0.50 m high, with light LT surface pottery, several obsidian artifacts, and moderate-to-heavy rock rubble.
  We made one collection from the entire surface of Feature B.
  Classification: Small Hamlet, 5–10 people.

SITE NO. Zu-LT-79 [Zu-LT-2(M); Location 3]
  Date of Survey: May 21, 1973
  Location: 477430 E, 2204320 N; 19.9352° N, 99.2157° W
  Natural Setting: 2280 m asl, on gently sloping ground in the Upper Salado Drainage; shallow to medium soil cover and moderate erosion.
  Modern Land Use: Rainfall-based agriculture, although the immediate site area is fallow. A modern dirt road crosses the center of the site.
  Archaeological Remains: Variable light, light-to-moderate, and moderate Late Toltec surface pottery over an area of ca. 2.90 ha. We noted several green and gray obsidian artifacts (both blades and scrapers). There are no discernible structural remains.
  We made one surface collection (Location 3) over an area ca. 10 × 10 m in an unplowed area, with moderate LT surface pottery, several obsidian artifacts, and moderate-to-heavy rock rubble.
  Classification: Hamlet, 45–90 people.

Plate A100. Zu-LT-80, facing NW at Feature A.

SITE NO. Zu-LT-80 [Zu-LT-3(M); Location 1; Features A, C]
  Date of Survey: May 21, 1973
  Location: 478180 E, 2204130 N; 19.9334° N, 99.2085° W
  Natural Setting: 2270 m asl, on gently sloping ground in the Upper Salado Drainage; medium soil cover and slight erosion.
  Modern Land Use: Rainfall-based agriculture. A modern dirt road crosses the southern part of the site. There is an active rock quarry immediately to the west.
  Archaeological Remains: Variable light and light-to-moderate Late Toltec surface pottery over an area of ca. 11.50 ha. There are also traces of Aztec ceramics (no Az site designated). We noted several green and gray obsidian blades and debitage fragments.

We identified two definite mounds in the southern part of the site (Features A, C); the presence of vague, low, irregular mounding and substantial rock rubble throughout the site area may represent the remnants of other prehispanic structures.

Fea.	Area and Context	Height	Content
A	18 × 22 m, in unplowed field (Plate A100)	2.50 m	Light LT surface pottery, moderate rock rubble. Looter's pit shows rock-rubble fill and a possible stone wall; possible ceremonial-civic function (Plate A101).
C	10 × 15 m, in unplowed field (Plate A102)	1.50 m	Light LT surface pottery, moderate rock rubble. Shallow looter's pit in top.

We made one surface collection (Location 1) over an area ca. 10 × 10 m in an unplowed field (Plate A103), with moderate LT and traces of Az surface pottery, several obsidian artifacts, and moderate rock rubble.
  Discussion: The height of Feature A suggests a ceremonial-civic function. Although we doubt it, the trace of Aztec surface pottery could mean that Feature A may be a Late Aztec feature. If Features A and C are both LT structures, this site could have had more than purely local significance.
  Classification: Small Dispersed Village (?), 150–300 people.

SITE NO. Zu-LT-81 [Zu-LT-45(M); Location 48; Features CW, CX, CY, CZ, DA]
  Date of Survey: July 5, 1973
  Location: 477950 E, 2201600 N; 19.9106° N, 99.2107° W
  Natural Setting: 2270 m asl, on gently sloping ground in the Upper Salado Drainage; shallow soil cover and generally slight erosion, except along the the north-central side where erosion has been severe. Most of the immediate site area is covered with thick grass and closely spaced *pirule* trees.
  Modern Land Use: Unplowed pasture.
  Archaeological Remains: Variable light and light-to-moderate Late Toltec surface pottery over an area of ca. 3.30 ha. We noted several green and gray obsidian blades and some obsidian debitage.

We identified five mounds (Features CW, CX, CY, CZ, DA) in the southern part of the site:

Fea.	Area and Context	Height	Content
CW	20 × 25 m, in unplowed field	2.50 m	Light LT surface pottery, light rock rubble. Extensively pitted. One pit shows earth and rock-rubble fill, and possible stone wall.
CX	17 m dia., in unplowed field	1.00 m	Very light LT surface pottery, very little rock rubble. Flat top; possible stone wall base on east side.
CY	21 × 23 m, in unplowed field	2.00 m	Light LT surface pottery, light-to-moderate rock rubble. Pitting shows solid rock-rubble construction.
CZ	55 × 55 m, in unplowed field	2.00 m	Light LT surface pottery, very little rock rubble. Flat top, with traces of stone wall base.
DA	19 × 20 m, in unplowed field	2.00 m	Very light LT surface pottery, light-to-moderate rock rubble.

We made one surface collection (Location 48) over an area ca. 5 × 7 m in an unplowed area with light-to-moderate LT surface pottery, numerous obsidian and chert artifacts (including one trilobal eccentric), and light rock rubble.
  Discussion: The function(s) of the discernible mounds are unclear. The relative paucity of both surface pottery and obsidian artifacts might indicate a ceremonial-civic function, especially in the case of Feature CZ, which appears to have been a flat-topped temple platform. If ceremonial-civic architecture is present, this site, despite its small size, may have had more than purely local significance.
  Classification: Hamlet (?), 35–70 people.

Plate A101. Zu-LT-80, rubble fill in looter's pit at Feature A.

Plate A102. Zu-LT-80, facing east at Feature C.

Plate A103. Zu-LT-80, facing east over Location 1.

SITE NO. Zu-LT-82 [Zu-LT-44(M); Features CP, CQ, CR]
   Date of Survey: July 1, 1973
   Location: 477650 E, 2202000 N; 19.9142° N, 99.2135° W
   Natural Setting: 2270 m asl, on gently sloping ground in the Upper Salado Drainage; shallow soil cover and moderate erosion.
   Modern Land Use: Unplowed pasture. The immediate site area has a thick grass cover.
   Archaeological Remains: Variable light and light-to-moderate Late Toltec surface pottery over an area of ca. 4.10 ha. The LT material is mixed with a trace of Aztec ceramics (no Az site designated). The thick grass cover may obscure some surface pottery. We noted several green and gray obsidian blades and scrapers, and some obsidian debitage.

There are three discernible mounds (Features CP, CQ, CR); Feature CO is at the north end of the site, and Features CQ and CR lie along the site's west-central side. The two latter mounds rest on a supporting platform, or terrace, about 30 × 50 m in area; the north (downhill) side of this supporting platform rises ca. 1.50 m above the general ground level.

Fea.	Area and Context	Height	Content
CP	18 × 28 m, in unplowed area (Plate A104)	1.50 m	Light LT surface pottery, light rock rubble. Several fragmentary stone wall bases on surface.
CQ	12 × 18 m, in unplowed area (Plate A105)	2.00 m	Light LT surface pottery, light rock rubble. Three stone wall bases on surface.
CR	18 × 22 m, in unplowed area	2.00 m	Light LT, and trace of Az (Texcoco Fabric Marked). Looter's pit shows rock-rubble construction, with a stone wall exposed on east side.

   Discussion: The presence of Texcoco Fabric Marked pottery at this location so far from the lakeshore, and in the absence of significant Aztec-period occupation, is unusual. All three mounds appear to be ceremonial-civic features. If so, then despite its small size, this site may have more than purely local significance.
   Classification: Hamlet (?), 40–80 people.

SITE NO. Zu-LT-83 [Zu-LT-42(M)]
   Date of Survey: June 24, 1973
   Location: 482630 E, 2201000 N; 19.9052° N, 99.1660° W
   Natural Setting: 2250 m asl, on gently sloping ground, near the eastern base of Cerro de la Mesa Grande in the Upper Salado Drainage; shallow soil cover and moderate to severe erosion, with several patches of bare tepetate.
   Modern Land Use: Pasture.
   Archaeological Remains: Light Late Toltec surface pottery over an area of ca. 0.50 ha. The LT material is mixed with traces of Aztec ceramics (no Az site designated). There are no discernible structural remains.
   No surface collection made.
   Classification: Small Hamlet, 2–5 people.

SITE NO. Zu-LT-84 [Zu-LT-39(M)]
   Date of Survey: June 21, 1973
   Location: 483600 E, 2198720 N; 19.9052° N, 99.1567° W
   Natural Setting: 2280 m asl, on gently sloping ground at the eastern base of Cerro de la Mesa Grande in the Upper Salado Drainage; shallow soil cover and severe erosion, with some patches of bare tepetate.
   Modern Land Use: Rainfall-based agriculture. There is a railroad line about 25 m to the southeast.
   Archaeological Remains: Light Late Toltec surface pottery over an area of ca. 1.20 ha. We noted several obsidian artifacts. There are no discernible structural remains.
   No surface collection made.
   Discussion: This site probably represents an outlier of the larger Zu-LT-87 settlement to the east.
   Classification: Small Hamlet, 5–10 people.

SITE NO. Zu-LT-85 [Zu-LT-35(M); Feature BE]
   Date of Survey: June 21, 1973
   Location: 483780 E, 2199570 N; 19.8923° N, 99.1550° W

Plate A104. Zu-LT-82, facing west at Feature CP.

Plate A105. Zu-LT-82, facing north at Feature CQ.

Plate A106. Zu-LT-85, facing east at Feature BE.

Natural Setting: 2280 m asl, on gently sloping ground at the eastern base of Cerro de la Mesa Grande in the Upper Salado Drainage; medium soil cover and slight erosion.

Modern Land Use: Rainfall-based agriculture, with some stone-faced terracing. At the time of our survey, the site had been recently plowed and planted.

Archaeological Remains: Variable light and light-to-moderate Late Toltec surface pottery over an area of ca. 0.60 ha. There is a single discernible mound (Feature BE). This feature measures ca. 39 m in diameter and 0.50 m high, with light-to-moderate LT surface pottery, several obsidian and chert artifacts, and heavy rock rubble (Plate A106).

We made one surface collection from an area ca. 5 × 5 m on the surface of Feature BE.

Classification: Small Hamlet, 5–10 people.

SITE NO. Zu-LT-86 [Zu-LT-36(M); Location 44]
  Date of Survey: June 25, 1973
  Location: 484250 E, 2199650 N; 19.8930° N, 99.1505° W
  Natural Setting: 2270 m asl, on nearly level ground in the Upper Salado Drainage; shallow soil cover and severe erosion, with some patches of bare tepetate.
  Modern Land Use: Marginal rainfall-based agriculture. Some erosion control has been achieved by small terraces and check dams made of tepetate blocks. Modern houses encroach onto the site from the southeast, and may obscure some of the prehispanic occupation. A modern dirt road crosses the center of the site.
  Archaeological Remains: Variable light and light-to-moderate Late Toltec surface pottery over an area ca. 0.90 ha. The LT material is mixed with a trace of Aztec ceramics (no Az site designated). We noted several green and gray obsidian blades, one gray obsidian projectile point, and some obsidian debitage (which seems mostly gray). There are no discernible structural remains.

We made one surface collection (Location 44) over an area of unrecorded size in an unplowed, badly eroded area (Plate A107), with light-to-moderate LT and traces of Az surface pottery, several obsidian artifacts, and no rock rubble.

  Discussion: Because of modern occupation, the site area remains uncertain.
  Classification: Small Hamlet (?), 10–20 people.

SITE NO. Zu-LT-87 [Zu-LT-37(M); Features BF, BG, BL, BM, BN, BO, BQ]
  Date of Survey: June 21, 25, 1973
  Location: 484100 E, 2199070 N; 19.8878° N, 99.1519° W
  Natural Setting: 2255 m asl, on nearly level ground at the eastern base of Cerro de la Mesa Grande in the Upper Salado Drainage (Plate A108); shallow soil cover with severe erosion and numerous patches of bare tepetate.
  Modern Land Use: Marginal rainfall-based agriculture. At the time of our survey, the immediate site area had recently been plowed and planted. Some measure of erosion control has been achieved by small terraces and check dams made of stone and tepetate blocks. A railroad line passes through the site.
  Archaeological Remains: Variable light and light to moderate Late Toltec surface pottery over an area of ca. 10.70 ha. The LT material is mixed with partially overlapping Late Aztec ceramics (Zu-Az-119), and with heavier Classic pottery (Zu-Cl-58) in the south-central part of

Plate A107. Zu-LT-86, facing north over Location 44.

the site. We noted numerous green and gray obsidian blades, one green obsidian core, and some obsidian debitage.

We identified seven mounds within the central and southern parts of the site (Features BF, BG, BL, BM, BN, BO, BQ). The largest of these mounds, Feature BM, is at the approximate center of the site, and may represent a ceremonial-civic focus.

Fea.	Area and Context	Height	Content
BF	13 m dia., in unplowed field (Plate A109)	2.00 m	Light-to-moderate LT surface pottery; light rock rubble. Several looter's pits.
BG	22 × 30 m, in plowed field	Low	Light LT and Late Az surface pottery; light-to-moderate rock rubble.
BL	40 m dia., in unplowed field	1.00 m	Light-to-moderate LT and very light Late Az surface pottery; moderate rock rubble.
BM	30 × 35 m, in unplowed field (Plate A110)	3.30 m	Light LT surface pottery; light rock rubble.
BN	6 × 13 m, in unplowed field	1.50 m	Light-to-moderate Cl, light LT and very light Az surface pottery; light-to-moderate rock rubble.
BO	6 × 12 m, in unplowed field	1.50 m	Light Cl surface pottery.
BQ	25 × 28 m, in unplowed field	0.40 m	Light-to-moderate LT surface pottery.

We made two surface collections: one from an area of ca. 8 × 8 m on Feature BG, and another from an area of ca. 6 × 13 m on Feature BN.

Discussion: Despite the presence of substantial Classic surface pottery, we suspect all the mounds are of LT age. The presence of well-defined ceremonial-civic architecture suggests that this site had more than purely local significance.

Classification: Local Center, 200–400 people.

SITE NO. Zu-LT-88 [Zu-LT-37(M)]
Date of Survey: June 25, 1973
Location: 484720 E, 2199720 N; 19.8937° N, 99.1460° W
Natural Setting: 2245 m asl, on gently sloping ground in the Upper Salado Drainage; shallow soil cover and severe erosion, with several patches of bare tepetate.

Modern Land Use: Rainfall-based agriculture, with some maguey semi-terracing. Modern houses encroach onto the site from the north and east.

Archaeological Remains: Variable light and light-to-moderate Late Toltec surface pottery over an area of ca. 1.20 ha. Along the southern, eastern, and western edges of this site, the LT material is mixed with Late Aztec ceramics (Zu-Az-118). There are no discernible structural remains.

No surface collection made.

Discussion: The apparent absence of Early Aztec surface pottery suggests that this locality was abandoned after LT times and reoccupied during the Late Aztec period.

Classification: Small Hamlet, 10–20 people.

Plate A108. Zu-LT-87, facing SE over general site area.

Plate A109. Zu-LT-87, facing east at Feature BF.

Plate A110. Zu-LT-87, facing SW at Feature BM.

SITE NO. Zu-LT-89 [Zu-LT-41(M)]
Date of Survey: June 25, 1973
Location: 484680 E, 2200030 N; 19.8965° N, 99.1464° W
Natural Setting: 2245 m asl, on gently sloping ground in the Upper Salado Drainage; shallow soil cover, with severe erosion and several patches of bare tepetate.
Modern Land Use: Rainfall-based agriculture, with some maguey semi-terracing. Modern houses encroach onto the site from the west.
Archaeological Remains: Variable light and light-to-moderate Late Toltec surface pottery over an area of ca. 0.40 ha. In this central part of the site, the LT material is mixed with heavier and partially overlapping Late Aztec ceramics (Zu-Az-118). There are no discernible structural remains.
No surface collection made.
Discussion: The apparent absence of Early Aztec surface pottery suggests that this locality was abandoned after LT times and reoccupied during the Late Aztec period.
Classification: Hamlet, 40–80 people.

SITE NO. Zu-LT-90 [Zu-LT-52(M)]
Date of Survey: July 12, 1973
Location: 487130 E, 2199750 N; 19.8939° N, 99.1230° W
Natural Setting: 2300 m asl, on gently sloping ground in the Upper Salado Drainage; medium soil cover and slight erosion.
Modern Land Use: Rainfall-based agriculture.
Archaeological Remains: Variable light and light-to-moderate Late Toltec surface pottery over an area of ca. 2.10 ha. The LT material is mixed with traces of Aztec ceramics (no Az site designated). There are no discernible structural remains.
No surface collection made.
Classification: Hamlet, 20–40 people.

SITE NO. Zu-LT-91 [Zu-LT-48(M); Location 50]
Date of Survey: July 12, 1973
Location: 487320 E, 2199970 N; 19.8959° N, 99.1211° W
Natural Setting: 2265 m asl, on gently sloping ground in the Upper Salado Drainage; medium soil cover and slight erosion.
Modern Land Use: Rainfall-based agriculture. The site is surrounded by dispersed modern houses at the southeastern edge of Teoloyucan. These modern buildings encroach slightly onto the site, but do not appear to cover any of it.
Archaeological Remains: Light Late Toltec surface pottery over an area of ca. 1.70 ha. The LT material is mixed with approximately equal quantities of Classic (Zu-Cl-54) and Late Aztec (Zu-Az-115) ceramics. We noted numerous green obsidian blades and fragments, one gray obsidian blade and scraper, and one basalt mano fragment. There is light rock rubble but no discernible structural remains.
We made one surface collection (Location 50) over an area ca. 20 × 20 m in a plowed field, with light-to-moderate Cl and light LT and Az surface pottery, numerous obsidian artifacts, and light rock rubble.
Discussion: The apparent absence of Early Aztec surface pottery suggests that this locality was abandoned after LT times and reoccupied during the Late Aztec period.
Classification: Small Hamlet, 10–20 people.

SITE NO. Zu-LT-92 [Zu-LT-46(M); Location 49]
Date of Survey: July 9, 1973
Location: 486650 E, 2202000 N; 19.9143° N, 99.1276° W
Natural Setting: 2250 m asl, on gently sloping ground in the Upper Salado Drainage; shallow soil cover and moderate erosion.
Modern Land Use: Mixed pasture and rainfall-based agriculture.
Archaeological Remains: Variable light, light-to-moderate, and moderate Late Toltec surface pottery over an area of ca. 4.40 ha. In the northeastern corner of the site, the LT material is mixed with lighter Late Aztec ceramics (Zu-Az-110). We noted numerous green and gray blades, scrapers, and some obsidian debitage, and one green obsidian trilobal eccentric. There are no discernible structural remains.

We made one surface collection (Location 49) over an area ca. 10 × 10 m in an unplowed field, with light-to-moderate LT and light Late Az surface pottery, numerous obsidian artifacts (including one trilobal eccentric of gray obsidian), and light rock rubble.
Discussion: The apparent absence of Early Aztec surface pottery suggests that this locality was abandoned after LT times and reoccupied during the Late Aztec period.
Classification: Small Nucleated Village, 75–150 people.

SITE NO. Zu-LT-93 [Zu-LT-47(M)]
Date of Survey: July 9, 1973
Location: 487780 E, 2201950 N; 19.9143° N, 99.1168° W
Natural Setting: 2275 m asl, on gently sloping ground in the Upper Salado Drainage; shallow soil cover and moderate erosion.
Modern Land Use: Mixed pasture and rainfall-based agriculture. Two modern dirt roads cross the site.
Archaeological Remains: Variable light and light-to-moderate Late Toltec surface pottery over an area of ca. 3.40 ha. In the southern part of the site, the LT material is mixed with traces of Aztec ceramics (no Az site defined). There are no discernible structural remains.
No surface collection made.
Classification: Hamlet, 35–70 people.

SITE NO. Zu-LT-94 [Zu-LT-53(M); Location 62]
Date of Survey: July 9, 1973
Location: 488150 E, 2201550 N; 19.9102° N, 99.1132° W
Natural Setting: 2280 m asl, on gently sloping ground in the Upper Salado Drainage; shallow soil cover and moderate erosion. There is a major *barranca* running northeast-southwest immediately to the west.
Modern Land Use: Mixed pasture and rainfall-based agriculture.
Archaeological Remains: Light-to-moderate Late Toltec surface pottery over an area of ca. 0.40 ha. In the southwestern part of this site, the LT material is mixed with traces of Aztec ceramics (no Az site defined). We noted several obsidian artifacts, one chert fragment, and one maguey spindle whorl. There are no discernible structural remains.

We made one surface collection (Location 62) over an area ca. 15 × 15 m in an unplowed area with light-to-moderate LT surface pottery, several obsidian artifacts, and light-to-moderate rock rubble.
Classification: Small Hamlet, 5–10 people.

SITE NO. Zu-LT-95 [Zu-LT-56(J)]
Date of Survey: July 5, 1973
Location: 489100 E, 2201630 N; 19.9109° N, 99.1041° W
Natural Setting: 2315 m asl, on gently sloping ground in the Upper Salado Drainage; shallow soil cover and slight to moderate erosion.
Modern Land Use: Rainfall-based agriculture. The site is presently fallow.
Archaeological Remains: Light-to-moderate Late Toltec surface pottery over an area of ca. 1.00 ha. The LT material is mixed with approximately equal quantities of Late Aztec ceramics (Zu-Az-106). There are no discernible structural remains.
No surface collection made.
Discussion: The apparent absence of Early Aztec surface pottery suggests that this locality was abandoned after LT times and reoccupied during the Late Aztec period.
Classification: Hamlet, 15–30 people.

SITE NO. Zu-LT-96 [Zu-LT-50(J); Feature BQ]
Date of Survey: July 5, 1973
Location: 488850 E, 2201100 N; 19.9062° N, 99.1065° W
Natural Setting: 2305 m asl, on gently sloping ground in the Upper Salado Drainage; shallow soil cover and severe erosion. A major *barranca* borders the western edge of the site.
Modern Land Use: Rainfall-based agriculture.
Archaeological Remains: Variable light and light-to-moderate Late Toltec surface pottery over an area of ca. 6.40 ha. The LT material is mixed with traces of Aztec ceramics (no Az site designated). We noted a few obsidian artifacts.

We identified one mound in the northern part of the site (Feature BQ). This feature measures ca. 20 m in diameter and 0.50 m high, with light-to-moderate LT surface pottery, several obsidian artifacts, and light-to-moderate rock rubble. A looter's pit reveals solid rock-rubble construction.
No surface collection made.
Classification: Small Dispersed Village, 65–130 people.

SITE NO. Zu-LT-97 [Zu-LT-51(J)]
Date of Survey: July 5, 1973
Location: 489500 E, 2200600 N; 19.9016° N, 99.1003° W
Natural Setting: 2350 m asl, on gently sloping ground in the Upper Salado Drainage; medium soil cover and slight erosion.
Modern Land Use: Rainfall-based agriculture.
Archaeological Remains: Light Late Toltec surface pottery over an area of ca. 0.60 ha. The LT material is mixed with approximately equal quantities of Late Aztec ceramics (Zu-Az-128).
No surface collection made.
Discussion: The apparent absence of Early Aztec surface pottery suggests that this locality was abandoned after LT times and reoccupied during the Late Aztec period.
Classification: Small Hamlet, 2–5 people.

SITE NO. Zu-LT-98 [Zu-LT-52(J)]
Date of Survey: July 5, 1973
Location: 489850 E, 2200530 N; 19.9010° N, 99.0970° W
Natural Setting: 2355 m asl, on gently sloping ground in the Upper Salado Drainage; medium soil cover and slight erosion.
Modern Land Use: Rainfall-based agriculture.
Archaeological Remains: Light Late Toltec surface pottery over an area of ca. 0.90 ha. The LT material is mixed with heavier and much more extensive Late Aztec ceramics (Zu-Az-129). There are no definite structural remains, although substantial rock rubble in the southern part of the site may represent the remnants of prehispanic architecture.
No surface collection made.
Discussion: The apparent absence of Early Aztec surface pottery suggests that this locality was abandoned after LT times and reoccupied during the Late Aztec period.
Classification: Small Hamlet, 5–10 people.

Plate A111. Zu-LT-101, stone wall base on Feature AJ.

SITE NO. Zu-LT-99 [Zu-LT-41(J)]
  Date of Survey: June 21, 1973
  Location: 490900 E, 2200650 N; 19.9021° N, 99.0869° W
  Natural Setting: 2340 m asl, on gently sloping ground in the Upper Salado Drainage; shallow soil cover and severe erosion.
  Modern Land Use: Rainfall-based agriculture. The immediate site area is fallow.
  Archaeological Remains: Variable light and light-to-moderate Late Toltec surface pottery over an area of ca. 2.20 ha. The LT material is mixed with approximately equal quantities of Late Aztec ceramics (Zu-Az-130). No surface collection.
  Discussion: The apparent absence of Early Aztec surface pottery suggests that this locality was abandoned after LT times and reoccupied during the Late Aztec period.
  Classification: Hamlet, 20–40 people.

SITE NO. Zu-LT-100 [Zu-LT-53(J)]
  Date of Survey: July 5, 1973
  Location: 489930 E, 2199880 N; 19.8951° N, 99.0962° W
  Natural Setting: 2355 m asl, on gently sloping ground in the Upper Salado Drainage; shallow soil cover and slight erosion.
  Modern Land Use: Rainfall-based agriculture.
  Archaeological Remains: Variable light and light-to-moderate Late Toltec surface pottery over an area of ca. 1.50 ha. This small LT site is located at the northern end of a larger Aztec site (Zu-Az-161), and in this area the dominant LT material is mixed with lighter Late Az ceramics. There are no discernible structural remains.
  No surface collection made.
  Discussion: The apparent absence of Early Aztec surface pottery suggests that this locality was abandoned after LT times and reoccupied during the Late Aztec period.
  Classification: Hamlet, 15–30 people.

SITE NO. Zu-LT-101 [Zu-LT-40(J); Feature AJ]
  Date of Survey: June 21, 1973
  Location: 490470 E, 2199630 N; 19.8929° N, 99.0910° W
  Natural Setting: 2350 m asl, on gently sloping ground in the Upper Salado Drainage; shallow soil cover and severe erosion.
  Modern Land Use: Pasture.
  Archaeological Remains: Light and light-to-moderate Late Toltec surface pottery over an area of ca. 0.40 ha. We noted one maguey spindle whorl. There are also traces of Late Aztec ceramics—the LT site is within the borders of a larger Aztec site (Zu-Az-130).
  We identified one badly eroded mound (Feature AJ) in an unplowed area. This feature measures ca. 10 m in diameter and 0.10 m high, with light-to-moderate LT surface pottery and moderate rock rubble, with one partially exposed stone wall base (Plate A111).
  Discussion: The age of Feature AJ is uncertain; it could be an Aztec-period structure. The apparent absence of Early Aztec surface pottery suggests that this locality was abandoned after LT times and reoccupied during the Late Aztec period.
  Classification: Small Hamlet, 5–10 people.

SITE NO. Zu-LT-102 [Zu-LT-49(J)]
  Date of Survey: June 27, 1973
  Location: 490550 E, 2198850 N; 19.8858° N, 99.0903° W
  Natural Setting: 2350 m asl, on moderately sloping ground in the Upper Salado Drainage, just north of the divide between the Upper Salado and the Basin of Mexico drainages; shallow soil cover and severe erosion.
  Modern Land Use: Primarily marginal pasture, with minor rainfall-based agriculture where there is sufficient soil in scattered small fields.
  Archaeological Remains: Variable light and light-to-moderate Late Toltec surface pottery over an area of ca. 0.90 ha. The LT material

Plate A112. Zu-LT-106, facing NW at Feature AS.

is mixed with approximately equal quantities of Late Aztec ceramics (Zu-Az-155). There are no discernible structural remains.

No surface collection made.

Discussion: The apparent absence of Early Aztec surface pottery suggests that this locality was abandoned after LT times and reoccupied during the Late Aztec period.

Classification: Small Hamlet, 10–20 people.

SITE NO. Zu-LT-103 [Zu-LT-39(J); Location 25]
   Date of Survey: June 21, 1973
   Location: 491530 E, 2199530 N; 19.8920° N, 99.0809° W
   Natural Setting: 2320 m asl, on gently sloping ground in the Upper Salado Drainage; medium to deep soil cover and moderate erosion.
   Modern Land Use: Mixed pasture and rainfall-based agriculture. A modern dirt road crosses the center of the site.
   Archaeological Remains: Variable light and light-to-moderate Late Toltec surface pottery over an area of ca. 8.60 ha. In the southwestern part of the site, the LT material is mixed with approximately equal quantities of Late Aztec ceramics (Zu-Az-156). We noted two spindle whorls, several obsidian artifacts, and one basalt metate fragment. There are no discernible structural remains.

We made one surface collection (Location 25) over an area ca. 15 × 15 m in a plowed field, with light-to-moderate LT surface pottery, several obsidian artifacts, and moderate rock rubble.

Discussion: The apparent absence of Early Aztec surface pottery suggests that this locality was abandoned after LT times and reoccupied during the Late Aztec period.

Classification: Small Dispersed Village, 85–170 people.

SITE NO. Zu-LT-104 [Zu-LT-37(J)]
   Date of Survey: June 23, 1973
   Location: 492200 E, 2199780 N; 19.8942° N, 99.0745° W
   Natural Setting: 2305 m asl, on moderately sloping ground in the Upper Salado Drainage; shallow soil cover and severe erosion.
   Modern Land Use: Rainfall-based agriculture.
   Archaeological Remains: Variable light and light-to-moderate Late Toltec surface pottery over an area of ca. 5.60 ha. The LT material is mixed with approximately equal quantities of Late Aztec ceramics (Zu-Az-132). There are no discernible structural remains.

No surface collection made.

Discussion: The apparent absence of Early Aztec surface pottery suggests that this locality was abandoned after LT times and reoccupied during the Late Aztec period.

Classification: Small Dispersed Village, 60–120 people.

SITE NO. Zu-LT-105 [Zu-LT-36(J)]
   Date of Survey: June 23, 1973
   Location: 492650 E, 2199750 N; 19.8940° N, 99.0702° W
   Natural Setting: 2310 m asl, on moderately sloping ground in the Upper Salado Drainage; shallow soil cover and severe erosion.
   Modern Land Use: Pasture and rainfall-based maguey cultivation.
   Archaeological Remains: Variable light and light-to-moderate Late Toltec surface pottery over an area of ca. 0.60 ha. The LT material is mixed with lighter Late Aztec ceramics (Zu-Az-132). There are no discernible structural remains.

No surface collection made.

Discussion: The apparent absence of Early Aztec surface pottery suggests that this locality was abandoned after LT times and reoccupied during the Late Aztec period.

Classification: Small Hamlet, 5–10 people.

SITE NO. Zu-LT-106 [Zu-LT-35(J); Feature AS]
   Date of Survey: June 23, 1973
   Location: 493430 E, 2199470 N; 19.8914° N, 99.0628° W
   Natural Setting: 2330 m asl, on gently sloping ground in the Upper Salado Drainage, just west of the divide between the Upper Salado and Basin of Mexico drainages; shallow soil cover and severe erosion.
   Modern Land Use: Rainfall-based agriculture.
   Archaeological Remains: This site consists of a single mound (Feature AS). This unplowed feature measures ca. 10 m in diameter and 0.10 m high, with moderate rock rubble and light to moderate Late Toltec surface pottery (Plate A112). We noted several obsidian blades.

No surface collection made.

Classification: Small Hamlet, 2–5 people.

Plate A113. Zu-LT-109, facing SE at Feature BB.

SITE NO. Zu-LT-107 [Zu-LT-47(J)]
Date of Survey: July 1, 1973
Location: 492470 E, 2199180 N; 19.8888° N, 99.0719° W
Natural Setting: 2340 m asl, on moderately sloping ground in the Upper Salado Drainage; shallow soil cover and severe erosion.
Modern Land Use: Pasture and rainfall-based maguey cultivation.
Archaeological Remains: Variable light and light-to-moderate Late Toltec surface pottery over an area of ca. 2.10 ha. The LT material is mixed with heavier Late Aztec ceramics (Zu-Az-132). There are no discernible structural remains.
No surface collection made.
Discussion: The apparent absence of Early Aztec surface pottery suggests that this locality was abandoned after LT times and reoccupied during the Late Aztec period.
Classification: Hamlet, 20–40 people.

SITE NO. Zu-LT-108 [Zu-LT-48(J); Feature BI]
Date of Survey: July 1, 1973
Location: 492970 E, 2199150 N; 19.8886° N, 99.0672° W
Natural Setting: 2340 m asl, on gently sloping ground atop a small, mesa-like erosional remnant in the Upper Salado Drainage, just west of the divide between the Upper Salado and Basin of Mexico drainages; shallow soil cover and severe erosion.
Modern Land Use: Mixed pasture and rainfall-based agriculture.
Archaeological Remains: The site consists of a single, badly eroded mound (Feature BI). This feature measures ca. 15 m in diameter and 0.20 m high, with light-to-moderate Late Toltec surface pottery and moderate rock rubble. Several stone wall bases are preserved in the mound's surface. These walls appear to rest directly on the tepetate subsoil. We noted several green and gray obsidian blades and scrapers.
No surface collection made.
Classification: Small Hamlet, 2–5 people.

SITE NO. Zu-LT-109 [Zu-LT-46a(J); Feature BB]
Date of Survey: July 1, 1973
Location: 492720 E, 2198880 N; 19.8861° N, 99.0695° W
Natural Setting: 2350 m asl, on gently sloping ground in the Upper Salado Drainage, just northwest of the divide between the Upper Salado and Basin of Mexico drainages; shallow soil cover and severe erosion.
Modern Land Use: Mixed pasture and rainfall-based agriculture.
Archaeological Remains: Variable light and light-to-moderate Late Toltec surface pottery over an area of ca. 1.00 ha. We noted several obsidian blades and scrapers. There is one badly eroded mound (Feature BB) (Plate A113). This feature measures ca. 10 × 15 m in area and 0.50 m high, with light-to-moderate LT surface pottery, several obsidian artifacts, and moderate rock rubble.
No surface collection made.
Classification: Hamlet, 15–30 people.

SITE NO. Zu-LT-110 [Zu-LT-46b(J)]
Date of Survey: July 1, 1973
Location: 492970 E, 2198880 N; 19.8861° N, 99.0672° W
Natural Setting: 2350 m asl, on gently sloping ground in the Upper Salado Drainage, just northwest of the divide between the Upper Salado and Basin of Mexico drainages; shallow soil cover and severe erosion.
Modern Land Use: Mixed pasture and rainfall-based agriculture.
Archaeological Remains: Variable light and light-to-moderate Late Toltec surface pottery over an area of ca. 1.00 ha. The LT material is mixed with lighter Late Aztec ceramics (Zu-Az-136). There are no discernible structural remains.
No surface collection made.
Discussion: The apparent absence of Early Aztec surface pottery suggests that this locality was abandoned after LT times and reoccupied during the Late Aztec period.
Classification: Hamlet, 15–30 people.

SITE NO. Zu-LT-111 [Zu-LT-42(J)]
  Date of Survey: July 1, 1973
  Location: 493600 E, 2199070 N; 19.8878° N, 99.0611° W
  Natural Setting: 2345 m asl, on gently sloping ground in the Upper Salado Drainage, just west of the divide between the Upper Salado and Basin of Mexico drainages; shallow soil cover and severe erosion.
  Modern Land Use: Pasture.
  Archaeological Remains: Light Late Toltec surface pottery over an area of ca. 1.90 ha. The LT material is mixed with approximately equal quantities of Late Aztec ceramics (Zu-Az-135). There are no discernible structural remains.
  No surface collection made.
  Discussion: The apparent absence of Early Aztec surface pottery suggests that this locality was abandoned after LT times and reoccupied during the Late Aztec period.
  Classification: Small Hamlet, 10–20 people.

SITE NO. Zu-LT-112 [Zu-LT-64(J)]
  Date of Survey: July 15, 1973
  Location: 495450 E, 2198930 N; 19.8866° N, 99.0435° W
  Natural Setting: 2345 m asl, on nearly level ground atop a low, broad ridge in the Basin of Mexico Lower Piedmont, just south of the divide between the Upper Salado and Basin of Mexico drainages; shallow soil cover and moderate erosion.
  Modern Land Use: Rainfall-based agriculture.
  Archaeological Remains: Light Late Toltec surface pottery over an area of ca. 0.80 ha. There are no definite structural remains, but one area of moderate rock rubble in the southern part of the site may represent the remnants of prehispanic architecture.
  No surface collection made.
  Classification: Small Hamlet, 5–10 people.

SITE NO. Zu-LT-113 [Zu LT 65a(J)]
  Date of Survey: July 15, 1973
  Location: 495970 E, 2198430 N; 19.8821° N, 99.0385° W
  Natural Setting: 2340 m asl, on gently sloping ground in the Basin of Mexico Lower Piedmont, just south of the divide between the Upper Salado and Basin of Mexico drainages; shallow soil cover and moderate erosion.
  Modern Land Use: Rainfall-based agriculture.
  Archaeological Remains: Light Late Toltec surface pottery over an area of ca. 0.50 ha. There are no discernible structural remains.
  No surface collection made.
  Classification: Small Hamlet, 2–5 people.

SITE NO. Zu-LT-114 [Zu-LT-65b(J)]
  Date of Survey: July 15, 1973
  Location: 496220 E, 2198430 N; 19.8821° N, 99.0361° W
  Natural Setting: 2335 m asl, on gently sloping ground in the Basin of Mexico Lower Piedmont, just south of the divide between the Upper Salado and Basin of Mexico drainages; shallow soil cover and moderate erosion.
  Modern Land Use: Rainfall-based agriculture.
  Archaeological Remains: Variable very light and light Late Toltec surface pottery over an area of ca. 1.50 ha.
  No surface collection made.
  Classification: Small Hamlet, 10–20 people.

SITE NO. Zu-LT-115 [Zu-LT-43a(J); Feature BL]
  Date of Survey: July 2, 1973
  Location: 493570 E, 2197900 N; 19.8773° N, 99.0614° W
  Natural Setting: 2355 m asl, on gently sloping ground in the Upper Salado Drainage, very close to the divide between the Upper Salado and Basin of Mexico drainages; shallow soil cover and severe erosion.
  Modern Land Use: Rainfall-based agriculture.
  Archaeological Remains: Variable light and light-to-moderate Late Toltec surface pottery over an area of ca. 1.20 ha. The LT material is mixed with a trace of Aztec ceramics (no Az site designated). We noted a few obsidian artifacts.
  There is a single mound near the eastern edge of the site (Feature BL). This unplowed feature measures ca. 20 m in diameter and 0.20 m high, with light-to-moderate LT surface pottery, several obsidian artifacts, and moderate rock rubble.
  No surface collection made.
  Classification: Hamlet, 15–30 people.

SITE NO. Zu-LT-116 [Zu-LT-43b(J); Feature BM]
  Date of Survey: July 2, 1973
  Location: 493570 E, 2198150 N; 19.8795° N, 99.0614° W
  Natural Setting: 2360 m asl, on gently sloping ground in the Basin of Mexico Lower Piedmont, very close to the divide between the Upper Salado and Basin of Mexico drainages; shallow soil cover and severe erosion.
  Modern Land Use: Rainfall-based agriculture.
  Archaeological Remains: Variable light and light-to-moderate Late Toltec surface pottery over an area of ca. 4.00 ha. We noted a few obsidian artifacts.
  There is a single mound (Feature BM) near the eastern edge of the site. This unplowed feature measures ca. 15 m in diameter and 0.30 m high, with light-to-moderate surface pottery, several obsidian artifacts, and moderate rock rubble.
  No surface collection made.
  Classification: Hamlet, 50–100 people.

SITE NO. Zu-LT-117 [Zu-LT-45(J); Features BC, BD, BE]
  Date of Survey: July 1, 1973
  Location: 492630 E, 2198030 N; 19.8784° N, 99.0704° W
  Natural Setting: 2370 m asl, on gently sloping ground in the Upper Salado Drainage, just north of the divide between the Upper Salado and Basin of Mexico drainages; shallow soil cover and severe erosion, with patches of bare tepetate.
  Modern Land Use: Rainfall-based agriculture.
  Archaeological Remains: Variable light and light-to-moderate Late Toltec surface pottery over an area of ca. 2.10 ha. We noted numerous obsidian artifacts.
  There are three preserved mounds (Features BC, BD, BE) in the southern part of the site:

Fea.	Area and Context	Height	Content
BC	15 m dia., in unplowed field	0.30 m	Light-to-moderate LT surface pottery, numerous obsidian artifacts, moderate rock rubble.
BD	15 m dia., in unplowed field (Plate A114)	0.30 m	Light-to-moderate LT surface pottery, numerous obsidian artifacts, moderate rock rubble.
BE	15 m dia., in unplowed field	0.30 m	Light-to-moderate LT surface pottery, numerous obsidian artifacts, moderate rock rubble

  No surface collection made.
  Classification: Hamlet, 20–40 people.

Plate A114. Zu-LT-117, facing SE at Feature BD.

SITE NO. Zu-LT-118 [Zu-LT-44(J)]
Date of Survey: July 2, 1973
Location: 492820 E, 2197430 N; 19.8730° N, 99.0686° W
Natural Setting: 2370 m asl, on gently sloping ground in the Basin of Mexico Lower Piedmont, very close to the divide between the Upper Salado and Basin of Mexico drainages; shallow soil cover and severe erosion.
Modern Land Use: Rainfall-based agriculture.
Archaeological Remains: Variable light and light-to-moderate Late Toltec surface pottery over an area of ca. 4.30 ha. The LT material is mixed with lighter Late Aztec ceramics (Zu-Az-147). There are no discernible structural remains.
No surface collection made.
Discussion: The apparent absence of Early Aztec surface pottery suggests that this locality was abandoned after LT times and reoccupied during the Late Aztec period.
Classification: Hamlet, 45–90 people.

SITE NO. Zu-LT-119 [Zu-LT-69(J); Feature CW]
Date of Survey: July 25, 1973
Location: 492220 E, 2196100 N; 19.8610° N, 99.0743° W
Natural Setting: 2370 m asl, on gently sloping ground in the Basin of Mexico Lower Piedmont, just south of the divide between the Upper Salado and Basin of Mexico drainages; shallow soil cover and severe erosion.
Modern Land Use: Pasture and rainfall-based maguey cultivation. A modern dirt road crosses the site.
Archaeological Remains: Variable light and light-to-moderate Late Toltec surface pottery over an area of ca. 4.30 ha. The LT material is mixed with approximately equal quantities of Late Aztec ceramics (Zu-Az-149). We noted several obsidian blades and one basalt mano fragment.
There is a single mound (Feature CW) in the east-central part of the site. This unplowed feature measures ca. 30 m in diameter and 0.30 m high, with moderate rock rubble and light-to-moderate LT surface pottery. We made one surface collection from the eastern half of the mound.
Discussion: The apparent absence of Early Aztec surface pottery suggests that this locality was abandoned after LT times and reoccupied during the Late Aztec period.
Classification: Hamlet, 45–90 people.

SITE NO. Zu-LT-120 [Zu-LT-70(J)]
Date of Survey: July 19–20, 1973
Location: 492880 E, 2195300 N; 19.8538° N, 99.0680° W
Natural Setting: 2395 m asl, on nearly level ground atop a broad, low ridge in the Basin of Mexico Lower Piedmont; severe erosion and shallow soil cover, with some patches of bare tepetate.
Modern Land Use: Unplowed pasture.
Archaeological Remains: Light-to-moderate Late Toltec surface pottery over an area of ca. 0.20 ha. The LT material is mixed with approximately equal quantities of Late Aztec ceramics (Zu-Az-172). There are no discernible structural remains.
No surface collection made.
Discussion: The apparent absence of Early Aztec surface pottery suggests that this locality was abandoned after LT times and reoccupied during the Late Aztec period.
Classification: Small Hamlet, 2–5 people.

SITE NO. Zu-LT-121 [Zu-LT-71(J)]
Date of Survey: July 19, 22, 1973
Location: 492930 E, 2194950 N; 19.8506° N, 99.0675° W
Natural Setting: 2390 m asl, on nearly level ground atop a broad,

low ridge in the Basin of Mexico Lower Piedmont; shallow soil cover and severe erosion, with patches of bare tepetate.
Modern Land Use: Unplowed pasture.
Archaeological Remains: Variable light and light-to-moderate Late Toltec surface pottery over an area of ca. 3.50 ha. The LT material is mixed with lighter Late Aztec ceramics (Zu-Az-172). There are no discernible structural remains.
No surface collection made.
Discussion: The apparent absence of Early Aztec surface pottery suggests that this locality was abandoned after LT times and reoccupied during the Late Aztec period.
Classification: Hamlet, 35–70 people.

SITE NO. Zu-LT-122 [Zu-LT-72(J)]
Date of Survey: July 19, 22, 1973
Location: 492570 E, 2194400 N; 19.8456° N, 99.0710° W
Natural Setting: 2370 m asl, on gently sloping ground in the Basin of Mexico Lower Piedmont; shallow soil cover and severe erosion.
Modern Utilization: Rainfall-based agriculture.
Archaeological Remains: Variable light and light-to-moderate Late Toltec surface pottery over an area of ca. 1.90 ha. The LT material is mixed with lighter Late Aztec ceramics (Zu-Az-180). There are no discernible structural remains.
No surface collection made.
Discussion: The apparent absence of Early Aztec surface pottery suggests that this locality was abandoned after LT times and reoccupied during the Late Aztec period.
Classification: Hamlet, 20–40 people.

SITE NO. Zu-LT-123 [Zu-LT-66(J)]
Date of Survey: July 22, 1973
Location: 493750 E, 2194500 N; 19.8465° N, 99.0597° W
Natural Setting: 2350 m asl, on nearly level ground atop a broad, low ridge in the Basin of Mexico Lower Piedmont; shallow soil cover and severe erosion, with patches of bare tepetate.
Modern Land Use: Wasteland and marginal pasture.
Archaeological Remains: Variable light and light-to-moderate Late Toltec surface pottery over an area of ca. 0.50 ha. The LT material is mixed with approximately equal quantities of Classic ceramics (Zu-Cl-46) and lighter Late Aztec pottery (Zu-Az-172). There are no discernible structural remains.
No surface collection made.
Discussion: The apparent absence of Early Aztec surface pottery suggests that this locality was abandoned after LT times and reoccupied during the Late Aztec period.
Classification: Small Hamlet, 5–10 people.

SITE NO. Zu-LT-124 [Zu-LT-67a(J)]
Date of Survey: July 22, 1973
Location: 493700 E, 2194350 N; 19.8452° N, 99.0602° W
Natural Setting: 2345 m asl, on nearly level ground atop a broad, low ridge in the Basin of Mexico Lower Piedmont; shallow soil cover and severe erosion, with patches of bare tepetate.
Archaeological Remains: Light Late Toltec surface pottery over an area of ca. 0.10 ha. The LT material is mixed with approximately equal quantities of Classic pottery (Zu-Cl-46). There are no discernible structural remains.
No surface collection made.
Classification: Small Hamlet, 2–5 people.

SITE NO. Zu-LT-125 [Zu-LT-67b(J)]
Date of Survey: July 22, 1973
Location: 493800 E, 2194350 N; 19.8452° N, 99.0592° W
Natural Setting: 2340 m asl, on nearly level ground atop a broad, low ridge in the Basin of Mexico Lower Piedmont; shallow soil cover and severe erosion, with patches of bare tepetate.
Modern Land Use: Wasteland and marginal pasture. A modern dirt road crosses the site.
Archaeological Remains: Light Late Toltec surface pottery over an area of ca. 0.10 ha. There are no discernible structural remains.
No surface collection made.
Classification: Small Hamlet, 2–5 people.

SITE NO. Zu-LT-126 [Zu-LT-68(J)]
Date of Survey: July 23, 1973
Location: 494470 E, 2193350 N; 19.8361° N, 99.0528° W
Natural Setting: 2320 m asl, on gently sloping ground in the Basin of Mexico Lower Piedmont; medium soil cover and slight to moderate erosion. A major *barranca* borders the southwestern edge of the site.
Modern Land Use: Rainfall-based agriculture.
Archaeological Remains: Variable light and light-to-moderate Late Toltec surface pottery over an area of ca. 0.70 ha. There are no discernible structural remains.
No surface collection made.
Classification: Small Hamlet, 5–10 people.

SITE NO. Zu-LT-127 [Zu-LT-75(J)]
Date of Survey: July 30, 1973
Location: 493200 E, 2193200 N; 19.8348° N, 99.0649° W
Natural Setting: 2340 m asl, on gently sloping ground in the Basin of Mexico Lower Piedmont; shallow soil cover and moderate erosion.
Modern Land Use: Mixed pasture and rainfall-based agriculture.
Archaeological Remains: Variable light and light-to-moderate Late Toltec surface pottery over an area of ca. 1.00 ha. There are no discernible structural remains.
No surface collection made.
Classification: Small Hamlet, 10–20 people.

SITE NO. Zu-LT-128 [Zu-LT-74(J)]
Date of Survey: July 30, 1973
Location: 493300 E, 2193400 N; 19.8366° N, 99.0640° W
Natural Setting: 2345 m asl, on gently sloping ground in the Basin of Mexico Lower Piedmont; shallow soil cover and moderate erosion.
Modern Land Use: Rainfall-based agriculture.
Archaeological Remains: Variable light and light-to-moderate Late Toltec surface pottery over an area of ca. 0.90 ha. There are no definite structural remains, although a moderate concentration of rock rubble in the central site area may represent the remnants of prehispanic architecture.
No surface collection made.
Classification: Small Hamlet, 10–20 people.

SITE NO. Zu-LT-129 [Zu-LT-73(J)]
Date of Survey: July 24, 1973
Location: 492720 E, 2193750 N; 19.8398° N, 99.0695° W
Natural Setting: 2360 m asl, on gently sloping ground in the Basin of Mexico Lower Piedmont; medium soil cover and severe erosion.
Modern Land Use: Mixed pasture and rainfall-based agriculture. A modern dirt road borders the northern edge of the site.

Archaeological Remains: Light Late Toltec surface pottery over an area of ca. 7.30 ha. The LT material is mixed with approximately equal quantities of Late Aztec ceramics (Zu-Az-181). There are no discernible structural remains.

Discussion: The apparent absence of Early Aztec surface pottery suggests that this locality was abandoned after LT times and reoccupied during the Late Aztec period.

Classification: Hamlet, 35–70 people.

SITE NO. Zu-LT-130 [Zu-LT-77a(J)]
Date of Survey: Aug. 1, 1973
Location: 490880 E, 2195070 N; 19.8517° N, 99.0871° W
Natural Setting: 2355 m asl, on gently sloping ground in the Basin of Mexico Lower Piedmont; shallow soil cover and moderate erosion.
Modern Land Use: Unplowed pasture. There is a large nopal orchard just south of the site.
Archaeological Remains: Light Late Toltec surface pottery over an area of ca. 0.10 ha. The LT material is mixed with approximately equal quantities of Late Aztec ceramics (Zu-Az-170). There are no discernible structural remains.
No surface collection made.
Discussion: The apparent absence of Early Aztec surface pottery suggests that this locality was abandoned after LT times and reoccupied during the Late Aztec period.
Classification: Small Hamlet, 2–5 people.

SITE NO. Zu-LT-131 [Zu-LT-77b(J)]
Date of Survey: Aug. 1, 1973
Location: 490780 E, 2194970 N; 19.8508° N, 99.0881° W
Natural Setting: 2355 m asl, on gently sloping ground in the Basin of Mexico Lower Piedmont; shallow soil cover and moderate erosion.
Modern Land Use: Unplowed pasture. There is a large nopal orchard just south of the site.
Archaeological Remains: Light-to-moderate Late Toltec surface pottery over an area of ca. 0.10 ha. There are no discernible structural remains.
No surface collection made.
Classification: Small Hamlet, 2–5 people.

SITE NO. Zu-LT-132 [Zu-LT-55(J)]
Date of Survey: July 10, 1973
Location: 488970 E, 2198500 N; 19.8827° N, 99.1054° W
Natural Setting: 2340 m asl, on moderately sloping ground in the Upper Salado Drainage, just north of the divide between the Upper Salado and Basin of Mexico drainages; shallow soil cover and severe erosion.
Modern Land Use: Rainfall-based agriculture. Scattered modern houses encroach onto the southern edge of the site.
Archaeological Remains: Variable light and light-to-moderate Late Toltec surface pottery over an area of ca. 1.10 ha. There are no discernible structural remains. The southern limits of the site may be obscured by modern occupation.
No surface collection made.
Discussion: Because of modern occupation, site size is uncertain.
Classification: Small Hamlet (?), 10–20 people.

SITE NO. Zu-LT-133 [Zu-LT-54(J); Locations 34, 35, 36; Features BT, BU]
Date of Survey: July 10, 1973
Location: 488800 E, 2197880 N; 19.8771° N, 99.1070° W

Natural Setting: 2340 m asl, on nearly level ground atop a broad, low ridge in the Upper Salado Drainage, just north of the divide between the Upper Salado and Basin of Mexico drainages; medium soil cover and slight erosion. Approximately a fifth of the site area is on moderately sloping ground on the north side of the ridge, where there is shallow soil cover and severe erosion.
Modern Land Use: Rainfall-based agriculture on the ridge top; marginal pasture on the hillslope.
Archaeological Remains: Variable light and light-to-moderate Late Toltec surface pottery over an area of ca. 10.30 ha. In the western part of the site, the LT material is mixed with approximately equal quantities of Classic (Zu-Cl-52) and Early Toltec (Zu-ET-17) ceramics. We noted several scrapers, points, blades, and flakes of green and gray obsidian, and one basalt mano fragment.

Two mounds (Features BT, BU) are visible in the western part of the site:

Fea.	Area and Context	Height	Content
BT	15 m dia., in unplowed field	0.75 m	Very light Cl and light LT surface pottery; several obsidian artifacts; moderate rock rubble.
BU	20 m dia., in unplowed field	1.00 m	Light LT and Cl surface pottery; several obsidian artifacts; moderate rock rubble.

We made three surface collections (Locations 34, 35, 36):

Location	Area and Context	Content
34	10 × 15 m, in plowed field	Light-to-moderate LT and light Cl and ET surface pottery; several obsidian artifacts; moderate rock rubble.
35	10 × 10 m, in fallow field	Moderate Cl and ET and very light LT surface pottery; several obsidian artifacts; moderate rock rubble.
36	15 × 15 m, in fallow field	Light-to-moderate LT, light Cl and ET surface pottery; several obsidian artifacts; light-to-moderate rock rubble.

Discussion: It is uncertain whether the construction and use of the two mounds are Cl or LT; we suspect they are primarily LT features.
Classification: Small Dispersed Village, 105–210 people.

SITE NO. Zu-LT-134 [Zu-LT-38(M); Feature BP]
Date of Survey: June 25, 1973
Location: 484720 E, 2198280 N; 19.8806° N, 99.1460° W
Natural Setting: 2260 m asl, on gently sloping ground in the Upper Salado Drainage; deep soil cover and slight erosion.
Modern Land Use: Rainfall-based agriculture, with secondary irrigated agriculture in the general area. The site area is presently fallow. A modern dirt road crosses the western part of the site.
Archaeological Remains: Variable light, light-to-moderate, and moderate Late Toltec surface pottery over an area of ca. 4.10 ha. The LT material is mixed with heavier Late Aztec ceramics (Zu-Az-120). We noted numerous obsidian blades, several obsidian scrapers, one obsidian projectile point, and one obsidian "chunk" measuring about 7 cm in diameter.

There is a single mound (Feature BP) in the central part of the site (Plate A115). This feature measures ca. 25 m in diameter and 1.0 m high, with moderate LT surface pottery and moderate rock rubble.
No surface collection made.
Discussion: The apparent absence of Early Aztec surface pottery suggests that this locality was abandoned after LT times and reoccupied during the Late Aztec period.
Classification: Small Nucleated Village, 80–160 people.

Plate A115. Zu-LT-134, facing west at Feature BP.

SITE NO. Zu-LT-135 [Zu-LT-73(M); Feature EI]
   Date of Survey: Nov. 6–7, 1973
   Location: 479820 E, 2196750 N; 19.8668° N, 99.1928° W
   Natural Setting: 2280m asl, on gently sloping ground in the Upper Salado Drainage (Plate A116); shallow to medium soil cover and moderate to severe erosion, with patches of bare tepetate. A major *barranca* borders the northern edge of the site.
   Modern Land Use: Rainfall-based agriculture, except in the severely eroded northeastern sector that is used only as marginal pasture.
   Archaeological Remains: Variable light and light-to-moderate Late Toltec surface pottery over an area of ca. 34.50 ha. In the central part of the site, the LT material is mixed with lighter Late Aztec ceramics (Zu-Az-211). Obsidian blades and debitage are common.
   A single mound (Feature EI) is preserved in the central part of the site (Plate A117). This feature is ca. 20 × 40 m in area and 1.50 m high, with a flat top surface. A modern dirt road cuts into the mound on two of its sides. These road cuts, and a looter's pit in another part of the structure, have exposed solid earth and rock-rubble construction. Surface pottery on and around the mound is light LT. The size and shape of the mound suggest that it functioned as a temple platform.
   There are no other definite structural remains, but a concentration of moderate rock rubble ca. 150 m southwest of Feature EI may represent the plowed-down remnants of other prehispanic architecture.
   No surface collection made.
   Discussion: This is one of the largest LT sites in the Zumpango Region. The probable temple platform at this site suggests a regional sociopolitical significance. The apparent absence of Early Aztec surface pottery suggests that this locality was abandoned after LT times and reoccupied during the Late Aztec period.
   Classification: Local Center, 600–1200 people.

SITE NO. Zu-LT-136 [Zu-LT-71(M)]
   Date of Survey: Nov. 6, 1973
   Location: 478070 E, 2197600 N; 19.8744° N, 99.2095° W
   Natural Setting: 2270 m asl, on gently sloping ground in the Upper Salado Drainage; medium soil cover and moderate erosion.
   Modern Land Use: Rainfall-based agriculture. On lower ground to the east and south of the site, there are the extensive remnants of an abandoned floodwater irrigation system, probably dating to the late nineteenth and early twentieth centuries.
   Archaeological Remains: Variable light and light-to-moderate Late Toltec surface pottery over an area of ca. 1.10 ha. In the northwestern part of the site, the LT material is mixed with lighter Late Aztec ceramics (Zu-Az-215). There are no discernible structural remains.
   No surface collection made.
   Discussion: The apparent absence of Early Aztec surface pottery suggests that this locality was abandoned after LT times and reoccupied during the Late Aztec period.
   Classification: Small Hamlet, 10–20 people.

SITE NO. Zu-LT-137 [Zu-LT-72(M)]
   Date of Survey: Dec. 5, 1973
   Location: 476820 E, 2197630 N; 19.8747° N, 99.2214° W
   Natural Setting: 2265 m asl, on gently sloping ground in the Upper Salado Drainage; shallow soil cover and severe erosion, with patches of bare tepetate.
   Modern Land Use: Unplowed pasture, with a thick grass cover over much of the site.
   Archaeological Remains: Light Late Toltec surface pottery over an area of ca. 1.40 ha. The LT material is mixed with heavier Late Aztec ceramics (Zu-Az-216). There are no discernible structural remains.
   No surface collection made.
   Discussion: The apparent absence of Early Aztec surface pottery suggests that this locality was abandoned after LT times and reoccupied during the Late Aztec period.
   Classification: Small Hamlet, 10–20 people.

Plate A116. Zu-LT-135, facing west over general site area.

Plate A117. Zu-LT-135, facing south at Feature EI.

SITE NO. Zu-LT-138 [Zu-LT-75(M)]
Date of Survey: Late Nov., 1973
Location: 474970 E, 2193820 N; 19.8402° N, 99.2390° W
Natural Setting: 2305 m asl, on gently sloping ground in the Upper Salado Drainage; shallow soil cover and severe erosion, with patches of bare tepetate. Some erosional gullies in the area are up to 15 m deep and 30 m wide.
Modern Land Use: Mainly wasteland, with some use as marginal pasture.
Archaeological Remains: Variable light and light-to-moderate Late Toltec surface pottery over an area of ca. 1.70 ha. The LT material is mixed with traces of Aztec pottery (no Az site designated). There are no discernible structural remains.
No surface collection made.
Discussion: The site is at the western border of the survey area and may extend an unknown distance to the west.
Classification: Hamlet (?), 15–30 people.

SITE NO. Zu-LT-139 [Zu-LT-76(M)]
Date of Survey: Late Nov., 1973
Location: 474900 E, 2193450 N; 19.8369° N, 99.2397° W
Natural Setting: 2295 m asl, on gently sloping ground in the Upper Salado Drainage; shallow soil cover and severe erosion, with patches of bare tepetate. Several erosional gullies in the general area are up to 15 m deep and 30 m wide.
Modern Land Use: Primarily wasteland, with some marginal rainfall-based pasture.
Archaeological Remains: Variable light and light-to-moderate Late Toltec surface pottery over an area of ca. 1.50 ha. The LT material is mixed with approximately equal quantities of Late Aztec ceramics (Zu-Az-218). There are no discernible structural remains.
No surface collection made.
Discussion: The site is at the western edge of the survey area, and may extend farther to the west. The apparent absence of Early Aztec surface pottery suggests that this locality was abandoned after LT times and reoccupied during the Late Aztec period.
Classification: Hamlet (?), 15–30 people.

SITE NO. Zu-LT-140 [Zu-LT-77(M)]
Date of Survey: Late Nov., 1973
Location: 475350 E, 2193400 N; 19.8364° N, 99.2354° W
Natural Setting: 2280 m asl, on gently sloping ground in the Upper Salado Drainage; shallow soil cover and severe erosion, with patches of bare tepetate. The southwestern and southeastern corners of the site are virtually destroyed by a large *barranca*.
Modern Land Use: Primarily wasteland, with some marginal pasture.
Archaeological Remains: Variable light and light-to-moderate Late Toltec surface pottery over an area of ca. 2.60 ha. The LT material is mixed with approximately equal quantities of Late Aztec ceramics (Zu-Az-218). There are no discernible structural remains.
No surface collection made.
Discussion: The apparent absence of Early Aztec surface pottery suggests that this locality was abandoned after LT times and reoccupied during the Late Aztec period.
Classification: Hamlet, 25–50 people.

SITE NO. Zu-LT-141 [Zu-LT-78(M)]
Date of Survey: Late Nov., 1973
Location: 475220 E, 2192680 N; 19.8299° N, 99.2366° W
Natural Setting: 2270 m asl, on gently sloping ground in the Upper Salado Drainage; medium soil cover and moderate to severe erosion.
Modern Land Use: Rainfall-based agriculture.
Archaeological Remains: Light Late Toltec surface pottery over an area of ca. 1.40 ha. The LT material is mixed with approximately equal quantities of Late Aztec ceramics (Zu-Az-218). There are no discernible structural remains.
No surface collection made.
Discussion: The apparent absence of Early Aztec surface pottery suggests that this locality was abandoned after LT times and reoccupied during the Late Aztec period.
Classification: Small Hamlet, 10–20 people.

SITE NO. Zu-LT-142 [Zu-LT-79(M)]
Date of Survey: Late Nov., 1973
Location: 475350 E, 2192320 N; 19.8267° N, 99.2354° W
Natural Setting: 2270 m asl, on gently sloping ground in the Upper Salado Drainage; medium soil cover and moderate to severe erosion.
Modern Land Use: Rainfall-based agriculture.
Archaeological Remains: Light Late Toltec surface pottery over an area of ca. 2.00 ha. The LT material is mixed with lighter Late Aztec ceramics (Zu-Az-218). There are no discernible structural remains.
No surface collection made.
Discussion: The apparent absence of Early Aztec surface pottery suggests that this locality was abandoned after LT times and reoccupied during the Late Aztec period.
Classification: Small Hamlet, 10–20 people.

SITE NO. Zu-LT-143 [Zu-LT-74(M)]
Date of Survey: Nov. 14, 1973
Location: 481000 E, 2193030 N; 19.8332° N, 99.1814° W
Natural Setting: 2320 m asl, on gently sloping ground in the Upper Salado Drainage, very close to the divide between the Upper Salado and Basin of Mexico drainages; shallow soil cover and severe erosion. A major *barranca* borders the southern edge of the site.
Modern Land Use: Rainfall-based agriculture with maguey semi-terracing.
Archaeological Remains: Variable light and light-to-moderate Late Toltec surface pottery over an area of ca. 1.70 ha. There are no discernible structural remains.
No surface collection made.
Classification: Hamlet, 15–30 people.

SITE NO. Zu-LT-144 [Zu-LT-58(M)]
Date of Survey: July 20, 1973
Location: 482530 E, 2196220 N; 19.8620° N, 99.1669° W
Natural Setting: 2295 m asl, on gently sloping ground in the Upper Salado Drainage; medium soil cover and slight erosion.
Modern Land Use: Rainfall-base agriculture. A modern dirt road borders the southern edge of the site.
Archaeological Remains: Variable light and light-to-moderate Late Toltec surface pottery over an area of ca. 0.40 ha. There are no discernible structural remains.
No surface collection made.
Classification: Small Hamlet, 5–10 people.

SITE NO. Zu-LT-145 [Zu-LT-57(M)]
Date of Survey: July 20, 1973
Location: 482550 E, 2196000 N; 19.8600° N, 99.1667° W

Natural Setting: 2295 m asl, on gently sloping ground in the Upper Salado Drainage; medium soil cover and slight erosion.
Modern Land Use: Rainfall-based agriculture.
Archaeological Remains: Variable light, light-to-moderate, and moderate Late Toltec surface pottery over an area of ca. 1.10 ha. There are no discernible structural remains.
No surface collection made.
Classification: Hamlet, 15–30 people.

SITE NO. Zu-LT-146 [Zu-LT-86(M)]
Date of Survey: Nov. 12, 1973
Location: 481750 E, 2195000 N; 19.8510° N, 99.1743° W
Natural Setting: 2290 m asl, on gently sloping ground in the Upper Salado Drainage; shallow to medium soil cover and moderate to severe erosion.
Modern Land Use: Rainfall-based agriculture. Some erosion control has been achieved by the construction of earth *bancales* in the general area. On lower ground to the east are the abandoned remnants of an extensive floodwater irrigation system that probably date to the late nineteenth and early twentieth centuries.
Archaeological Remains: Light Late Toltec surface pottery over an area of ca. 1.10 ha. There are no discernible structural remains.
No surface collection made.
Classification: Small Hamlet, 5–10 people.

SITE NO. Zu-LT-147 [Zu-LT-56(M); Feature DP]
Date of Survey: July 23, 1973
Location: 483250 E, 2196220 N; 19.8620° N, 99.1600° W
Natural Setting: 2320 m asl, in the Upper Salado Drainage; medium soil cover and slight erosion.
Modern Land Use: Rainfall-based agriculture.
Archaeological Remains: Variable light, light-to-moderate, and moderate Late Toltec surface pottery over an area of ca. 0.80 ha. The LT material is mixed with a trace of Classic pottery (no Cl site designated). We noted one probable LT Plumbate sherd. Obsidian blades (mostly green), scrapers (mostly gray), and debitage are common, and this site is unusual for the large quantity of white chert debris (flakes, chunks [up to 7 × 5 × 5 cm], and debitage). We noted two Cl figurine fragments, two basalt metate fragments, and two basalt mano fragments.

There is a single mound (Feature DP) in the southeast corner of the site. This plowed feature measures ca. 30 × 40 m in area and 1.50 m high. The mound's surface is covered with light rock rubble, light-to-moderate LT surface pottery, and several obsidian artifacts. We made one surface collection over an area ca. 20 × 20 m on the mound surface.
Discussion: The unusual quantity of chert debris here suggests a specialized chert processing locale.
Classification: Small Hamlet, 10–20 people.

SITE NO. Zu-LT-148 [Zu-LT-59(M)]
Date of Survey: July 20, 1973
Location: 482430 E, 2194280 N; 19.8445° N, 99.1678° W
Natural Setting: 2345 m asl, on gently sloping ground in the Upper Salado Drainage; medium soil cover and slight erosion.
Modern Land Use: Rainfall-based agriculture.
Archaeological Remains: Light Late Toltec surface pottery over an area of ca. 0.50 ha. There are no discernible structural remains.
No surface collection made.
Classification: Small Hamlet, 2–5 people.

SITE NO. Zu-LT-149 [Zu-LT-55(M); Feature DH]
Date of Survey: July 18, 1973
Location: 485250 E, 2195280 N; 19.8535° N, 99.1409° W
Natural Setting: 2400 m asl, on gently sloping ground in the Basin of Mexico Lower Piedmont, just south of the divide between the Upper Salado and Basin of Mexico drainages; medium soil cover and slight erosion.
Modern Land Use: Pasture.
Archaeological Remains: Light Late Toltec surface pottery over an area of ca. 0.10 ha. The LT material is mixed with traces of Aztec ceramics (no Aztec site designated). We noted one green obsidian blade. This site contains two closely spaced stone wall remnants (Feature DH) that may represent the remains of prehispanic terracing.
No surface collection made.
Discussion: This site is difficult to classify. However, the presence of surface pottery suggests a residential function.
Classification: Small Hamlet (?), 2–5 people.

SITE NO. Zu-LT-150 [Zu-LT-54(M); Features DD, DE, DF]
Date of Survey: July 18, 1973
Location: 485630 E, 2195400 N; 19.8546° N, 99.1372° W
Natural Setting: 2380 m asl, on gently sloping ground in the Basin of Mexico Lower Piedmont, just south of the divide between the Upper Salado and Basin of Mexico drainages; medium soil cover and slight erosion.
Modern Land Use: Rainfall-based agriculture.
Archaeological Remains: Light Late Toltec surface pottery over an area of ca. 0.50 ha. We noted a few obsidian artifacts. The LT material is mixed with approximately equal quantities of Late Aztec ceramics (Zu-Az-204, Zu-Az-205).

There are three mounds (Features DD, DE, DF) in the western part of the LT site:

Fea.	Area and Context	Height	Content
DD	14 × 16, in unplowed field	1.50 m	Light LT and trace of Aztec surface pottery, several obsidian artifacts, very light rock rubble. Exposed wall of rock and tepetate blocks.
DE	8 × 16 m, in plowed field	1.50 m	Very light LT surface pottery, several obsidian artifacts, very light rock rubble.
DF	19 × 24 m, in unplowed field	1.50 m	Very light LT and trace of Az surface pottery, several obsidian artifacts, very light rock rubble.

No surface collection made.
Discussion: Age of the mounds remains uncertain. They may be primarily Aztec features. The apparent absence of Early Aztec surface pottery suggests that this locality was abandoned after LT times and reoccupied during the Late Aztec period.
Classification: Small Hamlet, 5–10 people.

SITE NO. Zu-LT-151 [Zu-LT-49(M); Location 56; Feature DG]
Date of Survey: July 18, 1973
Location: 485720 E, 2195030 N; 19.8513° N, 99.1364° W
Natural Setting: 2385 m asl, in the Basin of Mexico Lower Piedmont, just southeast of the divide between the Upper Salado and Basin of Mexico drainages; medium soil cover and slight erosion.
Modern Land Use: Rainfall-based agriculture. Field borders in this area are delineated by stone walls; the construction of these walls may have damaged ancient architecture.

Plate A118. Zu-LT-151, facing SW at Feature DG.

Archaeological Remains: Variable light and light-to-moderate Late Toltec surface pottery over an area of ca. 3.60 ha. Obsidian blades (mostly green), scrapers (mostly gray), and debris are common. We noted one basalt mano fragment.

A single mound (Feature DG) is preserved near the western edge of the site. This feature measures 20 × 27 m in area and up to ca. 3.00 m high (Plate A118). A large looter's pit in the mound's center reveals solid earth and rock-rubble construction. There is moderate rock rubble and light LT pottery on the mound's surface.

We made one surface collection (Location 56) over an area ca. 9 × 15 m in an unplowed field near Feature DG, with light-to-moderate LT surface pottery, numerous obsidian artifacts, and moderate rock rubble.

Discussion: Feature DG probably functioned as a temple platform. If so, then this small site may have had regional sociopolitical significance. The relatively heavy density of surface pottery also suggests a significant domestic function.

Classification: Hamlet (?), 35–70 people.

SITE NO. Zu-LT-152 [Zu-LT-50(M)]
   Date of Survey: July 18, 1973
   Location: 486550 E, 2195630 N; 19.8567° N, 99.1285° W
   Natural Setting: 2350 m asl, on gently sloping ground in the Basin of Mexico Lower Piedmont, just south of the divide between the Upper Salado and Basin of Mexico drainages; medium soil cover and slight erosion.
   Modern Land Use: Rainfall-based agriculture.
   Archaeological Remains: Light-to-moderate Late Toltec surface pottery over an area of ca. 1.30 ha. There are no definite structural remains.
   No surface collection made.
   Classification: Hamlet, 20–40 people.

SITE NO. Zu-LT-153 [Zu-Az-80(M); Feature DW]
   Date of Survey: July 25, 1973
   Location: 484070 E, 2192030 N; 19.8242° N, 99.1521° W
   Natural Setting: 2340 m asl, on gently sloping ground in the Basin of Mexico Lower Piedmont, just south of the divide between the Upper Salado and Basin of Mexico drainages; shallow to medium soil cover and severe erosion.
   Modern Land Use: Marginal pasture.
   Archaeological Remains: The site consists of a single mound (Feature DW). This feature measures 10 × 20 m in area and 0.60 m high. Its surface pottery is very light Late Toltec and light-to-moderate Late Aztec (Zu-Az-228). The principal construction and use of this feature probably dates to Late Az times.
   No surface collection made.
   Discussion: The LT occupation here may be insignificant. The apparent absence of Early Aztec surface pottery suggests that this locality was abandoned after LT times and reoccupied during the Late Aztec period.
   Classification: Small Hamlet (?), 2–5 people.

SITE NO. Zu-LT-154 [Zu-LT-60(M); Features DS, DT]
   Date of Survey: July 25, 1973
   Location: 484550 E, 2191880 N; 19.8228° N, 99.1475° W
   Natural Setting: 2350 m asl, on gently sloping ground in the Basin of Mexico Lower Piedmont; shallow to medium soil cover and slight erosion.
   Modern Land Use: Rainfall-based agriculture.
   Archaeological Remains: Light Late Toltec surface pottery over an area of ca. 0.40 ha. We noted several green and gray obsidian artifacts and some obsidian debitage.
   There are two mounds (Features DS, DT), situated about 40 m apart, in the central part of the site:

Fea.	Area and Context	Height	Content
DS	25 × 30 m, in plowed field	0.50 m	Light LT surface pottery, several obsidian artifacts, light-to-moderate rock rubble.
DT	12 × 14 m, in plowed field	0.30 m	Light LT surface pottery, several obsidian artifacts, light-to-moderate rock rubble.

No surface collection made.
Classification: Small Hamlet, 5–10 people.

SITE NO. Zu-LT-155 [Zu-LT-64(M)]
  Date of Survey: July 27, 1973
  Location: 485800 E, 2192430 N; 19.8278° N, 99.1356° W
  Natural Setting: 2345 m asl, on gently sloping ground in the Basin of Mexico Lower Piedmont; shallow soil cover and moderate erosion.
  Modern Land Use: Rainfall-based agriculture.
  Archaeological Remains: Variable light and light-to-moderate Late Toltec surface pottery over an area of ca. 0.70 ha. There are no discernible structural remains.
  No surface collection made.
  Classification: Small Hamlet, 10–20 people.

SITE NO. Zu-LT-156 [Zu-LT-62(M); Location 65; Feature DY]
  Date of Survey: July 25, 1973
  Location: 486470 E, 2193000 N; 19.8329° N, 99.1292° W
  Natural Setting: 2340 m asl, in the Basin of Mexico Lower Piedmont; shallow soil cover and severe erosion, with patches of bare tepetate.
  Modern Land Use: Mixed marginal pasture and rainfall-based agriculture (in small scattered fields where there is sufficient soil).
  Archaeological Remains: Variable light, light-to-moderate, and moderate Late Toltec surface pottery over an area of ca. 4.10 ha. The LT material is mixed with traces of Aztec ceramics (no Az site designated). We noted several green obsidian blades and flakes, one basalt mano fragment, and one basalt metate fragment.
  There is a single mound (Feature DY) in the northern part of the site. This well-preserved feature measures ca. 8 × 13 m in area and 1.00 m high. Its surface is covered with light LT surface pottery, several obsidian artifacts, and light-to-moderate rock rubble.
  We made one surface collection (Location 65) over an area ca. 4 × 8 m, with light-to-moderate LT surface pottery, several obsidian artifacts, one basalt mano fragment, one basalt metate fragment, and very light rock rubble.
  Classification: Hamlet, 50–100 people.

SITE NO. Zu-LT-157 [Zu-LT-61(M); Location 64; Features DZ, EA]
  Date of Survey: July 29, 1973
  Location: 486900 E, 2193350 N; 19.8361° N, 99.1251° W
  Natural Setting: 2335 m asl, on gently sloping ground in the Basin of Mexico Lower Piedmont; medium soil cover and slight erosion.
  Modern Land Use: Rainfall-based agriculture.
  Archaeological Remains: Variable light and light-to-moderate Late Toltec surface pottery over an area of ca. 5.00 ha. We noted numerous green and gray obsidian blades, scrapers, flakes, and some obsidian debitage, and two basalt mano fragments.
  Two mounds (Features DZ, EA) are preserved in the east-central part of the site:

Fea.	Area and Context	Height	Content
DZ	12 × 15 m, in unplowed field	1.00 m	Very light LT surface pottery, light rock rubble. Looter's pit shows solid earth and rock-rubble construction.
EA	20 × 20 m	1.00 m	Light-to-moderate LT surface pottery, light rock rubble. Looter's pit shows solid earth and rock-rubble construction.

We made one surface collection (Location 64) over an area ca. 10 × 10 m in a plowed field with light-to-moderate LT surface pottery, several obsidian artifacts, and light-to-moderate rock rubble.
  Classification: Hamlet, 50–100 people.

SITE NO. Zu-LT-158 [Zu-LT-65(M)]
  Date of Survey: July 27, 1973
  Location: 486470 E, 2192380 N; 19.8273° N, 99.1292° W
  Natural Setting: 2320 m asl, on gently sloping ground in the Basin of Mexico Lower Piedmont; medium soil cover and slight erosion.
  Modern Land Use: Rainfall-based agriculture.
  Archaeological Remains: Light-to-moderate surface Late Toltec pottery over an area of ca. 0.30 ha. There are no discernible structural remains.
  No surface collection made.
  Classification: Small Hamlet, 2–5 people.

SITE NO. Zu-LT-159 [Zu-LT-63(M)]
  Date of Survey: July 27, 1973
  Location: 487050 E, 2192950 N; 19.8325° N, 99.1237° W
  Natural Setting: 2330 m asl, on gently sloping ground in the Basin of Mexico Lower Piedmont; shallow soil cover and moderate to severe erosion. A major *barranca* appears to have destroyed about one-third of the prehispanic occupation.
  Modern Land Use: Rainfall-based agriculture where soil cover is sufficiently well preserved.
  Archaeological Remains: Light Late Toltec surface pottery over an area of ca. 1.00 ha. The LT material is mixed with traces of Aztec pottery (no Az site designated). There are no discernible structural remains.
  No surface collection made.
  Classification: Small Hamlet, 2–5 people.

SITE NO. Zu-LT-160 [Zu-LT-66(M)]
  Date of Survey: July 27, 1973
  Location: 487500 E, 2192550 N; 19.8289° N, 99.1194° W
  Natural Setting: 2315 m asl, on gently sloping ground in the Basin of Mexico Lower Piedmont; medium soil cover and slight erosion.
  Modern Land Use: Rainfall-based agriculture.
  Archaeological Remains: Light Late Toltec surface pottery over an area of ca. 1.20 ha. The LT material is mixed with traces of Aztec pottery in the eastern part of the site (no Az site designated). There are no discernible structural remains.
  No surface collection made.
  Classification: Small Hamlet, 5–10 people.

SITE NO. Zu-LT-161 [Zu-LT-80(J)]
  Date of Survey: Early Aug., 1973
  Location: 487750 E, 2192220 N; 19.8259° N, 99.1170° W
  Natural Setting: 2310 m asl, on nearly level ground in the Basin of Mexico Lower Piedmont; medium soil cover and slight erosion.
  Modern Land Use: Rainfall-based agriculture.

Archaeological Remains: Light Late Toltec surface pottery over an area of ca. 0.80 ha. There are no discernible structural remains. No surface collection made.
Classification: Small Hamlet, 5–10 people.

SITE NO. Zu-LT-162 [Zu-LT-51(M); Location 59]
Date of Survey: July 19, 1973
Location: 487780 E, 2194680 N; 19.8481° N, 99.1167° W
Natural Setting: 2320 m asl, on nearly level ground in the Basin of Mexico Lower Piedmont; shallow soil cover and severe erosion.
Modern Land Use: Rainfall-based agriculture.
Archaeological Remains: Light-to-moderate Late Toltec surface pottery over an area of ca. 0.80 ha. The LT material is mixed with traces of Terminal Formative, Classic, and Aztec ceramics (no TF, Cl, or Az sites designated). We noted several green and gray obsidian blades, scrapers, and debitage. There are no discernible structural remains.

We made one surface collection (Location 59) over an area ca. 10 × 15 m, with light-to-moderate LT surface pottery, traces of Az and Cl surface pottery, several obsidian artifacts, and light-to-moderate rock rubble.
Classification: Small Hamlet, 10–20 people.

SITE NO. Zu-LT-163 [Zu-LT-87(J); Locations 64-J, 66-M]
Date of Survey: July 30, Sept. 18, 1973
Location: 487800 E, 2191000 N; 19.8149° N, 99.1165° W
Natural Setting: 2270 m asl, on gently sloping ground on the Lakeshore Plain, just below the lower edge of the Basin of Mexico Lower Piedmont; medium soil cover and slight erosion. The site is situated on what appears to be a natural terrace face along the shoreline of the former shore of Lake Xaltocán-Zumpango.
Modern Land Use: Rainfall-based agriculture. A modern dirt road borders the southern edge of the site.
Archaeological Remains: Variable light and light-to-moderate Late Toltec surface pottery over an area of ca. 2.30 ha. The LT material is mixed with approximately equal quantities of Aztec ceramics (Zu-Az-236; including Aztec II-III Black/Orange), and there is a trace of Classic pottery (no Cl site designated). We noted numerous green and gray obsidian blades, scrapers, and debitage. There are no discernible structural remains.

We made two surface collections (Locations 64-J, 66-M):

Location	Area and Context	Content
64-J	6 × 10 m, in unplowed field	Light-to-moderate LT and Az (with Az II-III B/O) surface pottery, moderate rock rubble.
66-M	10 × 10 m, in plowed field	Light LT and light-to-moderate Az surface pottery, Cl figurine.

Discussion: The presence of Az II-III Black/Orange pottery suggests possible occupation continuity at this locality between LT and Aztec times.
Classification: Hamlet, 25–50 people.

SITE NO. Zu-LT-164 [Zu-LT-86(J)]
Date of Survey: Sept. 18, 1973
Location: 487970 E, 2191030 N; 19.8151° N, 99.1149° W
Natural Setting: 2265 m asl, on gently sloping ground atop what appears to be a natural terrace face along a former shoreline of Lake Xaltocán-Zumpango on the Lakeshore Plain; medium soil cover and slight erosion.
Modern Land Use: Rainfall-based agriculture.
Archaeological Remains: Light Late Toltec surface pottery over an area of ca. 0.70 ha. There are no discernible structural remains. No surface collection made.
Classification: Small Hamlet, 5–10 people.

SITE NO. Zu-LT-165 [Zu-LT-88(J)]
Date of Survey: Sept. 25, 1973
Location: 491820 E, 2190700 N; 19.8122° N, 99.0781° W
Natural Setting: 2280 m asl, on gently sloping ground at the upper edge of the Lakeshore Plain, just below the juncture with the Basin of Mexico Lower Piedmont; deep soil cover and slight erosion. The Río Zumpango, presently a small stream, flows just south of the site.
Modern Land Use: Rainfall-based agriculture. A modern dirt road borders the site on the southeast.
Archaeological Remains: Light Late Toltec surface pottery over an area of ca. 2.90 ha. There are no discernible structural remains. No surface collection made.
Classification: Hamlet, 15–30 people.

SITE NO. Zu-LT-166 [Zu-LT-89(J)]
Date of Survey: Sept. 25, 1973
Location: 492200 E, 2190650 N; 19.8117° N, 99.0745° W
Natural Setting: 2270 m asl, on gently sloping ground at the upper edge of the Lakeshore Plain, just north of the Río Zumpango (now a small stream); deep soil cover and slight erosion.
Modern Land Use: Rainfall-based agriculture. The immediate site area is presently unplowed, but surface pottery has been brought to the surface in the course of maguey cultivation.
Archaeological Remains: Light Late Toltec surface pottery over an area of ca. 1.90 ha. The LT material is mixed with approximately equal quantities of Late Aztec pottery (Zu-Az-240). There are no discernible structural remains.
No surface collection made.
Discussion: The apparent absence of Early Aztec surface pottery suggests that this locality was abandoned after LT times and reoccupied during the Late Aztec period.
Classification: Small Hamlet, 10–20 people.

SITE NO. Zu-LT-167 [Zu-LT-90(J)]
Date of Survey: Sept. 25, 1973
Location: 491880 E, 2190400 N; 19.8095° N, 99.0775° W
Natural Setting: 2270 m asl, on gently sloping ground at the upper edge of the Lakeshore Plain, immediately north of the Río Zumpango, just below the juncture with the Basin of Mexico Lower Piedmont; deep soil cover and slight erosion.
Modern Land Use: Rainfall-based maguey cultivation. The immediate site area is unplowed, but potsherds have been brought to the surface through digging pits for maguey planting.
Archaeological Remains: Light Late Toltec surface pottery over an area of ca. 1.10 ha. The LT material is mixed with approximately equal quantities of Late Aztec ceramics (Zu-Az-240). There are no discernible structural remains.
No surface collection made.
Discussion: The apparent absence of Early Aztec surface pottery suggests that this locality was abandoned after LT times and reoccupied during the Late Aztec period.
Classification: Small Hamlet, 5–10 people.

SITE NO. Zu-LT-168 [Zu-LT-99(J)]
Date of Survey: Oct. 1, 1973
Location: 494100 E, 2188200 N; 19.7896° N, 99.0563° W

Plate A119. Zu-LT-169, facing north over Location 70.

Natural Setting: 2260 m asl, on nearly level ground on the Lakeshore Plain, near the north shore of Lake Xaltocán-Zumpango; medium soil cover and no erosion.
Modern Land Use: Rainfall-based agriculture.
Archaeological Remains: Light Late Toltec surface pottery over an area of ca. 0.80 ha. There are no discernible structural remains.
No surface collection made.
Classification: Small Hamlet, 5–10 people.

SITE NO. Zu-LT-169 [Zu-LT-102(J); Location 70]
Date of Survey: Oct. 4, 1973
Location: 494600 E, 2188150 N; 19.7892° N, 99.0516° W
Natural Setting: 2300 m asl, on gently sloping ground on the western side of a low hill that rises to a maximum elevation of ca. 20 m above the level of the surrounding Lakeshore Plain; medium soil cover and slight erosion.
Modern Land Use: Rainfall-based agriculture. Modern occupation may obscure part of the northwestern part of the site. A modern dirt road crosses the western side of the site.
Archaeological Remains: Variable light and light-to-moderate Late Toltec surface pottery over an area of ca. 5.90 ha. We noted several green and gray obsidian artifacts. There are no definite structural remains, although an area of moderate rock rubble near the north edge of the site may represent the remains of prehispanic architecture.
We made one surface collection (Location 70) over an area ca. 15 × 15 m in a plowed maize field (Plate A119), with light-to-moderate LT surface pottery, several obsidian artifacts, and light rock rubble.
Discussion: The site may be slightly larger if modern occupation covers part of the northwestern site area.
Classification: Small Dispersed Village (?), 75–150 people.

SITE NO. Zu-LT-170 [Zu-LT-101(J)]
Date of Survey: Oct. 4, 1973
Location: 495180 E, 2187470 N; 19.7830° N, 99.0460° W

Natural Setting: 2260 m asl, on nearly level ground on the Lakeshore Plain, near the north shore of Lake Xaltocán-Zumpango; medium soil cover and slight erosion. Together with sites Zu-LT-171–Zu-LT-194, this site occupies a topographic elevation (ancient beach ridges and intervening strand plain) several meters above the general level of the surrounding Lakeshore Plain (Frederick et al. 2005:75) (Fig. 2.4).
Modern Land Use: Rainfall-based agriculture. The northern edge of modern San Sebastian encroaches onto the southwestern edge of the site.
Archaeological Remains: Light Late Toltec surface pottery over an area of ca. 0.60 ha. There are no discernible structural remains.
No surface collection made.
Classification: Small Hamlet, 2–5 people.

SITE NO. Zu-LT-171 [Zu-LT-100(J)]
Date of Survey: Early Oct., 1973
Location: 494600 E, 2187070 N; 19.7794° N, 99.0516° W
Natural Setting: 2250 m asl, on nearly level ground on the Lakeshore Plain, near the upper edge of Lake Xaltocán-Zumpango; medium soil cover and slight erosion. Together with sites Zu-LT-170 and Zu-LT-172–Zu-LT-194, this site occupies a topographic elevation (ancient beach ridges and intervening strand plain) several meters above the general level of the surrounding Lakeshore Plain (Frederick et al. 2005:75) (Fig. 2.4).
Modern Land Use: Rainfall-based agriculture. The modern town of San Sebastian encroaches onto site from all sides.
Archaeological Remains: Variable light and light-to-moderate Late Toltec surface pottery over an area of ca. 0.80 ha. There are no discernible structural remains.
No surface collection made.
Discussion: Modern occupation makes it virtually impossible to define the limits of this site.
Classification: Small Hamlet (?), 5–10 people.

SITE NO. Zu-LT-172 [Zu-LT-104(J)]
    Date of Survey: Oct. 9, 1973
    Location: 495680 E, 2186900 N; 19.7779° N, 99.0412° W
    Natural Setting: 2245 m asl, on nearly level ground on the Lakeshore Plain, near the upper edge of Lake Xaltocán-Zumpango; medium soil cover and slight erosion. Together with sites Zu-LT-170, Zu-LT-171 and Zu-LT-173–Zu-LT-194, this site occupies a topographic elevation (ancient beach ridges and intervening strand plain) several meters above the general level of the surrounding Lakeshore Plain (Frederick et al. 2005:75) (Fig. 2.4).
    Modern Land Use: Rainfall-based agriculture.
    Archaeological Remains: Light Late Toltec surface pottery over an area of ca. 1.10 ha. There are no discernible structural remains.
    No surface collection made.
    Classification: Small Hamlet, 5–10 people.

SITE NO. Zu-LT-173 [Zu-LT-103(J)]
    Date of Survey: Oct. 8, 1973
    Location: 496280 E, 2187030 N; 19.7790° N, 99.0355° W
    Natural Setting: 2245 m asl, on nearly level ground on the Lakeshore Plain, near the upper edge of Lake Xaltocán-Zumpango; deep soil cover and no erosion. Together with sites Zu-LT-170–Zu-LT-172 and Zu-LT-174–Zu-LT-194, this site occupies a topographic elevation (ancient beach ridges and intervening strand plain) several meters above the general level of the surrounding Lakeshore Plain (Frederick et al. 2005:75) (Fig. 2.4).
    Modern Land Use: Rainfall-based agriculture. A paved highway crosses the northern side of the site.
    Archaeological Remains: Light Late Toltec surface pottery over an area of ca. 1.30 ha. There are no discernible structural remains.
    No surface collection made.
    Classification: Small Hamlet, 5–10 people.

SITE NO. Zu-LT-174 [Zu-LT-107(J); Locations 73, 74]
    Date of Survey: Oct. 10, 1973
    Location: 495320 E, 2186400 N; 19.7733° N, 99.0447° W
    Natural Setting: 2245 m asl, on nearly level ground atop a low, almost imperceptible rise (natural or artificial?) on the Lakeshore Plain, near the shore of Lake Xaltocán-Zumpango; medium to deep soil cover and no erosion. Together with sites Zu-LT-170–Zu-LT-173 and Zu-LT-175–Zu-LT-194, this site occupies a topographic elevation (ancient beach ridges and intervening strand plain) several meters above the general level of the surrounding Lakeshore Plain (Frederick et al. 2005:75) (Fig. 2.4).
    Modern Land Use: Rainfall-based agriculture. A modern dirt road borders the western edge of the site.
    Archaeological Remains: Variable light and light-to-moderate Late Toltec surface pottery over an area of ca. 8.90 ha. In the southwestern part of the site, the LT material is mixed with Terminal Formative (Zu-TF-21) and Classic (Zu-Cl-76) ceramics. We noted several obsidian blades (both green and gray), and several obsidian fragments. There is light rock rubble and no definite structural remains, although the low rise that supports the site raises the possibility of subsurface architecture.
    We made two surface collections (Locations 73, 74):

Location	Area and Context	Content
73	20 × 20 m, in plowed maize field	Light-to-moderate Cl and LT and light TF surface pottery, several obsidian artifacts, light rock rubble.
74	10 × 15 m, in plowed maize field (Plate A120)	Light-to-moderate LT and light Cl and TF surface pottery, several obsidian artifacts, light rock rubble.

    Discussion: The deep soil, lack of erosion, and the possibility of subsurface architecture make this an excellent location for future testing through excavation. The long-term occupation here may mean that the slight elevation is partly or wholly artificial in origin.
    Classification: Small Dispersed Village, 90–180 people.

SITE NO. Zu-LT-175 [Zu-LT-109(J)]
    Date of Survey: Oct. 14, 1973
    Location: 494630 E, 2185630 N; 19.7664° N, 99.0513° W
    Natural Setting: 2245 m asl, on nearly level ground on the Lakeshore Plain, near the shore of Lake Xaltocán-Zumpango; medium to deep soil cover and no erosion. Together with sites Zu-LT-170–Zu-LT-174 and Zu-LT-176–Zu-LT-194, this site occupies a topographic elevation (ancient beach ridges and intervening strand plain) several meters above the general level of the surrounding Lakeshore Plain (Frederick et al. 2005:75) (Fig. 2.4).
    Modern Land Use: Rainfall-based agriculture. Modern occupation at the eastern edge of San Sebastian encroaches onto the site from the east and northeast.
    Archaeological Remains: Light Late Toltec surface pottery over an area of ca. 2.10 ha. There are no discernible structural remains.
    No surface collection made.
    Discussion: Because of modern occupation, the eastern limits of the site could not be accurately defined.
    Classification: Small Hamlet (?), 10–20 people.

SITE NO. Zu-LT-176 [Zu-LT-108(J); Locations 76, 77]
    Date of Survey: Oct. 11, 1973
    Location: 493400 E, 2185050 N; 19.7611° N, 99.0630° W
    Natural Setting: 2245 m asl, on nearly level ground on the Lakeshore Plain, near the shore of Lake Xaltocán-Zumpango; deep soil cover and no erosion. The site rests atop a slightly elevated, barely perceptible ridge (natural or artificial?) that rises a few cm above the general level of the surrounding plain (Plate A121). Together with sites Zu-LT-170–Zu-LT-175 and Zu-LT-176–Zu-LT-194, this site occupies a topographic elevation (ancient beach ridges and intervening strand plain) several meters above the general level of the surrounding Lakeshore Plain (Frederick et al. 2005:75) (Fig. 2.4).
    Modern Land Use: Primarily rainfall-based agriculture, with some fields of irrigated alfalfa. A modern dirt road crosses the central site area.
    Archaeological Remains: Variable light and light-to-moderate Late Toltec surface pottery over an area of ca. 16.80 ha. The LT material is mixed with Terminal Formative ceramics in two localities (Zu-TF-23, Zu-TF-24). We noted several green and gray obsidian blades and some obsidian debitage. There are no definite structural remains, but if the supporting ridge is artificial, there may be subsurface architecture.
    We made two surface collections (Locations 76, 77):

Location	Area and Context	Content
76	20 × 20 m, in fallow field (Plate A122)	Light-to-moderate LT and light TF surface pottery; several obsidian artifacts; very little rock rubble.
77	8 × 10 m, in plowed maize field	Light-to-moderate LT, and trace TF surface pottery; several obsidian artifacts; no rock rubble.

    Discussion: The deep soil, lack of erosion, and the possibility of subsurface architecture make this an excellent location for future testing through excavation.
    Classification: Small Dispersed Village, 170–340 people.

Plate A120. Zu-LT-174, facing east over Location 74.

Plate A121. Zu-LT-176, facing SE over general site area.

Plate A122. Zu-LT-176, facing NE over Location 76.

Plate A123. Zu-LT-178, facing north over Location 82.

SITE NO. Zu-LT-177 [Zu-LT-110(J)]
Date of Survey: Oct. 24, 1976
Location: 492930 E, 2184070 N; 19.7523° N, 99.0675° W
Natural Setting: 2245 m asl, on level ground on the Lakeshore Plain, near the shore of Lake Xaltocán-Zumpango; deep soil cover and no erosion. Together with sites Zu-LT-170–Zu-LT-176 and Zu-LT-178–Zu-LT-194, this site occupies a topographic elevation (ancient beach ridges and intervening strand plain) several meters above the general level of the surrounding Lakeshore Plain (Frederick et al. 2005:75) (Fig. 2.4).
Modern Land Use: Rainfall-based agriculture.
Archaeological Remains: Variable light and light-to-moderate Late Toltec surface pottery over an area of ca. 2.10 ha. There are no discernible structural remains.
No surface collection made.
Classification: Hamlet, 20–40 people.

SITE NO. Zu-LT-178 [Zu-LT-106(J); Location 82]
Date of Survey: Oct. 17, 1973
Location: 492100 E, 2183570 N; 19.7478° N, 99.0754° W
Natural Setting: 2240 m asl, on level ground at or near the juncture of the Lakeshore Plain and the former bed of Lake Xaltocán-Zumpango; deep soil cover and no erosion. Together with sites Zu-LT-170–Zu-LT-177 and Zu-LT-179–Zu-LT-194, this site occupies a topographic elevation (ancient beach ridges and intervening strand plain) several meters above the general level of the surrounding Lakeshore Plain (Frederick et al. 2005:75) (Fig. 2.4).
Modern Land Use: Rainfall-based agriculture. Except for magueys, the immediate site area is presently fallow.
Archaeological Remains: Light to moderate Late Toltec surface pottery over an area of ca. 1.40 ha. The LT material is mixed with a trace of Classic ceramics (no Cl site designated). We noted several green obsidian blades and gray obsidian blades and scrapers. There are no discernible structural remains.

We made one surface collection (Location 82) over an area ca. 8 × 10 m in a fallow field (Plate A123), with light-to-moderate LT surface pottery, several obsidian artifacts, and very little rock rubble.
Classification: Hamlet, 20–40 people.

SITE NO. Zu-LT-179, -180, -181, -182, -183 [Zu-LT-105(J); Location 79]
Date of Survey: Oct. 15, 1973
Location: 491800 E, 2185180 N; 19.7623° N, 99.0783° W
Natural Setting: 2245 m asl, on level ground at or near the juncture of the Lakeshore Plain and the former bed of Lake Xaltocán-Zumpango; deep soil cover and no erosion. Together with sites Zu-LT-170–Zu-LT-178 and Zu-LT-184–Zu-LT-194, this site occupies a topographic elevation (ancient beach ridges and intervening strand plain) several meters above the general level of the surrounding Lakeshore Plain (Frederick et al. 2005:75) (Fig. 2.4).
Modern Land Use: Rainfall-based agriculture.
Archaeological Remains: The site consists of a cluster of five discrete areas, each area containing concentrations of variable light and light-to-moderate Late Toltec surface pottery; the locational coordinates above are for their approximate aggregate midpoint. Their aggregate surface area is 11.40 ha. Each cluster is separated by 50–100 m of "empty" ground. We noted several green obsidian blades and some obsidian debitage, a little chert debitage, and a few apparently marine shells. There are no discernible structural remains.

We made one surface collection (Location 79) over an area ca. 10 × 10 m in a fallow field (Plate A124), with light-to-moderate LT surface pottery, several obsidian artifacts, and a few fragments of marine shell.
Discussion: We originally designated each of the five occupational clusters a separate site (Parsons et al. 1983:128-29). However, because they are so closely spaced, we now prefer to consider them as a single site.
Classification: Small Dispersed Village, 115–230 people.

Plate A124. Zu-LT-179/-180/-181/-182/-183, facing SE over Location 79.

SITE NO. Zu-LT-184 [Zu-LT-96(J)]
Date of Survey: Oct. 1, 1973
Location: 492450 E, 2186280 N; 19.7722° N, 99.0721° W
Natural Setting: 2245 m asl, on nearly level ground on the Lakeshore Plain; medium to deep soil cover and slight erosion. Together with sites Zu-LT-170–Zu-LT-183 and Zu-LT-185–Zu-LT-194, this site occupies a topographic elevation (ancient beach ridges and intervening strand plain) several meters above the general level of the surrounding Lakeshore Plain (Frederick et al. 2005:75) (Fig. 2.4).
Modern Land Use: Rainfall-based agriculture.
Archaeological Remains: Variable very light and light Late Toltec surface pottery over an area of ca. 0.50 ha. There are no discernible structural remains.
No surface collection made.
Classification: Small Hamlet, 2–5 people.

SITE NO. Zu-LT-185 [Zu-LT-95(J)]
Date of Survey: Oct. 1, 1973
Location: 492100 E, 2186600 N; 19.7751° N, 99.0754° W
Natural Setting: 2250 m asl, on nearly level ground on the Lakeshore Plain; medium to deep soil cover and slight erosion. Together with sites Zu-LT-170–Zu-LT-184 and Zu-LT-186–Zu-LT-194, this site occupies a topographic elevation (ancient beach ridges and intervening strand plain) several meters above the general level of the surrounding Lakeshore Plain (Frederick et al. 2005:75) (Fig. 2.4).
Modern Land Use: Rainfall-based agriculture. There is a modern house in the middle of the site. A modern dirt road skirts the eastern edge of the site.
Archaeological Remains: Variable light, and light-to-moderate Late Toltec surface pottery over an area of ca. 1.50 ha. There are no discernible structural remains.
No surface collection made.
Classification: Hamlet, 15–30 people.

SITE NO. Zu-LT-186 [Zu-LT-94(J)]
Date of Survey: Oct. 1, 1973
Location: 492250 E, 2186880 N; 19.7777° N, 99.0740° W
Natural Setting: 2250 m asl, on gently sloping ground on the Lakeshore Plain; medium soil cover and slight erosion. Together with sites Zu-LT-170–Zu-LT-185 and Zu-LT-187–Zu-LT-194, this site occupies a topographic elevation (ancient beach ridges and intervening strand plain) several meters above the general level of the surrounding Lakeshore Plain (Frederick et al. 2005:75) (Fig. 2.4).
Modern Land Use: Rainfall-based agriculture. A modern dirt road borders the eastern edge of the site.
Archaeological Remains: Light Late Toltec surface pottery over an area of ca. 0.60 ha. There are no discernible structural remains.
No surface collection made.
Classification: Small Hamlet, 2–5 people.

SITE NO. Zu-LT-187 [Zu-LT-93(J)]
Date of Survey: Oct. 3, 1973
Location: 492500 E, 2187030 N; 19.7790° N, 99.0716° W
Natural Setting: 2250 m asl, on gently sloping ground on the Lakeshore Plain; medium soil cover and slight erosion. Together with sites Zu-LT-170–Zu-LT-186 and Zu-LT-188–Zu-LT-194, this site occupies a topographic elevation (ancient beach ridges and intervening strand plain) several meters above the general level of the surrounding Lakeshore Plain (Frederick et al. 2005:75) (Fig. 2.4).
Modern Land Use: Rainfall-based agriculture. At the time of our survey, the site area had been freshly plowed. Modern dirt roads border the eastern and southern edges of the site.
Archaeological Remains: Variable light and light-to-moderate Late Toltec surface pottery over an area of ca. 0.90 ha. There are no discernible structural remains.
No surface collection made.
Classification: Small Hamlet, 10–20 people.

SITE NO. Zu-LT-188 [Zu-LT-91(J)]
Date of Survey: Oct. 1, 1973
Location: 492200 E, 2187750 N; 19.7855° N, 99.0745° W
Natural Setting: 2250 m asl, on gently sloping ground on the Lakeshore Plain; medium soil cover and slight erosion. Together with sites Zu-LT-170–Zu-LT-187 and Zu-LT-189–Zu-LT-194, this site

Plate A125. Zu-LT-191, facing north over Location 80, illustrating extreme conditions of thick maize we sometimes faced in detecting and collecting surface pottery.

occupies a topographic elevation (ancient beach ridges and intervening strand plain) several meters above the general level of the surrounding Lakeshore Plain (Frederick et al. 2005:75) (Fig. 2.4).

Modern Land Use: Rainfall-based agriculture. Modern occupation on the southeastern edge of Zumpango encroaches onto the northern side of the site.

Archaeological Remains: Variable light and light-to-moderate Late Toltec surface pottery over an area of ca. 1.10 ha. There are no discernible structural remains.

No surface collection made.

Discussion: Because of modern occupation, the northern limits of the site could not be accurately defined.

Classification: Small Hamlet (?), 10–20 people.

SITE NO. Zu-LT-189 [Zu-LT-92(J)]
  Date of Survey: Oct. 1, 1973
  Location: 491850 E, 2187530 N; 19.7835° N, 99.0778° W
  Natural Setting: 2245 m asl, on gently sloping ground on the Lakeshore Plain; medium soil cover and slight erosion. Together with sites Zu-LT-170–Zu-LT-188 and Zu-LT-190–Zu-LT-194, this site occupies a topographic elevation (ancient beach ridges and intervening strand plain) several meters above the general level of the surrounding Lakeshore Plain (Frederick et al. 2005:75) (Fig. 2.4).
  Modern Land Use: Rainfall-based agriculture. A modern dirt road borders the northwestern side of the site.
  Archaeological Remains: Variable light and light-to-moderate Late Toltec surface pottery over an area of ca. 1.10 ha. The LT material is mixed with a trace of Aztec ceramics (no Az site designated). There are no discernible structural remains.
  No surface collection made.
  Classification: Small Hamlet, 10–20 people.

SITE NO. Zu-LT-190 [Zu-LT-97(J)]
  Date of Survey: Oct. 3, 1973
  Location: 491470 E, 2187250 N; 19.7810° N, 99.0814° W

  Natural Setting: 2250 m asl, on gently sloping ground on the Lakeshore Plain; medium soil cover and slight erosion. Together with sites Zu-LT-170–Zu-LT-189 and Zu-LT-191–Zu-LT-194, this site occupies a topographic elevation (ancient beach ridges and intervening strand plain) several meters above the general level of the surrounding Lakeshore Plain (Frederick et al. 2005:75) (Fig. 2.4).
  Modern Land Use: Rainfall-based agriculture. There is a modern house at the southwestern edge of the site.
  Archaeological Remains: Light Late Toltec surface pottery over an area of ca. 0.60 ha. There are no discernible structural remains.
  No surface collection made.
  Classification: Small Hamlet, 5–10 people.

SITE NO. Zu-LT-191 [Zu-LT-98(J); Location 80]
  Date of Survey: Oct. 16, 1973
  Location: 490220 E, 2186050 N; 19.7702° N, 99.0934° W
  Natural Setting: 2245 m asl, on level ground on the Lakeshore Plain; deep soil cover and no erosion. Together with sites Zu-LT-170–Zu-LT-190 and Zu-LT-192–Zu-LT-194, this site occupies a topographic elevation (ancient beach ridges and intervening strand plain) several meters above the general level of the surrounding Lakeshore Plain (Frederick et al. 2005:75) (Fig. 2.4).
  Modern Land Use: Rainfall-based agriculture. A modern dirt road crosses the southwestern corner of the site.
  Archaeological Remains: Variable light and light-to-moderate Late Toltec surface pottery over an area of ca. 8.50 ha. The LT material is mixed with traces of Aztec ceramics (no Az site designated). We noted several green obsidian blades, a little obsidian debitage, and one maguey spindle whorl. There are no discernible structural remains.
  We made one surface collection (Location 80) over an area ca. 5 × 10 m in a field with mature maize up to 2 m high (Plate A125), with moderate LT surface pottery, one maguey spindle whorl, several obsidian artifacts, a few chert fragments, and very little rock rubble.
  Classification: Small Dispersed Village, 85–170 people.

SITE NO. Zu-LT-192 [Zu-LT-85(J)]
  Date of Survey: Sept. 20, 1973
  Location: 489500 E, 2186750 N; 19.7765° N, 99.1002° W
  Natural Setting: 2245 m asl, on nearly level ground on the Lakeshore Plain, close to the former shore of Lake Xaltocán-Zumpango; medium to deep soil cover and no erosion. Together with sites Zu-LT-170–Zu-LT-191, Zu-LT-193, and Zu-LT-194, this site occupies a topographic elevation (ancient beach ridges and intervening strand plain) several meters above the general level of the surrounding Lakeshore Plain (Frederick et al. 2005:75) (Fig. 2.4).
  Modern Land Use: Rainfall-based agriculture. Houses on the western edge of the modern town of Zumpango encroach onto the site from the east. A modern dirt road borders the site on the west.
  Archaeological Remains: Variable light and light-to-moderate Late Toltec surface pottery over an area of ca. 12.00 ha. The LT material is mixed with traces of Aztec ceramics in the central part of the site (no Az site designated). There are no discernible structural remains.
  No surface collection made.
  Discussion: Because of modern occupation, the western limits of the site could not be defined.
  Classification: Small Dispersed Village (?), 120–240 people.

SITE NO. Zu-LT-193 [Zu-LT-78(J)]
  Date of Survey: Aug. 9, 1973
  Location: 487780 E, 2185570 N; 19.7658° N, 99.1166° W
  Natural Setting: 2245 m asl, on level ground on the Lakeshore Plain, close to the northern edge of Lake Xaltocán-Zumpango; deep soil cover and no erosion. Together with sites Zu-LT-170–Zu-LT-192 and Zu-LT-194, this site occupies a topographic elevation (ancient beach ridges and intervening strand plain) several meters above the general level of the surrounding Lakeshore Plain (Frederick et al. 2005:75) (Fig. 2.4).
  Modern Land Use: Rainfall-based agriculture.
  Archaeological Remains: Variable light and light-to-moderate Late Toltec surface pottery over an area of ca. 1.60 ha. The LT material is mixed with lighter Late Aztec ceramics (Zu-Az-250, Zu-Az-251, Zu-Az-252). No discernible structural remains.
  No surface collection made.
  Discussion: The apparent absence of Early Aztec surface pottery suggests that this locality was abandoned after LT times and reoccupied during the Late Aztec period.
  Classification: Hamlet, 15–30 people.

SITE NO. Zu-LT-194 [Zu-LT-79(J); Location 49]
  Date of Survey: Aug. 9, 1973
  Location: 488050 E, 2185100 N; 19.7616° N, 99.1141° W
  Natural Setting: 2245 m asl, on level ground on the Lakeshore Plain, near the northern edge of Lake Xaltocán-Zumpango; deep soil cover and no erosion. Together with sites Zu-LT-170–Zu-LT-193, this site occupies a topographic elevation (ancient beach ridges and intervening strand plain) several meters above the general level of the surrounding Lakeshore Plain (Frederick et al. 2005:75) (Fig. 2.4).
  Modern Land Use: Rainfall-based agriculture.
  Archaeological Remains: Light-to-moderate Late Toltec surface pottery over an area of ca. 0.30 ha. The LT material is mixed with lighter Late Aztec ceramics (Zu-Az-249). A few weathered human bones were noted, suggesting that modern plowing may have disturbed a prehispanic burial. There are no discernible structural remains in the LT site area.
  We made one surface collection (Location 49) over an area 10 × 15 m in a plowed field with light-to-moderate LT and light Late Aztec surface pottery, several obsidian artifacts, and very little rock rubble. We noted fragments of several human long bones.
  Discussion: The apparent absence of Early Aztec surface pottery suggests that this locality was abandoned after LT times and reoccupied during the Late Aztec period.
  Classification: Small Hamlet, 5–10 people.

SITE NO. Zu-LT-195 [Zu-LT-67(M); Location 68]
  Date of Survey: Aug. 2, 1973
  Location: 482680 E, 2189630 N; 19.8025° N, 99.1654° W
  Natural Setting: 2280 m asl, on level ground on the Lakeshore Plain, near the lower edge of the Basin of Mexico Lower Piedmont; deep soil cover and no erosion. Together with sites Zu-LT-170–Zu-LT-194, Zu-LT-196, and Zu-LT-197, this site occupies a topographic elevation (ancient beach ridges and intervening strand plain) several meters above the general level of the surrounding Lakeshore Plain (Frederick et al. 2005:75) (Fig. 2.4).
  Modern Land Use: Rainfall-based agriculture. A modern dirt road crosses the western part of the site.
  Archaeological Remains: Variable light-to-moderate and moderate Late Toltec surface pottery over an area of ca. 0.80 ha. The site is immediately next to a gap in airphoto coverage, and the site may extend farther to the west. The LT material is mixed with traces of Aztec ceramics (no Az site designated). We noted several green obsidian blades and a few pieces of green and gray obsidian debitage. There are no discernible structural remains.
  We made one surface collection (Location 68) over an area ca. 5 × 10 m in a plowed field, with moderate LT and traces of Aztec surface pottery, several obsidian artifacts, one basalt mano fragment, and very light rock rubble.
  Discussion: Owing to circumstances beyond our control, the western limits of the site could not be defined.
  Classification: Hamlet (?), 15–30 people.

SITE NO. Zu-LT-196 [Zu-LT-87(M); Location 90]
  Date of Survey: Dec. 2, 1973
  Location: 482030 E, 2189680 N; 19.8029° N, 99.1716° W
  Natural Setting: 2280 m asl, on level ground on the Lakeshore Plain, close to the lower edge of the Basin of Mexico Lower Piedmont; deep soil cover and no erosion. Together with sites Zu-LT-170–Zu-LT-195 and Zu-LT-198, this site occupies a topographic elevation (ancient beach ridges and intervening strand plain) several meters above the general level of the surrounding Lakeshore Plain (Frederick et al. 2005:75) (Fig. 2.4).
  Modern Land Use: Irrigated cultivation of maize and alfalfa.
  Archaeological Remains: Variable light and light-to-moderate Late Toltec surface pottery over an area of ca. 1.30 ha. The LT material is mixed with traces of Aztec ceramics (no Az site designated). We noted several green obsidian blades and some green obsidian debitage, and one maguey spindle whorl. There are no definite structural remains, but one area of moderate rock rubble may represent the remnants of prehispanic architecture.
  We made one surface collection (Location 90) over an area ca. 10 × 20 m in a recently harvested maize field (Plate A126), with light-to-moderate LT and traces of Late Az surface pottery, several obsidian artifacts, and moderate rock rubble.
  Classification: Hamlet, 20–40 people.

Plate A126. Zu-LT-196, facing west over Location 90.

SITE NO. Zu-LT-197 [Zu-LT-88(M); Locations 91, 93, 94]
  Date of Survey: Dec. 3, 1973
  Location: 481000 E, 2189180 N; 19.7984° N, 99.1814° W
  Natural Setting: 2260 m asl, on nearly level ground atop a broad, low knoll (natural or artificial?) that rises to a maximum height of ca. 5.00 m above the level of the surrounding Lakeshore Plain; deep soil cover and slight erosion. Together with sites Zu-LT-170–Zu-LT-196, this site occupies a topographic elevation (ancient beach ridges and intervening strand plain) several meters above the general level of the surrounding Lakeshore Plain (Frederick et al. 2005:75) (Fig. 2.4).
  Modern Land Use: The supporting knoll is devoted to rainfall-based agriculture. Much of the surrounding lower ground is irrigated for the production of maize and alfalfa. Remnants of a large floodwater irrigation network occur throughout the general area—probably dating to the late nineteenth or early twentieth centuries.
  Archaeological Remains: Variable light and light-to-moderate Late Toltec surface pottery over an area of ca. 5.10 ha atop the supporting knoll. The LT material is mixed with heavier Classic (Zu-Cl-83) and Early Toltec (Zu-ET-23) ceramics, and with lighter Late Aztec pottery (Zu-Az-259, Zu-Az-260). We noted several obsidian blades and scrapers, mostly green in color. There is very little rock rubble, and no definite structural remains, although the supporting knoll itself could be partially artificial.
  We made three surface collections in the area of the LT site (Locations 91, 93, 94):

Location	Area and Context	Content
91	15 × 15 m, in harvested maize field	Light-to-moderate Cl and ET, light LT and very light Az surface pottery; several obsidian artifacts; very little rock rubble.
93	8 × 20 m, in harvested maize field	Light-to-moderate Cl and ET, light LT and very light Az surface pottery; several obsidian artifacts; very little rock rubble.
94	10 × 15 m, in harvested maize field	Light-to-moderate Cl and ET, light LT and very light Az surface pottery; no rock rubble.

  Discussion: The long-term occupation of this locality is unusual in the Zumpango Region. This might indicate that the supporting knoll is wholly or partially artificial—a tell-like feature that has built up over many centuries of settlement. This possibility, together with the deep soil cover and generally good preservation, indicate that this would be an excellent locality for excavation to clarify problems of ceramic stratigraphy (among other things).
  Note: By the late 1980s, this area had begun to be heavily settled by new urban occupation, and this urbanization process has accelerated greatly over the subsequent decades. It is unlikely that this promising archaeological site still exists.
  The apparent absence of Early Aztec surface pottery suggests that this locality was abandoned after LT times and reoccupied during the Late Aztec period.
  Classification: Hamlet, 50–100 people.

SITE NO. Zu-LT-198 [Zu-LT-84(M)]
  Date of Survey: Late Nov., 1973
  Location: 479150 E, 2188930 N; 19.7961° N, 99.1991° W
  Natural Setting: 2255 m asl, on level ground on the Lakeshore Plain, near the northwestern shore of Lake Xaltocán-Zumpango; deep soil cover and no erosion.
  Modern Land Use: Irrigated maize cultivation. Numerous irrigation canals crisscross the general area.
  Archaeological Remains: Light Late Toltec surface pottery over an area of ca. 1.30 ha. The LT material is mixed with approximately equal quantities of Late Aztec ceramics (Zu-Az-261). There are no discernible structural remains.
  No surface collection made.
  Discussion: The apparent absence of Early Aztec surface pottery suggests that this locality was abandoned after LT times and reoccupied during the Late Aztec period.
  Classification: Small Hamlet, 5–10 people.

SITE NO. Zu-LT-199 [Zu-LT-85(M)]
Date of Survey: Late Nov., 1973
Location: 478570 E, 2188600 N; 99.2046° N, 99.2046° W
Natural Setting: 2255 m asl, on nearly level ground, atop a slight rise (natural or artificial?) that is elevated a few cm above the general level of the surrounding Lakeshore Plain, near the northwestern shore of Lake Xaltocán-Zumpango; deep soil cover and no erosion.
Modern Land Use: Irrigated agriculture. Numerous irrigation canals crisscross the general area.
Archaeological Remains: Light Late Toltec surface pottery over an area of ca. 1.10 ha. The LT material is mixed with a trace of Terminal Formative ceramics (no TF site designated). There are no definite structural remains, although the slight rise may represent subsurface architecture.
No surface collection made.
Discussion: The deep soil cover and slight elevation hint at the presence of well-preserved subsurface archaeological deposits. This might be an excellent locality for future excavation.
Classification: Small Hamlet, 5–10 people.

SITE NO. Zu-LT-200 [Zu-LT-83(M)]
Date of Survey: Late Nov., 1973
Location: 478650 E, 2189220 N; 19.7987° N, 99.2038° W
Natural Setting: 2255 m asl, on nearly level ground on the Lakeshore Plain, near the northwestern shore of Lake Xaltocán-Zumpango; deep soil cover and no erosion.
Modern Land Use: Irrigated agriculture. A network of irrigation canals crisscross the general area.
Archaeological Remains: Light Late Toltec surface pottery over an area of ca. 0.30 ha. The LT material is mixed with lighter Late Aztec ceramics (Zu-Az-262). There are no definite structural remains.
No surface collection made.
Discussion: The apparent absence of Early Aztec surface pottery suggests that this locality was abandoned after LT times and reoccupied during the Late Aztec period.
Classification: Small Hamlet, 2–5 people.

SITE NO. Zu-LT-201 [Zu-LT-82(M)]
Date of Survey: Nov. 28, 1973
Location: 476320 E, 2189280 N; 19.7992° N, 99.2261° W
Natural Setting: 2305 m asl, on gently sloping ground in the Upper Salado Drainage, on the side of a spur of higher ground that extends into the Lakeshore Plain, just north of the divide between the USD and Basin of Mexico drainages; shallow soil cover, with severe erosion with patches of bare tepetate.
Modern Land Use: The immediate site area is unplowed pasture. The surrounding lower ground is devoted to rainfall-based agriculture.
Archaeological Remains: Light Late Toltec surface pottery over an area of ca. 0.80 ha. The LT material is mixed with a trace of Aztec ceramics (no Az site designated). There are no discernible structural remains.
No surface collection made.
Classification: Small Hamlet, 5–10 people.

SITE NO. Zu-LT-202 [Zu-LT-81(M)]
Date of Survey: Nov. 28, 1973
Location: 475800 E, 2189220 N; 19.7987° N, 99.2311° W
Natural Setting: 2295 m asl, on gently sloping ground in the Basin of Mexico Lower Piedmont, on the north slope of a spur of higher ground that extends out into the Lakeshore Plain; shallow soil cover and moderate erosion.
Modern Land Use: Rainfall-based agriculture in the immediate site area. Lower ground to the east is devoted to irrigated maize.
Archaeological Remains: Light Late Toltec surface pottery over an area of ca. 1.40 ha. The LT material is mixed with a trace of Aztec ceramics (no Az site designated). There are no discernible structural remains.
No surface collection made.
Classification: Small Hamlet, 5–10 people.

SITE NO. Zu-LT-203 [Zu-LT-80(M); Locations 86, 87; Feature EJ]
Date of Survey: Nov. 28, 1973
Location: 475280 E, 2189550 N; 19.8017° N, 99.2360° W
Natural Setting: 2285 m asl, on gently sloping ground in the Basin of Mexico Lower Piedmont; medium soil cover and slight erosion.
Modern Land Use: Rainfall-based agriculture. A large canal (irrigation?) borders the eastern edge of the site. The Mexico City-to-Queretaro highway crosses the eastern part of the site. There is an active modern quarry in the southeastern corner of the site.
Archaeological Remains: Variable light, light-to-moderate, and moderate Late Toltec surface pottery over an area of ca. 11.50 ha. The LT material is mixed with approximately equal quantities of Late Aztec ceramics (Zu-Az-269), and there is also a possible trace of Classic and Late Formative pottery (no Cl or LF sites designated). We noted several green and gray obsidian blades, scrapers, and some obsidian debitage, and one LT figurine body.

A single mound (Feature EJ) is preserved in an unplowed area in the western part of the site. This feature measures ca. 15 m in diameter and 0.75 m high. Two looter's pits reveal solid earth and rock-rubble construction. The mound's surface pottery is light LT and Late Az, so its age is uncertain.

We made two surface collections (Locations 86, 87):

Location	Area and Context	Content
86	5 × 6 m, in harvested maize field (Plate A127)	Light-to-moderate LT and light Late Az surface pottery, several obsidian artifacts, and light-to-moderate rock rubble.
87	15 × 20 m, in harvested maize field	Light-to-moderate LT and light Late Az surface pottery, several obsidian artifacts, and moderate rock rubble.

Discussion: The apparent absence of Early Aztec surface pottery suggests that this locality was abandoned after LT times and reoccupied during the Late Aztec period.
Classification: Small Nucleated Village, 200–400 people.

SITE NO. Zu-LT-204 [Zu-LT-90(M)]
Date of Survey: Dec. 4, 1973
Location: 478900 E, 2184250 N; 19.7538° N, 99.2014° W
Natural Setting: 2280 m asl, on gently sloping ground at the upper edge of the Lakeshore Plain, near the northwestern shore of Lake Xaltocán-Zumpango; medium soil cover and moderate to severe erosion.
Modern Land Use: Rainfall-based agriculture. A modern dirt road borders the eastern edge of the site.
Archaeological Remains: Variable light and light-to-moderate Late Toltec surface pottery over an area of ca. 1.20 ha. There are no discernible structural remains.
No surface collection made.
Classification: Small Hamlet, 10–20 people.

SITE NO. Zu-LT-205 [Zu-LT-89(M)]
Date of Survey: Dec. 4, 1973
Location: 480250 E, 2185500 N; 19.7651° N, 99.1885° W

Plate A127. Zu-LT-203, facing SE over Location 86.

Natural Setting: 2260 m asl, on gently sloping ground on the Lakeshore Plain, near the northwestern shore of Lake Xaltocán-Zumpango; shallow to medium soil cover and moderate to severe erosion.

Modern Land Use: Rainfall-based agriculture, with abundant maguey semi-terracing.

Archaeological Remains: Light Late Toltec surface pottery over an area of ca. 5.00 ha. The LT material is mixed with approximately equal quantities of Late Aztec ceramics (Zu-Az-272). There are no discernible structural remains.

No surface collection made.

Discussion: The apparent absence of Early Aztec surface pottery suggests that this locality was abandoned after LT times and reoccupied during the Late Aztec period.

Classification: Hamlet, 25–50 people.

SITE NO. Zu-LT-206 [Zu-LT-91(M); Location 96]
   Date of Survey: Dec. 5, 1973
   Location: 479850 E, 2182900 N; 19.7416° N, 99.1923° W
   Natural Setting: 2260 m asl, on gently sloping ground on the Lakeshore Plain, near the northwestern shore of Lake Xaltocán-Zumpango; medium soil cover and moderate erosion.
   Modern Land Use: Rainfall-based agriculture. The modern town of Teoloyucan encroaches onto the site from the northeast.
   Archaeological Remains: Light-to-moderate Late Toltec surface pottery over most of the site, with sherd density declining to light around the site margins (including the northeastern side, where site borders could not be accurately defined because of modern occupation). The site area is ca. 13.50 ha. We noted several green obsidian blades. There are no discernible structural remains.
   We made one surface collection (Location 96) over an area ca. 10 × 10 m in a harvested maize field, with light-to-moderate LT surface pottery, several obsidian artifacts, and light-to-moderate rock rubble.
   Discussion: Because of modern occupation on its northeastern side, we may have underestimated the site size. However, because the sherd density appears to be declining to the northeast, we believe that 13.50 ha is a reasonable estimate of site area.
   Classification: Small Nucleated Village, 200–400 people.

SITE NO. Zu-LT-207 [Zu-LT-68(M); Location 75]
   Date of Survey: Aug. 16, 1973
   Location: 484280 E, 2178550 N; 19.7023° N, 99.1500° W
   Natural Setting: 2250 m asl, on level ground at the base of Cerro Tultepec in the Lakeshore Plain, on the shore of Lake Xaltocán-Zumpango; deep soil cover, no erosion.
   Modern Land Use: Rainfall-based alfalfa cultivation.
   Archaeological Remains: Variable light and light-to-moderate Late Toltec surface pottery over an area of ca. 1.70 ha. At the center of the site, the LT material is mixed with lighter Late Aztec ceramics (Zu-Az-285). We noted several green obsidian blades, one green obsidian scraper, and a few gray obsidian blades. There are no discernible structural remains.
   We made one surface collection (Location 75) over an area ca. 12 × 16 m in a recently harvested alfalfa field, with light-to-moderate LT and very light Aztec surface pottery, several obsidian artifacts, and no rock rubble.
   Discussion: The apparent absence of Early Aztec surface pottery suggests that this locality was abandoned after LT times and reoccupied during the Late Aztec period.
   Classification: Hamlet, 15–30 people.

SITE NO. Zu-LT-208 [Zu-LT-69(M); Location 76]
   Date of Survey: Aug. 16, 1973
   Location: 484630 E, 2178880 N; 19.7053° N, 99.1467° W
   Natural Setting: 2260 m asl, on gently sloping ground at the western base of Cerro Tultepec in the Lakeshore Plain, on the shore of Lake Xaltocán-Zumpango; deep soil cover and slight erosion.
   Modern Land Use: Rainfall-based agriculture. Outlying houses at the northern edge of the modern town of Melchor Ocampo encroach slightly

Plate A128. Zu-LT-209, facing SW over Location 51.

onto the site from the south. Two modern dirt roads cross the eastern part of the site, and there is a large active quarry on the south side.

Archaeological Remains: Variable light and light-to-moderate Late Toltec surface pottery over an area of ca. 2.80 ha. The LT material is mixed with approximately equal quantities of Late Aztec ceramics (Zu-Az-284), and there are significant numbers of modern potsherds in the site area. There are no discernible structural remains.

We made one surface collection (Location 76) over an area ca. 20 m in diameter in a plowed maize field, with light-to-moderate LT and light Late Az surface pottery, several obsidian artifacts, and no rock rubble.

Discussion: Despite the encroaching modern occupation, we were able to define the site limits reasonably well. The apparent absence of Early Aztec surface pottery suggests that this locality was abandoned after LT times and reoccupied during the Late Aztec period.

Classification: Hamlet, 30–60 people.

SITE NO. Zu-LT-209 [Zu-LT-81(J); Location 51]
 Date of Survey: Aug. 16, 1973
 Location: 486970 E, 2179720 N; 19.7129° N, 99.1243° W
 Natural Setting: 2250 m asl, on level to gently sloping ground at the edge of Cerro Tultepec in the the Lakeshore Plain on the shore of Lake Xaltocán-Zumpango; medium to deep soil cover and slight erosion.
 Modern Land Use: Rainfall-based agriculture. Modern occupation encroaches onto the site from both the west (modern town of Visitación) and the east (modern town of Tenopalco). A modern dirt road crosses the center of the site.
 Archaeological Remains: Variable light and light-to-moderate Late Toltec surface pottery over an area of ca. 10.60 ha. The site may be significantly larger if significant parts of it extend beneath modern occupation to the east or west. The LT material is mixed with traces of Aztec ceramics (no Az site defined). We noted several green and gray obsidian blades. There are no definite structural remains, although an area of moderate rock rubble in the north-central part of the site may represent the remnants of prehispanic architecture.

We made one surface collection (Location 51) over an area ca. 15 × 15 m in a plowed field (Plate A128), with light-to-moderate LT surface pottery, several obsidian artifacts, and very little rock rubble.

Discussion: Because of modern occupation, the site limits could not be defined.
 Classification: Small Dispersed Village (?), 150–300 people.

SITE NO. Zu-LT-210 [Zu-LT-84(J); Location 62; Features DG, DH, DI]
 Date of Survey: Sept. 16, 1973
 Location: 488630 E, 2177800 N; 19.6956° N, 99.1085° W
 Natural Setting: 2305 m asl, on gently sloping ground on the eastern flank of Cerro Tultepec (Plate A129) in the Lakeshore Plain, near the shore of Lake Xaltocán-Zumpango; shallow soil cover and slight to moderate erosion.
 Modern Land Use: Rainfall-based agriculture.
 Archaeological Remains: Variable light, light-to-moderate, and moderate Late Toltec surface pottery over an area of ca. 9.50 ha. The LT material is mixed with traces of Aztec ceramics (no Az site defined), and we saw one TF (Tzacaulli phase) ceramic figurine (no TF site defined). We noted several green obsidian blades and a few pieces of gray obsidian.

There are three preserved mounds (Features DG, DH, DI), and concentrations of amorphous rock rubble in several other places may represent the remnants of prehispanic architecture.

Fea.	Area and Context	Height	Content
DG	5 × 10 m, in unplowed field (Plate A130)	1.00 m	Very light LT and very light Late Az surface pottery, several obsidian artifacts, very little rock rubble. A looter's pit shows rock-rubble construction.
DH	20 m dia., in unplowed ground next to maize field	1.00 m	Light LT surface pottery, several obsidian artifacts, moderate rock rubble.
DI	12 m dia., in unplowed ground next to maize field	1.00 m	Light LT surface pottery, heavy rock rubble. A looter's pit shows rock-rubble fill.

We made one surface collection (Location 62) over an area ca. 10 × 10 m in a fallow field with light-to-moderate LT and traces of Aztec and TF (Tzacualli figurine) surface pottery, and moderate rock rubble.
 Classification: Small Nucleated Village, 200–400 people.

Plate A129. Zu-LT-210, facing east over general site area.

Plate A130. Zu-LT-210, facing east at Feature DG.

Plate A131. Zu-LT-211, facing north at Feature EG.

SITE NO. Zu-LT-211 [Zu-LT-70(M); Locations 78, 79, 80, 81, 82; Features EG, EH]

Date of Survey: Aug. 20–22, 1973
Location: 484800 E, 2175700 N; 19.6766° N, 99.1450° W
Natural Setting: 2245 m asl, on level ground along the southern base of Cerro Tultepec, in the Lakeshore Plain on the shore of Lake Xaltocán-Zumpango; deep soil cover and slight erosion.
Modern Land Use: The modern town of Tultepec encroaches onto the entire eastern side of the site. The terrain not presently occupied by modern buildings is used for the rainfall-based agriculture. Some prehispanic occupation has definitely been covered by the modern town. However, we estimate that not more than 10% of the total site area has been obscured in this way.
Archaeological Remains: Variable light and light-to-moderate Late Toltec surface pottery over an area of ca. 97.50 ha. In the central part of the site, the LT material is mixed with Early Toltec ceramics (Zu-ET-29), and there are also traces of Aztec pottery throughout the site area (no Az site designated). Sherd densities are fairly uniform over most of the site, except for an area in the southeastern (lakeshore) part of the site where LT sherd concentrations are moderate and even heavy in a few places. These heavy concentrations occur around two preserved mounds (Features EG, EH), and also at Location 81. Virtually all the sherds in this latter area are distinctive large ollas with scraped exteriors—we suspect they were associated with saltmaking at this locality during LT times. We noted numerous obsidian artifacts and a little obsidian debitage.

We identified only two distinct mounds (Features EG and EH), and we saw no other notable concentrations of rock rubble that might suggest the former presence of prehispanic architecture. However, extensive field clearing and building construction in modern times may well have removed such debris from the ground surface.

Fea.	Area and Context	Height	Content
EG	10 × 13 m, in unplowed area (Plate A131)	Irregular, 0.50-1.50 m	Heavy LT surface pottery; nearly all large scraped basins.
EH	5 × 9 m, in unplowed area (Plate A132)	Irregular, ca. 1.00 m	Moderate-to-heavy LT surface pottery; several obsidian artifacts; moderate rock rubble. Looter's pits reveal several large stones in fill.

We made five surface collections (Locations 78, 79, 80, 81, 82):

Location	Area and Context	Content
78	7 × 10 m, in plowed field	Moderate LT and traces of Az surface pottery; several obsidian artifacts; very little rock rubble.
79	5 × 8 m, in fallow field	Moderate-to-heavy LT and traces of Az surface pottery; several obsidian artifacts; light rock rubble.
80	Area size not recorded, in plowed field	Light-to-moderate LT and traces of Az surface pottery; several obsidian artifacts; very little rock rubble.
81	3 × 4 m, in plowed field	Heavy LT surface pottery, nearly all large scraped basins (Plate A133); several obsidian artifacts; very little rock rubble.
82	5 × 8 m, in fallow field	Moderate LT and traces of Az surface pottery; several obsidian artifacts; very little rock rubble.

Discussion: This is the largest LT site in the Zumpango Region survey area. It may once have contained substantial public architecture,

Plate A132. Zu-LT-211, facing east at Feature EH.

Plate A133. Zu-LT-211, heavy sherd cover at Location 81.

although modern occupation has greatly obscured whatever prehispanic structures may have existed. The possible presence of intensive saltmaking at the southeastern corner of the site suggests that this settlement may have played an important role in the production and exchange of salt during LT times. The linkage between this site and Tula (the major Early Postclassic center in this part of Mexico, situated ca. 45 km to the northwest of this site) needs to be further explored.

Classification: Regional Center, 1500–3000 people.

Plate A134. Zu-LT-212, facing west over site.

SITE NO. Zu-LT-212 [Zu-LT-83(J); Location 61]
Date of Survey: Sept. 13, 1973
Location: 487550 E, 2174220 N; 19.6632° N, 99.1188° W
Natural Setting: 2245 m asl, on level ground atop a low elevation (natural or artificial?) that attains a maximum height of ca. 1.50 m above the general level of the surrounding bed of Lake Xaltocán-Zumpango (Plate A134); deep soil cover and slight erosion.
Modern Land Use: Rainfall-based agriculture. A railroad line runs southwest-northeast about 50 m to the west of the site.
Archaeological Remains: Variable light, light-to-moderate, moderate, and moderate-to-heavy Late Toltec surface pottery over an area of ca. 1.40 ha. The LT material is mixed with lighter Classic (Zu-Cl-90) and Early Toltec (Zu-ET-30), and Late Aztec (Zu-Az-297) ceramics. The high proportion of large ollas with scraped exterior surfaces in the LT ceramic assemblage suggests a saltmaking function (similar to that noted at nearby Zu-LT-211). We noted a few green obsidian blades and a little obsidian debitage. There are no definite structural remains, although the supporting elevated area hints at the presence of subsurface architecture or fill.
We made one surface collection (Location 61) over an area ca. 5 × 7 m in a plowed field with moderate-to-heavy LT and traces of Cl and Aztec surface pottery.
Discussion: The long-term occupation, deep soil cover, possibility of well-preserved subsurface cultural material, and likelihood of intensive saltmaking all make this an ideal locality for further testing through excavation.
The apparent absence of Early Aztec surface pottery suggests that this locality was abandoned after LT times and reoccupied during the Late Aztec period.
Classification: Hamlet, 30–60 people.

SITE NO. Zu-LT-213 [Zu-LT-82(J); Location 53]
Date of Survey: Aug. 22, 1973
Location: 488000 E, 2173650 N; 19.6581° N, 99.1145° W
Natural Setting: 2245 m asl, on nearly level ground atop a low elevation (natural or artificial?) that attains a maximum height of ca. 1.00 m above the general level of the surrounding bed of Lake Xaltocán-Zumpango (Plate A135); deep soil cover and slight erosion.
Modern Land Use: Most of the site area is unplowed pasture. There is rainfall-based agriculture along the southern edges of the site. A modern dirt road borders the northern edge of the site.
Archaeological Remains: Variable light, light-to-moderate, and moderate Late Toltec surface pottery over an area of ca. 4.40 ha. The LT material is mixed with approximately equal quantities of Late Aztec ceramics (Zu-Az-298). As at nearby sites 211 and 212, large basins with scraped exterior surfaces are especially common in the LT ceramic assemblage, although other ceramic types are also present. We noted a few green obsidian blades and one gray obsidian scraper. There are no definite structural remains, although vague, irregular mounded areas suggestive of subsurface cultural features are visible in several places.
We made one surface collection (Location 53) over an area ca. 10 × 10 m in a fallow field, with moderate LT (including a high proportion of large basins with scraped exterior surfaces) and traces of Az surface pottery, several obsidian artifacts, and no rock rubble.
Discussion: A possible LT saltmaking site. The supporting elevation, deep soil cover, and multicomponent occupation suggest that this would be a good locality for future excavation.
The apparent absence of Early Aztec surface pottery suggests that this locality was abandoned after LT times and reoccupied during the Late Aztec period.
Classification: Hamlet, 50–100 people.

Plate A135. Zu-LT-213, facing SW over site.

Aztec Sites (Fig. A8)

Diagnostic Early Aztec surface pottery (defined primarily by the presence of Aztec I and II Black/Orange) is unusually scarce in the Zumpango Region. Because Early Aztec Red Wares and especially plainwares are less well defined than their Late Aztec counterparts, it remains very difficult to plot the boundaries of Early Aztec occupation within sites where both Early and Late Aztec components co-occur. And, since what Early Aztec surface pottery we have identified invariably co-occurs in sites with a great preponderance of Late Aztec material, we have seldom been able to assess the size and character of the few Early Aztec sites we do have.

Another potential problem was our tendency to take proportionately fewer surface collections at Aztec sites relative to those of earlier periods. This was primarily due to two factors:

(1) Many Aztec sites are single component occupations, and thus presented fewer difficulties in sorting out the different chronological components.

(2) It is relatively easy to identify Late Aztec surface pottery while walking over it on the ground surface.

In retrospect, we realize that this under-sampling may have made it more difficult for us to recognize the presence of low frequencies of Early Aztec surface pottery in localities where they might exist. We do not think this is a serious problem, but it may have exaggerated our impression of a minimal Early Aztec presence in the Zumpango Region.

SITE NO. Zu-Az-1 [No field number]
Date of Survey: June 11, 1973
Location: 494320 E, 2210850 N; 19.9943° N, 99.0543° W
Natural Setting: 2405 m asl, on gently sloping ground in Upper Salado Drainage; shallow soil cover and severe erosion.
Modern Land Use: Marginal pasture.
Archaeological Remains: Light Late Aztec surface pottery over an area of ca. 0.50 ha. There are no structural remains.
No surface collection made.
Classification: Small hamlet, 2–5 people.

SITE NO. Zu-Az-2 [Zu-Az-19(J); Feature V]
Date of Survey: June 11, 1973
Location: 496050 E, 2210720 N; 19.9931° N, 99.0378° W
Natural Setting: 2405 m asl, on gently sloping ground in the Upper Salado Drainage; shallow soil cover and severe erosion, with abundant (natural?) rock rubble.
Modern Land Use: Marginal pasture.
Archaeological Remains: This site comprises a single distinct mound (Feature V) and a scatter of variable light and light-to-moderate Late Aztec surface pottery over an area ca. 100 m in diameter (0.80 ha). Feature V measures ca. 15 m in diameter and 0.75 m high, with light Late Az surface pottery and heavy rock rubble.
No surface collection made.
Discussion: The general abundance of rock rubble may indicate the former presence of other ancient structures.
Classification: Small Hamlet, 5–10 people.

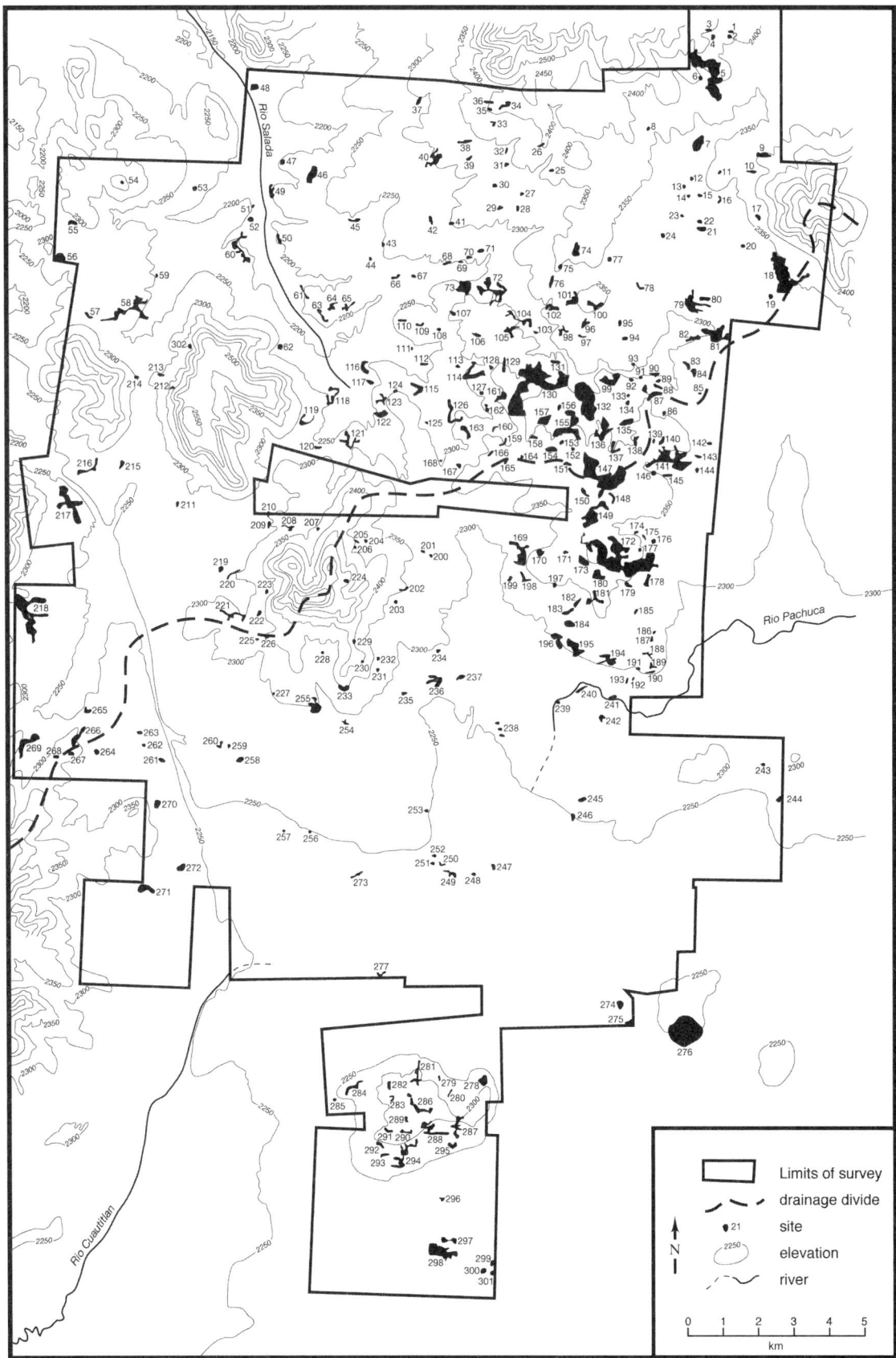

Figure A8. Map of Aztec sites in the Zumpango Region.

Plate A136. Zu-Az-5, facing south over Location 21.

SITE NO. Zu-Az-3 [No field number]
Date of Survey: June 11, 1973
Location: 495650 E, 2210800 N; 19.9938° N, 99.0416° W
Natural Setting: 2450 m asl, on gently sloping ground in the Upper Salado Drainage; shallow soil cover, with moderate erosion.
Modern Land Use: Pasture.
Archaeological Remains: Variable light and light-to-moderate Late Aztec surface pottery over an area of ca. 0.40 ha. There are no structural remains.
No surface collection made.
Classification: Small Hamlet, 5–10 people.

SITE NO. Zu-Az-4 [Zu-Az-18(J); Feature U]
Date of Survey: June 11, 1973
Location: 495650 E, 2210700 N; 19.9929° N, 99.0416° W
Natural Setting: 2445 m asl, on gently sloping ground atop a low hill in the Upper Salado Drainage; shallow soil cover and moderate erosion, with substantial (natural?) rock rubble.
Modern Land Use: Pasture.
Archaeological Remains: Variable light and light-to-moderate Late Aztec surface pottery over an area of ca. 1.10 ha. We identified one fairly well preserved mound (Feature U), measuring ca. 10 × 12 m in area and 0.50 m high with light Late Az and traces of Colonial-period surface pottery, numerous obsidian artifacts, and moderate rock rubble.
No surface collection made.
Discussion: Feature U probably represents the remnant of a domestic residence, although a ceremonial-civic function at this hilltop location cannot be ruled out.
Classification: Small Hamlet, 10–20 people.

SITE NO. Zu-Az-5, Zu-Az-6 [Zu-Az-17(J); Locations 19, 21]
Date of Survey: June 11, 1973
Location:
Zu-Az-5: 495380 E, 2209800 N; 19.9848° N, 99.0442° W;
Zu-Az-6 (a detached location ca. 0.70 ha, situated ca. 150 m west of Zu-Az-5): 495000 E, 2209570 N; 19.9827° N, 99.0478° W
Natural Setting: 2400 m asl, on gently sloping ground in the Upper Salado Drainage; shallow to medium soil cover and moderate erosion. There is a major *barranca* along the western side of the site.
Modern Land Use: Pasture and maguey cultivation. Some of the site area has been used for rainfall-based agriculture, but all fields are presently fallow. The northern edge of the modern town of Santa María Ajoloapan lies about 100 m from the site's western and southern borders. Several modern dirt roads extend from Ajoloapan across the northern and southern sections of the site.
Archaeological Remains: Variable light and light-to-moderate Late Aztec surface pottery over an area of ca. 53.10 ha. Obsidian blades are common, and we noted a few large spindle whorls. There are no definite structural remains, but several concentrations of amorphous rock rubble may represent the remnants of ancient buildings—especially near the southern edge of the site. The Late Az material is mixed with Late Toltec surface pottery in three discrete areas (Zu-LT-3, Zu-LT-4, and Zu-LT-5), and there is a single Classic component in the east-central part of the Aztec site (Zu-Cl-1).
We made two surface collections (Locations 19, 21):

Location	Area and Context	Content
19	10 × 15 m, in plowed field	Light-to-moderate Late Az, light LT, and traces of Cl surface pottery; several obsidian artifacts; and moderate rock rubble.
21	15 m dia., in fallow field (Plate A136)	Light-to-moderate LT and light Late Az surface pottery; several obsidian artifacts; one maguey spindle whorl; and moderate rock rubble.

Discussion: This site does not appear to extend beneath the modern town of Santa María Ajoloapan. The apparent absence of Early Aztec surface pottery suggests that this locality was abandoned after LT times and reoccupied during the Late Aztec period.
Classification: Large Dispersed Village, 600–1200 people.

SITE NO. Zu-Az-7 [Zu-Az-16(J)]
   Date of Survey: June 11, 1973
   Location: 495030 E, 2207650 N; 19.9654° N, 99.0475° W
   Natural Setting: 2340 m asl, on gently sloping round in the Upper Salado Drainage; medium soil cover and moderate erosion.
   Modern Land Use: Rainfall-based agriculture. The modern town of Santa María Ajoloapan encroaches onto the western side of the site
   Archaeological Remains: Variable light and light-to-moderate Late Aztec surface pottery over an area of ca. 9.70 ha. There are no definite structural remains, but several concentrations of amorphous rock rubble may represent the remnants of ancient buildings.
   No surface collection made.
   Discussion: Because of modern occupation, we were unable to define the western limits of this site. It may be significantly larger than the area we were able to measure.
   Classification: Small Dispersed Village (?), 100–200 people.

SITE NO. Zu-Az-8 [Zu-Az-20(J); Feature X]
   Date of Survey: June 13, 1973
   Location: 493720 E, 2208100 N; 19.9694° N, 99.0600° W
   Natural Setting: 2360 m asl, on gently sloping ground in the Upper Salado Drainage; medium to deep soil cover and slight to moderate erosion.
   Modern Land Use: Rainfall-based agriculture. The southwestern edge of the modern town of Santa María Ajoloapan is about 25 m east of the site area.
   Archaeological Remains: Variable light and light-to-moderate Late Aztec surface pottery over an area ca. 0.50 ha. The Az material is mixed with roughly equivalent quantities of Late Toltec ceramics (Zu-LT-7). There is a single discernible mound (Feature X), measuring ca. 20 m in diameter and 0.25 m high. The mound's surface is covered with mixed Late Az and LT surface pottery, in about equal proportions, and moderate rock rubble. There is very little surface pottery in the immediately surrounding area.
   No surface collection made.
   Discussion: The site does not appear to extend below the modern town, and it probably represents a single domestic residence. The apparent absence of Early Aztec surface pottery suggests that this locality was abandoned after LT times and reoccupied during the Late Aztec period.
   Classification: Small Hamlet, 5–10 people.

SITE NO. Zu-Az-9 [Zu-Az-15(J)]
   Date of Survey: June 13, 1973
   Location: 497050 E, 2207300 N; 19.9622° N, 99.0282° W
   Natural Setting: 2405 m asl, on gently sloping ground in the Upper Salado Drainage; shallow soil cover and severe erosion.
   Modern Land Use: Marginal pasture.
   Archaeological Remains: Variable light and light-to-moderate Late Aztec surface pottery over an area of ca. 3.70 ha. There are no distinct structural remains, although an area of moderate rock rubble in the eastern part of the site may represent the remains of one or two ancient buildings.
   No surface collection made.
   Classification: Hamlet, 25–50 people.

SITE NO. Zu-Az-10 [Zu-Az-14(J); Location 16]
   Date of Survey: June 6, 1973
   Location: 496700 E, 2206800 N; 19.9677° N, 99.0315° W
   Natural Setting: 2380 m asl, on gently sloping ground in the Upper Salado Drainage; shallow soil cover and moderate erosion.
   Modern Land Use: Pasture.
   Archaeological Remains: Variable light and light-to-moderate Late Aztec surface pottery over an area of ca. 1.10 ha. Obsidian artifacts are abundant. The Late Az material is mixed with heavier and more extensive Early Toltec ceramics (Zu-ET-1). There are no recognizable structural remains.
   We made one surface collection (Location 16) in an unplowed field over an area of ca. 15 × 20 m, with light-to-moderate ET and light Late Az surface pottery, several obsidian artifacts, and moderate rock rubble.
   Classification: Small Hamlet, 10–20 people.

SITE NO. Zu-Az-11 [Zu-Cl-6(J); Feature O]
   Date of Survey: June 6, 1973
   Location: 495850 E, 2206750 N; 19.9572° N, 99.0397° W
   Natural Setting: 2355 m asl, on gently sloping ground in the Upper Salado Drainage; shallow to medium soil cover and moderate to severe erosion.
   Modern Land Use: Rainfall-based agriculture. A modern dirt road crosses the central site area.
   Archaeological Remains: Light Late Aztec surface pottery over an area of ca. 0.50 ha. The Late Az material is mixed with Classic (Zu-Cl-8) and Late Toltec (Zu-LT-38) ceramics.
   There is one definite mound (Feature O) in a plowed field, measuring ca. 35 m in diameter and 1.50 m high, with light Cl, LT, and Late Az surface pottery, and numerous obsidian artifacts. We made a surface collection from an area ca. 10 × 10 m on the mound surface.
   Discussion: The apparent absence of Early Aztec surface pottery suggests that this locality was abandoned after LT times and reoccupied during the Late Aztec period. The age of Feature O is uncertain, but its main construction and use probably date to the Late Aztec period.
   Classification: Small Hamlet, 5–10 people.

SITE NO. Zu-Az-12 [Zu-Az-1(J)]
   Date of Survey: May 29, 1973
   Location: 495030 E, 2206570 N; 19.9556° N, 99.0475° W
   Natural Setting: 2340 m asl, on gently sloping ground in the Upper Salado Drainage; medium soil cover and slight to moderate erosion.
   Modern Land Use: Rainfall-based agriculture. The site area had been plowed and planted immediately prior to our survey.
   Archaeological Remains: Variable light and light-to-moderate Late Aztec surface pottery over an area of ca. 0.50 ha. There are no discernible structural remains and very little rock rubble.
   No surface collection made.
   Classification: Small Hamlet, 2–5 people.

SITE NO. Zu-Az-13 [Zu-Az-2(J)]
   Date of Survey: May 29, 1973
   Location: 494800 E, 2206380 N; 19.9539° N, 99.0497° W
   Natural Setting: 2340 m asl, on gently sloping ground in the Upper Salado Drainage; shallow soil cover and moderate to severe erosion.
   Modern Land Use: Marginal pasture.
   Archaeological Remains: Variable light and light-to-moderate Late Aztec surface pottery over an area of ca. 0.70 ha. There are no recognizable structural remains and very little rock rubble.
   No surface collection made.
   Classification: Small Hamlet, 5–10 people.

SITE NO. Zu-Az-14 [Zu-Az-3(J)]
Date of Survey: May 29, 1973
Location: 494900 E, 2206070 N; 19.9511° N, 99.0487° W
Natural Setting: 2340 m asl, on gently sloping ground in the Upper Salado Drainage; shallow soil cover and severe erosion.
Modern Land Use: The immediate site area is situated on a severely eroded patch of wasteland that is surrounded on all sides by fields devoted to rainfall-based agriculture.
Archaeological Remains: Variable very light, light, and light-to-moderate Late Aztec surface pottery over an area of ca. 0.70 ha. There are no recognizable structural remains and very little rock rubble.
No surface collection made.
Classification: Small Hamlet, 5–10 people.

SITE NO. Zu-Az-15 [Zu-Az-4(J)]
Date of Survey: May 29, 1973
Location: 494600 E, 2206100 N; 19.9514° N, 99.0516° W
Natural Setting: 2340 m asl, on gently sloping ground in the Upper Salado Drainage; shallow soil cover and moderate erosion.
Modern Land Use: Rainfall-based agriculture. The site area had been recently plowed and planted at the time of our survey. A modern dirt road skirts the western edge of the site.
Archaeological Remains: Light-to-moderate Late Aztec surface pottery over an area of ca. 0.60 ha. There are no recognizable structures, although a concentration of amorphous rock rubble in the center of the site may represent the remnants of ancient buildings.
No surface collection made.
Classification: Small Hamlet, 10–20 people.

SITE NO. Zu-Az-16 [No field number]
Date of Survey: May 29, 1973
Location: 495900 E, 2206000 N; 19.9505° N, 99.0392° W
Natural Setting: 2345 m asl, on gently sloping ground in the Upper Salado Drainage; shallow soil cover and moderate erosion.
Modern Land Use: Rainfall-based agriculture. A modern dirt road borders the north edge of the site.
Archaeological Remains: Light Late Aztec surface pottery over an area of ca. 0.70 ha. There is very little rock rubble and no discernible structural remains.
No surface collection made.
Classification: Small Hamlet, 2–5 people.

SITE NO. Zu-Az-17 [Zu-Az-13(J)]
Date of Survey: June 6, 1973
Location: 497000 E, 2205450 N; 19.9455° N, 99.0287° W
Natural Setting: 2375 m asl, on moderately sloping ground in the Upper Salado Drainage; shallow soil cover and moderate erosion.
Modern Land Use: Pasture. A modern dirt road skirts the western side of the site.
Archaeological Remains: Variable light and light-to-moderate Late Aztec surface pottery over an area of ca. 1.60 ha. No recognizable structural remains.
No surface collection made.
Classification: Small Hamlet, 15–30 people.

SITE NO. Zu-Az-18 [Zu-Az-12(J); Locations 12, 13, 14, 15]
Date of Survey: June 5, 1973
Location: 497900 E, 2203680 N; 19.9295° N, 99.0201° W
Natural Setting: 2345 m asl, on gently sloping ground in the Upper Salado Drainage; shallow to medium soil cover, with moderate to severe erosion and numerous patches of bare tepetate along the eastern and western sides of the site. A major *barranca* borders the western edge of the site.
Modern Land Use: Rainfall-based agriculture in relatively uneroded areas. The modern town of Nopala encroaches onto the site from the northeast. There are large pirule trees scattered over the general site area.
Archaeological Remains: Variable light and light-to-moderate Late Aztec surface pottery over an area of ca. 50.00 ha. Obsidian blades are common, and we noted several large spindle whorls. The Aztec material is mixed with less extensive remains of Classic (Zu-Cl-7) and Late Toltec (Zu-LT-37, Zu-LT-38) ceramics. Because of modern occupation, the northeastern limits of the prehispanic site could not be defined, and as much as one-third of the original site area may extend below the modern town of Nopala. There are no recognizable structural remains, although the presence of concentrations of amorphous rock rubble in some areas may be the remnants of ancient buildings.
We made four surface collections (Locations 12, 13, 14, 15):

Location	Area and Context	Content
12	15 × 15 m, in plowed field with slight mounding (Plate A137)	Light-to-moderate Late Az and LT, and light Cl surface pottery; one spindle whorl; several obsidian artifacts; light rock rubble.
13	5 × 5 m, in plowed field	Moderate-to-heavy Cl and very light Late Az surface pottery; several obsidian artifacts; moderate-to-heavy rock rubble.
14	10 × 10 m, in plowed field	Light Late Az and light-to-moderate LT surface pottery; several obsidian artifacts; light-to-moderate rock rubble.
15	10 × 10 m, in plowed field	Light-to-moderate Late Az and very light LT surface pottery; several obsidian artifacts; light-to-moderate rock rubble.

Discussion: Because of modern occupation, the site size cannot be accurately estimated. The original site area may have been up to ca. 80 ha. Obviously this site represents a substantial Late Aztec settlement. The apparent absence of Early Aztec surface pottery indicates that this locality was abandoned at the end of LT times and reoccupied in the Late Aztec period.
Classification: Large Dispersed Village (?), 750–1500 people.

SITE NO. Zu-Az-19 [Zu-Az-11(J); Feature O]
Date of Survey: June 4, 1973
Location: 497530 E, 2203070 N; 19.9240° N, 99.0236° W
Natural Setting: 2330 m asl, on gently sloping ground in the Upper Salado Drainage; medium to deep soil cover and slight erosion.
Modern Land Use: Rainfall-based agriculture. Much of the entire site area had been recently plowed and planted at the time of our survey.
Archaeological Remains: Variable light and light-to-moderate Late Aztec surface pottery over an area of ca. 1.20 ha. We noted numerous green obsidian blades. The Late Aztec material is mixed with partially overlapping Classic (Zu-Cl-7) and Late Toltec (Zu-LT-38) ceramics.
There is a single recognizable mound (Feature O) in a plowed field near the northern edge of the site. This feature measures ca. 35 m in diameter and 0.35 cm high (Plate A138), and is covered with mixed Cl, LT, and Late Az surface pottery and moderate rock rubble. There is a large looter's pit in the center of the mound; most of the Cl pottery

Plate A137. Zu-Az-18, facing SE over Location 12.

seems to occur around the edges of the pit. The pit profiles indicate solid earth and rock rubble construction (Plate A139).

We made a single surface collection from an area ca. 10 × 10 m around the looter's pit atop Feature O and on the western side of the mound.

Discussion: This site probably represents a detached component of the larger Zu-Az-18 site to the northeast. The apparent absence of Early Aztec surface pottery indicates that this locality was abandoned at the end of LT times and reoccupied in the Late Aztec period.

Classification: Small Hamlet, 15–30 people.

SITE NO. Zu-Az-20 [No field number]
Date of Survey: June 4, 1973
Location: 496630 E, 2204550 N; 19.9374° N, 99.0322° W
Natural Setting: 2340 m asl, on gently sloping ground in the Upper Salado Drainage; shallow soil cover and severe erosion, with patches of bare tepetate. A major *barranca* cuts north-south across the site area.
Modern Land Use: Marginal pasture and marginal rainfall-based agriculture.
Archaeological Remains: Light Late Aztec surface pottery over an area of ca. 0.40 ha. There are no discernible structural remains and very little rock rubble.
No surface collection made.
Classification: Small Hamlet, 2–5 people.

SITE NO. Zu-Az-21 [Zu-Az-6(J)]
Date of Survey: May 30, 1973
Location: 495130 E, 2205050 N; 19.9419° N, 99.0465° W
Natural Setting: 2340 m asl, on gently sloping ground in the Upper Salado Drainage; shallow soil cover and moderate to severe erosion.
Modern Land Use: Rainfall-based agriculture. The site area had recently been plowed and planted at the time of our survey. A modern dirt road borders the western edge of the site.

Archaeological Remains: Variable light and light-to-moderate Late Aztec surface pottery over an area ca. 3.00 ha. The Late Az material is mixed with lighter and partially overlapping Late Toltec ceramics (Zu-LT-33). There are no definite structural remains, but a concentration of amorphous rock rubble in the eastern part of the site may represent the remnants of ancient architecture.
No surface collection made.
Discussion: The apparent absence of Early Aztec surface pottery indicates that this locality was abandoned at the end of LT times and reoccupied in the Late Aztec period.
Classification: Hamlet, 30–60 people.

SITE NO. Zu-Az-22 [Zu-Az-5(J)]
Date of Survey: May 30, 1973
Location: 495220 E, 2205280 N; 19.9440° N, 99.0457° W
Natural Setting: 2340 m asl, on gently sloping ground in the Upper Salado Drainage; shallow soil cover and moderate to severe erosion.
Modern Land Use: Rainfall-based agriculture. The site area had recently been plowed and planted at the time of our survey. A modern dirt road borders the western edge of the site.
Archaeological Remains: Variable light, light-to-moderate, and moderate Late Aztec surface pottery over an area of ca. 1.40 ha. The Late Aztec material is mixed with approximately equal amounts of Late Toltec surface pottery (Zu-LT-33). There are no recognizable structural remains, although two concentrations of amorphous rock rubble may represent the remnants of ancient architecture.
No surface collection made.
Discussion: The apparent absence of Early Aztec surface pottery indicates that this locality was abandoned at the end of LT times and reoccupied in the Late Aztec period.
Classification: Hamlet, 30–60 people.

Plate A138. Zu-Az-19, facing east at Feature O.

Plate A139. Zu-Az-19, looter's pit in Feature O.

Plate A140. Zu-Az-24, facing NW over Location 3.

SITE NO. Zu-Az-23 [No field number]
Date of Survey: May 30, 1973
Location: 494750 E, 2205450 N; 19.9455° N, 99.0502° W
Natural Setting: 2340 m asl, on gently sloping ground in the Upper Salado Drainage; shallow soil cover and moderate erosion.
Modern Land Use: Rainfall-based agriculture.
Archaeological Remains: Variable light and light-to-moderate Late Aztec surface pottery over an area of ca. 0.40 ha. There are no definite structural remains, but concentrations of amorphous rock rubble may represent the remnants of one or more ancient buildings.
No surface collection made.
Classification: Small Hamlet, 5–10 people.

SITE NO. Zu-Az-24 [Zu-Az-7(J); Location 3]
Date of Survey: May 27, 1973
Location: 494100 E, 2204850 N; 19.9401° N, 99.0564° W
Natural Setting: 2335 m asl, on gently sloping ground in the Upper Salado Drainage; shallow to medium soil cover and moderate erosion.
Modern Land Use: Rainfall-based agriculture. The site area was partially plowed but fallow at the time of our survey. A modern dirt road skirts the eastern edge of the site.
Archaeological Remains: Variable light and light-to-moderate Late Aztec surface pottery over an area of ca. 1.00 ha. We noted numerous green obsidian blades, one obsidian scraper, and one maguey spindle whorl. There are no definite structural remains, although several concentrations of amorphous rock rubble probably represent the remnants of ancient buildings. There are also traces of Late Toltec pottery (no LT site defined here).
We made one surface collection (Location 3) over an area of ca. 10 × 10 m in a slightly mounded area that had recently been plowed (Plate A140), with light-to-moderate Late Az surface pottery, several obsidian artifacts, and moderate rock rubble.
Classification: Small Hamlet, 10–20 people.

SITE NO. Zu-Az-25 [Zu-Az-29(J); Feature AH]
Date of Survey: June 20, 1973
Location: 490950 E, 2206850 N; 19.9582° N, 99.0865° W
Natural Setting: 2370 m asl, on gently sloping ground in the Upper Salado Drainage; shallow soil cover and moderate erosion.
Modern Land Use: Rainfall-based agriculture. Much of the site area had been recently plowed at the time of our survey.
Archaeological Remains: This site comprises a single poorly preserved, slightly elevated mound (Feature AH) in a plowed field. This feature measures ca. 20 m in diameter, with light-to-moderate Late Aztec surface pottery, numerous obsidian blades, one obsidian scraper, one ceramic spindle whorl, and moderate rock rubble.
No surface collection made.
Classification: Small Hamlet, 5–10 people.

SITE NO. Zu-Az-26 [Zu-Az-30(J)]
Date of Survey: June 20, 1973
Location: 490450 E, 2207550 N; 19.9645° N, 99.0913° W
Natural Setting: 2380 m asl, on gently sloping ground in the Upper Salado Drainage; shallow soil cover and moderate erosion.
Modern Land Use: Rainfall-based agriculture. The site area was fallow at the time of our survey.
Archaeological Remains: Variable light and light-to-moderate Late Aztec surface pottery over an area of ca. 1.10 ha. There are no discernible structural remains and very little rock rubble.
No surface collection made.
Classification: Small Hamlet, 10–20 people.

SITE NO. Zu-Az-27 [Zu-Az-28(J)]
Date of Survey: June 20, 1973
Location: 490030 E, 2206100 N; 19.9513° N, 99.0953° W
Natural Setting: 2330 m asl, on gently sloping ground atop a broad, low hilltop in the Upper Salado Drainage; shallow soil cover and moderate to severe erosion.
Modern Land Use: Pasture and marginal rainfall-based agriculture.
Archaeological Remains: Light-to-moderate Late Aztec surface pottery over an area of ca. 0.40 ha. There are no discernible structural remains, although several concentrations of amorphous rock rubble may represent the remains of ancient buildings.
No surface collection made.
Classification: Small Hamlet, 5–10 people.

SITE NO. Zu-Az-28 [Zu-Az-27(J)]
Date of Survey: June 18, 1973
Location: 489900 E, 2205630 N; 19.9471° N, 99.0965° W
Natural Setting: 2320 m asl, on gently sloping ground in the Upper Salado Drainage; shallow soil cover and severe erosion, with patches of bare tepetate.
Modern Land Use: Marginal pasture.
Archaeological Remains: Light Late Aztec surface pottery over an area of ca. 1.00 ha. There are no discernible structural remains.
No surface collection made.
Classification: Small Hamlet, 5–10 people.

SITE NO. Zu-Az-29 [Zu-Az-17(M); Features AU, AV; Location 36]
Date of Survey: June 17, 1973
Location: 489250 E, 2205900 N; 19.9495° N, 99.1027° W
Natural Setting: 2330 m asl, on gently sloping ground in the Upper Salado Drainage; shallow soil cover and severe erosion, with patches of bare tepctate.
Modern Land Use: Marginal rainfall-based agriculture, with maguey semi-terracing. Several small stone-brush check dams have been constructed in an attempt to control sheet wash.
Archaeological Remains: Variable light and light-to-moderate Late Aztec surface pottery over an area of ca. 0.90 ha. The Late Az material is mixed with heavier Classic (Zu-Cl-11) and Late Toltec (Zu-LT-25) ceramics; there is also a small quantity of Terminal Formative surface pottery at the far western edge of the site (Zu-TF-1). See Zu-Cl-11 for description of two preserved mounds and surface collection.
Discussion: The apparent absence of Early Aztec surface pottery indicates that this locality was abandoned at the end of LT times and reoccupied in the Late Aztec period.
Classification: Small Hamlet, 10–20 people.

SITE NO. Zu-Az-30 [Zu-Az-40(M)]
Date of Survey: June 12, 1973
Location: 489070 E, 2206320 N; 19.9533° N, 99.1045° W
Natural Setting: 2335 m asl, on nearly level ground in the Upper Salado Drainage; medium soil cover and moderate erosion.
Modern Land Use: Rainfall-based agriculture.
Archaeological Remains: Variable light and light-to-moderate Late Aztec surface pottery over an area of ca. 0.60 ha. There are no discernible structural remains.
No surface collection made.
Classification: Small Hamlet, 5–10 people.

SITE NO. Zu-Az-31 [Zu-Az-34(M)]
Date of Survey: June 12, 1973
Location: 489430 E, 2206950 N; 19.9590° N, 99.1010° W
Natural Setting: 2335 m asl, on nearly level ground in the Upper Salado Drainage; medium soil cover and moderate erosion.
Modern Land Use: Rainfall-based agriculture.
Archaeological Remains: Light Late Aztec surface pottery over an area of ca. 1.00 ha. There are no discernible structural remains and very little rock rubble
No surface collection made.
Classification: Small Hamlet, 5–10 people.

SITE NO. Zu-Az-32 [Zu-Az-33(M)]
Date of Survey: June 12, 1973
Location: 489530 E, 2207400 N; 19.9631° N, 99.1001° W
Natural Setting: 2345 m asl, on nearly level ground in the Upper Salado Drainage; medium soil cover and moderate erosion.
Modern Land Use: Rainfall-based agriculture.
Archaeological Remains: Light Late Aztec surface pottery over an area of ca. 0.70 ha. There are no discernible structural remains and very little rock rubble.
No surface collection made.
Classification: Small Hamlet, 5-10 people.

SITE NO. Zu-Az-33 [Zu-Az-32(M)]
Date of Survey: June 12, 1973
Location: 489050 E, 2208180 N; 19.9701° N, 99.1047° W
Natural Setting: 2370 m asl, on gently sloping ground in the Upper Salado Drainage; shallow soil cover and severe erosion, with numerous patches of bare tepetate
Modern Land Use: Wasteland.
Archaeological Remains: Variable light and light-to-moderate Late Aztec surface pottery over an area of ca. 1.30 ha. There are no structural remains and very little rock rubble.
No surface collection made.
Classification: Small Hamlet, 10–20 people.

SITE NO. Zu-Az-34 [Zu-Az-30(M)]
Date of Survey: June 12, 1973
Location: 489350 E, 2208750 N; 19.9753° N, 99.1018° W
Natural Setting: 2410 m asl, on gently sloping ground in the Upper Salado Drainage; shallow soil cover and severe erosion, with numerous patches of bare tepetate.
Modern Land Use: Wasteland, previously used only for maguey cultivation.
Archaeological Remains: Light Late Aztec surface pottery over an area of ca. 3.00 ha. There are no structural remains and very little rock rubble.
No surface collection made.
Classification: Hamlet, 15–30 people.

SITE NO. Zu-Az-35 [Zu-Az-31(M); Location 32]
Date of Survey: June 12, 1973
Location: 488850 E, 2208630 N; 19.9742° N, 99.1066° W
Natural Setting: 2395 m asl, on gently sloping ground in the Upper Salado Drainage; shallow soil cover and severe erosion, with numerous patches of bare tepetate.
Modern Land Use: Marginal pasture and wasteland. The area was formerly used for maguey cultivation.

Plate A141. Zu-Az-35, facing north over Location 32.

Archaeological Remains: Variable light and light-to-moderate Late Aztec surface pottery over an area of ca. 0.70 ha. There is also trace of Late Toltec pottery (no LT site defined). We noted numerous green obsidian blades, one gray obsidian scraper, one green obsidian trilobal eccentric, and one maguey spindle whorl. There are no discernible structural remains.

We made a single surface collection (Location 32) over an area of ca. 5 × 7 m in a badly eroded area (Plate A141) with light-to-moderate Late Az surface pottery, numerous obsidian artifacts, and very little rock rubble.

Classification: Small Hamlet, 5–10 people.

SITE NO. Zu-Az-36 [Zu-Az-29(M); Feature AQ]
Date of Survey: June 12, 1973
Location: 488750 E, 2208850 N; 19.9762° N, 99.1075° W
Natural Setting: 2400 m asl, on gently sloping ground in the Upper Salado Drainage; shallow soil cover and severe erosion, with numerous patches of bare tepetate.
Modern Land Use: Marginal pasture and wasteland.
Archaeological Remains: Light Late Aztec surface pottery over an area of ca. 1.30 ha. We noted several green obsidian blades. There is a definite architectural remnant (Feature AQ) in the central site area where erosion has partially exposed the stone bases of the walls of two structures (Plate A142). These structures appear to have been rather small, the better preserved one measuring ca. 1.50 × 3.00 m in area and 0.50 m high (Fig. A9).

No surface collection made.

Classification: Small Hamlet, 10–20 people.

SITE NO. Zu-Az-37 [Zu-Az-25(M); Features AK, AL, AM, AN, AO]
Date of Survey: June 10, 1973
Location: 487200 E, 2208850 N; 19.9762° N, 99.1223° W
Natural Setting: 2295 m asl, on gently sloping ground in the Upper Salado Drainage; medium soil cover and moderate erosion.
Modern Land Use: Rainfall-based agriculture. A modern dirt road borders the eastern edge of the site.
Archaeological Remains: Light Late Aztec surface pottery over an area of ca. 1.60 ha. There are five fairly well preserved mounds (Features AK, AL, AM, AN, AO) clustered in the northern half of the site; surface pottery is more abundant on and immediately around these features than elsewhere in the site.

Fea.	Area and Context	Height	Content
AK	30 × 50 m, in plowed field	0.20 m	Light Late Az surface pottery, numerous obsidian artifacts, light-to-moderate rock rubble.
AL	15 × 30 m, in plowed field (Plate A143)	0.30 m	Light Late Az surface pottery, several obsidian artifacts, light rock rubble.
AM	15 × 18 m, in plowed field	0.35 m	Light Late Az surface pottery, several obsidian artifacts, light rock rubble. One surface collection taken from the entire mound surface.
AN	25 × 30 m, in plowed field	0.20 m	Light Late Az surface pottery, several obsidian artifacts, light-to-moderate rock rubble.
AO	20 × 25 m, in plowed field	0.15 m	Light Late Az surface pottery, several obsidian artifacts, one basalt mano fragment, light rock rubble.

Classification: Hamlet, 35–50 people.

Appendix A: Site Descriptions

Plate A142. Zu-Az-36, facing north at Feature AQ.

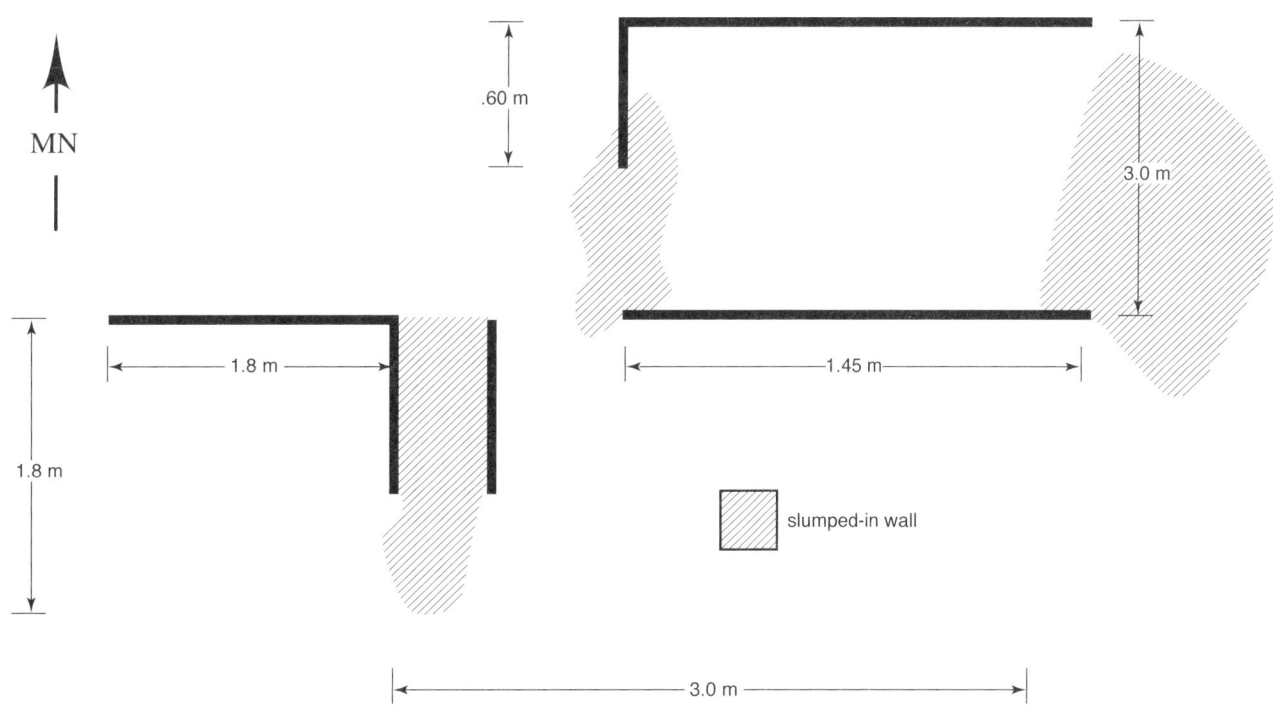

Feature AQ

Figure A9. Zu-Az-36, sketch plan of base of structure at Feature AQ.

SITE NO. Zu-Az-38 [Zu-Az-28(M)]
Date of Survey: June 12, 1973
Location: 487970 E, 2207630 N; 19.9652° N, 99.1150° W
Natural Setting: 2335 m asl, on gently sloping ground in the Upper Salado Drainage; shallow to medium soil cover and moderate to severe erosion.
Modern Land Use: Rainfall-based agriculture.
Archaeological Remains: Variable light and light-to-moderate Late Aztec surface pottery over an area of ca. 1.70 ha. There are no discernible structural remains and very little rock rubble.
No surface collection made.
Classification: Small Hamlet, 15–30 people.

SITE NO. Zu-Az-39 [Zu-Az-27(M); Feature AR]
Date of Survey: June 13, 1973
Location: 488300 E, 2207100 N; 19.9604° N, 99.1118° W
Natural Setting: 2320 m asl, on gently sloping ground in the Upper Salado Drainage; medium soil cover and moderate erosion.
Modern Land Use: Rainfall-based agriculture and pasture.
Archaeological Remains: Variable light and light-to-moderate Late Aztec surface pottery over an area of ca. 1.10 ha. There is one discernible mound (Feature AR) in a plowed field in the southwestern part of the site. This feature measures ca. 25 m in diameter and 0.40 m high (Plate A144), with light Late Az surface pottery, several green and gray obsidian blades and scrapers, and light-to-moderate rock rubble.
No surface collection made.
Classification: Small Hamlet, 10–20 people.

SITE NO. Zu-Az-40 [Zu-Az-26(M); Feature AP]
Date of Survey: June 11, 1973
Location: 487150 E, 2207100 N; 19.9604° N, 99.1228° W
Natural Setting: 2305 m asl, on gently sloping ground in the Upper Salado Drainage; shallow to medium soil cover and severe erosion, with numerous patches of bare tepetate.
Modern Land Use: Rainfall-based agriculture. A modern dirt road skirts the eastern edge of the site.
Archaeological Remains: Variable light and light-to-moderate Late Aztec surface pottery over an area of ca. 8.60 ha. There is one discernible mound (Feature AP) in a plowed field in the southwestern part of the site. This feature measures ca. 15 m in diameter and 0.20 m high. The mound surface has light Late Az surface pottery, several obsidian artifacts, and light-to-moderate rock rubble.
No surface collection made.
Classification: Small Dispersed Village, 85–170 people.

SITE NO. Zu-Az-41 [Zu-Az-16(M); Feature AS]
Date of Survey: June 14, 1973
Location: 487900 E, 2205150 N; 19.9427° N, 99.1156° W
Natural Setting: 2310 m asl, on nearly level ground in the Upper Salado Drainage; medium soil cover and moderate erosion.
Modern Land Use: Rainfall-based agriculture.
Archaeological Remains: Light Late Aztec surface pottery over an area of ca. 0.80 ha. There is one discernible mound (Feature AS) in a plowed field in the eastern site area. This feature measures ca. 14 × 21 m in area and 0.30 m high, with light Late Az surface pottery, several green obsidian blades and chips, two basalt mano fragments, and light rock rubble.
No surface collection made.
Classification: Small Hamlet, 5–10 people.

SITE NO. Zu-Az-42 [Zu-Az-15(M)]
Date of Survey: June 14, 1973
Location: 487150 E, 2205220 N; 19.9434° N, 99.1228° W
Natural Setting: 2270 m asl, on level ground in the Upper Salado Drainage; medium soil cover and moderate erosion.
Modern Land Use: Rainfall-based agriculture.
Archaeological Remains: Variable light and light-to-moderate Late Aztec surface pottery over an area of ca. 1.80 ha. There are no discernible structural remains, although several concentrations of amorphous rock rubble may represent the remnants of ancient buildings.
No surface collection made.
Classification: Hamlet, 20–40 people.

SITE NO. Zu-Az-43 [Zu-Az-12(M)]
Date of Survey: June 20, 1973
Location: 485700 E, 2204470 N; 19.9366° N, 99.1366° W
Natural Setting: 2250 m asl, on gently sloping ground in the Upper Salado Drainage; medium soil cover and moderate erosion.
Modern Land Use: Rainfall-based agriculture.
Archaeological Remains: Light Late Aztec surface pottery over an area of ca. 0.60 ha. There is a small Classic site (Zu-Cl-30) just west of the Aztec site. There are no discernible structural remains and very little rock rubble.
No surface collection made.
Classification: Small Hamlet, 2–5 people.

SITE NO. Zu-Az-44 [Zu-Az-39(M); Feature BC]
Date of Survey: June 20, 1973
Location: 485350 E, 2204050 N; 19.9328° N, 99.1400° W
Natural Setting: 2240 m asl, on gently sloping ground in the Upper Salado Drainage; medium soil cover and moderate erosion.
Modern Land Use: Rainfall-based agriculture. Much of the site area had recently been plowed at the time of our survey.
Archaeological Remains: The site consists of a single mound (Feature BC) in a plowed field (Plate A145). This feature measures ca. 15 × 23 m in area and 1.00 m high, with light Late Aztec surface pottery, several green and gray obsidian blades and flakes, and light rock rubble. Numerous looter's pits reveal construction of earth and rock-rubble fill, with a plastered stone wall exposed on the north side of one pit (Plate A146).
No surface collection made.
Classification: Small Hamlet, 5–10 people.

SITE NO. Zu-Az-45 [Zu-Az-11(M)]
Date of Survey: June 20, 1973
Location: 484850 E, 2205180 N; 19.9430° N, 99.1448° W
Natural Setting: 2245 m asl, on gently sloping ground in the Upper Salado Drainage; shallow to medium soil cover and moderate to severe erosion.
Modern Land Use: Rainfall-based agriculture.
Archaeological Remains: Variable light and light-to-moderate Late Aztec surface pottery over an area of ca. 1.80 ha. There is a trace of Late Toltec surface pottery in the south-central part of the site (no LT site defined here). There are no discernible structural remains.
No surface collection made.
Classification: Hamlet, 20–40 people.

Plate A143. Zu-Az-37, facing NE at Feature AL.

Plate A144. Zu-Az-39, facing west at Feature AR.

Plate A145. Zu-Az-44, facing west at Feature BC.

Plate A146. Zu-Az-44, stone wall exposed in looter's pit at Feature BC.

SITE NO. Zu-Az-46 [Zu-Az-9(M); Locations 20, 27]
Date of Survey: June 5, 1973
Location: 483450 E, 2206500 N; 19.9549° N, 99.1582° W
Natural Setting: 2235 m asl, on nearly level ground in the Upper Salado Drainage; shallow soil cover and moderate to severe erosion.
Modern Land Use: Rainfall-based agriculture.
Archaeological Remains: Variable light, light-to-moderate, and moderate Aztec surface pottery over an area of ca. 8.10 ha. Both Early and Late Aztec pottery occur. The Az material is mixed with approximately equal quantities of Late Toltec ceramics (Zu-LT-70); there are also a few traces of Classic surface pottery (no Classic site defined here). Obsidian blades and scrapers are abundant. There are no discernible structural remains, but amorphous rock rubble throughout the site probably represents the remnants of several ancient buildings.

We made two surface collections (Locations 20, 27):

Location	Surface Area and Context	Content
20	20 × 15 m, in fallow field	Light-to-moderate Az II, II-III and III, and light LT surface pottery; several obsidian artifacts; light-to-moderate rock rubble.
27	10 × 10 m, in fallow field	Moderate Az III and traces of LT surface pottery; numerous obsidian artifacts; one basalt mano fragment; one maguey spindle whorl; light rock rubble.

Discussion: This is one of the more substantial Aztec-period settlements in this part of the survey area. The presence of Az II and II-III Black/Orange suggests continuous occupation between Late Toltec and Late Aztec times. The Early Aztec settlement is not well defined.
Classification: Late Aztec: Small Dispersed Village, 150–300 people. Early Aztec: ?

SITE NO. Zu-Az-47 [Zu-Az-10(M); Feature AE]
Date of Survey: June 5, 1973
Location: 482450 E, 2206930 N; 19.9588° N, 99.1677° W
Natural Setting: 2205 m asl, on gently sloping ground in the Upper Salado Drainage; medium soil cover and moderate erosion.
Modern Land Use: Rainfall-based agriculture.
Archaeological Remains: This site consists of a complex mounded area measuring ca. 90 × 100 m (Feature AE), covering an area of ca. 1.00 ha. The height of this feature averages 1.00–2.50 m above the general level of the surrounding fields.

There are three distinct sub-areas (Fig. A10):
(1) an area of high mounding, up to 2.5 m high, in the northeast part of the site;
(2) an irregularly shaped area of partially exposed and well-preserved plaster floor, running diagonally from northwest to southeast across the central site area;
(3) an area of low mounding, up to 2.0 m high, near the western and southwestern edges of the site.

Appendix A: Site Descriptions

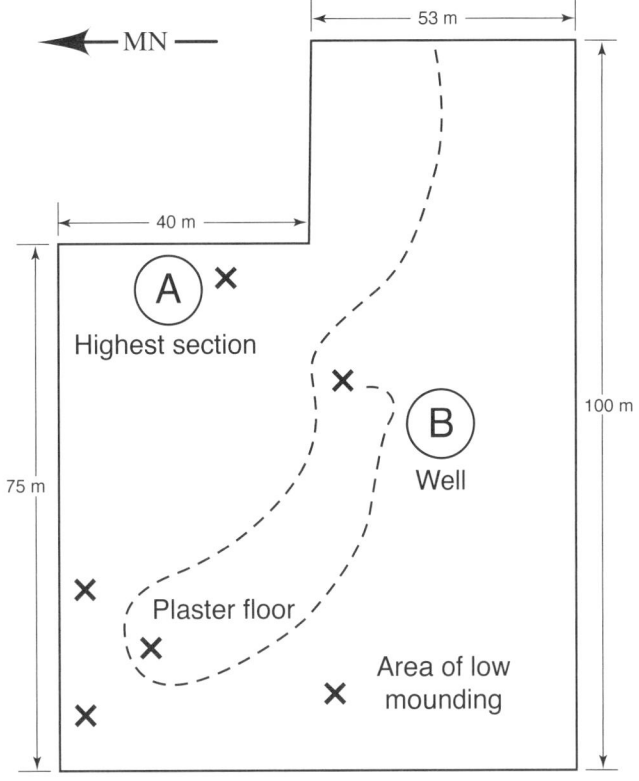

Feature AE

Figure A10. Zu-Az-47, sketch plan of site areas.

Plate A147. Zu-Az-47, stucco floor exposed in looter's pit at Feature AE.

Plate A148. Zu-Az-47, stucco floor in plaza area.

Most of the site has been extensively pitted by looters. A pit ca. 2 m deep in sub-area No. 1 has exposed at least two stucco floors in stratigraphic sequence. A lens of carbon and ash rests upon the upper floor (Plate A147). Two vertical plastered stone walls are exposed in the eastern and southern pit profiles.

The plaster flooring in the central part of the site (sub-area No. 2) appears to be approximately 10 cm thick (Plate A148). A modern well has been dug to a depth of about 2 m immediately south of the plaster flooring. The upper 90 cm of the well profile show earth and rock-rubble fill, and solid tepetate appears in this profile at about 90 cm below ground level. This well profile suggests that the central plaster surface was constructed upon a base of solid earth and rock-rubble fill, and probably functioned as an open plaza.

The entire site is covered with light-to-moderate rock rubble and substantial quantities of modern refuse. Human bones appear at several places, although there is no clear indication of formal burials. Prehispanic surface pottery is scarce, and appears to be exclusively light Late Aztec.

Discussion: This unusual site appears to represent an important ceremonial-civic complex, the largest and most complex architectural feature in this general region.

Classification: Isolated Ceremonial-Civic Precinct.

SITE NO. Zu-Az-48 [Zu-Az-24(M); Location 25]
Date of Survey: June 5, 1973
Location: 481570 E, 2209220 N; 19.9795° N, 99.1761° W
Natural Setting: 2175 m asl, on nearly level ground in the Upper Salado Drainage; medium to deep soil cover and slight to moderate erosion.
Modern Land Use: Rainfall-based agriculture. The modern town of Apaxco encroaches onto the site from the south.

Archaeological Remains: Light Late Aztec surface pottery over an area of ca. 1.90 ha. There are no structural remains, but several concentrations of amorphous rock rubble may represent the remnants of ancient buildings. We noted several green obsidian blades, a few pieces of gray obsidian debitage, and three basalt mano fragments. The Late Az material is mixed with Classic (Zu-Cl-17) and Early Toltec (Zu-ET-6) ceramics.

We made one surface collection (Location 25) over an area of ca. 8 × 10 m in a fallow field, with light Late Aztec surface pottery.

Discussion: The southern limits of this site could not be defined. It may extend southward below the modern town of Apaxco.

Classification: Small Hamlet (?), 10–20 people.

SITE NO. Zu-Az-49 [Zu-Az-8(M); Feature X]
Date of Survey: June 4, 1973
Location: 481250 E, 2206030 N; 19.9506° N, 99.1792° W
Natural Setting: 2200 m asl, on gently sloping ground in the Upper Salado Drainage; shallow soil cover and severe erosion.
Modern Land Use: The immediate site area is wasteland. The lower ground to the west is devoted to irrigation-based maize agriculture (irrigated with *agua negra*), while higher ground to the east is used for rainfall-based agriculture. The modern paved road between Apaxco and Tequixquiac crosses the northern part of the site.

Archaeological Remains: Variable light and light-to-moderate Late Aztec surface pottery over an area of ca. 3.90 ha. There is also a trace of Late Toltec ceramics (no LT site defined here). There is one definite mound (Feature X), measuring ca. 20 m in diameter and 0.50 cm high, with light Late Aztec surface pottery and moderate rock rubble (Plate A149).

No surface collection made.

Classification: Hamlet, 25–50 people.

Plate A149. Zu-Az-49, facing south at Feature X, with Cerro de la Mesa Grande in background.

SITE NO. Zu-Az-50 [Zu-Az-7(M)]
  Date of Survey: June 4, 1973
  Location: 482470 E, 2204600 N; 19.9377° N, 99.1675° W
  Natural Setting: 2205 m asl, on gently sloping ground in the Upper Salado Drainage; medium soil cover and moderate erosion.
  Modern Land Use: Irrigation-based (*agua negra*) agriculture.
  Archaeological Remains: Light Late Aztec surface pottery over an area of ca. 2.00 ha. There are no discernible structural remains and very little rock rubble.
  No surface collection made.
  Classification: Small Hamlet, 10–20 people.

SITE NO. Zu-Az-51 [Zu-Az-6(M); Location 12]
  Date of Survey: May 30, 1973
  Location: 481570 E, 2206250 N; 19.9526° N, 99.1761° W
  Natural Setting: 2195 m asl, on gently sloping ground in the Upper Salado Drainage; shallow soil cover and moderate erosion.
  Modern Land Use: Irrigation-based agriculture, using *agua negra* distributed from a storage tank ca. 800 m to the southwest of the site. A railroad line runs north-south ca. 25 m to the east of the site.
  Archaeological Remains: Light Late Aztec surface pottery over an area of ca. 0.50 ha. There are no discernible structural remains, but a concentration of amorphous rock rubble may represent the remnants of one or more ancient buildings. We noted several green obsidian blades.
  We made one surface collection (Location 12) over an area ca. 20 m in diameter in a fallow field, with light Late Aztec surface pottery, several obsidian artifacts, and moderate rock rubble.
  Classification: Small Hamlet, 5–10 people.

SITE NO. Zu-Az-52 [Zu-Az-35(M); Location 17; Feature W]
  Date of Survey: June 3, 1973
  Location: 481550 E, 2205180 N; 19.9430° N, 99.1763° W
  Natural Setting: 2195 m asl, on gently sloping ground in the Upper Salado Drainage; medium soil cover and moderate erosion.
  Modern Land Use: Rainfall-based agriculture. The site area was fallow at the time of our survey. A railroad line borders the western edge of the site.
  Archaeological Remains: Variable light and light-to-moderate Aztec surface pottery (including Az II-III and III Black/Orange ceramics) over an area of ca. 1.40 ha. The Az material is mixed with a trace of Late Toltec pottery (no LT site defined here). We noted several green and gray obsidian artifacts (mostly blades) and one maguey spindle whorl.
  There is one definite mound (Feature W) that measures ca. 16 × 24 m in area and 1.30 m high, with moderate rock rubble. Although we could discern no other structural remains, several concentrations of amorphous rock rubble may represent the remnants of ancient buildings.
  We made one surface collection (Location 17) over an area 15 × 20 m in a fallow field, with light-to-moderate Aztec surface pottery, one maguey spindle whorl, several obsidian artifacts, and light-to-moderate rock rubble.
  Discussion: The presence of Az II-III B/O suggests a possible Early Aztec occupation, but the nature of this occupation is uncertain.
  Classification: Late Aztec: Hamlet, 20–40 people. Early Aztec: ?

SITE NO. Zu-Az-53 [Zu-Az-5(M)]
  Date of Survey: May 30, 1973
  Location: 479780 E, 2206100 N; 19.9513° N, 99.1932° W
  Natural Setting: 2225 m asl, on gently sloping ground in the Upper Salado Drainage; medium soil cover and moderate erosion.
  Modern Land Use: Rainfall-based agriculture, with maguey semi-terracing. The modern town of Santa María Apaxco encroaches onto the site from the south.
  Archaeological Remains: Variable light and light-to-moderate Late Aztec surface pottery over an area of ca. 1.30 ha. There are no discernible structural remains. Because of modern occupation, we were unable to determine the southern limits of the site.
  No surface collection made.
  Discussion: This site area is uncertain.
  Classification: Hamlet (?), 20–40 people.

Plate A150. Zu-Az-56, example of earth-faced terrace.

SITE NO. Zu-Az-54 [Zu-Az-3(M); Feature M]
Date of Survey: May 28, 1973
Location: 477570 E, 2206320 N; 19.9532° N, 99.2144° W
Natural Setting: 2355 m asl, on gently sloping ground atop a prominent low hill in the Upper Salado Drainage; shallow soil cover and moderate to severe erosion.
Modern Land Use: Pasture.
Archaeological Remains: The site consists of a single mound (Feature M) that measures ca. 25 m in diameter and 1.50 m high, with very light Late Aztec surface pottery and moderate rock rubble. There is a nineteenth-century stone hacienda marker atop the mound. We noted the poorly preserved remnants of several possible prehispanic stone-faced terraces downslope from Feature M.
No surface collection made.
Discussion: The height of the mound, its hilltop setting, and the scarcity of surface pottery suggest a ceremonial-civic, rather than a domestic residential, function.
Classification: Isolated Ceremonial-Civic Precinct.

SITE NO. Zu-Az-55 [Zu-Az-1(M)]
Date of Survey: May 21, 1973
Location: 476070 E, 2205030 N; 19.9416° N, 99.2287° W
Natural Setting: 2295 m asl, on gently sloping ground in the Upper Salado Drainage; medium soil cover and moderate erosion.
Modern Land Use: Rainfall-based agriculture. A railroad line runs north-south along the eastern edge of the site area.
Archaeological Remains: Variable light and light-to-moderate Late Aztec surface pottery over an area of ca. 2.00 ha. There are no discernible structural remains and very little rock rubble.
No surface collection made.
Classification: Small Hamlet, 15–30 people.

SITE NO. Zu-Az-56 [Zu-Az-2(M); Location 2]
Date of Survey: May 21, 1973
Location: 475700 E, 2203970 N; 19.9320° N, 99.2322° W
Natural Setting: 2280 m asl, on moderately sloping ground in the Upper Salado Drainage; shallow soil cover and severe erosion, with patches of bare tepetate.
Modern Land Use: Marginal rainfall-based agriculture.
Archaeological Remains: Variable light, light-to-moderate, and moderate Late Aztec surface pottery over an area of ca. 4.50 ha. There is also a trace of Late Toltec material (no LT site defined here). There are no discernible prehispanic structural remains, but the site area contains several large earth terraces of uncertain age (Plate A150)—we suspect they are Colonial or nineteenth-century constructions, but they could be older. The terraces measure 1.0–1.5 m high on the downhill side, ca. 10 m wide, and extend for considerable distances across the entire site area. There is very little rock rubble.
We made a surface collection (Location 2) over an area ca. 15 × 20 m across three terraces, with light-to-moderate Late Az surface pottery, several obsidian artifacts, one basalt mano fragment, and very little rock rubble. Virtually all surface pottery occurs along the terrace faces.
Discussion: The age of the terracing is uncertain. Because this site lies on the far western edge of our survey airphoto, its western limits could not be defined.
Classification: Hamlet (?), 45–90 people.

SITE NO. Zu-Az-57 [Zu-Az-44b(M)]
Date of Survey: July 5, 1973
Location: 476650 E, 2205070 N; 19.9419° N, 99.2231° W
Natural Setting: 2275 m asl, on gently sloping ground in the Upper Salado Drainage; shallow soil cover and moderate erosion.
Modern Land Use: Rainfall-based agriculture.

Archaeological Remains: Light Late Aztec surface pottery over an area of ca. 1.50 ha. There are no discernible structural remains.

No surface collection made.

Discussion: This site is probably a detached component of the larger Late Aztec settlement to the east (Zu-Az-58).

Classification: Small Hamlet, 10–20 people.

SITE NO. Zu-Az-58 [Zu-Az-44a(M); Location 47; Feature DB]
Date of Survey: July 5, 1973
Location: 477820 E, 2205070 N; 19.9419° N, 99.2120° W
Natural Setting: 2260 m asl, on gently sloping ground in the Upper Salado Drainage; shallow soil cover and moderate to severe erosion.

Modern Land Use: Pasture and rainfall-based agriculture. A modern lime quarry cuts into the south-central part of the site, and has probably destroyed some prehispanic features.

Archaeological Remains: Variable light and light-to-moderate Late Aztec surface pottery over an area of ca. 21.00 ha. There are also traces of glazed Colonial ceramics.

There is one definite mound (Feature DB) in a plowed field at the northern tip of the site (the mound itself is unplowed). This feature measures ca. 10 × 15 m in area and 0.20 m high, with light and light-to-moderate Late Az surface pottery, a few obsidian blades and scrapers, three basalt mano fragments, three basalt metate fragments, and light-to-moderate rock rubble.

We made one surface collection (Location 47) from an area of ca. 15 × 15 m in an unplowed area in the central part of the site, with light Late Aztec surface pottery and numerous obsidian artifacts.

Discussion: The site may originally have extended another 50–100 m farther south, into the area now covered by the modern limestone quarry. This is the most substantial Late Aztec settlement in this part of the survey area.

Classification: Large Dispersed Village (?), 400–800 people.

SITE NO. Zu-Az-59 [Zu-Az-43(M)]
Date of Survey: July 8, 1973
Location: 478700 E, 2203500 N; 19.9278° N, 99.2035° W
Natural Setting: 2245 m asl, on gently sloping ground in the Upper Salado Drainage; shallow soil cover and moderate erosion.

Modern Land Use: Rainfall-based agriculture. A modern dirt road borders the western edge of the site.

Archaeological Remains: Light Late Aztec surface pottery over an area of ca. 0.30 ha. There are no discernible structural remains.

No surface collection made.

Discussion: Probably a detached segment of the larger Late Aztec settlement (Zu-Az-58) farther west.

Classification: Small Hamlet, 5–10 people.

SITE NO. Zu-Az-60 [Zu-Az-4(M); Features N, O, P, Q]
Date of Survey: May 31, 1973
Location: 481220 E, 2204300 N; 19.9350° N, 99.1795° W
Natural Setting: 2205 m asl, on gently sloping ground in the Upper Salado Drainage; shallow soil cover and moderate to severe erosion. A major *barranca* cuts through the northern part of the site.

Modern Land Use: Rainfall-based agriculture. A railroad line runs through the length of the site, and there is a modern dirt road along the site's eastern edge.

Archaeological Remains: Variable light and light-to-moderate Late Aztec surface pottery over an area of ca. 10.40 ha, with some slightly overlapping admixture of Late Toltec material (Zu-LT-72) on the southwestern edge of the site. Both Aztec III and IV Black/Orange surface pottery occur.

There are four discernible mounds (Features N, O, P, Q):

Fea.	Area and Context	Height	Content
N	20 × 15 m, in unplowed field	0.30 m	Light-to-moderate Late Az surface pottery, several green obsidian blades, light-to-moderate rock rubble. Surface collection made over area 10 × 20 m.
O	14 × 10 m, in unplowed field, ca. 50 m SSE of Fea. N	0.20 m	Light Late Az surface pottery, several green and gray obsidian blades, two basalt mano fragments, light-to-moderate rock rubble.
P	9 × 12 m, in unplowed field, ca. 60 m south of Fea. N	0.30 m	Light Late Az surface pottery, several green obsidian artifacts, one ground stone scraper, one ground stone pestle, light-to-moderate rock rubble.
Q	8 × 8 m, in unplowed field	0.10 m	Light Late Az pottery, several green obsidian blades, light-to-moderate rock rubble.

Discussion: The presence of both Az III and IV Black/Orange surface pottery indicates that this locality was occupied from Late Az times into the Early Colonial period.

Classification: Small Dispersed Village, 150–300 people.

SITE NO. Zu-Az-61 [Zu-Az-66(M)]
Date of Survey: July 16, 1973
Location: 483300 E, 2203000 N; 19.9233° N, 99.1596° W
Natural Setting: 2200 m asl, on gently sloping ground in the Upper Salado Drainage; medium soil cover and moderate erosion.

Modern Land Use: Irrigation-based agriculture (using *agua negra*).

Archaeological Remains: Light Late Aztec surface pottery over an area of ca. 1.40 ha, partially overlapping with Classic occupation (Zu-Cl-27) in the northern part of the Az site. There are no discernible structural remains.

No surface collection made.

Classification: Small Hamlet, 5–10 people.

SITE NO. Zu-Az-62 [Zu-Az-70(M)]
Date of Survey: ca. June 26, 1973
Location: 482700 E, 2201350 N; 19.9084° N, 99.1653° W
Natural Setting: 2245 m asl, on gently sloping ground in the Upper Salado Drainage; medium soil cover and moderate erosion.

Modern Land Use: Rainfall-based agriculture.

Archaeological Remains: Light Late Aztec surface pottery over an area of ca. 1.50 ha. There are no discernible structural remains, although a concentration of amorphous rock rubble in the central part of the site may represent the remnants of an ancient building.

No surface collection made.

Classification: Small Hamlet, 10–20 people.

SITE NO. Zu-Az-63 [Zu-Az-67(M)]
Date of Survey: July 16, 1973
Location: 483880 E, 2202250 N; 19.9165° N, 99.1540° W
Natural Setting: 2210 m asl, on gently sloping ground in the Upper Salado Drainage; medium soil cover and moderate erosion.

Modern Land Use: Irrigation-based agriculture (using *agua negra*). A modern irrigation canal crosses the northern tip of the site.

Archaeological Remains: Variable light and light-to-moderate Late Aztec surface pottery over an area of ca. 2.10 ha. There are no discernible structural remains.
No surface collection made.
Classification: Hamlet, 20–40 people.

SITE NO. Zu-Az-64 [Zu-Az-68(M)]
Date of Survey: July 16, 1973
Location: 484130 E, 2202570 N; 19.9194° N, 99.1516° W
Natural Setting: 2215 m asl, on gently sloping ground in the Upper Salado Drainage; medium soil cover and moderate erosion.
Modern Land Use: Irrigation-based agriculture (using *agua negra*). A modern irrigation canal cuts across the southeastern edge of the site.
Archaeological Remains: Light Late Aztec surface pottery over an area of ca. 2.40 ha. There are no discernible structural remains.
No surface collection made.
Classification: Small Hamlet, 15–30.

SITE NO. Zu-Az-65 [Zu-Az-69(M)]
Date of Survey: July 16, 1973
Location: 484680 E, 2202630 N; 19.9200° N, 99.1464° W
Natural Setting: 2210 m asl, on gently sloping ground in the Upper Salado Drainage; medium soil cover and moderate erosion.
Modern Land Use: Irrigation-based agriculture (using *agua negra*). A modern irrigation canal cuts across the northwestern tip of the site.
Archaeological Remains: Variable light and light-to-moderate Late Aztec surface pottery over an area of ca. 2.80 ha. There are no discernible structural remains.
No surface collection made.
Classification: Hamlet, 25–50 people.

SITE NO. Zu-Az-66 [Zu-Az-13(M); Features AZ, BA; Location 39]
Date of Survey: June 18, 1973
Location: 486200 E, 2203530 N; 19.9281° N, 99.1319° W
Natural Setting: 2225 m asl, on gently sloping ground in the Upper Salado Drainage; deep soil cover and slight erosion.
Modern Land Use: Rainfall-based agriculture.
Archaeological Remains: Variable light and light-to-moderate Late Aztec surface pottery over an area of ca. 1.90 ha. The Late Az material is mixed with partially overlapping Classic (Zu-Cl-32) and Early Toltec (Zu-ET-9) ceramics. Both Aztec III and IV Black/Orange surface pottery occur.
There are two discernible mounds (Features AZ, BA):

Fea.	Area and Context	Height	Content
AZ	20 × 13 m, in plowed field	0.50 m	Light Cl and ET and very light Az surface pottery, several obsidian artifacts, moderate rock rubble.
BA	24 m dia., in partly plowed field	1.50 m	Very light Aztec surface pottery, several obsidian artifacts.

We made one surface collection (Location 39) over an area of ca. 10 × 15 m in an unplowed field, with light-to-moderate Cl and ET and light Late Az surface pottery, several obsidian artifacts, and moderate rock rubble.
Discussion: The presence of both Aztec III and IV Black/Orange surface pottery indicates that this locality was occupied from Late Az times into the Early Colonial period.
Classification: Small Hamlet, 10–20 people.

SITE NO. Zu-Az-67 [Zu-Az-14(M)]
Date of Survey: June 18, 1973
Location: 486680 E, 2203550 N; 19.9283° N, 99.1273° W
Natural Setting: 2230 m asl, on gently sloping ground in the Upper Salado Drainage; deep soil cover and slight erosion.
Modern Land Use: Rainfall-based agriculture.
Archaeological Remains: Light Late Aztec surface pottery over an area of 0.50 ha. There are no discernible structural remains.
No surface collection made.
Classification: Small Hamlet, 5–10 people.

SITE NO. Zu-Az-68 [Zu-Az-21(M); Location 35]
Date of Survey: June 14, 1973
Location: 487720 E, 2203950 N; 19.9319° N, 99.1173° W
Natural Setting: 2250 m asl, on gently sloping ground in the Upper Salado Drainage; medium soil cover and moderate erosion.
Modern Land Use: Rainfall-based agriculture, with maguey semi-terracing.
Archaeological Remains: Variable light and light-to-moderate Late Aztec and partially overlapping Late Toltec (Zu-LT-61) surface pottery over an area of ca. 1.10 ha. We noted several green obsidian blades, one maguey spindle whorl, and one basalt metate fragment. There are no discernible structural remains, but several concentrations of amorphous rock rubble may represent the remnants of ancient buildings.
We made one surface collection (Location 35) over an area of 15 × 15 m in a fallow field, with light-to-moderate LT and light Late Az surface pottery, several obsidian artifacts, and moderate-to-heavy rock rubble (Plate A151).
Discussion: The apparent absence of Early Aztec material indicates that this locality was abandoned after LT times and reoccupied during the Late Aztec period.
Classification: Small Hamlet, 10–20 people.

SITE NO. Zu-Az-69 [Zu-Az-20(M)]
Date of Survey: June 14, 1973
Location: 488100 E, 2203970 N; 19.9321° N, 99.1137° W
Natural Setting: 2245 m asl, on gently sloping ground in the Upper Salado Drainage; medium soil cover and slight to moderate erosion.
Modern Land Use: Rainfall-based agriculture, with maguey semi-terracing. A modern paved road borders the south edge of the site.
Archaeological Remains: Variable light and light-to-moderate Late Aztec surface pottery over an area of ca. 0.40 ha. There are no discernible structural remains.
No surface collection made.
Classification: Small Hamlet, 5–10 people.

SITE NO. Zu-Az-70 [Zu-Az-19(M)]
Date of Survey: June 14, 1973
Location: 488400 E, 2204130 N; 19.9335° N, 99.1108° W
Natural Setting: 2255 m asl, on gently sloping ground in the Upper Salado Drainage; medium soil cover and slight to moderate erosion.
Modern Land Use: Rainfall-based agriculture. A modern paved road borders the southern side of the site.
Archaeological Remains: Variable light and light-to-moderate Late Aztec surface pottery over an area of ca. 0.90 ha. There are no discernible structural remains.
No surface collection made.
Classification: Small Hamlet, 10–20 people.

Plate A151. Zu-Az-68, facing west over Location 35.

SITE NO. Zu-Az-71 [Zu-Az-18(M); Location 9]
  Date of Survey: June 3, 14, 1973
  Location: 488780 E, 2204320 N; 19.9353° N, 99.1072° W
  Natural Setting: 2260 m asl, on gently sloping ground in the Upper Salado Drainage; deep soil cover and slight erosion.
  Modern Land Use: Rainfall-based agriculture, with some drainage ditches and earth terracing in the general site area. The modern town of Tlapanaloya encroaches onto the site from the east. A modern dirt road crosses the central site area, and there is a modern paved road bordering the southern edge of the site.
  Archaeological Remains: Variable light and light-to-moderate Late Aztec surface pottery over an area of ca. 1.40 ha. The Late Az material is mixed with more substantial Classic (Zu-Cl-33) and Late Toltec (Zu-LT-60) ceramics. We noted numerous green obsidian blades and scrapers.
  No discernible structural remains can be associated with the Aztec occupation (see Zu-Cl-33 and LT-LT-60 site descriptions for mounds that probably date to those earlier periods).
  We made one surface collection (Location 9) over an area of ca. 8 × 10 m in a fallow field (Plate A152), with light Late Az and light-to-moderate Cl and LT surface pottery, several obsidian artifacts, and light-to-moderate rock rubble. There is some Aztec II-III Black/Orange.
  Discussion: The site may extend farther to the east below modern Tlapanaloya.
  Classification: Small Hamlet (?), 15–30 people.

SITE NO. Zu-Az-72 [Zu-Az-22(M), Zu-Az-144(J); Locations 37-M, 88-J]
  Date of Survey: June 18, Oct. 31, 1973
  Location: 489070 E, 2203100 N; 19.9242° N, 99.1044° W
  Natural Setting: 2300 m asl, on gently sloping ground atop a broad, low ridge in the Upper Salado Drainage; medium soil cover and moderate erosion.
  Modern Land Use: Rainfall-based agriculture. The modern town of Tlapanaloya encroaches onto the site from the east. Several modern dirt roads cross the site area.
  Archaeological Remains: Variable light and light-to-moderate Aztec surface pottery over an area of ca. 17.20 ha; both Early and Late Aztec material is present. We noted several green and gray obsidian artifacts. The northern section of the Aztec site contains lighter Late Toltec surface pottery (Zu-LT-59) and also partially overlaps with Classic occupation (Zu-Cl-34).
  We made two surface collections in the Aztec site (Locations 37-M, 88-J):

Location	Area and Context	Content
37-M	15 m dia., in fallow field (Plate A153)	Light LT and light Az surface pottery, including Aztec II B/O; numerous obsidian artifacts; light rock rubble.
88-J	10 × 10 m, in maize field	Light-to-moderate Cl and light Az surface pottery; several obsidian blades; moderate rock rubble.

  Discussion: This is one of the few Aztec sites in the Zumpango Region that contains both Early and Late Aztec surface pottery. There appears to have been continuous occupation here from LT through Late Az times. The Early Az occupation remains poorly defined. Because of modern occupation, we were unable to determine the eastern limits of the Az site.
  Classification: Late Aztec: Small Dispersed Village (?), 170–340 people. Early Aztec: ?

Plate A152. Zu-Az-71, facing NE over Location 9.

Plate A153. Zu-Az-72, facing NE over Location 37-M.

Plate A154. Zu-Az-73, facing north over Location 38.

SITE NO. Zu-Az-73 [Zu-Az-23(M); Location 38]
  Date of Survey: June 18, 1973
  Location: 488280 E, 2203180 N; 19.9249° N, 99.1120° W
  Natural Setting: 2280 m asl, on gently sloping ground atop a low, broad ridge in the Upper Salado Drainage; medium soil cover and moderate erosion.
  Modern Land Use: Rainfall-based agriculture, with maguey semi-terracing.
  Archaeological Remains: Variable light and light-to-moderate Late Aztec surface pottery over an area of ca. 15.20 ha; there may also be a little Az II-III and traces of Late Toltec ceramics (no LT site defined at this locality). There are no definite structural remains.
  We made one surface collection (Location 38) over an area ca. 5 × 10 m in a fallow field (Plate A154), with light-to-moderate Late Az surface pottery (including some Panuco VI tradeware), numerous obsidian artifacts, and light rock rubble.
  Discussion: Like nearby site Zu-Az-72, this site is one of the few Aztec sites in the Zumpango Region that contains Az II-III B/O ceramics. The possible Early Az occupation remains poorly defined.
  Classification: Late Aztec: Small Dispersed Village, possibly an outlier of Aztec Tlapanaloya, 150–300 people. Early Aztec: ?

SITE NO. Zu-Az-74 [Zu-Az-25(J); Feature AD]
  Date of Survey: June 14, 1973
  Location: 491350 E, 2204400 N; 19.9360° N, 99.0827° W
  Natural Setting: 2360 m asl, on nearly level ground in the Upper Salado Drainage; medium soil cover and moderate erosion.
  Modern Land Use: Rainfall-based agriculture. A modern dirt road crosses the northern end of the site.
  Archaeological Remains: Light Late Aztec surface pottery over an area of ca. 5.10 ha. The northern section of the Az site overlaps onto the southern part of a more extensive Late Toltec site (Zu-LT-30). There is one discernible mound (Feature AD) in the northern part of the site. This feature measures ca. 20 m in diameter and 0.50 m high, with moderate rock rubble and light Late Az and LT surface pottery.
  We made one surface collection from the entire surface of Feature AD.
  Discussion: The apparent absence of Early Aztec pottery suggests that this locality was abandoned after LT times and reoccupied during the Late Aztec period.
  Classification: Hamlet, 25–50 people.

SITE NO. Zu-Az-75 [Zu-Az-23(J); Feature AC]
  Date of Survey: June 17, 1973
  Location: 491130 E, 2203900 N; 19.9315° N, 99.0848° W
  Natural Setting: 2350 m asl, on gently sloping ground in the Upper Salado Drainage; shallow soil cover and severe erosion.
  Modern Land Use: Marginal pasture and wasteland.
  Archaeological Remains: The site consists of a single low mound (Feature AC), measuring ca. 20 m in diameter and 0.15 m high, with light-to-moderate Late Aztec surface pottery (Az IV B/O abundant) and moderate rock rubble.
  No surface collection made.
  Discussion: The abundance of both Az III and IV B/O pottery indicates continuous occupation from Late Az into Early Colonial times.
  Classification: Small Hamlet, 5–10 people.

SITE NO. Zu-Az-76 [Zu-Az-22(J); Feature AB]
   Date of Survey: June 17, 1973
   Location: 490850 E, 2203470 N; 19.9276° N, 99.0874° W
   Natural Setting: 2340 m asl, on gently sloping ground in the Upper Salado Drainage; shallow soil cover and severe erosion.
   Modern Land Use: Rainfall-based agriculture.
   Archaeological Remains: Light Late Aztec surface pottery over an area of ca. 2.60 ha. The Late Az material is mixed with approximately equal quantities of Late Toltec ceramics (Zu-LT-56). There is a single low mound (Feature AB) in a plowed field in the central part of the site. This feature measures ca. 25 m in diameter and 0.20 m high, with light Late Az and LT surface pottery and moderate rock rubble.

   A concentration of amorphous rock rubble near the northern edge of the site may represent the remnants of another prehispanic structure. No surface collection made.
   Discussion: The apparent absence of Early Aztec surface pottery suggests that this locality was abandoned after LT times and reoccupied during the Late Aztec period.
   Classification: Hamlet, 20–40 people.

SITE NO. Zu-Az-77 [Zu-Az-24(J)]
   Date of Survey: June 14, 1973
   Location: 492570 E, 2204150 N; 19.9337° N, 99.0710° W
   Natural Setting: 2345 m asl, on nearly level ground in the Upper Salado Drainage; medium soil cover and moderate erosion.
   Modern Land Use: Rainfall-based agriculture.
   Archaeological Remains: Light-to-moderate Late Aztec surface pottery over an area of ca. 0.90 ha. There are no discernible structural remains, but several concentrations of amorphous rock rubble may represent the remnants of one or more ancient buildings. No surface collection made.
   Classification: Small Hamlet, 15–30 people.

SITE NO. Zu-Az-78 [Zu-Az-8(J); Features K, L]
   Date of Survey: May 28, 1973
   Location: 493530 E, 2203200 N; 19.9252° N, 99.0618° W
   Natural Setting: 2330 m asl, on gently sloping ground in the Upper Salado Drainage; medium soil cover and moderate erosion.
   Modern Land Use: Rainfall-based agriculture. The site area had been recently plowed and planted at the time of our survey. A modern dirt road borders the western edge of the site.
   Archaeological Remains: Variable light and light-to-moderate Late Aztec surface pottery over an area of ca. 1.80 ha. There are also traces of Late Toltec ceramics (no LT site designated here).

   We identified two mounds (Features K and L) at either end of the site, and a concentration of amorphous rock rubble in the central part of the site may represent the remnants of another prehispanic building.

Fea.	Area and Context	Height	Content
K	ca. 20 m dia., in plowed field	Very low	Light-to-moderate Late Az surface pottery (mainly Az IV B/O, some Az III B/O), numerous obsidian artifacts, moderate rock rubble.
L	ca. 20 m dia., in plowed field (Plate A155)	0.15 m	Light Late Az pottery (both Az III and IV B/O noted), several obsidian artifacts, one basalt mano, moderate rock rubble.

No surface collection made.
   Discussion: The abundance of Az IV Black/Orange pottery suggests that the dominant occupation may be Early Colonial period.
   Classification: Hamlet, 25–50 people.

SITE NO. Zu-Az-79 [Zu-Az-9(J); Location 2; Features B, D, E, F, G, H, I, J]
   Date of Survey: May 24, 1973
   Location: 495130 E, 2202950 N; 19.9229° N, 99.0465° W
   Natural Setting: 2310 m asl, on gently sloping ground in the Upper Salado Drainage; medium soil cover and moderate to severe erosion.
   Modern Land Use: Rainfall-based agriculture.
   Archaeological Remains: Variable light, light-to-moderate, and moderate Late Aztec surface pottery over an area of ca. 19.80 ha (both Aztec III and IV Black/Orange pottery occur). The Late Az material is mixed with approximately equal proportions of Late Toltec ceramics in the northern part of the Aztec site (Zu-LT-42).

   We identified eight mounds (Features B, D, E, F, G, H, I, J) throughout the site area. Three of these are clustered in the east-central site area; the other five are located along the southern edge of the site (where Features G, H, I, and J are tightly clustered). Several concentrations of amorphous rock rubble in other parts of the site may represent the remnants of other ancient buildings.

Fea.	Area and Context	Height	Content
B	ca. 20 m dia., in unplowed field	0.75 m	Very light Late Az and Colonial surface pottery, moderate rock rubble. A questionable feature—may be a modern rock pile.
D	ca. 20 m dia., in plowed field (Plate A156)	1.00 m	Light-to-moderate Late Az surface pottery, moderate rock rubble.
E	ca. 15 m dia., in plowed field	0.30 m	Light Late Az surface pottery, moderate rock rubble.
F	ca. 15 m dia., in plowed field	0.25 m	Light-to-moderate Late Az surface pottery (Az IV B/O noted), a little obsidian, moderate rock rubble.
G	ca. 20 m dia., in plowed field	0.25 m	Light-to-moderate Late Az surface pottery (both Az III and IV B/O), several obsidian artifacts, heavy rock rubble.
H	ca. 15 m dia., in plowed field	Very low	Moderate Late Az surface pottery (both Az III and IV B/O), several obsidian artifacts, one basalt mano, one maguey spindle whorl, light rock rubble.
I	ca. 15 m dia., in plowed field	0.10 m	Moderate Late Az surface pottery, one basalt mano, several obsidian artifacts, heavy rock rubble.
J	ca. 20 m dia., in plowed field	0.10 m	Moderate Late Az surface pottery (both Az III and IV B/O), numerous obsidian artifacts, several basalt manos, moderate rock rubble. Surface collection made over an area 10 × 10 m at the center of the mound.

In addition to the surface collection at Feature J, we made a second surface collection (Location 2), over an area of 10 × 10 m in a plowed field in the northern part of the site, in an area of mixed light Late Az and LT occupation.
   Discussion: The presence of Aztec IV Black/Orange surface pottery indicates some Early Colonial-period occupation. This is one of the largest Aztec-period sites in this part of the Zumpango Region. The apparent absence of Early Az surface pottery suggests that this locality was abandoned after LT times and reoccupied during the Late Az period.
   Classification: Large Nucleated Village, 500–1000 people.

Plate A155. Zu-Az-78, facing SW at Feature L.

Plate A156. Zu-Az-79, facing south at Feature D.

Plate A157. Zu-Az-80, facing north at Feature A.

SITE NO. Zu-Az-80 [Zu-Az-10(J); Features A, C]
  Date of Survey: May 24, 1973
  Location: 495470 E, 2202970 N; 19.9231° N, 99.0433° W
  Natural Setting: 2315 m asl, on gently sloping ground in the Upper Salado Drainage; medium soil cover and moderate erosion.
  Modern Land Use: Rainfall-based agriculture.
  Archaeological Remains: Variable light and light-to-moderate Late Aztec surface pottery over an area of ca. 2.80 ha; both Aztec III and IV Black/Orange ceramics occur, and there are some glazed Colonial-period sherds. We noted several obsidian artifacts.

There are two discernible mounds (Features A, C) in the western part of the site, and several concentrations of amorphous rock rubble elsewhere may represent the remnants of other ancient buildings.

Fea.	Area and Context	Height	Content
A	15 m dia., in plowed field (Plate A157)	0.50 m	Light-to-moderate Late Az surface pottery (plus a few glazed Colonial-period sherds), one maguey spindle whorl, one basalt mano fragment, several green obsidian blades, moderate rock rubble. Surface collection made over entire mound surface.
C	20 m dia., in plowed field	0.30 m	Light-to-moderate Late Az surface pottery, several obsidian blades, moderate rock rubble.

  Discussion: This site probably represents a detached segment of the larger nearby Zu-Az-79 settlement. The presence of both Aztec III and IV Black/Orange surface pottery indicates that this locality was occupied from Late Az times into the Early Colonial period.
  Classification: Hamlet, 40–80 people.

SITE NO. Zu-Az-81 [Zu-Az-65(J); Features CE, CF, CG]
  Date of Survey: July 12, 1973
  Location: 495900 E, 2201880 N; 19.9132° N, 99.0392° W
  Natural Setting: 2310 m asl, on gently sloping ground in the Upper Salado Drainage, just northwest of the divide between the Upper Salado and BOM drainages; medium to deep soil cover and moderate erosion.
  Modern Land Use: Rainfall-based agriculture. A modern dirt road borders the southern edge of the site.
  Archaeological Remains: Variable light and light-to-moderate Late Aztec surface pottery over an area of ca. 20.30 ha. The Late Az material is mixed with partially overlapping Late Toltec ceramics in the eastern part of the site (Zu-LT-43). There are three discernible mounds (Features CE, CF, CG), and several concentrations of amorphous rock rubble elsewhere in the site area may represent a few other ancient buildings.

Fea.	Area and Context	Height	Content
CE	20 m dia., in unplowed field	0.30 m	Light-to-moderate Late Az and very light LT surface pottery, several obsidian artifacts.
CF	20 m dia., in unplowed field	0.25 m	Light-to-moderate Late Az and light LT surface pottery, several obsidian artifacts.
CG	15 m dia., in plowed field	Very low	Light-Late Az and very light LT surface pottery, several obsidian artifacts.

No surface collection made.
  Discussion: Because the site is at the eastern edge of our survey area, its eastern limits could not be defined. The apparent absence of Early Aztec surface pottery suggests that this locality was abandoned after LT times and reoccupied during the Late Aztec period.
  Classification: Small Dispersed Village (?), 250–500 people.

SITE NO. Zu-Az-82 [Zu-Az-66(J); Feature CD]
Date of Survey: July 11, 1973
Location: 495380 E, 2201780 N; 19.9123° N, 99.0441° W
Natural Setting: 2300 m asl, on gently sloping ground in the Upper Salado Drainage, just northwest of the divide between the Upper Salado and BOM drainages; shallow soil cover and severe erosion.
Modern Land Use: Marginal pasture.
Archaeological Remains: Variable light and light-to-moderate Late Aztec surface pottery over an area of ca. 5.20 ha. The Late Az material is mixed with partially overlapping Late Toltec ceramics (Zu-LT-45) in the south-central part of the site.

There is one low mound (Feature CD) in the south-central part of the site. This feature measures ca. 15 m in diameter and up to 10 cm high, with moderate LT and very light Aztec surface pottery. We made a surface collection from the entire mound surface.

Several concentrations of amorphous rock rubble in the northwestern part of the site may represent the remnants of a few other ancient buildings.
Discussion: The apparent absence of Early Aztec surface pottery suggests that this locality was abandoned after LT times and reoccupied during the Late Aztec period.
Classification: Hamlet, 50–100 people.

SITE NO. Zu-Az-83, Zu-Az-84 [Zu-Az-63a, 63b(J); Features BZ, CA, CB, CC]
Date of Survey: July 11, 1973
Location:
Zu-Az-83: 494970 E, 2201000 N; 19.9053° N, 99.0481° W;
Zu-Az-84: 495220 E, 2200750 N; 19.9030° N, 99.0457° W
Natural Setting: 2330 m asl, on gently sloping ground in the Upper Salado Drainage, near the divide between the Upper Salado and BOM drainages; medium soil cover and moderate erosion.
Modern Land Use: Rainfall-based agriculture. Much of the site area was fallow at the time of our survey.
Archaeological Remains: This site consists of two closely spaced concentrations of variable light and light-to-moderate Late Aztec surface pottery and rock rubble: a northern area (Zu-Az-83), extending over ca. 1.80 ha, and a southern area (Zu-Az-84) extending over ca. 3.10 ha. The two sub-areas are separated by a gap of ca. 150 m that lacks Aztec surface pottery.

The Aztec occupation is mixed with partially overlapping Classic (Zu-Cl-39) and Late Toltec (Zu-LT-47) surface pottery in the northern and southern sub-areas, respectively.

There are four discernible mounds (Features BZ, CA, CB, CC) with Aztec surface pottery in that part of the site with overlapping Late Toltec occupation.

Fea.	Area and Context	Height	Content
BZ	40 m dia., in unplowed field	0.20 m	Light-to-moderate LT and very light Az surface pottery, moderate rock rubble.
CA	15 m dia., in unplowed field	0.15 m	Light-to-moderate LT and very light Az surface pottery, moderate rock rubble.
CB	15 m dia., in unplowed field	0.10 m	Light LT and Late Az surface pottery, moderate rock rubble.
CC	8 × 10 m, in plowed field	0.20 m	Light-to-moderate LT and very light Az surface pottery, moderate rock rubble. Surface collection made over entire mound area.

Discussion: The apparent absence of Az II B/O pottery suggests that this locality was abandoned after LT times and reoccupied during the Late Aztec period.
Classification: Hamlet, 50–100 people.

SITE NO. Zu-Az-85 [Zu-ET-1(J); Location 40?]
Date of Survey: July 16, 1973
Location: 495450 E, 2200130 N; 19.8974° N, 99.0435° W
Natural Setting: 2330 m asl, on nearly level ground atop a broad, low ridge in the Upper Salado Drainage, very close to the divide between the Upper Salado and BOM drainages; shallow soil cover and moderate erosion.
Modern Land Use: Rainfall-based agriculture.
Archaeological Remains: Variable light and light-to-moderate Late Aztec surface pottery over an area of ca. 0.40 ha. The Late Az material is mixed with much more extensive Classic (Zu-Cl-40) and Early Toltec (Zu-ET-16) ceramics. No discernible structural remains can be associated with the Aztec occupation.

No surface collection made.
Classification: Small Hamlet, 5–10 people.

SITE NO. Zu-Az-86 [Zu-Az-69(J)]
Date of Survey: July 15, 1973
Location: 494400 E, 2202030 N; 19.9146° N, 99.0535° W
Natural Setting: 2350 m asl, on gently sloping ground in the Upper Salado Drainage; shallow soil cover and moderate erosion.
Modern Land Use: Pasture.
Archaeological Remains: Variable light and light-to-moderate Late Aztec surface pottery over an area of ca. 1.00 ha. There are no discernible structural remains, but a concentration of amorphous rock rubble in the southern part of the site may represent an ancient building.

No surface collection made.
Classification: Small Hamlet, 10–20 people.

SITE NO. Zu-Az-87 [Zu-Az-31(J), Zu-Az-68(J); Features AR, CM, CN]
Date of Survey: June 23, July 18, 1973
Location: 493500 E, 2202720 N; 19.9208° N, 99.0621° W
Natural Setting: 2340 m asl, on gently to moderately sloping ground in the Upper Salado Drainage, very near the divide between the Upper Salado and BOM drainages; shallow soil cover and severe erosion.
Modern Land Use: Pasture.
Archaeological Remains: Variable light and light-to-moderate Late Aztec surface pottery (both Aztec III and IV Black/Orange) over an area of ca. 8.00 ha. There are three discernible mounds (Features AR, CM, CN), and concentrations of amorphous rock rubble in three other places may represent the remnants of other ancient buildings. We noted the possible remnants of a badly disturbed human burial (scattered human bones and portions of four plainware bowls) ca. 50 m NW of Feature CM.

Fea.	Area and Context	Height	Content
AR	20 m dia.	0.15 m	Light-to-moderate Late Az surface pottery (Az IV B/O). Section of stone wall base.
CM	15 m dia. (Plate A158)	0.50 m	Light-to-moderate Late Az surface pottery (Az III and IV B/O), numerous obsidian artifacts, one basalt mano fragment, moderate rock rubble.
CN	10 m dia.	0.10 m	Light-to-moderate Late Az surface pottery, several obsidian artifacts, moderate rock rubble.

No surface collection made.
Discussion: The presence of both Aztec III and IV Black/Orange pottery suggests that occupation continued from Late Az times into the Colonial period.
Classification: Small Dispersed Village, 100–200 people.

Plate A158. Zu-Az-87, facing NW at Feature CM.

SITE NO. Zu-Az-88 [Zu-Az-67(J)]
Date of Survey: July 15, 1973
Location: 494180 E, 2200300 N; 19.8989° N, 99.0556° W
Natural Setting: 2320 m asl, on gently sloping ground in the Upper Salado Drainage; shallow soil cover and severe erosion, with patches of bare tepetate.
Modern Land Use: Marginal pasture.
Archaeological Remains: Variable light and light-to-moderate Late Aztec surface pottery over an area of ca. 2.00 ha. There are two discernible mounds (Features CH, CJ), one at either end of the site.

Fea.	Area and Context	Height	Content
CH	15 m dia., in unplowed land	0.25 m	Light-to-moderate Late Az surface pottery (Az III and IV B/O), several obsidian artifacts, moderate rock rubble.
CJ	15 m dia., in unplowed land	0.15 m	Light-to-moderate Late Az surface pottery (Az III and IV B/O), several obsidian artifacts, moderate rock rubble.

No surface collection made.
Discussion: The presence of Aztec IV Black/Orange surface pottery suggests that occupation continued from Late Az times into the Early Colonial period.
Classification: Small Hamlet, 10–20 people.

SITE NO. Zu-Az-89 [Zu-Az-64b(J)]
Date of Survey: July 15, 1973
Location: 494220 E, 2200470 N; 19.9005° N, 99.0552° W
Natural Setting: 2310 m asl, on gently sloping ground in the Upper Salado Drainage, near the divide between the Upper Salado and BOM drainages; shallow soil cover and severe erosion, with patches of bare tepetate.
Modern Land Use: Marginal pasture.
Archaeological Remains: Light Late Aztec surface pottery over an area of ca. 0.90 ha. There are no discernible structures, although a concentration of amorphous rock rubble near the northern edge of the site may represent the remnants of an ancient building.

No surface collection.
Discussion: This site might be considered part of nearby Zu-Az-90.
Classification: Small Hamlet, 5–10 people.

SITE NO. Zu-Az-90 [Zu-Az-64a(J)]
Date of Survey: July 15, 1973
Location: 494180 E, 2200600 N; 19.9017° N, 99.0556° W
Natural Setting: 2305 m asl, on gently sloping ground in the Upper Salado Drainage, just north of the divide between the Upper Salado and BOM drainages; shallow soil cover and severe erosion, with patches of bare tepetate.
Modern Land Use: Marginal pasture.
Archaeological Remains: Variable light and light-to-moderate Late Aztec surface pottery over an area of ca. 2.30 ha. There are no discernible structures, although a concentration of amorphous rock rubble near the southern edge of the site may represent the remnants of an ancient building.
No surface collection made.
Discussion: This site might be considered part of the same settlement as nearby Zu-Az-89.
Classification: Hamlet, 25–50 people.

SITE NO. Zu-Az-91 [Zu-Az-36(J)]
Date of Survey: June 26, 1973
Location: 493530 E, 2201100 N; 19.9062° N, 99.0618° W
Natural Setting: 2305 m asl, on gently sloping ground in the Upper Salado Drainage, near the divide between the Upper Salado and BOM drainages; shallow soil cover and severe erosion.
Modern Land Use: Marginal pasture.
Archaeological Remains: Light-to-moderate Late Aztec surface pottery over an area of ca. 0.40 ha. There are no discernible structural remains and very little rock rubble.
No surface collection made.
Classification: Small Hamlet, 5–10 people.

SITE NO. Zu-Az-92 [Zu-Az-32(J)]
Date of Survey: June 26, 1973
Location: 493180 E, 2200500 N; 19.9008° N, 99.0652° W
Natural Setting: 2305 m asl, on gently sloping ground in the Upper Salado Drainage, near the divide between the Upper Salado and BOM drainages; shallow soil cover and severe erosion.
Modern Land Use: Pasture.
Archaeological Remains: Variable light and light-to-moderate Late Aztec surface pottery over an area of ca. 1.60 ha. The Late Az material is mixed with a trace of Late Toltec surface pottery near the southwestern edge of the site (no LT site defined here). There are no discernible structural remains, although a concentration of amorphous rock rubble near the eastern edge of the site may represent the remnants of an ancient building.
No surface collection made.
Classification: Hamlet, 15–30 people.

SITE NO. Zu-Az-93 [Zu-Az-38(J)]
Date of Survey: June 26, 1973
Location: 493180 E, 2200550 N; 19.9012° N, 99.0652° W
Natural Setting: 2305 m asl, on gently sloping ground in the Upper Salado Drainage; shallow soil cover and severe erosion.
Modern Land Use: Marginal pasture.
Archaeological Remains: Light Late Aztec surface pottery over an area of ca. 0.60 ha. There are no discernible structural remains and very little rock rubble.
No surface collection made.
Classification: Small Hamlet, 2–5 people.

SITE NO. Zu-Az-94, Zu-Az-95, Zu-Az-97, Zu-Az-98 [Zu-Az-139b-1, -2, -3, -4(J); Location 27]
Date of Survey: Oct. 21, 1973
Location:
Zu-Az-94: 492930 E, 2201720 N; 19.9118° N, 99.0675° W;
Zu-Az-95: 492900 E, 2202180 N; 19.9159° N, 99.0678° W;
Zu-Az-97: 491680 E, 2201780 N; 19.9123° N, 99.0795° W;
Zu-Az-98: 491130 E, 2201900 N; 19.9134° N, 99.0847° W
Natural Setting: 2320 m asl, on gently sloping ground in the Upper Salado Drainage; shallow soil cover and severe erosion.
Modern Land Use: Marginal pasture and marginal rainfall-based agriculture. The modern town of Hueypoxtla encroaches onto the sites from the west and north.
Archaeological Remains: Variable light and light-to-moderate Late Aztec surface pottery at four scattered locations around the peripheries of modern Hueypoxtla, covering an aggregate area of ca. 8.20 ha. All the identifiable B/O pottery is Aztec III. The eastern segment (Zu-Az-94) partially overlaps onto a Late Toltec site (Zu-LT-53).
We made one surface collection (Location 27) in an area of light-to-moderate Late Az and LT surface pottery in the Zu-Az-94 site area. There may be a trace of Aztec II Black/Orange ceramics in this collection.
Discussion: These four small sites are grouped together because they probably represent extensions along the northern edge of the Aztec settlement that appears to underlie the modern town of Hueypoxtla. These four small "sites" may originally have been continuous with the larger Zu-Az-99 site at the southern edge of modern Hueypoxtla.
The possible trace of Aztec II Black/Orange surface pottery may indicate a significant Early Aztec occupation, but the nature of such an occupation remains uncertain.
Classification: Late Aztec: Uncertain. The visible occupation may represent a Small Dispersed Village with ca. 80–160 inhabitants. A much larger Late Az settlement may underlie modern Hueypoxtla. Early Aztec: ?

SITE NO. Zu-Az-96 [Zu-Az-139a(J)]
Date of Survey: Oct. 21, 1973
Location: 491900 E, 2202200 N; 19.9161° N, 99.0774° W
Natural Setting: 2335 m asl, on gently sloping ground in the Upper Salado Drainage; shallow soil cover and severe erosion.
Modern Land Use: Rainfall-based agriculture.
Archaeological Remains: Variable light and light-to-moderate Late Aztec surface pottery over an area of ca. 2.70 ha. No discernible structural remains.
No surface collection made.
Discussion: This small site probably represents a detached segment of the Aztec settlement underlying the modern town of Hueypoxtla, and so might be grouped with sites Zu-Az-94, -95, -97, -98, and -99.
Classification: Hamlet, 30–60 people.

SITE NO. Zu-Az-99 [Zu-Az-34(J); Features AP, AQ, AT, AU, AV]
Date of Survey: June 23, 26, 1973
Location: 492780 E, 2200400 N; 19.8998° N, 99.0690° W
Natural Setting: 2310 m asl, on gently sloping ground in the Upper Salado Drainage; shallow to medium soil cover and moderate to severe erosion.
Modern Land Use: Pasture and some rainfall-based agriculture, with maguey semi-terracing. The modern town of Hueypoxtla encroaches onto the site from the north.
Archaeological Remains: Variable light and light-to-moderate Late Aztec surface pottery over an area of ca. 15.70 ha. The Late Az material is mixed with partially overlapping Classic (Zu-Cl-39) and Late Toltec (Zu-LT-50, Zu-LT-51) surface pottery.
We distinguished five mounds (Features AP, AQ, AT, AU, and AV):

Fea.	Area and Context	Height	Content
AP	10 m dia.	0.10 m	Light-to-moderate Late Az surface pottery (Az III and IV B/O), moderate rock rubble.
AQ	15 m dia.	0.15 m	Light-to-moderate Late Az surface pottery, moderate rock rubble. One surface collection made over entire mound surface.
AT	20 m dia.	0.15 m	Light-to-moderate Late Az surface pottery (Az III and IV B/O), moderate rock rubble.
AU	10 m dia., in unplowed maguey field (Plate A159)	0.40 m	Light-to-moderate Late Az surface pottery, moderate rock rubble.
AV	10 m dia.	0.50 m	Light-to-moderate Late Az surface pottery, moderate rock rubble.

Discussion: This site probably extends below the modern town of Hueypoxtla, and may originally have been continuous with sites Zu-Az-94, Zu-Az-95, Zu-Az-97, and Zu-Az-98 along the northern and eastern sides of the modern town. The presence of Aztec IV Black/Orange surface pottery indicates that occupation continued from Late Az times into the Early Colonial period.
Classification: Uncertain. The visible occupation appears to represent a Small Dispersed Village of 150–300 inhabitants.

Plate A159. Zu-Az-99, facing north at Feature AU.

SITE NO. Zu-Az-100 [Zu-Az-26(J)]
  Date of Survey: June 17, 1973
  Location: 489250 E, 2205630 N; 19.9471° N, 99.1027° W
  Natural Setting: 2355 m asl, on gently sloping ground in the Upper Salado Drainage; shallow soil cover and severe erosion.
  Modern Land Use: Pasture.
  Archaeological Remains: Variable light and light-to-moderate Late Aztec surface pottery over an area of ca. 4.50 ha. The Late Az material is mixed with overlapping Late Toltec ceramics (Zu-LT-54). There are no discernible structural remains, but a concentration of amorphous rock rubble in the northwestern corner of the site may represent the remnants of an ancient building.
  No surface collection made.
  Discussion: The apparent absence of Early Aztec surface pottery suggests that this locality was abandoned after LT times and reoccupied during the Late Aztec period.
  Classification: Hamlet, 50–100 people.

SITE NO. Zu-Az-101 [Zu-Az-21(J); Feature AA]
  Date of Survey: June 17, 1973
  Location: 489250 E, 2202900 N; 19.9224° N, 99.1027° W
  Natural Setting: 2345 m asl, on gently sloping ground in the Upper Salado Drainage; shallow soil cover and severe erosion.
  Modern Land Use: Marginal pasture.
  Archaeological Remains: Variable light and light-to-moderate Late Aztec surface pottery over an area of ca. 6.00 ha. There are traces of Late Toltec surface pottery near the southwestern edge of the site (no LT site defined here).
  There is a single discernible mound (Feature AA) in a fallow field near the northern edge of the site. This feature measures ca. 20 m in diameter and 0.20 m high, with light-to-moderate Late Aztec surface pottery, several obsidian artifacts, and moderate rock rubble.
  No surface collection made.
  Classification: Hamlet, 60–120 people.

SITE NO. Zu-Az-102 [Zu-Az-138(J)]
  Date of Survey: Oct. 21, 1973
  Location: 490950 E, 2202750 N; 19.9211° N, 99.0865° W
  Natural Setting: 2310 m asl, on gently sloping ground atop a low ridge between two major *barrancas* in the Upper Salado Drainage; shallow soil cover and severe erosion, with patches of bare tepetate.
  Modern Land Use: Rainfall-based agriculture and pasture.
  Archaeological Remains: Variable light and light-to-moderate Late Aztec surface pottery over an area of ca. 4.70 ha. The Late Az material is mixed with partially overlapping Classic ceramics (Zu-Cl-36) in the western part of the site. There are no discernible structural remains.
  No surface collection made.
  Classification: Hamlet, 50–100 people.

SITE NO. Zu-Az-103, Zu-Az-104 [Zu-Az-140a, b(J); Features DR, DS, DT]
  Date of Survey: Oct. 21, 1973
  Location:
  Zu-Az-103: 490450 E, 2201900 N; 19.9134° N, 99.0912° W;
  Zu-Az-104: 489930 E, 2202220 N; 19.9163° N, 99.0962° W
  Natural Setting: 2295 m asl, on gently sloping ground along a long, low ridge in the Upper Salado Drainage (Plate A160); shallow soil cover and severe erosion.
  Modern Land Use: Marginal rainfall-based agriculture, with maguey semi-terracing.
  Archaeological Remains: Variable light and light-to-moderate Late Aztec surface pottery over an area of ca. 9.10 ha. The Late Az material is mixed with partially overlapping Late Toltec ceramics (Zu-LT-57). Three discernible mounds (Features DR, DS, DT) are tightly clustered in the southern part of the site where Late Toltec surface pottery is dominant—these features have both Late Aztec and Late Toltec surface pottery, and their precise chronology is uncertain. Their height suggests a nonresidential function.

Plate A160. Zu-Az-103/-104, facing north over general site area.

Fea.	Area and Context	Height	Content
DR	15 m dia., in unplowed area (Plate A161)	3.75 m	Very light LT and Az surface pottery, heavy rock rubble. Probably a temple platform.
DS	15 m dia., in unplowed area	1.75 m	Very light LT and Az surface pottery, moderate rock rubble. A looter's pit reveals tepetate-block construction.
DT	15 m dia., in unplowed area (Plate A162)	2.00 m	Light LT surface pottery, abundant obsidian, moderate rock rubble.

Discussion: The presence of a possible ceremonial-civic complex suggests that, despite its modest size, this site may have supra-local significance. In terms of its apparent area and population, this would be a Small Dispersed Village.

The apparent absence of Early Aztec pottery suggests that this locality was abandoned after LT times and reoccupied during the Late Aztec period.

Classification: Small Dispersed Village (?), 100–200 people.

SITE NO. Zu-Az-105 [Zu-Az-143(J); Features DQ, DW]
Date of Survey: Oct. 21, Nov. 1, 1973
Location: 489650 E, 2201930 N; 19.9137° N, 99.0989° W
Natural Setting: 2310 m asl, on gently sloping ground along a long, low ridge in the Upper Salado Drainage; shallow soil cover and severe erosion, with patches of bare tepetate.
Modern Land Use: Rainfall-based agriculture, with maguey semi-terracing in the western part of the site; the more severely eroded eastern section is marginal pasture.
Archaeological Remains: Variable light and light-to-moderate Late Aztec surface pottery over an area of ca. 5.00 ha. The Late Az material is mixed with traces of Late Toltec ceramics in the west-central part of the site (no LT site defined here). There are two discernible mounds (Features DQ, DW) in the north-central part of the site; concentrations of amorphous rock rubble in the southern site area may represent the remnants of other ancient buildings.

Fea.	Area and Context	Height	Content
DQ	15 m dia., in unplowed field (Plate A163)	0.50 m	Light-to-moderate Late Az surface pottery (both Az III and IV B/O, with a possible trace of Aztec II-III B/O); numerous obsidian artifacts and a few chert fragments; several stone wall bases. Surface collection made from entire mound surface.
DW	15 m dia., in unplowed field	0.60 m	Moderate Late Aztec pottery (both Az III and IV B/O); numerous obsidian artifacts and a few chert fragments.

Discussion: The apparent absence of well-defined Early Aztec pottery suggests that this locality was abandoned after LT times and reoccupied during the Late Aztec period. The presence of Aztec IV Black/Orange pottery indicates that occupation here continued from Late Az into the Early Colonial period.

Classification: Late Aztec: Hamlet, 50–100 people.

SITE NO. Zu-Az-106 [Zu-Az-50(J)]
Date of Survey: July 5, 1973
Location: 488750 E, 2201750 N; 19.9120° N, 99.1075° W
Natural Setting: 2310 m asl, on gently sloping ground in the Upper Salado Drainage; medium soil cover and slight to moderate erosion.
Modern Land Use: Rainfall-based agriculture. The site area was fallow at the time of our survey.
Archaeological Remains: Variable light and light-to-moderate Late Aztec surface pottery over an area of ca. 2.00 ha. The Late Az material is mixed with heavier and more extensive Late Toltec ceramics (Zu-LT-95). There are no discernible structural remains, although a concentration of amorphous rock rubble in the southeastern part of the site area may represent the remnants of an ancient building.

No surface collection made.

Discussion: The apparent absence of Early Aztec pottery suggests that this locality was abandoned after LT times and reoccupied during the Late Aztec period.

Classification: Hamlet, 20–40 people.

Plate A161. Zu-Az-103/-104, facing south at Feature DR.

Plate A162. Zu-Az-103/-104, facing SE at Feature DT.

Plate A163. Zu-Az-105, facing north at Feature DQ.

SITE NO. Zu-Az-107 [Zu-Az-145(J)]
Date of Survey: Oct. 31, 1973
Location: 487930 E, 2202430 N; 19.9182° N, 99.1153° W
Natural Setting: 2305 m asl, on gently sloping ground along a long, low ridge in the Upper Salado Drainage; shallow soil cover and moderate to severe erosion, with patches of bare tepetate.
Modern Land Use: Rainfall-based agriculture and pasture, with maguey semi-terracing.
Archaeological Remains: Light Late Aztec surface pottery over an area of ca. 1.40 ha. Obsidian artifacts are common. There are no discernible structural remains, although a concentration of amorphous rock rubble in the northern part of the site may represent the remnants of an ancient building.
No surface collection made.
Classification: Small Hamlet, 10–20 people.

SITE NO. Zu-Az-108 [Zu-Az-51(M)]
Date of Survey: July 8, 1973
Location: 487600 E, 2202130 N; 19.9155° N, 99.1185° W
Natural Setting: 2270 m asl, on gently sloping ground in the Upper Salado Drainage; shallow soil cover and moderate erosion.
Modern Land Use: Rainfall-based agriculture.
Archaeological Remains: Variable light and light-to-moderate Late Aztec surface pottery over an area of ca. 1.00 ha. There are no discernible structural remains.
No surface collection made.
Classification: Small Hamlet, 10–20 people.

SITE NO. Zu-Az-109 [Zu-Az-50(M)]
Date of Survey: July 8, 1973
Location: 487000 E, 2202070 N; 19.9149° N, 99.1242° W
Natural Setting: 2270 m asl, on gently sloping ground in the Upper Salado Drainage; shallow soil cover and slight to moderate erosion.
Modern Land Use: Rainfall-based agriculture.
Archaeological Remains: Variable light and light-to-moderate Late Aztec surface pottery over an area of ca. 1.40 ha. There are no discernible structural remains.
No surface collection made.
Classification: Small Hamlet, 15–30 people.

SITE NO. Zu-Az-110 [Zu-Az-49(M); Location 49)]
Date of Survey: July 8, 1973
Location: 486450 E, 2202050 N; 19.9147° N, 99.1295° W
Natural Setting: 2255 m asl, on gently sloping ground in the Upper Salado Drainage; shallow soil cover and moderate erosion.
Modern Land Use: Rainfall-based agriculture.
Archaeological Remains: Light Late Aztec surface pottery over an area of ca. 0.60 ha. Both Aztec III and IV Black/Orange occur. Green obsidian blades are abundant, and a few gray obsidian blades, one gray obsidian projectile point, and one gray obsidian trilobal eccentric were noted. The Late Az material is mixed with heavier and more extensive Late Toltec surface pottery (Zu-LT-92) in the western part of the site. There are no structural remains.
We made one surface collection (Location 49) over an area ca. 10 m in diameter in an unplowed field in the central site area, with light-to-moderate LT and light Late Az surface pottery, numerous obsidian artifacts (including a trilobal eccentric), and very little rock rubble.
Discussion: The apparent absence of Early Az surface pottery suggests that this locality was abandoned after LT times and reoccupied during the Late Aztec period. The presence of both Aztec III and IV B/O surface pottery suggests that this locality was occupied from Late Az times into the Early Colonial period.
Classification: Small Hamlet, 5–10 people.

SITE NO. Zu-Az-111 [Zu-Az-52(M)]
Date of Survey: July 10, 1973
Location: 486720 E, 2201350 N; 19.9084° N, 99.1269° W
Natural Setting: 2245 m asl, on gently sloping ground in the Upper Salado Drainage; medium soil cover and moderate erosion.
Modern Land Use: Rainfall-based agriculture. The site area is surrounded by scattered modern settlement on the northern edge of the modern town of Tequixquiac.
Archaeological Remains: Light Late Aztec surface pottery over an area of ca. 0.60 ha. The Late Az material is mixed with some Colonial-period glazed pottery. There are no structural remains.
No surface collection made.
Classification: Small Hamlet, 5–10 people.

SITE NO. Zu-Az-112 [Zu-Az-53(M)]
Date of Survey: July 9, 1973
Location: 487070 E, 2200880 N; 19.9042° N, 99.1235° W
Natural Setting: 2245 m asl, on gently sloping ground in the Upper Salado Drainage, ca. 25 m east of the confluence of two major *barrancas*; medium soil cover and slight to moderate erosion.
Modern Land Use: Rainfall-based agriculture. To the east and west of the site there are scattered modern houses at the eastern edge of the modern town of Tequixquiac.
Archaeological Remains: Light Late Aztec surface pottery over an area of ca. 0.90 ha. There are no discernible structural remains, although a concentration of amorphous rock rubble near the western edge of the site may represent the remnants of an ancient building.
No surface collection made.
Classification: Small Hamlet, 5–10 people.

SITE NO. Zu-Az-113 [Zu-Az-54(J); Location 30]
Date of Survey: July 7, 1973
Location: 488180 E, 2200820 N; 19.9036° N, 99.1129° W
Natural Setting: 2275 m asl, on gently sloping ground in the Upper Salado Drainage; shallow soil cover and severe erosion, with patches of bare tepetate.
Modern Land Use: Pasture and marginal rainfall-based agriculture.
Archaeological Remains: Light Late Aztec surface pottery over an area of ca. 0.70 ha. The Late Az material is mixed with partially overlapping and more extensive Classic ceramics (Zu-Zl-53). There are numerous obsidian artifacts. There are no discernible structural remains, although a concentration of amorphous rock rubble near the southwestern corner of the site may represent the remnants of an ancient building.
We made one surface collection (Location 30) over an area of ca. 15 × 25 m in a plowed field with light-to-moderate Cl and light Late Az surface pottery.
Classification: Small Hamlet, 5–10 people.

SITE NO. Zu-Az-114 [Zu-Az-53(J); Features BO, BP, BR, BS]
Date of Survey: July 5, 8, 1973
Location: 488470 E, 2200600 N; 19.9016° N, 99.1102° W
Natural Setting: 2320 m asl, on gently sloping ground in the Upper Salado Drainage; shallow soil cover and severe erosion, with patches of bare tepetate.

Modern Land Use: Pasture. The eastern edge of the modern town of Tequixquiac encroaches onto the southwestern corner of the site.

Archaeological Remains: Variable light and light-to-moderate Late Aztec surface pottery over an area of ca. 15.10 ha. There is also a trace of Classic surface pottery (no Cl site defined here).

There are four discernible mounds (Features BO, BP, BR, BS) clustered in the northern part of the site:

Fea.	Area and Context	Height	Content
BO	20 m dia., in unplowed field	0.20 m	Light Late Az surface pottery; numerous obsidian blades; moderate rock rubble.
BP	15 m dia., in unplowed field	0.20 m	Light Late Az surface pottery; numerous obsidian blades; moderate rock rubble.
BR	15 m dia., in unplowed field	0.20 m	Light Late Az surface pottery; numerous obsidian blades; moderate rock rubble.
BS	15 m dia., in unplowed field	0.20 m	Light-to-moderate Late Az surface pottery, trace of Classic pottery; numerous obsidian blades; moderate rock rubble.

No surface collection made.

Discussion: Some of the site probably underlies the modern town of Tequixquiac.

Classification: Small Dispersed Village (?), 150–300 people.

SITE NO. Zu-Az-115 [Zu-Az-48(M); Locations 50, 51]
Date of Survey: July 10–11, 1973
Location: 487000 E, 2200130 N; 19.8974° N, 99.1242° W
Natural Setting: 2270 m asl, on gently sloping ground in the Upper Salado Drainage; medium soil cover and moderate erosion.
Modern Land Use: Rainfall-based agriculture, with maguey semi-terracing. There are a few modern houses just north of the site, but they do not appear to overlie any of the prehispanic remains.
Archaeological Remains: Variable light and light-to-moderate Late Aztec surface pottery over an area of ca. 7.30 ha. The Late Az material is mixed with substantial Classic (Zu-Cl-54) and Late Toltec (Zu-LT-91) surface pottery; there is also a trace of Early Toltec surface pottery (we did not define an ET site at this locality).

There are no discernible structural remains, although amorphous concentrations of rock rubble throughout the site may represent the remnants of several ancient buildings.

We made two surface collections (Locations 50 and 51) in different parts of the site:

Location	Area and Context	Content
50	ca. 20 m dia., in plowed field	Light-to-moderate Cl and light Late Az and very light LT and a trace of ET surface pottery, numerous obsidian artifacts, one basalt mano fragment, moderate rock rubble.
51	ca. 10 m dia., in fallow field (Plate A164)	Moderate Late Az (at least one definite sherd of Az II B/O) (Plate A165) and very light LT surface pottery, numerous obsidian artifacts, moderate rock rubble.

Discussion: This is one of the few sites in the Zumpango Region with Aztec II Black/Orange surface pottery. The nature of the Early Aztec occupation is uncertain.

Classification: Late Aztec: Hamlet, 50–100 people. Early Aztec: ?

SITE NO. Zu-Az-116 [Zu-Az-46(M); Location 52]
Date of Survey: July 11, 1973
Location: 485350 E, 2200780 N; 19.9032° N, 99.1400° W
Natural Setting: 2240 m asl, on gently sloping ground in the Upper Salado Drainage; medium soil cover and moderate erosion.
Modern Land Use: The site is situated in a maize and maguey field surrounded by dispersed modern houses in the southeastern part of modern Tequixquiac. Parts of the site may underlie the modern town.
Archaeological Remains: Variable light and light-to-moderate Late Aztec surface pottery over an area of ca. 11.20 ha. Both Aztec III and IV Black/Orange pottery occur. There are also traces of Early Toltec and Late Toltec pottery in the western part of the site (no ET or LT sites defined here).

We made one surface collection (Location 52) over an area of ca. 10 × 20 m in a plowed field (Plate A166), with light-to-moderate Late Aztec and traces of Late Toltec and Early Toltec (no Aztec, LT, or ET sites designated), numerous obsidian artifacts, and little rock rubble.

Discussion: Because of modern occupation, the limits of this site could not be clearly defined. The presence of both Aztec III and IV Black/Orange surface pottery indicates that occupation here continued from Late Az times into the Early Colonial period.

Classification: Small Dispersed Village (?), 110–220 people.

SITE NO. Zu-Az-117 [Zu-Az-47(M)]
Date of Survey: July 11, 1973
Location: 485470 E, 2200300 N; 19.8989° N, 99.1388° W
Natural Setting: 2240 m asl, on gently sloping ground in the Upper Salado Drainage; medium soil cover and moderate erosion.
Modern Land Use: The site is situated in a maize and maguey field surrounded by dispersed modern houses in the southeastern part of Tequixquiac. Part of the site's original southeastern extent may underlie the modern houses.
Archaeological Remains: Light Late Aztec surface pottery over an area of ca. 2.90 ha. There are no discernible structural remains and very little rock rubble.

No surface collection made.

Discussion: Modern occupation makes it difficult to estimate the site's size.

Classification: Small Hamlet (?), 15–30 people.

SITE NO. Zu-Az-118 [Zu-Az-37(M)]
Date of Survey: June 25, 1973
Location: 484300 E, 2199820 N; 19.8946° N, 99.1500° W
Natural Setting: 2240 m asl, on gently sloping ground in the Upper Salado Drainage; shallow soil cover and severe erosion, with patches of bare tepetate.
Modern Land Use: Rainfall-based agriculture, with maguey semi-terracing. The eastern edge of the modern settlement of Colonia del Ejido (a detached segment of Tequixquiac) encroaches onto the site from the west. Part of the site may underlie the modern houses.
Archaeological Remains: Variable light and light-to-moderate Late Aztec surface pottery over an area of ca. 6.60 ha. The Late Az material is mixed with partially overlapping Late Toltec ceramics in the northwestern (Zu-LT-89) and southern (Zu-LT-88) parts of the site. There are no discernible structural remains.

No surface collection made.

Discussion: The apparent absence of Early Aztec pottery suggests that this locality was abandoned after LT times and reoccupied during the Late Aztec period.

Classification: Small Dispersed Village, 75–150 people.

(*above*) Plate A164. Zu-Az-115, facing west over Location 51.
(*right*) Plate A165. Zu-Az-115, example of Aztec II B/O sherd.
(*below*) Plate A166. Zu-Az-116, facing west over Location 52.

SITE NO. Zu-Az-119 [Zu-Az-36(M); Feature BG]
  Date of Survey: June 21, 1973
  Location: 483430 E, 2199070 N; 19.8878° N, 99.1583° W
  Natural Setting: 2280 m asl, on gently sloping ground in the Upper Salado Drainage, at the base of the steeper eastern slopes of Cerro de la Mesa Grande (Cerro Ahumada); medium soil cover and moderate to severe erosion.
  Modern Land Use: Rainfall-based agriculture. The site area had recently been plowed and planted at the time of our survey. A railroad line crosses the eastern part of the site.
  Archaeological Remains: Variable light and light-to-moderate Late Aztec surface pottery over an area of ca. 6.40 ha. The Late Az material is mixed with a partially overlapping and more extensive Late Toltec site (Zu-LT-87). The Az site contains one discernible mound (Feature BG) in a plowed field in that part of the site mixed with Late Toltec ceramics. There are six other mounds within the Zu-LT-87 site, where Aztec surface pottery is absent or present only in trace quantities (see Zu-LT-87 site description).
  Feature BG measures ca. 30 × 22 m in area and has very little vertical elevation. There is light LT and Late Az surface pottery, plus numerous obsidian artifacts and debitage, and moderate rock rubble.
  We made a surface collection from an area ca. 8 × 8 m on Feature BG in an area of mixed Late Toltec and Late Aztec surface pottery, including substantial Aztec IV Black/Orange.
  Discussion: The age of Feature BG is uncertain; it may have been occupied in both Late Toltec and Late Aztec times. The apparent absence of Early Aztec surface pottery suggests that this locality was abandoned after LT times and reoccupied during the Late Aztec period. The presence of Aztec IV Black/Orange surface pottery indicates that the site continued to be occupied from Late Az times into the Early Colonial period.
  Classification: Small Dispersed Village, 65–130 people.

SITE NO. Zu-Az-120 [Zu-Az-38(M)]
  Date of Survey: June 25, 1973
  Location: 483880 E, 2198300 N; 19.8808° N, 99.1540° W
  Natural Setting: 2275 m asl, on gently sloping ground in the Upper Salado Drainage; deep soil cover and slight erosion.
  Modern Land Use: Rainfall-based agriculture. The site area was fallow at the time of our survey. A modern dirt road borders the southeastern edge of the site.
  Archaeological Remains: Variable light and light-to-moderate Late Aztec surface pottery over an area of ca. 0.80 ha. The Late Az material is mixed with a partially overlapping, much larger Late Toltec site (Zu-LT-134). There are no discernible structural remains in the Late Az site. Zu-LT-134 contains one mound (Feature BG) that lacks Aztec surface pottery (see Zu-LT-134 site description).
  No surface collection made.
  Discussion: The apparent absence of Early Aztec surface pottery suggests that this locality was abandoned after LT times and reoccupied during the Late Aztec period.
  Classification: Small Hamlet, 10–20 people.

SITE NO. Zu-Az-121 [Zu-Az-61(M)]
  Date of Survey: July 14, 1973
  Location: 484900 E, 2198500 N; 19.8826° N, 99.1442° W
  Natural Setting: 2275 m asl, on gently sloping ground in the Upper Salado Drainage; shallow to medium soil cover and moderate severe erosion, with patches of bare tepetate.
  Modern Land Use: Rainfall-based agriculture, with maguey semi-terracing. Two modern dirt roads cross the western part of the site.
  Archaeological Remains: Variable light, light-to-moderate, and moderate Late Aztec surface pottery over an area of ca. 8.70 ha. There are also traces of Classic ceramics at the southern tip of the site (no Classic site defined here). There are no discernible structural remains.
  No surface collection made.
  Classification: Small Dispersed Village, 130–260 people.

SITE NO. Zu-Az-122 [Zu-Az-62(M)]
  Date of Survey: July 15, 1973
  Location: 485880 E, 2199320 N; 19.8901° N, 99.1349° W
  Natural Setting: 2275 m asl, on gently sloping ground in the Upper Salado Drainage; shallow to medium soil cover and severe erosion, with numerous patches of bare tepetate.
  Modern Land Use: Rainfall-based agriculture, with maguey semi-terracing. The site is situated in a maize field surrounded by dispersed modern houses in the southeastern part of Tequixquiac. Part of the site's original southeastern extent may underlie the modern houses.
  Archaeological Remains: Variable light and light-to-moderate Late Aztec surface pottery over an area of ca. 6.10 ha. There are no discernible structural remains.
  No surface collection made.
  Discussion: Because of modern occupation, it is difficult to estimate the site area.
  Classification: Small Dispersed Village (?), 75–150 people.

SITE NO. Zu-Az-123 [Zu-Az-63(M); Location 54]
  Date of Survey: July 15, 1973
  Location: 485820 E, 2199820 N; 19.8946° N, 99.1355° W
  Natural Setting: 2270 m asl, on moderately sloping ground in the Upper Salado Drainage; shallow to medium soil cover and severe erosion, with numerous patches of bare tepetate.
  Modern Land Use: Rainfall-based agriculture, with maguey semi-terracing. The modern town of Tequixquiac encroaches onto the western edge of the site.
  Archaeological Remains: Variable light and light-to-moderate Late Aztec surface pottery over an area of ca. 5.40 ha. There are no discernible structural remains.
  We made one surface collection (Location 54) in a severely eroded area over an area measuring ca. 5 × 5 m, with light-to-moderate Late Az surface pottery, numerous green obsidian blades, and very little rock rubble.
  Discussion: Because of modern occupation, we were unable to define the western limits of the site.
  Classification: Hamlet (?), 50–100 people.

SITE NO. Zu-Az-124 [Zu-Az-64(M)]
  Date of Survey: July 15, 1973
  Location: 486280 E, 2200030 N; 19.8965° N, 99.1311° W
  Natural Setting: 2300 m asl, on moderately sloping ground in the Upper Salado Drainage; shallow to medium soil cover and severe erosion, with patches of bare tepetate.
  Modern Land Use: Rainfall-based agriculture, with maguey semi-terracing. A modern dirt road crosses the site.
  Archaeological Remains: Variable light and light-to-moderate Late Aztec surface pottery over an area of ca. 1.50 ha. The Late Az material is mixed with traces of Late Toltec ceramics at the western tip of the site (no LT site defined here). There are no discernible structural remains.
  No surface collection made.
  Classification: Small Hamlet, 10–20 people.

SITE NO. Zu-Az-125 [Zu-Az-65(M); Feature DC]
  Date of Survey: July 12, 1973
  Location: 487250 E, 2199100 N; 19.8881° N, 99.1218° W
  Natural Setting: 2285 m asl, on gently sloping ground in the Upper Salado Drainage; shallow to medium soil cover and moderate to severe erosion. A major *barranca* (ca. 20 m deep) cuts north-south across the site area.
  Modern Land Use: Rainfall-based agriculture, with maguey semi-terracing.
  Archaeological Remains: Light Late Aztec surface pottery over an area of ca. 0.60 ha. There is one poorly preserved mound (Feature DC) in a plowed maize field. This severely eroded feature measures ca. 15 m in diameter and up to 2.00 m high, with light Late Aztec surface pottery, several obsidian artifacts, and light rock rubble; its height is probably exaggerated by the severe erosion.
  No surface collection made.
  Classification: Small Hamlet, 5–10 people.

SITE NO. Zu-Az-126 [Zu-Az-56(J); Feature BN]
  Date of Survey: July 3, 1973
  Location: 487930 E, 2199320 N; 19.8901° N, 99.1153° W
  Natural Setting: 2290 m asl, on gently sloping ground in the Upper Salado Drainage; shallow soil cover and severe erosion.
  Modern Land Use: Pasture.
  Archaeological Remains: Variable light and light-to-moderate Late Aztec surface pottery over an area of ca. 10.20 ha. There is one discernible mound (Feature BN) in an unplowed area. This feature measures ca. 10 m in diameter and 0.20 m high, with light-to-moderate Late Aztec surface pottery, several obsidian artifacts, and moderate rock rubble.
  No surface collection made.
  Classification: Small Dispersed Village, 100–200 people.

SITE NO. Zu-Az-127 [Zu-Az-62(J)]
  Date of Survey: July 5, 1973
  Location: 488750 E, 2200030 N; 19.8965° N, 99.1075° W
  Natural Setting: 2305 m asl, on gently sloping ground atop a broad, low ridge in the Upper Salado Drainage; shallow soil cover and severe erosion.
  Modern Land Use: Marginal pasture.
  Archaeological Remains: Light-to-moderate Late Aztec surface pottery and moderate rock rubble over an area of ca. 0.50 ha. There are no discernible structural remains.
  No surface collection made.
  Classification: Small Hamlet, 5–10 people.

SITE NO. Zu-Az-128 [Zu-Az-52(J)]
  Date of Survey: July 5, 1973
  Location: 489050 E, 2200800 N; 19.9034° N, 99.1046
  Natural Setting: 2350 m asl, on gently sloping ground in the Upper Salado Drainage; medium soil cover and slight to moderate erosion.
  Modern Land Use: Rainfall-based agriculture.
  Archaeological Remains: Light Late Aztec surface pottery over an area of ca. 1.00 ha. The Late Az material is mixed with partially overlapping Late Toltec surface pottery (Zu-LT-97) in the southeastern part of the site. There are no discernible structural remains.
  No surface collection made.
  Discussion: The apparent absence of Early Aztec surface pottery indicates that this locality was abandoned after LT times and reoccupied during the Late Aztec period.
  Classification: Small Hamlet, 5–10 people.

SITE NO. Zu-Az-129 [Zu-Az-51(J)]
  Date of Survey: July 5, 1973
  Location: 489380 E, 2200850 N; 19.9039° N, 99.1015° W
  Natural Setting: 2350 m asl, on gently sloping ground in the Upper Salado Drainage; medium soil cover and slight to moderate erosion.
  Modern Land Use: Rainfall-based agriculture.
  Archaeological Remains: Variable light and light-to-moderate Late Aztec surface pottery over an area of ca. 4.30 ha. The Late Az material is mixed with lighter Late Toltec ceramics (Zu-LT-98) in the southern part of the site. There are no discernible structural remains, although several concentrations of amorphous rock rubble at the southern end of the site may represent one or more ancient buildings.
  No surface collection made.
  Discussion: The apparent absence of Early Aztec surface pottery suggests that this locality was abandoned after LT times and reoccupied during the Late Aztec period.
  Classification: Hamlet, 40–80 people.

SITE NO. Zu-Az-130, Zu-Az-131 [Zu-Az-41a, b(J); Features AI, AK, AL, AM, AN, AO, AZ]
  Date of Survey: June 21, 1973
  Location:
  Zu-Az-130: 491000 E, 2201000 N; 19.9053° N, 99.0860° W;
  Zu-Az-131: 491500 E, 2201750 N; 19.9120° N, 99.0812° W
  Natural Setting: 2350 m asl, on gently sloping ground in the Upper Salado Drainage (Plate A167); shallow soil cover and severe erosion.
  Modern Land Use: Pasture. The site area has not been plowed in recent years.
  Archaeological Remains: Variable light and light-to-moderate Late Aztec surface pottery over an area of ca. 107.80 ha. Both Aztec III Black/Orange and Aztec IV Black/Orange occur. Small concentrations of Late Toltec ceramics are present at two localities (Zu-LT-99, Zu-LT-101).
  There are seven discernible mounds (Features AI, AK, AL, AM, AN, AO, and AZ), and several concentrations of amorphous rock rubble elsewhere in the site may represent the remnants of other ancient buildings. The two clearly nonresidential structures (Features AM and AN) are closely spaced in the northern part of the site.

Fea.	Area and Context	Height	Content
AI	30 m dia., in unplowed area	0.15 m	Light-to-moderate Late Az surface pottery, numerous obsidian artifacts, moderate rock rubble.
AK	10 m dia., in unplowed area (Plate A168)	0.50 m	Light-to-moderate Late Az surface pottery, numerous obsidian artifacts, moderate rock rubble.
AL	15 m dia., in unplowed area	0.50 m	Moderate Late Az surface pottery, numerous obsidian artifacts, moderate rock rubble.
AM	40 m dia., in a plowed area (Plate A169)	6.00 m	Very light Az surface pottery. A looter's pit shows solid rock-rubble fill. Close to Fea. AN.
AN	30 m dia., in a plowed area	2.00 m	Very light Az surface pottery. Close to Fea. AM.
AO	20 m dia., in plowed field	0.20 m	Light-Late Az surface pottery, numerous obsidian artifacts, moderate rock rubble.
AZ	20 m dia, in plowed field	0.20 m	Light-to-moderate Late Az surface pottery, numerous obsidian artifacts, moderate rock rubble.

No surface collection made.

Discussion: This is the largest Aztec site in this part of the Zumpango Region, and Feature AM is the largest mound we identified in the region. The apparent absence of Early Aztec surface pottery indicates that this locality was abandoned after LT times and reoccupied during the Late Aztec period.

Classification: Regional Center, 1100–2200 people.

SITE NO. Zu-Az-132 [Zu-Az-35(J); Features AP, AQ, AT]
Date of Survey: June 23, 1973
Location: 491820 E, 2199880 N; 19.8951° N, 99.0781° W
Natural Setting: 2330 m asl, on moderately sloping ground in the Upper Salado Drainage; shallow soil cover and severe erosion.
Modern Land Use: Mixed pasture and rainfall-based agriculture. A modern dirt road crosses the eastern side of the site.
Archaeological Remains: Variable light and light-to-moderate Late Aztec surface pottery over an area of ca. 53.60 ha; both Aztec III and IV Black/Orange ceramics occur. The Late Az material is mixed with small Late Toltec ceramics in different parts of the site (Zu-LT-104, Zu-LT-105, Zu-LT-107). Obsidian artifacts are abundant throughout the site.

We identified three mounds (Features AP, AQ, AT), all seemingly of residential function. Several concentrations of amorphous rock rubble elsewhere in the site may represent the remnants of other ancient structures.

Fea.	Area and Context	Height	Content
AP	10 m dia., in unplowed area	0.50 m	Light-to-moderate Late Az surface pottery, numerous obsidian artifacts, moderate rock rubble.
AQ	15 m dia., in unplowed area	0.15 m	Light-to-moderate Late Az surface pottery, numerous obsidian artifacts, moderate rock rubble. Surface collection made over entire mound surface.
AT	20 m dia., in unplowed area	0.15 m	Light-to-moderate Late Az surface pottery, numerous obsidian artifacts, moderate rock rubble.

Discussion: One of the larger Late Aztec settlements in this part of the Zumpango Region. Its close proximity to the Local Center at Zu-Az-130/Zu-Az-131 (a few hundred meters to the west) may mean that Zu-Az-132 is a detached component of the latter site.

The apparent absence of Early Aztec surface pottery suggests that this locality was abandoned after LT times and reoccupied during the Late Aztec period. The presence of both Aztec III and IV Black/Orange pottery indicates that this locality continued to be occupied from Late Az times into the Early Colonial period.

Classification: Large Dispersed Village, 750–1500 people.

SITE NO. Zu-Az-133 [Zu-Az-37(J)]
Date of Survey: June 23, 1973
Location: 493150 E, 2200050 N; 19.8967° N, 99.0654° W
Natural Setting: 2335 m asl, on gently sloping ground in the Upper Salado Drainage, just northwest of the divide between the Upper Salado and BOM drainages; shallow soil cover and severe erosion.
Modern Land Use: Marginal pasture.
Archaeological Remains: Light-to-moderate Late Aztec surface pottery over an area of ca. 0.50 ha. There are no discernible structural remains, although a concentration of amorphous rock rubble may represent the remnants of an ancient building.
No surface collection made.
Classification: Small Hamlet, 5–10 people.

SITE NO. Zu-Az-134 [Zu-Az-33(J)]
Date of Survey: June 23, 1973
Location: 493130 E, 2199850 N; 19.8949° N, 99.0656° W
Natural Setting: 2330 m asl, on gently sloping ground in the Upper Salado Drainage, just west of the divide between the Upper Salado and BOM drainages; shallow soil cover and severe erosion.
Modern Land Use: Marginal pasture.
Archaeological Remains: Variable light and light-to-moderate Late Aztec surface pottery over an area of ca. 1.30 ha. There are also traces of Late Toltec and Classic ceramics (no LT or Classic sites defined here).
No surface collection made.
Classification: Small Hamlet, 10–20 people.

SITE NO. Zu-Az-135 [Zu-Az-42(J)]
Date of Survey: July 2, 1973
Location: 493100 E, 2199250 N; 19.8895° N, 99.0659° W
Natural Setting: 2350 m asl, on gently sloping ground in the Upper Salado Drainage, just west of the divide between the Upper Salado and BOM drainages; shallow soil cover and severe erosion.
Modern Land Use: Marginal pasture.
Archaeological Remains: Variable light and light-to-moderate Late Aztec surface pottery over an area of ca. 6.10 ha. The Late Az material is mixed with approximately equal amounts of Late Toltec ceramics (Zu-LT-111). There are no discernible structural remains.
No surface collection made.
Discussion: The apparent absence of Early Aztec surface pottery suggests that this locality was abandoned after LT times and reoccupied during the Late Aztec period.
Classification: Small Dispersed Village, 60–120 people.

SITE NO. Zu-Az-136 [Zu-Az-43(J); Features BG, BH]
Date of Survey: July 1, 1973
Location: 492400 E, 2198970 N; 19.8869° N, 99.0726° W
Natural Setting: 2350 m asl, on gently sloping ground in the Upper Salado Drainage, just northwest of the divide between the Upper Salado and BOM drainages; shallow soil cover and severe erosion.
Modern Land Use: Pasture and rainfall-based agriculture.
Archaeological Remains: Variable light and light-to-moderate Late Aztec surface pottery and abundant obsidian artifacts over an area of ca. 18.60 ha. Both Aztec III and IV Black/Orange pottery are present. The Late Az material is mixed with heavier Late Toltec ceramics over parts of the northern site area (Zu-LT-108, -109, -110).

There are two discernible mounds (Features BG, BH), and amorphous concentrations of rock rubble in other parts of the site may represent the remnants of several other ancient buildings.

Fea.	Area and Context	Height	Content
BG	15 m dia., in unplowed field	0.20 m	Light-to-moderate Late Az surface pottery, abundant obsidian, moderate rock rubble.
BH	15 m dia., in unplowed field	0.15 m	Light-to-moderate Late Az surface pottery, abundant obsidian, moderate rock rubble.

No surface collection made.
Discussion: The apparent absence of Early Aztec surface pottery suggests that this locality was abandoned after LT times and reoccupied during the Late Aztec period. The presence of Aztec IV Black/Orange surface pottery indicates that the site continued to be occupied from Late Az times into the Early Colonial period.
Classification: Small Dispersed Village, 200–400 people.

Plate A167. Zu-Az-130/-131, facing SW over general site area.

Plate A168. Zu-Az-130/-131, facing west at Feature AK.

SITE NO. Zu-Az-137 [Zu-Az-44(J)]
Date of Survey: July 2, 1973
Location: 492950 E, 2205950 N; 19.9500° N, 99.0674° W
Natural Setting: 2355 m asl, on gently sloping ground in the Upper Salado Drainage, just north of the divide between the Upper Salado and BOM drainages; shallow soil cover and severe erosion.
Modern Land Use: Pasture and rainfall-based agriculture.
Archaeological Remains: Variable light and light-to-moderate Late Aztec surface pottery over an area of ca. 6.30 ha. The Late Az material is mixed with traces of Late Toltec ceramics at the eastern edge of the site (no LT site defined here). There are no discernible structural remains, although several concentrations of amorphous rock rubble may represent the remnants of ancient buildings.
No surface collection made.
Classification: Hamlet, 50–100 people.

SITE NO. Zu-Az-138 [Zu-Az-74(J); Features CK, CL]
Date of Survey: July 18, 1973
Location: 493530 E, 2198680 N; 19.8843° N, 99.0618° W
Natural Setting: 2355 m asl, on gently sloping ground in the Upper Salado Drainage, just west of the divide between the Upper Salado and BOM drainages; shallow soil cover and severe erosion.
Modern Land Use: Pasture and rainfall-based agriculture.
Archaeological Remains: Variable light and light-to-moderate Late Aztec surface pottery over an area of ca. 3.70 ha. Both Aztec III and IV Black/Orange pottery occur.
There are two discernible mounds (Features CK, CL):

Fea.	Area and Context	Height	Content
CK	15 m dia., in unplowed field	0.20 m	Light-to-moderate Late Az surface pottery, numerous obsidian blades and scrapers, moderate rock rubble.
CL	15 m dia., in unplowed field (Plate A170)	0.10 m	Light-to-moderate Late Az surface pottery, numerous obsidian blades and scrapers, moderate rock rubble.

No surface collection made.
Discussion: The presence of both Aztec III and IV Black/Orange ceramics indicates that the site continued to be occupied from Late Az times into the Early Colonial period.
Classification: Hamlet, 40–80 people.

SITE NO. Zu-Az-139 [Zu-Az-73(J)]
Date of Survey: July 15, 1973
Location: 494130 E, 2198700 N; 19.8845° N, 99.0561° W
Natural Setting: 2360 m asl, on gently sloping ground in the BOM Lower Piedmont, very close to the divide between the Upper Salado and BOM drainages; shallow soil cover and moderate erosion.
Modern Land Use: Rainfall-based agriculture.
Archaeological Remains: Light Late Aztec surface pottery over an area of ca. 0.80 ha. There are no discernible structural remains and very little rock rubble.
No surface collection made.
Classification: Small Hamlet, 5–10 people.

SITE NO. Zu-Az-140 [Zu-Az-71(J)]
Date of Survey: July 15, 1973
Location: 494470 E, 2198700 N; 19.8845° N, 99.0528° W
Natural Setting: 2355 m asl, on gently sloping ground in the BOM Lower Piedmont, very close to the divide between the Upper Salado and BOM drainages; shallow soil cover and severe erosion.
Modern Land Use: Rainfall-based agriculture.
Archaeological Remains: Light Late Aztec surface pottery over an area of ca. 1.90 ha. There are no discernible structural remains and very little rock rubble.
No surface collection made.
Classification: Small Hamlet, 10–20 people.

SITE NO. Zu-Az-141, Zu-Az-143, Zu-Az-144, Zu-Az-145 [Zu-Az-70a, b, c(J), Zu-Az-75(J)]
Date of Survey: July 18, 1973
Location: 494720 E, 2198130 N; 19.8793° N, 99.0504° W
Natural Setting: 2340 m asl, on gently sloping ground in the BOM Lower Piedmont, just southeast of the divide between the Upper Salado and BOM drainages; shallow soil cover and severe erosion.
Modern Land Use: Pasture and rainfall-based agriculture, with maguey semi-terracing.
Archaeological Remains: Variable light, and light-to-moderate Late Aztec surface pottery at four localities over an aggregate area of ca. 42.20 ha. Obsidian artifacts are common. The Late Az material is mixed with traces of Late Toltec ceramics along the western edge of the site (no LT site defined here). There are no discernible structural remains, although several concentrations of amorphous rock rubble may represent the remnants of ancient buildings.
No surface collection made.
Discussion: This is a very diffuse site, with occupational remnants separated by gaps with little or no surface pottery; its definition is more arbitrary than is usual. What we originally defined as sites Zu-Az-143, -144, and -145 are clearly small outliers of the much larger Zu-Az-141 site, and so we combine them for descriptive purposes.
Classification: Large Dispersed Village, 400–800 people.

SITE NO. Zu-Az-142 [Zu-Az-72(J)]
Date of Survey: July 15, 1973
Location: 495900 E, 2198650 N; 19.8840° N, 99.0392° W
Natural Setting: 2340 m asl, on gently sloping ground in the BOM Lower Piedmont; shallow soil cover and moderate erosion.
Modern Land Use: Rainfall-based agriculture.
Archaeological Remains: Light-to-moderate Late Aztec surface pottery and moderate rock rubble over an area of ca. 0.40 ha. There are no discernible structural remains.
No surface collection made.
Classification: Small Hamlet, 5–10 people.

SITE NO. Zu-Az-146 [Zu-Az-75a(J)]
Date of Survey: July 18, 1973
Location: 494200 E, 2197720 N; 19.8756° N, 99.0554° W
Natural Setting: 2350 m asl, on gently sloping ground in the Basin of Mexico Lower Piedmont, just southeast of the divide between the Upper Salado and Basin of Mexico drainages; shallow soil cover and severe erosion.
Modern Land Use: Wasteland.
Archaeological Remains: Light Late Aztec surface pottery over an area of ca. 2.20 ha. There are no structural remains and very little rock rubble.
No surface collection made.
Classification: Small Hamlet, 10–20 people.

Plate A169. Zu-Az-130/-131, Feature AM.

Plate A170. Zu-Az-138, facing NW at Feature CL.

SITE NO. Zu-Az-147, Zu-Az-148 [Zu-Az-45(J), Zu-Az-92(J); Features BF, BJ, BK]
Date of Survey: July 1–2, 1973
Location: 492630 E, 2204750 N; 19.9392° N, 99.0704° W
Natural Setting: 2390 m asl, on gently sloping ground at the divide between the Upper Salado and Basin of Mexico drainages; shallow soil cover and severe erosion.
Modern Land Use: Pasture and rainfall-based agriculture. The modern towns of Jilotzingo and Cuevas encroach onto the site from the southeast and west, respectively. A modern dirt road crosses the western part of the site.
Archaeological Remains: Variable light, and light-to-moderate Late Aztec surface pottery over an area of ca. 73.40 ha. Both Aztec III and Az IV Black/Orange pottery are present. The Late Az material is mixed with Late Toltec ceramics over a limited area in the central part of the site (Zu-LT-118).

There are three discernible mounds (Features BF, BJ, BK), and several concentrations of amorphous rock rubble elsewhere in the site may represent the remnants of other ancient buildings.

Fea.	Area and Context	Height	Content
BF	15 m dia., in unplowed field	0.20 m	Light-to-moderate Late Az surface pottery (both Az III and IV B/O, including some glazed ceramics), several obsidian artifacts, moderate rock rubble.
BJ	20 m dia., in unplowed field	0.20 m	Light-to-moderate Late Az surface pottery, abundant obsidian, moderate rock rubble. Close to Fea. BK, and may have been continuous with it before severe erosion.
BK	30 m dia., in unplowed field	0.20 m	Light-to-moderate Late Az surface pottery, one basalt mano, abundant obsidian, moderate rock rubble. Close to Fea. BJ, and may have been continuous with it before severe erosion.

No surface collection made.
Discussion: Like nearby site Zu-Az-141, this is a very diffuse site, with occupational remnants separated by gaps with little or no surface pottery; its definition is somewhat more arbitrary than usual. What we originally defined as site Zu-Az-148 is obviously a small outlier of the larger Zu-Az-147 site, and so we combine them for descriptive purposes.

The apparent absence of Early Aztec surface pottery suggests that this locality was abandoned after LT times and reoccupied during the Late Aztec period. The presence of both Aztec III and IV Black/Orange pottery, and some glazed ceramics, indicates that this area continued to be occupied from Late Az times into the Early Colonial period, and perhaps later.
Classification: Large Dispersed Village, 750–1500 people

SITE NO. Zu-Az-149 [Zu-Az-93(J)]
Date of Survey: July 25, 1973
Location: 492300 E, 2196500 N; 19.8646° N, 99.0735° W
Natural Setting: 2365 m asl, on gently sloping ground in the Basin of Mexico Lower Piedmont; shallow soil cover and severe erosion.
Modern Land Use: Pasture. There is a modern cemetery on the north edge of the site. Two modern dirt roads cross the southern and northeastern parts of the site.
Archaeological Remains: Variable light and light-to-moderate Late Aztec surface pottery over an area of ca. 25.20 ha. The Late Az material is mixed with partially overlapping Late Toltec ceramics (Zu-LT-119). There are no discernible structural remains in the Aztec site, although several concentrations of amorphous rock rubble may represent the remnants of ancient buildings.

No surface collection made.
Discussion: The apparent absence of Early Aztec surface pottery suggests that this locality was abandoned after LT times and reoccupied during the Late Aztec period.
Classification: Large Dispersed Village, 400–800 people.

SITE NO. Zu-Az-150 [Zu-Az-91(J)]
Date of Survey: July 25, 1973
Location: 492030 E, 2197100 N; 19.8700, 99.0761° W
Natural Setting: 2390 m asl, on gently sloping ground in the Basin of Mexico Lower Piedmont, just south of the divide between the Upper Salado and Basin of Mexico drainages; shallow soil cover and severe erosion.
Modern Land Use: Pasture. The eastern edge of the modern town of Cuevas is near the western edge of the site area.
Archaeological Remains: Light Late Aztec surface pottery over an area of ca. 2.90 ha. There are no discernible structural remains.
No surface collection made.
Classification: Hamlet, 20–40 people.

SITE NO. Zu-Az-151 [Zu-Az-47(J)]
Date of Survey: June 27, 1973
Location: 491470 E, 2200450 N; 19.9003° N, 99.0815° W
Natural Setting: 2370 m asl, on gently sloping ground at the divide between the Upper Salado and BOM drainages; shallow soil cover and moderate erosion.
Modern Land Use: Rainfall-based agriculture, with maguey semi-terracing.
Archaeological Remains: Variable light and light-to-moderate Late Aztec surface pottery over an area of ca. 1.80 ha. There are no discernible structural remains.
No surface collection made.
Classification: Hamlet, 20–40 people.

SITE NO. Zu-Az-152 [Zu-Az-46c(J); Feature AX]
Date of Survey: June 27, 1973
Location: 491600 E, 2198400 N; 19.8818° N, 99.0802° W
Natural Setting: 2405 m asl, on gently sloping ground in the Upper Salado Drainage, just north of the divide between the Upper Salado and BOM drainages; shallow soil cover and severe erosion.
Modern Land Use: Pasture.
Archaeological Remains: Variable light-to-moderate and moderate Late Aztec surface pottery (both Aztec III and IV Black/Orange) over an area of ca. 1.00 ha. There is one discernible mound (Feature AX), measuring ca. 10 m in diameter and 0.20 m high, with light-to-moderate Late Az surface pottery, numerous obsidian artifacts, and moderate rock rubble.
No surface collection made.
Discussion: The presence of both Aztec III and IV Black/Orange ceramics indicates that this site was occupied from Late Az times into the Early Colonial period.
Classification: Hamlet, 20–40 people.

SITE NO. Zu-Az-153 [Zu-Az-46a(J)]
Date of Survey: June 27, 1973
Location: 491200 E, 2198570 N; 19.8333° N, 99.0841° W
Natural Setting: 2365 m asl, on gently sloping ground in the Upper Salado Drainage, just north of the divide between the Upper Salado and BOM drainages; medium soil cover and moderate erosion.
Modern Land Use: Rainfall-based agriculture.

Plate A171. Zu-Az-155, facing SE at Feature AW.

Archaeological Remains: Light-to-moderate Late Aztec surface pottery over an area of ca. 1.50 ha. There are no discernible structural remains, although a concentration of amorphous rock rubble may represent the remnants of an ancient building.

No surface collection made.

Classification: Hamlet, 20–40 people.

SITE NO. Zu-Az-154 [Zu-Az-46b(J)]
  Date of Survey: June 27, 1973
  Location: 491000 E, 2198350 N; 19.8813° N, 99.0860° W
  Natural Setting: 2370 m asl, on gently sloping ground in the Upper Salado Drainage, very close to the divide between the Upper Salado and BOM drainages; medium soil cover and moderate erosion.
  Modern Land Use: Rainfall-based agriculture.
  Archaeological Remains: Variable light and light-to-moderate Late Aztec surface pottery over an area of ca. 5.50 ha. There are no discernible structural remains, but several concentrations of amorphous rock rubble in the western part of the site may represent the remnants of ancient buildings.
  No surface collection made.
  Classification: Small Dispersed Village, 75–150 people.

SITE NO. Zu-Az-155 [Zu-Az-39(J); Location 28; Features AV, AW]
  Date of Survey: June 22, 27, 1973
  Location: 491530 E, 2199050 N; 19.8876° N, 99.0809° W
  Natural Setting: 2355 m asl, on moderately sloping ground in the Upper Salado Drainage, just north of the divide between the Upper Salado and Basin of Mexico drainages; shallow soil cover and severe erosion.
  Modern Land Use: Pasture and marginal rainfall-based agriculture.
  Archaeological Remains: Variable light and light-to-moderate Late Aztec surface pottery over an area of ca. 28.70 ha. Both Aztec III and IV Black/Orange ceramics are present. The Late Az material is mixed with partially overlapping Late Toltec ceramics (Zu-LT-102). Obsidian blades and scrapers are common.
  There are two discernible mounds (Features AV, AW), and several concentrations of amorphous rock rubble may represent the remnants of other ancient buildings.

Fea.	Area and Context	Height	Content
AV	30 m dia., in plowed field	0.15 m	Light-to-moderate Late Az surface pottery (both Az III and IV B/O), numerous obsidian artifacts, moderate rock rubble.
AW	10 m dia., in badly eroded pasture (Plate A171)	0.50 m	Light Late Az surface pottery, numerous obsidian artifacts, moderate rock rubble. One preserved stone wall base with corner extends for ca. 3.5 m (Plate A172).

We made one surface collection (Location 28) over an area of 5 × 8 m in a badly eroded area (Plate A173) with moderate Late Az surface pottery (both Aztec III and IV Black/Orange), moderate rock rubble, and numerous obsidian artifacts

Discussion: The presence of both Aztec III and IV Black/Orange ceramics indicates that this site was occupied from Late Az times into the Early Colonial period. The apparent absence of Early Aztec pottery suggests that this locality was abandoned after LT times and reoccupied during the Late Aztec period.

Classification: Large Dispersed Village, 400–800 people.

SITE NO. Zu-Az-156 [Zu-Az-40(J)]
  Date of Survey: June 22, 1975
  Location: 491180 E, 2199650 N; 19.8931° N, 99.0843° W
  Natural Setting: 2330 m asl, on gently sloping ground in the Upper Salado Drainage; medium to deep soil cover and moderate erosion.
  Modern Land Use: Rainfall-based agriculture.
  Archaeological Remains: Light Late Aztec surface pottery over an area of ca. 0.60 ha. The Late Az material is mixed with heavier and more extensive Late Toltec ceramics (Zu-LT-103). There are no discernible structural remains, although a concentration of amorphous rock rubble in the central site area may represent the remnants of an ancient building.
  No surface collection made.
  Discussion: The apparent absence of Early Aztec surface pottery indicates that this locality was abandoned after LT times and reoccupied during the Late Aztec period.
  Classification: Small Hamlet, 5–10 people.

Plate A172. Zu-Az-155, stone wall base at Feature AW, with person standing at corner.

SITE NO. Zu-Az-157 [Zu-Az-49(J); Feature BA]
  Date of Survey: June 28, 1973
  Location: 490820 E, 2199250 N; 19.8894° N, 99.0877° W
  Natural Setting: 2340 m asl, on gently sloping ground in the Upper Salado Drainage; shallow soil cover and severe erosion.
  Modern Land Use: Pasture.
  Archaeological Remains: Variable light and light-to-moderate Late Aztec surface pottery over an area of ca. 8.80 ha. Both Aztec III and IV Black/Orange ceramics occur, and obsidian blades and scrapers are common.
  There is one discernible mound (Feature BA) in an unplowed area (Plate A174). This feature measures ca. 10 m in diameter and 0.25 m high, with light-to-moderate Late Az surface pottery (both Az III and IV B/O), numerous obsidian artifacts, and moderate rock rubble. A section of stone wall base is preserved on the mound's surface (Plate A175).
  Several other concentrations of amorphous rock rubble may represent the remnants of ancient buildings.
  No surface collection made.
  Discussion: The presence of both Aztec III and IV Black/Orange surface pottery indicates that this locality continued to be occupied from Late Az times into the Early Colonial period.
  Classification: Small Dispersed Village, 100–200 people.

SITE NO. Zu-Az-158 [Zu-Az-48(J); Feature AY]
  Date of Survey: June 27, 1973
  Location: 490380 E, 2198720 N; 19.8847° N, 99.0919° W
  Natural Setting: 2355 m asl, on gently sloping ground in the Upper Salado Drainage, just north of the divide between the Upper Salado and BOM drainages; shallow soil cover and severe erosion, with patches of bare tepetate.
  Modern Land Use: Pasture.
  Archaeological Remains: Variable light and light-to-moderate Late Aztec surface pottery over an area of ca. 2.60 ha. There is a single discernible badly eroded mound (Feature AY) in an unplowed area near the western edge of the site. This feature measures ca. 10 m in diameter and 0.25 m high, with light-to-moderate Late Az surface pottery, numerous obsidian artifacts, and moderate rock rubble.
  No surface collection made.
  Classification: Hamlet, 25–50 people.

SITE NO. Zu-Az-159 [no field number]
  Date of Survey: July 9, 1973
  Location: 489630 E, 2198550 N; 19.8831° N, 99.0991° W
  Natural Setting: 2350 m asl, on gently sloping ground in the Upper Salado Drainage, just north of the divide between the Upper Salado and BOM drainages; shallow soil cover and severe erosion.
  Modern Land Use: Marginal pasture.
  Archaeological Remains: Light Late Aztec surface pottery over an area of ca. 1.00 ha. There are no discernible structural remains.
  No surface collection made.
  Classification: Small Hamlet, 5–10 people.

SITE NO. Zu-Az-160 [Zu-Az-59(J)]
  Date of Survey: July 9, 1973
  Location: 489150 E, 2198970 N; 19.8869° N, 99.1036° W
  Natural Setting: 2340 m asl, on gently sloping ground in the Upper Salado Drainage; shallow soil cover and severe erosion.
  Modern Land Use: Marginal pasture.
  Archaeological Remains: Variable light and light-to-moderate Late Aztec surface pottery, with traces of Late Toltec ceramics (no LT site defined here), over an area of ca. 1.70 ha. There are no discernible structural remains.
  No surface collection made.
  Classification: Small Hamlet, 15–30 people.

SITE NO. Zu-Az-161 [Zu-Az-55(J)]
  Date of Survey: July, 1973
  Location: 489650 E, 2200000 N; 19.8962° N, 99.0989° W
  Natural Setting: 2355 m asl, on gently sloping ground in the Upper Salado Drainage; shallow soil cover and moderate erosion.
  Modern Land Use: Pasture and rainfall-based agriculture.
  Archaeological Remains: Variable light and light-to-moderate Late Aztec surface pottery over an area of ca. 6.40 ha, mixed with partially overlapping Late Toltec ceramics in the northern part of the site (Zu-LT-100). There are no discernible structural remains, but several concentrations of amorphous rock rubble may represent the remnants of ancient buildings.
  No surface collection made.
  Discussion: The apparent absence of Early Aztec surface pottery indicates that this locality was abandoned after LT times and reoccupied during the Late Aztec period.
  Classification: Small Dispersed Village, 75–150 people.

Plate A173. Zu-Az-155, surface collecting in progress at Location 28.

Plate A174. Zu-Az-157, facing SW at Feature BA.

Plate A175. Zu-Az-157, wall base at Feature BA.

SITE NO. Zu-Az-162 [Zu-Az-57(J)]
 Date of Survey: July 3, 1973
 Location: 489030 E, 2199600 N; 19.8926° N, 99.1048° W
 Natural Setting: 2305 m asl, on gently sloping ground in the Upper Salado Drainage; shallow soil cover and severe erosion. A major *barranca* runs SE-NW along the northern edge of the site area.
 Modern Land Use: Pasture.
 Archaeological Remains: Variable light and light-to-moderate Late Aztec surface pottery over an area of ca. 2.40 ha. There are no discernible structural remains, although a concentration of amorphous rock rubble at the southwestern edge of the site may represent the remnants of an ancient building.
 No surface collection made.
 Classification: Hamlet, 25–50 people.

SITE NO. Zu-Az-163 [Zu-Az-58(J)]
 Date of Survey: July 9, 1973
 Location: 488470 E, 2198900 N; 19.8863° N, 99.1101° W
 Natural Setting: 2325 m asl, on gently sloping ground in the Upper Salado Drainage; shallow soil cover and severe erosion. A major *barranca* cuts through the central part of the site.
 Modern Land Use: Pasture. A modern dirt road crosses the northwest corner of the site.
 Archaeological Remains: Variable light and light-to-moderate Late Aztec surface pottery over an area of ca. 4.80 ha. There are no structural remains.
 No surface collection made.
 Classification: Hamlet, 40–80 people.

SITE NO. Zu-Az-164 [no field number]
 Date of Survey: July 9, 1973
 Location: 490100 E, 2198130 N; 19.8793° N, 99.0946° W
 Natural Setting: 2360 m asl, on gently sloping ground at the divide between the Upper Salado and BOM drainages; shallow soil cover and severe erosion.
 Modern Land Use: Rainfall-based agriculture. There is a modern cemetery just northwest of the site.
 Archaeological Remains: Light Late Aztec surface pottery over an area of ca. 0.70 ha. There are no structural remains.
 No surface collection made.
 Classification: Small Hamlet, 5–10 people.

SITE NO. Zu-Az-165 [no field number]
 Date of Survey: July 9, 1973
 Location: 489550 E, 2198000 N; 19.8781° N, 99.0998° W
 Natural Setting: 2360 m asl, on gently sloping ground at the divide between the Upper Salado and BOM drainages; shallow soil cover and severe erosion.
 Modern Land Use: Rainfall-based agriculture. The northern edge of the modern town of Cuevas encroaches onto the southern part of the site area.
 Archaeological Remains: Light Late Aztec surface pottery over an area of ca. 0.60 ha. There are no structural remains.
 No surface collection made.
 Discussion: Because of modern occupation, it is difficult to estimate the site area.
 Classification: Small Hamlet (?), 5–10 people.

SITE NO. Zu-Az-166 [no field number]
 Date of Survey: July 9, 1973
 Location: 489130 E, 2198220 N; 19.8801° N, 99.1038° W
 Natural Setting: 2355 m asl, on gently sloping ground in the Upper Salado Drainage, very close to the divide between the Upper Salado and BOM drainages; shallow soil cover, moderate to severe erosion.
 Modern Land Use: Rainfall-based agriculture. The northern edge of the modern town of Cuevas lies just west of the site.
 Archaeological Remains: Light Late Aztec surface pottery over an area of ca. 0.80 ha. There are also traces of Late Toltec ceramics at the northern end of the site (no LT site defined here). There are no structural remains.
 No surface collection made.
 Classification: Small Hamlet, 5–10 people.

SITE NO. Zu-Az-167 [Zu-Az-61(J)]
 Date of Survey: July 9, 1973
 Location: 488350 E, 2197820 N; 19.8765° N, 99.1113° W
 Natural Setting: 2355 m asl, on gently sloping ground in the Upper Salado Drainage; shallow soil cover and severe erosion.
 Modern Land Use: Marginal pasture.
 Archaeological Remains: Variable light and light-to-moderate Late Aztec surface pottery over an area of ca. 1.40 ha. There are traces of

Plate A176. Zu-Az-169, facing east over general site area.

Plate A177. Zu-Az-169, facing north at Feature DA.

Classic surface pottery in the northern part of the site (no Cl site defined here). There are no structural remains.
No surface collection made.
Classification: Small Hamlet, 10–20 people.

SITE NO. Zu-Az-168 [Zu-Az-60(J)]
Date of Survey: July 9, 1973
Location: 487680 E, 2197970 N; 19.8779° N, 99.1177° W
Natural Setting: 2300 m asl, on gently sloping ground in the Upper Salado Drainage; shallow soil cover and severe erosion.
Modern Land Use: Marginal pasture.
Archaeological Remains: Light Late Aztec surface pottery over an area of ca. 0.60 ha. The Late Az material is mixed with a trace of Classic ceramics (no Classic site defined here). There are no structural remains.
No surface collection made.
Classification: Small Hamlet, 2–5 people.

SITE NO. Zu-Az-169 [Zu-Az-102(J); Feature DA]
Date of Survey: Aug. 2, 1973
Location: 490200 E, 2195250 N; 19.8533° N, 99.0936° W
Natural Setting: 2340 m asl, on gently sloping ground along the top of a broad, low ridge, in the BOM Lower Piedmont (Plate A176); shallow soil cover and severe erosion, with patches of bare tepetate.
Modern Land Use: Pasture.
Archaeological Remains: Variable light and light-to-moderate Late Aztec surface pottery over an area of ca. 18.10 ha. There are traces of Late Toltec ceramics in the west-central part of the site (no LT site defined here). There is one discernible mound (Feature DA) in an unplowed area (Plate A177). This feature measures ca. 15 m in diameter and 0.50 m high, with light-to-moderate Late Az surface pottery, several obsidian blades, and moderate rock rubble. Several other concentrations of amorphous rock rubble may represent the remnants of ancient buildings in other parts of the site.
No surface collection made.
Classification: Small Dispersed Village, 200–400 people.

Plate A178. Zu-Az-172, facing west over general site area.

SITE NO. Zu-Az-170 [Zu-Az-106(J)]
Date of Survey: Aug. 7, 1973
Location: 490720 E, 2195300 N; 19.8538° N, 99.0887° W
Natural Setting: 2355 m asl, on gently sloping ground in the BOM Lower Piedmont; shallow soil cover and moderate erosion.
Modern Land Use: Primarily pasture, with minor rainfall-based agriculture in the southern part of the site.
Archaeological Remains: Variable light and light-to-moderate Late Aztec surface pottery over an area of ca. 3.60 ha. The Late Az material is mixed with Late Toltec ceramics in the southwestern corner of the site area (Zu-LT-130, Zu-LT-131). There are no discernible structures, although two concentrations of amorphous rock rubble along the northeastern edge of the site may represent the remnants of ancient buildings.
No surface collection made.
Discussion: The apparent absence of Early Aztec surface pottery suggests that this locality was abandoned after LT times and reoccupied during the Late Aztec period.
Classification: Hamlet, 35–70 people.

SITE NO. Zu-Az-171 [Zu-Az-108(J)]
Date of Survey: Aug. 7, 1973
Location: 491450 E, 2195320 N; 19.8539° N, 99.0817° W
Natural Setting: 2365 m asl, on gently sloping ground in the BOM Lower Piedmont; shallow soil cover and moderate erosion.
Modern Land Use: Rainfall-based agriculture.
Archaeological Remains: Variable light and light-to-moderate Late Aztec surface pottery over an area of ca. 1.00 ha. There are no structural remains.
No surface collection made.
Classification: Small Hamlet, 10–20 people.

SITE NO. Zu-Az-172 [Zu-Az-76(J), Zu-Az-77(J); Locations 42, 43; Features CO, CP, CQ, CR, CS, CT, CU, CV]
Date of Survey: July 19, 22, 1973
Location: 493130 E, 2195130 N; 19.8522° N, 99.0656° W
Natural Setting: 2365 m asl, on gently sloping ground atop a broad, low hill in the BOM Lower Piedmont (Plate A178); shallow soil cover and severe erosion, with patches of bare tepetate.
Modern Land Use: Wasteland and marginal pasture. A modern dirt road cuts across the southeastern part of the site.
Archaeological Remains: Variable light and light-to-moderate Late Aztec surface pottery over an area of ca. 115.30 ha. Obsidian artifacts are abundant throughout the site. There are three small Late Toltec sites (Zu-LT-120, Zu-LT-121, and Zu-LT-123) scattered across the Aztec site, and there is a partially overlapping Classic site (Zu-Cl-46) in the south-central part of the Aztec site.

We identified 8 mounds clustered in three groups: (1) Features CO and CP near the eastern edge of the site; (2) Features CQ, CR, CS, and CT in the south-central part of the site; and (3) Features CU and CV near the west-central edge of the site. Several concentrations of amorphous rock rubble in other parts of the site may represent the remnants of other ancient buildings.

Fea.	Area and Context	Height	Content
CO	15 m dia., unplowed, badly eroded	Low	Light-to-moderate Late Az surface pottery, numerous obsidian artifacts, moderate rock rubble.
CP	20 m dia., unplowed, badly eroded	0.50 m	Light-to-moderate Late Az surface pottery, numerous obsidian artifacts, moderate rock rubble.
CQ	15 m dia., unplowed, badly eroded	0.10 m	Light-to-moderate Late Az and traces of Cl and LT surface pottery, numerous obsidian artifacts, moderate rock rubble.
CR	20 × 10 m, unplowed	0.50 m	Light-to-moderate Late Az surface pottery, numerous obsidian artifacts, moderate rock rubble.
CS	20 m dia., unplowed (Plate A179)	0.30 m	Light-to-moderate Late Az and traces of Cl and LT surface pottery, numerous obsidian artifacts, moderate rock rubble.
CT	15 × 30 m, unplowed	0.20 m	Light-to-moderate Late Az surface pottery, numerous obsidian artifacts, moderate rock rubble.
CU	15 m dia., unplowed (Plate A180)	0.30 m	Light-to-moderate Late Az surface pottery, several obsidian artifacts, moderate rock rubble
CV	20 m dia., unplowed (Plate A180)	3.50 m	Very little surface pottery. Moderate-to-heavy rock rubble. Looter's pit shows rock-rubble fill (Plate A181).

Plate A179. Zu-Az-172, facing south at Feature CS.

Plate A180. Zu-Az-172, facing south at Features CU (foreground) and CV (background).

We made two surface collections (Locations 42, 43):

Location	Area and Context	Content
42	10 × 10 m, in unplowed area just north of Fea. CP	Light-to-moderate Late Az pottery, green obsidian blades, one basalt mano fragment, light rock rubble.
43	5 × 5 m, in unplowed area	Moderate Cl and light Late Az pottery, moderate rock rubble.

Discussion: Most of the preserved mounds appear to represent domestic residential functions, but Feature CV is clearly a ceremonial-civic structure. The size of this site and the presence of an unusually high mound suggest a supra-local significance during Late Aztec times.

The apparent absence of Early Aztec ceramics suggests that this locality was abandoned after LT times and reoccupied during the Late Aztec period.

Classification: Local Center, 1200–2400 people.

Plate A181. Zu-Az-172, pitted surface of Feature CV.

SITE NO. Zu-Az-173 [Zu-Az-95(J)]
   Date of Survey: July 25, 1973
   Location: 492000 E, 2195050 N; 19.8515° N, 99.0764° W
   Natural Setting: 2385 m asl, on gently sloping ground in the BOM Lower Piedmont; shallow soil cover and severe erosion.
   Modern Land Use: Rainfall-based agriculture, with maguey semi-terracing.
   Archaeological Remains: Light Late Aztec surface pottery over an area of ca. 6.30 ha. The Late Az material is mixed with traces of Late Toltec ceramics in the southwest corner of the site (no LT site defined here). There are no discernible structural remains.
   No surface collection made.
   Classification: Hamlet, 30–60 people.

SITE NO. Zu-Az-174 [Zu-Az-81(J)]
   Date of Survey: July 22, 1973
   Location: 493570 E, 2195950 N; 19.8596° N, 99.0614° W
   Natural Setting: 2345 m asl, on gently sloping ground atop a broad, low hill in the BOM Lower Piedmont; shallow soil cover and severe erosion, with patches of bare tepetate.

   Modern Land Use: Marginal pasture.
   Archaeological Remains: Variable light and light-to-moderate Late Aztec surface pottery over an area of ca. 1.60 ha. There are no discernible structural remains.
   No surface collection made.
   Classification: Small Hamlet, 15–30 people.

SITE NO. Zu-Az-175 [Zu-Az-80(J)]
   Date of Survey: July 22, 1973
   Location: 493850 E, 2195800 N; 19.8583° N, 99.0587° W
   Natural Setting: 2340 m asl, on gently sloping ground atop a broad, low hill, in the BOM Lower Piedmont; shallow soil cover and severe erosion, with patches of bare tepetate.
   Modern Land Use: Marginal pasture.
   Archaeological Remains: Light Late Aztec surface pottery over an area of ca. 0.60 ha. There are no discernible structural remains.
   No surface collection made.
   Classification: Small Hamlet, 5–10 people.

SITE NO. Zu-Az-176 [Zu-Az-79(J)]
  Date of Survey: July 22, 1973
  Location: 494130 E, 2195720 N; 19.8576° N, 99.0561° W
  Natural Setting: 2340 m asl, on gently sloping ground atop a broad, low hill, in the BOM Lower Piedmont; shallow soil cover and severe erosion, with patches of bare tepetate.
  Modern Land Use: Marginal pasture.
  Archaeological Remains: Light Late Aztec surface pottery over an area of ca. 1.30 ha. There are no discernible structural remains.
  No surface collection made.
  Classification: Small Hamlet, 10–20 people.

SITE NO. Zu-Az-177 [Zu-Az-78(J)]
  Date of Survey: July 22, 1973
  Location: 493700 E, 2195430 N; 19.8549° N, 99.0602° W
  Natural Setting: 2355 m asl, on gently sloping ground atop a broad, low hill in the BOM Lower Piedmont; shallow soil cover and severe erosion, with patches of bare tepetate.
  Modern Land Use: Marginal pasture.
  Archaeological Remains: Light Late Aztec surface pottery over an area of ca. 0.70 ha. There are no discernible structural remains.
  No surface collection made.
  Classification: Small Hamlet, 5–10 people.

SITE NO. Zu-Az-178 [Zu-Az-82(J)]
  Date of Survey: July 22, 1973
  Location: 493970 E, 2194500 N; 19.8465° N, 99.0576° W
  Natural Setting: 2330 m asl, on gently sloping ground in the BOM Lower Piedmont; shallow soil cover and severe erosion, with patches of bare tepetate.
  Modern Land Use: Marginal pasture. A modern dirt road crosses the southern tip of the site.
  Archaeological Remains: Light Late Aztec surface pottery over an area of ca. 4.10 ha. There are no discernible structural remains.
  No surface collection made.
  Classification: Hamlet, 25–50 people.

SITE NO. Zu-Az-179 [Zu-Az-83(J)]
  Date of Survey: July 22, 1973
  Location: 493400 E, 2194380 N; 19.8454° N, 99.0630° W
  Natural Setting: 2340 m asl, on gently sloping ground atop a broad, low hill in the BOM Lower Piedmont; shallow soil cover and severe erosion, with patches of bare tepetate.
  Modern Land Use: Marginal pasture. A modern dirt road crosses the eastern part of the site.
  Archaeological Remains: Variable light and light-to-moderate Late Aztec surface pottery over an area of ca. 2.40 ha. The Late Az material is mixed with traces of Classic ceramics in the eastern part of the site (no Cl site defined here). There are no discernible structural remains.
  No surface collection made.
  Classification: Hamlet, 25–50 people.

SITE NO. Zu-Az-180 [Zu-Az-94(J)]
  Date of Survey: July 22, 1973
  Location: 492470 E, 2194650 N; 19.8479° N, 99.0719° W
  Natural Setting: 2370 m asl, on gently sloping ground in the BOM Lower Piedmont; shallow soil cover and severe erosion, with patches of bare tepetate.
  Modern Land Use: Pasture and marginal rainfall-based agriculture.
  Archaeological Remains: Light Late Aztec surface pottery over an area of ca. 9.20 ha. The Late Az material is mixed with partially overlapping Late Toltec ceramics (Zu-LT-122) in the southwestern part of the site. There are no discernible structural remains.
  No surface collection made.
  Discussion: The apparent absence of Early Aztec surface pottery suggests that this locality was abandoned after LT times and reoccupied during the Late Aztec period.
  Classification: Hamlet, 50–100 people.

SITE NO. Zu-Az-181 [Zu-Az-97(J)]
  Date of Survey: July 30, 1973
  Location: 492250 E, 2193800 N; 19.8402° N, 99.0740° W
  Natural Setting: 2355 m asl, on gently sloping ground in the BOM Lower Piedmont; shallow soil cover and severe erosion.
  Modern Land Use: Rainfall-based agriculture, with maguey semi-terracing. A modern dirt road cuts across the northern end of the site.
  Archaeological Remains: Variable light and light-to-moderate Late Aztec surface pottery over an area of ca. 11.20 ha. The Late Az material is mixed with partially overlapping Late Toltec (Zu-LT-129), Classic (Zu-Cl-47), and Terminal Formative (Zu-TF-5) ceramics in the northern part of the Aztec site area. There are no discernible structural remains, but several concentrations of amorphous rock rubble may represent the remnants of ancient buildings.
  No surface collection made.
  Discussion: The apparent absence of Early Aztec surface pottery suggests that this locality was abandoned after LT times and reoccupied during the Late Aztec period.
  Classification: Small Dispersed Village, 150–300 people.

SITE NO. Zu-Az-182 [Zu-Az-96(J); Features CY, CZ]
  Date of Survey: July 30, 1973
  Location: 491700 E, 2195130 N; 19.8522° N, 99.0793° W
  Natural Setting: 2335 m asl, on gently sloping ground in the BOM Lower Piedmont; shallow soil cover and severe erosion.
  Modern Land Use: Rainfall-based agriculture. There is a modern house in the southern part of the site.
  Archaeological Remains: Variable light and light-to-moderate Late Aztec surface pottery over an area of ca. 6.20 ha. The western limits of the site could not be defined because the local landowner denied us access to that area.
  There are two discernible mounds (Features CY, CZ) in the central site area:

Fea.	Area and Context	Height	Content
CY	15 m dia., in unplowed field	0.30 m	Light-to-moderate Late Az surface pottery (both Aztec III and IV Black/Orange), several obsidian artifacts, moderate rock rubble.
CZ	12 m dia., in unplowed field, a few m from Fea. CY	0.15 m	Light-to-moderate Late Az surface pottery (both Aztec III and IV Black/Orange), several obsidian artifacts, moderate rock rubble.

  No surface collection made.
  Discussion: The presence of both Aztec III and IV Black/Orange surface pottery indicates that this site continued to be occupied from Late Az times into the Early Colonial period. The site area remains uncertain.
  Classification: Small Dispersed Village (?), 75–150 people.

SITE NO. Zu-Az-183 [Zu-Az-98(J)]
Date of Survey: July 30, 1973
Location: 491700 E, 2193130 N; 19.8341° N, 99.0793° W
Natural Setting: 2330 m asl, on gently sloping ground in the BOM Lower Piedmont; shallow soil cover and severe erosion.
Modern Land Use: Pasture and maguey semi-terracing.
Archaeological Remains: Variable light and light-to-moderate Late Aztec surface pottery over an area of ca. 3.60 ha. The western limits of the site could not be defined because the local landowner denied us access to that area. There are no discernible structural remains, although a concentration of amorphous rock rubble in the southern part of the site may represent the remnants of an ancient building.
No surface collection made.
Discussion: The site area remains uncertain.
Classification: Hamlet (?), 40–80 people.

SITE NO. Zu-Az-184 [Zu-Az-99(J)]
Date of Survey: July 30, 1973
Location: 491650 E, 2192720 N; 19.8304° N, 99.0797° W
Natural Setting: 2325 m asl, on gently sloping ground in the BOM Lower Piedmont; shallow soil cover and severe erosion.
Modern Land Use: Pasture and maguey semi-terracing.
Archaeological Remains: Variable light and light-to-moderate Late Aztec surface pottery over an area of ca. 6.20 ha. There are no discernible structural remains.
No surface collection made.
Classification: Small Dispersed Village, 65–130 people.

SITE NO. Zu-Az-185 [Zu-Az-84(J)]
Date of Survey: July 22, 1973
Location: 493650 E, 2193030 N; 19.8332° N, 99.0606° W
Natural Setting: 2320 m asl, on gently sloping ground in the BOM Lower Piedmont; medium soil cover and slight to moderate erosion.
Modern Land Use: Rainfall-based agriculture.
Archaeological Remains: Light Late Aztec surface pottery over an area of ca. 0.50 ha. There are no structural remains.
No surface collection made.
Classification: Small Hamlet, 2–5 people.

SITE NO. Zu-Az-186, Zu-Az-187 [Zu-Az-85a, b(J)]
Date of Survey: July 29, 1973
Location:
Zu-Az-186: 494180 E, 2192380 N; 19.8333° N, 99.0556° W;
Zu-Az-187: 494180 E, 2192220 N; 19.8259° N, 99.0556° W
Natural Setting: 2310 m asl, on moderately sloping ground in the BOM Lower Piedmont; shallow soil cover and moderate erosion.
Modern Land Use: Rainfall-based agriculture.
Archaeological Remains: There are two clusters of light Late Aztec surface pottery separated by a gap of ca. 75 m. The northern cluster (Zu-Az-186) covers an area of ca. 0.40 ha; the southern cluster (Zu-Az-187) covers ca. 0.70 ha. There are no discernible structural remains.
No surface collection made.
Classification: Small Hamlet, 5–10 people.

SITE NO. Zu-Az-188 [Zu-Az-86(J)]
Date of Survey: July 29, 1973
Location: 494030 E, 2191750 N; 19.8217° N, 99.0570° W
Natural Setting: 2310 m asl, on gently sloping ground in the BOM Lower Piedmont; shallow soil cover and moderate erosion.
Modern Land Use: Rainfall-based agriculture, with maguey semi-terracing.
Archaeological Remains: Light Late Aztec surface pottery over a poorly defined area of ca. 1.50 ha. There are no discernible structural remains.
No surface collection.
Classification: Small Hamlet, 10–20 people.

SITE NO. Zu-Az-189 [Zu-Az-87(J)]
Date of Survey: July 29, 1973
Location: 494130 E, 2191400 N; 19.8185° N, 99.0561° W
Natural Setting: 2305 m asl, on gently sloping ground in the BOM Lower Piedmont; medium soil cover and moderate erosion.
Modern Land Use: Rainfall-based agriculture. The site area was fallow at the time of our survey.
Archaeological Remains: Light Late Aztec surface pottery over a poorly defined area of ca. 2.10 ha. The Late Az material is mixed with partially overlapping Terminal Formative ceramics (Zu-TF-7) at the southern edge of the site. There are also traces of Late Toltec surface pottery (no LT site defined here). There are no discernible structural remains.
No surface collection made.
Classification: Small Hamlet, 10–20 people.

SITE NO. Zu-Az-190 [Zu-Az-89(J)]
Date of Survey: July 29, 1973
Location: 494030 E, 2191200 N; 19.8167° N, 99.0570° W
Natural Setting: 2305 m asl, on gently sloping ground in the BOM Lower Piedmont; medium soil cover and moderate erosion.
Modern Land Use: Rainfall-based agriculture, with maguey semi-terracing.
Archaeological Remains: Light Late Aztec surface pottery over an area of ca. 0.90 ha. The Late Az material is mixed with partially overlapping Terminal Formative ceramics (Zu-TF-7) in the central part of the site.
No surface collection.
Classification: Small Hamlet, 5–10 people.

SITE NO. Zu-Az-191 [Zu-Az-88(J)]
Date of Survey: July 29, 1973
Location: 493720 E, 2191300 N; 19.8176° N, 99.0600° W
Natural Setting: 2300 m asl, on gently sloping ground in the BOM Lower Piedmont; medium soil cover and moderate erosion.
Modern Land Use: Rainfall-based agriculture, with maguey semi-terracing.
Archaeological Remains: Light Late Aztec surface pottery over an area of ca. 0.40 ha. The Late Az material is mixed with partially overlapping Terminal Formative ceramics (Zu-TF-7) in the central part of the site. There are no discernible structural remains.
No surface collection made.
Classification: Small Hamlet, 2–5 people.

SITE NO. Zu-Az-192, Zu-Az-193 [Zu-Az-90a, b(J)]
Date of Survey: July 29, 1973
Location:
Zu-Az-192: 493530 E, 2191000 N; 19.8149° N, 99.0618° W;
Zu-Az-193: 493430 E, 2191000 N; 19.8149° N, 99.0627° W
Natural Setting: 2285 m asl, on gently sloping ground at the lowermost edge of the BOM Lower Piedmont, near the upper edge of the Lakeshore Plain; medium soil cover and moderate erosion.

Plate A182. Zu-Az-196, facing north at Feature DB.

Modern Land Use: Rainfall-based agriculture.

Archaeological Remains: Two concentrations of variable light and light-to-moderate Late Aztec surface pottery separated by a gap of ca. 100 m. The eastern sherd concentration (Zu-Az-192) measures ca. 0.50 ha; the western sherd concentration measures ca. 0.60 ha. There are also traces of Late Toltec surface pottery along the southern edges of the Aztec occupation (no LT site defined here). There are no discernible structural remains.

No surface collection made.

Classification: Small Hamlet, 10–20 people.

SITE NO. Zu-Az-194 [Zu-Az-101(J)]

Date of Survey: July 31, 1973
Location: 492880 E, 2191570 N; 19.8201° N, 99.0680° W
Natural Setting: 2305 m asl, on gently sloping ground in the BOM Lower Piedmont, near the upper edge of the Lakeshore Plain; shallow soil cover and severe erosion.

Modern Land Use: Rainfall-based agriculture, with maguey semi-terracing. A modern dirt road cuts across the western end of the site.

Archaeological Remains: Variable light and light-to-moderate Late Aztec surface pottery over an area of ca. 10.80 ha. There are no discernible structural remains.

No surface collection made.

Classification: Small Dispersed Village, 110–220 people.

SITE NO. Zu-Az-195 [Zu-Az-100(J)]

Date of Survey: July 31, 1973
Location: 491880 E, 2191900 N; 19.8230° N, 99.0775° W
Natural Setting: 2305 m asl, on gently sloping ground in the BOM Lower Piedmont, near the upper edge of the Lakeshore Plain; shallow soil cover and severe erosion.

Modern Land Use: Pasture and maguey semi-terracing. A modern dirt road crosses the northern end of the site.

Archaeological Remains: Variable light and light-to-moderate Late Aztec surface pottery over an area of ca. 15.40 ha. The Late Az material is mixed with traces of Late Toltec ceramics near the western edge of the site (no LT site defined here). There are no discernible structural remains.

No surface collection made.

Classification: Small Dispersed Village, 150–300 people.

SITE NO. Zu-Az-196 [Zu-Az-112(J); Features DB, DC]

Date of Survey: Aug. 8, 1973
Location: 491320 E, 2192250 N; 19.8262° N, 99.0829° W
Natural Setting: 2300 m asl, on gently sloping ground in the BOM Lower Piedmont, near the upper edge of the Lakeshore Plain; shallow soil cover and severe erosion.

Modern Land Use: Pasture and maguey semi-terracing. A modern dirt road crosses the northwestern part of the site.

Archaeological Remains: Variable light and light-to-moderate Late Aztec surface pottery over an area of ca. 8.10 ha. There are two discernible, but badly destroyed, mounds (Features DB, DC): one (DB) in the northern part of the site, and another (DC) near the site's southeastern edge. Two concentrations of amorphous rock rubble in the south-central part of the site may represent the remnants of other ancient buildings.

Fea.	Area and Context	Height	Content
DB	15 m dia., in unplowed field (Plate A182)	0.20 m	Light-to-moderate Late Az surface pottery (both Az III and IV B/O), several green obsidian blades, moderate rock rubble.
DC	15 m dia., in unplowed field	0.10 m	Light-to-moderate Late Az surface pottery (both Az III and IV B/O), several green obsidian blades, moderate rock rubble.

No surface collection made.

Discussion: The presence of both Aztec III and IV Black/Orange pottery indicates that occupation here continued from Late Az times into the Early Colonial period.

Classification: Small Dispersed Village, 80–160 people.

SITE NO. Zu-Az-197 [Zu-Az-107(J)]
Date of Survey: Aug. 7, 1973
Location: 491180 E, 2194320 N; 19.8449° N, 99.0842° W
Natural Setting: 2345 m asl, on gently sloping ground in the BOM Lower Piedmont; shallow soil cover and moderate erosion.
Modern Land Use: Rainfall-based agriculture. A modern dirt road cuts across the southern part of the site.
Archaeological Remains: Variable light and light-to-moderate Late Aztec surface pottery over an area of ca. 0.50 ha. There are no discernible structural remains. The western limits of the site could not be determined because the local landowner denied us access to that area.
No surface collection made.
Discussion: The site may be somewhat larger than our estimate.
Classification: Small Hamlet (?), 5–10 people.

SITE NO. Zu-Az-198 [Zu-Az-103(J)]
Date of Survey: Aug. 1, 1973
Location: 490250 E, 2194530 N; 19.8468° N, 99.0931° W
Natural Setting: 2320 m asl, on gently sloping ground atop a broad, low ridge in the BOM Lower Piedmont; shallow soil cover and severe erosion, with patches of bare tepetate.
Modern Land Use: Pasture.
Archaeological Remains: Variable light and light-to-moderate Late Aztec surface pottery over an area of ca. 2.90 ha. There are no discernible structural remains. The southeastern limits of the site could not be determined because our survey team was denied access to that area.
No surface collection made.
Discussion: The site may be somewhat larger than our estimate.
Classification: Hamlet (?), 30–60 people.

SITE NO. Zu-Az-199 [Zu-Az-104(J)]
Date of Survey: Aug. 1, 1973
Location: 489820 E, 2194470 N; 19.8462° N, 99.0972° W
Natural Setting: 2305 m asl, on gently sloping ground atop a broad, low ridge in the BOM Lower Piedmont; shallow soil cover and severe erosion, with patches of bare tepetate.
Modern Land Use: Pasture and maguey semi-terracing.
Archaeological Remains: Light Late Aztec surface pottery over an area of ca. 1.70 ha. There are no discernible structural remains.
No surface collection made.
Classification: Small Hamlet, 10–20 people.

SITE NO. Zu-Az-200 [Zu-Az-59(M)]
Date of Survey: July 19, 1973
Location: 479880 E, 2195130 N; 19.8521° N, 99.1922° W
Natural Setting: 2330 m asl, on gently sloping ground in the BOM Lower Piedmont; shallow soil cover and moderate erosion.
Modern Land Use: Rainfall-based agriculture.
Archaeological Remains: Variable light and light-to-moderate Late Aztec surface pottery over an area of ca. 0.80 ha. There are no discernible structural remains.
No surface collection made.
Classification: Small Hamlet, 10–20 people.

SITE NO. Zu-Az-201 [Zu-Az-60(M)]
Date of Survey: July 19, 1973
Location: 479650 E, 2195250 N; 19.8532° N, 99.1944° W
Natural Setting: 2340 m asl, on gently sloping ground in the BOM Lower Piedmont; shallow soil cover and moderate erosion.
Modern Land Use: Rainfall-based agriculture.
Archaeological Remains: Variable light and light-to-moderate Late Aztec surface pottery over an area of ca. 0.60 ha. There are no discernible structural remains.
No surface collection made.
Classification: Small Hamlet, 5–10 people.

SITE NO. Zu-Az-202 [Zu-Az-58(M); Location 57]
Date of Survey: July 19, 1973
Location: 486550 E, 2194070 N; 19.8426° N, 99.1285° W
Natural Setting: 2345 m asl, on gently sloping ground in the BOM Lower Piedmont; shallow soil cover and severe erosion, with patches of bare tepetate.
Modern Land Use: Marginal pasture.
Archaeological Remains: Variable light and light-to-moderate Late Aztec surface pottery over an area of ca. 2.30 ha. There are no discernible structural remains.
We made one surface collection (Location 57) over an area of ca. 5 × 5 m in an unplowed area, with light-to-moderate Late Aztec surface pottery and moderate rock rubble. We noted numerous green obsidian blades, several obsidian scrapers, one obsidian projectile point, one obsidian trilobal eccentric, and one maguey spindle whorl.
Classification: Hamlet, 25–50 people.

SITE NO. Zu-Az-203 [Zu-Az-87(M); Feature EB]
Date of Survey: July 29, 1973
Location: 486280 E, 2193780 N; 19.8400° N, 99.1311° W
Natural Setting: 2340 m asl, on gently sloping ground in the BOM Lower Piedmont; shallow soil cover and severe erosion, with patches of bare tepetate.
Modern Land Use: Wasteland.
Archaeological Remains: The site consists of a single mound (Feature EB) measuring ca. 5.00 m in diameter and 1.00 m high in an unplowed area, with light Late Aztec surface pottery and light rock rubble. The mound rests on bare tepetate.
No surface collection made.
Classification: Small Hamlet, 2–5 people.

SITE NO. Zu-Az-204 [Zu-Az-56(M); Features DD, DE, DF]
Date of Survey: July 18, 1973
Location: 485380 E, 2195570 N; 19.8562° N, 99.1396° W
Natural Setting: 2360 m asl, on gently sloping ground in the BOM Lower Piedmont, just east of the divide between the Upper Salado and BOM drainages; medium soil cover and moderate erosion.
Modern Land Use: Rainfall-based agriculture.
Archaeological Remains: Variable very light and light Late Aztec surface pottery over an area of ca. 0.40 ha. The Late Az material is mixed with heavier and more extensive Late Toltec ceramics (Zu-LT-150). We identified three mounds (Features DD, DE, DF)—it is uncertain whether these are primarily of Late Toltec or Aztec date.

Fea.	Area and Context	Height	Content
DD	14 × 16 m, in unplowed field	1.50 m	Light LT and trace Az surface pottery, light rock rubble, exposed wall of rock and tepetate blocks.
DE	16 × 18 m, in plowed field	1.50 m	Very light LT and Az surface pottery and very light rock rubble.
DF	19 × 24 m, in unplowed field (Plate A183)	1.50 m	Very light LT and Az surface pottery and very light rock rubble.

Plate A183. Zu-Az-204, facing south at Feature DF.

No surface collection made.

Discussion: This cluster of relatively high mounds with sparse surface pottery may have had a nonresidential function. Apparently this complex was in use during both Late Toltec and Late Aztec times; we suspect the final form and appearance of the three structures is Late Aztec in age. The apparent absence of Early Aztec surface pottery suggests that this locality was abandoned after LT times and reoccupied during the Late Aztec period.

Classification: Isolated Ceremonial-Civic Precinct (?). No permanent population.

SITE NO. Zu-Az-205 [Zu-Az-55(M)]
  Date of Survey: July 18, 1973
  Location: 485150 E, 2195550 N; 19.8560° N, 99.1418° W
  Natural Setting: 2380 m asl, on gently sloping ground in the BOM Lower Piedmont, just east of the divide between the Upper Salado and BOM drainages; shallow soil cover and moderate erosion.
  Modern Land Use: Pasture.
  Archaeological Remains: Light Late Aztec surface pottery over an area of ca. 0.90 ha. The Late Az material is mixed with partially overlapping and more extensive Late Toltec ceramics (Zu-LT-150). There are no discernible structural remains.

No surface collection made.

Discussion: The apparent absence of Early Aztec surface pottery suggests that this locality was abandoned after LT times and reoccupied during the Late Aztec period.

Classification: Small Hamlet, 10–20 people.

SITE NO. Zu-Az-206 [Zu-Az-57(M)]
  Date of Survey: July 18, 1973
  Location: 485000 E, 2195430 N; 19.8549° N, 99.1433° W
  Natural Setting: 2405 m asl, on gently sloping ground in the BOM Lower Piedmont, just east of the divide between the Upper Salado and BOM drainages; medium soil cover and moderate erosion.
  Modern Land Use: Pasture.
  Archaeological Remains: The site consists of a single structural remnant (Feature DH): a pair of stone wall bases that form the corner of a structure measuring at least 9 × 11 m in area, with very light Late Toltec (Zu-LT-149) and Late Aztec surface pottery and light rock rubble. We noted several green obsidian blades.

No surface collection made.

Discussion: The age of Feature DH is uncertain; it may be either Late Toltec or Late Aztec in age, or both. The apparent absence of Early Aztec surface pottery suggests that this locality was abandoned after LT times and reoccupied during the Late Aztec period.

Classification: Small Hamlet, 2–5 people.

SITE NO. Zu-Az-207 [Zu-Az-75(M); Features DN, DO]
  Date of Survey: July 22, 1973
  Location: 483900 E, 2195900 N; 19.8591° N, 99.1538° W
  Natural Setting: 2360 m asl, on gently sloping ground in the Upper Salado Drainage, just west of the divide between the Upper Salado and BOM drainages; shallow soil cover and severe erosion, with patches of bare tepetate. A major *barranca* cuts through the southern part of the site.

Modern Land Use: Pasture.
Archaeological Remains: Light Late Aztec surface pottery over an area of ca. 0.40 ha. There are two discernible, badly damaged mounds (Features DN, DO) in the southern part of the site:

Fea.	Area and Context	Height	Content
DN	10 × 20 m, in unplowed field	2.50 m	Very light to light Late Az surface pottery, several obsidian artifacts, light rock rubble on mound surface, moderate rock rubble around base.
DO	14 × 20 m, in unplowed field	1.75 m	Very light to light Late Az surface pottery, several obsidian artifacts, light rock rubble on mound surface, moderate rock rubble around base.

No surface collection made.
Discussion: The relatively high mounds and comparatively scarce surface pottery suggests a non-domestic function.
Classification: Isolated Ceremonial-Civic Precinct (?), probably no permanent population.

SITE NO. Zu-Az-208 [Zu-Az-72(M); Features DR, DQ]
Date of Survey: July 23–24, 1973
Location: 483100 E, 2195930 N; 19.8594° N, 99.1614° W
Natural Setting: 2340 m asl, on gently sloping ground in the Upper Salado Drainage; medium soil cover and moderate erosion.
Modern Land Use: Rainfall-based agriculture.
Archaeological Remains: Variable light and light-to-moderate Late Aztec surface pottery over an area of ca. 2.80 ha. The Late Az material is mixed with heavier Classic ceramics in the western part of the site (Zu-Cl-60). There are two discernible, badly destroyed mounds (Features DR, DQ) in the central part of the site. These features have Az and Cl surface pottery, plus traces of Early Toltec, so their age is uncertain.

Fea.	Area and Context	Height	Content
DR	8 × 10 m, in unplowed field	0.40 m	Light Cl, very light ET, and very light Late Az surface pottery; moderate rock rubble; heavy grass cover.
DQ	10 × 10 m, in unplowed field	0.40 m	Light Cl and ET, and very light Late Az surface pottery; moderate-to-heavy rock rubble; heavy grass cover; looter's pit shows rock-rubble fill.

No surface collection made.
Classification: Hamlet, 30–60 people.

SITE NO. Zu-Az-209 [Zu-Az-73(M)]
Date of Survey: July 20, 1973
Location: 482380 E, 2196000 N; 19.8600° N, 99.1683° W
Natural Setting: 2300 m asl, on gently sloping ground in the Upper Salado Drainage; medium soil cover and moderate erosion.
Modern Land Use: Rainfall-based agriculture. A modern dirt road borders the north edge of the site.
Archaeological Remains: Light Late Aztec surface pottery over an area of ca. 1.50 ha. There are no discernible structural remains.
No surface collection made.
Classification: Small Hamlet, 10–20 people.

SITE NO. Zu-Az-210 [Zu-Az-74(M)]
Date of Survey: July 20, 1973
Location: 482380 E, 2196250 N; 19.8623° N, 99.1683° W
Natural Setting: 2295 m asl, on gently sloping ground in the Upper Salado Drainage; medium soil cover and moderate erosion.
Modern Land Use: Rainfall-based agriculture.
Archaeological Remains: Light Late Aztec surface pottery over an area of ca. 0.70 ha. The Late Az material is mixed with traces of Late Toltec ceramics in the northern part of the site (no LT site defined here). There are no discernible structural remains. The northern limits of the site could not be defined because of a gap in airphoto coverage on that side.
No surface collection made.
Discussion: Site area remains uncertain.
Classification: Small Hamlet (?), 5–10 people.

SITE NO. Zu-Az-211 [Zu-Az-100(M)]
Date of Survey: Nov. 7, 1973
Location: 479570 E, 2196600 N; 19.8654° N, 99.1951° W
Natural Setting: 2275 m asl, on gently sloping ground in the Upper Salado Drainage; medium soil cover and moderate to severe erosion.
Modern Land Use: Rainfall-based agriculture, with maguey semi-terracing.
Archaeological Remains: Light Late Aztec surface pottery over an area of ca. 1.40 ha. The Late Az material is mixed with much heavier and more extensive Late Toltec ceramics (Zu-LT-135). No discernible structural remains can be associated with the Aztec-period occupation.
No surface collection made.
Discussion: The apparent absence of Early Aztec surface pottery suggests that this locality was abandoned after LT times and reoccupied during the Late Aztec period.
Classification: Small Hamlet, 10–20 people.

SITE NO. Zu-Az-212 [Zu-Az-41(M)]
Date of Survey: July 2, 1973
Location: 479320 E, 2205100 N; 19.9422° N, 99.1977° W
Natural Setting: 2380 m asl, on gently sloping ground in the Upper Salado Drainage; shallow to medium soil cover, moderate to severe erosion.
Modern Land Use: Pasture.
Archaeological Remains: Variable light and light-to-moderate Late Aztec surface pottery (both Aztec III and IV Black/Orange seen) over an area of ca. 0.60 ha. We noted several green obsidian blades and scrapers.
There is one discernible mound (Feature CS):

Fea.	Area and Context	Height	Content
CS	4 × 11 m, in unplowed area	0.50 m	Very little surface pottery on mound itself; light-to-moderate Late Az surface pottery (Az IV Black/Orange noted, but no Az III) around base and in surrounding area, mixed with glazed Colonial-period ceramics; light-to-moderate rock rubble. Two stone wall sections visible.

No surface collection made.
Discussion: The presence of Aztec IV Black/Orange surface pottery, together with the presence of some glazed ceramics, indicates that occupation continued from Late Az times into the Early Colonial period and perhaps beyond.
Classification: Small Hamlet, 5–10 people.

SITE NO. Zu-Az-213 [Zu-Az-42(M)]
Date of Survey: July 2, 1973
Location: 479000 E, 2200500 N; 19.9007° N, 99.2006° W

Plate A184. Zu-Az-214, facing east over general site area.

Natural Setting: 2315 m asl, on gently sloping ground in the Upper Salado Drainage; shallow to medium soil cover and severe erosion, with patches of bare tepetate.
Modern Land Use: Pasture.
Archaeological Remains: Light-to-moderate Late Aztec surface pottery, mixed with lighter Colonial-period glazed ceramics, over an area of ca. 0.80 ha. There are no discernible structural remains.
No surface collection made.
Classification: Small Hamlet, 10–20 people.

SITE NO. Zu-Az-214 [Zu-Az-45(M); Features CT, CU, CV]
Date of Survey: July 4, 1973
Location: 478300 E, 2202900 N; 19.9223° N, 99.2073° W
Natural Setting: 2295 m asl, on gently sloping ground in the Upper Salado Drainage; shallow soil cover and severe erosion, with patches of bare tepetate (Plate A184).
Modern Land Use: Pasture. A railroad line borders the eastern edge of the site, and there is a large borrow-pit for obtaining construction fill at the northern edge of the site.
Archaeological Remains: Light Late Aztec surface pottery over an area of ca. 1.00 ha, plus a cluster of three badly eroded mounds (Features CT, CU, CV), and the possible remnants of a fourth structure, in the central site area.

Fea.	Area and Context	Height	Content
CT	12 m dia., in unplowed area	1.00 m	Very light Late Az surface pottery, and moderate rock rubble.
CU	12 m dia., in unplowed area	1.00 m	Very light Late Az surface pottery, and moderate rock rubble.
CV	4 m dia., in unplowed area	1.00 m	Very light Late Az surface pottery, and moderate rock rubble. Adjacent to the possible remnants of another structure (possibly another section of CV), now defined by amorphous rock rubble.

No surface collection made.
Discussion: The relatively high mounds, and sparse surface pottery, suggest a nonresidential function.
Classification: Isolated Ceremonial-Civic Precinct (?), few permanent inhabitants.

SITE NO. Zu-Az-215 [Zu-Az-97(M)]
Date of Survey: Nov. 6, 1973
Location: 477850 E, 2197780 N; 19.8761° N, 99.2116° W
Natural Setting: 2270 m asl, on gently sloping ground in the Upper Salado Drainage; medium soil cover and moderate to severe erosion.
Modern Land Use: Rainfall-based agriculture, with maguey semi-terracing.
Archaeological Remains: Light Late Aztec surface pottery over an area of ca. 2.50 ha. The Late Az material is mixed with partially overlapping Late Toltec ceramics (Zu-LT-136) in the southeastern part of the site. There are no discernible structural remains.
No surface collection made.
Discussion: The apparent absence of Early Aztec surface pottery suggests that this locality was abandoned after LT times and reoccupied during the Late Aztec period.
Classification: Hamlet, 20–40 people.

SITE NO. Zu-Az-216 [Zu-Az-98(M)]
Date of Survey: Nov. 5, 1973
Location: 476880 E, 2197720 N; 19.8755° N, 99.2208° W
Natural Setting: 2270 m asl, on gently sloping ground in the Upper Salado Drainage; shallow soil cover and severe erosion, with patches of bare tepetate. There is a fairly thick cover of pirule trees, wild nopal, and thorn brush.
Modern Land Use: Pasture.
Archaeological Remains: Light Late Aztec surface pottery over an area of ca. 7.40 ha. The Late Az material is mixed with partially

overlapping Late Toltec ceramics (Zu-LT-137) in the western part of the site. There are no discernible structural remains.

No surface collection made.

Discussion: The apparent absence of Early Aztec surface pottery suggests that this locality was abandoned after LT times and reoccupied during the Late Aztec period.

Classification: Hamlet, 50–100 people.

SITE NO. Zu-Az-217 [Zu-Az-99(M)]
  Date of Survey: Nov. 15, 1973
  Location: 476320 E, 2196570 N; 19.8651° N, 99.2262° W
  Natural Setting: 2270 m asl, on gently sloping ground in the Upper Salado Drainage; shallow soil cover and severe erosion, with numerous patches of bare tepetate.
  Modern Land Use: Pasture.
  Archaeological Remains: Variable very light, light, and light-to-moderate Late Aztec surface pottery over an area of ca. 31.80 ha. The Late Az material is mixed with traces of Classic and Late Toltec ceramics (no Cl or LT site defined here). There are no discernible structural remains.
  No surface collection made.
  Classification: Large Dispersed Village, 400–800 people.

SITE NO. Zu-Az-218 [Zu-Az-103(M)]
  Date of Survey: Nov. 15, 1973
  Location: 474930 E, 2193220 N; 19.8348° N, 99.2394° W
  Natural Setting: 2280 m asl, on gently sloping ground in the Upper Salado Drainage; shallow soil cover and severe erosion, with patches of bare tepetate. Two major *barrancas* cut across the site area.
  Modern Land Use: Pasture and wasteland.
  Archaeological Remains: Variable light and light-to-moderate Late Aztec surface pottery over an area of ca. 38.00 ha. The northwestern corner of the site abuts the western edge of the survey area, and so we did not determine the extent of the site in that direction. The Late Az material is mixed with smaller concentrations of Late Toltec ceramics in several parts of the site (Zu-LT-139, -140, -141, -142). There are no discernible structural remains.
  No surface collection made.
  Discussion: The apparent absence of Early Aztec surface pottery suggests that this locality was abandoned after LT times and reoccupied during the Late Aztec period. Because the western limits of the site were not defined, the full surface area remains uncertain.
  Classification: Large Dispersed Village (?), 400–800 people.

SITE NO. Zu-Az-219 [Zu-Cl-41(M)]
  Date of Survey: Nov. 13, 1973
  Location: 480950 E, 2194650 N; 19.8478° N, 99.1819° W
  Natural Setting: 2280 m asl, on gently sloping ground in the Upper Salado Drainage; medium soil cover and moderate erosion.
  Modern Land Use: Rainfall-based agriculture.
  Archaeological Remains: Light Late Aztec surface pottery over an area of ca. 3.50 ha. The Late Az material is mixed with heavier and more extensive Early Toltec ceramics (Zu-ET-20). There are no discernible structural remains.
  No surface collection made.
  Classification: Hamlet, 25–50 people.

SITE NO. Zu-Az-220 [Zu-Az-101(M)]
  Date of Survey: Nov. 13, 1973
  Location: 481250 E, 2194530 N; 19.8467° N, 99.1791° W
  Natural Setting: 2290 m asl, on gently sloping ground near in the Upper Salado Drainage; shallow soil cover and severe erosion, with patches of bare tepetate.
  Modern Land Use: Rainfall-based agriculture. There is some use of earth *bancales* to control sheet erosion.
  Archaeological Remains: Light Late Aztec surface pottery over an area of ca. 2.40 ha. There are no discernible structural remains.
  No surface collection made.
  Classification: Hamlet, 20–40 people.

SITE NO. Zu-Az-221 [Zu-Az-102(M)]
  Date of Survey: Nov. 14, 1973
  Location: 481280 E, 2193180 N; 19.8345° N, 99.1788° W
  Natural Setting: 2315 m asl, on gently sloping ground in the Upper Salado Drainage, just north of the divide between the Upper Salado and BOM drainages; shallow soil cover and severe erosion, with patches of bare tepetate.
  Modern Land Use: Rainfall-based agriculture, with maguey semi-terracing.
  Archaeological Remains: Light Late Aztec surface pottery over an area of ca. 7.80 ha. There are no discernible structural remains.
  No surface collection made.
  Classification: Hamlet, 40–80 people.

SITE NO. Zu-Az-222 [Zu-Az-77(M)]
  Date of Survey: July 20, 1973
  Location: 482100 E, 2192970 N; 19.8326° N, 99.1709° W
  Natural Setting: 2345 m asl, on gently sloping ground in the Upper Salado Drainage, just north of the divide between the Upper Salado and BOM drainages; shallow soil cover and moderate erosion.
  Modern Land Use: Rainfall-based agriculture, with maguey semi-terracing and some use of stone-faced terracing to control sheet erosion.
  Archaeological Remains: Light Late Aztec surface pottery over an area of ca. 0.80 ha. There are no discernible structural remains.
  No surface collection made.
  Classification: Small Hamlet, 5–10 people.

SITE NO. Zu-Az-223 [Zu-Az-76(M)]
  Date of Survey: July 20, 1973
  Location: 482380 E, 2194030 N; 19.8422° N, 99.1683° W
  Natural Setting: 2345 m asl, on gently sloping ground in the Upper Salado Drainage, just northwest of the divide between the Upper Salado and BOM drainages; medium soil cover and moderate erosion.
  Modern Land Use: Rainfall-based agriculture, with maguey semi-terracing.
  Archaeological Remains: Variable light and light-to-moderate Late Aztec surface pottery over an area of ca. 1.20 ha. There are no discernible structural remains.
  No surface collection made.
  Classification: Hamlet, 15–30 people.

SITE NO. Zu-Az-224 [Zu-Az-54(M); Feature DI]
  Date of Survey: July 18, 1973
  Location: 487280 E, 2194350 N; 19.8451° N, 99.1215° W
  Natural Setting: 2550 m asl, on nearly level ground atop a prominent ridge on the eastern flanks of Cerro Jalpa overlooking the BOM Lower Piedmont to the east and southeast, just east of the divide between the Upper Salado and BOM drainages; shallow soil cover and moderate erosion.
  Modern Land Use: Pasture.

Plate A185. Zu-Az-224, facing west at Feature DI.

Archaeological Remains: This site consists of a single mound (Feature DI) measuring ca. 10 × 10 m and 0.40 m high, covered with heavy rock rubble (Plate A185) and very light Late Aztec surface pottery.

Discussion: This site's hilltop location and sparse surface pottery suggest a non-domestic function.

Classification: Isolated Ceremonial-Civic Precinct, no permanent population.

SITE NO. Zu-Az-225 [Zu-Az-78(M); Feature DV]
  Date of Survey: July 20, 1973
  Location: 482050 E, 2192430 N; 19.8278° N, 99.1714° W
  Natural Setting: 2335 m asl, on gently sloping ground in the BOM Lower Piedmont, just south of the divide between the Upper Salado and BOM drainages; medium to deep soil cover and moderate erosion.
  Modern Land Use: Rainfall-based agriculture, with maguey semi-terracing.
  Archaeological Remains: Light Late Aztec surface pottery over an area of ca. 1.00 ha. There is one discernible mound (Feature DV) at the northeastern edge of the site. This feature measures ca. 13 × 17 m in area and 1.00 m high, with very light and light concentrations of Late Aztec surface pottery, several obsidian artifacts (blades, scrapers, debitage), one basalt mano fragment, and moderate rock rubble. Several small looter's pits show rock-rubble fill. There is also a trace of Late Toltec ceramics (no LT site defined here).
  We made a surface collection over an area ca. 10 × 20 m on the mound.
  Discussion: The artifact assemblage suggests a domestic function.
  Classification: Small Hamlet, 5–10 people.

SITE NO. Zu-Az-226 [Zu-Az-79(M)]
  Date of Survey: July 20, 1973
  Location: 482280 E, 2192500 N; 19.8284° N, 99.1692° W
  Natural Setting: 2355 m asl, on gently sloping ground at the divide between the Upper Piedmont and BOM drainages; medium to deep soil cover and slight erosion.
  Modern Land Use: Rainfall-based agriculture, with maguey semi-terracing.
  Archaeological Remains: Light Late Aztec surface pottery over an area of ca. 0.80 ha. There are no discernible structural remains, but a concentration of amorphous rock rubble may represent the remnants of an ancient building.
  No surface collection made.
  Classification: Small Hamlet, 5–10 people.

SITE NO. Zu-Az-227 [Zu-LT-67(M); Location 67]
Date of Survey: Aug. 2, 1973
Location: 482600 E, 2190780 N; 19.8128° N, 99.1661° W
Natural Setting: 2300 m asl, on nearly level ground in the BOM Lower Piedmont, just north of the upper edge of the Lakeshore Plain; deep soil cover, little or no erosion.
Modern Land Use: Rainfall-based agriculture. A modern dirt road crosses the western part of the site.
Archaeological Remains: Light Late Aztec surface pottery over an area of ca. 0.90 ha. The Late Az material is mixed with heavier and more extensive Late Toltec ceramics (Zu-LT-195). There are no discernible structural remains. The western limits of the site could not be defined due to a gap in the airphoto coverage.
We made no surface collection within the borders of the Aztec site. One surface collection (Location 67) was made in the Late Toltec site area (see Zu-LT-195 site description).
Discussion: The apparent absence of Early Aztec surface pottery suggests that this locality was abandoned after LT times and reoccupied during the Late Aztec period. The site area remains uncertain.
Classification: Small Hamlet (?), 5–10 people.

SITE NO. Zu-Az-228 [Zu-Az-80(M); Feature DW]
Date of Survey: July 25, 1973
Location: 484070 E, 2192030 N; 19.8242° N, 99.1521° W
Natural Setting: 2340 m asl, on gently sloping ground in the BOM Lower Piedmont, situated near the confluence of two major *barrancas*; medium soil cover and slight to moderate erosion.
Modern Land Use: Pasture.
Archaeological Remains: This site consists of a single mound (Feature DW), measuring 10 × 12 m in area and 0.60 m high, with light-to-moderate Late Aztec surface pottery and traces of Late Toltec ceramics (no LT site defined here). There is very little rock rubble, perhaps indicating that the mound's contents remain relatively intact. We noted several green and gray obsidian artifacts and one maguey spindle whorl.
We made one surface collection over an area of 4 × 8 m on the mound.
Classification: Small Hamlet, 2–5 people.

SITE NO. Zu-Az-229 [Zu-Az-81(M)]
Date of Survey: July 25, 1973
Location: 485070 E, 2192320 N; 19.8268° N, 99.1426° W
Natural Setting: 2390 m asl, on gently sloping ground atop a low hill in the saddle between two higher hills on the lower southern flanks of Cerro Jalpa in the BOM Lower Piedmont; shallow soil cover and severe erosion, with patches of bare tepetate.
Modern Land Use: Wasteland and marginal pasture.
Archaeological Remains: Variable light and light-to-moderate Late Aztec surface pottery over an area of ca. 0.50 ha. There are no discernible structural remains and only light rock rubble.
No surface collection made.
Classification: Small Hamlet, 5–10 people.

SITE NO. Zu-Az-230 [Zu-Az-85(M); Feature DX]
Date of Survey: July 25, 1973
Location: 485300 E, 2191750 N; 19.8216° N, 99.1404° W
Natural Setting: 2405 m asl, on gently sloping ground atop a low hill on the lower southeastern flanks of Cerro Jalpa in the BOM Lower Piedmont; shallow soil cover and moderate erosion.
Modern Land Use: Pasture.

Archaeological Remains: This site consists of a mound (Feature DX) situated on the south end of a flat, well defined open area with light rock rubble, probably a plaza, that measures ca. 15 × 21 m in area, with its long dimension extending in a north-south direction. The mound measures ca. 7 × 10 m in area and 0.50 m high, with heavy rock rubble and light Late Aztec surface pottery. A looter's pit has exposed rock rubble and earth fill.
We made a surface collection from the plaza area in an area of light Late Aztec surface pottery. We noted numerous sherds of Texcoco Molded and Texcoco Filleted pottery (fragments of long-handled incense burners), plus several green obsidian blades.
Discussion: This site's hilltop location and abundance of ritual ceramics (Texcoco Molded and Texcoco Filleted) suggest a nonresidential function.
Classification: Isolated Ceremonial-Civic Precinct, no permanent population.

SITE NO. Zu-Az-231, Zu-Az-232 [Zu-Az-82a, b(M)]
Date of Survey: July 25, 1973
Location:
Zu-Az-231: 485880 E, 2191600 N; 19.8203° N, 99.1348° W;
Zu-Az-232: 485880 E, 2191800 N; 19.8221° N, 99.1348° W
Natural Setting: 2340 m asl, on gently sloping ground in the BOM Lower Piedmont; medium soil cover and slight to moderate erosion.
Modern Land Use: Rainfall-based agriculture, with maguey semi-terracing. The modern settlement of Colonia Lázaro Cárdenas encroaches onto the site area from the north.
Archaeological Remains: Light Late Aztec surface pottery in two concentrations covering a total area of ca. 0.90 ha. The two sherd concentrations are separated by a gap of ca. 80 m. The southern concentration (designated Zu-Az-231) and the northern concentration (Zu-Az-232) are probably best regarded as a single settlement site. There are no discernible structural remains.
No surface collection made.
Discussion: Because of modern occupation, the site's northern limits could not be defined.
Classification: Small Hamlet (?), 10–20 people.

SITE NO. Zu-Az-233, Zu-Az-254, Zu-Az-255 [Zu-Az-92a, b, c(M); Features ED, EE, EF; Locations 70, 71]
Date of Survey: Aug. 5, 1973
Location:
Zu-Az-233: 484950 E, 2190880 N; 19.8138° N, 99.1437° W;
Zu-Az-254: 484880 E, 2189880 N; 19.8047° N, 99.1444° W;
Zu-Az-255: 483930 E, 2190380 N; 19.8092° N, 99.1534° W
Natural Setting: 2300 m asl, on gently sloping ground in the BOM Lower Piedmont, near the upper edge of the Lakeshore Plain; medium soil cover and slight to moderate erosion.
Modern Land Use: Rainfall-based agriculture around the margins of the nucleated modern town of Zitlaltepec. The modern settlement appears to cover most of the Aztec site.
Archaeological Remains: This site consists of three separate areas of variable light, light-to-moderate, and moderate Late Aztec surface pottery around the edges of modern Zitlaltepec. These locations are separated by considerable distances, but are here considered to represent the fringes of a single site: the Aztec urban settlement of Citlaltepec. The northern concentration is designated Zu-Az-233; the southern concentration is Zu-Az-254; the western concentration is Zu-Az-255. Together, they extend over an aggregate area of ca. 21.00 ha. We estimate that the archaeologically defined area of 21.00 ha represents roughly

Plate A186. Zu-Az-236, facing north over general site area.

one-fifth, or less, of the original Aztec center, and so we estimate this site area as ca. 100.0 ha.

The western site component (Zu-Az-255) partially overlaps with a small Classic site (Zu-Cl-66).

We identified a cluster of three mounds at a high point in the northern end of Zu-Az-255. These features appear to comprise a ceremonial-civic precinct at the edge of the Late Aztec center.

Fea.	Area and Context	Height	Content
ED	29 × 34 m, in unplowed field atop a low hill	3.00 m	Light Late Az and traces of Cl surface pottery, numerous obsidian artifacts. Four looter's pits show rock rubble and earth fill construction. A modern water tank has partially destroyed the mound.
EE	16 × 30 m, in unplowed field	1.00 m	Light-to-moderate Late Az and traces of Cl surface pottery, numerous obsidian artifacts. Extensively damaged by looters.
EF	8 × 12 m, in unplowed field	0.60 m	Light-to-moderate Late Az surface pottery, several obsidian artifacts.

We made two surface collections (Locations 70, 71):

Location	Area and Context	Content
70	8 × 10 m, in unplowed maguey field	Light-to-moderate Late Az and traces of Cl surface pottery, numerous obsidian artifacts, moderate rock rubble.
71	10 × 12 m, in unplowed field	Light-to-moderate Late Az surface pottery, several obsidian artifacts, light rock rubble.

Discussion: We could not determine the extent to which modern Zitlaltepec covers the ethnohistorically documented Aztec and Colonial center of Citlaltepec. We estimate that the archaeological remains visible to us around the periphery of the modern town may represent a population of ca. 300–600 people.

Classification: Local Center (?), ca. 100 ha, ca. 1000–2000 people. Obviously these estimates remain highly problematic.

SITE NO. Zu-Az-234 [Zu-Az-113(J)]
Date of Survey: Aug. 8, 1973
Location: 487680 E, 2192000 N; 19.8239° N, 99.1176° W
Natural Setting: 2290 m asl, on nearly level ground at the lower edge of the BOM Lower Piedmont, near the upper edge of the Lakeshore Plain; deep soil cover and slight erosion.
Modern Land Use: Rainfall-based agriculture. A modern dirt road crosses the center of the site.
Archaeological Remains: Light Late Aztec surface pottery over an area of ca. 0.50 ha. There are no discernible structural remains.
No surface collection made.
Classification: Small Hamlet, 2–5 people.

SITE NO. Zu-Az-235 [Zu-Az-86(M)]
Date of Survey: July 30, 1973
Location: 486650 E, 2190720 N; 19.8123° N, 99.1275° W
Natural Setting: 2270 m asl, on gently sloping ground on the Lakeshore Plain, near the northern shore of Lake Xaltocán-Zumpango; medium soil cover and moderate erosion.
Modern Land Use: Rainfall-based agriculture.
Archaeological Remains: Variable light and light-to-moderate Late Aztec surface pottery over an area of ca. 1.20 ha. There are no discernible structural remains.
No surface collection made.
Classification: Small Hamlet, 10–20 people.

SITE NO. Zu-Az-236 [Zu-Az-83(M); Locations 64-J, 66-M]
Date of Survey: July 25, Sept. 18, 1973
Location: 487680 E, 2191130 N; 19.8161° N, 99.1176° W
Natural Setting: 2260 m asl, on gently sloping ground on the Lakeshore Plain (Plate A186); medium to deep soil cover and slight erosion.
Modern Land Use: Rainfall-based agriculture.
Archaeological Remains: Variable light and light-to-moderate Aztec surface pottery over an area of ca. 11.80 ha. Both Aztec II and III Black/Orange pottery occur. The Az material is mixed with lighter Late Toltec ceramics (Zu-LT-163), and there are also traces of Classic surface pottery (no Cl site defined here). There are no discernible structural remains.

We made two surface collections (Locations 64-J, 66-M):

Location	Area and Context	Content
64-J	6 × 10 m, in fallow field	Light-to-moderate Az (both Az II and III B/O) and traces of LT surface pottery, several obsidian artifacts, moderate rock rubble.
66-M	10 × 10 m, in maize field	Light-to-moderate Az (both Az II and III B/O) and traces of Cl and LT surface pottery, several obsidian artifacts, light rock rubble.

Discussion: This is one of the few Aztec-period sites in the Zumpango Region with definite Aztec II Black/Orange surface pottery. The size and nature of the Early Aztec site is uncertain.

Classification: Late Aztec: Small Dispersed Village, 110–220 people. Early Aztec: ?

SITE NO. Zu-Az-237, Zu-Az-238 [Zu-Az-129a, b(J); Feature DL]
Date of Survey: Sept. 18, 24, 1973
Location:
Zu-Az-237: 488500 E, 2191180 N; 19.8165° N, 99.1098° W;
Zu-Az-238: 489570 E, 2189630 N; 19.8025° N, 99.09956° W
Natural Setting: 2260 m asl, on gently sloping ground on the Lakeshore Plain, near the northern shore of Lake Xaltocán-Zumpango; medium soil cover and moderate erosion.
Modern Land Use: Rainfall-based agriculture around the edges of the modern town of Zumpango. Most of the site is now covered by the nucleated modern town.
Archaeological Remains: We identified two localities of variable light and light-to-moderate Aztec surface pottery: one (site Zu-Az-237) extends over an area of ca. 2.60 ha at the far northern edge of the modern town of Zumpango; the other (site Zu-Az-238) is about 2 km to the southeast, covering an area of ca. 1.00 ha in an unused empty field surrounded by nucleated modern buildings. Although they are separated by a considerable distance, we include them both as remnants of the ethnohistorically documented Aztec town of Zumpango.

We identified one mound in the Zu-Az-238 component: Feature DL. This structure measures ca. 20 m diameter and 2.00 m high (Plate A187), with light Aztec surface pottery (including both Aztec II and III Black/Orange), plus traces of Classic ceramics (no Cl site defined here). A looter's pit shows a stuccoed floor and wall (Plate A188). The height of this mound and the presence of stuccoed architecture both suggest a ceremonial-civic function.

We made one surface collection from the entire surface of Feature DL.

Discussion: Although we could not define a Classic site at the Zu-Az-238 locality, the traces of Classic pottery in Feature DL suggest the possible presence here of a small Classic site. Like nearby site Zu-Az-236, this is one of the few Aztec-period sites in the Zumpango Region with definite Aztec II Black/Orange surface pottery. The size and nature of the Early Aztec site is uncertain.

It is difficult to know whether, as we have assumed, sites Zu-Az-237 and -238 are actually part of the same, much larger site now covered by modern Zumpango. We assume that the Late Aztec period settlement underlies much of the modern town, but this clearly needs to be evaluated by further field investigation. If so, the Late Aztec site may measure roughly 100 ha.

Classification: Late Aztec: Regional Center (?), 2000–4000 people (?). Early Aztec: ?

SITE NO. Zu-Az-239 [Zu-Az-130(J)]
Date of Survey: Sept. 25, 1973
Location: 491250 E, 2190350 N; 19.8090° N, 99.0835° W
Natural Setting: 2275 m asl, on gently sloping ground in the Lakeshore Plain, ca. 50 m south of the present course of the Río Zumpango (Avenidas de Pachuca); moderate to deep soil cover and slight erosion.
Modern Land Use: Rainfall-based agriculture, with maguey semi-terracing.
Archaeological Remains: Light Late Aztec surface pottery over an area of ca. 1.10 ha. There are no discernible structural remains.
No surface collection made.
Classification: Small Hamlet, 5–10 people.

SITE NO. Zu-Az-240 [Zu-Az-131(J)]
Date of Survey: Sept. 25, 1973
Location: 491950 E, 2190720 N; 19.8124° N, 99.0769° W
Natural Setting: 2275 m asl, on gently sloping ground in the Lakeshore Plain, ca. 50 m south of the present course of the Río Zumpango (Avenidas de Pachuca); moderate to deep soil cover and slight erosion.
Modern Land Use: Rainfall-based agriculture, primarily maguey.
Archaeological Remains: Light Late Aztec surface pottery over an area of ca. 1.80 ha. The Late Az material is mixed with approximately equal amounts of Late Toltec ceramics in the northeastern (Zu-LT-166) and southeastern (Zu-LT-167) parts of the site. There are no discernible structural remains.
No surface collection made.
Discussion: The apparent absence of Early Aztec pottery suggests an abandonment of this locality after LT times and a reoccupation during the Late Aztec period.
Classification: Small Hamlet, 10–20 people.

SITE NO. Zu-Az-241 [Zu-Az-133(J)]
Date of Survey: Sept. 24, 1973
Location: 492900 E, 2190430 N; 19.8098° N, 99.0678° W
Natural Setting: 2275 m asl, on gently sloping ground on the Lakeshore Plain, just south of the present course of the Río Zumpango (Avenidas de Pachuca); moderate to deep soil cover and moderate erosion.
Modern Land Use: The immediate site area is used only for pasture. The surrounding area is devoted to rainfall-based agriculture.
Archaeological Remains: Variable light and light-to-moderate Late Aztec surface pottery over an area of ca. 1.90 ha. The Late Az material is mixed with traces of Late Toltec ceramics (no LT site defined here). There are no discernible structural remains, although a concentration of amorphous rock rubble near the stream bed may represent the remnants of an ancient building.
No surface collection made.
Classification: Hamlet, 20–40 people.

SITE NO. Zu-Az-242 [Zu-Az-132(J)]
Date of Survey: Sept. 24, 1973
Location: 492570 E, 2189930 N; 19.8052° N, 99.0709° W
Natural Setting: 2270 m asl, on gently sloping ground on the Lakeshore Plain, ca. 50 m south of the present course of the Río Zumpango (Avenidas de Pachuca); moderate to deep soil cover and moderate erosion.
Modern Land Use: Rainfall-based agriculture.
Archaeological Remains: Variable light and light-to-moderate Late Aztec surface pottery over an area of ca. 2.50 ha. The Late Az material is mixed with traces of Classic ceramics (no Cl site defined here). There are no discernible structural remains.
No surface collection made.
Classification: Hamlet, 25–50 people.

Plate A187. Zu-Az-237, facing west at Feature DL.

Plate A188. Zu-Az-237, plastered surfaces at Feature DL. Note pen for scale.

SITE NO. Zu-Az-243 [Zu-Az-136(J)]
Date of Survey: Oct. 7, 1973
Location: 497450 E, 2188380 N; 19.7912° N, 99.0243° W
Natural Setting: 2260 m asl, on nearly level ground near on the Lakeshore Plain, in a broad saddle between two prominent low hills; medium soil cover and moderate erosion.
Modern Land Use: Rainfall-based agriculture. A modern dirt road borders the northern edge of the site.
Archaeological Remains: Light Late Aztec surface pottery over an area of ca. 1.00 ha. There are no discernible structural remains.
No surface collection made.
Discussion: This is one of the very few sites in the immediate area. The only other Aztec-period site within a radius of several km is Zu-Az-244, ca. 1.20 km to the southeast.
Classification: Small Hamlet, 5–10 people.

SITE NO. Zu-Az-244 [Zu-Az-137(J)]
Date of Survey: Oct. 7, 1973
Location: 498000 E, 2187380 N; 19.7822° N, 99.0191° W
Natural Setting: 2255 m asl, on nearly level ground on the Lakeshore Plain, near the northern shore of Lake Xaltocán-Zumpango; medium soil cover and moderate erosion.
Modern Land Use: Rainfall-based agriculture.
Archaeological Remains: Light Late Aztec surface pottery over an area of ca. 0.60 ha. There are no discernible structural remains. The site is at the eastern limit of the survey area, and its full eastern extent could not be determined.
No surface collection made.
Discussion: The site's surface area remains uncertain. Like site Zu-Az-243 ca. 1.2 km to the northwest, this is one of the very few sites in the immediate area.
Classification: Small Hamlet (?), 5–10 people.

SITE NO. Zu-Az-245 [Zu-Az-134(J)]
Date of Survey: Oct. 2, 1973
Location: 491950 E, 2187430 N; 19.7826° N, 99.0769° W
Natural Setting: 2255 m asl, on nearly level ground on the Lakeshore Plain, near the northern shore of Lake Xaltocán-Zumpango; deep soil cover and slight erosion.
Modern Land Use: Rainfall-based agriculture. Several modern drainage canals cross the site area.
Archaeological Remains: Variable light and light-to-moderate Late Aztec surface pottery over an area of ca. 3.50 ha. The Late Az material is mixed with approximately equal quantities of Terminal Formative ceramics in the central part of the site (Zu-TF-14). There are no discernible structural remains.
No surface collection made.
Classification: Hamlet, 35–70 people.

SITE NO. Zu-Az-246 [Zu-Az-135(J)]
Date of Survey: Oct. 1, 1973
Location: 491680 E, 2186930 N; 19.7781° N, 99.0794° W
Natural Setting: 2250 m asl, on nearly level ground on the Lakeshore Plain, near the northern shore of Lake Xaltocán-Zumpango; deep soil cover and slight erosion.
Modern Land Use: Rainfall-based agriculture.
Archaeological Remains: Light Late Aztec surface pottery over an area of ca. 1.00 ha. The Late Az material is mixed with approximately equal quantities of Terminal Formative ceramics (Zu-TF-16). There are no discernible structural remains.
No surface collection made.
Classification: Small Hamlet, 5–10 people.

SITE NO. Zu-Az-247 [Zu-Az-111(J)]
Date of Survey: Aug. 12, 1973
Location: 489280 E, 2185430 N; 19.7646° N, 99.1023° W
Natural Setting: 2245 m asl, on nearly level ground on the northern shore of Lake Xaltocán-Zumpango; deep soil cover, little or no erosion.
Modern Land Use: Rainfall-based agriculture. The southern outliers of the modern town of San Pedro de la Laguna encroach slightly onto the northern edge of the site. A modern dirt road crosses the site area.
Archaeological Remains: Variable light and light-to-moderate Late Aztec surface pottery over an area of ca. 1.30 ha. The Late Az material is mixed with traces of Late Toltec ceramics (no LT site defined here). There are no discernible structural remains.
No surface collection made.
Classification: Small Hamlet, 15–30 people.

SITE NO. Zu-Az-248 [no field number]
Date of Survey: Aug. 12, 1973
Location: 488250 E, 2185630 N; 19.7664° N, 99.1122° W
Natural Setting: 2245 m asl, on nearly level ground on the northern shore of Lake Xaltocán-Zumpango; deep soil cover, little or no erosion.
Modern Land Use: Rainfall-based agriculture. The Gran Canal de Desagüe is ca. 100 m to the west of the site.
Archaeological Remains: Light Late Aztec surface pottery over an area of ca. 0.30 ha. There are no discernible structural remains.
No surface collection made.
Classification: Small Hamlet, 2–5 people.

SITE NO. Zu-Az-249 [Zu-Az-110(J); Feature DD; Location 49]
Date of Survey: Aug. 9, 1973
Location: 488000 E, 2185300 N; 19.7634° N, 99.1145° W
Natural Setting: 2245 m asl, on nearly level ground on the shore of Lake Xaltocán-Zumpango, atop an ancient beach ridge (Plate A189); deep soil cover and little or no erosion.
Modern Land Use: Rainfall-based agriculture. The Gran Canal de Desagüe is ca. 50 m east of the site.
Archaeological Remains: Variable light and light-to-moderate Late Aztec surface pottery over an area of ca. 5.10 ha. The Late Az material is mixed with Late Toltec ceramics in the southwestern part of the site (Zu-LT-194).
There is one discernible mound (Feature DD) in a plowed field in the north-central site area. This poorly preserved feature measures ca. 15 m in diameter and 0.20 m high, with light-to-moderate Late Aztec surface pottery (both Aztec III and IV Black/Orange ceramics), several obsidian artifacts, and light rock rubble.
We made one surface collection (Location 49) over an area of 10 × 15 m in a maize field (Plate A190), with light Late Az (both Aztec III and IV Black/Orange ceramics) and light-to-moderate LT surface pottery, several green obsidian blades, and light rock rubble.
Discussion: The presence of both Aztec III and IV Black/Orange surface pottery indicates that this site continued to be occupied from Late Az times into the Early Colonial period. The apparent absence of Early Az surface pottery suggests that this locality was abandoned after LT times and reoccupied during the Late Az period.
Classification: Hamlet, 50–100 people.

Plate A189. Zu-Az-249, facing NE over site area.

Plate A190. Zu-Az-249, facing north over Location 49.

Plate A191. Zu-Az-253, facing north over general site area at edge of Lake Zumpango.

SITE NO. Zu-Az-250, Zu-Az-251, Zu-Az-252 [Zu-Az-109a, b, c(J)]
Date of Survey: Aug. 9, 1973
Location:
Zu-Az-250: 487630 E, 2185630 N; 19.7663° N, 99.1181° W;
Zu-Az-251: 487500 E, 2185750 N; 19.7674° N, 99.1193° W;
Zu-Az-252: 487500 E, 2185820 N; 19.7681° N, 99.1193° W
Natural Setting: 2245 m asl, on nearly level ground on the northern shore of Lake Xaltocán-Zumpango; deep soil cover and little or no erosion. At the time of our survey, the southeastern shore of the water-filled Laguna de Zumpango was ca. 50 m to the west of the site area.
Modern Land Use: Rainfall-based agriculture.
Archaeological Remains: This site consists of three closely spaced concentrations (designated as Zu-Az-250, -251, and -252) of light-to-moderate Late Aztec surface pottery over a total aggregate area of ca. 1.60 ha (Zu-Az-250 = 0.90 ha; Zu-Az-251 = 0.40 ha; Zu-Az-252 = 0.30 ha). These three concentrations occur over a linear distance of ca. 500 m, and are separated by gaps of ca. 60 m. There are no discernible structural remains.

The Late Az material is mixed with partially overlapping Late Toltec ceramics (Zu-LT-193) in the southernmost part of the site (Zu-Az-250).
Discussion: The apparent absence of Early Aztec surface pottery suggests that this locality was abandoned after LT times and reoccupied during the Late Aztec period.
Classification: Hamlet, 20–40 people.

SITE NO. Zu-Az-253 [Zu-Az-128(J); Feature DK ("La Corona")]
Date of Survey: Sept. 19, 1973
Location: 487220 E, 2185650 N; 19.7665° N, 99.1220° W
Natural Setting: 2250 m asl, on level ground on the Lakeshore Plain, right at the edge of present-day water-filled Laguna de Zumpango (Plate A191), and very close to the northern shore of Lake Xaltocán-Zumpango; deep soil cover, no erosion.
Modern Land Use: Rainfall-based agriculture, except in the area of standing water to the west where a few fishermen still work (Aguilera 2001).

Archaeological Remains: This site consists of a single mound (Feature DK, locally called "La Corona"), measuring ca. 40 m in diameter and 0.75 m high, in the middle of a maize field. The mound is covered with light Late Aztec surface pottery, several green obsidian blades, and moderate rock rubble.

We made a surface collection from the entire mound surface.
Discussion: A local man told us that there are several other mounds in the area now covered by water in the Laguna de Zumpango, ca. 1.5 km west of Feature DK. One of these mounds, locally known as "Zatletelco," is said to be larger than Feature DK. This Zatletelco mound is also mentioned by a mid-nineteenth-century observer (Orozco y Berra 1864:171).

Despite its lakeshore location, there is no Texcoco Fabric Marked pottery at Feature DK, so saltmaking was apparently not one of its functions.
Classification: Small Hamlet, 5–10 people.

SITE NO. Zu-Az-254 [Zu-Az-92b(M)] [See Zu-Az-233]

SITE NO. Zu-Az-255 [Zu-Az-92c(M)] [See Zu-Az-233]

SITE NO. Zu-Az-256 [Zu-Az-89(M); Location 73]
Date of Survey: Aug. 12, 1973
Location: 483600 E, 2186600 N; 19.7751° N, 99.1566° W
Natural Setting: 2250 m asl, on level ground on the Lakeshore Plain, right at the edge of present-day water-filled Laguna de Zumpango, and close to the northern shore of Lake Xaltocán-Zumpango; deep soil cover and no erosion. At the time of our survey, part of the site area was covered with 5–15 cm of standing water.
Modern Land Use: Pasture and rainfall-based agriculture, except in the area of standing water to the north where a few fishermen still work (Aguilera 2001). A modern dike-road borders the western edge of the site.
Archaeological Remains: Light Late Aztec surface pottery (mostly Texcoco Fabric Marked) over an area of ca. 0.40 ha; there also are some

Plate A192. Zu-Az-259/-260, facing SE over general site area.

sherds of typical Late Aztec Red and Orange Ware, and we noted several obsidian artifacts. There are no discernible structural remains.

We made a surface collection (Location 73) over an area ca. 10 × 10 m in a fallow field with light Late Az surface pottery (including numerous Texcoco Fabric Marked sherds), several obsidian artifacts, and no rock rubble.

Discussion: The high proportion of Texcoco Fabric Marked surface pottery suggests a saltmaking function, possibly with some temporary or seasonal residence.

Classification: Small Hamlet, 2–5 people, probably temporary occupation at a saltmaking workshop.

SITE NO. Zu-Az-257 [Zu-Az-88(M); Location 74]
Date of Survey: Aug. 12, 1973
Location: 482800 E, 2186650 N; 19.7755° N, 99.1642° W
Natural Setting: 2245 m asl, on level ground at the juncture of the Lakeshore Plain and the northwestern shore of Lake Xaltocán-Zumpango; deep soil cover, no erosion.
Modern Land Use: Rainfall-based agriculture, except in the area of standing water to the north of the site area where a few fishermen still work (Aguilera 2001). Several large drainage canals cut through the general area.
Archaeological Remains: Variable light and light-to-moderate Late Aztec surface pottery over an area of ca. 0.60 ha. There is a high proportion of Texcoco Fabric Marked pottery, but also some standard Late Aztec Red and Orange Wares. We noted several green obsidian blades. There are no discernible structural remains, and no rock rubble.

We made a surface collection (Location 74) over an area ca. 15 × 15 m in a maize field (recently drowned out by rising water level) with moderate Late Az (predominantly Texcoco Fabric Marked ceramics) surface pottery and several obsidian artifacts.

Discussion: The high proportion of Texcoco Fabric Marked surface pottery suggests a saltmaking function, possibly with some temporary or seasonal residence.

Classification: Small Hamlet, 5–10 people, probably temporary occupation at a saltmaking workshop.

SITE NO. Zu-Az-258 [Zu-Az-114(M)]
Date of Survey: Dec. 3, 1973
Location: 481470 E, 2188850 N; 19.7954° N, 99.1769° W
Natural Setting: 2260 m asl, on gently sloping ground atop a low, broad knoll that rises about 3 m above the general level of the surrounding Lakeshore Plain, near the northwestern shore of Lake Xaltocán-Zumpango; deep soil cover and slight erosion.
Modern Land Use: Rainfall-based agriculture on the supporting knoll, and irrigated maize and alfalfa in the surrounding fields. A modern dirt road skirts the northern, western, and southern edges of the site.
Archaeological Remains: Light Late Aztec surface pottery over an area of ca. 1.00 ha. There are no discernible structural remains, and no rock rubble.

No surface collection made.

Classification: Small Hamlet, 5–10 people.

SITE NO. Zu-Az-259, Zu-Az-260 [Zu-Az-113a, b(M); Locations 91, 92, 93, 94]
Date of Survey: Dec. 3, 1973
Location:
Zu-Az-259: 481180 E, 2189250 N; 19.7990° N, 99.1797° W;
Zu-Az-260: 480880 E, 2189250 N; 19.7990° N, 99.1826° W
Natural Setting: 2260 m asl, on gently sloping ground atop a low, broad knoll that rises about 5 m above the general level of the surrounding Lakeshore Plain (Plate A192), near the northwestern shore of Lake Xaltocán-Zumpango; deep soil cover and slight erosion.
Modern Land Use: Rainfall-based agriculture on the supporting knoll, and irrigated maize and alfalfa cultivation in the surrounding fields.
Archaeological Remains: This site comprises two concentrations of variable light and light-to-moderate Aztec surface pottery separated by a gap of ca. 150 m. The western concentration (Zu-Az-260) measures ca. 1.30 ha, and the eastern (Zu-Az-259) covers ca. 0.40 ha, for a total site area of 1.90 ha. Both Aztec II-III and III Black/Orange pottery occur. The Aztec material is mixed with heavier Classic (Zu-Cl-83), Early Toltec (Zu-ET-23), and Late Toltec (Zu-LT-197) ceramics. There are no discernible structural remains, and rock rubble is scarce.

We made four surface collections (Locations 91, 92, 93, 94):

Plate A193. Zu-Az-259/-260, facing SE over Location 94.

Location	Area and Context	Content
91	15 × 15 m, in harvested maize field	Light Az and LT surface pottery (Az II-III, III, and IV B/O); several obsidian artifacts; little rock rubble.
92	15 × 15 m, in harvested maize field	Light Late Az, light-to-moderate Cl and light ET surface pottery; several obsidian artifacts; little rock rubble.
93	8 × 20 m, in harvested maize field	Light Late Az, light-to-moderate Cl, and traces of ET and LT surface pottery; several obsidian artifacts; one trapezoidal basalt maguey-fiber scraper; little rock rubble.
94	10 × 15 m, in harvested maize field (Plate A193)	Light Late Az, light-to-moderate Cl, and light ET surface pottery; several obsidian artifacts; one trapezoidal basalt maguey-fiber scraper; very little rock rubble.

Discussion: This site appears to have been continuously occupied from Classic through Early Colonial times—it may be the only such site in the entire Zumpango Region survey. Its deep soil and relatively good preservation (in 1973) make it an ideal location for future excavation. The low frequency of Texcoco Fabric Marked surface pottery suggests that saltmaking was not a primary activity at this location.

The nature of the Early Aztec site remains uncertain.

Classification: Early Aztec: ? Late Aztec: Hamlet, 20–40 people.

SITE NO. Zu-Az-261 [Zu-Az-112(M)]
Date of Survey: Nov. 28, 1973
Location: 479100 E, 2188850 N; 19.7954° N, 99.1995° W
Natural Setting: 2255 m asl, on level ground on the Lakeshore Plain; deep soil cover, no erosion.
Modern Land Use: Irrigated maize agriculture. Numerous irrigation and drainage canals cut across the general site area.
Archaeological Remains: Light Late Aztec surface pottery over an area of ca. 1.50 ha. The Late Az material is mixed with partially overlapping Late Toltec ceramics (Zu-LT-198). There are no discernible structural remains.

No surface collection made.
Discussion: The apparent absence of Early Az surface pottery suggests that this locality was abandoned after LT times and reoccupied during the Late Aztec period.
Classification: Small Hamlet, 10–20 people.

SITE NO. Zu-Az-262 [Zu-Az-111(M)]
Date of Survey: Nov. 28, 1973
Location: 478570 E, 2189300 N; 19.7994° N, 99.2046° W
Natural Setting: 2255 m asl, on level ground in the Lakeshore Plain; deep soil cover and no erosion.
Modern Land Use: Irrigated maize agriculture. Numerous irrigation and drainage canals cut across the general site area.
Archaeological Remains: Light Late Aztec surface pottery over an area of ca. 0.30 ha. The Late Az material is mixed with heavier Late Toltec ceramics (Zu-LT-200). There are no discernible structural remains, although amorphous rock rubble may represent the remnants of ancient architecture.

No surface collection made.
Discussion: The apparent absence of Early Aztec surface pottery suggests an abandonment of this locality after LT times and a reoccupation during the Late Aztec period.
Classification: Small Hamlet, 2–5 people.

SITE NO. Zu-Az-263 [Zu-Az-110(M)]
Date of Survey: Nov. 28, 1973
Location: 478430 E, 2189550 N; 19.8017° N, 99.2059° W
Natural Setting: 2255 m asl, on level ground in the Lakeshore Plain; deep soil cover and no erosion.
Modern Land Use: Irrigated maize agriculture. Numerous irrigation and drainage canals cut across the general site area.
Archaeological Remains: Variable light and light-to-moderate Late Aztec surface pottery over an area of ca. 0.80 ha. There are no discernible structural remains.

No surface collection made.
Classification: Small Hamlet, 10–20 people.

SITE NO. Zu-Az-264 [Zu-Az-109(M)]
Date of Survey: Nov. 28, 1973
Location: 477150 E, 2189100 N; 19.7976° N, 99.2182° W
Natural Setting: 2260 m asl, on gently sloping ground on the Lakeshore Plain; shallow soil cover and severe erosion, with patches of bare tepetate.
Modern Land Use: Rainfall-based agriculture. A modern paved road crosses the center of the site.
Archaeological Remains: Variable light and light-to-moderate Late Aztec surface pottery over an area of ca. 1.70 ha. We noted several obsidian blades. There are no discernible structural remains.
No surface collection made.
Classification: Hamlet, 20–40 people.

SITE NO. Zu-Az-265 [Zu-Az-108(M)]
Date of Survey: Nov. 28, 1973
Location: 476880 E, 2190350 N; 19.8089° N, 99.2208° W
Natural Setting: 2255 m asl, on gently sloping ground atop a low ridge spur that juts out into the Lakeshore Plain; shallow soil cover and moderate erosion.
Modern Land Use: Rainfall-based agriculture in the immediate site area; the surrounding fields are devoted to irrigated maize and alfalfa cultivation.
Archaeological Remains: Variable very light and light Late Aztec surface pottery over an area of ca. 3.00 ha. There are no discernible structural remains.
No surface collection made.
Classification: Hamlet, 20–40 people.

SITE NO. Zu-Az-266 [Zu-Az-107(M)]
Date of Survey: Nov. 28, 1973
Location: 476500 E, 2189570 N; 19.8019° N, 99.2244° W
Natural Setting: 2300 m asl, on gently sloping ground in the BOM Lower Piedmont, atop a low ridge spur that projects into the edge of the Lakeshore Plain; shallow soil cover and severe erosion, with patches of bare tepetate.
Modern Land Use: Rainfall-based agriculture.
Archaeological Remains: Variable light and light-to-moderate Late Aztec surface pottery over an area of ca. 5.30 ha. The Late Az material is mixed with Classic ceramics at the northern edge of the site (Zu-Cl-84) and Late Toltec ceramics at the southern edge (Zu-LT-201). There are no discernible structural remains.
No surface collection made.
Discussion: The apparent absence of Early Aztec surface pottery suggests that this locality was abandoned after LT times and reoccupied during the Late Aztec period.
Classification: Hamlet, 50–100 people.

SITE NO. Zu-Az-267 [Zu-Az-106(M)]
Date of Survey: Nov. 28, 1973
Location: 476320 E, 2189050 N; 19.7971° N, 99.2261° W
Natural Setting: 2310 m asl, on gently sloping ground atop a low ridge spur in the BOM Lower Piedmont; shallow to medium soil cover and moderate to severe erosion, with patches of bare tepetate.
Modern Land Use: Rainfall-based agriculture, with maguey semi-terracing.
Archaeological Remains: Light Late Aztec surface pottery over an area of ca. 1.70 ha. There are no discernible structural remains.
No surface collection made.
Classification: Small Hamlet, 10–20 people.

SITE NO. Zu-Az-268 [Zu-Az-105(M)]
Date of Survey: Nov. 28, 1973
Location: 475820 E, 2189000 N; 19.7967° N, 99.2309° W
Natural Setting: 2305 m asl, on gently sloping ground atop a broad, low ridge in the BOM Lower Piedmont, near the upper edge of the Lakeshore Plain; shallow soil cover and moderate to severe erosion.
Modern Land Use: Rainfall-based agriculture. The modern paved highway between Mexico City and Queretaro borders the western edge of the site.
Archaeological Remains: Variable light and light-to-moderate Late Aztec surface pottery over an area of ca. 1.50 ha. We noted several obsidian blades. There are no discernible structural remains, although a concentration of amorphous rock rubble in the central part of the site may represent the remnants of an ancient building.
No surface collection made.
Classification: Small Hamlet, 15–30 people.

SITE NO. Zu-Az-269 [Zu-Az-104(M); Feature EJ; Locations 86, 87]
Date of Survey: Nov. 28, 1973
Location: 474950 E, 2189430 N; 19.8006° N, 99.2392° W
Natural Setting: 2280 m asl, on gently sloping ground atop a broad, low ridge in the BOM Lower Piedmont; medium soil cover and moderate erosion.
Modern Land Use: Rainfall-based agriculture. The modern paved highway between Mexico City and Queretaro borders the eastern edge of the site.
Archaeological Remains: Light Late Aztec surface pottery over an area of ca. 13.60 ha. The Late Az material is mixed with heavier quantities of Late Toltec ceramics (Zu-LT-203) and lighter Early Toltec surface pottery (Zu-ET-22). We noted several green and gray obsidian blades and scrapers.

There is one discernible mound (Feature EJ) in an unplowed area. This feature measures ca. 15 m in diameter and 0.75 m high, with moderate rock rubble and very light Late Az and LT surface pottery. Two small looter's pits reveal solid earth-rock rubble construction. Because of the admixture of Aztec and Late Toltec surface pottery, the age of this mound's construction and use is uncertain.

We made two surface collections (Locations 86 and 87):

Location	Area and Context	Content
86	5 × 6 m, in harvested maize field	Light Late Az (including Az II-III B/O) and light-to-moderate LT surface pottery (including one LT figurine body), and numerous obsidian artifacts.
87	15 × 20 m, in harvested maize field	Light Late Az and and light-to-moderate LT surface pottery, and numerous obsidian artifacts.

Discussion: The apparent absence of Early Aztec surface pottery suggests that this locality was abandoned after LT times and reoccupied during the Late Aztec period.
Classification: Small Dispersed Village, 100–200 people.

SITE NO. Zu-Az-270 [Zu-Cl-46(M)]
Date of Survey: Dec. 4, 1973
Location: 478800 E, 2185600 N; 19.7660° N, 99.2024° W
Natural Setting: 2280 m asl, on gently sloping ground at the lower edge of the BOM Lower Piedmont, just above the upper edge of the Lakeshore Plain; shallow soil cover and severe erosion, with patches of bare tepetate.
Modern Land Use: Pasture and maguey semi-terracing. The modern town of Coyotepec encroaches onto the site from all sides.

Archaeological Remains: Variable light and light-to-moderate Late Aztec surface pottery over an area of ca. 2.80 ha. Because of modern occupation, we were unable to determine the full extent of the site. The Late Az material is mixed with partially overlapping and somewhat heavier Classic (Zu-Cl-86) and Terminal Formative (Zu-TF-11) ceramics. We noted several green and gray obsidian artifacts.

We made one surface collection in the partially overlapping Classic/Terminal Formative site (Location 95), but none in the Aztec site area (see Zu-Cl-86 site description).

Discussion: This site could be substantially larger if any significant part of it extends beneath modern Coyotepec.

Classification: Hamlet (?), 25–50 people.

SITE NO. Zu-Az-271 [Zu-Az-116(M)]
Date of Survey: Dec. 5, 1973
Location: 478450 E, 2185050 N; 19.7610° N, 99.2057° W
Natural Setting: 2275 m asl, on gently sloping ground at the upper edge of the Lakeshore Plain; medium soil cover and moderate erosion.
Modern Land Use: Rainfall-based agriculture, with maguey semi-terracing.
Archaeological Remains: Variable light and light-to-moderate Late Aztec surface pottery over an area of ca. 6.50 ha. We noted several obsidian artifacts. There are no discernible structural remains.
No surface collection made.
Classification: Small Dispersed Village, 65–130 people.

SITE NO. Zu-Az-272 [Zu-Az-115(M)]
Date of Survey: Dec. 4, 1973
Location: 479550 E, 2187550 N; 19.7836° N, 99.1952° W
Natural Setting: 2260 m asl, on gently sloping ground in the Lakeshore Plain, near the eastern base of Cerro de Coyotepec; medium soil cover and moderate to severe erosion.
Modern Land Use: Rainfall-based agriculture, with maguey semi-terracing.
Archaeological Remains: Light Late Aztec surface pottery over an area of ca. 3.10 ha. The Late Az material is mixed with partially overlapping Late Toltec ceramics (Zu-LT-205). There are no discernible structural remains.
No surface collection made.
Discussion: The apparent absence of Early Aztec surface pottery suggests that this locality was abandoned after LT times and reoccupied during the Late Aztec period.
Classification: Hamlet, 20–40 people.

SITE NO. Zu-Az-273 [Zu-Az-90(M); Location 72]
Date of Survey: Aug. 9, 1973
Location: 485050 E, 2185280 N; 19.7632° N, 99.1427° W
Natural Setting: 2245 m asl, on level ground on the shore of Lake Xaltocán-Zumpango; deep soil cover and no erosion. The southern edge of the present-day water-filled Laguna de Zumpango borders the site area on the north.
Modern Land Use: Normally pasture and rainfall-based agriculture. At the time of our survey, the water level in the Laguna de Zumpango had recently risen so as to flood part of the site area. A modern earth dike (2–3 m high) crosses the center of the site.
Archaeological Remains: Light Late Aztec surface pottery over an area of ca. 1.40 ha; there are also traces of Classic and Late Toltec ceramics (no Cl or LT sites defined here). There are no discernible structural remains.

We made one surface collection (Location 72) over an area ca. 20 m in diameter along the edge of the modern dike. There is light Late Az surface pottery, plus traces of Colonial-period ceramics. We noted several green obsidian blades and one obsidian scraper. There is no Texcoco Fabric Marked surface pottery.
Discussion: The absence of Texcoco Fabric Marked surface pottery indicates that this was probably not a saltmaking locality.
Classification: Small Hamlet, 5–10 people.

SITE NO. Zu-Az-274 [Zu-Az-141(J); Feature DU]
Date of Survey: Oct. 24, 1973
Location: 493000 E, 2181320 N; 19.7274° N, 99.0668° W
Natural Setting: 2245 m asl, on level ground on the bed of Lake Xaltocán-Zumpango, ca. 100 m west of Xaltocán Island; deep soil cover (with a notably sandy soil texture) and no erosion.
Modern Land Use: Pasture in the immediate site area and to the south; rainfall-based agriculture to the north.
Archaeological Remains: Variable light and light-to-moderate and moderate-to-heavy Late Aztec surface pottery over an area of ca. 3.20 ha. The site contains a large, irregular mounded area (Feature DU) measuring ca. 50 × 100 m and elevated ca. 1.50 m above the general level of the surrounding plain (Plate A194). This may be an artificial island. The heaviest surface pottery is found at the north end of the mounded area. Both Aztec III and IV Black/Orange pottery occur. Substantial quantities of Texcoco Fabric Marked ceramics are present, and we noted a few pieces of Huastec Black/White tradeware. Green obsidian blades are abundant.

We made a surface collection from an area ca. 3 × 3 m in the area of heaviest surface pottery at the north end of Feature DU.
Discussion: The presence of both Aztec III and IV Black/Orange surface pottery indicates that this locality continued to be occupied from Late Az times into the Early Colonial period. This site may have been an outlier of Aztec Xaltocán partly devoted to saltmaking.
Classification: Hamlet, 30–60 people.

SITE NO. Zu-Az-275 [Zu-Az-142(J); Feature DV]
Date of Survey: Oct. 24, 1973
Location: 493320 E, 2180800 N; 19.7227° N, 99.0637° W
Natural Setting: 2245 m asl, on level ground on the former bed of Lake Xaltocán-Zumpango, ca. 75 m west of Xaltocán Island; deep soil cover (with a notably sandy texture) and no erosion.
Modern Land Use: Pasture in the immediate site area and to the south; rainfall-based agriculture to the north.
Archaeological Remains: Variable light, light-to-moderate, and moderate Late Aztec surface pottery over an area of ca. 3.20 ha. The site abuts the edges of the survey area on the east and south, and so we did not determine its full southeastern extent—however, it appears that the site does not extend far in that direction. Green obsidian blades are abundant.

There is a single mound (Feature DV), measuring ca. 10 m in diameter and 0.50 m high, with moderate Late Aztec surface pottery and light rock rubble (Plate A195).

We made a surface collection from the entire surface of Feature DV. There are only a few sherds of Texcoco Fabric Marked pottery.
Discussion: The low proportion of Texcoco Fabric Marked surface pottery suggests that saltmaking was not an important activity at this locality.
Classification: Hamlet, 30–60 people.

Appendix A: Site Descriptions 325

Plate A194. Zu-Az-274, facing south at Feature DU.

Plate A195. Zu-Az-275, surface at Feature DV.

SITE NO. Zu-Az-276 [Zu-Az-146(J), Aztec Xaltocán; Locations 89, 90]
   Date of Survey: Dec. 6, 1973
   Note: We were unable to include this site within the borders of our systematic survey area. Our observations were confined to driving through and around the modern town, and in making two quick surface collections (Locations 89 and 90) at the eastern and western edges, respectively, of the modern town. Since the time of our survey, this site has been intensively studied by Elizabeth Brumfiel and her colleagues (Brumfiel 2005). This description does not incorporate any of the latter study's findings.
   Location: 494900 E, 2180500 N; 19.7200° N, 99.0487° W
   Natural Setting: 2250 m asl on gently sloping to level ground atop a broad, low elevation on the former bed of Lake Xaltocán-Zumpango. The supporting elevated area attains a maximum elevation of 7 to 8 m above the general level of the surrounding lakebed (e.g., Plate A196).
   Modern Land Use: Most of the Aztec site is covered by the modern town of Xaltocán (Plate A197). The peripheries of the archaeological site around the edges of the modern town are primarily devoted to pasture (Plate A198), with some rainfall-based agriculture in fields to the west.
   Archaeological Remains: There are abundant archaeological remains within and around the modern town. The archaeological site clearly underlies the entire modern settlement, and extends significantly beyond its present-day borders. We noted numerous mounded areas (up to 3 m high) and concentrations of variable light, light-to-moderate, and moderate Early and Late Aztec surface pottery throughout the site area—both Aztec II and III Black/Orange pottery occur in abundance, and stone rubble is abundant throughout, as are a diversity of green and gray obsidian artifacts. We estimate that the site area is 69.30 ha, including the entirety of the modern town.
   We made two surface collections (Locations 89, 90):

Location	Area and Context	Content
89	25 × 25 m, in pasture at east edge of modern town	Light-to-moderate Early and Late Az surface pottery (II and III B/O), numerous green obsidian blades and a few gray obsidian scrapers.
90	15 × 15 m, in pasture at western edge of modern town	Light-to-moderate Early and Late Az surface pottery (II and III B/O), numerous green obsidian blades and a few gray obsidian scrapers.

   Discussion: Subsequent study by Elizabeth Brumfiel and her colleagues (Brumfiel 2005) has revealed that the supporting elevation that underlies the modern town of Xaltocán is actually an artificial island, a tell-like feature that represents several centuries of occupation at this lakebed locality. Brumfiel's investigation showed that Aztec I Black/Orange pottery is abundant in the lower levels of the Aztec-period occupation of Xaltocán—something that our survey did not reveal. Obviously, our limited 1973 survey could only sketch the outlines of this important Late Postclassic regional center.
   The abundance of Aztec I and II Black/Orange pottery found at Xaltocán is virtually unique within the Zumpango Region survey area.
   Classification: Early Aztec: Regional Center, 1500–3000 people. Late Aztec: Regional Center, 1750–3500 people.

SITE NO. Zu-Az-277 [Zu-Az-91(M)]
   Date of Survey: Aug. 10, 1973
   Location: 485800 E, 2182300 N; 19.7362° N, 99.1355° W
   Natural Setting: 2240 m asl, on level ground on the former bed of Lake Xaltocán-Zumpango; deep soil cover and no erosion.
   Modern Land Use: Rainfall-based agriculture. Several modern drainage ditches cut through the site area.
   Archaeological Remains: Light Late Aztec surface pottery over an area of ca. 1.30 ha. There are no discernible structural remains.
   No surface collection made.
   Classification: Small Hamlet, 5–10 people.

SITE NO. Zu-Az-278 [Zu-Az-114(J)]
   Date of Survey: Aug. 17, 1973
   Location: 488800 E, 2179150 N; 19.7078° N, 99.1069° W
   Natural Setting: 2270 m asl, on gently sloping ground near the northeastern flank of Tultepec Island on the western shore of Lake Xaltocán-Zumpango; shallow to medium soil cover and slight to moderate erosion.
   Modern Land Use: Pasture and rainfall-based agriculture. The southeastern edge of the modern town of Tenopalco encroaches onto the northwestern part of the site.
   Archaeological Remains: Variable light and light-to-moderate Late Aztec surface pottery over an area of ca. 5.70 ha. There are no discernible structural remains.
   No surface collection made.
   Discussion: Part of this site may extend beneath the modern town.
   Classification: Small Dispersed Village (?), 60–120 people.

SITE NO. Zu-Az-279 [no field number]
   Date of Survey: Aug. 17, 1973
   Location: 487500 E, 2179200 N; 19.7082° N, 99.11923° W
   Natural Setting: 2280 m asl, on gently sloping ground near the northeastern flank of Tultepec Island, on the western shore of Lake Xaltocán-Zumpango; shallow soil cover and moderate erosion.
   Modern Land Use: Pasture. The modern town of Tenopalco encroaches slightly onto the northern end of the site.
   Archaeological Remains: Light Late Aztec surface pottery over an area of ca. 0.80 ha. There are no discernible structural remains, but a concentration of amorphous rock rubble in the northern part of the site may represent the remnants of ancient buildings.
   No surface collection made.
   Discussion: Part of the site may extend beneath the modern town.
   Classification: Small Hamlet (?), 5–10 people.

SITE NO. Zu-Az-280 [no field number]
   Date of Survey: Aug. 17, 1973
   Location: 487800 E, 2178750 N; 19.7042° N, 99.1164° W
   Natural Setting: 2275 m asl, on gently sloping ground on the eastern flanks of Tultepec Island, on the western shore of Lake Xaltocán-Zumpango; shallow soil cover and moderate erosion.
   Modern Land Use: Pasture.
   Archaeological Remains: Light Late Aztec surface pottery over an area of ca. 0.80 ha. There are no discernible structural remains.
   No surface collection made.
   Classification: Small Hamlet, 5–10 people.

SITE NO. Zu-Az-281 [Zu-Az-115(J)]
   Date of Survey: Aug. 16, 1973
   Location: 486820 E, 2179280 N; 19.7090° N, 99.1258° W
   Natural Setting: 2305 m asl, on moderately sloping ground on the northern flank of Tultepec Island, on the western shore of Lake Xaltocán-Zumpango; shallow soil cover and moderate erosion.
   Modern Land Use: Pasture.
   Archaeological Remains: Variable light and light-to-moderate Late Aztec surface pottery over an area of ca. 7.50 ha. There are no discernible structural remains.
   No surface collection made.
   Classification: Small Dispersed Village, 75–150 people.

Plate A196. Zu-Az-276, facing south over part of Xaltocán Island, from adjacent lakebed.

Plate A197. Zu-Az-276, facing NE at modern Xaltocán.

Plate A198. Zu-Az-276, facing east across old lakebed east of Xaltocán.

SITE NO. Zu-Az-282 [Zu-Az-94a(M)]
Date of Survey: Aug. 16, 1973
Location: 485930 E, 2179030 N; 19.7067° N, 99.1343° W
Natural Setting: 2310 m asl, on gently sloping ground on the northwestern flanks of Tultepec Island, on the western shore of Lake Xaltocán-Zumpango; medium soil cover and moderate erosion.
Modern Land Use: Rainfall-based agriculture.
Archaeological Remains: Variable light and light-to-moderate Late Aztec surface pottery over an area of ca. 2.90 ha. There are no discernible structural remains.
No surface collection made.
Classification: Hamlet, 30–60 people.

SITE NO. Zu-Az-283 [Zu-Az-94b(M)]
Date of Survey: Aug. 16, 1973
Location: 486070 E, 2178600 N; 19.7028° N, 99.1329° W
Natural Setting: 2310 m asl, on gently sloping ground on the northwestern flanks of Tultepec Island, on the western shore of Lake Xaltocán-Zumpango; medium soil cover and moderate erosion.
Modern Land Use: Rainfall-based agriculture.
Archaeological Remains: Light Late Aztec surface pottery over an area of ca. 1.60 ha. There are no discernible structural remains.
No surface collection made.
Classification: Small Hamlet, 10–20 people.

SITE NO. Zu-Az-284 [Zu-Az-93(M); Location 76]
Date of Survey: Aug. 16, 1973
Location: 484800 E, 2179000 N; 19.7064° N, 99.1450° W
Natural Setting: 2260 m asl, on gently sloping ground on the lower northwestern flanks of Tultepec Island, on the western shore of Lake Xaltocán-Zumpango; deep soil cover and slight erosion.
Modern Land Use: Rainfall-based agriculture, with maguey semi-terracing. The northern edge of the modern town of Melchor Ocampo encroaches onto the southwestern edge of the site, and a large gravel quarry has destroyed part of the northeastern sector of the site.
Archaeological Remains: Light Late Aztec surface pottery over an area of ca. 5.40 ha. The Late Az material is mixed with partially overlapping Late Toltec ceramics (Zu-LT-208).
We made a surface collection (Location 76) in a plowed field over an area ca. 20 m in diameter with light Late Az and light-to-moderate LT surface pottery and no rock rubble.
Discussion: Part of the site may underlie the modern town.
Classification: Hamlet (?), 40–80 people.

SITE NO. Zu-Az-285 [Zu-LT-68(M); Location 75]
Date of Survey: Aug. 16, 1973
Location: 484280 E, 2178630 N; 19.7031° N, 99.1500° W
Natural Setting: 2245 m asl, on level ground at the western edge of Tultepec Island, on the western shore of Lake Xaltocán-Zumpango; deep soil cover, little or no erosion.
Modern Land Use: Rainfall-based agriculture.
Archaeological Remains: Light Late Aztec surface pottery over an area of ca. 0.10 ha. The Late Az material is mixed with heavier and more extensive Late Toltec ceramics (Zu-LT-207). Both Aztec III and IV Black/Orange surface pottery occur. There are no discernible structural remains.
We made one surface collection (Location 75) in a recently cut alfalfa field over an area of ca. 12 × 16 m, with light-to-moderate LT and light Late Az surface pottery, several obsidian artifacts, and no rock rubble.

Discussion: The apparent absence of Early Aztec surface pottery suggests that this locality was abandoned after LT times and reoccupied during the Late Aztec period. The presence of both Aztec III and IV B/O indicates that this locality continued to be occupied from Late Az times into the Early Colonial period.
Classification: Small Hamlet, 2–5 people.

SITE NO. Zu-Az-286 [Zu-Az-95(M)]
Date of Survey: Aug. 16, 1973
Location: 486750 E, 2178280 N; 19.6999° N, 99.1264° W
Natural Setting: 2330 m asl, on gently sloping ground near the top of Tultepec Island, on the western shore of Lake Xaltocán-Zumpango; medium soil cover and moderate erosion.
Modern Land Use: Rainfall-based agriculture.
Archaeological Remains: Light Late Aztec surface pottery over an area of ca. 10.10 ha. Mixed with heavier and more extensive Classic ceramics (Zu-Cl-89) in the central part of the Aztec site. There are no discernible structural remains in the Aztec site area, although there is a definite temple platform (Feature DE) in the Classic site.
No surface collection made in the Aztec site, although we did make a collection from the Classic site (Location 50) (see Zu-Cl-89 site description).
Classification: Small Dispersed Village, 75–150 people.

SITE NO. Zu-Az-287 [Zu-Az-117b(J)]
Date of Survey: Aug. 20, 1973
Location: 487930 E, 2177720 N; 19.6949° N, 99.1152° W
Natural Setting: 2280 m asl, on gently sloping ground on the upper southern flanks of Tultepec Island, on the western shore of Lake Xaltocán-Zumpango; shallow soil cover and moderate erosion.
Modern Land Use: Rainfall-based agriculture. A modern dirt road crosses the southwestern corner of the site.
Archaeological Remains: Variable light and light-to-moderate Late Aztec surface pottery over an area of ca. 8.50 ha. There are no discernible structural remains, but a concentration of amorphous rock rubble near the northern edge of the site may represent the remnants of ancient buildings.
No surface collection made.
Classification: Small Dispersed Village, 85–170 people.

SITE NO. Zu-Az-288 [Zu-Az-117a(J)]
Date of Survey: Aug. 20, 1973
Location: 487150 E, 2177650 N; 19.6942° N, 99.1226° W
Natural Setting: 2290 m asl, on gently sloping ground on the upper southern flanks of Tultepec Island, on the western shore of Lake Xaltocán-Zumpango; shallow soil cover and moderate erosion.
Modern Land Use: Rainfall-based agriculture. A modern dirt road crosses the southern part of the site.
Archaeological Remains: Variable light and light-to-moderate Late Aztec surface pottery over an area of ca. 14.50 ha. The Late Az material is mixed with traces of Late Toltec ceramics (no LT site defined here). There are no discernible structural remains.
No surface collection made.
Classification: Small Dispersed Village, 150–300 people.

SITE NO. Zu-Az-289 [Zu-Az-124(J); Feature DJ; Location 63]
Date of Survey: Sept. 17, 1973
Location: 486450 E, 2178000 N; 19.6974° N, 99.1293° W

Plate A199. Zu-Az-289, facing north over site area.

Natural Setting: 2330 m asl, on gently sloping ground at the top of Tultepec Island (Plate A199), on the western shore of Lake Xaltocán-Zumpango; medium soil cover and moderate erosion.

Modern Land Use: Rainfall-based agriculture. A modern dirt road skirts the eastern edge of the site.

Archaeological Remains: Variable light and light-to-moderate Late Aztec surface pottery over an area of ca. 1.50 ha. There is a large mound (Feature DJ) at the highest point on Tultepec Island in the southern part of the site. This feature measures ca. 25 m in diameter and 3.00 m high (Plate A200), with very light Late Aztec surface pottery, several obsidian artifacts, and moderate-to-heavy rock rubble. A large looter's pit ca. 7 m in diameter and 1.6 m deep in the center of the mound reveals earth and rock-rubble fill (Plate A201).

We made one surface collection (Location 63) over an area ca. 10 × 15 m in a fallow field, with light-to-moderate Late Aztec surface pottery, numerous obsidian blades, and light rock rubble.

Discussion: Its height, construction, scarcity of surface pottery, and location at the highest point in the local landscape all suggest that Feature DJ had a ceremonial-civic, not a domestic residential, function. The presence of this major public structure suggests that this site, despite its small area, may have had more than purely local significance.

Classification: Isolated Ceremonial-Civic precinct, possibly with a small resident population of ca. 25–50 people.

SITE NO. Zu-Az-290 [Zu-Az-127(J)]
Date of Survey: Sept. 17, 1973
Location: 486430 E, 2177600 N; 19.6938° N, 99.1295° W
Natural Setting: 2320 m asl, on gently sloping ground on the upper southern flank of Tultepec Island, on the western shore of Lake Xaltocán-Zumpango; medium soil cover and moderate erosion.
Modern Land Use: Rainfall-based agriculture, with maguey semi-terracing.
Archaeological Remains: Variable light and light-to-moderate Late Aztec surface pottery over an area of ca. 1.70 ha. There are no discernible structural remains.
No surface collection made.
Classification: Hamlet, 20–40 people.

SITE NO. Zu-Az-291 [Zu-Az-126(J)]
Date of Survey: Sept. 17, 1973
Location: 485950 E, 2177600 N; 19.6938° N, 99.1341° W
Natural Setting: 2310 m asl, on gently sloping ground on the upper western flank of Tultepec Island, on the western shore of Lake Xaltocán-Zumpango; medium soil cover and moderate erosion.
Modern Land Use: Rainfall-based agriculture, with maguey semi-terracing.
Archaeological Remains: Light Late Aztec surface pottery over an area of ca. 2.00 ha; there are also traces of Classic ceramics (no Cl site defined here). There are no discernible structural remains.
No surface collection made.
Classification: Small Hamlet, 10–20 people.

SITE NO. Zu-Az-292, Zu-Az-293, Zu-Az-294 [Zu-Az-96a, b, c(M); Location 77]
Date of Survey: Aug. 20, 1973
Location:
Zu-Az-292: 485630 E, 2177250 N; 19.6906° N, 99.1371° W;
Zu-Az-293: 485780 E, 2176930 N; 19.6877° N, 99.1357° W;
Zu-Az-294: 486450 E, 2177000 N; 19.6884° N, 99.1293° W
Natural Setting: 2275 m asl, on gently sloping ground at the lower southern flanks of Tultepec Island, on the western shore of Lake Xaltocán-Zumpango; medium soil cover and moderate erosion.
Modern Land Use: Most of the archaeological site appears to underlie the nucleated modern town of Tultepec. Rainfall-based

Plate A200. Zu-Az-289, facing west at Feature DJ.

Plate A201. Zu-Az-289, looter's pit in Feature DJ.

agriculture is practiced around the peripheries of the modern town where the visible archaeological remains occur.

Archaeological Remains: This site comprises three separate concentrations of variable light and light-to-moderate Late Aztec surface pottery around the peripheries of modern Tultepec; the modern settlement encroaches onto the archaeological remains in all three localities. The northern segment (Zu-Az-294) measures ca. 15.20 ha; the southern segment (Zu-Az-292) measures ca. 2.40 ha; and the southeastern segment (Zu-Az-293) measures ca. 1.60 ha. There are no discernible structural remains.

We made one surface collection (Location 77) in a maize field over an area ca. 16 m in diameter, with light Late Az surface pottery, numerous obsidian artifacts (mostly blades, plus one scraper and one projectile point fragment), with very little rock rubble. Most of the surface pottery is Aztec III, although there is also a trace of Aztec II Black/Orange, and one very unusual Black/Orange sherd that may be post-Hispanic.

Discussion: Because all three site segments appear to extend underneath the modern town, we suspect that the site originally extended over the area occupied by modern Tultepec. The area visible to us covers a total of 19.20 ha. The trace of Aztec II Black/Orange indicates an Early Aztec occupation, but its character remains uncertain.

Classification: Early Aztec: ? Late Aztec: Small Dispersed Village (??), ca. 200–400 people. However, possibly a much larger site.

SITE NO. Zu-Az-295 [Zu-Az-118(J)]
Date of Survey: Aug. 20, 1973
Location: 487700 E, 2177150 N; 19.6897° N, 99.1174° W
Natural Setting: 2265 m asl, on gently sloping ground on the lower southeastern flank of Tultepec Island, on the western shore of Lake Xaltocán-Zumpango; shallow soil cover and moderate erosion.
Modern Land Use: Rainfall-based agriculture.
Archaeological Remains: Variable light and light-to-moderate Late Aztec surface pottery over an area of ca. 4.10 ha. There is a possible trace of Terminal Formative ceramics in the south-central part of the site (no TF site defined here). There are no discernible structural remains.
No surface collection made.
Classification: Hamlet, 40–80 people.

SITE NO. Zu-Az-296 [Zu-Az-119(J)]
Date of Survey: Aug. 21, 1973
Location: 487380 E, 2175550 N; 19.6753° N, 99.1204° W
Natural Setting: 2245 m asl, on level ground on the bed of Lake Xaltocán-Zumpango, ca. 120 m south of Tultepec Island; medium soil depth and little or no erosion.
Modern Land Use: The immediate site area underlies a modern soccer field. The surrounding area is devoted to rainfall-based agriculture.
Archaeological Remains: Light Late Aztec surface pottery over an area of ca. 0.60 ha. There are no discernible structural remains. There are also traces of Late Toltec ceramics on the western edge of the site (no LT site defined here).
No surface collection made.
Classification: Small Hamlet, 2–5 people.

SITE NO. Zu-Az-297 [Zu-Az-123(J); Locations 55, 57, 58, 59]
Date of Survey: Aug. 23, Sept. 13, 1973
Location: 487650 E, 2174320 N; 19.6641° N, 99.1178° W
Natural Setting: 2245 m asl, on level ground atop a broad, slightly elevated area on the bed of Lake Xaltocán-Zumpango, ca. 200 m south of Tultepec Island. The supporting elevation raises ca. 0.50 above the general level of the surrounding lakebed plain, and may be partly, or wholly, artificial.
Modern Land Use: Pasture and marginal rainfall-based agriculture. Several modern dirt roads and drainage ditches cut through the site area.
Archaeological Remains: Variable light and light-to-moderate, moderate, and heavy Late Aztec surface pottery over an area of ca. 4.60 ha. The Late Az material is mixed with partially overlapping Classic (Zu-Cl-90), Early Toltec (Zu-ET-30), and Late Toltec (Zu-LT-212) ceramics in the southwestern and western parts of the Aztec site. Texcoco Fabric Marked surface pottery is abundant in those parts of the site area with the heaviest surface pottery. We noted several green and gray obsidian artifacts, including blades and a few projectile points.

There are no definite structural remains, although there is light-to-moderate and moderate rock rubble over much of the site, and there is vague, irregular mounding throughout the site; the entire supporting ridge may be largely artificial.

We made four surface collections (Locations 55, 57, 58, 59) in the area of the Aztec site:

Location	Area and Context	Content
55	10 × 10 m, in unplowed area	Moderate Cl, light ET, and light Late Az surface pottery; several green obsidian blades; light rock rubble.
57	10 × 10 m, in fallow field	Moderate Cl, light ET, and light Late Az surface pottery; several green obsidian blades; light rock rubble.
58	2 × 4 m, along ditch in pasture area; only selected sherds collected	Moderate-to-heavy Cl, light ET, and light Late Az surface pottery; several green obsidian blades; light rock rubble.
59	5 × 5 m, in pasture area	Moderate-to-heavy Cl, light ET, and very light Late Az surface pottery; several green obsidian blades; light rock rubble.

Discussion: The great abundance of Texcoco Fabric Marked surface pottery indicates that this was a saltmaking site. The presence of significant quantities of typical Aztec Orange Wares and Red Wares suggests that there was also some significant residential occupation.

The high proportions of large Classic and Late Toltec ollas or basins suggest that these ceramic forms had a similar function related to saltmaking during these two earlier periods; the Early Toltec situation is less clear. This site was apparently continuously associated with saltmaking from Classic through Late Aztec times, although the apparent absence of Early Aztec surface pottery suggests that this locality was abandoned after LT times and reoccupied during the Late Aztec period.

Classification: Hamlet, 45–90 people, probably dedicated primarily to saltmaking.

SITE NO. Zu-Az-298 [Zu-Az-120(J); Locations 54, 56]
Date of Survey: Aug. 22–23, 1973
Location: 487380 E, 2173970 N; 19.6610° N, 99.12034° W
Natural Setting: 2245 m asl, on level ground on the bed of Lake Xaltocán-Zumpango, ca. 225 m south of Tultepec Island. The eastern part of the site is atop a low rise that is elevated ca. 1.00 m above the general level of the surrounding plain; this rise may be partly or wholly artificial (Plate A202). There is deep soil cover and little or no erosion.
Modern Land Use: The lower, western part of the site is devoted to rainfall-based agriculture; the higher, eastern end is uncultivated pasture. Several modern dirt roads and drainage canals cross the site area.

Plate A202. Zu-Az-298, facing north over site area.

Archaeological Remains: Variable light and light-to-moderate Late Aztec surface pottery over an area of ca. 23.70 ha. An abundance of Texcoco Fabric Marked pottery in the central site area suggests that saltmaking was an important function. However, the presence of other standard Late Aztec Orange and Red Wares indicates a residential occupation as well. The Late Aztec material is mixed with partially overlapping Classic (Zu-Cl-90), Early Toltec (Zu-ET-30), and Late Toltec (Zu-LT-213) sites.

We made two surface collections (Locations 54, 56):

Location	Area and Context	Content
54	10 × 10 m, in unplowed area	Light-to-moderate Cl, light ET, and light Late Az surface pottery; several green obsidian blades; light-to-moderate rock rubble.
56	10 × 12 m, in unplowed area	Moderate Late Az and light Cl surface pottery; several green obsidian blades; light rock rubble.

Discussion: The abundance of Texcoco Fabric Marked surface pottery indicates that this was a saltmaking site. The presence of significant quantities of typical Aztec Orange Wares and Red Wares suggests that there was also some significant residential occupation.

The high proportions of large Cl and LT ollas or basins suggest that these ceramic forms had functions related to saltmaking during these two earlier periods; the Early Toltec situation is less clear. This site was apparently continuously associated with saltmaking from Classic through Late Aztec times, although the apparent absence of Early Aztec surface pottery suggests that this locality was abandoned after LT times and reoccupied during the Late Aztec period.

Classification: Small Dispersed Village, 250–500 people.

SITE NO. Zu-Az-299 [no field number; Feature DF]
Date of Survey: Aug. 22, 1973
Location: 488050 E, 2173600 N; 19.6576° N, 99.1140° W
Natural Setting: 2245 m asl, on level ground on the bed of Lake Xaltocán-Zumpango; deep soil cover, little or no erosion.
Modern Land Use: Pasture and marginal rainfall-based agriculture.

Archaeological Remains: The site consists of a single low, irregular mound (Feature DF) measuring ca. 10 m in diameter with only a slight elevation (Plate A203). The mound surface is covered with moderate Late Aztec surface pottery, virtually all of which is Texcoco Fabric Marked.

No surface collection made.

Discussion: Probably a specialized saltmaking locality, with little or no residential occupation.

Classification: Specialized Saltmaking Workshop, no permanent population.

SITE NO. Zu-Az-300 [Zu-Az-121(J); Location 52]
Date of Survey: Aug. 22, 1973
Location: 488680 E, 2173400 N; 19.6558° N, 99.1080° W
Natural Setting: 2245 m asl, on level ground on the bed of Lake Xaltocán-Zumpango; deep soil cover and no erosion. The site rests atop an amorphous low elevation that raises ca. 0.20 m above the general level of the surrounding lakebed plain (Plate A204).
Modern Land Use: The immediate site area is uncultivated pasture. The surrounding plain is devoted to rainfall- and irrigation-based maize cultivation. A modern drainage canal cuts through the eastern side of the site.
Archaeological Remains: Variable light and light-to-moderate Late Aztec surface pottery over an area of ca. 1.40 ha. Most of the surface pottery is Texcoco Fabric Marked. There are no definite structural remains, although the amorphous elevation that supports the site may be partly, or wholly, artificial. There is very little rock rubble.

We made one surface collection (Location 52) in an uncultivated area over an area of ca. 10 × 10 m, with light-to-moderate Late Az surface pottery (mainly Texcoco Fabric Marked), a few green obsidian blades, and no rock rubble.

Discussion: The high proportion of Texcoco Fabric Marked surface pottery suggests that this site functioned primarily as a specialized saltmaking locality.

Classification: Specialized Saltmaking Workshop, with little or no permanent residence.

Appendix A: Site Descriptions 333

Plate A203. Zu-Az-299, view of Feature DF.

Plate A204. Zu-Az-300, facing north over site.

Plate A205. Zu-Az-302, facing SE at Feature CM.

SITE NO. Zu-Az-301 [Zu-Az-122(J)]
  Date of Survey: Aug. 23, 1973
  Location: 488950 E, 2173350 N; 19.6554° N, 99.1054° W
  Natural Setting: 2245 m asl, on level ground on the bed of Lake Xaltocán-Zumpango; deep soil cover and no erosion.
  Modern Land Use: Rainfall-based agriculture. Several modern drainage canals cut through the area.
  Archaeological Remains: Light Late Aztec surface pottery (mostly Texcoco Fabric Marked) over an area of ca. 1.00 ha. There are no discernible structural remains.
  No surface collection made.
  Discussion: The high proportion of Texcoco Fabric Marked surface pottery suggests that this site functioned primarily as a specialized saltmaking locality.
  Classification: Specialized Saltmaking Workshop, little or no permanent residence.

SITE NO. Zu-Az-302 [Zu-Az-71(M); Feature CM]
  Note: This site was mistakenly overlooked until the Aztec-site numbering sequence was completed; thus, it is "out of place" according to our usual numbering procedure.
  Date of Survey: July 1, 1973
  Location: 479800 E, 2201320 N; 19.9081° N, 99.1930° W
  Natural Setting: 2350 m asl, on moderately sloping ground in the Upper Salado Drainage; medium soil cover and moderate erosion.
  Modern Land Use: Pasture. There is some stone-faced terracing in the area, obviously old, but of uncertain age.
  Archaeological Remains: The site consists of a single mound (Feature CM), measuring ca. 15 × 18 m in area and 2.00 m high, which blends into the hillslope on its uphill side (Plate A205). The mound surface has very light Late Aztec, with a few obsidian artifacts and light-to-moderate rock rubble.
  No surface collection made.
  Discussion: Feature CM appears to be largely intact. Its height might indicate a non-domestic function, but most of the height is on the downslope side, and so may be exaggerated by the local topography.
  Classification: Small Hamlet (?), 2–5 people.

Table A1. Summary of Zumpango Region site data.

Site Number	Elevation (m asl)	Zone	Classification	Hectares	Population Minimum	Maximum
Late Formative Sites						
Zu-LF-1	2345	USD	H	3.00	15	30
			Totals:	3.00	15	30
Terminal Formative Sites (Tzacualli Phase)						
Zu-TF-1	2310	USD	SH	0.10	2	5
Zu-TF-2	2260	USD	SH	0.50	2	5
Zu-TF-3	2320	USD	H	2.90	20	40
Zu-TF-4	2305	USD	SH	0.50	5	10
Zu-TF-5	2355	BOMLP	H	3.50	35	70
Zu-TF-6	2320	BOMLP	H	2.30	15	30
Zu-TF-7	2305	BOMLP	H	7.80	50	100
Zu-TF-8	2260	LP	H	4.20	20	40
Zu-TF-9	2260	LP	SH	0.70	5	10
Zu-TF-10	2295	BOMLP	SH	0.10	2	5
Zu-TF-11	2290	BOMLP	H?	2.40	30	60
Zu-TF-12	2280	LP	SH?	0.80	5	10
Zu-TF-13	2260	LP	SH	1.30	5	15
Zu-TF-14	2260	LP	SH	1.30	5	15
Zu-TF-15	2255	LP	SH	1.10	5	10
Zu-TF-16	2250	LP	SH	1.80	10	20
Zu-TF-17	2260	LP	H	3.50	20	40
Zu-TF-18	2255	LP	SH	1.00	5	10
Zu-TF-19	2250	LP	SH	0.80	5	10
Zu-TF-20	2245	LP	H	3.00	30	60
Zu-TF-21	2245	LP	SH	0.80	5	10
Zu-TF-22	2245	LP	SH	1.20	15	30
Zu-TF-23	2245	LP	SH	0.90	5	10
Zu-TF-24	2245	LP	SH	1.40	10	20
Zu-TF-25	2245	LP	H	4.00	50	100
Zu-TF-26	2245	LP	SH	0.50	2	5
			Totals:	48.40	363	740
Classic Sites						
Zu-Cl-1	2390	USD	SDV	5.70	55	110
Zu-Cl-2	2360	USD	SNV	8.20	130	260
Zu-Cl-3	2350	USD	SNV	5.10	100	200
Zu-Cl-4	2340	USD	H	1.70	30	60
Zu-Cl-5	2340	USD	H	3.00	15	30
Zu-Cl-6	2345	USD	SNV	4.40	70	140
Zu-Cl-7	2340	USD	H	3.50	40	80
Zu-Cl-8	2330	USD	SH	0.50	5	10
Zu-Cl-9	2355	USD	SH	1.80	10	20
Zu-Cl-10	2345	USD	H	3.00	35	70
Zu-Cl-11	2320	USD	H	2.40	25	50
Zu-Cl-12	2320	USD	SH	0.40	2	5
Zu-Cl-13	2290	USD	H	2.10	20	40
Zu-Cl-14	2260	USD	SH?	1.20	5	10
Zu-Cl-15	2240	USD	H?	2.40	20	40
Zu-Cl-16	2240	USD	H	1.60	15	30
Zu-Cl-17	2170	USD	SH	1.10	10	20
Zu-Cl-18	2200	USD	SH	0.70	5	10

Table A1 cont.

Site Number	Elevation (m asl)	Zone	Classification	Hectares	Population Minimum	Population Maximum
Zu-Cl-19	2270	USD	SH	1.00	5	10
Zu-Cl-20	2260	USD	SH	0.50	2	5
Zu-Cl-21	2240	USD	H	4.50	50	100
Zu-Cl-22	2255	USD	SH	0.70	10	20
Zu-Cl-23	2230	USD	SH	0.70	5	10
Zu-Cl-24	2230	USD	SH	0.90	5	10
Zu-Cl-25	2190	USD	SH	0.40	5	10
Zu-Cl-26	2190	USD	H	4.40	20	40
Zu-Cl-27	2195	USD	H	1.40	15	30
Zu-Cl-28	2210	USD	SH	0.40	2	5
Zu-Cl-29	2235	USD	SH	0.20	2	5
Zu-Cl-30	2245	USD	SH	1.50	5	10
Zu-Cl-31	2220	USD	H	2.40	25	50
Zu-Cl-32	2230	USD	H	3.90	40	80
Zu-Cl-33	2260	USD	H	3.80	40	80
Zu-Cl-34	2320	USD	H	3.50	35	70
Zu-Cl-35	2330	USD	H	1.70	20	40
Zu-Cl-36	2305	USD	H	4.00	40	80
Zu-Cl-37	2310	USD	H(?)	2.10	25	50
Zu-Cl-38	2305	USD	H	5.30	50	100
Zu-Cl-39	2325	USD	SH	0.60	5	10
Zu-Cl-40	2320	USD	LDV	17.20	300	600
Zu-Cl-41	2330	BOMLP	SH	0.60	10	20
Zu-Cl-42	2340	BOMLP	LNV	16.40	350	700
Zu-Cl-43	2310	BOMLP	H	1.50	15	30
Zu-Cl-44	2310	BOMLP	SH	0.30	2	5
Zu-Cl-45	2310	BOMLP	SH	0.40	5	10
Zu-Cl-46	2345	BOMLP	H	3.90	40	80
Zu-Cl-47	2355	BOMLP	H	2.70	30	60
Zu-Cl-48	2295	BOMLP	H	2.90	15	30
Zu-Cl-49	2330	BOMLP	SH	0.30	5	10
Zu-Cl-50	2325	BOMLP	SH	0.40	2	5
Zu-Cl-51	2335	BOMLP	SH	0.60	2	5
Zu-Cl-52	2330	USD	SDV	11.80	160	320
Zu-Cl-53	2280	USD	SDV	8.20	120	240
Zu-Cl-54	2280	USD	H	3.10	15	30
Zu-Cl-55	2305	USD	H	3.40	35	70
Zu-Cl-56	2230	USD	SH	0.20	2	5
Zu-Cl-57	2255	USD	SH	0.10	2	5
Zu-Cl-58	2260	USD	SH	0.50	5	10
Zu-Cl-59	2270	USD	H	1.40	20	40
Zu-Cl-60	2330	USD	LC	19.50	500	1000
Zu-Cl-61	2265	USD	SNV	5.90	100	200
Zu-Cl-62	2270	USD	H	2.30	25	50
Zu-Cl-63	2260	USD	SNV	3.90	75	150
Zu-Cl-64	2280	BOMLP	H	2.70	25	50
Zu-Cl-65	2295	BOMLP	H	2.50	25	50
Zu-Cl-66	2300	BOMLP	H	3.60	35	70
Zu-Cl-67	2505	BOMLP (CJ)	SH	1.00	10	20
Zu-Cl-68	2260	LP	H	1.70	20	40
Zu-Cl-69	2265	LP	SH	1.30	5	10

Table A1 cont.

Site Number	Elevation (m asl)	Zone	Classification	Hectares	Population Minimum	Maximum
Zu-Cl-70	2270	LP	SDV	5.60	60	120
Zu-Cl-71	2320	BOMLP	H	3.10	15	30
Zu-Cl-72	2295	BOMLP	H	2.40	25	50
Zu-Cl-73	2310	LP	SDV	6.50	60	120
Zu-Cl-74	2260	LP	SH	0.80	5	10
Zu-Cl-75	2280	LP	SH(?)	1.90	10	20
Zu-Cl-76	2245	LP	SDV?	6.30	60	120
Zu-Cl-77	2270	LP	SDV	5.50	60	120
Zu-Cl-78	2270	LP	SH	0.70	5	10
Zu-Cl-79	2245	LP	SH	2.20	10	20
Zu-Cl-80	2245	LP	H	3.30	30	60
Zu-Cl-81	2245	LP	H	2.90	30	60
Zu-Cl-82	2245	LP	SNV	5.30	80	160
Zu-Cl-83	2260	LP	SNV	10.10	150	300
Zu-Cl-84	2295	USD	H	2.00	20	40
Zu-Cl-85	2275	USD	H	2.10	20	40
Zu-Cl-86	2285	BOMLP	H??	2.30	30	60
Zu-Cl-87	2270	LP	H?	2.00	15	30
Zu-Cl-88	2270	LP	SH	0.70	2	5
Zu-Cl-89	2310	LP (TI)	LC	21.00	400	800
Zu-Cl-90	2245	LB	SDV	7.60	100	200
			Totals:	307.3	4140	8290
Early Toltec Sites						
Zu-ET-1	2380	USD	SNV	10.00	200	400
Zu-ET-2	2340	USD	SNV	4.40	100	200
Zu-ET-3	2345	USD	H	3.00	45	90
Zu-ET-4	2260	USD	SH	0.50	10	20
Zu ET-5	2245	USD	H?	2.40	25	50
Zu-ET-6	2170	USD	SH?	1.10	10	20
Zu-ET-7	2245	USD	SNV	4.50	75	150
Zu-ET-8	2250	USD	SH	0.30	2	5
Zu-ET-9	2240	USD	H	3.90	40	80
Zu-ET-10	2225	USD	H	2.40	25	50
Zu-ET-11	2230	USD	SH	0.70	5	10
Zu-ET-12	2510	USD (CMG)	RC	28.60	750	1500
Zu-ET-13	2270	USD	H	1.40	20	40
Zu-ET-14	2280	USD	SDV	6.50	75	150
Zu-ET-15	2290	USD	H	2.10	20	40
Zu-ET-16	2325	USD	SDV	13.40	150	300
Zu-ET-17	2325	USD	H	3.30	35	70
Zu-ET-18	2290	BOMLP	H	3.60	20	40
Zu-ET-19	2330	USD	LNV??	19.50	400	800
Zu-ET-20	2290	USD	H	3.40	35	70
Zu-ET-21	2280	LP	SH	0.80	10	20
Zu-ET-22	2280	USD	H	1.00	15	30
Zu-ET-23	2260	LP	H	3.80	40	80
Zu-ET-24	2305	BOMLP	H	1.80	20	40
Zu-ET-25	2505	BOMLP (CJ)	SH?	1.10	10	20
Zu-ET-26	2260	LP	SDV	5.50	60	120
Zu-ET-27	2310	LP	SDV?	6.50	65	130
Zu-ET-28	2245	LP	H	3.30	35	70

Table A1 cont.

Site Number	Elevation (m asl)	Zone	Classification	Hectares	Population Minimum	Maximum
Zu-ET-29	2270	LP	SDV?	7.20	75	150
Zu-ET-30	2245	LP	SNV?	10.40	200	400
			Totals:	156.4	2582	5145
Late Toltec Sites						
Zu-LT-1	2390	USD	SDV	6.40	65	130
Zu-LT-2	2445	USD	SH	0.70	5	10
Zu-LT-3	2430	USD	SDV	7.90	80	160
Zu-LT-4	2400	USD	SH	1.40	5	10
Zu-LT-5	2380	USD	SH	0.80	10	20
Zu-LT-6	2405	USD	SH	0.60	5	10
Zu-LT-7	2360	USD	SH?	0.50	10	20
Zu-LT-8	2400	USD	H	2.00	20	40
Zu-LT-9	2420	USD	H	1.30	15	30
Zu-LT-10	2350	USD	H	1.40	15	30
Zu-LT-11	2340	USD	SH	0.40	5	10
Zu-LT-12	2365	USD	SH	0.40	5	10
Zu-LT-13	2360	USD	SH	0.10	2	5
Zu-LT-14	2255	USD	SH	0.40	2	5
Zu-LT-15	2300	USD	SH	0.90	10	20
Zu-LT-16	2305	USD	H	1.50	20	40
Zu-LT-17	2245	USD	SDV	5.40	80	160
Zu-LT-18	2260	USD	H	2.50	25	50
Zu-LT-19	2270	USD	H	1.60	15	30
Zu-LT-20	2280	USD	H	1.90	30	60
Zu-LT-21	2300	USD	SH	0.60	5	10
Zu-LT-22	2300	USD	SH	0.50	5	10
Zu-LT-23	2310	USD	SH	0.80	10	20
Zu-LT-24	2315	USD	SH	0.30	5	10
Zu-LT-25	2310	USD	SH	1.00	10	20
Zu-LT-26	2300	USD	SH	0.30	5	10
Zu-LT-27	2315	USD	SH	0.60	5	10
Zu-LT-28	2320	USD	SH	0.10	2	5
Zu-LT-29	2295	USD	H	2.00	30	60
Zu-LT-30	2360	USD	LNV	16.80	340	680
Zu-LT-31	2340	USD	H	1.40	25	50
Zu-LT-32	2340	USD	SH	1.10	10	20
Zu-LT-33	2335	USD	SDV	10.70	125	250
Zu-LT-34	2345	USD	SDV	6.80	100	200
Zu-LT-35	2345	USD	H	2.60	25	50
Zu-LT-36	2345	USD	H?	1.30	15	30
Zu-LT-37	2350	BOMLP	H	2.30	25	50
Zu-LT-38	2340	USD	SNV	15.70	250	500
Zu-LT-39	2340	BOMLP	SDV	7.00	75	150
Zu-LT-40	2340	BOMLP	H?	4.40	45	90
Zu-LT-41	2320	USD	SNV	10.80	200	400
Zu-LT-42	2310	USD	SNV	5.70	85	170
Zu-LT-43	2305	USD	SDV	8.20	80	160
Zu-LT-44	2315	USD	H	1.40	15	30
Zu-LT-45	2310	USD	H	2.90	30	60
Zu-LT-46	2335	USD	SDV	10.40	105	210
Zu-LT-47	2325	USD	SDV	8.70	90	180

Table A1 cont.

Site Number	Elevation (m asl)	Zone	Classification	Hectares	Population Minimum	Maximum
Zu-LT-48	2335	BOMLP	SNV	5.10	100	200
Zu-LT-49	2330	USD	SDV	5.60	55	110
Zu-LT-50	2310	USD	SH	0.40	5	10
Zu-LT-51	2300	USD	SH	1.40	5	10
Zu-LT-52	2310	USD	H	2.20	20	40
Zu-LT-53	2320	USD	H?	3.00	30	60
Zu-LT-54	2350	USD	SDV	5.90	60	120
Zu-LT-55	2340	USD	H	1.40	15	30
Zu-LT-56	2330	USD	H	1.50	15	30
Zu-LT-57	2300	USD	SDV?	6.00	100	200
Zu-LT-58	2315	USD	H	2.30	25	50
Zu-LT-59	2370	USD	SH	0.80	5	10
Zu-LT-60	2255	USD	H	3.10	30	60
Zu-LT-61	2250	USD	SH	0.60	5	10
Zu-LT-62	2245	USD	IOW	0.10	-	-
Zu-LT-63	2270	USD	SH	0.40	5	10
Zu-LT-64	2270	USD	SH	0.20	2	5
Zu-LT-65	2260	USD	SH	0.40	5	10
Zu-LT-66	2250	USD	SH	0.90	5	10
Zu-LT-67	2220	USD	SH	0.10	2	5
Zu-LT-68	2200	USD	SH	0.40	2	5
Zu-LT-69	2215	USD	SDV	5.50	60	120
Zu-LT-70	2230	USD	H	0.80	15	30
Zu-LT-71	2200	USD	SH	0.90	2	5
Zu-LT-72	2205	USD	SDV	6.10	60	120
Zu-LT-73	2225	USD	SH	0.70	5	10
Zu-LT-74	2255	USD	H	4.10	40	80
Zu-LT-75	2240	USD	LC	10.70	300	600
Zu-LT-76	2245	USD	SH?	0.10	5	10
Zu-LT-77	2260	USD	SH	0.80	10	20
Zu-LT-78	2350	USD	SH	0.80	5	10
Zu-LT-79	2280	USD	H	2.90	45	90
Zu-LT-80	2270	USD	SDV?	11.50	150	300
Zu-LT-81	2270	USD	H?	3.30	35	70
Zu-LT-82	2270	USD	H?	4.10	40	80
Zu-LT-83	2250	USD	SH	0.50	2	5
Zu-LT-84	2280	USD	SH	1.20	5	10
Zu-LT-85	2280	USD	SH	0.60	5	10
Zu-LT-86	2270	USD	SH?	0.90	10	20
Zu-LT-87	2255	USD	LC	10.70	200	400
Zu-LT-88	2245	USD	SH	1.20	10	20
Zu-LT-89	2245	USD	H	0.40	40	80
Zu-LT-90	2300	USD	H	2.10	20	40
Zu-LT-91	2265	USD	SH	1.70	10	20
Zu-LT-92	2250	USD	SNV	4.40	75	150
Zu-LT-93	2275	USD	H	3.40	35	70
Zu-LT-94	2280	USD	SH	0.40	5	10
Zu-LT-95	2315	USD	H	1.00	15	30
Zu-LT-96	2305	USD	SDV	6.40	65	130
Zu-LT-97	2350	USD	SH	0.60	2	5
Zu-LT-98	2355	USD	SH	0.90	5	10

Table A1 cont.

Site Number	Elevation (m asl)	Zone	Classification	Hectares	Population Minimum	Maximum
Zu-LT-99	2340	USD	H	2.20	20	40
Zu-LT-100	2355	USD	H	1.50	15	30
Zu-LT-101	2350	USD	SH	0.40	5	10
Zu-LT-102	2350	USD	SH	0.90	10	20
Zu-LT-103	2320	USD	SDV	8.60	85	170
Zu-LT-104	2305	USD	SDV	5.60	60	120
Zu-LT-105	2310	USD	SH	0.60	5	10
Zu-LT-106	2330	USD	SH	0.10	2	5
Zu-LT-107	2340	USD	H	2.10	20	40
Zu-LT-108	2340	USD	SH	0.10	2	5
Zu-LT-109	2350	USD	H	1.00	15	30
Zu-LT-110	2350	USD	H	1.00	15	30
Zu-LT-111	2345	USD	SH	1.90	10	20
Zu-LT-112	2345	BOMLP	SH	0.80	5	10
Zu-LT-113	2340	BOMLP	SH	0.50	2	5
Zu-LT-114	2335	BOMLP	SH	1.50	10	20
Zu-LT-115	2355	USD	H	1.20	15	30
Zu-LT-116	2360	BOMLP	H	4.00	50	100
Zu-LT-117	2370	USD	H	2.10	20	40
Zu-LT-118	2370	BOMLP	H	4.30	45	90
Zu-LT-119	2370	BOMLP	H	4.30	45	90
Zu-LT-120	2395	BOMLP	SH	0.20	2	5
Zu-LT-121	2390	BOMLP	H	3.50	35	70
Zu-LT-122	2370	BOMLP	H	1.90	20	40
Zu-LT-123	2350	BOMLP	SH	0.50	5	10
Zu-LT-124	2345	BOMLP	SH	0.10	2	5
Zu-LT-125	2340	BOMLP	SH	0.10	2	5
Zu-LT-126	2320	BOMLP	SH	0.70	5	10
Zu-LT-127	2340	BOMLP	SH	1.00	10	20
Zu-LT-128	2345	BOMLP	SH	0.90	10	20
Zu-LT-129	2360	BOMLP	H	7.30	35	70
Zu-LT-130	2355	BOMLP	SH	0.10	2	5
Zu-LT-131	2355	BOMLP	SH	0.10	2	5
Zu-LT-132	2340	USD	SH?	1.10	10	20
Zu-LT-133	2340	USD	SDV	10.30	105	210
Zu-LT-134	2260	USD	SNV	4.10	80	160
Zu-LT-135	2280	USD	LC	34.50	600	1200
Zu-LT-136	2270	USD	SH	1.10	10	20
Zu-LT-137	2265	USD	SH	1.40	10	20
Zu-LT-138	2305	USD	H?	1.70	15	30
Zu-LT-139	2295	USD	H?	1.50	15	30
Zu-LT-140	2280	USD	H	2.60	25	50
Zu-LT-141	2270	USD	SH	1.40	10	20
Zu-LT-142	2270	USD	SH	2.00	10	20
Zu-LT-143	2320	USD	H	1.70	15	30
Zu-LT-144	2295	USD	SH	0.40	5	10
Zu-LT-145	2295	USD	H	1.10	15	30
Zu-LT-146	2290	USD	SH	1.10	5	10
Zu-LT-147	2320	USD	SH	0.80	10	20
Zu-LT-148	2345	USD	SH	0.50	2	5
Zu-LT-149	2400	BOMLP	SH?	0.10	2	5

Table A1 cont.

Site Number	Elevation (m asl)	Zone	Classification	Hectares	Population	
					Minimum	*Maximum*
Zu-LT-150	2380	BOMLP	SH	0.50	5	10
Zu-LT-151	2385	BOMLP	H?	3.60	35	70
Zu-LT-152	2350	BOMLP	H	1.30	20	40
Zu-LT-153	2340	BOMLP	SH?	0.10	2	5
Zu-LT-154	2350	BOMLP	SH	0.40	5	10
Zu-LT-155	2345	BOMLP	SH	0.70	10	20
Zu-LT-156	2340	BOMLP	H	4.10	50	100
Zu-LT-157	2335	BOMLP	H	5.00	50	100
Zu-LT-158	2320	BOMLP	SH	0.30	2	5
Zu-LT-159	2330	BOMLP	SH	1.00	2	5
Zu-LT-160	2315	BOMLP	SH	1.20	5	10
Zu-LT-161	2310	BOMLP	SH	0.80	5	10
Zu-LT-162	2320	BOMLP	SH	0.80	10	20
Zu-LT-163	2270	LP	H	2.30	25	50
Zu-LT-164	2265	LP	SH	0.70	5	10
Zu-LT-165	2280	LP	H	2.90	15	30
Zu-LT-166	2270	LP	SH	1.90	10	20
Zu-LT-167	2270	LP	SH	1.10	5	10
Zu-LT-168	2260	LP	SH	0.80	5	10
Zu-LT-169	2300	LP (hill)	SDV	5.90	75	150
Zu-LT-170	2260	LP	SH	0.60	2	5
Zu-LT-171	2250	LP	SH?	0.80	5	10
Zu-LT-172	2245	LP	SH	1.10	5	10
Zu-LT-173	2245	LP	SH	1.30	5	10
Zu-LT-174	2245	LP	SDV	8.90	90	180
Zu-LT-175	2245	LP	SH?	2.10	10	20
Zu-LT-176	2245	LP	SDV	16.80	170	340
Zu-LT-177	2245	LP	H	2.10	20	40
Zu-LT-178	2240	LB	H	1.40	20	40
Zu-LT-179, -180, -181, -182, -183	2245	LB	SDV	11.40	115	230
Zu-LT-184	2245	LP	SH	0.50	2	5
Zu-LT-185	2250	LP	H	1.50	15	30
Zu-LT-186	2250	LP	SH	0.60	2	5
Zu-LT-187	2250	LP	SH	0.90	10	20
Zu-LT-188	2250	LP	SH?	1.10	10	20
Zu-LT-189	2245	LP	SH	1.10	10	20
Zu-LT-190	2250	LP	SH	0.60	5	10
Zu-LT-191	2245	LP	SDV	8.50	85	170
Zu-LT-192	2245	LP	SDV?	12.00	120	240
Zu-LT-193	2245	LP	H	1.60	15	30
Zu-LT-194	2245	LP	SH	0.30	5	10
Zu-LT-195	2280	LP	H?	0.80	15	30
Zu-LT-196	2280	LP	H	1.30	20	40
Zu-LT-197	2260	LP	H	5.10	50	100
Zu-LT-198	2255	LP	SH	1.30	5	10
Zu-LT-199	2255	LP	SH	1.10	5	10
Zu-LT-200	2255	LP	SH	0.30	2	5
Zu-LT-201	2305	USD	SH	0.80	5	10
Zu-LT-202	2295	BOMLP	SH	1.40	5	10
Zu-LT-203	2285	BOMLP	SNV	11.50	200	400

Table A1 cont.

Site Number	Elevation (m asl)	Zone	Classification	Hectares	Population Minimum	Maximum
Zu-LT-204	2280	LP	SH	1.20	10	20
Zu-LT-205	2260	LP	H	5.00	25	50
Zu-LT-206	2260	LP	SNV	13.50	200	400
Zu-LT-207	2250	LP (TI)	H	1.70	15	30
Zu-LT-208	2260	LP (TI)	H	2.80	30	60
Zu-LT-209	2250	LP (TI)	SDV?	10.60	150	300
Zu-LT-210	2305	LP (TI)	SNV	9.50	200	400
Zu-LT-211	2245	LP (TI)	RC	97.50	1500	3000
Zu-LT-212	2245	LB	H	1.40	30	60
Zu-LT-213	2245	LB	H	4.40	50	100
			Totals:	703.3	9,017	18,060
Aztec Sites						
Zu-Az-1	2405	USD	SH	0.50	2	5
Zu-Az-2	2405	USD	SH	0.80	5	10
Zu-Az-3	2450	USD	SH	0.40	5	10
Zu-Az-4	2445	USD	SH	1.10	10	20
Zu-Az-5, -6	2400	USD	LDV	53.10	600	1200
Zu-Az-7	2340	USD	SDV?	9.70	100	200
Zu-Az-8	2360	USD	SH	0.50	5	10
Zu-Az-9	2405	USD	H	3.70	25	50
Zu-Az-10	2380	USD	SH	1.10	10	20
Zu-Az-11	2355	USD	SH	0.50	5	10
Zu-Az-12	2340	USD	SH	0.50	2	5
Zu-Az-13	2340	USD	SH	0.70	5	10
Zu-Az-14	2340	USD	SH	0.70	5	10
Zu-Az-15	2340	USD	SH	0.60	10	20
Zu-Az-16	2345	USD	SH	0.70	2	5
Zu-Az-17	2375	USD	SH	1.60	15	30
Zu-Az-18	2345	USD	LDV?	50.00	750	1500
Zu-Az-19	2330	USD	SH	1.20	15	30
Zu-Az-20	2340	USD	SH	0.40	2	5
Zu-Az-21	2340	USD	H	3.00	30	60
Zu-Az-22	2340	USD	H	1.40	30	60
Zu-Az-23	2340	USD	SH	0.40	5	10
Zu-Az-24	2335	USD	SH	1.00	10	20
Zu-Az-25	2370	USD	SH	0.10	5	10
Zu-Az-26	2380	USD	SH	1.10	10	20
Zu-Az-27	2330	USD	SH	0.40	5	10
Zu-Az-28	2320	USD	SH	1.00	5	10
Zu-Az-29	2330	USD	SH	0.90	10	20
Zu-Az-30	2335	USD	SH	0.60	5	10
Zu-Az-31	2335	USD	SH	1.00	5	10
Zu-Az-32	2345	USD	SH	0.70	5	10
Zu-Az-33	2370	USD	SH	1.30	10	20
Zu-Az-34	2410	USD	H	3.00	15	30
Zu-Az-35	2395	USD	SH	0.70	5	10
Zu-Az-36	2400	USD	SH	1.30	10	20
Zu-Az-37	2295	USD	H	1.60	35	50
Zu-Az-38	2335	USD	SH	1.70	15	30
Zu-Az-39	2320	USD	SH	1.10	10	20
Zu-Az-40	2305	USD	SDV	8.60	85	170

Table A1 cont.

Site Number	Elevation (m asl)	Zone	Classification	Hectares	Population Minimum	Maximum
Zu-Az-41	2310	USD	SH	0.80	5	10
Zu-Az-42	2270	USD	H	1.80	20	40
Zu-Az-43	2250	USD	SH	0.60	2	5
Zu-Az-44	2240	USD	SH	0.10	5	10
Zu-Az-45	2245	USD	H	1.80	20	40
Zu-Az-46	2235	USD	SDV	8.10	150	300
Zu-Az-47	2205	USD	ICCP	1.00	-	-
Zu-Az-48	2175	USD	SH?	1.90	10	20
Zu-Az-49	2200	USD	H	3.90	25	50
Zu-Az-50	2205	USD	SH	2.00	10	20
Zu-Az-51	2195	USD	SH	0.50	5	10
Zu-Az-52	2195	USD	H	1.40	20	40
Zu-Az-53	2225	USD	H?	1.30	20	40
Zu-Az-54	2355	USD	ICCP	0.10	-	-
Zu-Az-55	2295	USD	SH	2.00	15	30
Zu-Az-56	2280	USD	H?	4.50	45	90
Zu-Az-57	2275	USD	SH	1.50	10	20
Zu-Az-58	2260	USD	LDV?	21.00	400	800
Zu-Az-59	2245	USD	SH	0.30	5	10
Zu-Az-60	2205	USD	SDV	10.40	150	300
Zu-Az-61	2200	USD	SH	1.40	5	10
Zu-Az-62	2245	USD	SH	1.50	10	20
Zu-Az-63	2210	USD	H	2.10	20	40
Zu-Az-64	2215	USD	SH	2.40	15	30
Zu-Az-65	2210	USD	H	2.80	25	50
Zu-Az-66	2225	USD	SH	1.90	10	20
Zu-Az-67	2230	USD	SH	0.50	5	10
Zu-Az-68	2250	USD	SH	1.10	10	20
Zu-Az-69	2245	USD	SH	0.40	5	10
Zu-Az-70	2255	USD	SH	0.90	10	20
Zu-Az-71	2260	USD	SH?	1.40	15	30
Zu-Az-72	2300	USD	SDV?	17.20	170	340
Zu-Az-73	2280	USD	SDV	15.20	150	300
Zu-Az-74	2360	USD	H	5.10	25	50
Zu-Az-75	2350	USD	SH	0.10	5	10
Zu-Az-76	2340	USD	H	2.60	20	40
Zu-Az-77	2345	USD	SH	0.90	15	30
Zu-Az-78	2330	USD	H	1.80	25	50
Zu-Az-79	2310	USD	LNV	19.80	500	1000
Zu-Az-80	2315	USD	H	2.80	40	80
Zu-Az-81	2310	USD	SDV?	20.30	250	500
Zu-Az-82	2300	USD	H	5.20	50	100
Zu-Az-83, -84	2330	USD	H	1.80	50	100
Zu-Az-85	2330	USD	SH	0.40	5	10
Zu-Az-86	2350	USD	SH	1.00	10	20
Zu-Az-87	2340	USD	SDV	8.00	100	200
Zu-Az-88	2320	USD	SH	2.00	10	20
Zu-Az-89	2310	USD	SH	0.90	5	10
Zu-Az-90	2305	USD	H	2.30	25	50
Zu-Az-91	2305	USD	SH	0.40	5	10
Zu-Az-92	2305	USD	H	1.60	15	30

Table A1 cont.

Site Number	Elevation (m asl)	Zone	Classification	Hectares	Population Minimum	Maximum
Zu-Az-93	2305	USD	SH	0.60	2	5
Zu-Az-94, -95, -97, -98	2330	USD	SDV??	8.20	80	160
Zu-Az-96	2335	USD	H	2.70	30	60
Zu-Az-99	2310	USD	SDV??	15.70	150	300
Zu-Az-100	2355	USD	H	4.50	50	100
Zu-Az-101	2345	USD	H	6.00	60	120
Zu-Az-102	2310	USD	H	4.70	50	100
Zu-Az-103, -104	2295	USD	SDV?	9.10	100	200
Zu-Az-105	2310	USD	H	5.00	50	100
Zu-Az-106	2310	USD	H	2.00	20	40
Zu-Az-107	2305	USD	SH	1.40	10	20
Zu-Az-108	2270	USD	SH	1.00	10	20
Zu-Az-109	2270	USD	SH	1.40	15	30
Zu-Az-110	2255	USD	SH	0.60	5	10
Zu-Az-111	2245	USD	SH	0.60	5	10
Zu-Az-112	2245	USD	SH	0.90	5	10
Zu-Az-113	2275	USD	SH	0.70	5	10
Zu-Az-114	2320	USD	SDV?	15.10	150	300
Zu-Az-115	2270	USD	H	7.30	50	100
Zu-Az-116	2240	USD	SDV?	11.20	110	220
Zu-Az-117	2240	USD	SH?	2.90	15	30
Zu-Az-118	2240	USD	SDV	6.60	75	150
Zu-Az-119	2280	USD	SDV	6.40	65	130
Zu-Az-120	2275	USD	SH	0.80	10	20
Zu-Az-121	2275	USD	SDV	8.70	130	260
Zu-Az-122	2275	USD	SDV?	6.10	75	150
Zu-Az-123	2270	USD	H?	5.40	50	100
Zu-Az-124	2300	USD	SH	1.50	10	20
Zu-Az-125	2285	USD	SH	0.60	5	10
Zu-Az-126	2290	USD	SDV	10.20	100	200
Zu-Az-127	2305	USD	SH	0.50	5	10
Zu-Az-128	2350	USD	SH	1.00	5	10
Zu-Az-129	2350	USD	H	4.30	40	80
Zu-Az-130, -131	2350	USD	RC	107.80	1100	2200
Zu-Az-132	2330	USD	LDV	53.60	750	1500
Zu-Az-133	2335	USD	SH	0.50	5	10
Zu-Az-134	2330	USD	SH	1.30	10	20
Zu-Az-135	2350	USD	SDV	6.10	60	120
Zu-Az-136	2350	USD	SDV	18.60	200	400
Zu-Az-137	2355	USD	H	6.30	50	100
Zu-Az-138	2355	USD	H	3.70	40	80
Zu-Az-139	2360	BOMLP	SH	0.80	5	10
Zu-Az-140	2355	BOMLP	SH	1.90	10	20
Zu-Az-141, -143, -144, -145	2340	BOMLP	LDV	42.20	400	800
Zu-Az-142	2340	BOMLP	SH	0.40	5	10
Zu-Az-146	2350	BOMLP	SH	2.20	10	20
Zu-Az-147, -148	2390	BOMLP	LDV	73.40	750	1500
Zu-Az-149	2365	BOMLP	LDV	25.20	400	800
Zu-Az-150	2390	BOMLP	H	2.90	20	40
Zu-Az-151	2370	BOMLP	H	1.80	20	40

Table A1 cont.

Site Number	Elevation (m asl)	Zone	Classification	Hectares	Population Minimum	Maximum
Zu-Az-152	2405	USD	H	1.00	20	40
Zu-Az-153	2365	USD	H	1.50	20	40
Zu-Az-154	2370	USD	SDV	5.50	75	150
Zu-Az-155	2355	USD	LDV	28.70	400	800
Zu-Az-156	2330	USD	SH	0.60	5	10
Zu-Az-157	2340	USD	SDV	8.80	100	200
Zu-Az-158	2355	USD	H	2.60	25	50
Zu-Az-159	2350	USD	SH	1.00	5	10
Zu-Az-160	2340	USD	SH	1.70	15	30
Zu-Az-161	2355	USD	SDV	6.40	75	150
Zu-Az-162	2305	USD	H	2.40	25	50
Zu-Az-163	2325	USD	H	4.80	40	80
Zu-Az-164	2360	USD	SH	0.70	5	10
Zu-Az-165	2360	BOMLP	SH?	0.60	5	10
Zu-Az-166	2355	USD	SH	0.80	5	10
Zu-Az-167	2355	USD	SH	1.40	10	20
Zu-Az-168	2300	USD	SH	0.60	2	5
Zu-Az-169	2340	BOMLP	SDV	18.10	200	400
Zu-Az-170	2355	BOMLP	H	3.60	35	70
Zu-Az-171	2365	BOMLP	SH	1.00	10	20
Zu-Az-172	2365	BOMLP	LC	115.30	1200	2400
Zu-Az-173	2385	BOMLP	H	6.30	30	60
Zu-Az-174	2345	BOMLP	SH	1.60	15	30
Zu-Az-175	2340	BOMLP	SH	0.60	5	10
Zu-Az-176	2340	BOMLP	SH	1.30	10	20
Zu-Az-177	2355	BOMLP	SH	0.70	5	10
Zu-Az-178	2330	BOMLP	H	4.10	25	50
Zu-Az-179	2340	BOMLP	H	2.40	25	50
Zu-Az-180	2370	BOMLP	H	9.20	50	100
Zu-Az-181	2355	BOMLP	SDV	11.20	150	300
Zu-Az-182	2335	BOMLP	SDV?	6.20	75	150
Zu-Az-183	2330	BOMLP	H?	3.60	40	80
Zu-Az-184	2325	BOMLP	SDV	6.20	65	130
Zu-Az-185	2320	BOMLP	SH	0.50	2	5
Zu-Az-186, -187	2310	BOMLP	SH	1.10	5	10
Zu-Az-188	2310	BOMLP	SH	1.50	10	20
Zu-Az-189	2305	BOMLP	SH	2.10	10	20
Zu-Az-190	2305	BOMLP	SH	0.90	5	10
Zu-Az-191	2300	BOMLP	SH	0.40	2	5
Zu-Az-192, -193	2285	BOMLP	SH	1.10	10	20
Zu-Az-194	2305	BOMLP	SDV	10.80	110	220
Zu-Az-195	2305	BOMLP	SDV	15.40	150	300
Zu-Az-196	2300	BOMLP	SDV	8.10	80	160
Zu-Az-197	2345	BOMLP	SH?	0.50	5	10
Zu-Az-198	2320	BOMLP	H?	2.90	30	60
Zu-Az-199	2305	BOMLP	SH	1.70	10	20
Zu-Az-200	2330	BOMLP	SH	0.80	10	20
Zu-Az-201	2340	BOMLP	SH	0.60	5	10
Zu-Az-202	2345	BOMLP	H	2.30	25	50
Zu-Az-203	2340	BOMLP	SH	0.10	2	5
Zu-Az-204	2360	BOMLP	ICCP	0.40	-	-

Table A1 cont.

Site Number	Elevation (m asl)	Zone	Classification	Hectares	Population Minimum	Maximum
Zu-Az-205	2380	BOMLP	SH	0.90	10	20
Zu-Az-206	2405	BOMLP	SH	0.10	2	5
Zu-Az-207	2360	USD	ICCP?	0.40	-	-
Zu-Az-208	2340	USD	H	2.80	30	60
Zu-Az-209	2300	USD	SH	1.50	10	20
Zu-Az-210	2295	USD	SH?	0.70	5	10
Zu-Az-211	2275	USD	SH	1.40	10	20
Zu-Az-212	2380	USD	SH	0.60	5	10
Zu-Az-213	2315	USD	SH	0.80	10	20
Zu-Az-214	2295	USD	ICCP?	1.00	-	-
Zu-Az-215	2270	USD	H	2.50	20	40
Zu-Az-216	2270	USD	H	7.40	50	100
Zu-Az-217	2270	USD	LDV	31.80	400	800
Zu-Az-218	2280	USD	LDV?	38.00	400	800
Zu-Az-219	2280	USD	H	3.50	25	50
Zu-Az-220	2290	USD	H	2.40	20	40
Zu-Az-221	2315	USD	H	7.80	40	80
Zu-Az-222	2345	USD	SH	0.80	5	10
Zu-Az-223	2345	USD	H	1.20	15	30
Zu-Az-224	2550	BOMLP (CJ)	ICCP	0.10	-	-
Zu-Az-225	2335	BOMLP	SH	1.00	5	10
Zu-Az-226	2355	BOMLP	SH	0.80	5	10
Zu-Az-227	2300	BOMLP	SH?	0.90	5	10
Zu-Az-228	2340	BOMLP	SH	0.10	2	5
Zu-Az-229	2390	BOMLP (CJ)	SH	0.50	5	10
Zu-Az-230	2405	BOMLP (CJ)	ICCP	0.10	-	-
Zu-Az-231, -232	2340	BOMLP	SH?	0.90	10	20
Zu-Az-233, -254, -255	2300	BOMLP	LC?	100.00??	1000	2000
Zu-Az-234	2290	BOMLP	SH	0.50	2	5
Zu-Az-235	2270	LP	SH	1.20	10	20
Zu-Az-236	2260	LP	SDV	11.80	110	220
Zu-Az-237, -238	2260	LP	RC?	100.00??	2000	4000
Zu-Az-239	2275	LP	SH	1.10	5	10
Zu-Az-240	2275	LP	SH	1.80	10	20
Zu-Az-241	2275	LP	H	1.90	20	40
Zu-Az-242	2270	LP	H	2.50	25	50
Zu-Az-243	2260	LP	SH	1.00	5	10
Zu-Az-244	2255	LP	SH?	0.60	5	10
Zu-Az-245	2255	LP	H	3.50	35	70
Zu-Az-246	2250	LP	SH	1.00	5	10
Zu-Az-247	2245	LP	SH	1.30	15	30
Zu-Az-248	2245	LP	SH	0.30	2	5
Zu-Az-249	2245	LP	H	5.10	50	100
Zu-Az-250, -251, -252	2245	LP	H	1.60	20	40
Zu-Az-253	2250	LP	SH	0.10	5	10
Zu-Az-254 (see Zu-Az-233)	-	-	-	-	-	-
Zu-Az-255 (see Zu-Az-233)	-	-	-	-	-	-
Zu-Az-256	2250	LP	SH (ISMW)	0.40	2	5

Table A1 cont.

Site Number	Elevation (m asl)	Zone	Classification	Hectares	Population Minimum	Population Maximum
Zu-Az-257	2245	LP	SH (ISMW)	0.60	5	10
Zu-Az-258	2260	LP	SH	1.00	5	10
Zu-Az-259, -260	2260	LP	H	1.90	20	40
Zu-Az-261	2255	LP	SH	1.50	10	20
Zu-Az-262	2255	LP	SH	0.30	2	5
Zu-Az-263	2255	LP	SH	0.80	10	20
Zu-Az-264	2260	LP	H	1.70	20	40
Zu-Az-265	2255	LP	H	3.00	20	40
Zu-Az-266	2300	BOMLP	H	5.30	50	100
Zu-Az-267	2310	BOMLP	SH	1.70	10	20
Zu-Az-268	2305	BOMLP	SH	1.50	15	30
Zu-Az-269	2280	BOMLP	SDV	13.60	100	200
Zu-Az-270	2280	BOMLP	H?	2.80	25	50
Zu-Az-271	2275	LP	SDV	6.50	65	130
Zu-Az-272	2260	LP	H	3.10	20	40
Zu-Az-273	2245	LP	SH	1.40	5	10
Zu-Az-274	2245	LB	H	3.20	30	60
Zu-Az-275	2245	LB	H	3.20	30	60
Zu-Az-276	2250	LB	RC	69.30	1750	3500
Zu-Az-277	2240	LB	SH	1.30	5	10
Zu-Az-278	2270	LP (TI)	SDV?	5.70	60	120
Zu-Az-279	2280	LP (TI)	SH?	0.80	5	10
Zu-Az-280	2275	LP (TI)	SH	0.80	5	10
Zu-Az-281	2305	LP (TI)	SDV	7.50	75	150
Zu-Az-282	2310	LP (TI)	H	2.90	30	60
Zu-Az-283	2310	LP (TI)	SH	1.60	10	20
Zu-Az-284	2260	LP (TI))	H?	5.40	40	80
Zu-Az-285	2245	LP (TI)	SH	0.10	2	5
Zu-Az-286	2330	LP (TI)	SDV	10.10	75	150
Zu-Az-287	2280	LP (TI)	SDV	8.50	85	170
Zu-Az-288	2290	LP (TI)	SDV	14.50	150	300
Zu-Az-289	2330	LP (TI)	ICCP?	1.50	?	?
Zu-Az-290	2320	LP (TI)	H	1.70	20	40
Zu-Az-291	2310	LP (TI)	SH	2.00	10	20
Zu-Az-292, -293, -294	2275	LP (TI)	SDV??	19.20+?	200?	400?
Zu-Az-295	2265	LP (TI)	H	4.10	40	80
Zu-Az-296	2245	LB	SH	0.60	2	5
Zu-Az-297	2245	LB	H	4.60	45	90
Zu-Az-298	2245	LB	SDV	23.70	250	500
Zu-Az-299	2245	LB	ISMW	0.10	-	-
Zu-Az-300	2245	LB	ISMW	1.40	-	-
Zu-Az-301	2245	LB	ISMW	1.00	-	-
Zu-Az-302	2350	USD	SH?	0.10	2	5
			Totals:	1799.90	20,743	41,485

Key:

Zone:
USD = Upper Salado Drainage
BOMLP = Basin of Mexico Lower Piedmont
LP = Lakeshore Plain
LB = Lakebed
BOMLP (CJ) = Basin of Mexico (Cerro Jalpa)
USD (CMG) = Upper Salado Drainage (Cerro de la Mesa Grande)
BOMLP (CC) = Basin of Mexico (Cerro de Coyotepec)
LP (TI) = Lakeshore Plain (Tultepec Island)

Site Classification:
SH = Small Hamlet
H = Hamlet
SDV = Small Dispersed Village
LDV = Large Dispersed Village
SNV = Small Nucleated Village
LNV = Large Nucleated Village
LC = Local Center
RC = Regional Center
ICCP = Isolated Ceremonial Civic Precinct
ISMW = Isolated Saltmaking Workshop
IOW = Isolated Obsidian Workshop

Note: Question mark suffix indicates relative degree of uncertainty.

Appendix B

Ceramic Chronology

Jeffrey R. Parsons, Mary H. Parsons, and David J. Wilson

Here we do not attempt to describe the full range of pottery for each period. Rather, we focus on those ceramic categories that were most useful to us in making chronological assessments. Although we do describe several useful low-frequency types, in many cases these were not commonly encountered or recognized in our typically small and badly weathered surface collections. Our emphasis is on vessel form and surface decoration; we have less to say about paste or the full range of color and surface treatment.

Many nuances of vessel form, decoration, and surface treatment have facilitated the refinement of ceramic phases over the past four decades in and around the Valley of Mexico (e.g., Blucher 1970; Brumfiel 2005; Cobean 1978, 1990; García Chávez 1991, 2004; García Chávez and Córdoba 1994; Rattray 1966, 1973, 2001; Ramírez et al. 2000; Sugiura 2005). However, these nuances were often difficult to discern in our weathered surface samples. Consequently, we have been forced to "lump" rather than "split," and our chronology remains quite generalized. This is especially true for the long Classic period, which, unfortunately, we have been forced to treat as a single chronological unit—although it is often clear that either or both early and late phases are present in many of our surface collections.

In the following period-by-period descriptions, we distinguish three basic ceramic categories: Service Wares, Utilitarian Wares, and Specialty Wares (low-frequency types and tradewares). Relative to Utilitarian Wares, Service Wares are typically thinner walled, better finished, more frequently decorated, and sometimes (although not always) more highly fired and with finer pastes. We assume that the basic functions of the two wares were different: Utilitarian Wares were probably involved with basic domestic tasks (for example, food preparation, food storage, material storage and transport), while Service Wares probably would have functioned for serving prepared food and drink, signaling wealth or prestige, or for certain ritual activities.

We found no Early Formative or Middle Formative surface pottery in the Zumpango Region, and we know of no other reports of these ceramics from our survey region. The closest Early and Middle Formative occupation appears to be that reported by McBride (1974) and Gorenflo and Sanders (2007) in the neighboring Cuauhtitlan Region several kilometers to the southwest. We begin with the Late Formative period.

All plates appear at the end of this appendix. The scale bars are in centimeters.

The Late Formative

Gorenflo and Sanders (2007:48-59) report forty-two Late Formative sites from the neighboring Cuautitlan Region to the southwest, and there is also a modest, but significant, Late Formative occupation in the Teotihuacan Region to the southeast (Sanders et al. 1975); Mastache, Cobean, and Healan (2002:44-45) have reported a sizable (ca. 15 ha) Late Formative site near Tepeji del Río, approximately 15 km to the west of the western edge of the Zumpango Region. In marked contrast, we found only one small Late Formative site in the Zumpango Region. Our ceramic sample is thus correspondingly small, with few categories. The paste in all categories appears to be similar: gray-brown in color with relatively coarse temper.

We have classified our Late Formative pottery as follows:

I. Service Ware
    A. Red Shouldered Bowl
    B. Plain Shouldered Bowl
II. Utilitarian Ware
    A. Plainware Olla with Flaring Neck
    B. Plainware Bowl or Basin

Late Formative Service Ware: Shouldered Bowl (Fig. B1)

Although the original surface color is very difficult to discern in many of our sherds, enough usually remains to indicate that the upper walls of some were originally coated with a deep red paint (Fig. B1*a-f*), while others appear to have been unpainted (Fig. B1*g-m*). In a few cases, the upper exterior walls are decorated with two parallel lines of small, shallow punctates (Fig. B1*l, m*). Rim diameters range between 10 and 14 cm. Both interior and exterior walls tend to be well smoothed. We noted no associated supports or other appendages. Vessel height remains uncertain.

Similar vessels, some with tripod hollow supports, have been described from Late Formative sites throughout the Valley of Mexico (e.g., Vaillant 1930:94-95, 1931:380-81; Barba de Piña Chan 1956:72-73, Lam. 10; Blanton and Parsons 1971:263-66; Sanders et al. 1975:506-22; Niederberger 1976:203-5; Whalen and Parsons 1982:397-98; Müller 1990:122, 124; García Chávez and Córdoba 1994:106-9; Ramírez et al. 2000:103-11).

Late Formative Utilitarian Ware: Plainware Olla with Flaring Neck (Fig. B2a-h)

These low-necked vessels are thicker walled and less well smoothed than the shouldered bowls described above, and they appear to lack surface decoration of any kind. We have no evidence of supports, handles, or other appendages. Rim diameters range between 10 and 15 cm. Vessel height remains unknown. Similar vessels have been described from other Late Formative sites in the Valley of Mexico by Vaillant (1930:92-93; 1931:372-73), Blanton and Parsons (1971:263-65), Niederberger (1976:204), Whalen and Parsons (1982:397), Sanders et al. (1975:504-22), Müller (1990:124), García Chávez (1991:127-29), and Ramírez et al. (2000:100-102).

Late Formative Utilitarian Ware: Plainware Bowl or Basin (Fig. B2i)

These are less frequent than ollas in our sample, but appear to be a definite component of the Late Formative plainware assemblage. Rim diameters average 15 cm. Vessel height remains unknown. We noted no supports or other appendages.

Comparable material is reported from other Late Formative sites in the Valley of Mexico by Vaillant (1930:92-93; 1931:372-73), Blanton and Parsons (1971:263-65), McBride (1974:196), Sanders et al. (1975:502-22), Whalen and Parsons (1982:396-97), and Ramírez et al. (2000:100-102).

Terminal Formative (Tzacualli Phase)

All the Terminal Formative material we can identify seems to date to the Tzacaulli phase. Relative to the antecedent Late Formative there are many more sites but, like the Late Formative, the ceramic assemblage in our surface collections remains heavily dominated by only a few vessel-form categories. Although bowls tend to be thinner walled and better smoothed than ollas, all vessel categories appear to be constructed of similar gray-brown, relatively coarse paste. There are no supports or other appendages in our surface collections. Vessel height remains unknown.

Although it did not occur on a designated TF site, we did find one badly weathered Tzacualli ceramic figurine at Zu-LT-210 (Plate B1), in an area far from any other identified TF occupation.

We have classified our Terminal Formative pottery as follows:

I. Service Ware
   A. Plainware Simple Bowl
   B. Plainware Shouldered Bowl
II. Utilitarian Ware
   A. Plainware Wedge-Rim Olla
   B. Plainware Flaring-Rim Olla

Terminal Formative Service Ware: Plainware Simple Bowl (Fig. B3a-j)

These are simple, hemispherical vessels with rim diameters ranging from 11 to 15 cm. Similar vessels found in or near Teotihuacan are illustrated by Rattray (1973: Figs. 13, 35; 2001:473-74) and Sanders et al. (1975:542).

Terminal Formative Service Ware: Plainware Shouldered Bowl (Fig. B3k-o)

Similar to the simple bowls just described, except for a distinctive shoulder slightly below the rim. Similar sherds found in or near Teotihuacan are illustrated by Rattray (1973: Fig. 35; 2001:472-73) and Sanders et al. (1975:537, 549-51).

Terminal Formative Utilitarian Ware: Plainware Wedge-Rim Olla (Figs. B4a-p, B5a-g)

These are by far the most common vessel form at all TF sites in the Zumpango Region. Rim diameters range from 12 to 20 cm. Similar sherds located in and around Teotihuacan are described by Rattray (2001:468-71), and Sanders et al. (1975:533-34, 545), and from other parts of the Valley of Mexico by Blanton and Parsons (1971:272-74), McBride (1974:280), Whalen and Parsons (1982:401-3), and García Chávez (1991:141-42).

Terminal Formative Utilitarian Ware: Plainware Flaring-Rim Olla (Fig. B5h-n)

Although consistently present, these vessels are significantly less abundant than wedge-rim ollas in our TF surface collections. Similar sherds found in or near Teotihuacan are illustrated by Rattray (1973: Fig. 35; 2001:471) and Sanders et al. (1975:545), and in the Cuautitlan Region by McBride (1974:279).

Appendix B: Ceramic Chronology 351

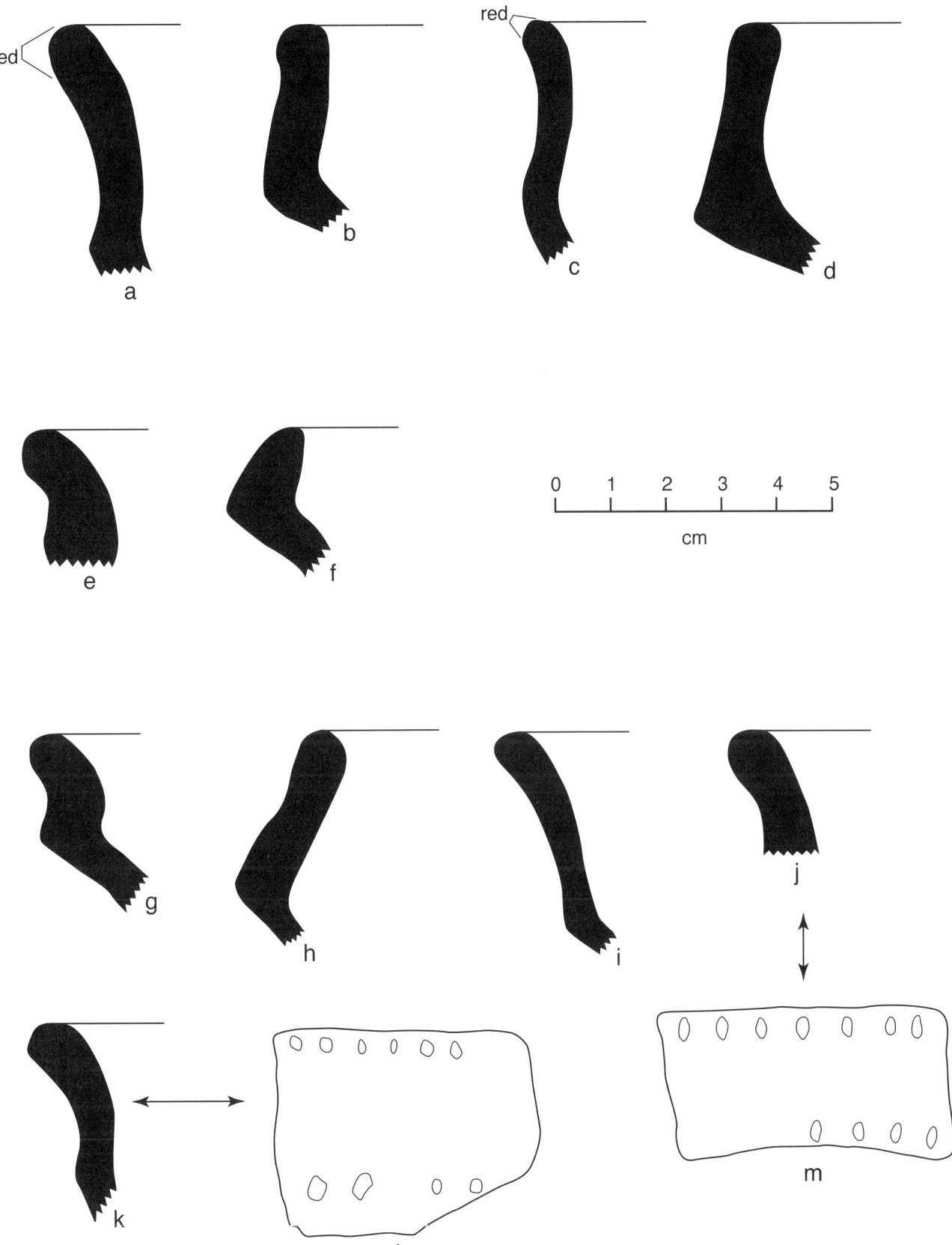

Figure B1. Late Formative Red shouldered bowls (*a-f*) and Plainware shouldered bowls (*g-m*). Proveniences: all from Zu-LF-1.

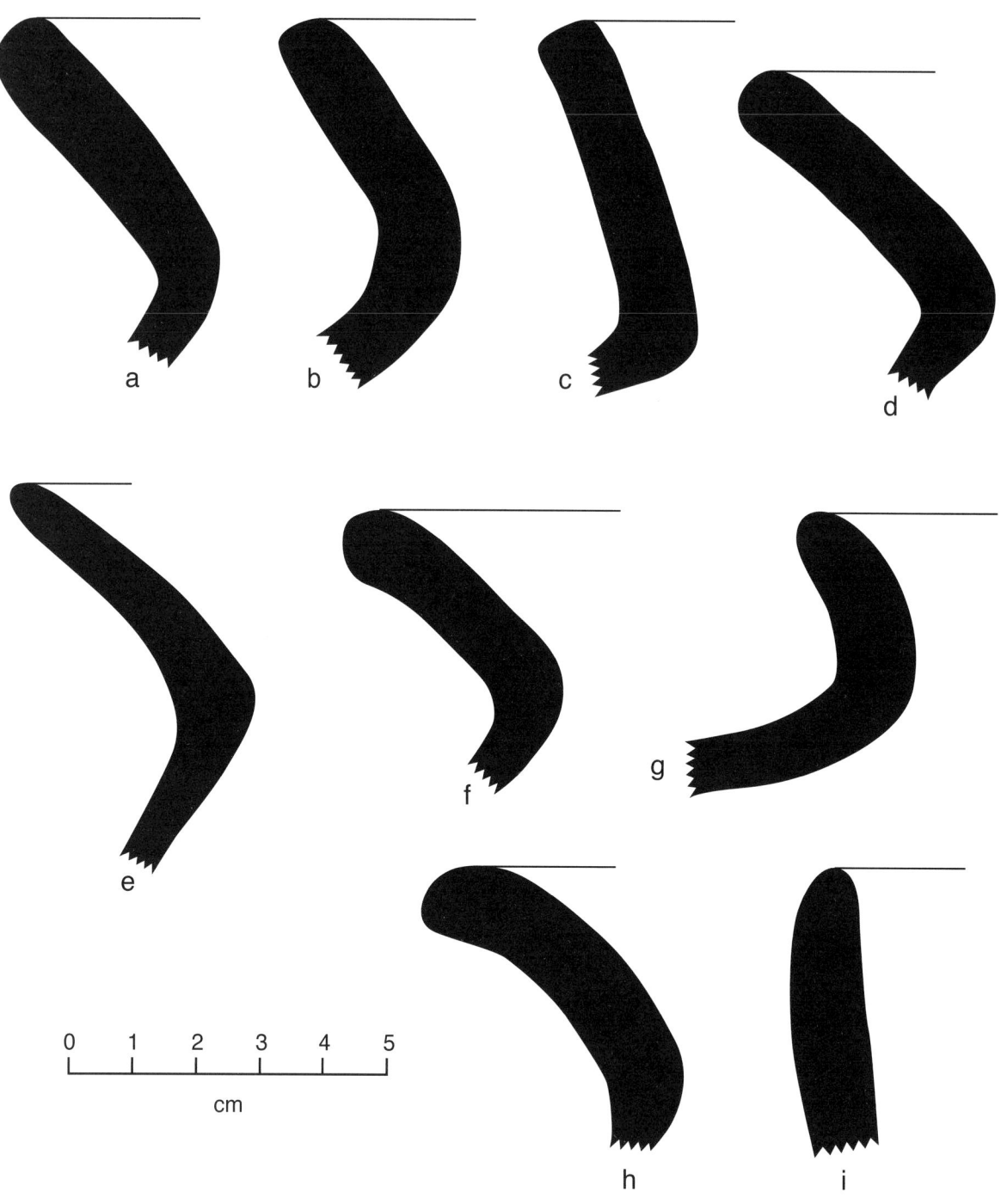

Figure B2. Late Formative Plainware ollas with flaring necks (*a-h*) and bowl-basin (*i*). Proveniences: all from Zu-LF-1.

Appendix B: Ceramic Chronology 353

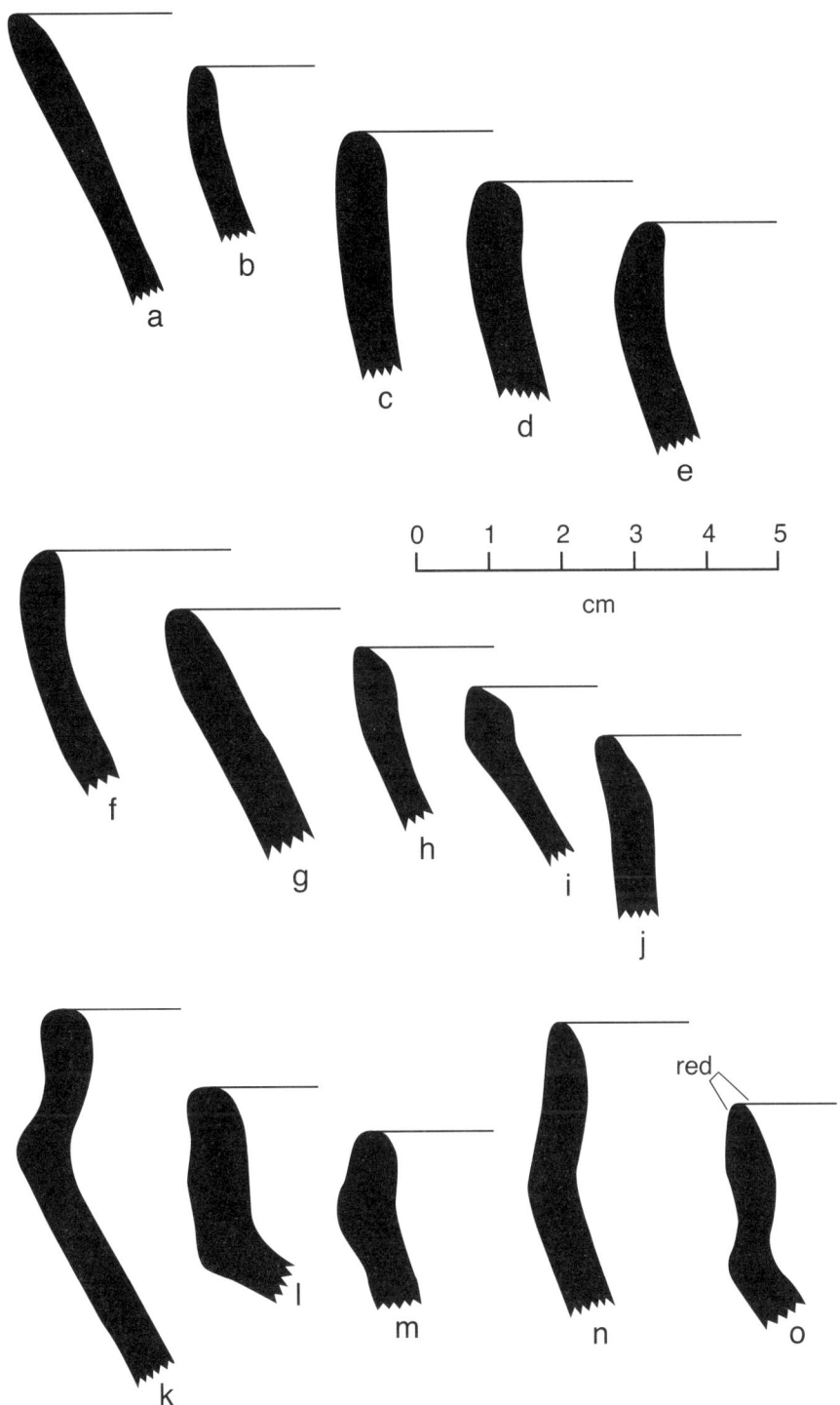

Figure B3. Terminal Formative (Tzacualli phase) Plainware simple bowls (*a-j*) and Plainware shouldered bowls (*k-o*). Proveniences: *a-e* (Zu-TF-22); *f-j* (Zu-TF-8); *k-m* (Zu-TF-22); *n* (Zu-TF-8); *o* (Zu-TF-20).

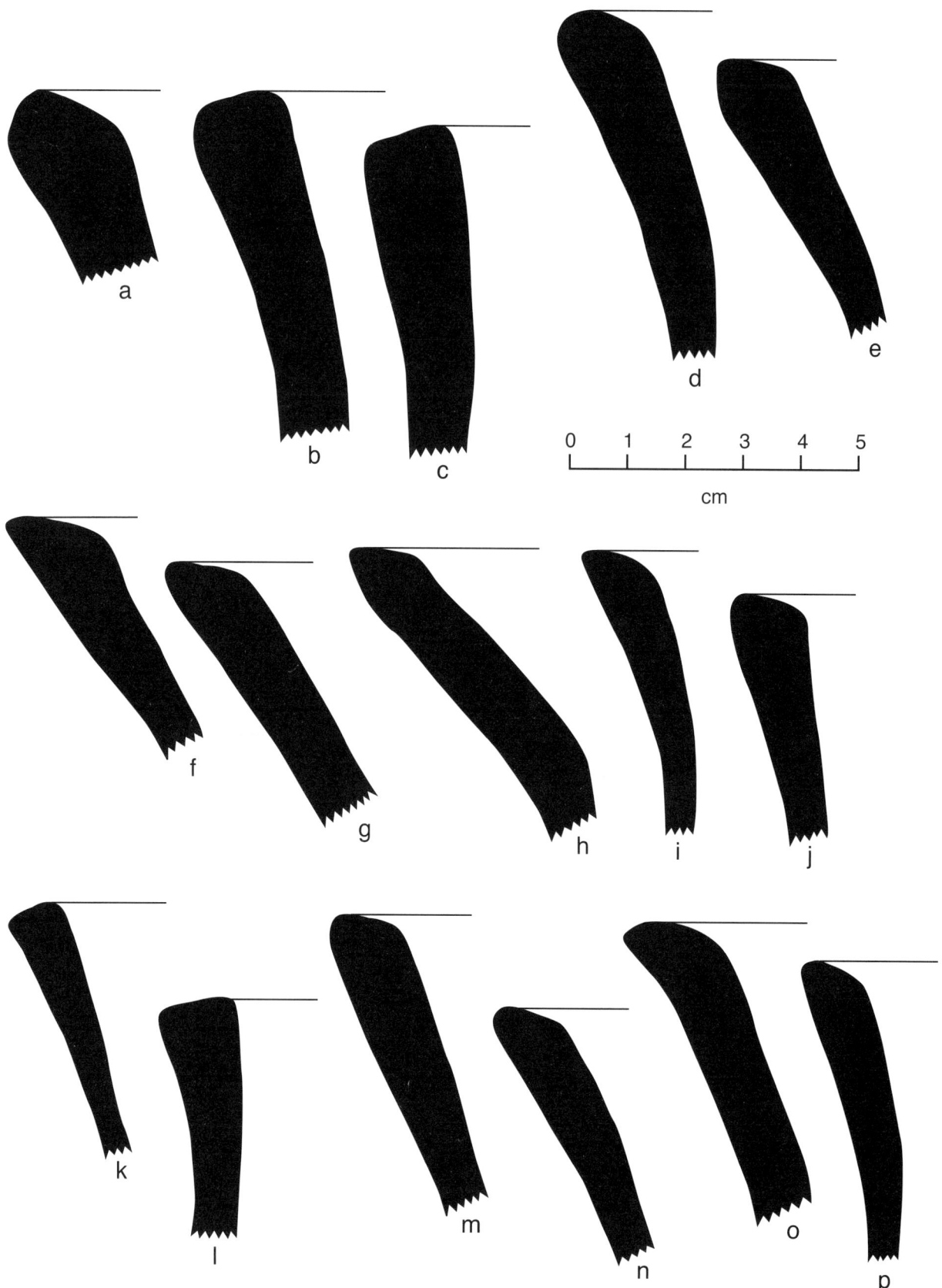

Figure B4. Terminal Formative (Tzacualli phase) Plainware wedge-rim ollas (*a-p*). Proveniences: *a, h, o* (Zu-TF-8); *b-g, i-n, p* (Zu-TF-22).

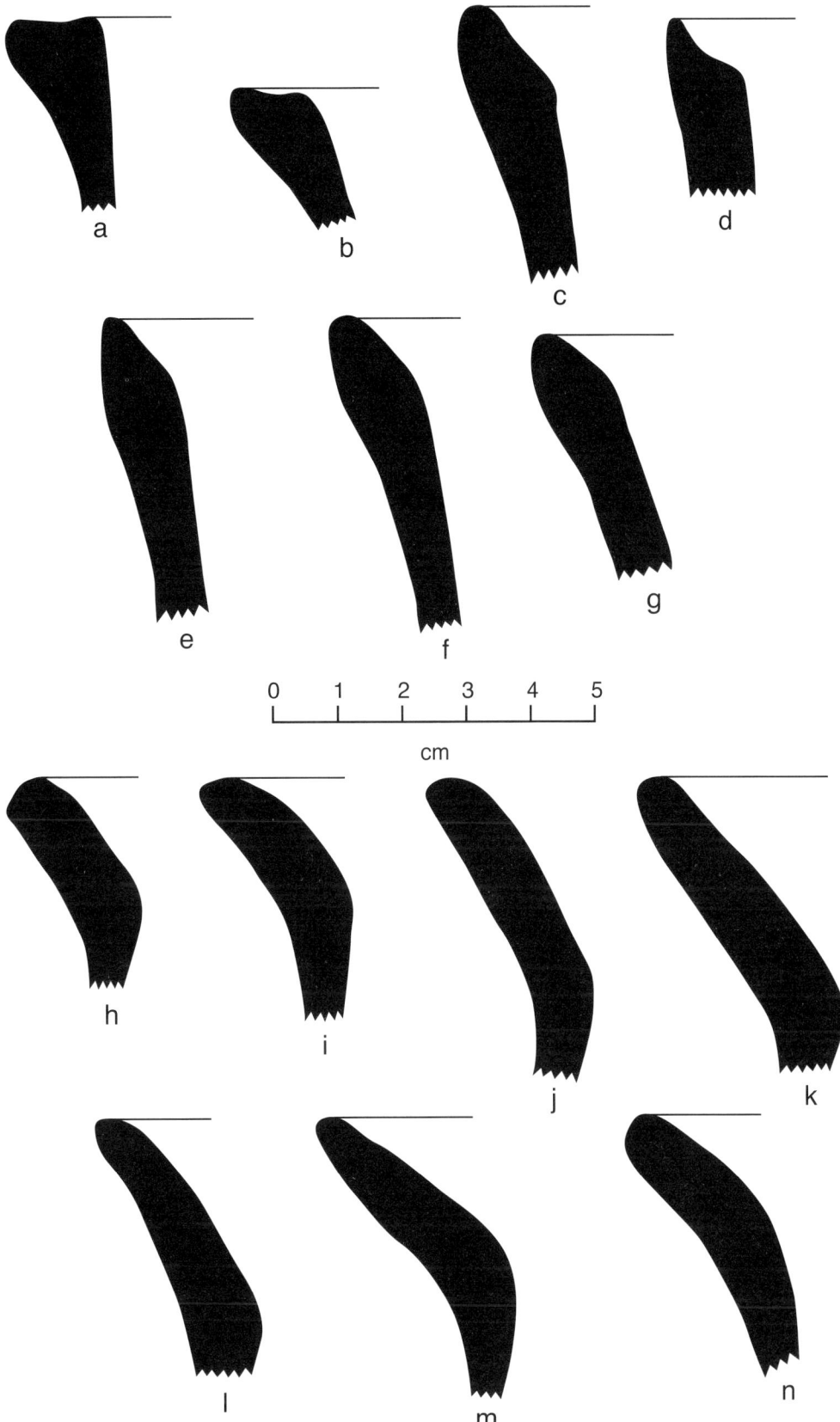

Figure B5. Terminal Formative (Tzacualli phase) Plainware wedge-rim ollas (*a-g*) and Plainware flaring-rim ollas (*h-n*). Proveniences: *a, c, e-m* (Zu-TF-22); *b, d* (Zu-TF-8); *n* (Zu-TF-20).

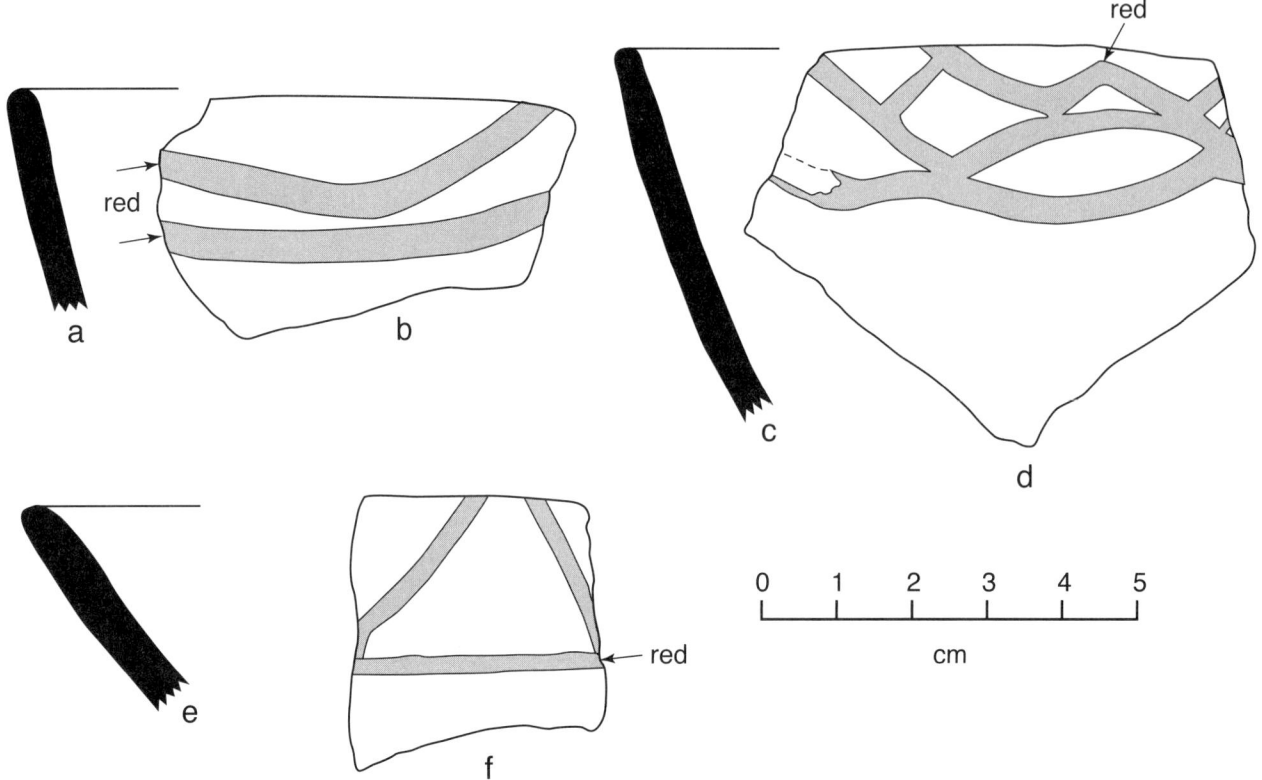

Figure B6. Classic Red/Buff hemispherical bowls. Proveniences: *a, b* (same sherd) (Zu-Cl-52); *c-f* (same two sherds) (Zu-Cl-60).

Classic

In this period there are many more sites and, for the first time, the ceramic assemblage is much more varied, with numerous ware and vessel-form categories. Nevertheless, utilitarian plainwares, especially large ollas, continue to dominate the Classic-period assemblages, just as they did in the antecedent Late Formative and Terminal Formative.

NOTE: Classic Red/Buff pottery is complicated and confusing. We have classified our Classic pottery as follows:

I. Service Ware
   A. Red/Buff Bowl
   B. Monochrome Bowl
II. Utilitarian Ware
   A. Monochrome Olla (slight-, medium-, and wide-everted rims)
   B. Red/Buff Olla
   C. Monochrome Basin
   D. Red/Buff Basin/Bowl
   E. Plainware Comal
   F. Rose-on-Granular Olla
III. Specialty Wares
   A. Thin Orange
   B. Censer Flange
   C. Figurines
   D. Candeleros
   E. Monochrome Matte Bowl (saltmaking?)

Classic Service Ware: Red/Buff Bowl (Figs. B6–B9)

These vessels occur in both direct-rim (Fig. B6) and flaring-rim variants (Figs. B7–B9). Vessels with direct-rims are less frequent than those with flaring-rims, and are quite similar to Epiclassic Coyotlatelco Red/Buff bowls (the examples we illustrate in Fig. B6 may actually be Coyotlatelco). The direct-rim variant appears to occur in the form of simple hemispherical bowls that lack supports or other appendages; the flaring-rim variant appears to have flat bottoms with sharp basal exterior angles and small, tripod nubbin supports (Plate B2). Both variants are well smoothed and polished on their exterior surfaces; interior surfaces are typically well smoothed, but not always polished. Exterior surfaces are decorated with a variety of bold curvilinear red designs (Plate B3). Some red paint is specular, and in some cases the red designs are outlined with incised lines (Plate B4). Rim diameters range between 11 and 16 cm. Vessel height (in those few cases where it can be determined) are about 9 to 10 cm.

Similar vessels found in and around Teotihuacan are illustrated by Rattray (2001:499-500, 514, 582-83) and Sanders (1995: Plates 38, 44, 51-52), and from other parts of the Valley of Mexico by Sejourne (1983: Lam. IV), Blanton and Parsons (1971:279-80), Whalen and Parsons (1982:409-12), and García Chávez (1991:170-75).

Appendix B: Ceramic Chronology 357

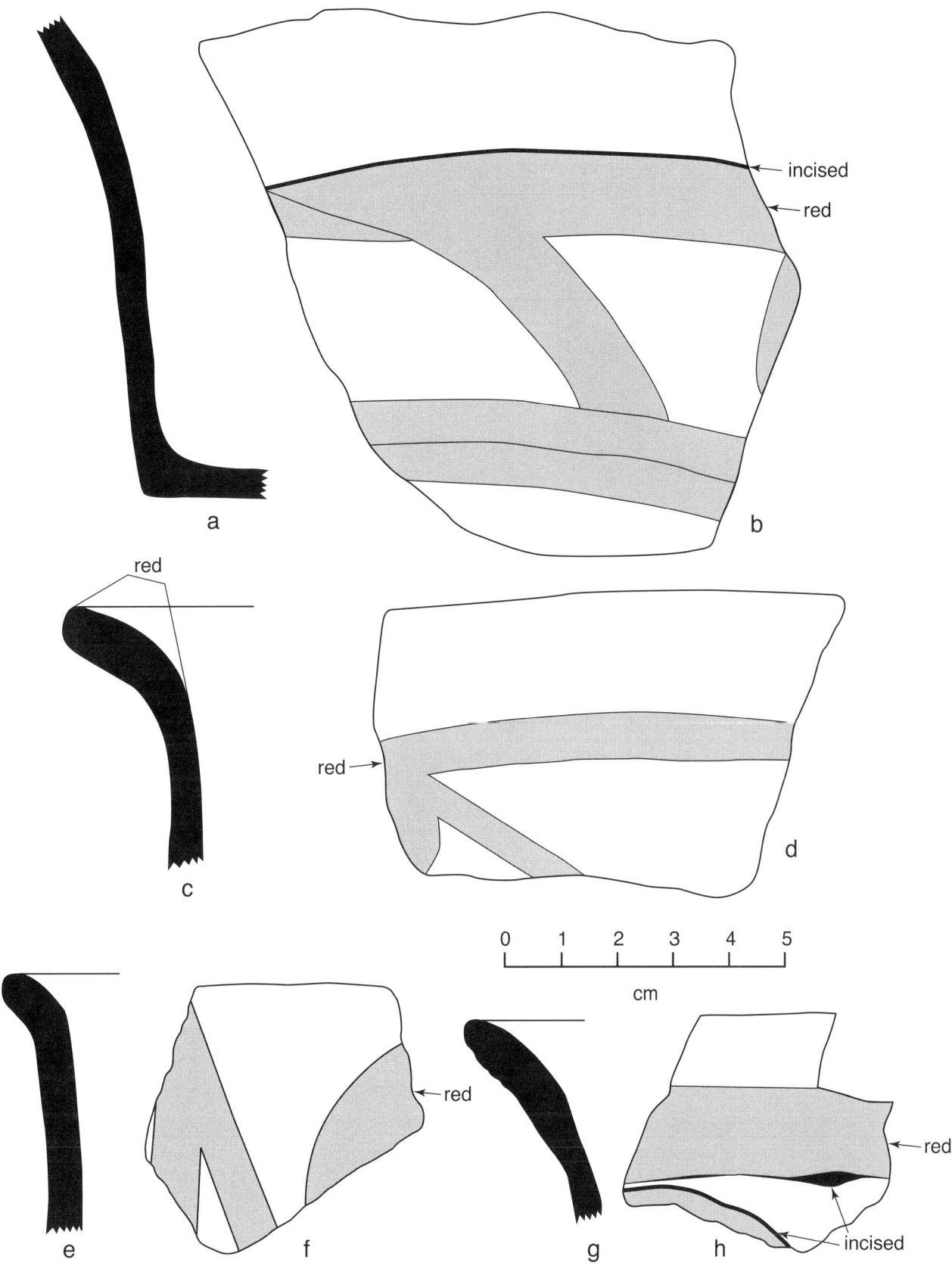

Figure B7. Classic Red/Buff flaring-rim bowls. Proveniences: *a*, *b* (same body sherd) (Zu-Cl-68); *c*, *d* (same sherd), *e*, *f* (same sherd), *g*, *h* (same sherd) (Zu-Cl-53).

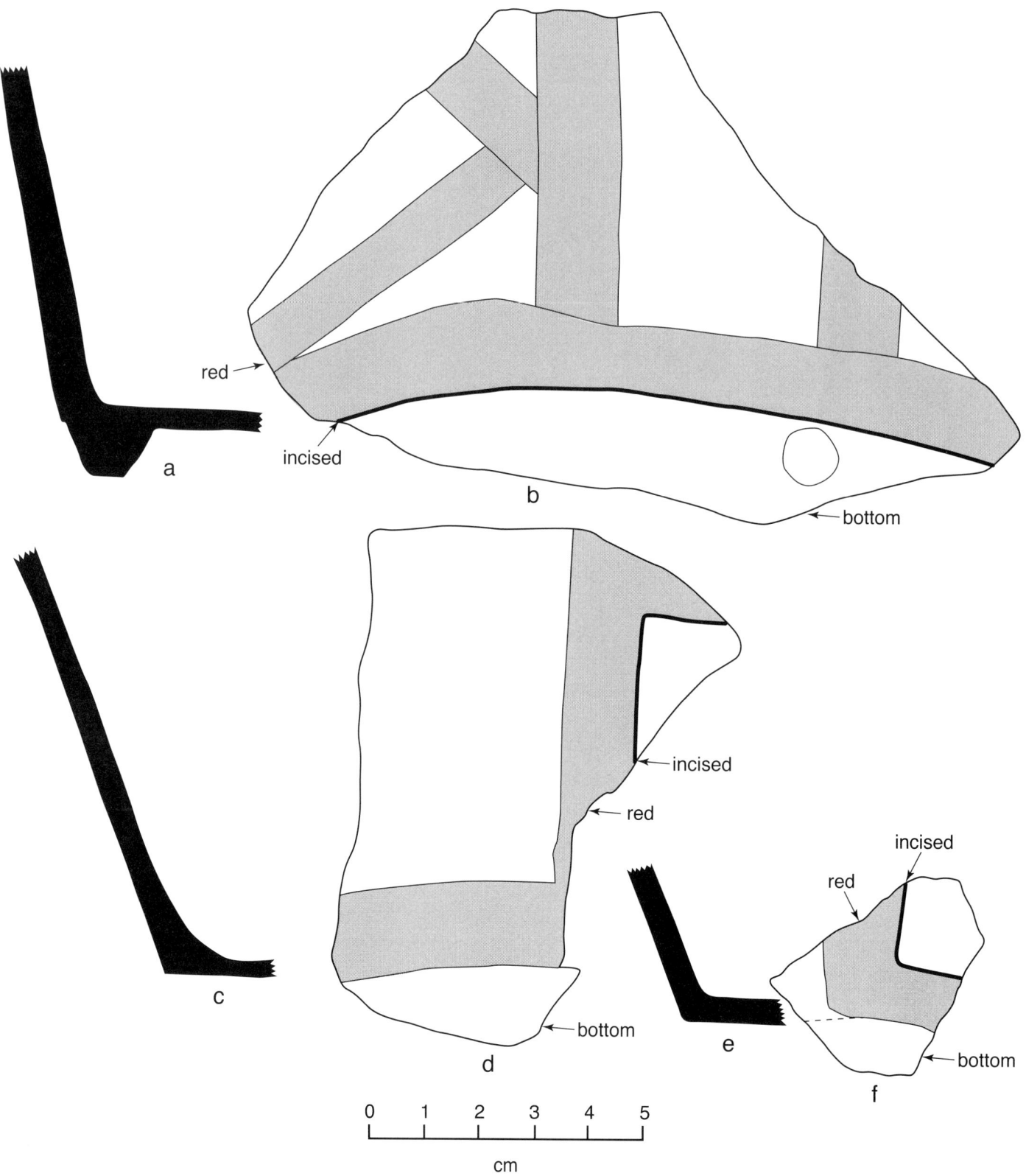

Figure B8. Classic Red/Buff flaring-rim bowls, no rim sherds. Proveniences: all from Zu-Cl-68.

Appendix B: Ceramic Chronology 359

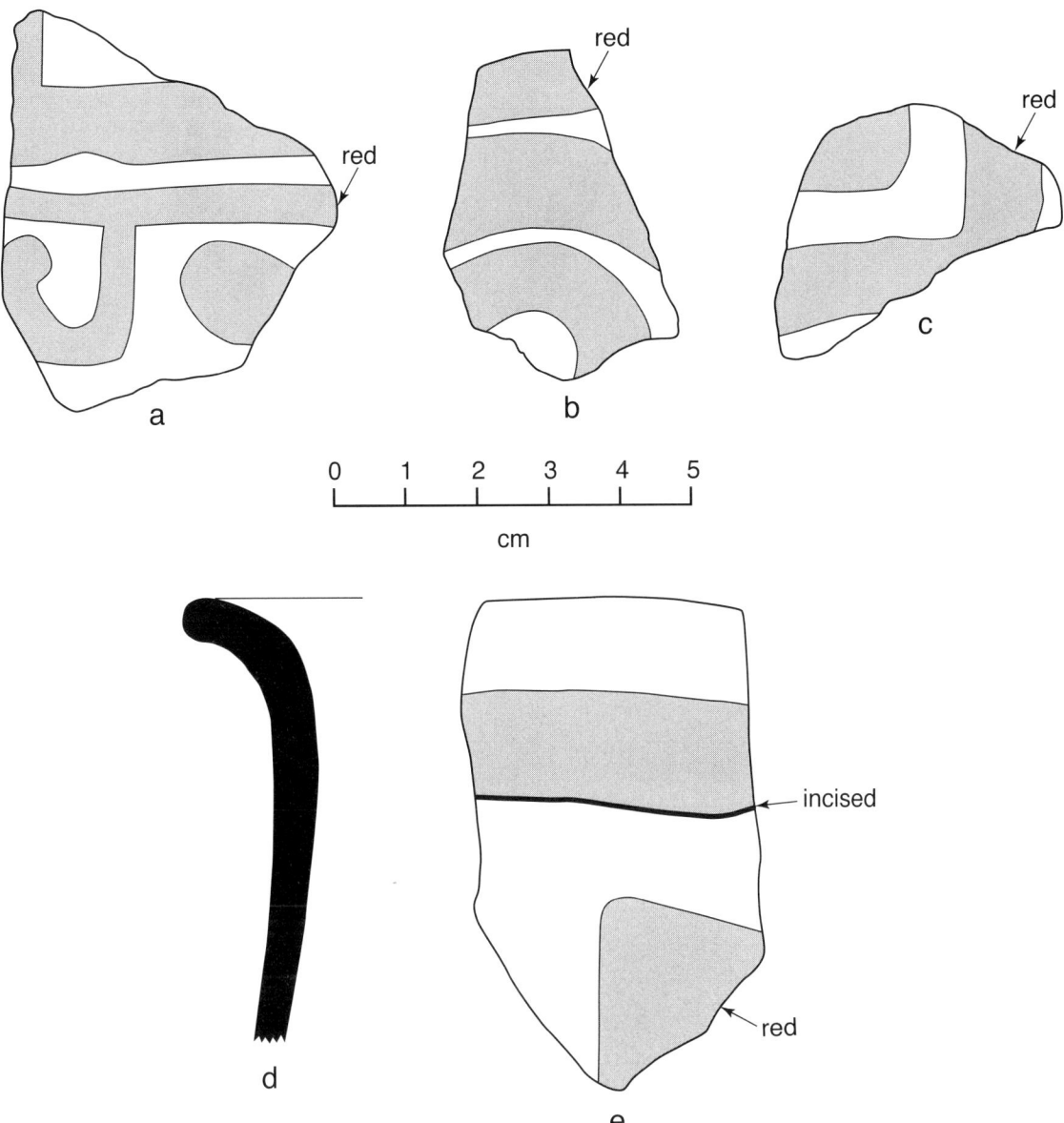

Figure B9. Classic Red/Buff flaring-rim bowls. Proveniences: *a, b, c* (all body sherds) (Zu-Cl-53); *d, e* (same sherd) (Zu-Cl-82).

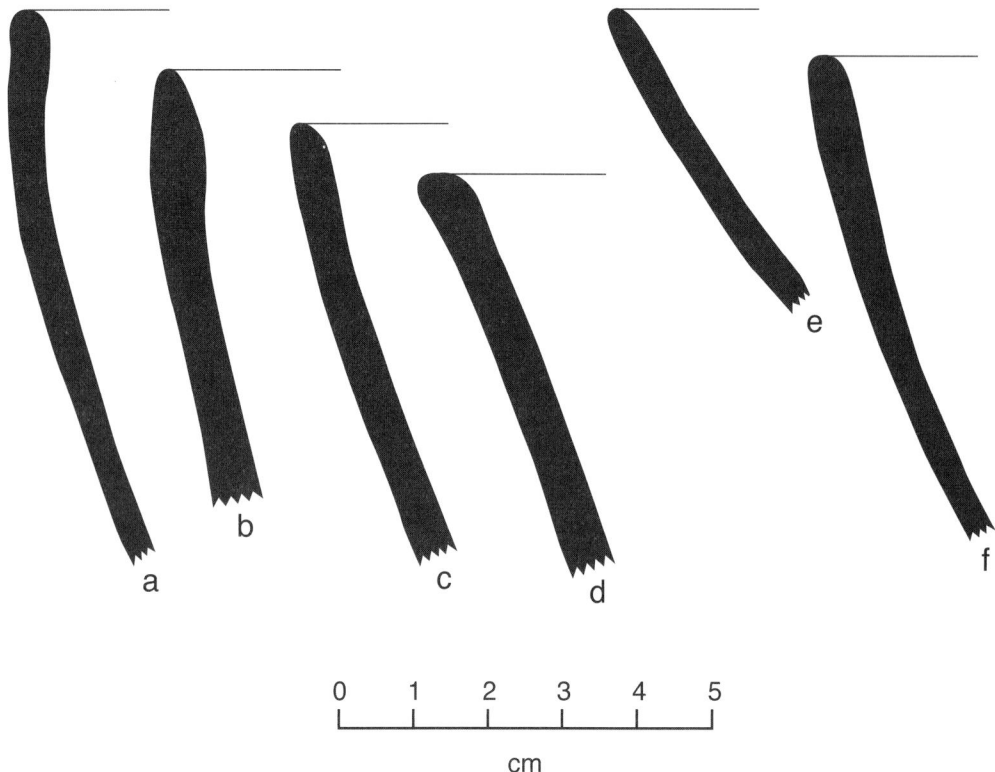

Figure B10. Classic Monochrome hemispherical bowls. Proveniences: all from Zu-Cl-60.

Classic Service Ware: Monochrome Bowl (Figs. B10, B11)

Like the Red/Buff bowls, these vessels occur in both direct-rim (Fig. B10) and flaring-rim variants (Fig. B11). Vessels with direct-rims are less frequent than those with flaring-rims, and are quite similar to Early Toltec monochrome bowls. The direct-rim variant appears to occur in the form of simple hemispherical vessels that lack supports or other appendages; the flaring-rim variant appears to have flat bottoms with sharp basal exterior angles and small, tripod nubbin supports. Surface color ranges from brown-black to medium brown to tan. Both variants are well smoothed and polished on their exterior surfaces; interior surfaces are typically well smoothed, but not always polished. Rim diameters range between 10 and 17 cm. Vessel heights could not be determined, but appear to be similar to Red/Buff bowls (ca. 9–10 cm).

Similar vessels in and around Teotihuacan are illustrated by Sanders (1995: Figs. 102-3, 107-9, 112-14, 120, 122) and Rattray (2001:480, 492, 508, 523-24, 572-73). Comparable material from other parts of the Valley of Mexico is illustrated by Blanton and Parsons (1971:274-75), Whalen and Parsons (1982:405-9), and García Chávez (1991:166-69).

Classic Utilitarian Ware: Monochrome Olla (Figs. B12–B14)

These occur with slight-everted rims (Fig. B12), medium-everted rims (Fig. B13), and wide-everted rims (Fig. B14). Vessels with wide-everted rims typically have a sharp, well-defined interior angle (Plate B5). In all cases they are relatively thick walled with similar gray-brown paste, have fairly well smoothed exterior and interior surfaces that are usually medium-brown to tan and gray-brown in color, and lack any painted or incised decoration. Neck height varies considerably. There are many low-necked vessels (Plate B6). Late Classic forms are often low-necked, with thickened rims that tend to be slightly rolled over (Plate B7). Rim diameters range from 10 to 19 cm. Neither vessel height nor basal form could be determined. The presence of handles or other appendages is uncertain. These are the dominant vessel forms at most Classic sites in the Zumpango Region.

Similar vessels found in and around Teotihuacan are illustrated by Rattray (2001:491, 505, 547, 571) and Sanders (1995: Figs. 116, 138-43), and from other parts of the Valley of Mexico by Blanton and Parsons (1971:275-76, 280-81), Whalen and Parsons (1982:405-8, 410-11), and García Chávez (1991:177-85, 274-75).

Classic Utilitarian Ware: Red/Buff Olla and Basin (Figs. B15, B16)

These vessels are not abundant, but usually occur at Classic sites in the Zumpango Region. In form they are quite similar to the monochrome ollas described above and below. The red designs are applied in several ways: sometimes there is a single band around the top or upper interior of the rim (Fig. B15*a*; Plate B8); sometimes there are wide bands applied to the upper interior and exterior surfaces (Fig. B15*c*; Plate B9); and in a few cases the entire upper exterior and interior surface wall surfaces are red (Fig. B15*b*; Plate B10).

Similar vessels in and around Teotihuacan are illustrated by Rattray (2001:499-500, 514, 582-83) and Sanders (1995: Plates 38, 44, 51-52), and from other parts of the Valley of Mexico by Blanton and Parsons (1971:279) and Whalen and Parsons (1982:410-11).

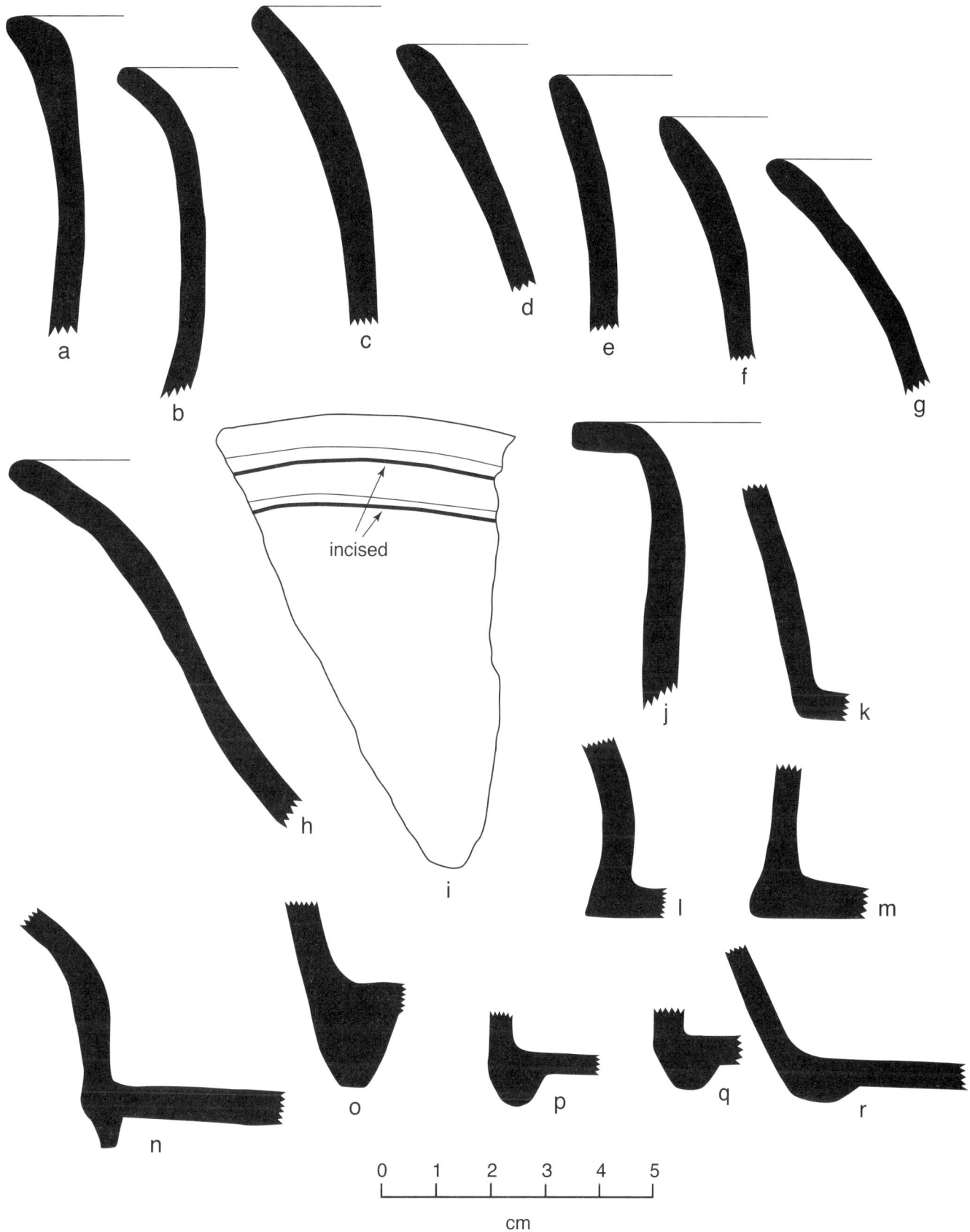

Figure B11. Classic Monochrome bowls with flaring rims. Proveniences: *a, b, j, n* (Zu-Cl-68); *c-i, k, r* (Zu-Cl-53); *l, o-q* (Zu-Cl-10); *m* (Zu-Cl-60).

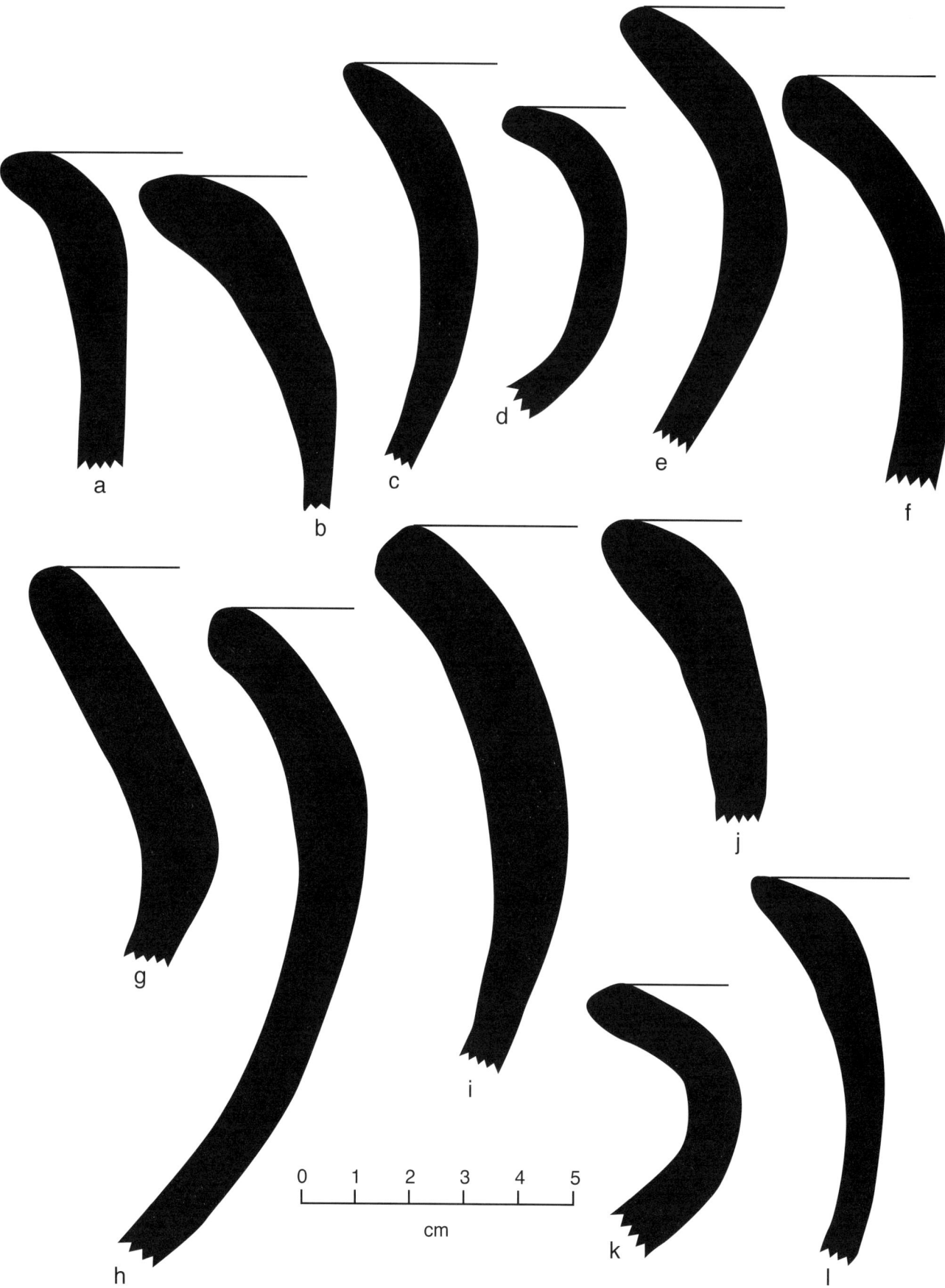

Figure B12. Classic Monochrome ollas with slight-everted rims. Proveniences: *a-e, g-i, k* (Zu-Cl-60); *f, j, l* (Zu-Cl-52).

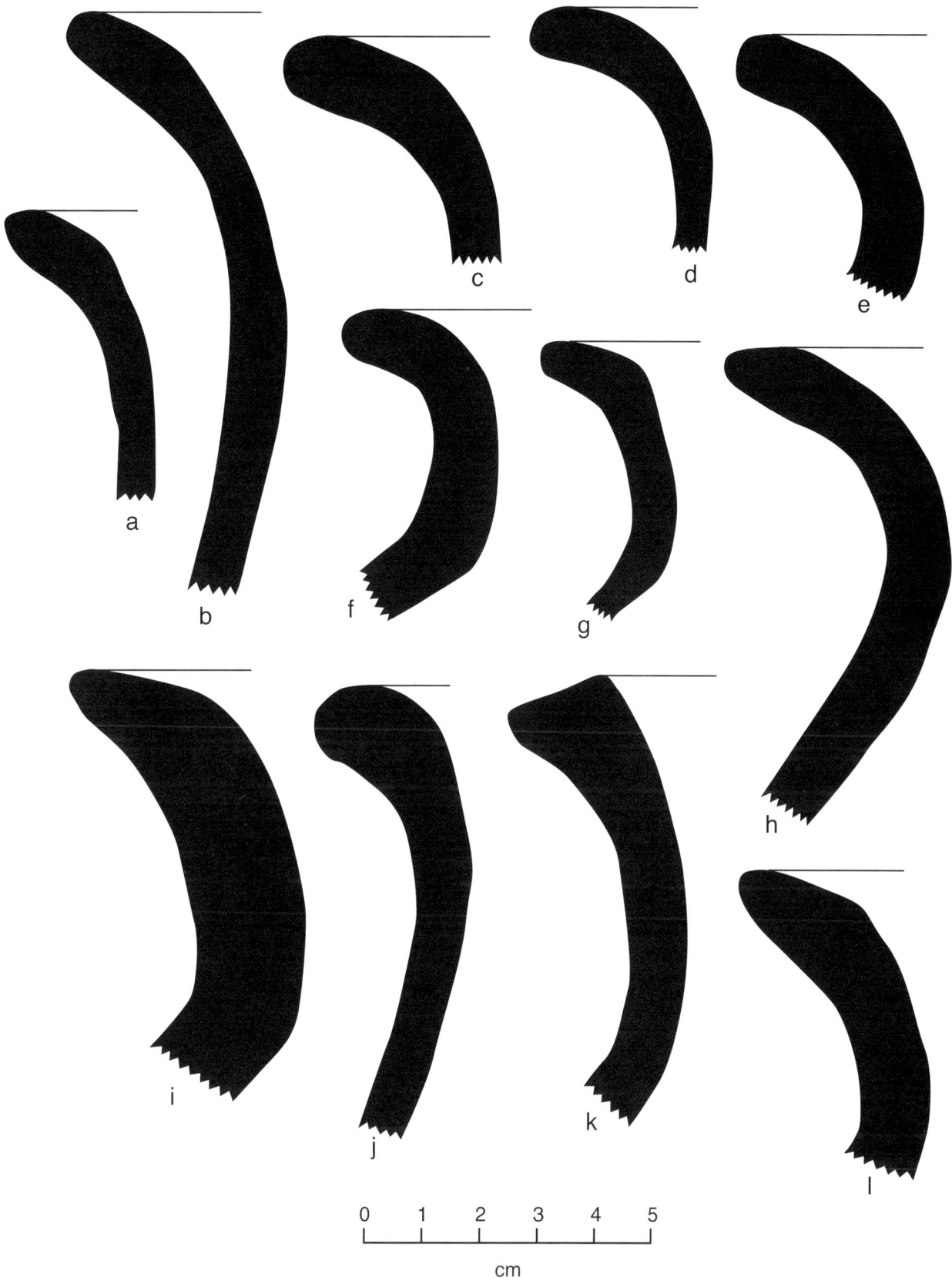

Figure B13. Classic Monochrome ollas with medium-everted rims. Proveniences: *a, h* (Zu-Cl-10); *b, f, g, h* (Zu-Cl-53); *c, d, e* (Zu-Cl-52); *i, k, l* (Zu-Cl-68); *j* (Zu-Cl-90).

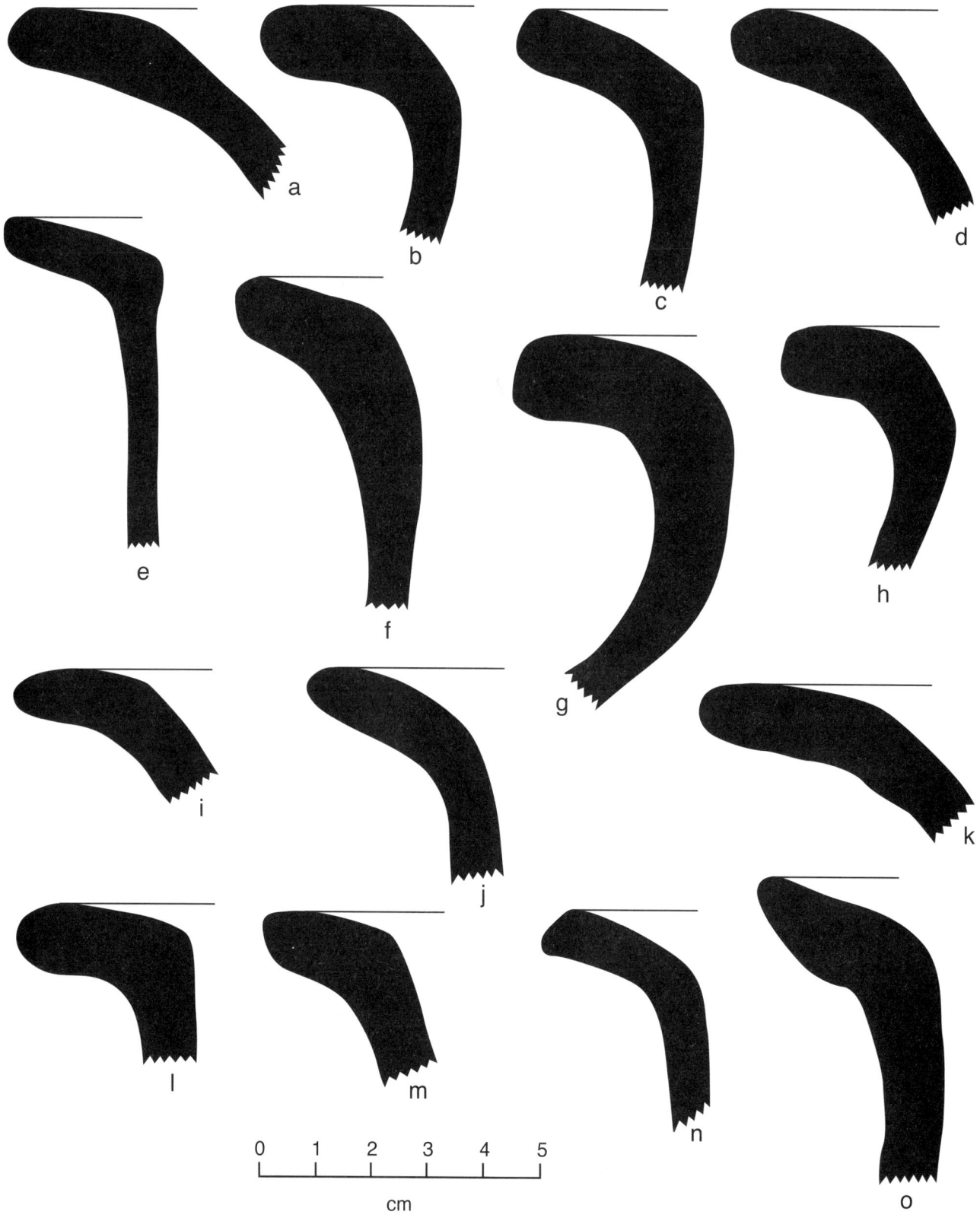

Figure B14. Classic Monochrome ollas with wide-everted rims. Proveniences: *a, i, k* (Zu-Cl-10); *b, g, h, j, l* (Zu-Cl-52); *c* (Zu-Cl-72); *d* (Zu-Cl-53); *e, m, n* (Zu-Cl-68); *f, o* (Zu-Cl-90).

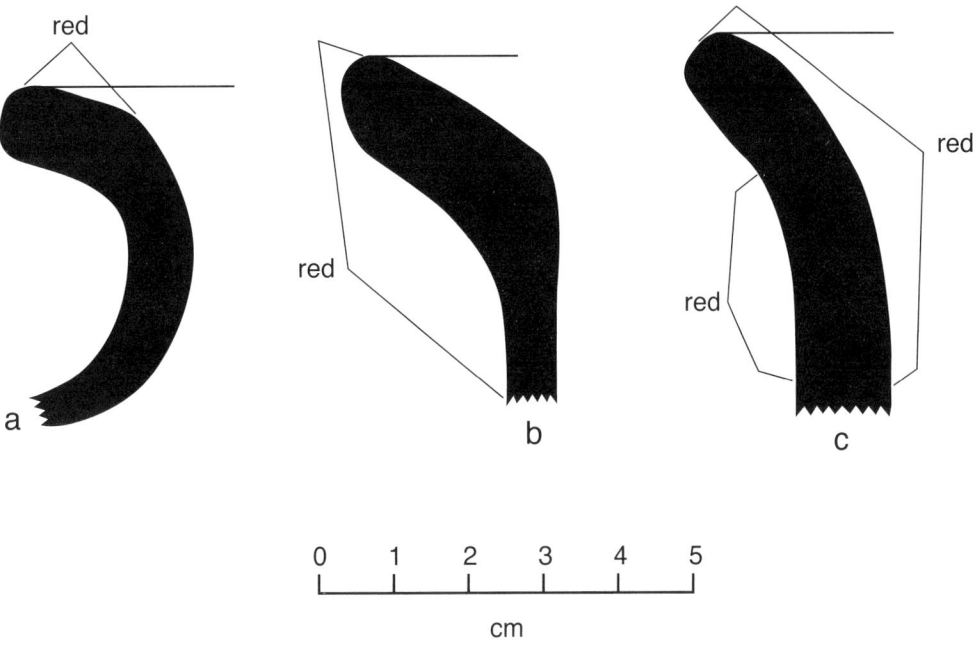

Figure B15. Classic Utilitarian Ware, Red/Buff olla/basins. All from Zu-Cl-60.

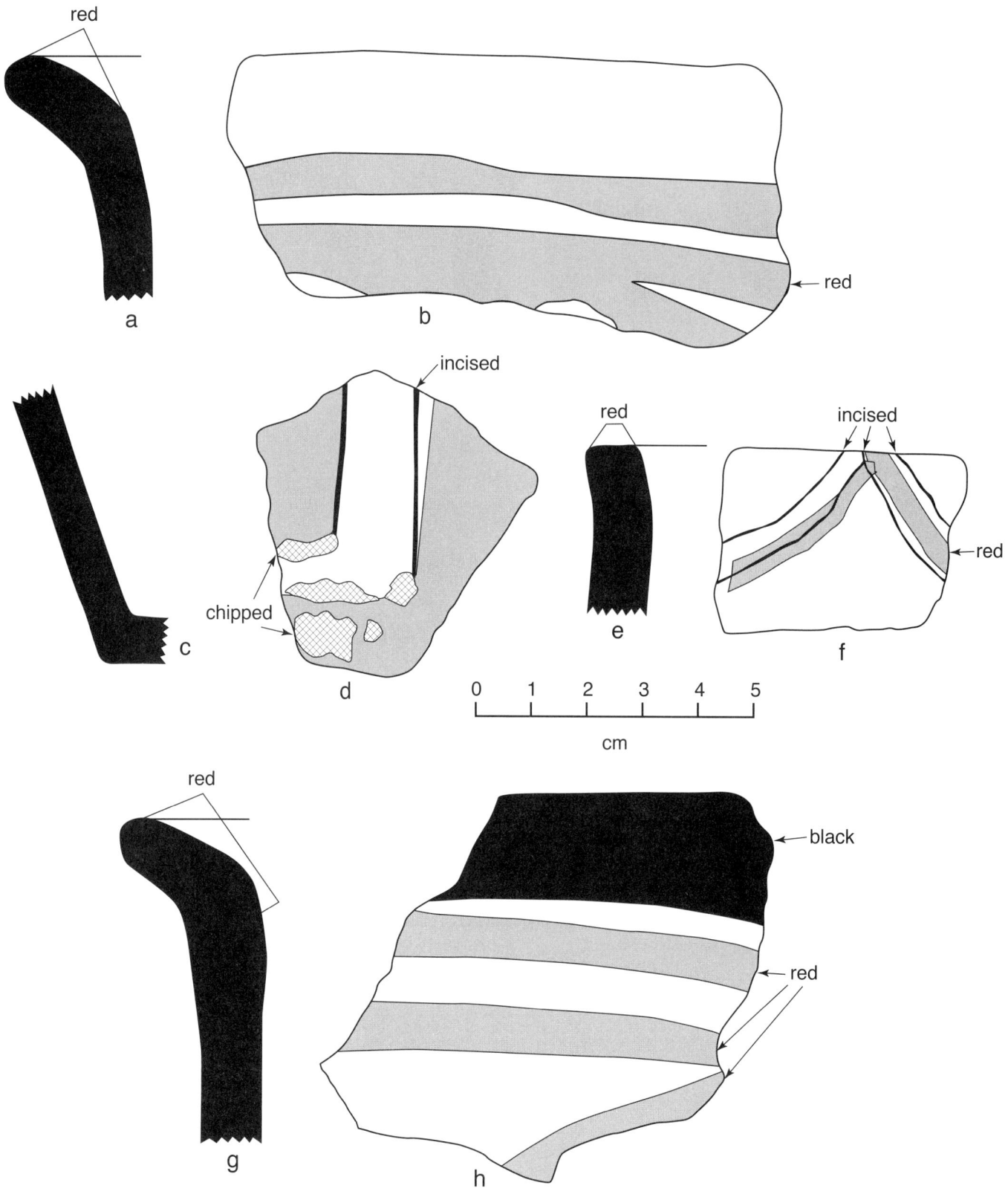

Figure B16. Classic Utilitarian Ware, Red/Buff olla/basins. Proveniences: *a-d* (Zu-Cl-60); *e, f* (Zu-Cl-72); *g, h* (Zu-Cl-1).

Classic Utilitarian Ware: Monochrome Basin (Fig. B17)

These vessels are larger and less well finished than the monochrome bowls described above. Surfaces are generally well smoothed; there is no surface decoration of any kind. Surface color ranges from gray-brown to tan. Rims are sometimes direct (Fig. B17*b, h*), but are usually slightly everted. Rim diameters range from 12 to 20 cm. We could not determine vessel height. We noted a few flat basal sections (Fig. B17*g*). As far as we could determine, there are no supports or other appendages.

Similar vessels in and around Teotihuacan are illustrated by Rattray (2001:491, 573). Blanton and Parsons (1971:276-77), Whalen and Parsons (1982:406-8), and García Chávez (1991:246-49) describe similar material from other parts of the Valley of Mexico.

Classic Utilitarian Ware: Comal (Fig. B18a-d)

These vessels are scarce, but sometimes occur in low frequencies. Although their form is like those of some better known and much more frequent Postclassic comales, their function is actually somewhat problematical—they may have served as lids or covers for jars, ollas, or basins. These vessels are essentially flat, with slightly elevated walls and slightly roughened flat bases. Rims and upper surfaces are fairly well smoothed, while the basal exterior is unfinished (or deliberately roughened). Rim diameters range from 17 to 20 cm.

Similar vessels in and around Teotihuacan are illustrated by Rattray (2001:477, 505, 570-71) and Sanders (1995: Figs. 125-26, 136-37). García Chávez (1991:160-61, 211-12, 277-78) describes comparable Classic comales near Atzcapotzalco in the western Valley of Mexico.

Classic Utilitarian Ware: Rose-on-Granular Olla (Fig. B18e)

These vessels occur consistently in low frequencies at many Classic sites. Because the paste is more friable than that of most other Classic ceramics, a relatively high proportion of these vessels may have disintegrated and thus remained unrecognizable to us on the ground surface. If so, they may have been more abundant than we now perceive them to have been. All the sherds in our surface collections are quite small, and we have no information on basal form, appendages, or vessel height. The vessel surfaces are poorly finished, with slightly smoothed exteriors; the vessel interior is typically very rough and unfinished (Plate B11*a*). A thin band of dull red paint has usually been applied around the rim, and occasionally in diamond-shaped patterns on the upper exterior walls (Plate B11*b*) (e.g., Blanton and Parsons 1971:279; Rattray 2001:613). Typical rim diameter is approximately 12 cm.

The function of these vessels is uncertain, although a reconstructed, near complete, three-handled vessel of this type from Teotihuacan suggests they may have served to carry and store water (Linne 1934:95, Fig. 126).

Similar vessels from Teotihuacan have been described by Rattray (2001:608-15), and from other parts of the Valley of Mexico by Blanton and Parsons (1971:279-80) and Whalen and Parsons (1982:413-14).

Classic Specialty Ware: Thin Orange (Fig. B19)

This is one of the archaeological hallmarks of the Classic period in central Mexico, and it has been the subject of considerable study over the past 50 years (e.g., Rattray 2001). Although there are numerous Thin Orange vessel forms known at urban Teotihuacan, including a few thicker walled jar and basin forms (sometimes referred to as "Thick Thin Orange"), nearly all the Thin Orange sherds in our surface collections from the Zumpango Region come from simple, thin walled, hemispherical bowls, typically with low annular supports (Fig. B19*m-r*; Plate B12*a*). Exterior walls sometimes have simple curvilinear incised designs (Fig. B19*b, j*; Plate B12*b*), and a few exterior surfaces are distinctly "rippled" (Plate B12*c*). The thin walls, pale-to-medium orange surface color, and pale tan-orange paste with tabular calcitic tempering are all highly distinctive. This paste is unique in the Valley of Mexico. Rattray's research (1990) has demonstrated conclusively what had been suspected for some time: Thin Orange pottery was made in southern Puebla, about 100 to 150 km to the southeast of the Valley of Mexico. Thin Orange pottery in finished form was apparently transported in bulk from Puebla to Teotihuacan, and redistributed from there throughout the Valley of Mexico during the Classic period.

Thin Orange pottery in and around Teotihuacan has been exhaustively discussed and described by Rattray (2001:305-35, 591-604) and Sanders (1995:143-44, Figs. 94-96, 144), and more briefly described by Blanton and Parsons (1971:277-78) and Whalen and Parsons (1982:412-13) from other parts of the Valley of Mexico.

Classic Specialty Ware: Censer Flange (Fig. B20a, b)

These highly distinctive sherds come from collars applied around the rims of large, poorly finished vessels that presumably functioned for ritual purposes. Fragments of these collars are the only part of the vessels that we recognized and collected. They occur in very low frequency, but are consistently present at many Classic sites throughout the Zumpango Region.

Rattray (2001:488, 517-18, 542, 566) and Sanders (1995: Plate 67) describe "Coarse Matte Ware Incensarios" and "Heavy Matte Censers," respectively, from Teotihuacan and nearby sites that correspond closely to this material from the Zumpango Region. García Chávez (1991:244-45, 269, 272) illustrates similar material near Atzcapotzalco in the western Valley of Mexico.

Classic Specialty Ware: Figurines (Fig. B20c, d)

Mold-made ceramic figurines from the Classic period at and around Teotihuacan have been extensively studied and described (e.g., Barbour 1976; Sanders 1995:392-465, Figs. 148-51, Plates 70-101). In our surface collections from the Zumpango Region, figurines identical to those at Teotihuacan occur consistently in low frequencies at many Classic sites (we recognized them primarily as heads detached from bodies and limbs). Both early (Fig. B20*d*) and later (Fig. B20*c*) phases of the Classic period are represented (Plate B13).

Classic Specialty Ware: Candeleros (Plate B14)

These distinctive artifacts consistently occur in low frequencies at many Classic sites throughout the Zumpango Region. They are crudely made, typically with unfinished surfaces except for occasional smoothing and burnishing on the top surfaces of some vessels, and with crude impressions on the exterior walls (Plate B14).

Identical candelero artifacts in and around Teotihuacan have been described by Linne (1934:113), Sanders (1996: Figs. 285-87), and Rattray (2001:503, 519, 543). Similar material has also been reported by García Chávez (1991:359-60) near Atzcapotzalco in the western Valley of Mexico.

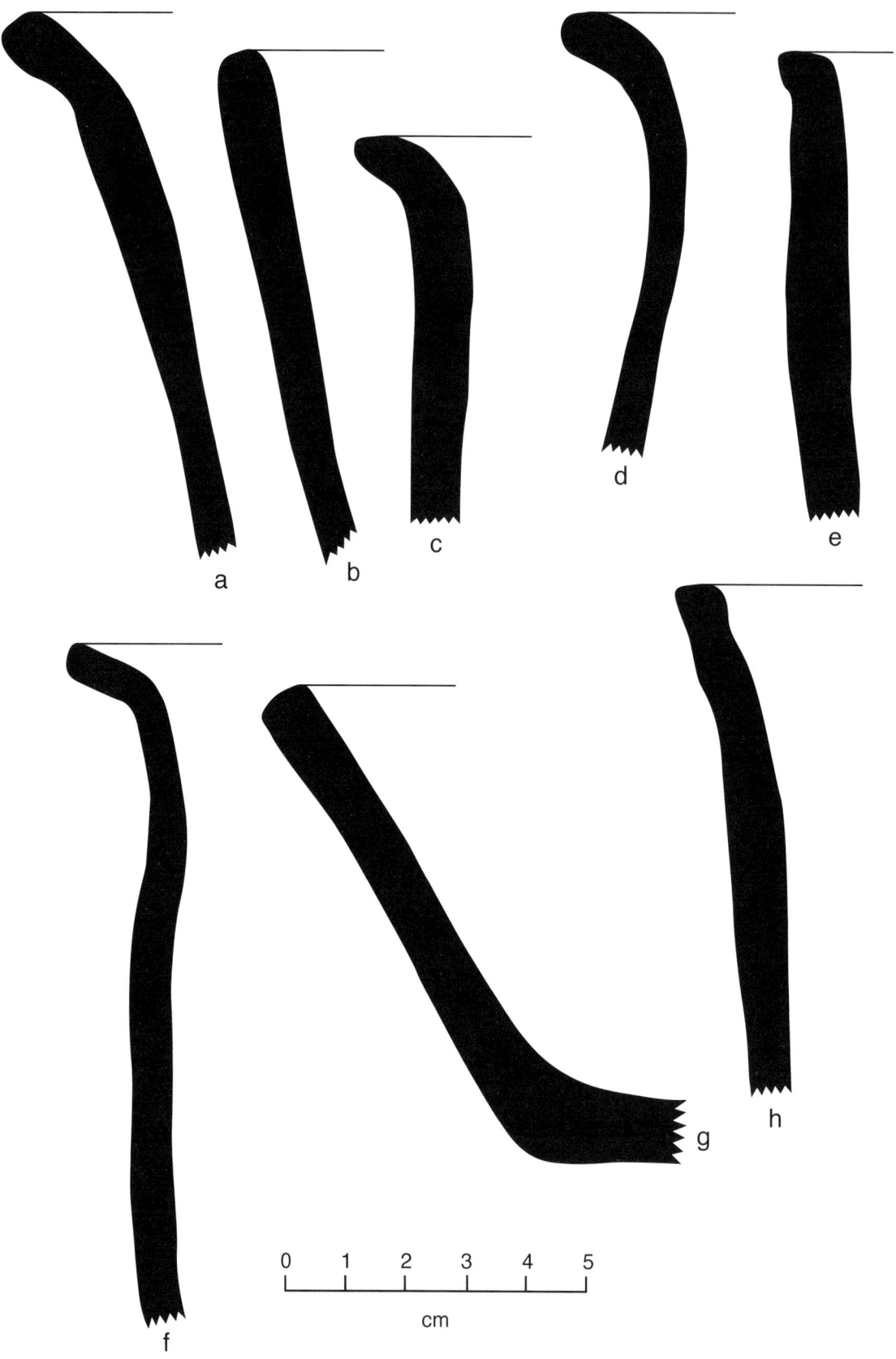

Figure B17. Classic Utilitarian Ware, Monochrome basins. Proveniences: *a-c* (Zu-Cl-53); *d, e* (Zu-Cl-60); *f* (Zu-Cl-82); *g, h* (Zu-Cl-60).

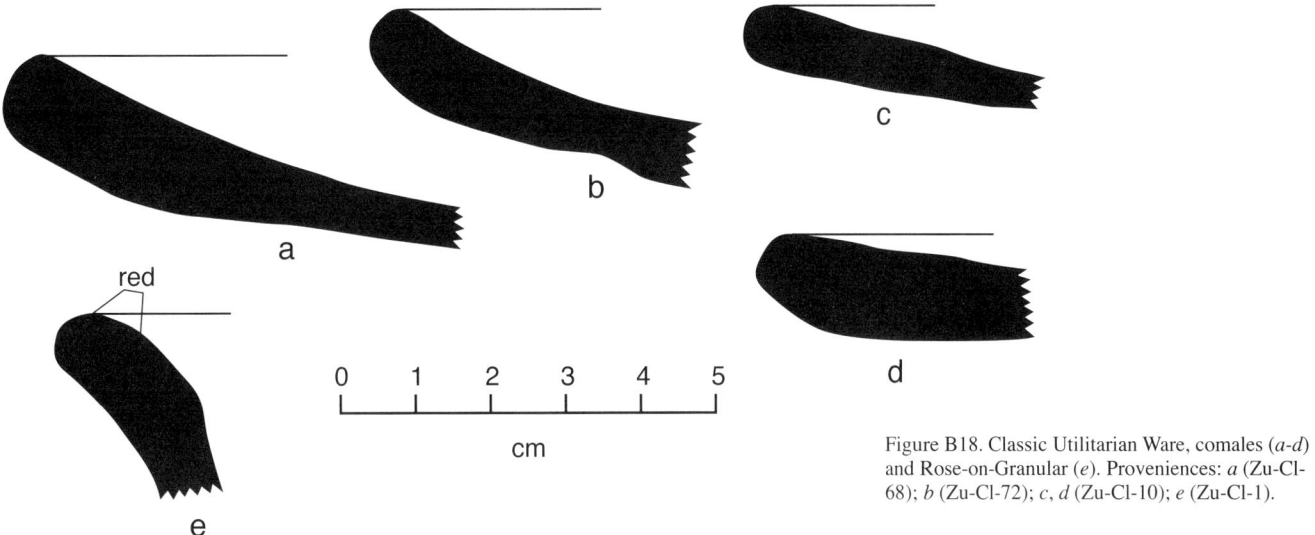

Figure B18. Classic Utilitarian Ware, comales (*a-d*) and Rose-on-Granular (*e*). Proveniences: *a* (Zu-Cl-68); *b* (Zu-Cl-72); *c*, *d* (Zu-Cl-10); *e* (Zu-Cl-1).

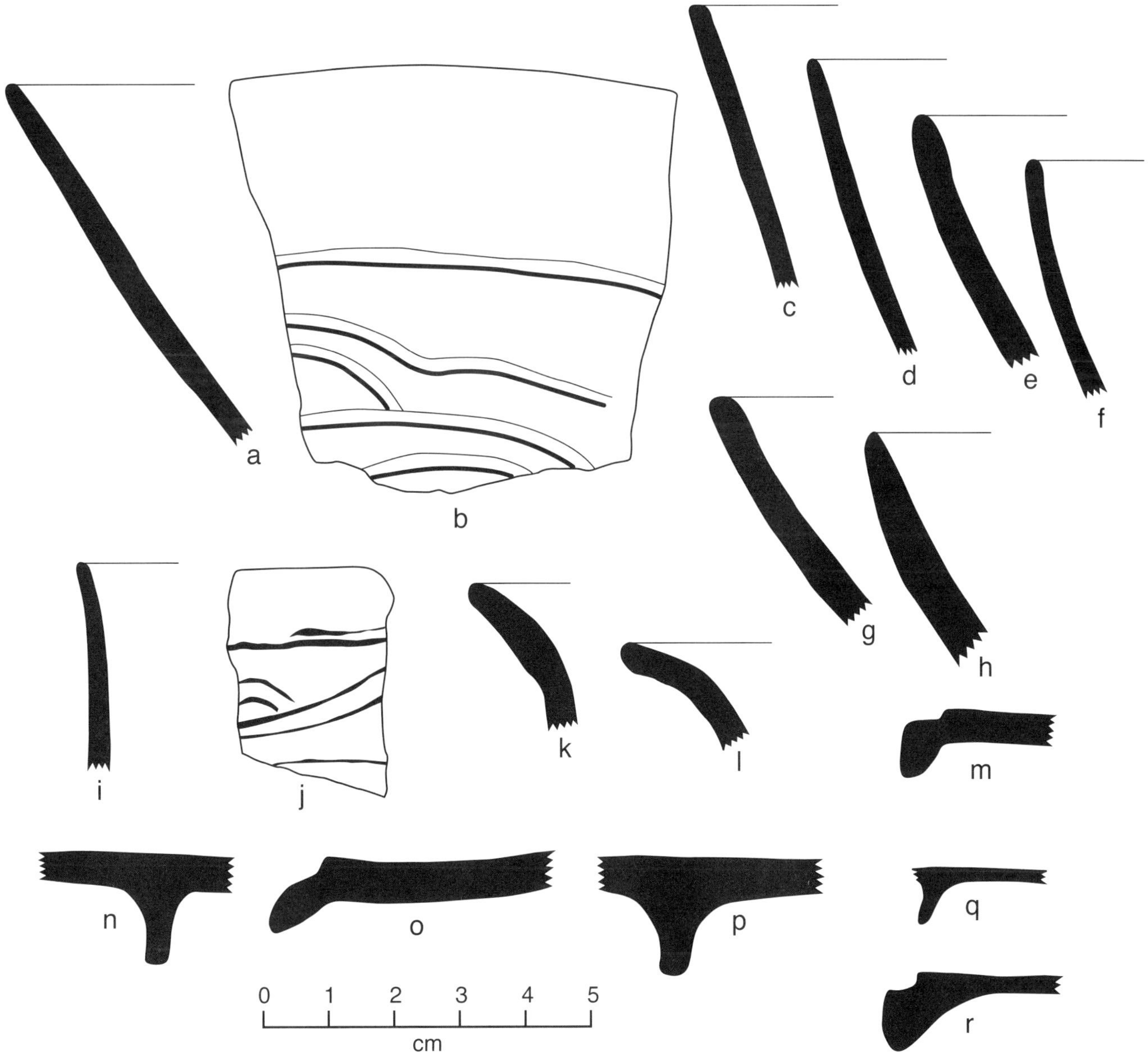

Figure B19. Classic Specialty Ware, Thin Orange. Proveniences: *a-e* (Zu-Cl-60); *f*, *p* (Zu-Cl-52); *g*, *h*, *l* (Zu-Cl-10); *i-k*, *m*, *q*, *r* (Zu-Cl-82); *n*, *o* (Zu-Cl-72).

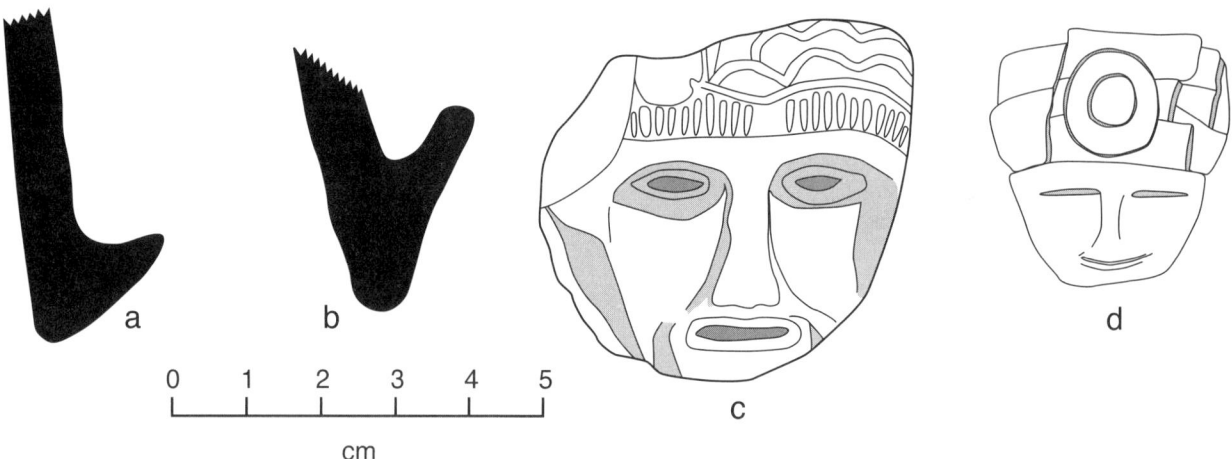

Figure B20. Classic Specialty Ware, censer flange (*a, b*) and figurines (*c, d*). Proveniences: *a, d* (Zu-Cl-10); *b* (Zu-Cl-53); *c* (Zu-Cl-60).

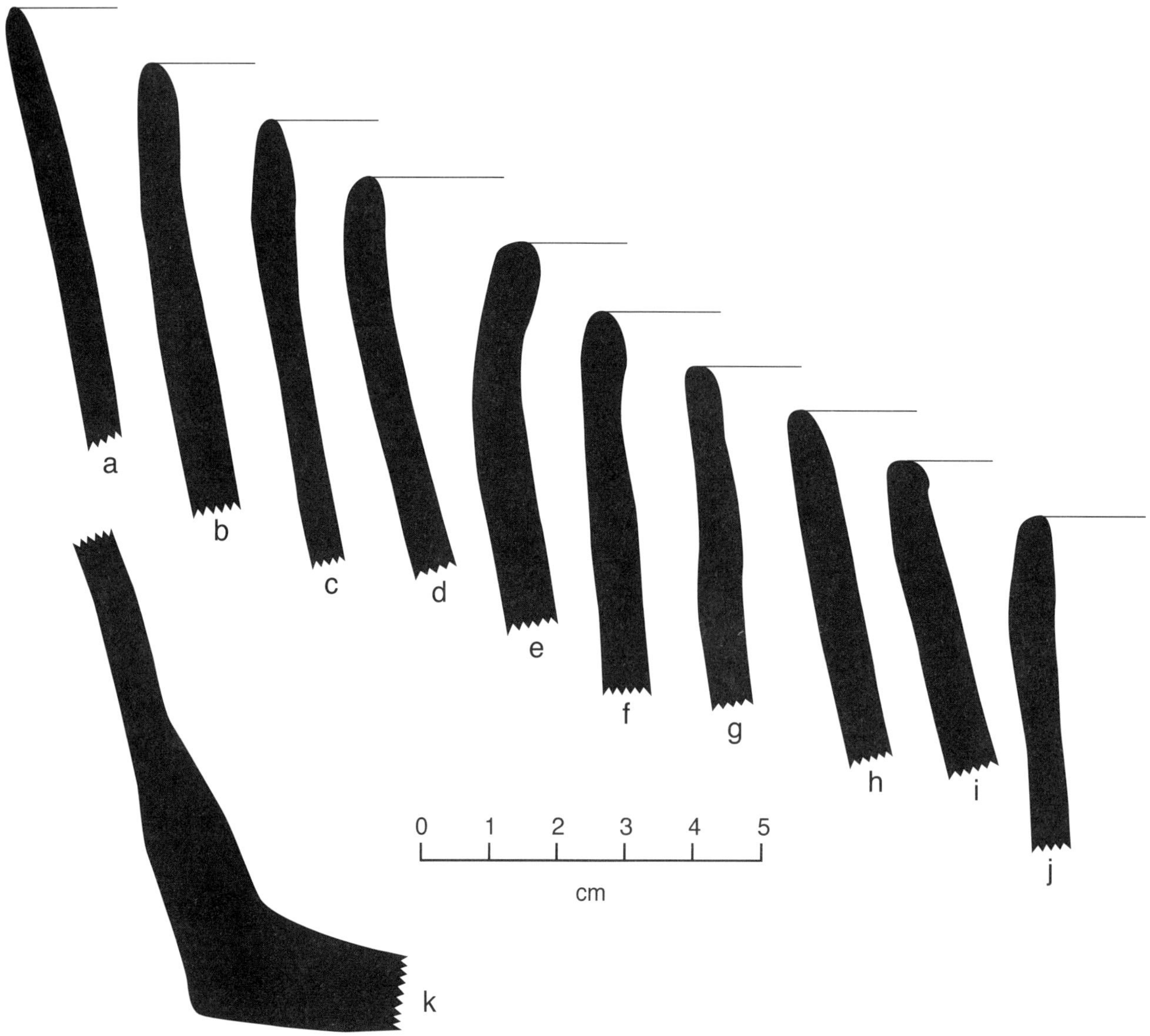

Figure B21. Classic Specialty Ware, Monochrome Matte bowls. All from Zu-Cl-90.

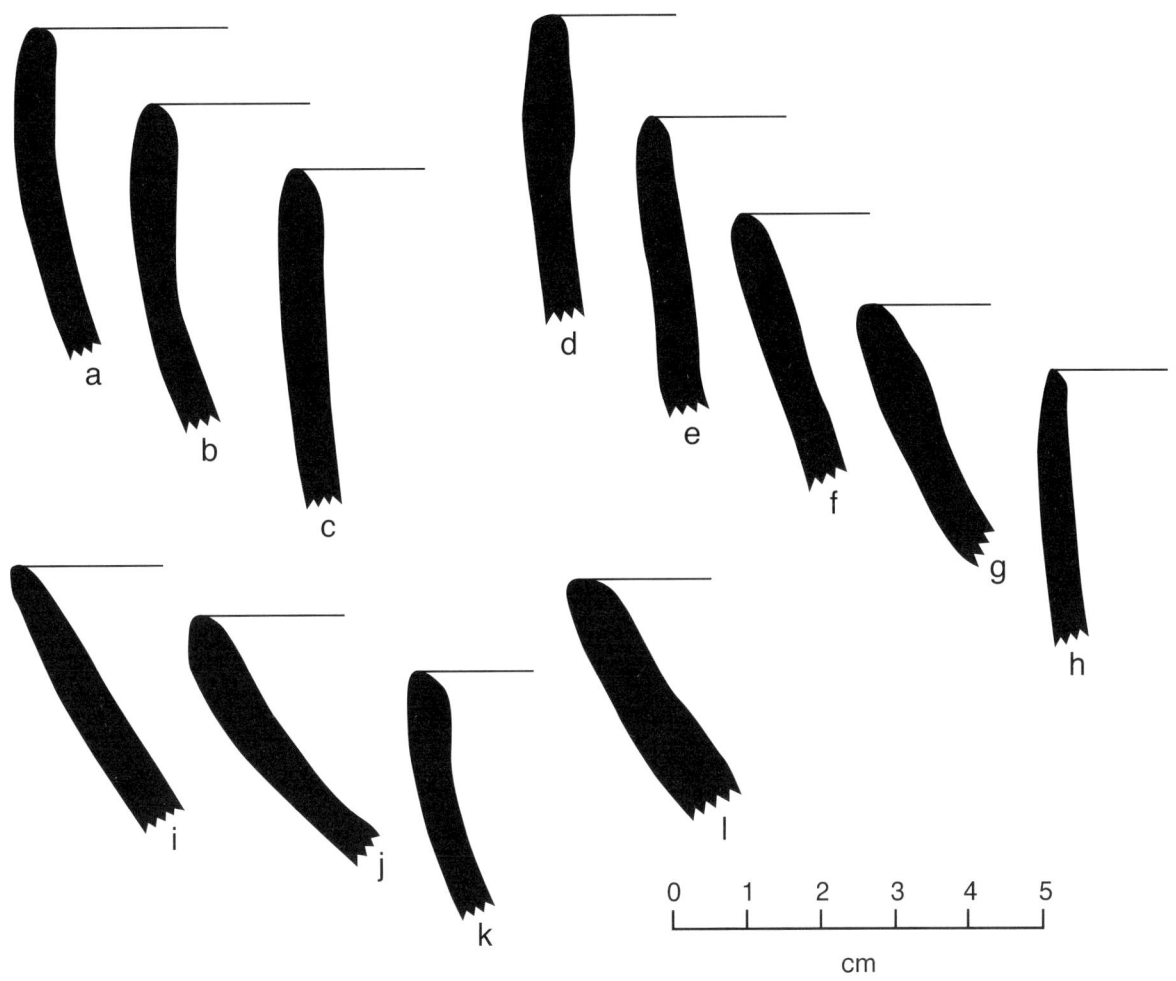

Figure B22. Early Toltec Service Ware, Monochrome bowls. Proveniences: *a, b, d, f-j* (Zu-ET-1); *c, e, k, l* (Zu-ET-12).

Classic Specialty Ware: Monochrome Matte Bowl (Fig. B21)

As far as we know, this distinctive type of pottery has never been described in the Valley of Mexico. In the Zumpango Region we found it at only one site: Zu-Cl-90, on the bed of Lake Xaltocán-Zumpango—the southernmost Classic site in the Zumpango Region—where it occurs in high frequency along with other Classic pottery types. We believe these vessels may have had something to do with saltmaking, although this inference is based exclusively on two factors: (1) their abundance and unusually high frequency at this single site, and (2) the location of Zu-Cl-90 in a lakebed setting that would have been suitable for salt production, and where there are clear indications that saltmaking was carried out in Postclassic and Colonial times.

The vessels are simple hemispherical bowls, fairly well fired, and with relatively thin walls, pale to medium brown surface color, direct-rims and flat bottoms, and rim diameters between 10 and 15 cm. We were unable to determine vessel height. There is no decoration or appendages of any kind. What is most distinctive about these vessels is that their interior and exterior surfaces are unsmoothed, with a unique matte texture.

Early Toltec

The Early Toltec is our most problematic period in terms of ceramic chronology. The most distinctive decorated type (Coyotlatelco Red/Buff) (Tozzer 1921; Rattray 1966; Vargas 1975; Solar 2006; Sugiura 2005)—which has served as the hallmark of Epiclassic occupation throughout other surveyed regions in the Valley of Mexico and some neighboring regions—is present in abundance at only two ET sites in the Zumpango Region (Zu-ET-1 and Zu-ET-12 [Cerro de Mesa Grande]), and in very low frequencies at only three others (Zu-ET-3, Zu-ET-19, Zu-ET-23). Other highly distinctive ET ceramic types are also quite scarce in the Zumpango Region: for example, incised Red/Buff bowls (Plate B15*a*), stamped Red/Buff bowls, stamped Plainware bowls (Plate B15*b*), incised Monochrome Brown bowls (Plate B15*c*), and double-handles on basins and ollas.

Except for Zu-ET-12, most Early Toltec sites in the Zumpango Region also have Classic occupations, and at such multicomponent sites it has often proved difficult to disentangle the two periods ceramically when we have had to depend mainly on less distinctive ET ceramic types to distinguish between them. In this task we have depended heavily on our surface collections from Zu-ET-12—apparently a pure Epiclassic assemblage—for our identification of diagnostic ET ceramic categories; unfortunately, surface pottery is not particularly abundant at this seldom-plowed hilltop locality.

Given all these difficulties, we make no attempt to differentiate in our surface collections between earlier and later phases of the Epiclassic that have been proposed by some authors (for example, the early Epiclassic Oxtotipac phase defined by Sanders [1986:232-66]). We simply lump everything identifiable as Epiclassic into a single chronological unit.

The Epiclassic constitutes a sort of transition between Classic and Postclassic ceramics in terms of firing and paste color: except for Aztec Red Wares, Postclassic vessels tend to be fired at higher temperatures, with orange-brown pastes; Classic-period vessels tend to be fired at lower temperatures, typically with gray-brown pastes. Epiclassic vessels tend to be intermediate in terms of these characteristics.

We have classified our Early Toltec pottery as follows:

I. Service Ware
  A. Monochrome Bowl
  B. Red/Buff Bowl (Coyotlatelco)
II. Utilitarian Ware
  A. Beveled-Rim Basin with Scraped Exterior
  B. Wedge-Rim Olla
  C. Everted-Rim Olla
  D. Low Neck, Rolled-Rim Olla

Early Toltec Service Ware: Monochrome Bowl (Fig. B22)

These are simple hemispherical bowls with direct-rims. Appendages of any sort appear to be lacking. Vessel height is indeterminate. Rim diameter ranges from 10 to 14 cm. Interior and exterior surfaces tend to be well smoothed, occasionally burnished, but unpolished. Surface color is typically pale brown to light orange-brown.

Comparable material has been described by Sanders (1986:161-64) from excavations in the Teotihuacan Valley, by Rattray (1966:118-20) from excavations at Cerro Tenayo in the western Valley of Mexico, and by Cobean (1990:201-5) from excavations at Tula. Whalen and Parsons (1982:418-19) described similar vessels from the southern Valley of Mexico, with some illustrations (p. 419) from Zu-ET-1 and Zu-ET-12 in the Zumpango Region (their Fig. 89).

Early Toltec Service Ware: Red/Buff Bowl (Coyotlatelco) (Figs. B23, B24)

This type is the hallmark of Epiclassic occupation in the Valley of Mexico and along its northern and western borders, and over the past century several authors have provided extensive descriptions of it from excavated sites (Tozzer 1921; Noguera 1935; Rattray 1966; Cobean 1990; Sanders 1986; Sugiura 2005; Solar 2006). Like the monochrome bowls described above, these are simple hemispherical bowls with direct-rims. Appendages of any sort appear to be lacking. Vessel height is indeterminate. Rim diameter ranges from 10 to 16 cm. Interior and exterior surfaces tend to be well smoothed, occasionally burnished, but unpolished. Surface color is typically pale brown to light orange-brown. Geometric and curvilinear red designs are usually applied directly to the unpainted buff-colored vessel surfaces (often on both interiors and exteriors) (Plate B16*a-e*), although in a few cases a thick cream slip underlies the red designs (Plate B16*f*).

Comparable material has been described in detail from excavations at the Xometla site in the Teotihuacan Valley (Sanders 1986:132, 147-55), and by Rattray (1966:158-79) from excavations at Cerro Tenayo in the western Valley of Mexico. Noguera (1935:151-55), Sejourne (1970: Figs. 25, 27; 1983: Lam. VIII), Blanton and Parsons (1971:286-87), Whalen and Parsons (1982:422-23), and García Chávez (1991:305-17) provide descriptions from other parts of the Valley of Mexico. Branstetter-Hardesty (1978) describes this material from excavations at Portesuelo south of Texcoco, and Tovalín (1998:137) notes its presence at Tlapizahuac, near Chalco in the southeastern Valley of Mexico. Cobean (1990:130-72) thoroughly describes very similar material from several excavations at Tula, and Sugiura (2005:125-202) provides an exhaustive discussion of the variants and distribution of comparable Coyotlatelco ceramics in the Toluca Region to the west of the Valley of Mexico.

Early Toltec Utilitarian Ware: Beveled-Rim Basin with Scraped Exterior (Fig. B25)

These vessels are similar in form to some vessels found elsewhere in the Valley of Mexico (e.g., Blanton and Parsons 1971:283), but seem to be unique in terms of their distinctive scraped exterior surfaces. In addition, the distinctive double-handles so characteristic of Epiclassic utilitarian ollas and basins elsewhere in the Valley of Mexico (e.g., Whalen and Parsons 1982:423) occur only infrequently in the Zumpango Region. These vessels in our surface collections appear to have rather undistinctive lug handles (Fig. B25*l*).

Rim diameters range from 12 to 20 cm. Surface color ranges from light brown to gray-brown. Vessel height and basal form are indeterminate. While the exterior surfaces seem to have been scraped prior to firing, while the drying vessels were leather hard, the interior walls tend to be fairly well smoothed.

Comparable vessels (apparently lacking scraped exterior walls) are described by Sanders (1986:245-46) from excavations in the Teotihuacan Valley, by García Chávez (1991:323-24) from excavations near Atzcapotzalco in the western Valley of Mexico, and by Cobean (1990:213-22) from excavations at Tula.

Early Toltec Utilitarian Ware: Wedge-Rim Olla (Fig. B26)

Except for the fact that exterior scraped walls are absent, small sherds of this form are difficult to distinguish from the basin forms described above. We lack information about appendages, vessel height, or basal form. Rim diameters range from 10 to 20 cm. Interior and exterior surfaces have been roughly smoothed. Surface color is typically pale brown to tan.

Comparable vessels are described by Sanders (1986:245-46) from excavations in the Teotihuacan Valley, and by Cobean (1990:213-22) from excavations at Tula. Blanton and Parsons (1971:283) and Whalen and Parsons (1982:415) describe similar material from other parts of the Valley of Mexico.

Early Toltec Utilitarian Ware: Everted-Rim Olla (Fig. B27)

We lack information about appendages, vessel height, or basal form. Rim diameters range from 12 to 19 cm. Interior and exterior surfaces have been roughly smoothed. Surface color is typically pale brown to tan.

Similar vessels are described by Sanders (1986:133-37) from excavations in the Teotihuacan Valley, and by Cobean (1990:227-32) from excavations at Tula. Blanton and Parsons (1971:283, Fig. 67*c*), Whalen and Parsons (1982:417), and García Chávez (1991:331-32) describe similar vessels from other parts of the Valley of Mexico.

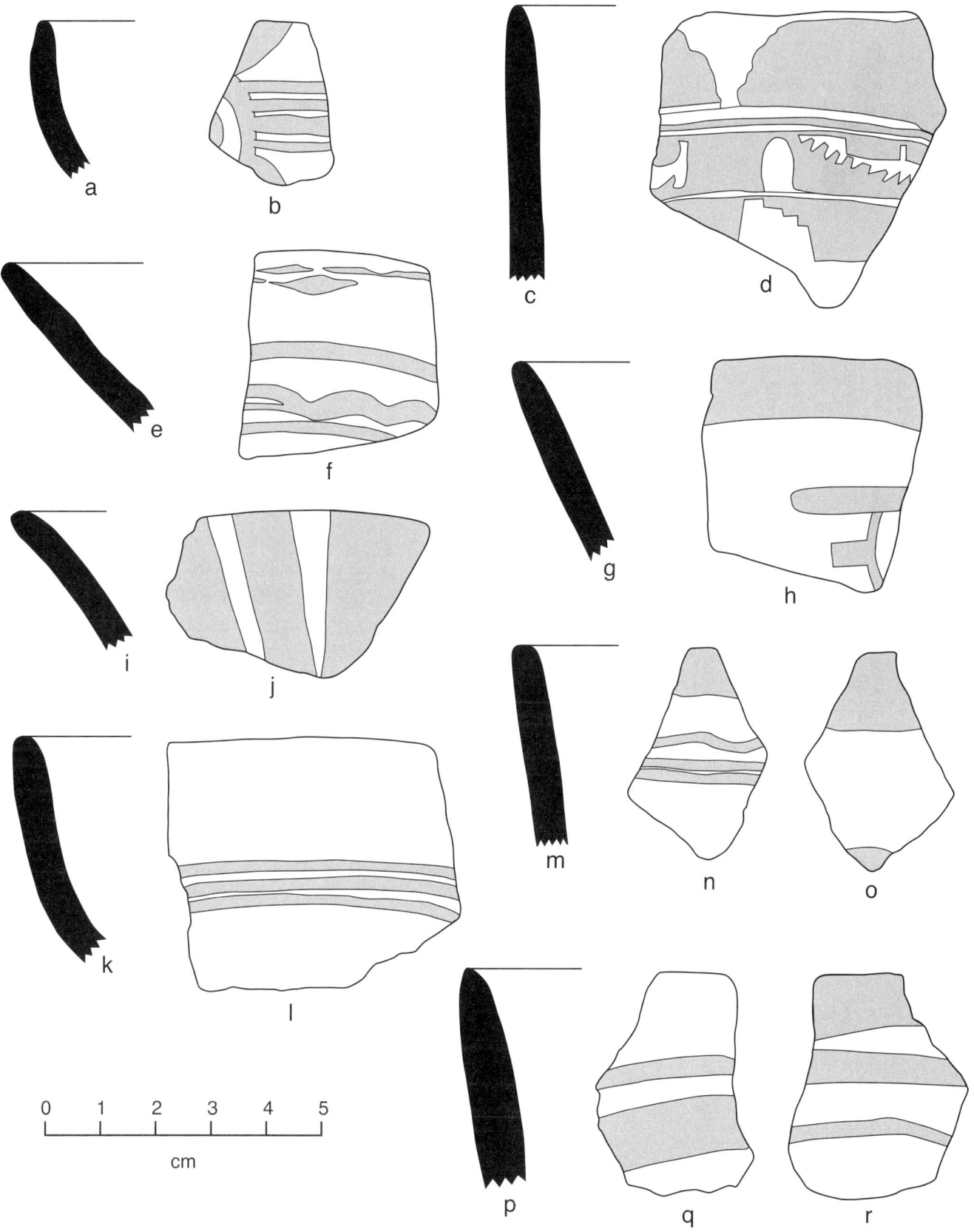

Figure B23. Early Toltec Service Ware, Red/Buff bowls (Coyotlatelco). All from Zu-ET-12.

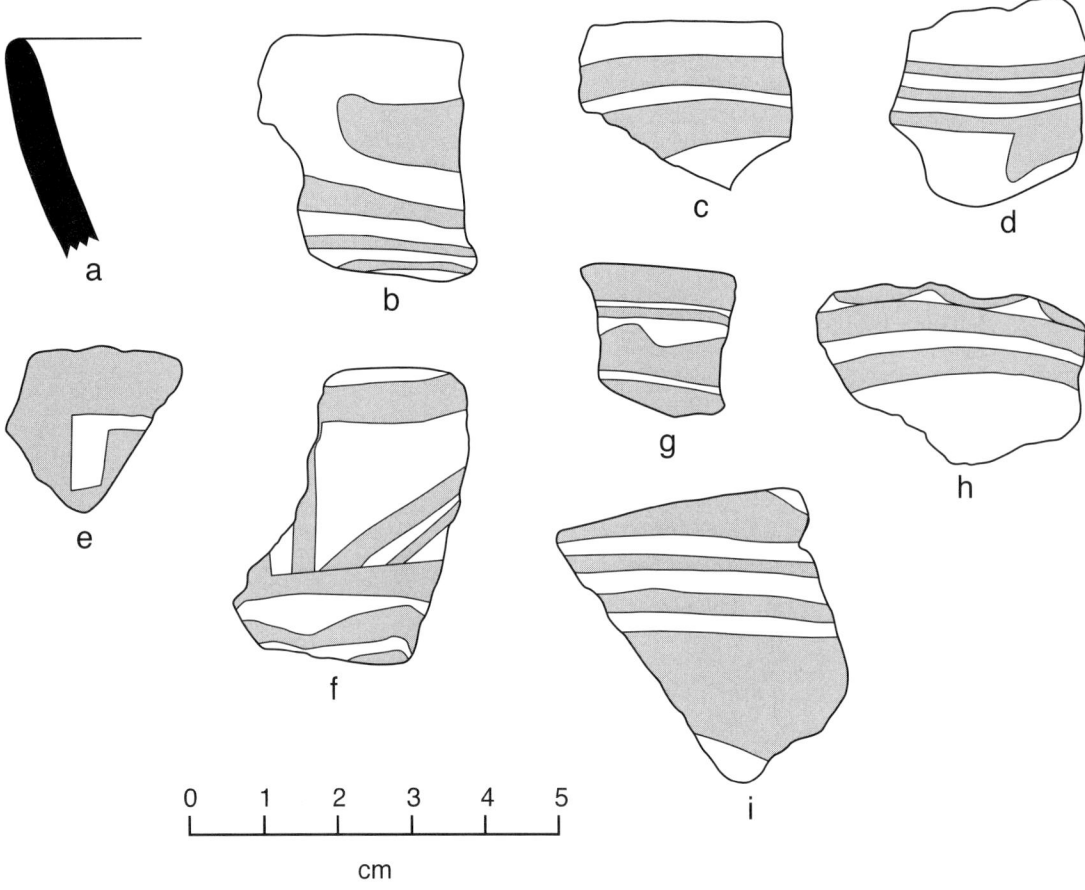

Figure B24. Early Toltec Service Ware, Red/Buff bowls (Coyotlatelco). All from Zu-ET-1. All except *a* and *b* (same sherd) are exterior body sherds.

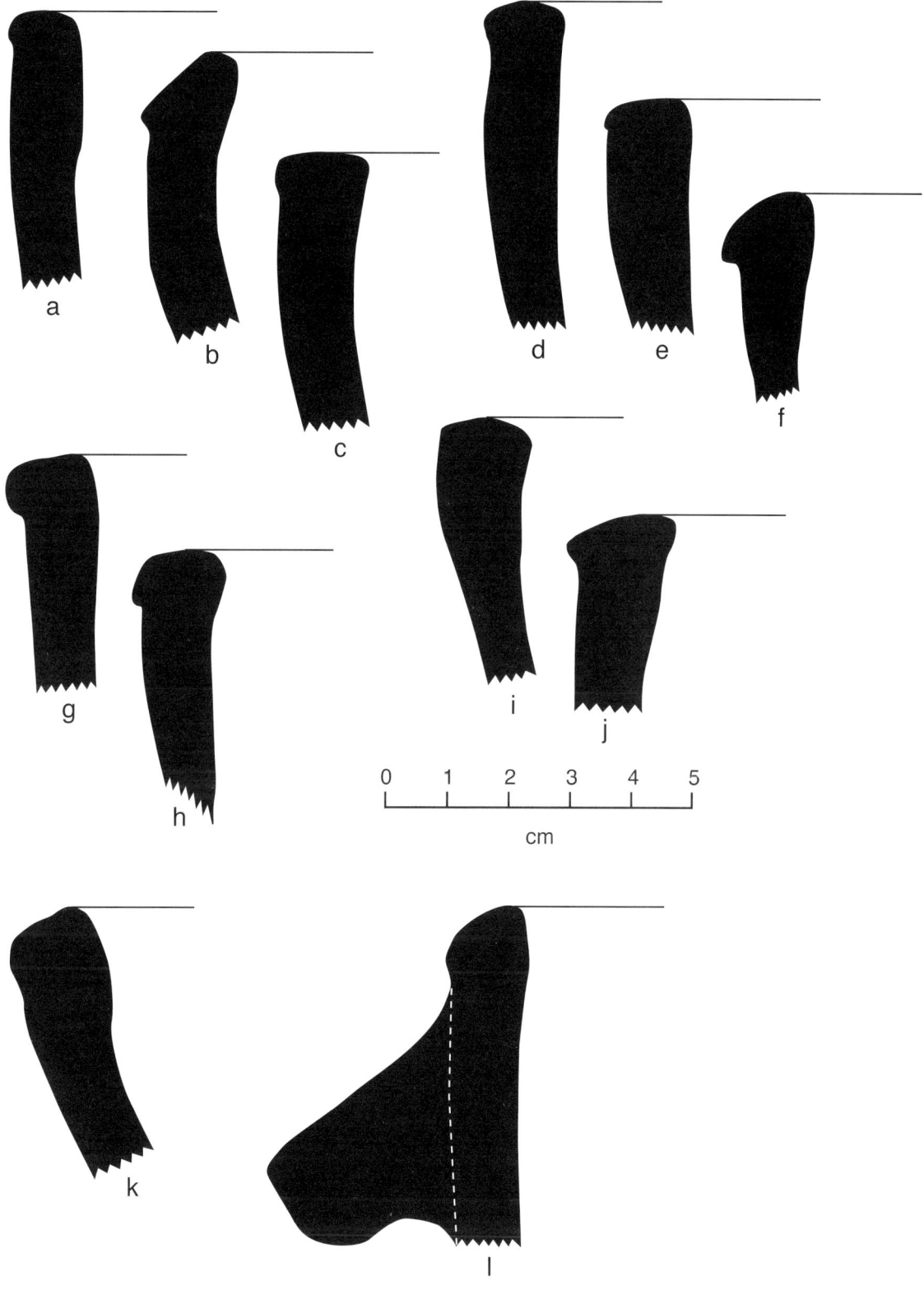

Figure B25. Early Toltec Utilitarian Ware, beveled-rim basins with scraped exterior. Proveniences: *a-h* (Zu-ET-1); *i-l* (Zu-ET-12).

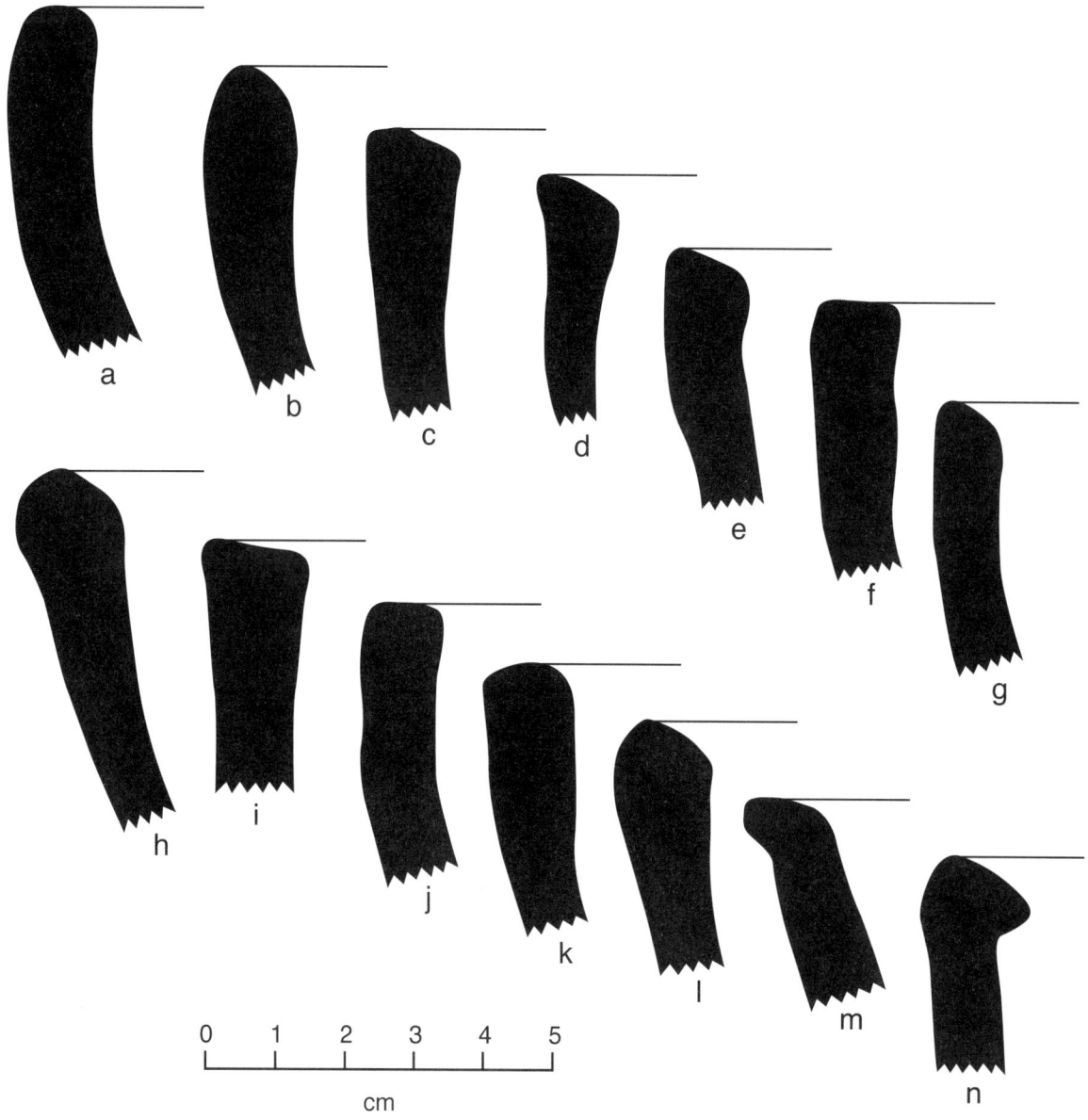

Figure B26. Early Toltec Utilitarian Ware, wedge-rim ollas. All from Zu-ET-1.

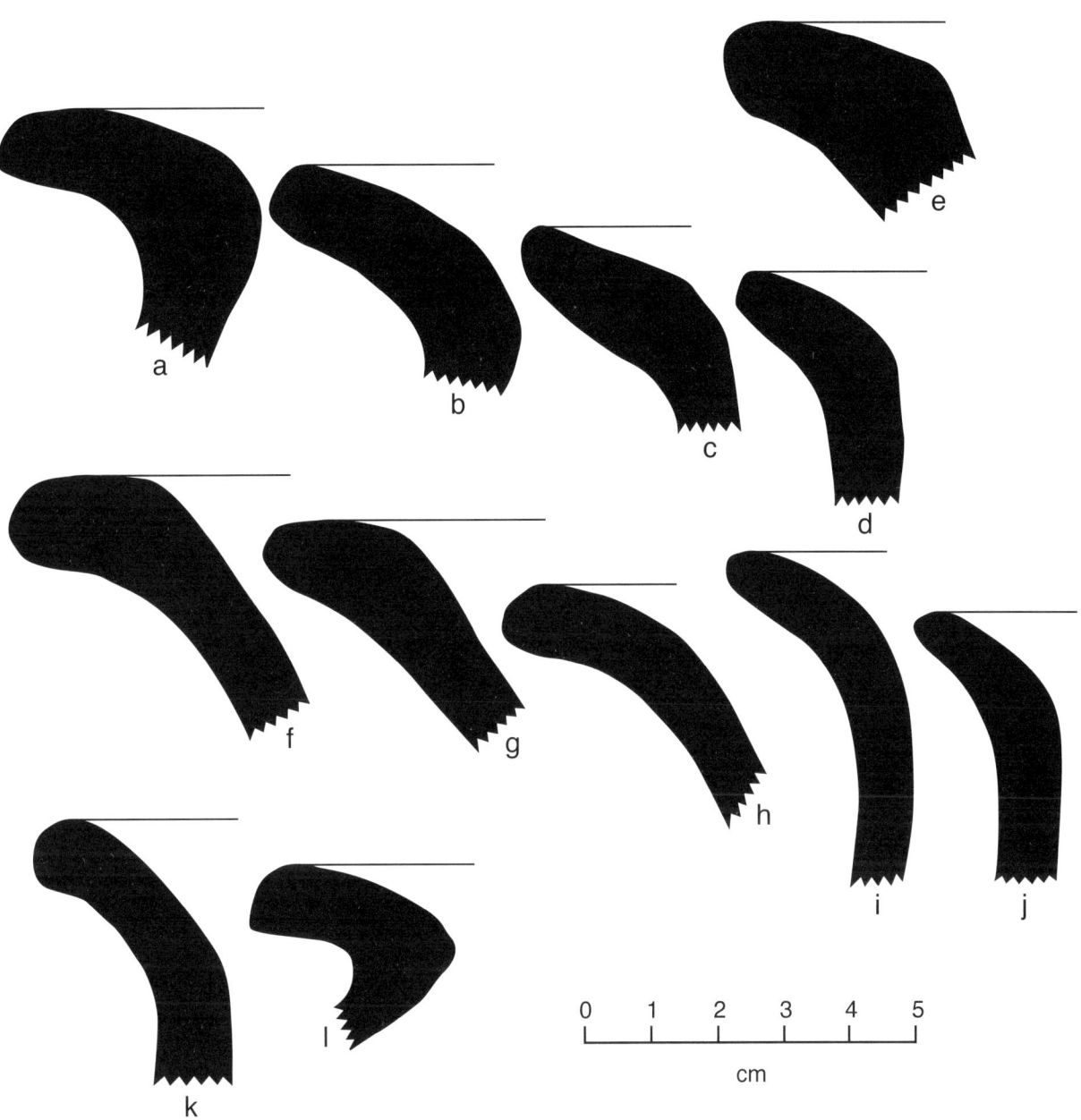

Figure B27. Early Toltec Utilitarian Ware, everted-rim ollas. Proveniences: *a-c*, *e-g*, *l* (Zu-ET-1); *d*, *h-k* (Zu-ET-12).

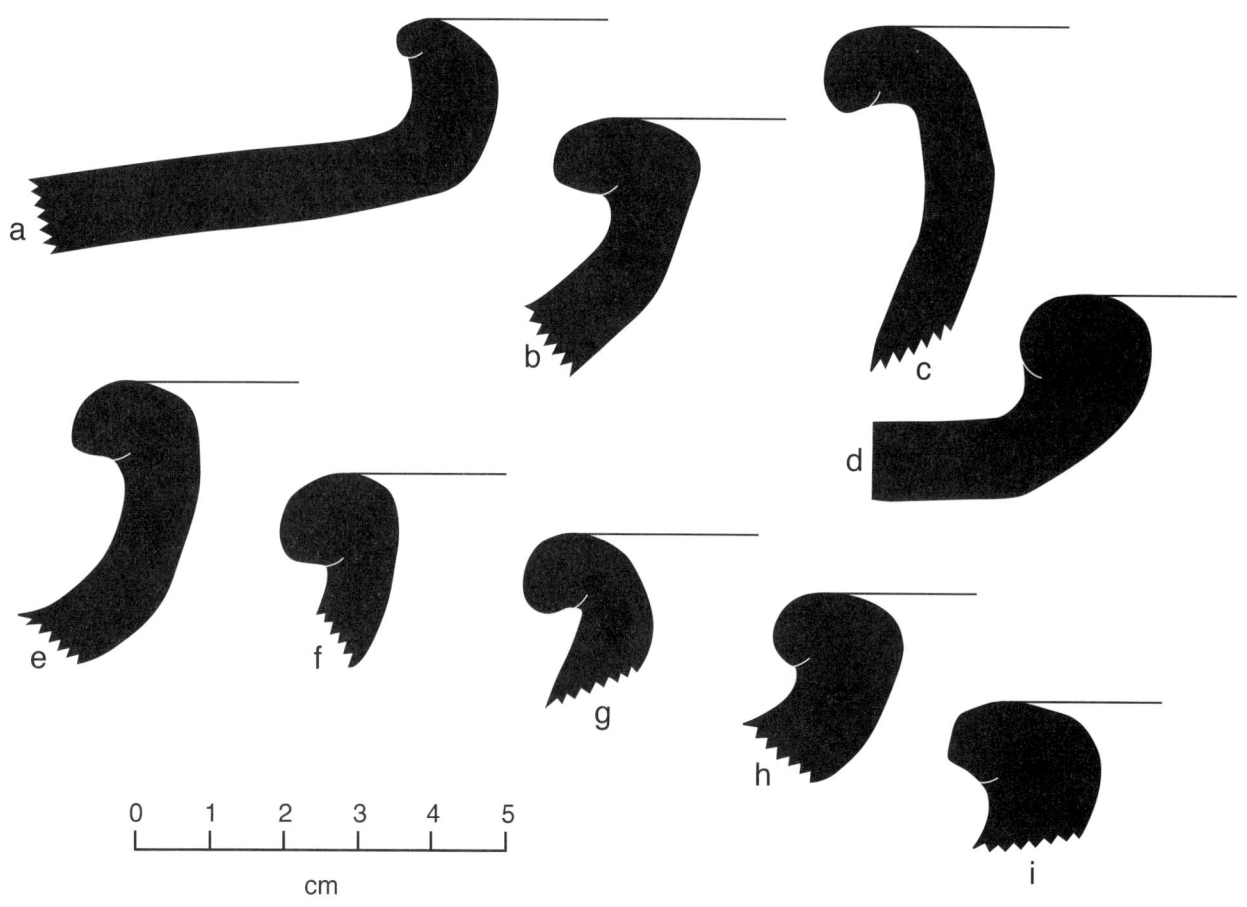

Figure B28. Early Toltec Utilitarian Ware, low-neck, rolled-rim ollas. All from Zu-ET-1.

Early Toltec Utilitarian Ware: Low Neck, Rolled-Rim Olla (Fig. B28)

These vessels are common throughout the Valley of Mexico during the Epiclassic. We lack information about appendages, vessel height, or basal form. Rim diameters range from 10 to 13 cm. Interior and exterior surfaces have been roughly smoothed. Surface color is typically pale to medium brown, gray-brown, and gray-orange.

Similar vessels are described by Sanders (1986:247) from excavations in the Teotihuacan Valley. Similar material is illustrated by Blanton and Parsons (1971:283, Fig. 67*a, b, d*) from the Texcoco Region in the east-central Valley of Mexico.

Late Toltec

For this period there is a great increase in the number of sites and the internal variety of the ceramic assemblage. Our Late Toltec ceramic categories correspond closely to many of those described by Cobean (1978, 1990) for his Tollan phase from Tula, approximately 20 km northwest of the northwestern corner of the Zumpango Region survey area. There are also close similarities with coeval types of the Mazapan phase in other parts of the Valley of Mexico (Parsons 1971; Blanton 1972; Parsons et al. 1982; Sanders 1986). We make no attempt to differentiate between earlier and later phases of the Early Postclassic period (that is, the terminal Mazapan Atlatongo subphase proposed by Sanders [1986:295] in the Teotihuacan Valley sequence).

We have classified our Early Postclassic pottery as follows:

Appendix B: Ceramic Chronology

I. Service Ware
   A. Monochrome Bowl
   B. Red/Buff Bowl, Wide-Band Variant
   C. Red/Buff Bowl, Wavy-Line Variant
   D. Orange/Cream Bowl (Joroba)
II. Utilitarian Ware
   A. Olla, with Square-Beveled Rim
   B. Basin, with Scraped Exterior
   C. Comal
   D. Ink-Stamped Jar
III. Specialty Ware
   A. Plumbate
   B. Sillon Incised Orange
   C. Orange Stamped
   D. Blanco Llevantado
   E. Figurines

Late Toltec Service Ware: Monochrome Bowl (Fig. B29)

These are simple hemispherical bowls with flat to gently rounded bases, and occasionally with small tripod nubbin supports; a very few examples of hollow stubby-conical, bulbous, or pinched-tip supports were also noted (Plate B17). A few of these vessels may have functioned as molcajetes, with patterned, diamond-shaped striations incised onto the interior basal surface (Plate B18). Rim diameters range from 10 to 18 cm. Vessel height appears to be in the range of 5 to 9 cm. Interior and exterior surfaces are well smoothed. Modal surface color ranges from pale orange to tan to orange-brown. Paste is typically light orange to orange-brown.

Similar material from excavations in the Teotihuacan Valley is described by Sanders (1986:342-44), and by Cobean (1990:335-50) from excavations at Tula. Whalen and Parsons (1982:433, Fig. 100*e*, *f*) describe comparable vessels from the southern Valley of Mexico.

Late Toltec Service Ware: Red/Buff Bowl,
Wide-Band Variant (Fig. B30)

Vessels in this category are quite common at LT sites in the Zumpango Region and throughout the eastern Valley of Mexico (Parsons 1971; Sanders 1986), and at Tula (Cobean 1990). These are simple hemispherical bowls, usually with hollow supports of bulbous (Plate B19*a*), pinched tip (Plate B19*b*), or bird-effigy (Plate B19*c*) form. Decoration is in the form of bold bands and circles of bright red, usually around the upper interior wall, but sometimes also on the exterior side (Plate B20). The red paint has been applied to an unpainted surface ranging from tan to orange-brown to light orange to (more rarely) dark gray-brown in color. Rim diameters range from 10 to 16 cm. Vessel height is indeterminate.

Similar material has been described by Sanders (1986:335-36, 354) from excavations in the Teotihuacan Valley, and by Cobean (1990:289-310, his "Macana Rojo sobre Café" type) from excavations at Tula. Blanton and Parsons (1971:290-94), Whalen and Parsons (1982:434-35), and Tovalín (1998:120) describe comparable vessels from other parts of the Valley of Mexico.

Late Toltec Service Ware: Red/Buff Bowl,
Wavy-Line Variant (Figs. B31, B32)

Vessels in this category are quite common at LT sites in the Zumpango Region and throughout the eastern Valley of Mexico (Parsons 1971; Sanders 1986). Vessel supports and vessel heights are uncertain. Decoration is in the form of groups of parallel bands of orange-red paint, usually wavy but sometimes straight, usually applied on the interior wall surfaces (Plate B21). There is considerable variability in these "wavy line" motifs, and there are a few unusual variants that resemble Early Toltec motifs (Plate B21*e*, *f*). The red paint is usually applied to unpainted surfaces ranging from tan to light orange to orange-brown in color. Rim diameters range from 12 to 20 cm. Vessel height is indeterminate.

Similar material has been described by Linne (1934:76-78) from Teotihuacan, by Sanders (1986:337-38, 355-56) from excavations in the Teotihuacan Valley, and by Cobean (1990:267-80, his "Mazapa Rojo sobre Café") from excavations at Tula. Blanton and Parsons (1971:290-94) and Whalen and Parsons (1982:434-35) describe comparable vessels from other parts of the Valley of Mexico.

Late Toltec Service Ware: Orange/Cream Bowl (Fig. B33)

This occurs throughout the eastern and northern Valley of Mexico. Vessels are simple hemispherical bowls, apparently lacking supports or other appendages. Typically narrow dull orange, gray-orange, or (less commonly) gray bands are applied atop a thick cream slip around the vessel rim (Plate B22*a*); occasionally, there are large circular designs on the interior vessel walls (Plate B22*b*). Rim diameters range from 11 to 17 cm. Vessel height is usually indeterminate in our surface collections, but a few large sherds suggest a height from 5 to 9 cm. Paste is typically pale orange to gray-orange.

Cobean (1990:282-89, 357-62) describes identical vessels from excavations at Tula, which he denotes as "Joroba Anaranajo sobre Crema" and "Proa Crema Pulido." Whalen and Parsons (1982:437) note this as a "minor type" in the southern Valley of Mexico, and it is reported from the Tlapizahuac site near Chalco in the southeastern Valley of Mexico (Tovalín 1998:120, 124).

Late Toltec Utilitarian Ware: Beveled-Rim Olla (Fig. B34)

These vessels are abundant at most Late Toltec sites in the Zumpango Region and throughout the Valley of Mexico. They have flaring rims with distinctly square-beveled tips. Rim diameters range from 13 to 20 cm. Neither vessel height nor basal form could be determined, and we are uncertain about handles or other appendages. Exterior surfaces and upper interior surfaces are fairly well smoothed. Surface color is typically pale brown to orange-brown. Paste is generally orange-brown.

Very similar material has been described by Sanders (1986:323-30) from excavations in the Teotihuacan Valley. Blanton and Parsons (1971:289) and Whalen and Parsons (1982:429) describe similar vessels from other parts of the Valley of Mexico.

Late Toltec Utilitarian Ware: Basin with Scraped
Exterior (Fig. B35; Plate B23)

As far as we know, this type of pottery, with its distinctive scraped exterior wall, has not been definitely reported from other parts of the Valley of Mexico. Cobean (1990:465-67, Fig. 212*A-C*) describes a few sherds from Tula that may correspond to our material, and Sanders (1986:351, Plate 4*c-f*) illustrates what may be four other sherds of this pottery from the Teotihuacan Valley. In the Zumpango Region, these distinctive vessels occur in abundance at only one site: Zu-LT-212—on the bed of Lake Xaltocán-Zumpango, near the far southern edge of our survey area; a few sherds are found in very low frequencies at a few other LT sites in the Zumpango Region.

Figure B29. Late Toltec Service Ware, Monochrome bowls. Provenances: *a, c, g-l, o-x* (Zu-LT-30); *b, d-f* (Zu-LT-33); *m, n* (Zu-LT-119).

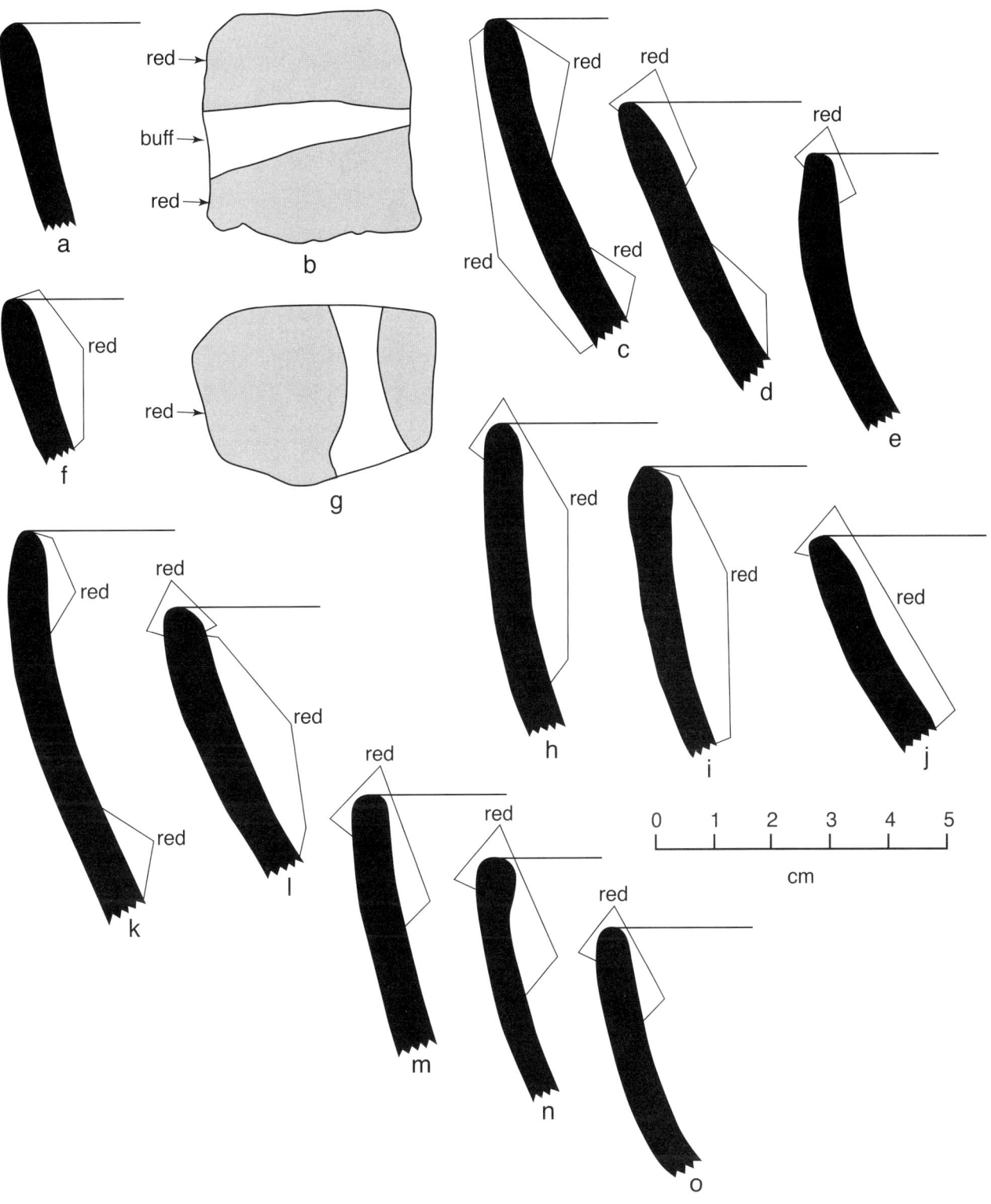

Figure B30. Late Toltec Service Ware, Red/Buff bowls, wide-band variant. Proveniences: *a*, *b*, *h-j*, *l-o* (Zu-LT-119); *c-g*, *k* (Zu-LT-30).

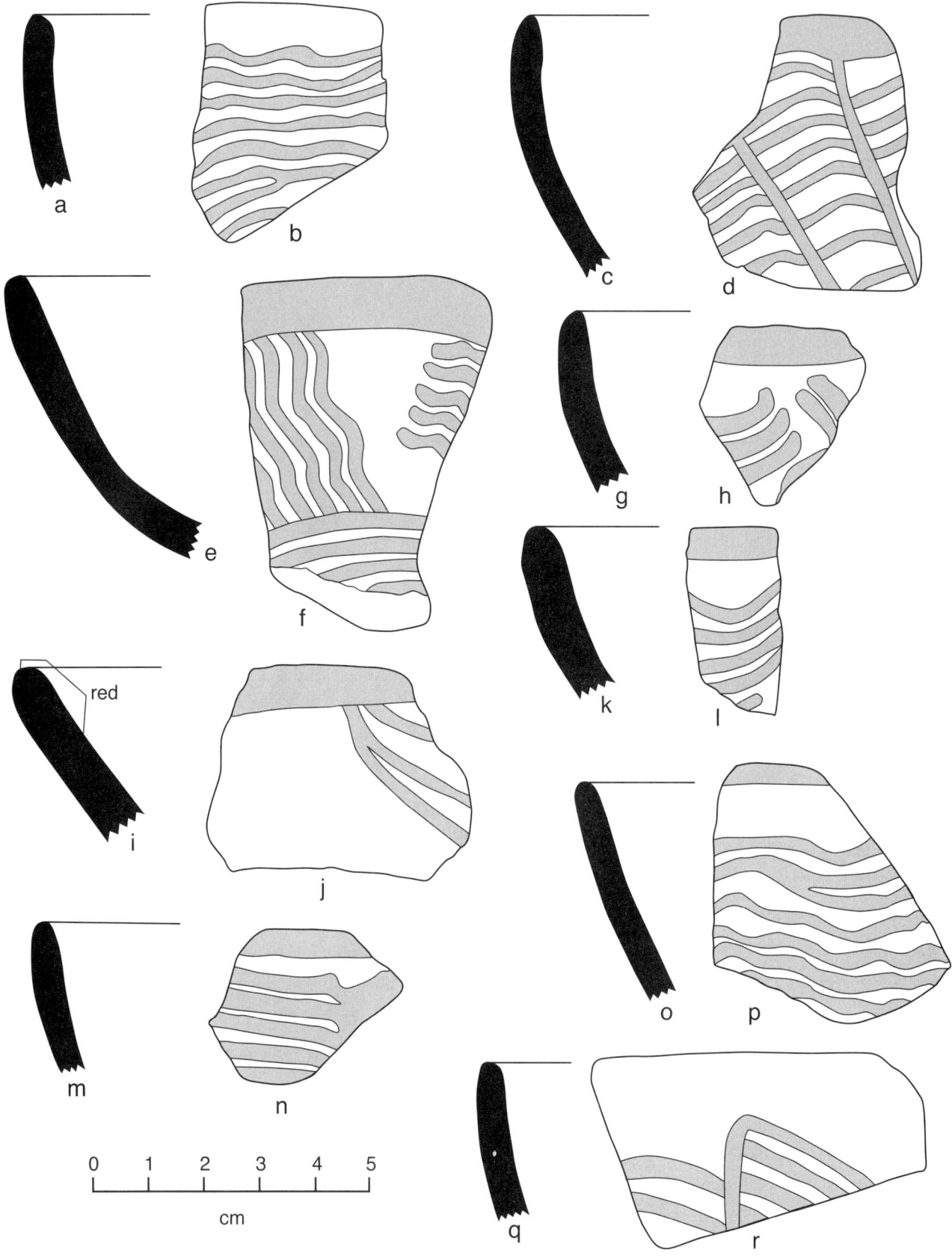

Figure B31. Late Toltec Service Ware, Red/Buff bowls, wavy-line variant. Proveniences: *a*, *b* (Zu-LT-212); *c-l* (Zu-LT-30); *m*, *n*, *q*, *r* (Zu-LT-33); *o*, *p* (Zu-LT-119).

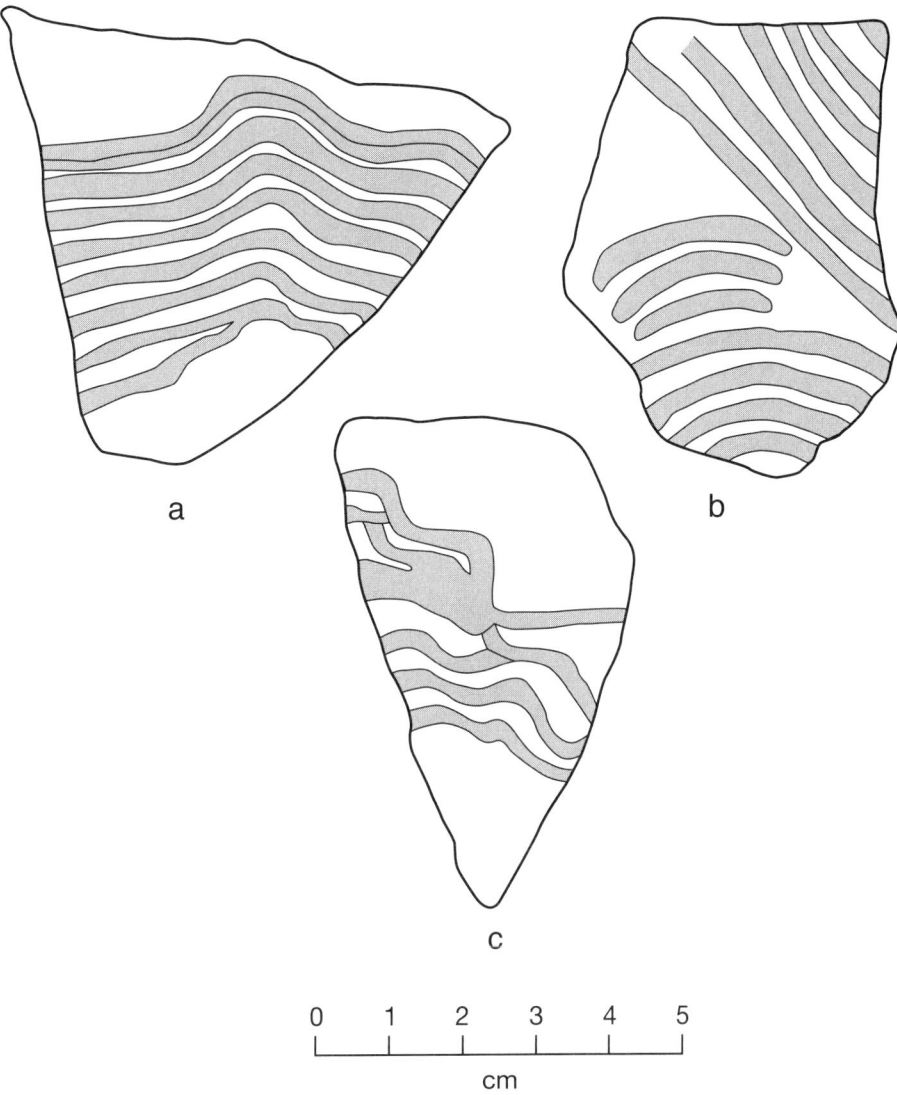

Figure B32. Late Toltec Service Ware, Red/Buff bowls, wavy-line variant. All interior-wall body sherds. Proveniences: *a*, *b* (Zu-LT-30); *c* (Zu-LT-212).

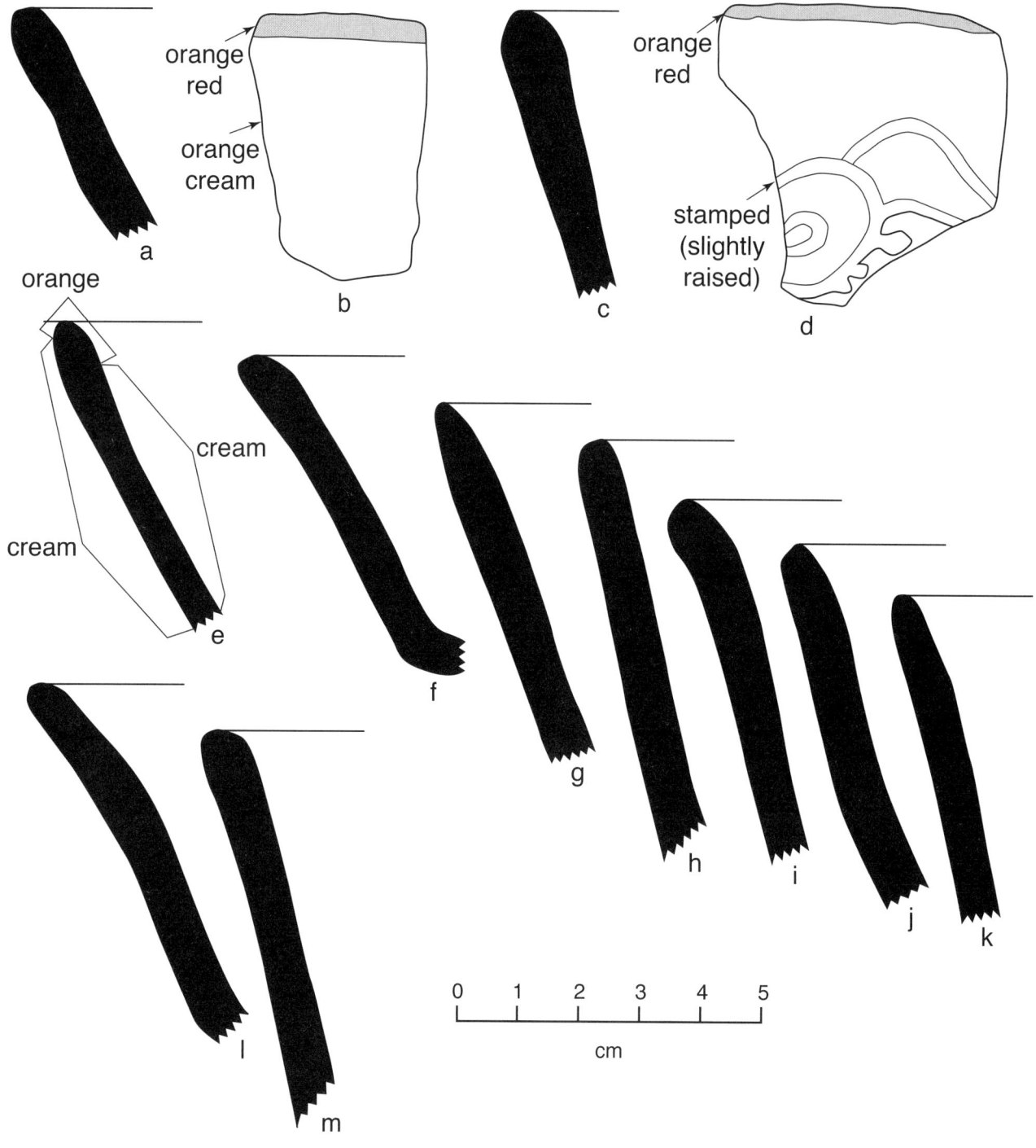

Figure B33. Late Toltec Service Ware, Orange/Cream (Joroba) bowls. Proveniences: *a-d*, *i* (Zu-LT-33); *e*, *f*, *h*, *j-m* (Zu-LT-30); *g* (Zu-LT-119).

Appendix B: Ceramic Chronology 385

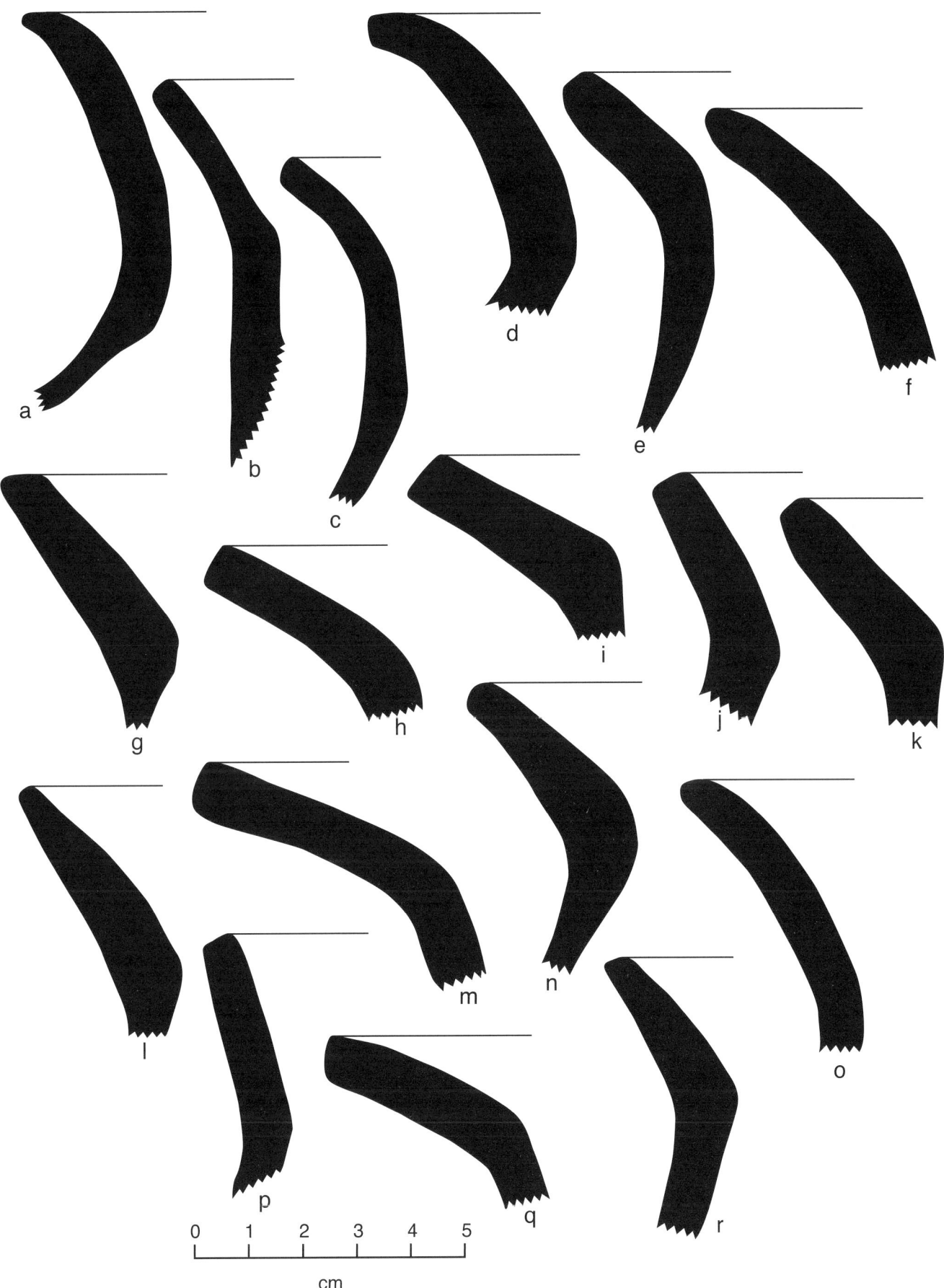

Figure B34. Late Toltec Utilitarian Ware, beveled-rim ollas. Proveniences: *a, f, h-l, q* (Zu-LT-33); *b-d, g, n, p, r* (Zu-LT-119); *e, o* (Zu-LT-30); *m* (Zu-LT-212).

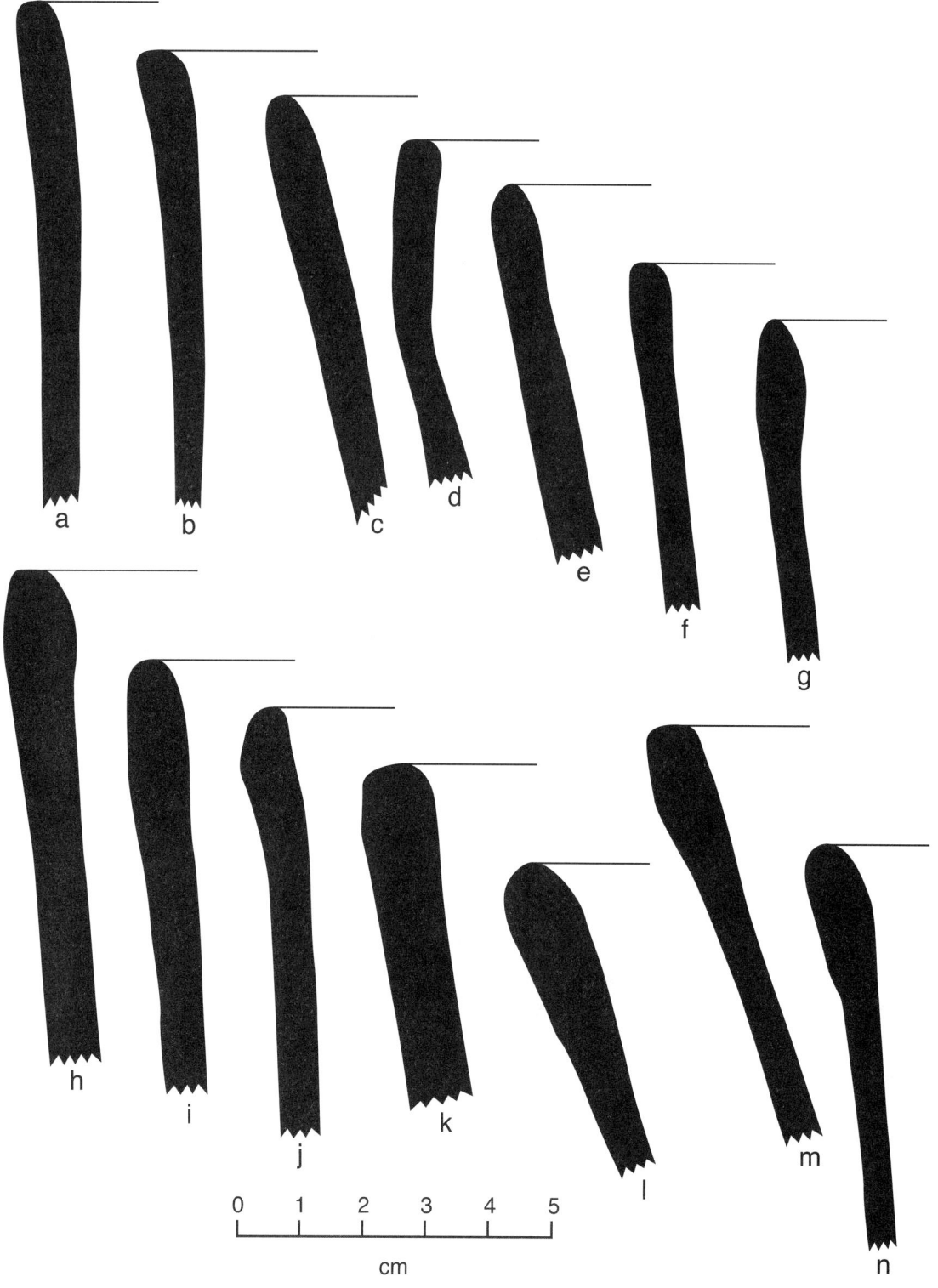

Figure B35. Late Toltec Utilitarian Ware, basins with scraped exterior. Proveniences: *e* (Zu-LT-30); all others from Zu-LT-212.

Because saltmaking was carried out in the lakebed-lakeshore area in later Postclassic and Colonial times, we infer that this pottery had something to do with saltmaking in the Early Postclassic. In fact, its regional distribution is much like that of Texcoco Fabric Marked pottery in Late Postclassic times: found in very high frequencies at certain lakebed-lakeshore sites, but only in very low frequencies at other sites on higher ground away from the lakeshore. Interestingly, Mayer-Oakes (1959:337, 339) found that his Early Postclassic "Texcoco Brown" type (also discussed as "Texcoco Dark Brown" by Tolstoy [1958:37-42]) had a complementary distribution over time to that of Texcoco Fabric Marked in his stratigraphic excavations at El Risco (near Ecatepec on the northwestern shore of Lake Texcoco): Texcoco Fabric Marked pottery tended to replace Texcoco Dark Brown over time at that lakeshore site. Mayer-Oakes' Texcoco Brown may include our scraped basin category. If so, this could be another indication that the scraped basins from the southern Zumpango Region had a saltmaking (or salt packaging) function.

Vessels are upright basins with simple direct-rims. Vessel height and basal form are indeterminate. Appendages of any sort appear to be absent. Typical surface color is a pale gray-brown, and the relatively coarse paste is much the same color. The interior wall surfaces have been roughly smoothed, while the vessel exteriors appear to have been scraped hard while leather-dry.

Late Toltec Utilitarian Ware: Comal (Fig. B36a, b)

While not abundant, these vessels usually occur in low frequencies at many Late Toltec sites in the Zumpango Region. By comparison with the much more abundant Late Postclassic comales, these are relatively high walled vessels with two small loop handles (Plate B24), situated on opposing sides (as far as we know, this is the only period in the Zumpango Region with handled comales); vessel walls typically rise 3 to 4 cm above the flat base. Rim diameters are approximately 20 cm. The interior surfaces are fairly well smoothed. Exterior walls are roughly smoothed, and exterior basal surfaces may be deliberately roughened. Surface color is typically light brown to gray-brown. The relatively coarse paste is gray-brown in color.

Similar material has been described by Sanders (1986:333-34) from excavations in the Teotihuacan Valley, and by Cobean (1990:391-97) from excavations at Tula. Blanton and Parsons (1971:289) and Whalen and Parsons (1982:433) describe similar vessels from other parts of the Valley of Mexico.

Late Toltec Utilitarian Ware: Ink-Stamped Jar (Fig. B36c-f; Plate B25)

This is a low-frequency type, but is highly diagnostic and consistently present at many Late Toltec sites in the Zumpango Region and throughout the northern Valley of Mexico and adjacent Tula Region. It is difficult to ascertain vessel form in our surface collections, but typical vessels appear to be high-necked jars with distinctive groupings of parallel black or dark gray lines (straight or wavy) applied on the upper parts of interior and exterior surfaces. The underlying color, apparently a thick slip, ranges from red-brown to gray. Modal rim diameter is about 10 cm. Vessel height, basal form, and appendages are indeterminate. The relatively coarse paste is gray-brown in color.

Similar material is described by Sanders (1986:364) from excavations in the Teotihuacan Valley, and by Cobean (1990:463-69, Figs. 212, 212D) from excavations at Tula (where it occurs in low frequency).

Late Toltec Specialty Wares

These low-frequency types do not occur at every LT site in the Zumpango Region. Nevertheless, a few sherds are to be found at many sites. When present, they help provide a measure of chronological control, and also are suggestive of linkages with urban Tula, where all occur in greater abundance (Cobean 1978, 1990). Some types (for instance, Plumbate) are known to be tradewares from Central America (e.g., Diehl et al. 1974); however, the provenance of other Early Postclassic specialty wares remains uncertain. We made no profile or design-motif drawings, but these materials are illustrated by accompanying photographs.

Late Toltec Specialty Ware: Plumbate (Plate B26)

All the sherds in our surface collections are too small to infer much about vessel form. Complete vessels from nearby Tula take the form of a variety of small jars and effigy jars, between 10 and 12 cm in height (Diehl et al. 1974; Cobean 1990:475-85). Interior and exterior surfaces are well burnished, with a characteristic gloss and color ranging from mottled dark gray-green to orange-brown.

Late Toltec Specialty Ware: Sillon Incised Orange (Plate B27)

Vessels are usually upright bowls with flaring rims and incised exterior decoration. Surfaces are typically deep red-orange to orange-brown, well burnished and sometimes slightly polished. Rim diameter, basal form, and appendages are uncertain.

Similar and identical material is described by Sanders (1986:365, Plate 18*f, h, i, m*) from excavations in the Teotihuacan Valley, and by Cobean (1990:375-83, his "Sillón Inciso" type) from excavations at Tula.

Late Toltec Specialty Ware: Orange Stamped (Plate B28)

Vessels are lightly flared bowls with curvilinear designs stamped into upper exterior surfaces prior to firing. Well smoothed exterior and interior surfaces are typically light orange-brown in color. Rim diameter, basal form, and appendages are uncertain.

Cobean (1990:350-57, his "Ira Anaranajado Sellado" type) describes this pottery from excavations at Tula.

Late Toltec Specialty Ware: Blanco Llevantado (Tula Watercolored) (Plate B29)

This distinctive pottery appears to be very scarce in the central and southern sectors of the Valley of Mexico, and only slightly more abundant in the Zumpango Region. Vessel form, rim diameter, and appendages are all uncertain. The distinctive designs (all on exterior surfaces) feature narrow linear bands of black, gray, or orange-brown overlaid atop a thick cream slip.

Comparable material is described by Tolstoy (1958:54-55, 80) from several locations in the northern Valley of Mexico, and by Sanders (1986:347) from excavations in the Teotihuacan Valley—both these authors use the term "Tula Watercolored" for this type. Cobean (1990:449-57) describes identical pottery from excavations at Tula.

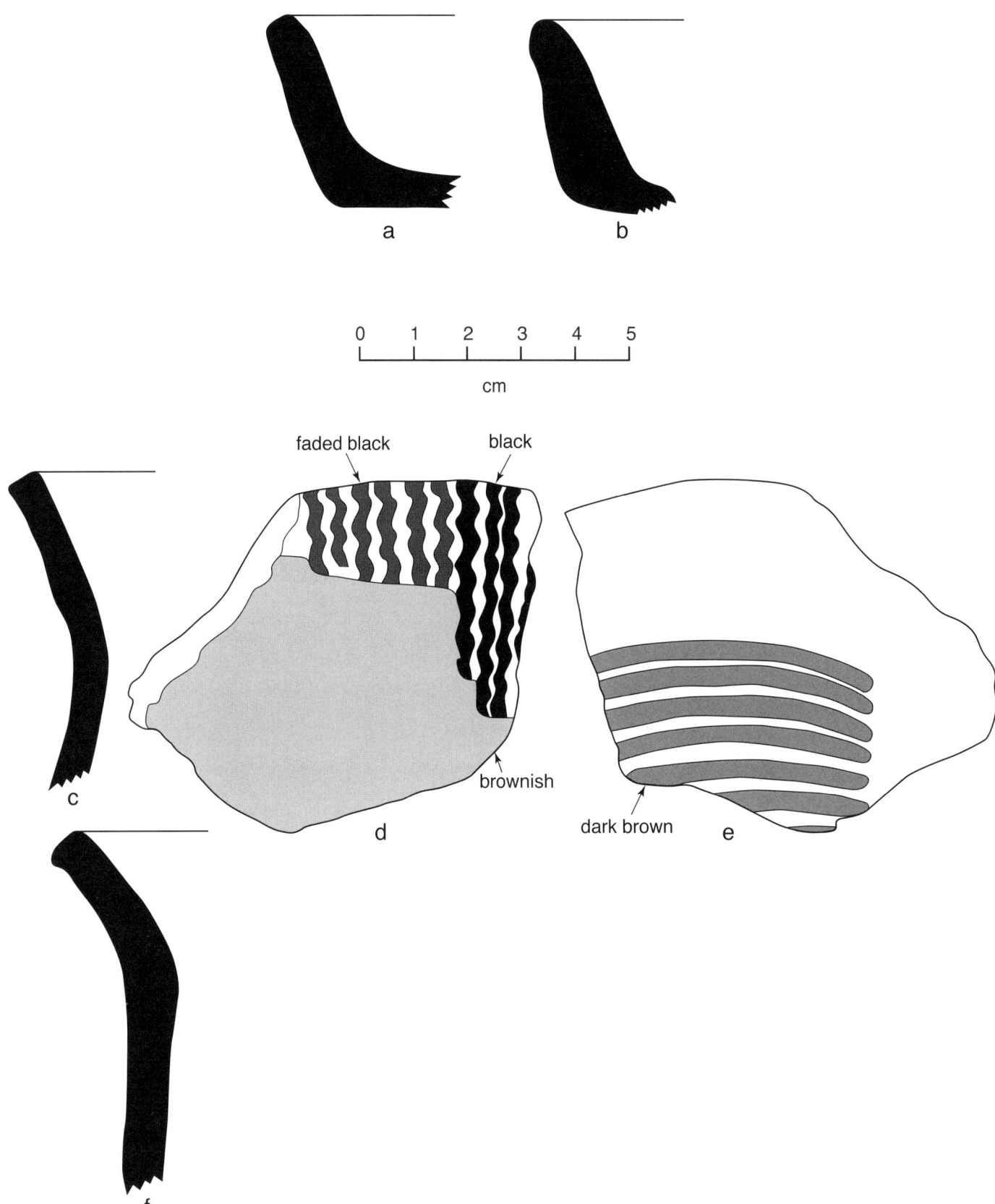

Figure B36. Late Toltec Utilitarian Ware, comales (*a, b*) and ink-stamped jars (*c-f*). Proveniences: *a, c-f* (Zu-LT-30), *b* (Zu-LT-119).

Late Toltec Specialty Ware: Figurines (Plate B30)

These distinctive thin, mold-made figurines are infrequent, but one or two typically show up in our surface collections from many Late Toltec sites in the Zumpango Region. They occur both as detached heads and as headless body fragments. The most distinctive are heads with goggle-eyes and simple headdresses (Plate B30*a*), although eyeless heads with different headdresses are also present (Plate B30*b*).

Comparable material is described by Koehler (1986:46), Barbour (1987:750), and Scott (1993) from excavations in the Teotihuacan Valley.

Early and Late Aztec

As previously noted in Sanders et al. (1979) and Parsons and Gorenflo (in press), what have been termed "Early Aztec" ceramics are very scarce in the Zumpango Region. This is most notable with the complete absence of Aztec I Black/Orange and the near-absence of Aztec II Black/Orange pottery—one or the other, or both, have long been considered the hallmarks of Early Aztec occupation in other surveyed parts of the Valley of Mexico. Interestingly, both Aztec I and II Black/Orange ceramics are abundant at Xaltocán (Zu-Az-276), just beyond the far southeastern corner of our survey area (Brumfiel 2005), although Aztec I Black/Orange is virtually absent from both the Teotihuacan and Texcoco Regions in the eastern Valley of Mexico (Parsons 1966, 1971), and becomes common only in the Ixtapalapa (Blanton 1972) and Chalco-Xochimilco Regions farther south (Parsons et al. 1982). Aztec II Black/Orange occurs throughout the Valley of Mexico south of the Zumpango Region (e.g., Minc et al. 1994; García Chávez 2004; Parsons and Gorenflo, in press), and small quantities have been reported from Tula (Franco 1945).

The most distinctive Aztec II Black/Orange variants (Vaillant 1938; Noguera 1935:140-47; Franco 1945; Griffin and Espejo 1947, 1950; Parsons 1966; Hodge and Minc 1991; Minc et al. 1994) are virtually absent in the Zumpango Region. However, what one might stylistically characterize as Aztec II-III Black/Orange does occur with some frequency in our survey area.[1] This II-III category includes what Vaillant (1938:541) termed "Black-on-Orange IIc, Late Aztec II," some of what Parsons designated as "Upright-Rim Bowls, Variants A, B, C" (1966:636, Plate 2), "Incurved-Rim Bowls, Variants A, B, C" (1966:646, Plate 12), "Upright-Rim Basins, Variants C, D, E" (1966:644, Plate 10), "Dish, Variant C" (1966:665, Plate 31), "Dish, Variant D, sub-variant 1" (1966:666, Plate 32), and "Plate, Variant C" (1966:679, Plate 45). Hodge and Minc (1991) provide a revised version of Parsons' original typology. Our Aztec II-III could represent a late phase of Aztec II.

Aztec III Black/Orange is abundant throughout the Zumpango Region, and there is also a fair amount of Aztec IV Black/Orange. Although Aztec IV Black/Orange may begin in the Late Postclassic, there is reason to suspect that much of it may also extend into the Early Colonial period; it is sometimes found at sites with clear hispanic-influenced surface pottery (Plate B31). The chronological distinction between Aztec III and IV Black/Orange is further complicated by the continuation of some variants of Aztec III into the Early Colonial period (Charlton et al. 2005; Garraty 2006). We cannot resolve the question of Aztec IV B/O chronology in this monograph, and so we simply assume that much of it is prehispanic, and we make no attempt to define a separate Early Colonial settlement pattern on the basis of this pottery type. We hope that eventually archaeologists will be able to clearly disentangle the Late Aztec and Early Colonial occupations that are now, in all likelihood, so inextricably mingled.

Although Red Ware is found at Aztec sites throughout the Zumpango Region, it occurs in lower frequencies and with less variation than farther south in the Valley of Mexico (Minc 1994).

In the following descriptions, we characterize our Aztec ceramics as a whole, referring where appropriate to those categories we regard as Aztec II or II-III Black/Orange. At our level of observation, this material corresponds closely to those coeval ceramics that have been described from other parts of the Valley of Mexico (e.g., Noguera 1935; Griffin and Espejo 1947, 1950; Tolstoy 1958; O'Neill 1962; Parsons 1966; Sejourne 1970, 1983; Blanton and Parsons 1971; Vega 1975; Whalen and Parsons 1982; Hodge and Minc 1991; Minc et al. 1994; García Chávez and Córdoba 1994; Castillo 1994; Lazcano 1995; García Chávez 2004; Brumfiel 2005; Ávila 2006).

We have classified our Aztec surface pottery as follows:

I. Orange Service Ware
   A. Monochrome Bowl
   B. Black/Orange Bowl
   C. Black/Orange Dish
   D. Black/Orange Molcajete

All Orange service wares have essentially the same paste: fired at relatively high temperature in an oxidizing atmosphere, pale orange-brown to orange-gray in color, with moderate quantities of temper. Bowls have upright walls and exterior decoration; dishes and molcajetes have outward sloping walls and interior decoration; molcajetes have very distinctive striated interior basal surfaces, often considerably worn by the pressure of circular grinding motion. Bowls lack supports, while dishes and molcajetes have tripod conical or slab supports.

II. Orange Utilitarian Ware
   A. Olla
   B. Basin
   C. Comal

Orange utilitarian wares have paste similar to that of Orange service wares, but typically somewhat coarser, with larger and slightly more abundant temper.

III. Red Service Ware
   A. Monochrome Bowl
   B. Black/Red Bowl
   C. Black-and-White/Red Bowl with Vertical Panels
   D. Black-and-White/Red Bowl with Triangular Panels
   E. Black-and-White/Red Bowl with Fugitive White Designs
   F. Yellow/Red Bowl

All Red service ware pottery types have essentially the same distinctive paste: gray to gray-brown in color, often with a notable dark gray to gray-black core indicating firing in an atmosphere of reduced oxygen. These vessels were obviously fired in a very different way than were the coeval Orange Wares.

---

[1] What we here refer to as Aztec II-III Black/Orange is much different from how Franco (1949, 1957) used the term (for material that we feel should be considered a variant of Axtec III).

IV. Specialty Ware
   A. Huastec Black-and-Purple/Cream Tradeware
   B. Texcoco Fabric Marked
   C. Chalco-Cholula Polychrome
   D. Texcoco Molded and Texcoco Filleted

Aztec Orange Service Ware: Monochrome Bowl (Fig. B37)

These are simple hemispherical vessels with upright, or slightly incurved, walls and direct-rims. Rim diameters range from 10 to 16 cm. Vessel height is indeterminate in our sample. Handles or appendages of any kind appear to be lacking. Both interior and exterior surfaces are generally well smoothed; surface color ranges from pale brown to pale orange to medium orange-brown. Very similar vessels have been described throughout the Valley of Mexico. They are similar to Late Toltec monochrome bowls, and it is sometimes difficult to distinguish between individual examples of this vessel form from the two periods.

Aztec Orange Service Ware: Black/Orange II-III Bowl-Basin (Fig. B38)

Here we make no attempt to distinguish between bowls and basins—in our surface samples, the latter appear to be simply slightly larger and thicker walled versions of the former. The sherd illustrated in Figure B38 is probably the single best example of something approximating Aztec II Black/Orange in our entire sample from the Zumpango Region. However, because it lacks the most typical Aztec II *zacate* (grassy) motif (that is, Variants A1, A2, and A3 as defined by Hodge and Minc [1991:146]), and because it occurs on a bowl form (a vessel form whose designs have sometimes been characterized as comparatively "archaic" relative to dish, plate, and molcajete forms [e.g., Parsons 1966]), we regard it as II-III, and assume it dates to the late part of the "Early Aztec" phase, or perhaps even slightly later.

Plate B32 illustrates the variability in what we designate Aztec II-III B/O Bowl-Basin decoration.

Exterior and interior surfaces are generally well smoothed, ranging in color from pale to medium orange to orange-brown, reddish brown, or gray-brown. Rim diameters range from 10 to 16 cm. Vessel height is indeterminate. Bowls seem to lack handles; basins may have small lug or horizontal loop handles. Supports are lacking.

Aztec Orange Service Ware: Aztec III Black/Orange Bowl-Basin (Figs. B39, B40)

Here we also lump bowls and basins. A few of the illustrated vessels might be characterized as Aztec II-III (e.g., Fig. B39*a-d*), but the great majority are clearly Aztec III variants. These are simple hemispherical bowls, apparently lacking appendages, with rim diameters between 10 and 15 cm.

Typical examples of Aztec III B/O bowls are illustrated in Plate B33.

Aztec Orange Service Ware: Aztec III Black/Orange Dish-Plate (Fig. B41)

Most of these are dishes, but a few are plates—in small sherds, it is sometimes difficult to distinguish between the two forms. In any case, the decorative motifs are essentially equivalent. Plate B34 illustrates fragments of two Aztec II Black/Orange plates, the only definite Aztec II B/O vessel of this form category in our surface collections. One of the illustrated examples might be considered Aztec II-III (Fig. B41*a*); Plate B35 illustrates typical Aztec II-III B/O dish-plate vessels. These vessels typically have tripod conical or slab supports, and rim diameters range from 10 to 14 cm. Overall vessel height is uncertain.

Aztec III variants are shown in Plate B36.

Aztec Orange Service Ware: Aztec III Black/Orange Molcajete (Figs. B42, B43)

Molcajetes are essentially dishes that have been modified in order to grind soft foods with a stone or ceramic pestle. These vessels are easily recognizable by the worn interior surfaces. This wear, produced by the grinding motion, has sometimes nearly obliterated the painted decoration. Small rim sherds, lacking the lower walls showing the characteristic wear, can easily be confused with dishes. Like dishes, molcajetes have tripod conical or slab supports, and rim diameters range from 10 to 14 cm. One large sherd (Fig. B42*a*) has a vessel height of 7.5 cm. Similar vessels have been reported throughout the Valley of Mexico (e.g., Parsons 1966; Hodge and Minc 1991).

Plate B37 illustrates a Aztec II-III Black/Orange molcajete; Plate B38*a-c* shows typical Aztec III B/O vessels. Similar vessels continue into the post-hispanic Colonial period (Plate B38*d*).

Aztec Orange Service Ware: Aztec IV Black/Orange Dish and Molcajete (Fig. B44)

These vessels are similar to Aztec III Black/Orange dishes and molcajetes, but all seem to have tripod slab (instead of conical) supports, and the black designs are quite distinctive, typified by parallel thick black lines applied around the vessel interiors; occasionally, drawings of birds and abstract curvilinear motifs also occur. The two vessels illustrated in Figure B44 are very unusual, perhaps unique; most Aztec IV Black/Orange pottery in the Zumpango Region conforms to the typical decoration that has been described for this type at sites of this period throughout the Valley of Mexico. Aztec IV Black/Orange decoration may date mainly from the post-hispanic period, and, as indicated above, is sometimes found with obvious post-hispanic pottery in our surface collections. Plate B39 illustrates a unique B/O decoration, possibly of post-hispanic age.

Plate B40 illustrates typical Aztec IV Black/Orange dishes and molcajetes in our surface collections; Plate B41 shows typical decoration of slab supports.

Aztec Orange Utilitarian Ware: Olla or Jar (Fig. B45a, b)

These vessels are abundant in our surface collections. Most have flaring rims approximately 10 to 13 cm in diameter. The upper interior and exterior surfaces are generally well smoothed, ranging in color from pale orange to medium orange to pale brown. Vessel height and basal form are uncertain. We found no handles attached to jar rims, but numerous vertical loop handles in many of our surface collections suggest that individual vessels had one such handle attached to the upper rim. Similar vessels have been reported throughout the Valley of Mexico (Parsons 1966; Hodge and Minc 1991).

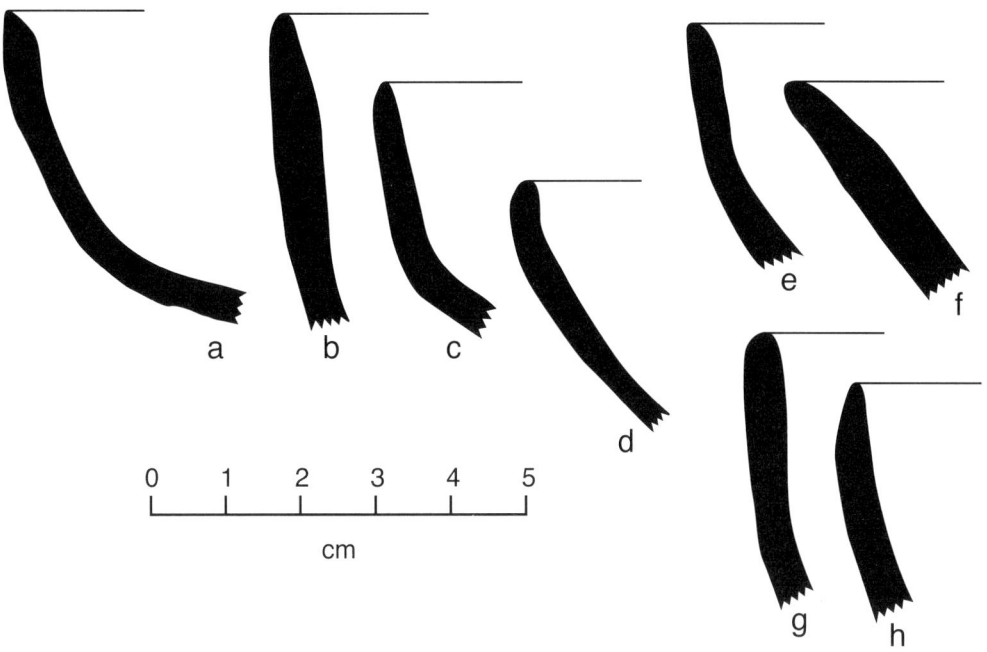

Figure B37. Aztec Orange Service Ware, Monochrome bowls. Proveniences: *a, c* (Zu-Az-292); *b, d-h* (Zu-Az-46).

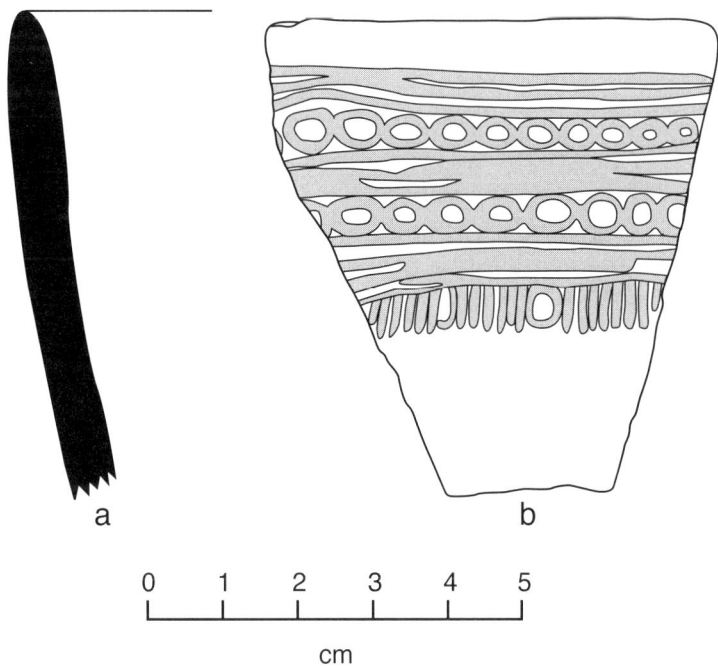

Figure B38. Aztec Orange Service Ware, Aztec II-III Black/Orange bowl-basin. Provenience: Zu-Az-18.

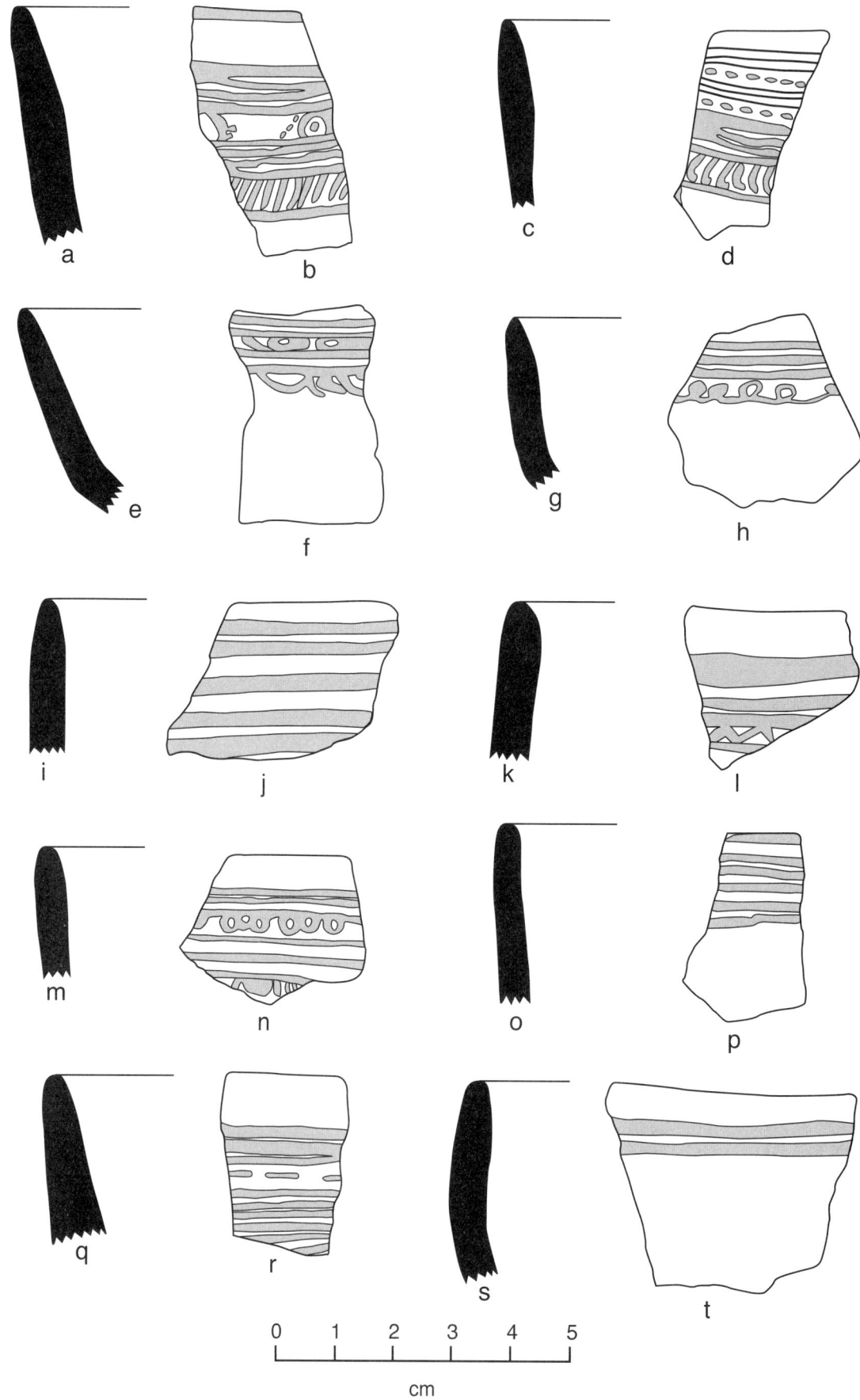

Figure B39. Orange Service Ware, Aztec III Black/Orange bowls. Proveniences: all from Zu-Az-46. All decoration is on exterior surfaces.

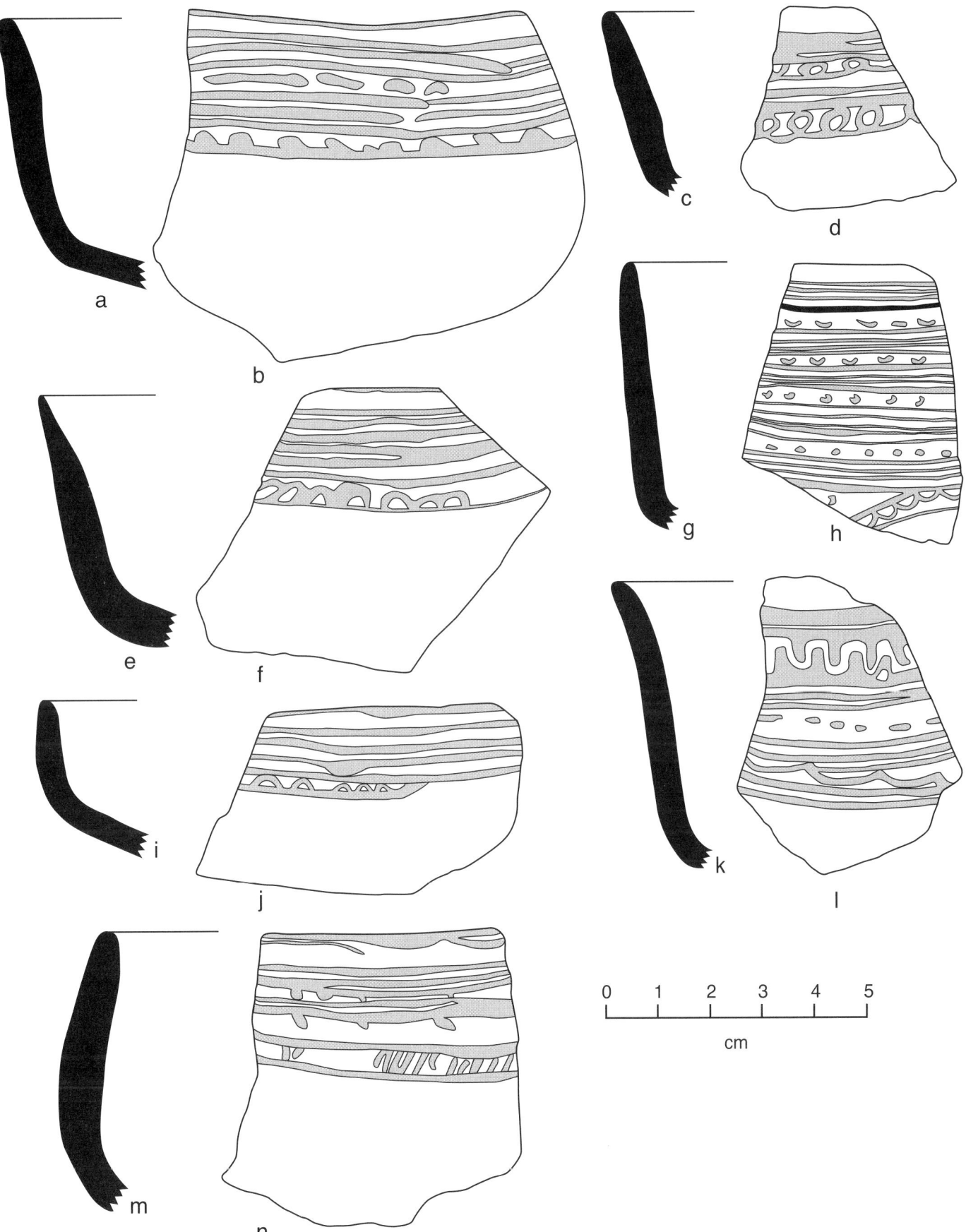

Figure B40. Aztec Orange Service Ware, Aztec III Black/Orange bowls. Proveniences: all from Zu-Az-73. All decoration is on exterior surfaces.

Figure B41. Aztec Orange Service Ware, Aztec III Black/Orange dishes. Proveniences: *a-f, i, j, m-p* (Zu-Az-46); *g, h, k, l, q, r* (Zu-Az-292). All decoration is on interior surfaces.

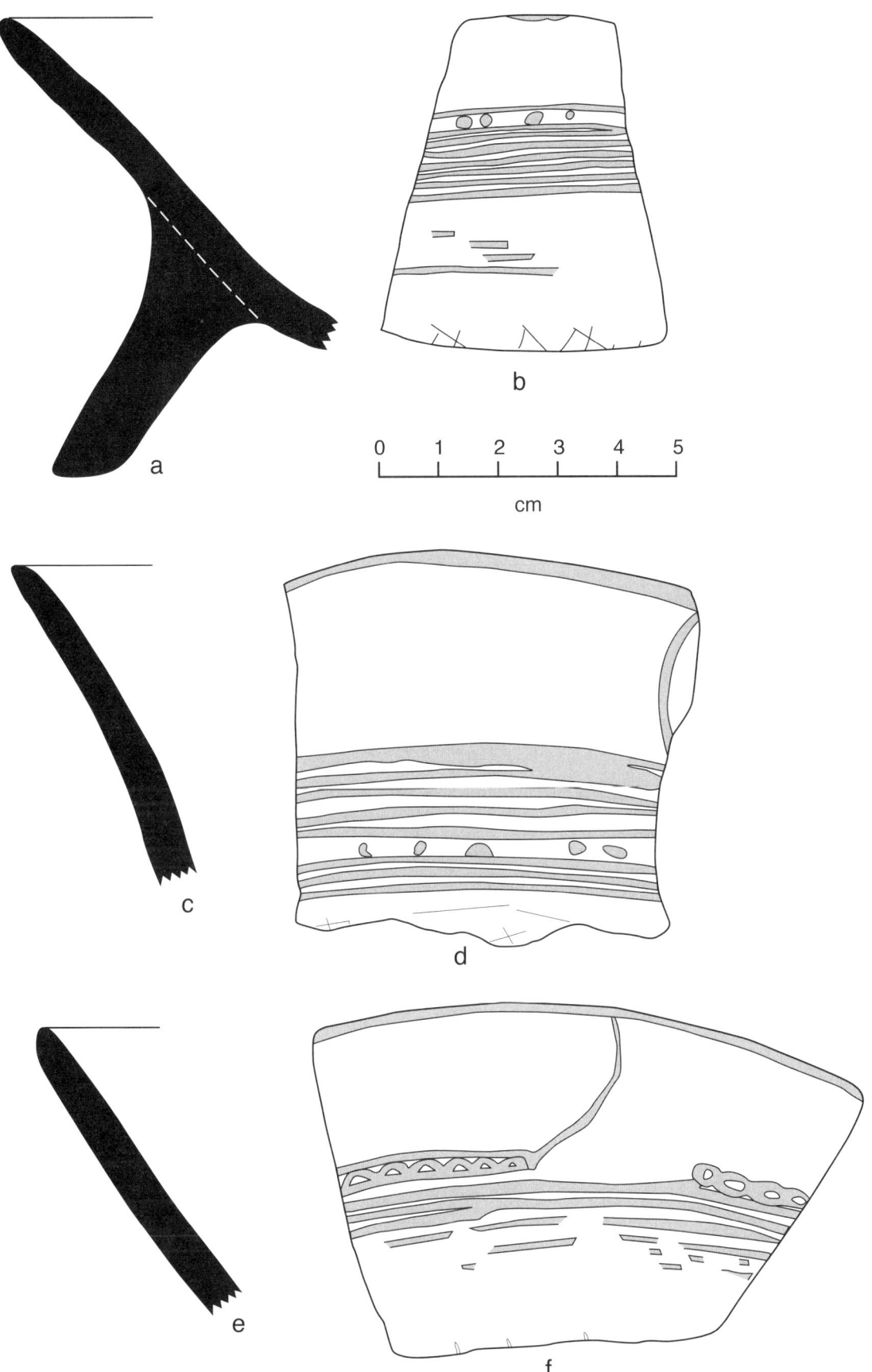

Figure B42. Aztec III Black/Orange molcajetes. Proveniences: all from Zu-Az-73. All decoration is on interior surfaces.

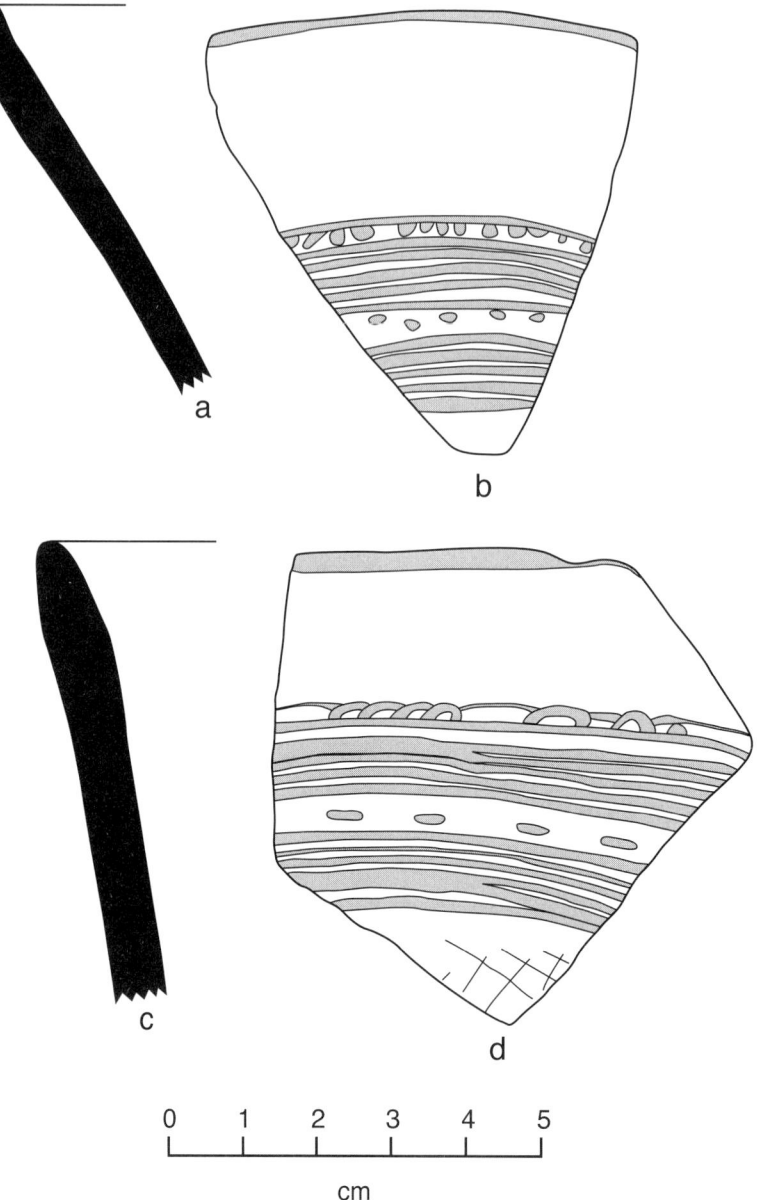

Figure B43. Aztec III Black/Orange molcajetes. Provenience: both from Zu-Az-292. All decoration is on interior surfaces.

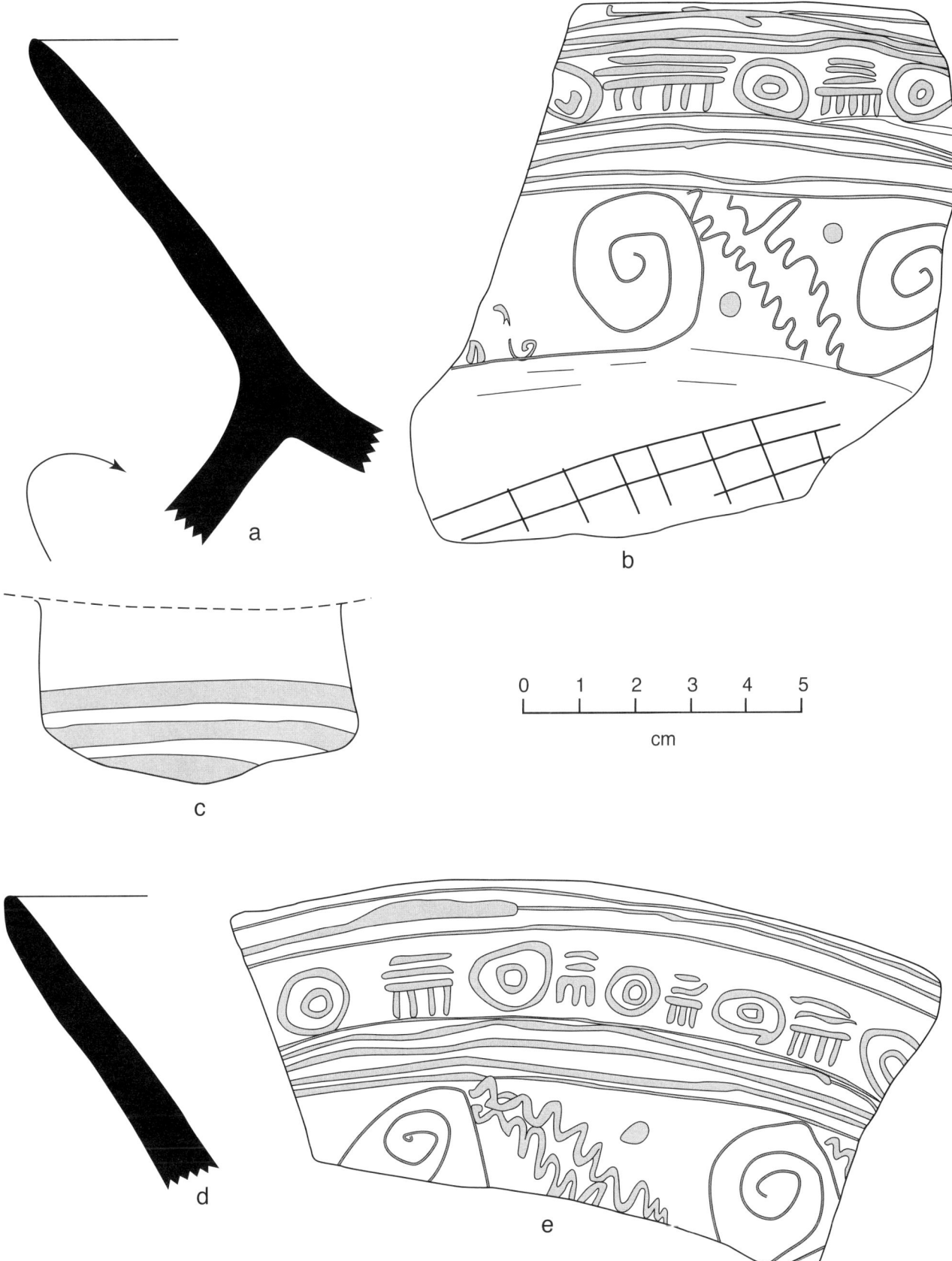

Figure B44. Aztec IV Black/Orange molcajetes. Proveniences: both from Zu-Az-292. All illustrated decoration is from interior surfaces. See Plate B39.

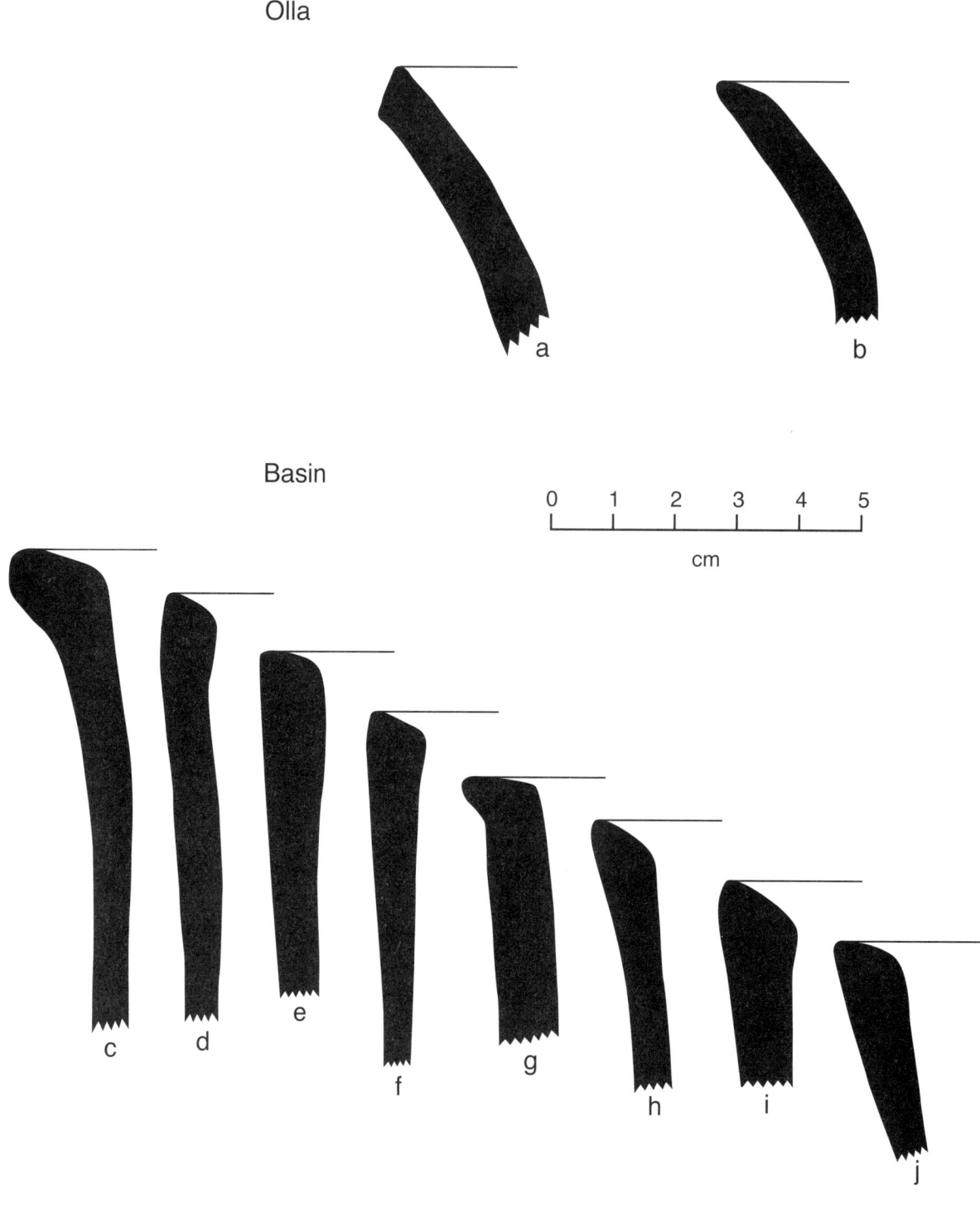

Figure B45. Aztec Orange Utilitarian Ware, jars (*a, b*) and basins (*c-j*). Proveniences: *a, b* (Zu-Az-292); *c-h* (Zu-Az-73); *i, j* (Zu-Az-46).

Aztec Orange Utilitarian Ware: Basin (Fig. B45c-j)

Like jars, these vessels are abundant in our surface collections. Most of them have upright walls and wedge-rims, about 10 to 16 cm in diameter. The upper interior and exterior surfaces are generally well smoothed, ranging in color from pale orange to medium orange to pale brown. Vessel height and basal form are uncertain. We are uncertain about the presence of handles or supports. Similar vessels have been reported throughout the Valley of Mexico (Parsons 1966; Hodge and Minc 1991).

Aztec Orange Utilitarian Ware: Comale (Fig. B46)

These distinctive vessels are abundant at Late Postclassic sites in the Zumpango Region, just as they are at coeval sites throughout the Valley of Mexico. Vessels are flat, with low walls that typically rise less than 2 cm above the level of the flat base, and with direct-rims that are sometimes slightly thickened. Interior surfaces are fairly well smoothed; exterior walls are roughly smoothed, while the bottom surfaces appear to have been deliberately roughened. Handles are lacking. Surface colors range from pale brown to pale orange-brown and gray-orange.

Aztec Red Service Ware: Monochrome Bowl (Fig. B47)

These are simple hemispherical bowls, typically with upright rounded walls, occasionally with more flaring walls, and with direct-rims. There are no supports or other appendages. Rim diameters range from 10 to 13 cm. Vessel heights are indeterminate in our sample. A bright red paint has been applied to upper exterior walls, and some upper interior walls; in most cases, the lower walls remain unpainted. Unpainted surfaces are typically pale to medium brown in color. Surfaces are well smoothed, sometimes burnished and even polished.

Aztec Red Service Ware: Black/Red Bowl (Figs. B48, B49)

These vessels are identical in form to the monochrome Red service ware bowls described above, with the addition of distinctive black decoration on the exterior surface. This decoration usually takes the form of simple bundles of thin parallel black lines applied on the vessel exterior below a narrow black band around the vessel rim (Plate B42). In some cases, more elaborate geometric designs have been applied onto the vessel exterior and/or interior surfaces (Fig. B49; Plate B43). Similar vessels have been widely reported from coeval sites throughout the Valley of Mexico (Parsons 1966; Hodge and Minc 1991).

Aztec Red Service Ware: Black-and-White/Red Bowl with Vertical Panels (Fig. B50a-h), Triangular Panels (Fig. B50i-p), or Complex Fugitive White Designs (Fig. B51)

In form, paste, and surface finish, these are identical to the Red Ware monochrome and Black/Red vessels described above. They differ in their much more elaborate polychrome decoration, usually on the exterior surface. This decoration typically takes one of two forms: (1) vertical panels formed by wide black bands, with thick, sometimes fugitive, white paint motifs applied between the panels (Plate B44); or (2) triangular panels formed by wide black bands, with thick, sometimes fugitive, white paint applied between the panels (Plate B45). In some cases, much more complex fugitive white curvilinear and geometric designs have been applied inside of, or overlapping onto, the black paint (Fig. B51; Plate B46).

Aztec Red Service Ware: Yellow/Red Bowl (Plate B47)

This is a very low-frequency type, but occurs with some consistency at many Late Postclassic sites in the Zumpango Region. We suspect that this type continued into the Early Colonial period, but at present there is no definitive information on this. Vessels are typical Red Ware simple hemispherical bowls, lacking appendages of any kind, on which thick curvilinear yellow designs have been applied to the upper exterior wall surfaces.

Aztec Specialty Ware: Huastec Black-and-Purple/Cream Tradeware (Fig. B52)

Sherds of this distinctive tradeware are scarce, but they do occur at several Aztec sites in the Zumpango Region, as elsewhere at coeval sites in the Valley of Mexico. These are bowls with upright walls and flared or incurved rims, and with distinctive black and purple designs painted around the upper interior and exterior surfaces, occasionally with incised lines around the rim (Plate B48); strap handles attached to the rim sometimes occur (Plate B49). The paste is highly distinctive: very fine, cream colored, with no added temper, completely unlike that of any other type from the Valley of Mexico. Vessel heights, basal form, and appendages are unknown. Rim diameters are about 10 cm.

Aztec Specialty Ware: Texcoco Fabric Marked (cerámica de impresión textil) (Plates B50, B51)

Almost all of this highly distinctive type in our surface collections comes from a handful of Late Aztec sites along the shoreline and on the lakebed of Lake Xaltocán-Zumpango, in the zone where documentary sources indicate saltmaking was important in the sixteenth century (see Chapter 3). A tiny number of fabric-marked sherds also occur at a few Late Postclassic sites well north of the lakeshore. This is a pattern that is replicated elsewhere in the Valley of Mexico. Several studies have described this unique ware and considered its distribution and significance (e.g., Holmes 1885; Tolstoy 1958; Mayer-Oakes 1959; Charlton 1969, 1971; Parsons 1971, 2001, 2006; Blanton 1972; Talavara 1979; Baños 1980; Sejourne 1970:74, Fig. 8; Sejourne 1983:144-47; Gonzalez Rul 1988; Sanchez 1989; Baños and Sanchez 1998; Minc 1999).

Because this ware is so friable and poorly fired, it disintegrates rapidly on the ground surface, and is usually found only as small sherds. Vessel form has been difficult to define, but several excavations (most importantly those reported by Baños and Sanchez, but including that of W. Holmes well over a century ago) have shown a range of open-mouthed vessels, with flat bases and upright to flaring walls, of variable but consistent volumes (Plate B51). The general consensus is that these quickly and cheaply made vessels served to package crystalline salt in standard volumes for redistribution through marketplaces, and that the ceramic packaging was meant to be discarded after a single use. This interpretation accounts well for the high frequencies of this ware in saltmaking/salt packaging production sites along the saline lakeshores, and its low frequencies at coeval salt-consuming sites elsewhere (e.g., Parsons 2001).

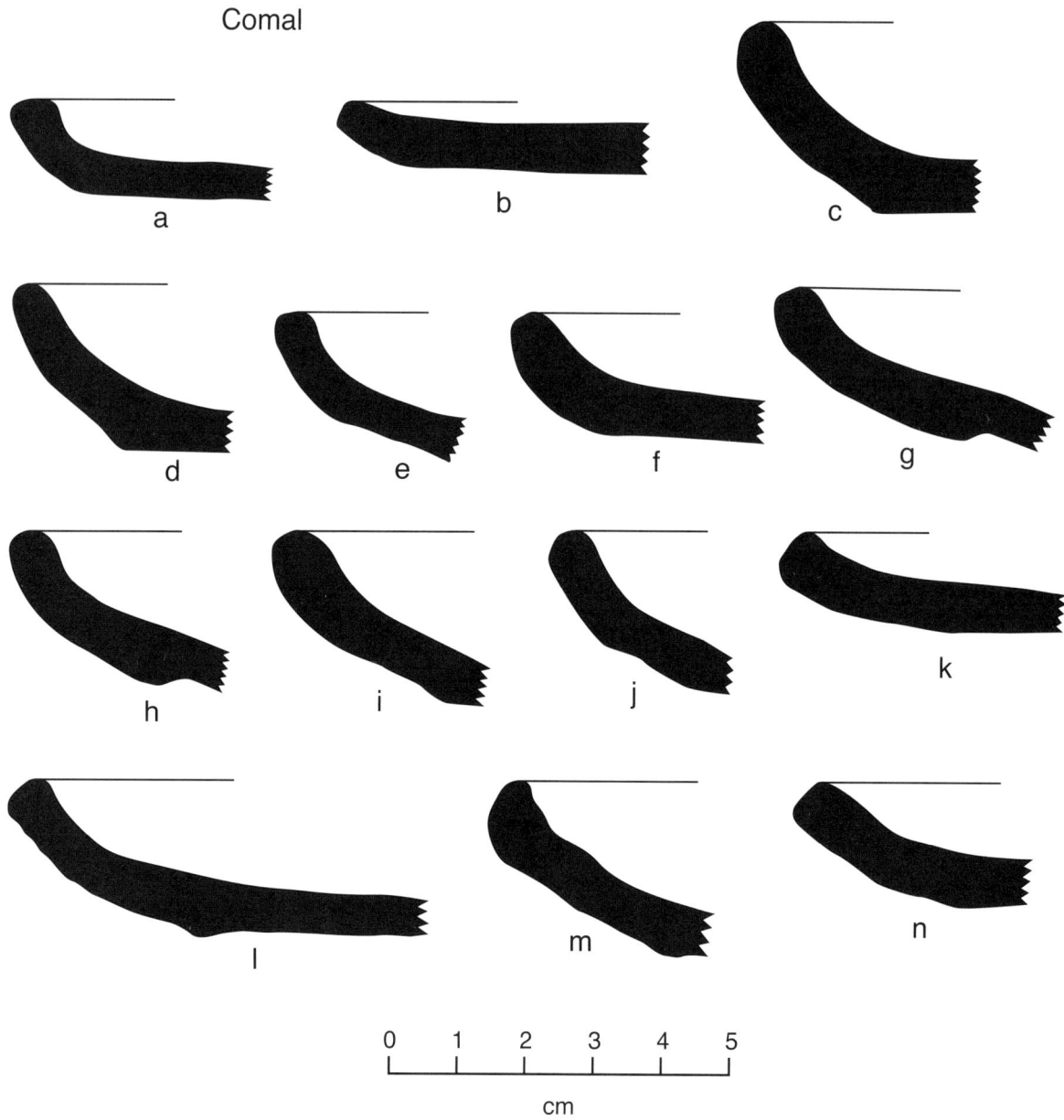

Figure B46. Aztec Orange Utilitarian Ware, comales. Proveniences: *a-c* (Zu-Az-292); *d-g* (Zu-Az-46); *h-n* (Zu-Az-73).

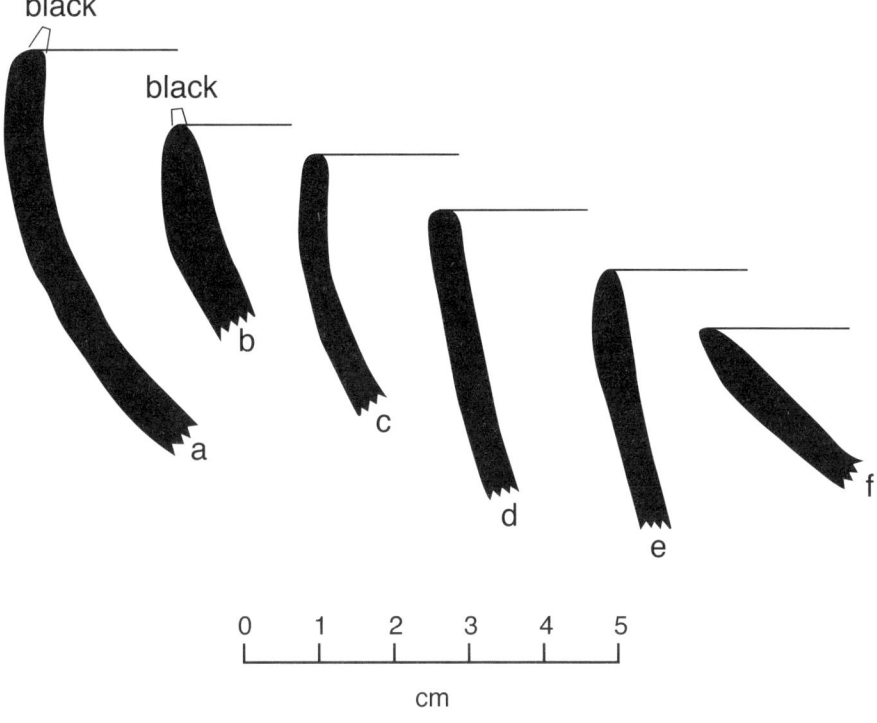

Figure B47. Aztec Red Service Ware, Monochrome bowls. Proveniences: *a, b* (Zu-Az-292); *c* (Zu-Az-46); *d-f* (Zu-Az-73).

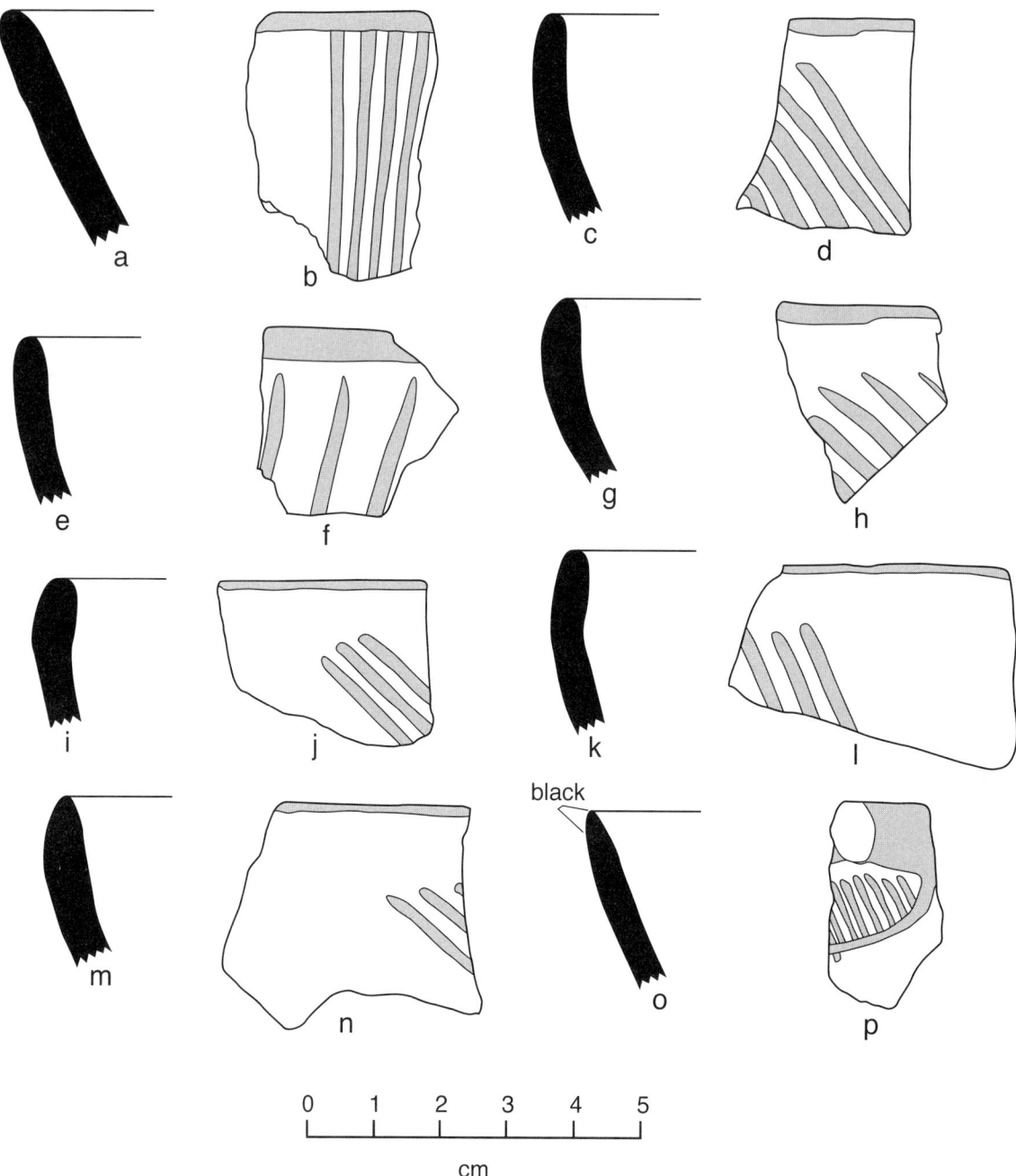

Figure B48. Aztec Red Service Ware, Black/Red bowls. Proveniences: *a, b, g, h, m, n* (Zu-Az-73); *c, d, o, p* (Zu-Az-292); *e, f, i-l* (Zu-Az-46). All designs are on exterior surfaces.

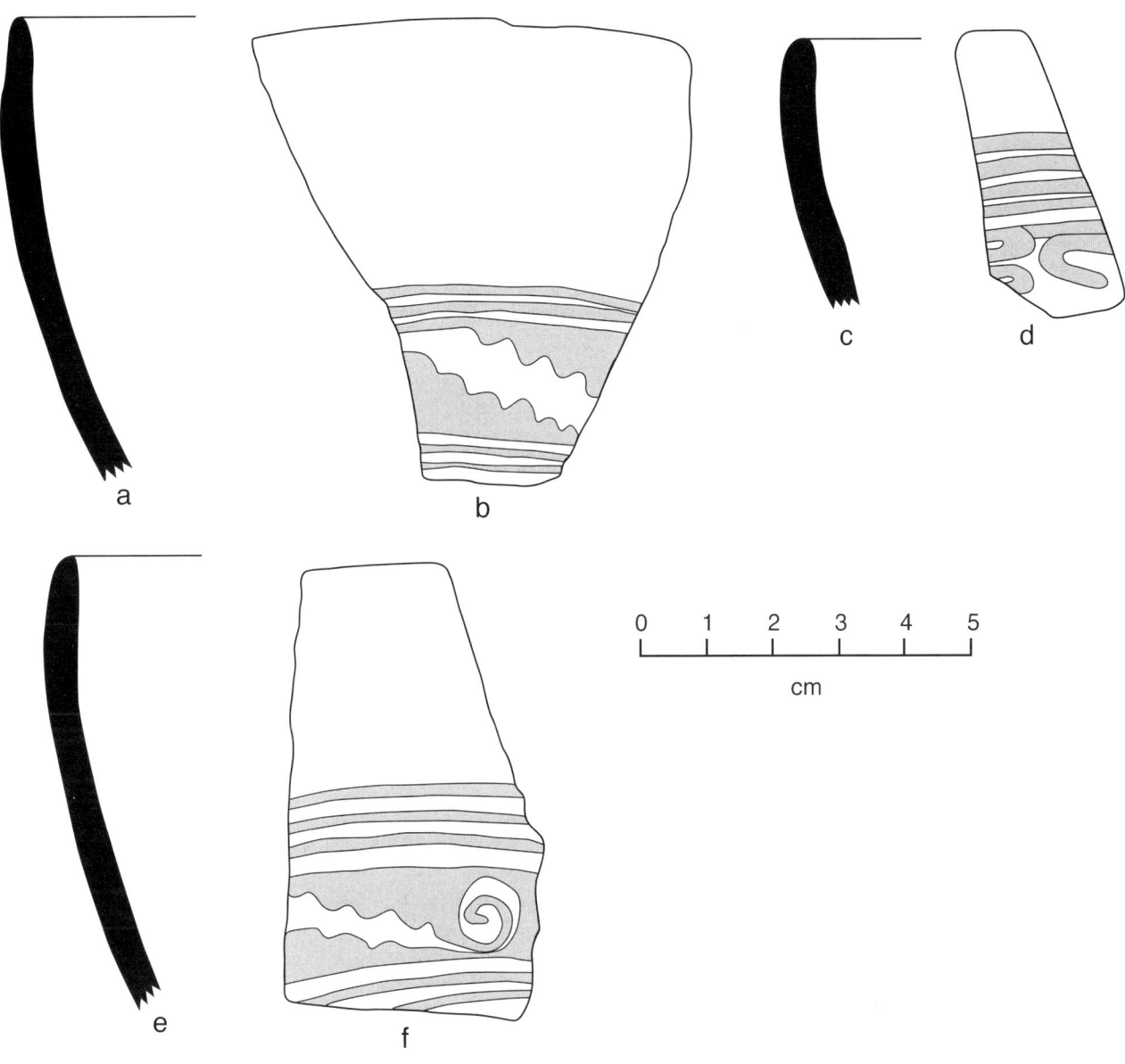

Figure B49. Aztec Red Service Ware, Black/Red bowls. Proveniences: *a*, *b*, *e*, *f* (Zu-Az-73); *c*, *d* (Zu-Az-46). All designs are on interior surfaces.

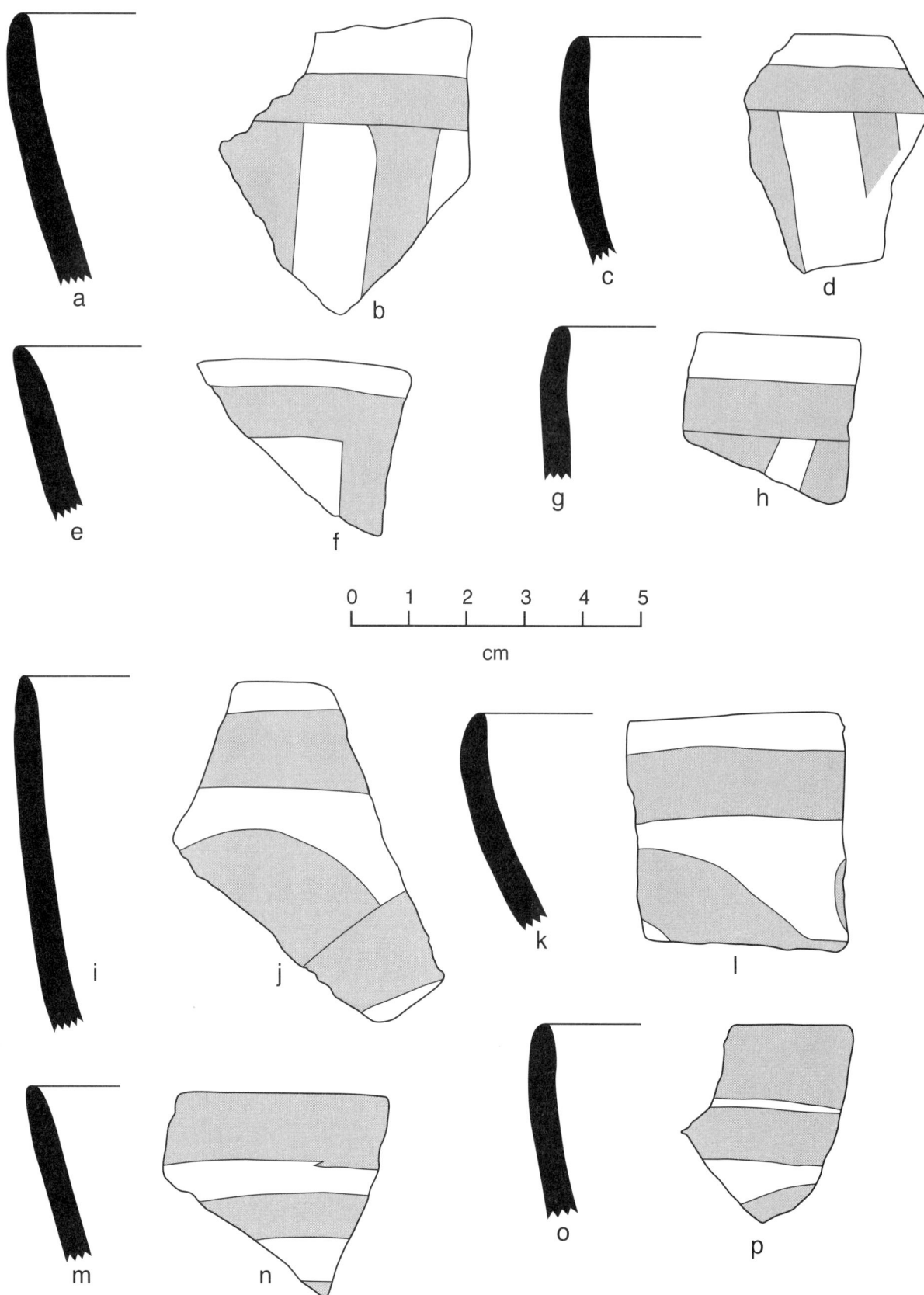

Figure B50. Aztec Red Service Ware, Black-and-White/Red bowls with vertical panels (*a-h*) and triangular panels (*i-p*). Proveniences: *a, b, i, j, m-p* (Zu-Az-292); *c-h* (Zu-Az-46); *k, l* (Zu-Az-73).

Appendix B: Ceramic Chronology

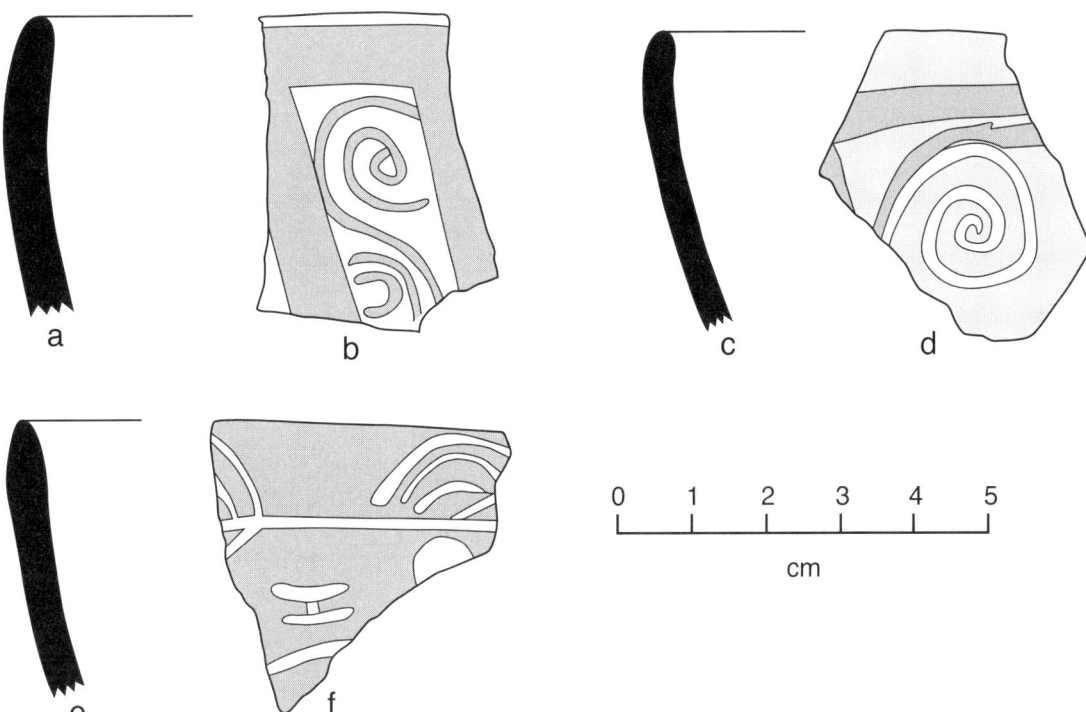

Figure B51. Aztec Red Service Ware, Black-and-White/Red bowls, with complex fugitive white designs. Proveniences: *a, b* (Zu-Az-46); *c, d* (Zu-Az-73); *e, f* (Zu-Az-292). All designs are on exterior surfaces.

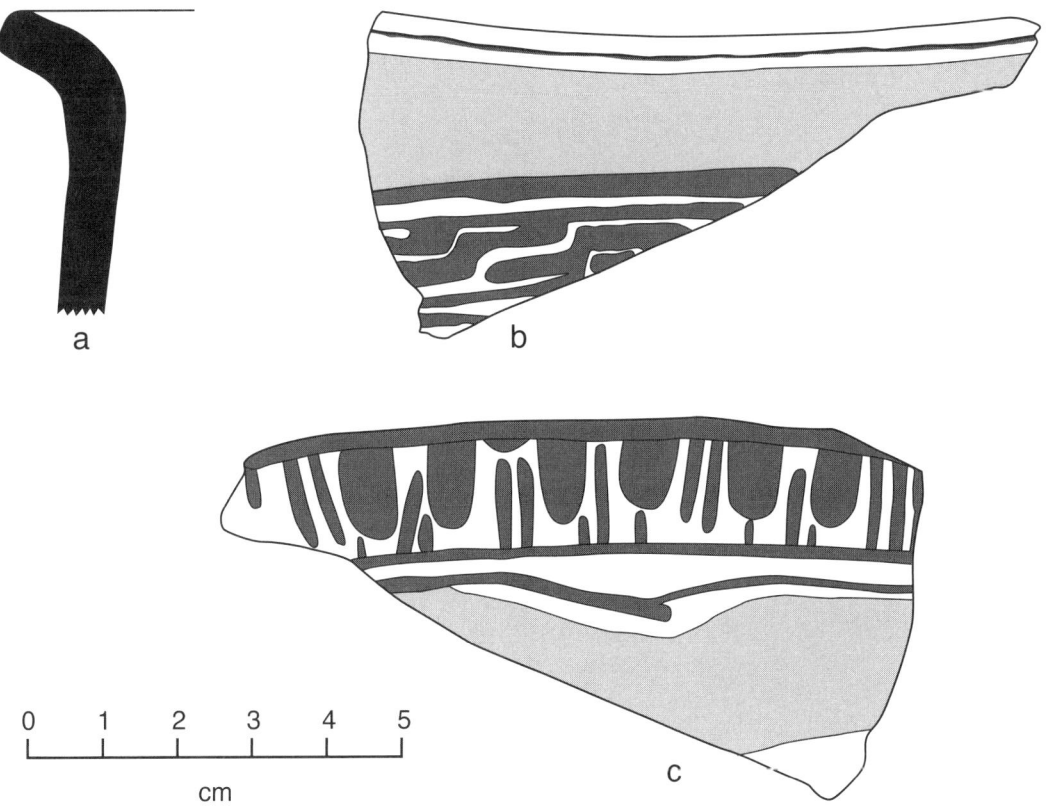

Figure B52. Aztec Specialty Ware, Huastec Black-and-Purple/Cream Tradeware. Provenience: Zu-Az-73. All are from the same sherd: *b* is the exterior surface, and *c* is the interior surface. See Plate B48.

Aztec Specialty Ware: Chalco-Cholula Polychrome (Plate B52)

A few sherds of this highly distinctive, but seldom seen, type occur in a handful of our surface collections from Late Postclassic sites in the Zumpango Region. All of what we have corresponds to what Hodge and Minc (1991:235-36, 247) classified as Variant C, a Late Postclassic type. In paste and form, this type corresponds closely to the Red Ware bowls described above: simple hemispherical bowls with upright walls, and painted designs of black, orange, and red applied on the upper exterior surface.

This polychrome material is much more abundant in the southern Valley of Mexico (Parsons et al. 1982), where Early Aztec types are also common. Frequencies of this type decline markedly northward in the Valley of Mexico, where the Early Aztec varieties of this ware are largely absent (as is Aztec I Black/Orange).

Aztec Specialty Ware: Texcoco Molded and Texcoco Filleted (Plates B53–B56)

These distinctive types occur only in low frequencies in our surface collections, but they are consistently present and chronologically diagnostic of the Late Postclassic. They are widely found at sites of this period throughout the Valley of Mexico, usually in small fragments. Excavations at the Templo Mayor in Tenochtitlan/Mexico City (Matos 1999), at a ritual shrine in central Lake Texcoco (Parsons and Morett 2004), and at a few other localities in the Valley of Mexico have shown that these are shallow, thin walled, flaring bowls with triangular cutout designs, attached to long, hollow handles (Plate B53). They appear to have been used for burning incense in ceremonial contexts. These vessels are typically smoothed, with a matte finish, sometimes with a fugitive white or cream slip, and occasionally with red-painted sections on the interior (upper) and exterior (bottom) surfaces (Plate B54). The characteristic linear (Plate B55) and pimpled (Plate B56) designs have often been termed Texcoco Filleted and Texcoco Molded, respectively.

Appendix B: Ceramic Chronology

Plate B1. Tzacualli figurine, Zu-LT-210.

Plate B2. Classic Red/Buff bowl with nubbin support, Zu-Cl-52.

Plate B3. Classic Red/Buff bowls, Zu-Cl-60.

Appendix B: Ceramic Chronology

Plate B5. Classic Monochrome olla, with wide-everted rim, Zu-Cl-72.

Plate B4. Classic Red/Buff bowl with incised lines, Zu-Cl-46.

Plate B6. Classic Monochrome olla, with low neck, Zu-Cl-46.

Plate B7. Classic Monochrome olla, with rolled rim, Zu-Cl-7.

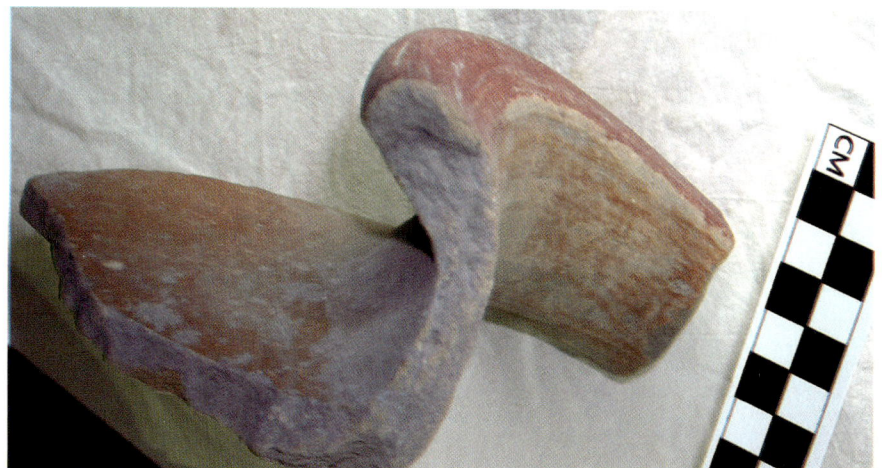

Plate B8. Classic Red/Buff olla, with single red band, Zu-Cl-53.

Plate B9. Classic Red/Buff olla, with wide red band, Zu-Cl-63.

Plate B10. Classic Red/Buff olla, rim with red upper surface, Zu-Cl-84.

Plate B11a. Classic Rose/Granular. *a*, interior, Zu-LT-53; *b*, exterior, Zu-LT-53.

Plate B12. Classic Thin Orange. *a*, annular base, Zu-Cl-46; *b*, Zu-Cl-60; *c*, Zu-LT-53.

Plate B13. Classic figurines. *a*, Early Classic, Zu-Cl-42; *b*, Late Classic, Zu-Cl-60.

Plate B14. Classic candelero, Zu-Cl-42.

Plate B15. Early Toltec, low frequency decorated types. *a*, Incised Red/Buff bowl, Zu-ET-23; *b*, Stamped Plainware bowl, Zu-ET-12; *c*, Incised Monochrome bowl, Zu-Cl-83.

Plate B16. Early Toltec Coyotlatelco Red/Buff. *a*, Zu-ET-3; *b-f*, Zu-ET-12.

Plate B17. Late Toltec Monochrome bowl supports. *a*, Zu-LT-87; *b*, Zu-LT-53; *c*, Zu-LT-49.

Plate B18. Late Toltec Monochrome bowl, striated interior base, Zu-LT-87.

Plate B19. Late Toltec Wide-Band Red/Buff bowl supports. *a*, bulbous, Zu-LT-211; *b*, pinched tip, Zu-LT-103; *c*, bird-effigy, Zu-LT-60.

Plate B20. Late Toltec Wide-Band Red/Buff bowl design variants. *a*, Zu-LT-36; *b*, Zu-LT-33; *c*, Zu-LT-211; *d*, Zu-LT-151.

Plate B21. Late Toltec Wavy-Line Red/Buff bowl design variants. *a*, Zu-LT-206; *b*, Zu-LT-30; *c*, Zu-LT-191; *d*, Zu-LT-203.

Plate B21. Late Toltec Wavy-Line Red/Buff bowl design variants. *e*, *f*, Zu-LT-176; *g*, Zu-LT-47.

Plate B22. Late Toltec Orange/Cream bowls. *a*, Zu-LT-75; *b*, Zu-LT-211.

Plate B23. Late Toltec Utilitarian basin with scraped exterior, Zu-LT-212.

Plate B24. Late Toltec comal with handle, Zu-LT-72.

Appendix B: Ceramic Chronology 421

Plate B25. Late Toltec Ink-Stamped jar, Zu-LT-58.

Plate B26. Late Toltec Plumbate Ware, Zu-LT-176.

Plate B27. Late Toltec Sillon Incised Orange, Zu-LT-169.

Plate B28. Late Toltec Orange Stamped, Zu-LT-2.

Plate B29. Late Toltec Blanco Llevantado (Tula Watercolored), Zu-LT-176.

Plate B31. Colonial glazed pottery, Zu-Col-1(J) (not described in text).

Plate B30. Late Toltec figurines. *a*, Zu-LT-69; *b*, Zu-LT-30.

Plate B32. Aztec II-III Black/Orange bowl/basins. *a*, Zu-Az-236; *b*, Zu-Az-5; *c*, Zu-Az-72.

Plate B33. Aztec III Black/Orange bowl/basin design variants, all Zu-Az-51.

Plate B34. Aztec II Black/Orange plates. *a*, Zu-Az-115; *b*, Zu-Az-46.

Plate B35. Aztec II-III Black/Orange dish/plates. *a*, Zu-Az-72; *b*, Zu-Az-292/-293/-294.

Plate B36. Aztec III Black/Orange dish/plates. *a*, Zu-Az-24; *b*, Zu-LT-52; *c*, Zu-Az-115.

Plate B37. Aztec II-III Black/Orange molcajete, Zu-Az-46.

Appendix B: Ceramic Chronology

Plate B38. Aztec III and IV Black/Orange molcajetes. *a*, Zu-Az-11; *b*, Zu-Az-155; *c*, Zu-Az-292/-293/-294; *d*, Zu-Col-1 (not described in text).

Plate B39. Aztec IV(?) Black/Orange molcajete (unique design), Zu-Az-292/-293/-294.

Plate B40. Aztec IV Black/Orange dishes and molcajetes. *a*, Zu-Az-132; *b*, Zu-Az-119; *c*, Zu-Az-119; *d*, Zu-LT-116.

Plate B41. Aztec IV Black/Orange slab supports. *a*, Zu-Az-51; *b*, Zu-Az-274; *c*, Zu-Az-11.

Plate B42. Aztec Black/Red bowls with comb design. *a*, Zu-Az-179; *b*, Zu-Az-249; *c*, Zu-Az-11; *d*, Zu-Az-11.

Appendix B: Ceramic Chronology 431

Plate B43. Aztec Black/Red bowls with geometric designs.
a, Zu-Az-234; *b*, Zu-Az-298; *c*, Zu-Az-116.

Plate B44. Aztec Black and White/Red bowls with vertical panels. *a*, Zu-Az-236; *b*, Zu-Az-12.

Appendix B: Ceramic Chronology 433

Plate B45. Aztec Black and White/Red bowls with triangular panels. *a*, Zu-Az-79; *b*, Zu-Az-72; *c*, Zu-Az-18.

Plate B46. Aztec Black and White/Red bowls with complex designs. *a*, Zu-Az-116; *b*, *c*, Zu-Az-274.

Plate B47. Aztec Yellow/Red bowl, Zu-Az-119.

Appendix B: Ceramic Chronology

Plate B48. Aztec Huastec Tradeware. *a*, Zu-Az-116; *b*, Zu-Az-18; *c*, Zu-Az-73; *d*, Zu-Az-73.

Plate B49. Aztec Huastec Tradeware with strap handle, Zu-LT-52.

Plate B50. Aztec Texcoco Fabric Marked. *a*, Zu-Az-300; *b*, Zu-Az-300.

Plate B51. Aztec Texcoco Fabric Marked, whole vessel, from recently excavated site near Ecatepec in the west-central Valley of Mexico.

Plate B52. Aztec Chalco-Cholula Polychrome. *a*, Zu-Az-236; *b*, Zu-Az-37.

Plate B53. Aztec censers, VLT-210, excavated site in central Lake Texcoco (Parsons and Morett 2004).

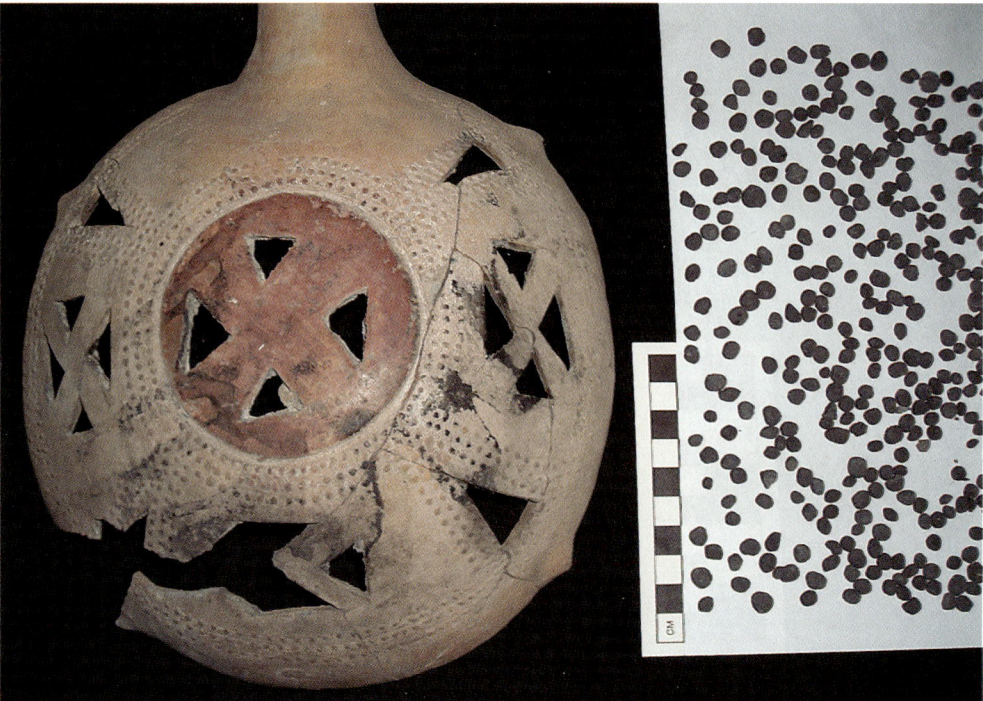

Plate B54. Aztec censer, VLT-210, excavated site in central Lake Texcoco (Parsons and Morett 2004).

Plate B55. Aztec censer, Zu-Az-230.

Plate B56. Aztec censer, Zu-Az-46.